PRENTICE-HALL

Grammar and Composition

Level 6

SERIES CONSULTANTS

Level 1
Ellen G. Manhire
English Consultant Coordinator
Fresno, California

Level 2
Elizabeth A. Nace
Supervisor, Language Arts
Akron, Ohio

Level 3
Jerry Reynolds
Supervisor, Language Arts
Rochester, Minnesota

Level 4
Marlene Corbett
Chairperson, Department of English
Charlotte, North Carolina

Level 5
Gilbert Hunt
Chairperson, Department of English
Manchester, Connecticut

Level 6
Margherite LaPota
Curriculum Specialist
Tulsa, Oklahoma

CRITIC READERS FOR LEVEL 6

Jewell Alexander
West Springfield High School
Springfield, Virginia

James E. Coomber
Concordia College
Moorhead, Minnesota

Harvey S. Farr
Elk Grove High School
Elk Grove, California

Ralph Gage
Hazen High School
Renton, Washington

Franklin E. May
Westside High School
Omaha, Nebraska

Howard D. Peet
North Dakota State University
Fargo, North Dakota

Janice Rayner
South High Community School
Worcester, Massachusetts

Gary C. Sedlacek
Westside High School
Omaha, Nebraska

James S. Sims
Columbus Public Schools
Columbus, Ohio

Kenneth D. White
R.B. Stall High School
Charleston Heights, South Carolina

Prentice-Hall

Grammar
and
Composition

Level 6

SERIES AUTHORS

Mary Beth Bauer, Language Arts Consultant, Houston, Texas

Lawrence Biener, Chairperson, Department of English, Locust Valley, New York

Linda Capo, Writer and English Teacher, Ithaca, New York

Gary Forlini, Writer and English Teacher, Pelham, New York

Karen L. Moore, English and Speech Teacher, Saratoga, California

Darla Shaw, Reading Coordinator, Ridgefield, Connecticut

Zenobia Verner, Professor of Curriculum and Instruction, Houston, Texas

PRENTICE-HALL, INC., Englewood Cliffs, New Jersey

SERIES TITLES

Prentice-Hall Grammar and Composition: Level 1
Prentice-Hall Grammar and Composition: Level 2
Prentice-Hall Grammar and Composition: Level 3
Prentice-Hall Grammar and Composition: Level 4
Prentice-Hall Grammar and Composition: Level 5
Prentice-Hall Grammar and Composition: Level 6

SUPPLEMENTARY MATERIALS

Annotated Teacher's Editions—Levels 1–6
Test Program—Levels 1–6

Acknowledgments: page 860

ISBN 0-13-696880-5

10 9 8 7 6 5 4

Prentice-Hall International, Inc., London
Prentice-Hall of Australia Pty. Ltd., Sydney
Prentice-Hall of Canada, Ltd., Toronto
Prentice-Hall of India Private Ltd., New Delhi
Prentice-Hall of Japan, Inc., Tokyo
Prentice-Hall of Southeast Asia Pte. Ltd., Singapore
Whitehall Books Limited, Wellington, New Zealand

Contents

Usage 149

Preface

This book has a single purpose—to help you deal more effectively with the English language. The content, organization, and special features have all been designed to help you reach this goal.

Content

Unit One, Grammar, covers parts of speech and the parts of sentences, while giving you a number of useful methods for correcting basic sentence faults. Unit Two, Usage, zeroes in on problems that may arise in using verbs, pronouns, adjectives, and adverbs. It also includes a special section listing one hundred common usage problems and a section on different levels of language. Unit Three, Mechanics, helps you decide when to capitalize, when to abbreviate, and when to use commas, quotation marks, and other forms of punctuation. Unit Four, Vocabulary and Spelling, provides strategies for building your knowledge of words and improving your spelling. Unit Five, Study Skills, offers numerous ideas for getting more out of the time you spend studying, listening to classroom lectures, organizing information, taking tests, and researching topics in the library. Unit Six, Composition, begins with ideas for making your sentences clearer and more interesting, moves on to steps for writing different kinds of paragraphs, and ends with steps and other useful methods for writing essays, library papers, literary analyses, letters, applications, précis, and answers to questions on essay examinations.

Organization

While your class may study any or all of the sections in the book in depth, you will find that the book has an equally important use as a reference work, not only in your English classes but also on any other occasions when you want to write or speak effectively.

As a Textbook. All the units are divided into chapters, each of which is divided into sections. The sections themselves are then divided into subsections. A glance at the Table of Contents, which begins on page 5 and a brief survey of a few of the text chapters should show you how this works.

The sections are short and can usually be covered in a day or two. Before beginning each section, you will find it useful to preview subsections. Which areas do you consider yourself strong in? Which areas are you weak in? As you work through the subsections, you will find one or more exercises at the end of each subsection. You can use these to preview or test your understanding of the topics covered. At the end of each section, you will find an Application which asks you to put all the skills you have reviewed or learned in the section to work in a practical exercise. This will give you a chance to check your overall understanding and ability to use the material in the section.

As a Reference Tool. In and out of school, you are likely to find situations in which knowing correct punctuation, correct spelling, and standard usage can make a difference. If you have questions on these matters there are three places you can go in this book to find the answers. You can check the Table of Contents at the front of the book, you can check the Key of Major Concepts at the back of the book, or you can use the Index. Note that the Index uses bold numbers to show you where to find rules and definitions.

Special Features

In addition to becoming familiar with the overall organization of the text, you may find it useful to explore some of the special features.

Clear Rules. All major rules and definitions are printed in bold type and written in easy-to-understand language. The bold numbers in the index indicate the pages where rules amd definitions can be found.

Numerous Examples. For most rules you will find a number of examples, each pointing out a different aspect of the rule. Whether you are studying a section or using it for quick reference, make sure you check all of the examples to be certain you understand all aspects of the rule.

Exercises for Each Subsection. Each subsection has one or more exercises. This will make it possible for you to tell what concepts you have mastered completely and what concepts you will need to review more thoroughly.

Applications for All Sections. The practical Application at the end of each section lets you put what you have been learning to work, generally in some writing exercise. At the same time, you will be checking your mastery of the ideas in the section.

Charts Covering Important Concepts. Throughout the book you will find important concepts highlighted in charts. This will make it possible for you quickly to identify and check your understanding and knowledge of essential ideas.

Charts Offering Useful Steps. Charts are also used to illustrate step by step processes: for identifying parts of speech, for preparing for an interview, for developing different materials in compositions, and for numerous other topics.

Checklists. One of the most important uses of charts is for revision checklists. What should you do when you have finished writing the first draft of a paragraph or essay? The checklists in the composition unit give some valuable suggestions.

Numerous Composition Models. One of the best ways to increase your own writing skill is to examine the works of professional writers and of other students. Throughout the composition unit are models by other writers with important elements clearly labeled.

A Special Unit on Study Skills. The study skills unit can help you review and develop a number of skills that will be immediately useful in a number of situations. You may want to look first at the suggestions for setting goals for school and life in Section 15.1

A Special Section on Manuscript Preparation. This section at the end of the book can be immensely useful any time you need to prepare a written work that you want to be well received.

Three Reference Aids. The Table of Contents, the Index, and the Key of Major Concepts at the back of the book all can help you zero in on the rules and examples you need when you are using the book for quick reference.

Chapter 1

The Parts of Speech

Every English word can be assigned to one of the following eight categories, called the *parts of speech*.

THE EIGHT PARTS OF SPEECH		
nouns	adjectives	prepositions
pronouns	adverbs	conjunctions
verbs		interjections

What determines a word's part of speech is its meaning and use within a sentence. This chapter discusses each of the eight parts of speech.

1.1 Nouns and Pronouns

Nouns are used to give labels to the people, places, objects, and ideas about which human beings communicate. Pronouns are the words that act as "stand-ins" for nouns, replacing them in sentences. Through careful use of nouns and pronouns, writers can avoid overworking particular nouns and can clarify possibly ambiguous references.

■ Nouns

Nouns constitute the largest of the parts of speech categories.

A noun is the name of a person, place, or thing.

Determining which words name *people* or *places* usually presents no problems.

PERSON: woman, infant, statesman, Dr. Sabes, Aunt Margaret

PLACE: university, Rowland Boulevard, desert, Chesapeake Bay, China

The classification *thing*, however, is as ambiguous as the word itself. It encompasses living things, nonliving things, ideas, actions, conditions, and qualities.

LIVING THINGS: fungus, shark, wheat

NONLIVING THINGS: plastic, refrigerator, water

IDEAS: abolition, welfarism, evolution

ACTIONS: dispute, construction, communication

CONDITIONS: pregnancy, loneliness, ownership

QUALITIES: integrity, assurance, vulgarity

Knowing the endings often found on nouns can sometimes aid in identification of the part of speech of these words. Some of the most common noun suffixes are *-dom, -ics, -ion, -ism, -ment, -ness,* and *-ship.*

EXAMPLES: freedom   entertainment

aeronautics   shyness

frustration   showmanship

socialism

Concrete and Abstract Nouns.   Nouns are sometimes grouped according to the characteristics of the things they name. A *concrete* noun names something that you can physically see, touch, taste, hear, or smell. An *abstract* noun names something that is nonphysical, that you cannot readily perceive through any of your five senses.

Concrete Nouns	Abstract Nouns
pitchfork	nationalism
garlic	era
critic	career
bruise	immortality

Singular and Plural Nouns.   Nouns can indicate number. *Singular* nouns name one person, place, or thing. *Plural* nouns name more than one. Most plural nouns are formed by the addition of *-s* or *-es* to the singular form. Some plural nouns, however, are formed irregularly and must be memorized. (For rules governing the formation of plural nouns, see Section 14.2.)

SINGULAR NOUNS	
Regular	**Irregular**
valley	mouse
lash	ox
sky	nucleus
PLURAL NOUNS	
valleys	mice
lashes	oxen
skies	nuclei

Collective Nouns.   Nouns that name *groups* of people or things are called *collective nouns*. Although a collective noun is singular in its base form, its meaning may be either singular or plural depending on how you use it in a sentence. (For rules governing the use of collective nouns in sentences, see Section 7.1.)

COLLECTIVE NOUNS	
council	orchestra
delegation	team
entourage	troop

Compound Nouns.   A noun that is composed of two or more words acting as a single unit is called a *compound noun.* For example, the noun *milk* and the noun *snake* can act together to name a particular animal—a *milk snake.* Compound nouns are usually entered in the dictionary because they name something other than what the individual words suggest. An expression such as *milk bottle,* on the other hand, is not generally considered a compound noun because it means nothing more than "a bottle for milk."

Compound nouns may appear in three forms: as separate words, as hyphenated words, or as combined words.

COMPOUND NOUNS	
Separate Words	sick leave, player piano, snake dance
Hyphenated Words	jack-in-the-box, light-year, sister-in-law
Combined Words	dragonfly, eardrum, starfish

If you are in doubt about the spelling of a compound noun, check a dictionary. If the noun is not entered in the dictionary, you can write it as separate words.

Common and Proper Nouns. All nouns can be categorized as either common or proper. A *common noun* names any one of a class of people, places, or things. A *proper noun* names a specific person, place, or thing.

Common Nouns	Proper Nouns
playwright	Lillian Hellman, Bernard Shaw
island	Maui, Sicily
building	World Trade Towers, Taj Mahal

As you can see from these examples, proper nouns are always capitalized, whereas common nouns are not. (For rules on capitalization, see Section 11.1.)

A *noun of direct address*—the name of a person you are directly talking to—is always proper, as is a family title before a personal name.

COMMON NOUN: My *aunt* is a taxi driver.

DIRECT ADDRESS: Please tell us, *Aunt*, about your trip to San Juan.

FAMILY TITLE: For many years *Aunt* Maria has managed a hotel in Miami.

EXERCISE A: **Identifying the Types of Nouns.** Copy the following list of nouns onto your paper. Identify each according to whether it (1) names a person, place, or thing, (2) is concrete or abstract, (3) is singular or plural, (4) is collective, (5) is compound, and (6) is common or proper.

EXAMPLE: gratitude   thing, abstract, singular, common

1. by-products
2. majority
3. Tuesday
4. New Mexico
5. short circuits
6. Lord Peter Wimsey

7. squadron
8. privileges
9. feudalism
10. Davis Cup
11. stitches
12. subcommittee
13. Hanging Gardens of Babylon

14. umbrella
15. geese
16. life preservers
17. jack-in-the-pulpit
18. honesty
19. Pearl Harbor
20. sundial

EXERCISE B: **Recognizing Compound Nouns.** Use a dictionary to determine which of the following expressions are compound nouns. Write the meaning for each compound noun and be prepared to explain why the other expressions do not need to be entered in the dictionary.

1. garden apartment
2. garden furniture
3. paper airplane
4. paper tiger
5. paper doll

6. storm warning
7. storm window
8. dog days
9. dog paddle
10. dog bone

■ Pronouns

Pronouns are the part of speech that helps speakers and writers avoid awkward repetition of nouns.

A **pronoun** is a word used to take the place of a noun or group of words acting as a noun.

In the following examples, the italicized words are pronouns. The arrows point to the words that the pronouns replace.

EXAMPLES: Jan and Ken went to the dance. *They* thought *it* was the best so far this year.

On May 3, 1810, Lord Byron succeeded in *his* attempt to swim the four miles across the Hellespont. *It* was a feat that Byron was proud of for the rest of his life.

In the preceding examples, the words that the arrows point to are called *antecedents*.

An **antecedent** is the noun (or group of words acting as a noun) for which a pronoun stands.

Although an antecedent usually precedes its pronoun, it can also follow the pronoun.

EXAMPLE: After *their* performance, the actors mingled with the audience.

There are several kinds of pronouns in English. Most have antecedents; a few do not. The rest of this section will describe the different kinds of pronouns and discuss their antecedents.

Personal Pronouns. Personal pronouns are used to refer to particular people, places, and things.

> **Personal pronouns** are used to refer to (1) the person speaking, (2) the person spoken to, or (3) the person, place, or thing spoken about.

All of the personal pronouns are listed in the following chart. First-person pronouns refer to the person speaking, second-person pronouns refer to the person spoken to, and third-person pronouns refer to the person, place, or thing spoken about. The personal pronouns in the chart that are italicized are sometimes called *possessive pronouns*.

PERSONAL PRONOUNS		
	Singular	**Plural**
First Person	I, me *my, mine*	we, us *our, ours*
Second Person	you *your, yours*	you *your, yours*
Third Person	he, she, it him, her *his, her, hers, its*	they, them *their, theirs*

The antecedent of a personal pronoun may or may not be clearly stated. In the following examples, only the last sentence, which has a third-person pronoun, has a stated antecedent. In the first two examples, the antecedents are implied.

FIRST PERSON: *We* practiced a rousing march for the parade.

SECOND PERSON: *You* must submit *your* application before December 15.

THIRD PERSON: The starlings have built *their* nest in the eaves of the house.

Reflexive and Intensive Pronouns.   Reflexive and intensive pronouns have the same form—both end in *-self* or *-selves*. Although these pronouns have the same form, their functions within sentences differ.

Reflexive pronouns are used to add information to a sentence by pointing back to a noun or pronoun near the beginning of the sentence.

Intensive pronouns are used simply to add emphasis to a noun or pronoun.

The eight reflexive and intensive pronouns are formed from personal pronouns.

REFLEXIVE AND INTENSIVE PRONOUNS		
	Singular	**Plural**
First Person	myself	ourselves
Second Person	yourself	yourselves
Third Person	himself, herself, itself	themselves

A reflexive pronoun adds essential information to a sentence. An intensive pronoun, on the other hand, can usually be removed from the sentence without changing the sentence's basic meaning.

REFLEXIVE: Cats clean *themselves* conscientiously after each meal.

INTENSIVE: You *yourself* admitted that the house needs painting.

Demonstrative Pronouns.   These pronouns are used to point out nouns.

A **demonstrative pronoun** is used to point out a specific person, place, or thing.

There are four demonstrative pronouns.

DEMONSTRATIVE PRONOUNS	
Singular	**Plural**
this, that	these, those

Demonstrative pronouns may be located before or after their antecedents.

BEFORE: *That* is an ambulance siren.

AFTER: A box of old photographs and my guitar—*these* were all I had been able to salvage from the fire.

Relative Pronouns.   These pronouns are used to relate a subordinate clause to another word in the same sentence. (For more information about relative pronouns and subordinate clauses, see Section 3.3.)

A **relative pronoun** is used to begin a subordinate clause and relate it to another idea in the sentence.

There are five relative pronouns.

RELATIVE PRONOUNS
that   which   who   whom   whose

As the following sentences show, the antecedent for a relative pronoun is located in another clause of the sentence. In the following chart, each relative pronoun links the information in a subordinate clause to a word in an independent clause.

Independent Clause	Subordinate Clause
We began reading *The Cyclops,*	*which* is a play by Euripides.
I wish to thank Leonard Cook	to *whom* we owe a debt of gratitude.
The show focused on people	*whose* discoveries have changed history.

Interrogative Pronouns.   These pronouns are used to ask questions.

An **interrogative pronoun** is used to begin a direct or indirect question.

There are five interrogative pronouns.

INTERROGATIVE PRONOUNS
what   which   who   whom   whose

The antecedent for an interrogative pronoun may not always be known, as the first of the following examples illustrates.

DIRECT QUESTION: *What* fell from that ledge?

INDIRECT QUESTION: The history professor cited two causes for the dispute. I asked *which* was the most influential.

Indefinite Pronouns.   Very similar in function to nouns, indefinite pronouns do not require specific antecedents.

Indefinite pronouns are used to refer to persons, places, or things, often without specifying which ones.

The following chart lists the most commonly used indefinite pronouns.

INDEFINITE PRONOUNS				
Singular			**Plural**	**Singular or Plural**
another	everyone	nothing	both	all
anybody	everything	one	few	any
anyone	little	other	many	more
anything	much	somebody	others	most
each	neither	someone	several	none
either	nobody	something		some
everybody	no one			such

NO SPECIFIC ANTECEDENT: *Nobody* was required to clean up, but *many* offered to assist.

SPECIFIC ANTECEDENT: I bought some new pillows for the couch; however, *none* was the right shade.

EXERCISE C: Recognizing Antecedents. One or more pronouns have been underlined in the following sentences. Write each pronoun and its antecedent on your paper. If a pronoun does not have an antecedent, mark an *X* on your paper after the pronoun.

1. Jo <u>herself</u> has had clairvoyant experiences at various times in <u>her</u> life.
2. The troops trudged through the thick forest. <u>Their</u> throats were parched and <u>they</u> yearned for some refreshment.
3. I think <u>nothing</u> is worse than a steak <u>that</u> is well-done.
4. <u>All</u> of the graduating seniors must pass proficiency tests. <u>Those</u> who fail will not receive a diploma.
5. A thick cloud of pollutants hung over the city. <u>Its</u> debilitating effects caused the schools to cancel <u>their</u> sports events.
6. *The City and the Stars* and *The Dispossessed* are both fine examples of science fiction. <u>Everyone</u> in class should read at least <u>one</u> of <u>them.</u>
7. It is inspirational to <u>me</u> to read stories of people <u>who</u> have overcome severe handicaps to lead successful lives.
8. Listening attentively is a valuable skill. Students should train <u>themselves</u> to do <u>it</u> effectively.
9. <u>I</u> asked Marcia <u>what</u> she meant by <u>her</u> mysterious remark.
10. <u>Both</u> of the actors gave superior performances. <u>They</u> captured the hearts of <u>their</u> audience.

EXERCISE D: Indentifying the Different Types of Pronouns. Most of the pronouns in the following sentences have been underlined. Decide what kind of pronoun each underlined item is and write your answer on your paper: *personal, reflexive, intensive, demonstrative, relative, interrogative,* or *indefinite.*

When over 130 million television viewers turned on (1) <u>their</u> sets to watch *Roots,* (2) <u>few</u> had any idea (3) <u>that</u> (4) <u>this</u> was the beginning of a new television era. Today, docudramas with (5) <u>their</u> colorful dramatizations of historical events make up a substantial portion of (6) <u>each</u> of the networks' programming. But even as American viewers treat (7) <u>themselves</u> to these television triumphs, there are (8) <u>those</u> (9) <u>who</u> denounce (10) <u>them.</u> Critics contend that docudramas mix fact with fiction without telling (11) <u>those</u> (12) <u>who</u> watch (13) <u>them</u> of this. The critics pose some disturbing questions: (14) <u>Who</u> verifies the historical accuracy of these tales? Are the networks doing a disservice by allowing the public to dupe (15) <u>themselves</u> into believing that these distorted accounts are true? (16) <u>Others</u> contend that the critics overstate the seriousness of the problem and insult the viewer (17) <u>who</u> is intelligent enough to distinguish reality from fiction. Nevertheless, the disquieting questions remain. When (18) <u>we</u> realize that the average television set is on for more than six hours a day, we (19) <u>ourselves</u>

must ponder the impact these shows may be exerting on us. If we do not, (20) <u>whose</u> version of past events will later fill our textbooks—the Hollywood producers' or the true historians'?

APPLICATION: Locating Nouns and Pronouns. List all of the nouns and pronouns each sentence contains, including nouns used as adjectives. Be prepared to identify each kind of noun and pronoun by name.

(1) As suburbs have prospered around our cities, many of the people in the cities have moved out of the less desirable inner neighborhoods, leaving behind them poverty-stricken areas. (2) For years, local governments left these areas withering on the vine, helpless to stop the mass exodus. (3) Now, times are changing; cities such as Baltimore, New York, and San Francisco can point with pride to inner-city areas that are now thriving and prosperous. (4) What is the reason? (5) Business people and homeowners have cleverly renovated old buildings with the help of strong economic incentives from local and federal governments. (6) In this way an old police station has become a popular cultural center for Italians, a former canning factory now houses a thriving group of small shops, and an old freight depot has been redressed as a health and racquet club. (7) In many locations the citizens themselves provide the catalyst for change. (8) As the pioneers of this century, they are venturing into the unknown regions of the city as urban homesteaders; here they can sometimes buy homes slated for destruction for one dollar, committing themselves to renovate the houses and live in them. (9) Realizing the potential for salvaging the inner city, many are working to lure potential businesses and homeowners to their communities. (10) Now, the future looks more optimistic for all of the inner cities as renovation brings in new blood.

1.2 Verbs

Every complete sentence contains at least one verb, which may consist of as many as four words.

A **verb** is a word or group of words that expresses time while showing an action, a condition, or the fact that something exists.

ACTION: The dog *whined* piteously.

CONDITION: The silk *felt* slippery to my touch.

EXISTENCE: The peacock *is* in the tree.

Because of the way they affect *syntax*—that is, the way words are put together and related to one another in sentences—verbs are divided into two main categories: *action verbs* and *linking verbs*.

■ Action Verbs and Linking Verbs

Action verbs, as their name suggests, express either physical or mental action—that is, what someone or something does, did, or will do. Linking verbs serve a more passive function, expressing a condition. Verbs used as linking verbs may also be used simply to show that something exists.

Action Verbs. Action verbs make up the majority of English verbs.

> An **action verb** tells what action someone or something is performing.

ACTION VERBS: The dancer *will attempt* a daring leap.

The kettle *whistled* incessantly.

In the first example, the verb tells what the dancer will do; in the second example, the verb tells what the kettle did. The person or thing that performs the action is called the *subject* of the verb: *Dancer* is the subject of *will attempt; kettle* is the subject of *whistled.*

Linking Verbs. Instead of expressing action, a linking verb expresses a subject's condition by linking the subject to another word in the sentence.

> A **linking verb** connects its subject with a word at or near the end of the sentence.

LINKING VERBS: Richard Howard *is* a poet.

Jack *was* a senior.

An oral recommendation *should be* sufficient.

I *am being* unkind.

The verb *be* is the most common linking verb. If you are not thoroughly familiar with the many forms of this verb, study the following chart.

THE FORMS OF *BE*			
am	am being	can be	have been
are	are being	could be	has been
is	is being	may be	had been
was	was being	might be	could have been
were	were being	must be	may have been
		shall be	might have been
		should be	must have been
		will be	shall have been
		would be	should have been
			will have been
			would have been

When the forms of *be* act as linking verbs, they express the condition of the subject. Sometimes, however, they may merely express existence, usually by working with other words to show where the subject is located.

EXAMPLES: The key *is* in the lock.

The photographer *will be* here soon.

Other verbs can also function as linking verbs.

OTHER LINKING VERBS		
appear	look	sound
become	remain	stay
feel	seem	taste
grow	smell	turn

EXAMPLES: After lunch she *became* sleepy.

The bride *looked* radiant.

Most of these verbs can also serve as action verbs. To determine the function of such a verb, insert *am, are,* or *is* in its place. If the resulting sentence makes sense while linking two words, then the verb is serving as a linking verb.

LINKING VERB: The man *looked* preoccupied. (The man *is* preoccupied.)

ACTION VERB: The man *looked* for a taxi.

EXERCISE A: **Identifying Action and Linking Verbs.** Identify each of the underlined verbs in the following sentences as either an *action verb* or a *linking verb.*

1. We <u>stayed</u> at charming roadside inns throughout our travels in England.
2. The conductor <u>grew</u> impatient when the audience continued coughing.
3. The reservoir <u>remained</u> empty even though a rain storm had broken the drought.
4. The actor's mannerisms <u>seemed</u> rehearsed and unnatural.
5. Following in the family tradition, she <u>became</u> a pharmacist.
6. The trail <u>looked</u> perilous to the novice hikers.
7. Brussels sprouts <u>taste</u> bitter to me.
8. The cat <u>appeared</u> from behind the woodshed.
9. The fighter <u>turned</u> sharply to avoid his opponent's blow.
10. After the strenuous exercises, I <u>felt</u> lightheaded.
11. You <u>are being</u> irrational about this issue.
12. I <u>flipped</u> the record onto the second side.
13. Health food enthusiasts often <u>grow</u> their own fruits and vegetables.
14. I <u>tasted</u> a hint of basil in the soup we were served.
15. The chartered bus <u>should have been</u> air conditioned.
16. Maples' leaves <u>turn</u> a vibrant shade of red in the fall.
17. The physician <u>felt</u> the child's swollen glands and diagnosed the illness as mumps.
18. The odd-looking contraption <u>stayed</u> airborne for about twenty seconds.
19. The canvas on the lawn chair <u>turned</u> light blue after exposure to the sun.
20. As I listened in awe, the words of the speaker <u>sounded</u> almost prophetic.

■ Transitive and Intransitive Verbs

All verbs can be described as either *transitive* or *intransitive,* depending on whether they transfer action to another word in a sentence.

A verb is **transitive** if it directs action toward someone or something named in the same sentence. It is **intransitive** if it does not direct action toward someone or something named in the same sentence.

The word toward which a transitive verb directs its action is called the *object* of the verb. Intransitive verbs never have objects. You can determine whether a verb has an object and is thus transitive by asking *What?* or *Whom?* after the verb. (For more about objects of verbs, see Section 2.3.)

TRANSITIVE: The company *published* his poems. (Published *what?* Answer: *poems*)

The doctor *examined* the patient. (Examined *whom?* Answer: *patient*)

INTRANSITIVE: The birds *migrated* south. → No object

She *sings* for the Metropolitan Opera. → No object

Notice in the examples that the action of the transitive verbs is done *to* something. The publishing is done to the poems, the examining is done to the patient. The action of the intransitive verbs, however, is just done. Nothing receives the action of the migrating or the singing.

Linking verbs, which do not express action, are always intransitive. Most action verbs, however, can be either transitive or intransitive, depending on their use in a sentence. Some are either always transitive or always intransitive.

TRANSITIVE OR INTRANSITIVE: The jockey *exercised* the horse.

I *exercise* at the health spa.

ALWAYS TRANSITIVE: A stone wall *encloses* the garden.

ALWAYS INTRANSITIVE: The child *cringed* in fear.

EXERCISE B: Identifying Transitive and Intransitive Verbs. Write the verbs in the following sentences on your paper and indicate if they are *transitive* or *intransitive*.

1. The wind buffeted the frail sapling.
2. At midnight the politician conceded the election.
3. I was there on Tuesday.
4. The glider soared dramatically close to the majestic cliffs.
5. I made an appointment with the dentist.
6. Our guests noticed the new landscaping around our home.

7. The agile squirrel scampered up the pine.
8. The oil spill polluted the local beaches.
9. After his vacation the President appeared rested.
10. The gymnast performed exceptionally well on the balance beam.

■ Verb Phrases

When a verb consists of more than one word, it is called a *verb phrase.*

A **verb phrase** is a verb with one, two, or three helping verbs before it.

Helping verbs, also known as *auxiliary verbs* or *auxiliaries,* add meaning to other verbs. Some helping verbs change the time expressed by the key verb; others, such as *should* and *might,* are used to indicate obligation, possibility, ability, or permission.

SINGLE VERB: The firm *employed* a new secretary today.

VERB PHRASES: The firm *will employ* a new secretary today.

The firm *should have employed* a new secretary today.

A new secretary *might have been employed* by the firm today.

Any of the forms of *be* listed on page 30 can be used as helping verbs, as can the words in the following chart.

HELPING VERBS OTHER THAN *BE*			
do	have	shall	can
does	has	should	could
did	had	will	may
		would	might
			must

Verb phrases are often interrupted by other words in the sentence. To find the complete verb in a sentence, locate the key verb first; then check for helping verbs that may precede it.

INTERRUPTED VERB PHRASES: The firm *will* probably not *hire* a secretary today.

Should the firm *hire* another secretary?

EXERCISE C: Using Verb Phrases. Complete each of the following sentences with an appropriate verb phrase that includes the verb in parentheses.

1. The American Kennel Club _____ _____ dogs into working dogs, sporting dogs, nonsporting dogs, hounds, terriers, and toys. (classified)
2. Euclid _____ _____ _____ the Father of Geometry. (called)
3. The profits from the song "God Bless America" by Irving Berlin _____ _____ to the Scouts. (donated)
4. Next year, professional golfers _____ _____ in any of four big tournaments—the U.S. Open, the Masters, the P.G.A., and the British Open. (participate)
5. _____ India, and Nepal _____ _____ _____ to put their flags atop Mount Everest? (permitted)
6. A person in the Navy with the rank of fleet admiral _____ _____ five stars. (attained)
7. The Jean Hersolt Humanitarian Award _____ always _____ at the Academy Awards. (presented)
8. Liberty Island, home of the Statue of Liberty, _____ formerly _____ as Bedloe's Island. (known)
9. We _____ _____ another astrological year on March 21. (begin)
10. Readers _____ _____ _____ by the eighty-four Perry Mason novels by Erle Stanley Gardner. (entertained)

APPLICATION: Writing Sentences with Different Kinds of Verbs. Use each of the following verbs in a sentence of your own, following the directions in parentheses.

1. taste (as an action verb)
2. taste (as a linking verb)
3. climb (as a transitive verb)
4. climb (as an intransitive verb)
5. prevent (with three helping verbs)

1.3 Adjectives and Adverbs

Adjectives and adverbs are the two parts of speech known as *modifiers*—that is, they slightly change the meaning of other words by adding description or by making them more precise.

Adjectives modify nouns and pronouns; adverbs modify verbs, adjectives, and other adverbs.

■ Adjectives

An adjective qualifies the meaning of a noun or pronoun by providing information about its appearance, location, characteristics, and so on.

An **adjective** is a word used to describe a noun or pronoun or to give it a more specific meaning.

An adjective can answer four questions regarding a noun or pronoun: *What kind? Which one? How many?* and *How much?*

EXAMPLES: *green* fields   (*What kind* of fields?)

the *left* window   (*Which* window?)

six lobsters   (*How many* lobsters?)

extensive rainfall   (*How much* rainfall?)

When an adjective modifies a noun, it usually precedes the noun. Occasionally, though, the adjective may follow the noun.

EXAMPLES: The banjo teacher was *tactful* about my talent.

I considered the teacher *tactful.*

When an adjective modifies a pronoun, it usually follows the pronoun. Sometimes, however, the adjective may precede the pronoun.

AFTER: They were *brokenhearted* by the verdict.

BEFORE: *Brokenhearted* by the verdict, they began immediate appeal proceedings.

Finally, more than one adjective may modify a single noun or pronoun.

EXAMPLE: We elected a *competent, enthusiastic* official.

Articles.   The three most common adjectives—*a, an,* and *the*—are known as *articles. A* and *an* are called *indefinite articles* because they refer to any one of a class of nouns. *The,* on the other hand, refers to a specific noun and, therefore, is called the *definite article.*

INDEFINITE: *a* dictator

an outrage

DEFINITE: *the* tarantula

Compound Adjectives.   Adjectives can be compound—that is, formed from more than one word. Most compound adjectives are hyphenated; some are written as combined words. A quick check in the dictionary should tell you which form to use.

HYPHENATED: *ready-made* clothes, *mail-order* catalogs

COMBINED: *crossword* puzzle, *warmhearted* invitation

Proper Adjectives.   Like nouns, some adjectives can be proper. Proper adjectives are formed from proper nouns and always begin with a capital letter.

PROPER NOUNS: Chaucer   Denmark
PROPER ADJECTIVES: *Chaucerian* scholar   *Danish* porcelain

Compound proper adjectives are usually written as two separate words.

EXAMPLE: *West German* embassy

Nouns, Pronouns, and Verbs Used as Adjectives.   Words that are usually nouns, pronouns, or verbs will occasionally act as adjectives. When functioning as adjectives, these words will answer one or more of the four questions for adjectives: *What kind? Which one? How many?* or *How much?*

When a noun functions as an adjective, it answers *What kind?* or *Which one?* about another noun.

NOUNS USED AS ADJECTIVES	
Common Nouns	
pencil	*pencil* sharpener
mail	*mail* clerk

Proper Nouns	
Monday	*Monday* morning
San Francisco	*San Francisco* streets

Certain pronouns can also function as adjectives, as the examples illustrate. The seven personal pronouns, known as either *possessive adjectives* or *possessive pronouns,* fill two capacities in the sentence. They act as pronouns because they have antecedents, but at the same time they also act as adjectives because they modify nouns by answering *Which one?*

PRONOUNS USED AS ADJECTIVES	
Possessive Adjectives	
my, your, his, her, its, our, their	The committee gave *its* report.
	Your hamstring is just pulled.
Demonstrative Adjectives	
this, that, these, those	*This* streetcar goes to Chinatown.
	These padlocks have rusted.
Interrogative Adjectives	
which, what, whose	*Which* orchard do you own?
	What handgrip is best in golf?
Indefinite Adjectives	
Used with singular nouns: another, each, either, little, much, neither, one	*Each* cruiser flew a flag.
Used with plural nouns: both, few, many, several	*Several* choirs competed for top honors.
Used with singular or plural nouns: all, any, more, most, other, some	Put on *any* record that you want.
	Any clothes you donate will be appreciated.

When a verb serves as an adjective, it usually ends in *-ed* or *-ing* and is called a *participle.*

VERBS USED AS ADJECTIVES

The *calculating* salesperson made a sizable profit.

They considered themselves *enlightened* parents.

Remember that nouns, pronouns, and verbs function as adjectives only when they modify other nouns or pronouns. Study the following examples to see how their function in a sentence can shift.

	Regular Function	**As an Adjective**
Noun	The *deck* of the boat tilted.	I sat in the *deck* chair.
Pronoun	*This* was an idyllic life.	*This* life was idyllic.
Verb	The grease *splattered* the walls.	I cleaned the *splattered* walls.

Order of Adjectives.   When two or more adjectives are used before a noun, they usually follow one another in a recognizable order, beginning with an article and ending with the noun.

TYPICAL ORDER OF ADJECTIVES	
Article or pronoun used as an adjective	a or your
Size	large
Age	old
Color	green
Participle	hand-blown
Proper adjective	French
Noun used as an adjective	wine
Noun	bottle

Though variations are possible, the general pattern will usually hold true. An article will always be first; a noun used as an adjective will always come directly before the noun.

EXERCISE A: **Identifying Adjectives.** The underlined words in the following paragraph are either nouns or pronouns. Copy each word onto your paper and write all of the adjectives, if any, that modify it. Be prepared to point out any nouns, pronouns, or verbs used as adjectives.

Dresden, an East German (1) <u>city</u>, houses some of the greatest art (2) <u>treasures</u> in the world. From the sixteenth (3) <u>century</u> to the eighteenth century, the Saxon (4) <u>electors</u> collected art from the four (5) <u>corners</u> of the globe and brought them to this (6) <u>location.</u> Though the Saxon (7) <u>reign</u> was short-lived, the treasures have not been; most (8) <u>pieces</u> even survived the Allied (9) <u>bombing</u> of Dresden during World War II. Today, the public can view the delicate Oriental (10) <u>porcelain</u> collected by Augustus the Strong and see the sensitive, moving (11) <u>paintings</u> of great (12) <u>masters</u> such as Rubens and Vermeer. The Green Vault holds the precious (13) <u>metals</u> and jewels created by the best European (14) <u>artisans.</u> One display contains shining diamond boot (15) <u>buckles</u> and jeweled shirt (16) <u>buttons.</u> To estimate the (17) <u>value</u> of these (18) <u>treasures</u> would prove virtually impossible; (19) <u>many</u> are priceless. For example, at one auction, eight Meissen china (20) <u>pieces</u> from the collection sold for $313,720.

EXERCISE B: **Putting Adjectives in Order.** Each of the following italicized words is a noun. Put the adjectives following it in proper order and write the entire phrase on your paper.

EXAMPLE: *jacket*—down-filled, new, winter, a

a new down-filled winter jacket

1. *sports car*—British, that, new, shiny, red
2. *road*—dirt, a, winding, narrow
3. *vase*—small, this, hand-painted, Japanese
4. *insects*—flying, iridescent, many
5. *coin*—bronze, ancient, the, Roman, battered

EXERCISE C: **Using Adjectives in Your Own Writing.** Pick one of the following items and use your imagination to describe it in five or six sentences. Use as many different adjectives as you effectively can. Try to be original; do not start your description with such words as "It looks like . . ." or "It was . . . ."

A well-known political figure
A national landmark or restored historical site
A piece of art
The aftermath of a disaster you have seen
A character from literature

■ Adverbs

Adverbs, like adjectives, describe other words or make other words more specific.

An **adverb** is a word that modifies a verb, an adjective, or another adverb.

When an adverb modifies a verb, it will answer any of the following questions: *Where? When? In what manner?* or *To what extent?* An adverb answers only one question, however, when modifying an adjective or another adverb: *To what extent?* Because it specifies the degree or intensity of the modified adjective or adverb, an adverb used in this manner is often called an *intensifier.*

The position of an adverb in relation to the word it modifies can vary in a sentence. If the adverb modifies a verb, it may precede or follow the verb or even interrupt a verb phrase. Normally, adverbs modifying adjectives and adverbs will immediately precede the word they modify.

Study the following chart, which shows adverbs in various positions modifying verbs, adjectives, and other adverbs.

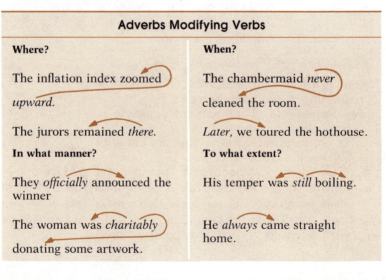

Adverbs Modifying Verbs	
Where?	**When?**
The inflation index zoomed *upward*.	The chambermaid *never* cleaned the room.
The jurors remained *there*.	*Later*, we toured the hothouse.
In what manner?	**To what extent?**
They *officially* announced the winner	His temper was *still* boiling.
The woman was *charitably* donating some artwork.	He *always* came straight home.

Adverbs Modifying Adjectives	Adverbs Modifying Adverbs
To what extent?	**To what extent?**
The solution was *quite* logical.	The dentist performed *very* competently.
I bit into an *extremely* sour orange.	The parachute did *not* completely open.

Adverbs as Parts of Verbs.   Some verbs require an adverb to complete their meaning. Adverbs used this way are considered part of the verb. An adverb functioning as an integral part of a verb does not answer the usual questions for adverbs.

EXAMPLES: The car *backed up* along the curb.

The fighter *knocked out* his opponent.

Nouns Functioning as Adverbs.   Several nouns can function as adverbs that answer the question *Where?* or *When?* Some of these words are *home, yesterday, today, tomorrow, mornings, afternoons, evenings, nights, week, month,* and *year.*

NOUNS USED AS ADVERBS	
Nouns	**As Adverbs**
Evenings are my favorite time of day.	I work *evenings.* (Work *when?*)
My *home* is five miles from here.	Let's head *home.* (Head *where?*)

Adverb or Adjective?   Adverbs usually have different forms from adjectives and thus are easily identified. Many adverbs are, in fact, formed by the addition of *-ly* to an adjective.

ADJECTIVE: Our professor looked *pensive.*

ADVERB: The professor looked at her notes *pensively.*

Some adjectives, however, also end in *-ly;* therefore, you cannot assume that every word ending in *-ly* is an adverb.

ADJECTIVES: a *grisly* scene

a *nightly* jaunt

Some adjectives and adverbs even share the same form. You can determine the part of speech of such words by checking their function in the sentence. An adverb will modify a verb, adjective, or adverb; an adjective will modify a noun or pronoun.

ADVERB: The concert ran *late*.

ADJECTIVE: We enjoyed the *late* dinners in Spain.

EXERCISE D: Identifying Adverbs. Each of the following sentences contains one to four adverbs. Copy the sentences onto your paper. Underline each adverb and then draw an arrow from it to the word it modifies.

1. Yesterday, the architects sketchily explained the plans they have for the office building.
2. A southerly storm approached quickly, drenching the area with an extremely heavy downpour.
3. Almost apologetically, the girl presented her handmade gift.
4. The roller coaster raced crazily up and down before eventually releasing its dizzy passengers.
5. Her ghastly pallor was attributed to the extremely long illness from which she had recently recovered.
6. My hand jerked involuntarily and sent my glass crashing violently to the floor.
7. The delivery person found my note but apparently did not read it carefully.
8. Though it was an uphill battle, I was extremely pleased with the final product.
9. His manly physique certainly helped him win the role in the repertory's newest production.
10. Yesterday, the guest speaker prattled continuously and monotonously for two hours.

EXERCISE E: Adding Adverbs to Sentences. Copy the following sentences onto your paper, adding at least one adverb. If necessary, change the wording of the sentence. Do not use the same adverb more than once.

1. Since the War of 1812, the symbol of Uncle Sam has characterized the American government.

2. This famous nickname was born from the initials put on barrels of salted meat by an army meat inspector.
3. Citizens in New York and Vermont liked the nickname and began to use it.
4. Uncle Sam achieved fame in 1813 when he was pictured in a Troy, New York, newspaper.
5. By 1830 Uncle Sam had donned his splashy costume of stars and stripes.
6. A clown dressed as Uncle Sam delighted crowds during the 1800's and helped to popularize the costume.
7. In 1813 most cartoonists depicted Uncle Sam as a young man.
8. By 1917 he had grown older.
9. During World War I, Uncle Sam pointed his wrinkled finger at the men across the country and declared, "I want you."
10. Congress made him a national symbol in 1961.

APPLICATION: **Writing Sentences with Adjectives and Adverbs.** The underlined word in each of the following sentences is either an adjective or an adverb. If the word is an adjective, write an original sentence of your own in which you use it as an adverb. If the word is an adverb, write a sentence using it as an adjective.

1. The <u>straight</u> ribbon of freeway led across the desert.
2. The shovel bit <u>deep</u> into the black soil.
3. I solved the <u>hard</u> algebra problem quite easily.
4. The flagman motioned the car <u>right</u>.
5. The building jutted <u>high</u> into the sky.
6. I left at six for an <u>early</u> appointment.
7. The boy consumed <u>more</u> spaghetti.
8. The vise will hold the wood <u>tight</u> until the glue dries.
9. She did <u>well</u> on her driver's examination.
10. We visited him <u>daily</u> in the hospital.

Prepositions, Conjunctions, and Interjections   1.4

Two of the final three parts of speech—prepositions and conjunctions—function in sentences as connectors. *Prepositions* express relationships between words or ideas, whereas *conjunctions* join words, groups of words, or even entire sentences.

The last part of speech, *interjections*, functions by itself, independent of other words in a sentence.

■ Prepositions

Prepositions enable a speaker or writer to show relationships between words. The relationships shown by prepositions may involve, for example, location, direction, time, cause, or possession.

A **preposition** relates the noun or pronoun following it to another word in the sentence.

Study the following chart so that you can recognize all prepositions on sight. Notice that some prepositions are *compound*—that is, they are made up of more than one word.

PREPOSITIONS			
aboard	before	in front of	over
about	behind	in place of	owing to
above	below	in regard to	past
according to	beneath	inside	prior to
across	beside	in spite of	regarding
after	besides	instead of	round
against	between	into	since
ahead of	beyond	in view of	through
along	but	like	throughout
alongside	by	near	till
along with	by means of	nearby	to
amid	concerning	next to	together with
among	considering	of	toward
apart from	despite	off	under
around	down	on	underneath
as of	during	on account of	until
aside from	except	onto	unto
at	for	on top of	up
atop	from	opposite	upon
barring	in	out	with
because of	in addition to	out of	within
	in back of	outside	without

In the following examples, notice how the prepositions relate the italicized words.

LOCATION: The brush fire *burned* **Prep** atop the *hill.*

DIRECTION: The brush fire *burned* **Prep** toward our *campsite.*

TIME: The fire *burned* **Prep** for three *days.*

CAUSE: The brush fire *started* **Prep** because of *carelessness.*

POSSESSION: *Smoke* **Prep** from the *fire* could be seen for miles.

Prepositional Phrases.   A preposition is always part of a *prepositional phrase.* These phrases are groups of words beginning with a preposition and ending with a noun or pronoun called the *object of the preposition.* The object may be preceded by one or more modifiers. A prepositional phrase may also contain more than one object.

EXAMPLES: I walked slightly *ahead of* **Obj** *her.*

The shampoo bottle *on the* **Obj** *shelf* was almost empty.

We were adopted *by a lovable, brown-eyed* **Obj** *mongrel.*

The new housing development is located *near stores and* **Obj** *schools.* **Obj**

In some sentences, especially questions, a prepositional phrase may be broken up.

EXAMPLES: *What* **Obj** were we talking *about?* **Prep**

Where **Obj** did this come *from?* **Prep**

For more information about prepositional phrases, see Section 3.1.

Preposition or Adverb?   Since prepositions and adverbs occasionally take the same form, they may be difficult to tell apart. Among the words that can function in either role are *around, behind, before, down, in, off, on, out, over,* and *up.* To determine the part of speech of these words, see if an object accompanies the word. If so, the word is used as a preposition.

PREPOSITION: The child ran *out the* **Obj** *door.*

ADVERB: The physician was *out.*

EXERCISE A: **Identifying Prepositional Phrases.** Write the prepositional phrases from each sentence in the following paragraph on your paper and circle each preposition.

(1) The thrill of cross-country skiing is infecting people around the globe. (2) The sport originated across the Atlantic Ocean in the Scandinavian countries and was brought to the United States by Scandinavian settlers. (3) According to recent figures, more than two million people are now cross-country skiers. (4) Cross-country skiers can compete for prizes in races held around the world. (5) A Norwegian race, the Birkenbeiner, honors two skiers who heroically carried a Norwegian prince to safety amid a civil war in the early thirteenth century. (6) The skiers were called "birch legs" or "birkenbeiner" because of the birch that they wrapped around their legs for warmth. (7) Californians hold the Snowshoe Thompson Race, named after a mail carrier. (8) By means of cross-country skiing, this man regularly carried the mail ninety miles through the Sierras. (9) The most popular cross-country race, however, is probably the one in Sweden called the Vasaloppet. (10) Ten thousand people gather every year for this competition.

EXERCISE B: **Distinguishing Between Prepositions and Adverbs.** Identify the underlined word in each of the following sentences as either a *preposition* or an *adverb*. If the word is a preposition, write its object on your paper as well.

1. A college student shimmied <u>up</u> the flagpole.
2. The sun went <u>down</u> behind the hill.
3. The lights were mistakenly left <u>on</u> overnight.
4. When she went <u>away</u>, we left as well.
5. The elephant suddenly turned <u>around</u> and charged.
6. We remained <u>behind</u> after the others had left.
7. A button on my blazer fell <u>off.</u>
8. The valley lies <u>below</u> sea level.
9. The antique chair was <u>in</u> good condition.
10. For dinner the couple went <u>out</u> and had a leisurely meal.

EXERCISE C: **Using Prepositional Phrases.** Copy the following sentences onto your paper, adding a prepositional phrase that provides the information requested in the parentheses. The last two sentences require the addition of more than one prepositional phrase.

1. I longingly watched the sailing vessels.   (location)
2. The porter carried the woman's valise.   (cause)
3. The snow level topped three feet.   (time)

4. The pungent odor assailed my senses. (possession)
5. Monorails will provide the transportation. (possession)
6. Several motel rooms were burglarized. (time)
7. The hound retrieved the fallen duck. (location)
8. We won the championship. (cause)
9. The bats flew erratically. (time, direction)
10. The dormitory had no electricity. (possession, cause)

■ Conjunctions

Conjunctions are the words that join other words within sentences.

A conjunction is a word used to connect other words or groups of words.

There are three main kinds of conjunctions in English: *co-ordinating, correlative,* and *subordinating.* Sometimes a kind of adverb, the *conjunctive adverb,* is considered a conjunction.

Coordinating Conjunctions. The seven coordinating conjunctions are used to connect similar parts of speech or groups of words of equal grammatical weight.

COORDINATING CONJUNCTIONS			
and	for	or	yet
but	nor	so	

WITH NOUNS AND PRONOUNS: Inge *and* I attended the lecture series together.

WITH VERBS: Our dog whined *and* scratched at the screen door.

WITH ADJECTIVES: The veal cutlet was tender, large, *yet* tasteless.

WITH ADVERBS: The man responded quickly *but* incorrectly.

WITH PREPOSITIONAL PHRASES: I will play at second base *or* in right field.

WITH DEPENDENT IDEAS: The agency indicated that jobs were available *but* that qualified personnel to fill them were not.

WITH COMPLETE IDEAS: He seemed distressed, *so* we discussed his problem.

Correlative Conjunctions.   Working in pairs, the five correlative conjunctions join elements of equal grammatical weight in sentences in much the same manner as coordinating conjunctions do.

CORRELATIVE CONJUNCTIONS
both . . . and   either . . . or   neither . . . nor
not only . . . but also   whether . . . or

WITH NOUNS: *Both* the employers *and* the employees agreed on Article 9.

WITH NOUNS AND PRONOUNS: Call *either* Bob *or* me if you need additional help.

WITH ADJECTIVES: The diamond was *not only* brilliant *but also* flawless.

WITH PREPOSITIONAL PHRASES: Put the check *either* in the drawer *or* beside the telephone.

WITH COMPLETE IDEAS: *Neither* did the swelling go down *nor* did the pain subside.

Subordinating Conjunctions.   Subordinating conjunctions join two complete ideas by making one of them subordinate—that is, dependent on the other.

SUBORDINATING CONJUNCTIONS			
after	because	lest	till
although	before	now that	unless
as	even if	provided	until
as if	even though	since	when

as long as	how	so that	whenever
as much as	if	than	where
as soon as	inasmuch as	that	wherever
as though	in order that	though	while

The dependent idea always begins with a subordinating conjunction and is known as a *subordinate clause.* (For more information about clauses, see Section 3.3.) A subordinate clause may precede or follow the main clause.

EXAMPLES:

               Indep Idea   Dep Idea

The referees watched carefully *lest* they miss a key play.

           Dep Idea   Indep Idea

Although the fumigator sprayed, the termites remained.

When trying to identify subordinating conjunctions, remember that some of these conjunctions can also function as prepositions or adverbs. *After, before, since, till,* and *until* often act as prepositions; *after, before, when,* and *where* often act as adverbs.

SUBORDINATING CONJUNCTION: *After* the billboards were removed, the area's natural beauty was restored.

PREPOSITION: The main course was served *after* the salad.

ADVERB: The parade began at noon and ended three hours *after.*

Conjunctive Adverbs. Conjunctive adverbs act as connectors between complete ideas by indicating comparisons, contrasts, results, and other relationships.

CONJUNCTIVE ADVERBS		
accordingly	for example	nevertheless
again	furthermore	on the other hand
also	however	otherwise
besides	in addition	then
consequently	indeed	therefore
finally	moreover	thus

As shown in the following examples, punctuation is usually required both before and after conjunctive adverbs. (For a more thorough discussion of the punctuation of conjunctive adverbs, see Sections 12.2 and 12.3.)

EXAMPLES: The doctor did help my back problem; *however,* I still experience occasional pain.

The earthquake damaged the wall structure. *Moreover,* it broke some water pipes.

My hay fever grew worse. I, *nevertheless,* refused to remain inside.

EXERCISE D: Identifying Conjunctions in Sentences. Each of the following sentences contains one conjunction. Write each conjunction on your paper and identify it as *coordinating, correlative,* or *subordinating.*

1. The physics instructor explained the theory, but I did not understand it.
2. Roger is significantly taller than Doug is.
3. You should eat salads, since they are good for your digestion.
4. I checked several banquet facilities before I finally chose this one.
5. Unless you reform, you will be dismissed.
6. I burned my tongue, for the soup was still too hot to eat.
7. Whenever the shepherd gave the order, the dog began to round up strays.
8. Not only can you do some packing, but you can also carry out some boxes.
9. Persimmons and pumpkins can be used to make excellent spice cookies.
10. Now that the harvest is behind them, the farmers can relax.

EXERCISE E: Distinguishing Between Subordinating Conjunctions, Prepositions, and Adverbs. Identify each underlined word in the following sentences as a *subordinating conjunction, preposition,* or *adverb.*

1. Shirley rented a typewriter <u>until</u> the end of the month.
2. <u>Where</u> do you keep the napkins?
3. They bought more exotic fish <u>after</u> they had experimented with goldfish.
4. My relatives had toured Europe four times <u>before</u>.
5. You should see Maine <u>where</u> the thick forests come right to the ocean's edge.
6. <u>When</u> did the school board vote on that issue?
7. I haven't skied <u>since</u> last February.
8. Louis stayed on board <u>till</u> the final warning bell forced him to leave.

9. We refinanced the house <u>because</u> we needed money.
10. We had dinner <u>before</u> the performance.

EXERCISE F: Using Conjunctive Adverbs. Rewrite the following pairs of sentences by adding an appropriate conjunctive adverb.

EXAMPLE: Many scholars believe that Homer wrote *The Iliad* and *The Odyssey*. Some scholars claim that he never existed.

EXAMPLE: Many scholars believe that Homer wrote *The Iliad* and *The Odyssey*. Some scholars, however, claim that he never existed.

1. The mythological gods had unearthly powers. They possessed many human frailties.
2. One of the most common themes in mythology is love. Many stories tell of lovers' betrayals, loyalties, passions, and jealousies.
3. Aphrodite refused Zeus' love. He gave her hand in marriage to his deformed son Hephaestus.
4. Hera, wife of Zeus, has been called mythology's most jealous wife. She spied on all of Zeus' actions.
5. Other gods participated in dramatic adventures. They often fought in battles against huge odds.
6. Herakles captured the Cretan bull. He strangled the Nemian lion.
7. Hades ruled the underworld. In literature hell is often referred to as Hades.
8. Upon his death Sisyphus was condemned to roll a stone up a hill in Hades. The stone always rolled back down.
9. The winged horse Pegasus has become a symbol of poetic inspiration. A constellation is named after him.
10. Phidias, a Greek, was inspired to sculpt the statue of Olympian Zeus. He did one of Athena Parthenos.

■ Interjections

Interjections express emotion. These words, however, have no grammatical connection to other words in a sentence.

An **interjection** is a word that expresses feeling or emotion and functions independently of a sentence.

Interjections can express a variety of sentiments, such as happiness, fear, anger, pain, surprise, sorrow, exhaustion, or hesitation.

SOME COMMON INTERJECTIONS				
ah	dear	help	oh	tsk
aha	goodness	hey	ouch	well
alas	gracious	hurray	psst	whew

Commas or exclamation marks usually set off an interjection from the rest of the sentence, as the following examples demonstrate.

EXAMPLES: *Ouch!* That bee sting throbs!

Goodness, if you don't leave now, I will be late!

EXERCISE G: **Using Interjections.** Write five sentences containing interjections that express the following general emotions. Underline the interjections in your sentences.

1. indecision
2. sorrow
3. urgency
4. exhaustion
5. fear

APPLICATION: **Using Prepositions and Conjunctions in Sentences.** Follow the instructions to write five sentences of your own.

1. Write a sentence containing two prepositions.
2. Write a sentence containing two coordinating conjunctions.
3. Write a sentence containing one preposition and one correlative conjunction.
4. Write a sentence containing two prepositions and one subordinating conjunction.
5. Write a sentence containing one coordinating conjunction and one subordinating conjunction.

1.5   Determining Parts of Speech by Function

Words are flexible, often serving as one part of speech in one sentence and as another part of speech in another. To assume, therefore, that once a word is identified as a noun it is always a noun will lead to confusion. A word's part of speech should be determined only by the way it is used in a sentence.

How a word is used in a sentence determines its part of speech.

Notice, for example the many functions of the word *outside.*

AS A NOUN: The *outside* of the house desperately needed painting.

AS AN ADJECTIVE: It was an *outside* chance, but I took it anyway.

AS AN ADVERB: The children played *outside.*

AS A PREPOSITION: We drove *outside* the city boundaries.

■ Recognizing Parts of Speech

The following chart suggests questions to ask yourself when you are trying to identify a word's part of speech in a sentence.

Part of Speech	Questions to Ask Yourself	Examples
Noun	Does the word name a person, place, or thing?	The *chancellor* at *Harvard University* carried the *mace.*
Pronoun	Does the word stand for a noun?	*You* lent *most* of *them* to *me.*
Verb	Does the word tell what someone or something did?	I *duplicated* the notes.
	Does the word link the noun or pronoun before it with an adjective or noun that follows?	The flag *was* colorful. She *sounded* sincere.
	Does the word merely indicate that something exists?	The plane *will be* there.
Adjective	Does the word tell what kind, which one, how many, or how much?	*A few singing* telegrams were ordered.
Adverb	Does the word tell where, when, in what manner, or to what extent?	This elevator goes *up.* We perform *next.* Talk very *softly.* The brooch was *certainly* exquisite.

Preposition	Is the word part of a phrase that ends with a noun or pronoun?	*Beyond our hedge* wild brush grows *in abundance.*
Conjunction	Does the word connect other words in the sentence?	*Because* the time changed, *both* you *and* I arrived late; *however*, the group waited.
Interjection	Does the word express emotion and function independently of the sentence?	*Oh,* report about 7:00; *well,* maybe that is too early.

EXERCISE A: Identifying Parts of Speech. In the following paragraph, words have been underlined and numbered. Identify the part of speech of each underlined word on your paper.

(1) Some say that creative minds are (2) restless minds, and (3) when they speak of Vincent van Gogh, (4) they may well be right. As a young child, (5) Vincent was not (6) very well-behaved and (7) often turned (8) upon himself. He started school rather late, (9) but, dissatisfied with the system, he eventually dropped out. Vincent started drawing at age eight, impressing (10) his family with his clever sketches. While he pursued his art career during the course of his life, he (11) was supported by his brother, Theo. (12) Restlessly, he sought his own style but was influenced largely by (13) the impressionist painters. It was not (14) until 1885 that a painting of his, *The Potato Eaters*, received (15) popular acclaim. But (16) alas, even (17) recognition did (18) not satisfy him. (19) Consequently, he experienced severe (20) mental disturbances, (21) and at one point, (22) entered a sanitarium at St. Remy. Vincent van Gogh (23) could not seem to escape the depression that gripped him, and (24) thus in 1890, this (25) talented painter committed suicide.

EXERCISE B: Identifying Troublesome Parts of Speech. In each of the following sentences, two words have been underlined. Identify the part of speech of each one on your paper.

1. We were bowling with a borrowed bowling ball.
2. I went early to avoid the early morning traffic.
3. Many of us felt that there were many injustices in the law.
4. Well, I think I will do well on the upcoming examination.
5. Put down that package and come down the steps.

6. I <u>left</u> the store and turned <u>left.</u>
7. <u>Goodness</u>, I really do hate to see such <u>goodness</u> go unpraised.
8. <u>Post</u> this notice in front of the <u>post</u> office.
9. We wanted <u>neither</u> of the choices offered, but <u>neither</u> Jim nor I was in a position to bargain.
10. We called in a <u>carpet</u> cleaner to clean our <u>carpet.</u>

APPLICATION: Using Words as Different Parts of Speech. Construct sentences of your own using the following words as indicated.

1. a. Use *dear* as an adjective.
   b. Use *dear* as an interjection.
2. a. Use *by* as an adverb.
   b. Use *by* as a preposition.
3. a. Use *several* as a pronoun.
   b. Use *several* as an adjective.
4. a. Use *sleep* as a verb.
   b. Use *sleep* as a noun.
5. a. Use *talking* as a noun.
   b. Use *talking* as an adjective.

2

Basic Sentence Parts and Patterns

When infants first begin to speak, they utter a single word to convey their needs. Later, children begin to compose sentences containing both a subject and an action. By the age of four or five, most children have become familiar with the basic sentence patterns. With time, their sentences take on greater complexity and sophistication. In studying a language, it often helps to view it as a child learns it—looking first at the basic parts of sentences and then using that knowledge to examine more difficult sentence patterns. This chapter will focus on how parts of speech are combined to form sentences.

2.1 Subjects and Verbs

Language is the tool with which people shape their ideas and communicate them to others. For the communication to be meaningful, a speaker or writer must choose appropriate words and put them in an order that the listener or reader can follow and understand. Unfortunately, many things can interfere with this process. A writer, for example, may use words that a reader does not understand. The resulting breakdown in communication is easily repaired if the reader takes the time to use a dictionary. But if the writer fails to put the words in an understandable order, the reader most likely will become hopelessly confused.

In any language, the basic order of words that expresses meaning is the sentence. In English, every sentence has two essential parts, a *complete subject* and a *complete predicate*, which in turn comprise other parts. Being aware of these parts and of how they are related can help you in your speaking and writing to avoid unintentionally letting the order of your words get in the way of your ideas.

■ Complete Subjects and Complete Predicates

A group of words in English is considered a sentence when it has two parts, either clearly stated or implied.

> A **sentence** is a group of words with two main parts: a **complete subject** and a **complete predicate.** Together, these parts express a complete thought.

The complete subject contains the noun, pronoun, or group of words acting as a noun, plus their modifiers, that tells *who* or *what* the sentence is about. Located in the complete predicate is the verb or verb phrase, plus any modifiers and complements, that tells what the complete subject *does* or *is*. (For more information about complements, see Section 2.3.) The length of a complete subject and complete predicate can vary greatly.

Complete Subject	Complete Predicate
Flowers	bloom.
A bell-clanging street car	moved through the intersection.
A soufflé or quiche	is a delicious main dish.
The candidate's pragmatic approach to fiscal problems	impressed the voters attending the rally and fund-raising party at Davis Park last Thursday.

In some sentences, a portion of the predicate may precede the complete subject. In the following example, *at noon* modifies *watched.*

EXAMPLE: At noon, we watched the changing of the guard.

Complete Subj

Complete Pred

EXERCISE A: Recognizing Complete Subjects and Complete Predicates. Recopy the following paragraph, drawing a slash between each complete subject and complete predicate. Some sentences may require more than one slash.

(1) Morning came quickly, much too early for our liking. (2) Long before sunrise, the alarm clock rang. (3) Sluggishly, we dragged ourselves from a restful sleep. (4) At 5:00 o'clock we left the dock. (5) We were sailing out of San Francisco Bay on an enormous yacht equipped with every modern convenience possible. (6) From bow to stern, the boat measured forty feet. (7) During the night, a fog had crept in. (8) Nestling on top of the ocean, it limited visibility and made the air very cold. (9) Sophisticated directional equipment led us through the fog, out to the open sea. (10) Inside the luxurious cabin we were warm and dry and eager to begin our day of deep-sea fishing.

■ Fragments

When either the complete subject or complete predicate is missing, the resulting group of words does not constitute a sentence; instead, it is called a *fragment,* which is usually considered an error in writing.

A **fragment** is a group of words that does not express a complete thought.

You can correct a fragment by adding the missing parts.

Fragments	Complete Sentences
People with respiratory ailments. (Complete predicate missing.)	People with respiratory ailments *should avoid smog-ridden cities.* (Complete predicate added.)
Swerved into a fire hydrant. (Complete subject missing.)	*The speeding car* swerved into a fire hydrant. (Complete subject added.)
In the new concert hall. (Complete subject and complete predicate missing.)	*Minor adjustments* in the new concert hall *improved the acoustics.* (Complete predicate and rest of complete subject added.)

In conversations, fragments usually do not present a problem since repetition, tone of voice, gestures, and facial expressions all help to communicate meaning. In writing, however, fragments should be avoided since the reader is alone with the words on the page and cannot go to the writer for clarification.

An exception, of course, is writing that represents speech, such as the dialogue in a play or short story. Even then, fragments must be used carefully so that the reader can follow the flow of ideas.

Another exception in writing is the occasional use of *elliptical sentences,* in which the missing word or words can be easily understood.

ELLIPTICAL SENTENCES: Until later.

Why the sad face?

For more information about fragments and how to correct them, see Section 4.1.

EXERCISE B: **Locating and Correcting Sentence Fragments.** For each of the following groups of words that is a sentence, write *complete* on your paper. If the group of words is a fragment, rewrite it, adding the necessary part to make it complete.

1. His mother, a gentle, yet strong woman.
2. Stepped from the boat after a rugged trip across the Atlantic.
3. Diane dipped her doughnut into her coffee before taking a bite.
4. Into the sky filled with dark thunderclouds.
5. The car's hood, hot from the sun's rays.
6. Sat around the campfire, roasting marshmallows.
7. The spider wove a beautiful, yet deadly web.
8. An old alligator with its thick, valuable hide.
9. My traveling companion carried a lightweight suitcase aboard the plane.
10. Under the weight of numerous responsibilities.

■ Simple Subjects and Simple Predicates

When all modifiers and complements are removed from a complete subject and complete predicate, an essential word or group of words remains in each. These essential elements, called the *simple subject* and *simple predicate,* are the core around which sentences are developed.

The **simple subject** is the essential noun, pronoun, or group of words acting as a noun that cannot be left out of the complete subject.

The **simple predicate** is the essential verb or verb phrase that cannot be left out of the complete predicate.

The following chart shows simple subjects underlined once and simple predicates underlined twice. Notice how any remaining words either modify the simple subject and simple predicate or enable the simple predicate to complete the meaning of the sentence.

SIMPLE SUBJECTS AND SIMPLE PREDICATES	
Complete Subject	**Complete Predicate**
Small pocket <u>calculators</u>	<u>fit</u> nicely into coat pockets.
<u>Ronald Reagan</u>	<u>starred</u> in many films in his early career.
<u>Pictures</u> of Saturn	<u>have</u> certainly <u>revealed</u> much about the planet.

Notice in the last example that the simple subject is *pictures*, not *Saturn*, which is the object of the preposition *of*. Objects of prepositions never function as simple subjects. In this same example, notice also that the simple predicate is a verb phrase interrupted by an adverb.

NOTE ABOUT TERMINOLOGY: From now on in this text, the term *subject* will be used to refer to a simple subject, and the term *verb* will be used to refer to a simple predicate. Whenever subjects and verbs need to be indicated in examples, subjects will be underlined once and verbs will be underlined twice.

Locating Subjects and Verbs.   You can employ either of two methods for locating subjects and verbs in sentences to help you check your own writing and avoid fragments. The first method involves locating the subject first. Ask, "What word tells what this sentence is about?" Once you have the answer—in other words, the subject—then ask, "What did the subject do?" This gives you the verb.

Some people, however, prefer to find the verb first. In this case, ask first, "What is the action verb or linking verb in the sentence?" This question should give you the verb. Then ask, "Who or what?" before it. The resulting word or words will be the subject.

Watch these methods applied to the following example.

EXAMPLE: African termites build huge mud castles up to twenty feet high.

To find the subject, first ask, "What word tells what this sentence is about?

ANSWER: termites (*Termites* is the subject.)

Then ask, "What did the termites do?"

ANSWER: build (*Build* is the verb.)

To find the verb first, ask, "What is the action verb or linking verb in this sentence?"

ANSWER: build (*Build* is an action verb.)

To find the subject using this answer, ask, "Who or what build?"

ANSWER: termites (*Termites* is the subject.)

Sometimes, a sentence contains numerous modifiers, making isolation of the subject and verb very difficult. Simplify these sentences by mentally crossing out adjectives, adverbs, and prepositional phrases.

EXAMPLE: The business of home computers should grow extensively in the next ten years.

With the skeletal sentence that remains, you can easily use one of the two methods just introduced to determine the subject and verb. (For information about subjects and verbs in more complicated sentences, see Sections 2.2, 3.3, and 3.4.)

More Than One Subject or Verb. So far, the examples in this section have contained only one subject and one verb. Sometimes, however, a sentence may contain a *compound subject* or *compound verb*.

A **compound subject** is two or more subjects that have the same verb and are joined by a conjunction such as *and* or *or*.

EXAMPLES: The <u>train</u> and <u>car</u> <u>collided</u> at the intersection.

<u>Nickels</u>, <u>dimes</u>, or <u>quarters</u> <u>are used</u> in these meters.

Like subjects, verbs can be compound.

A **compound verb** is two or more verbs that have the same subject and are joined by a conjunction such as *and* or *or*.

EXAMPLES: I neither <u>saw</u> them nor <u>overheard</u> their conversation.

The <u>sailors</u> <u>were stranded</u> by a storm and <u>shouted</u> frantically for help.

Some sentences may contain both a compound subject and a compound verb.

EXAMPLE: The private <u>plane</u> and the <u>airliner</u> <u>flew</u> too close, <u>touched</u> wing tips, and almost <u>crashed</u>.

EXERCISE C: **Identifying Subjects and Verbs.** Copy each of the following sentences onto your paper. Then, draw a slash between the complete subject and complete predicate. Finally, underline the subject once and the verb twice.

1. Some apes have been taught words and simple sentences.
2. Thomas Alva Edison invented the ticker tape machine, his first big moneymaker.
3. Many of the current television programs are airing sensitive, controversial issues.
4. Members of the Coast Guard rescued the passengers of the sinking ocean liner.
5. A glittering Monte Carlo lures the wealthy to its port.
6. The behavior of sharks has been studied by biologists.
7. Intricate ironwork decorated the outside of the stately New Orleans home.
8. People in stressful situations will often show symptoms of fatigue.
9. The longhaired Beatles from Liverpool changed the music of the Sixties.
10. New York is the setting for many pieces of American literature.

EXERCISE D: **Locating Compound Subjects and Compound Verbs.** Each of the following sentences contains either a compound subject, compound verb, or both. Write the subject and verb for each sentence on your paper.

1. The rod and reel stood in the corner ready for use.
2. We headed south for a mile and then turned east.
3. Either George Burns or Bob Hope would get my vote for best comedian.

4. Shoppers and salespersons felt the tension of the holidays and snapped at one another.
5. Both Sara and Blythe liked the story "The Lie" by Kurt Vonnegut, Jr.
6. The talented circus troupe balanced on high wires and swung from trapezes.
7. She stared at the problem and speculated on its answer.
8. Neither the Alaskan cruise nor the tour of English inns had tickets still available.
9. Both bees and hummingbirds gather nectar and pollinate flowers.
10. We built, sanded, and stained those tables.

APPLICATION: Developing Sentences from Subjects and Verbs. Write sentences of your own using the following kinds of subjects and verbs. Make sure the sentences are complete. Use adjectives, adverbs, prepositional phrases, and conjunctions where appropriate.

1. <u>fields</u> + verb phrase
2. compound subject + <u>were driven</u>
3. <u>President-elect</u> + compound verb
4. compound subject + <u>surfed and swam</u>
5. <u>the accountant and lawyer</u> + compound verb phrase

Subjects in Different Kinds of Sentences 2.2

Finding subjects and verbs enables you to check your sentences for logic, clarity, and completeness. Most often, the subject will precede the verb, making identification easy. Sometimes, however, the subject will assume another position in the sentence when the purpose of the sentence changes. This section will first explain the four functions of English sentences and then examine the positions that subjects can hold.

■ The Four Functions of Sentences

All complete sentences contain a subject and verb, but not all sentences function in the same way. Although they may share the same basic sentence parts, sentences have different patterns to convey different purposes. In English all sentences can be classified according to one of four functions: *declarative, interrogative, imperative,* and *exclamatory.*

A *declarative* sentence, the most common sentence in English, is used to express facts and opinions.

A **declarative** sentence states an idea and ends with a period.

EXAMPLES: The U.S. Postal Service issued a Carl Sandburg commemorative stamp.

Most people do not enjoy taking risks.

To pose a question, an *interrogative* sentence is used.

A **interrogative** sentence asks a question and ends with a question mark.

EXAMPLES: What harm did the delay cause?

Who designed the Guggenheim Museum?

Demands or requests are conveyed through *imperative* sentences.

An **imperative** sentence gives an order or direction and ends with a period or exclamation mark.

Since imperative sentences often express force or emotion, an exclamation mark rather than a period may be placed at the end of the sentence.

EXAMPLES: Call the insurance agent, please.

Watch out for that car!

The last type of sentence, the *exclamatory* sentence, is used to convey strong emotion.

An **exclamatory** sentence conveys emotion and ends with an exclamation mark.

As the first two of the following examples show, declarative and interrogative sentences are classified as exclamatory sentences when their primary purpose is to express strong emotion. Imperative sentences that show strong emotion can be classified as either imperative or exclamatory. Finally, some sentences such as the last of the following examples, a sentence with an understood subject and verb, are purely exclamatory.

EXAMPLES: The new baby just arrived! (declarative)

Isn't her voice magnificent! (interrogative)

Catch that thief! (imperative)

Ouch!

EXERCISE A: **Identifying the Four Functions of Sentences.** Read each sentence in the following account. Then, on your paper, write its function: *declarative, interrogative, imperative,* or *exclamatory.* Also indicate the end punctuation that you should use.

(1) "Hey, little runner (2) Come here (3) I bet you haven't had breakfast yet (4) Here—how about some granola muffins"

(5) I stopped in surprise as the garbage collector lobbed two packages of English muffins at me

(6) "Do you know how much perfectly good bread they throw away there " (7) He gestured to the grocery store that backed my apartment complex (8) "I always collect it and give it out to my friends along the route (9) What else can I get you "

(10) This dark-haired, beardless Santa Claus reached into the cabin of his truck (11) Two loaves of cinnamon raisin bread appeared

(12) "Do you mean they give you all of this for free"

(13) "Actually, I pull it out of their trash bins before I dump them (14) It is perfectly good, though—just a day or two old "

(15) I had to admit that the bread in my hand looked no different from the plastic-wrapped bread that lined the grocery shelves (16) I capitulated

(17) "Well, thanks very much (18) I have never eaten bread from a trash can before, but I'll give it a try (19) I run almost every day so maybe I will see you again soon "

(20) "Look for me (21) I don't always have this much loot, but whatever I've got, it's yours (22) And tell your neighbors " (23) He flashed me a smile and pointed upwards (24) "Don't you think we have a lot to be thankful for "

(25) I waved goodbye with the raisin bread

EXERCISE B: **Writing Sentences with Different Functions.** Write a sentence for each number in the following chart. Be sure that you use the subject indicated at the left and the function indicated at the top. For example, the first sentence should be a *declarative* sentence about the *media.*

	Declarative	Interrogative	Imperative	Exclamatory
Media	1	2		
Politics			3	4
Trivia	5			6
Basketball		7	8	
Subways	9			10

■ Hard-to-Find Subjects

The position of a subject in relation to its verb may vary according to the function of the sentence. Some subjects, therefore, are more difficult to find than others.

Subjects in Declarative Sentences. In most declarative sentences the subject precedes the verb, but there are two exceptions: sentences beginning with *there* or *here* and sentences that are inverted for emphasis.

When *there* or *here* begins a declarative sentence, it is often erroneously identified as the subject.

There or *here* is never the subject of a sentence.

This rule holds true as long as *there* or *here* is not referred to as a word, as in the wording of the preceding rule. These words usually serve as adverbs that modify the verb by explaining *where*. Sometimes, *there* may be an *expletive*, a device used merely to get the sentence started.

The most effective technique for making the subjects visible in these kinds of sentences is to rearrange the sentence in your mind so that *there* or *here* comes after the verb. If *there* sounds awkward after the verb, you can reasonably assume it is an expletive—in which case, simply drop it from the sentence.

Sentences Beginning with *There* or *Here*	Sentences Rearranged with Subject Before Verb
There are my prize orchids.	My prize orchids are there.
Here is your ticket to the concert.	Your ticket to the concert is here.
There were scholarships available.	Scholarships were available.

Sentences inverted for emphasis also vary from the regular subject-verb pattern of declarative sentences. In such sentences the subject is deliberately positioned at the end of the sentence to focus attention on it.

In some declarative sentences, the subject follows the verb in order to receive greater emphasis.

Often prepositional phrases begin such inverted sentences. Mentally shifting the words at the beginning of the sentence to the middle or to the end makes the subject easier to detect.

Sentences Inverted for Emphasis	Sentences Rephrased with Subject Before Verb
Deep into the cavernous hole <u>went</u> the <u>miners</u>.	The <u>miners</u> <u>went</u> deep into the cavernous hole.
Around my head <u>buzzed</u> the most persistent <u>fly</u>.	The most persistent <u>fly</u> <u>buzzed</u> around my head.

Subjects in Interrogative Sentences.   Many interrogative sentences follow the usual subject-verb order, making the subject easy to identify.

EXAMPLE: What television <u>shows</u> <u>have</u> the best ratings?

Almost as often, however, an inversion occurs, changing the subject's location within the sentence.

In interrogative sentences, the subject often follows the verb.

Inverted interrogative sentences will commonly begin with a verb, a helping verb, or one of the following words: *what, which, whose, who, when, why, where,* or *how.* When looking for the subject in these sentences, mentally change the interrogative sentence into a declarative sentence, as the following examples illustrate.

Question	Rephrased Question
<u>Is</u> the <u>coffee</u> ready?	The <u>coffee</u> <u>is</u> ready.
<u>Will</u> <u>you</u> <u>prepare</u> the monthly statements?	<u>You</u> <u>will</u> <u>prepare</u> the monthly statements.
How <u>should</u> this <u>line</u> <u>be</u> <u>delivered</u>?	This <u>line</u> <u>should</u> <u>be</u> <u>delivered</u> how.

Subjects in Imperative Sentences.   Subjects in imperative sentences are usually implied rather than specifically stated.

In imperative sentences, the subject is understood to be *you.*

In the following chart, the left side shows the imperative sentence in which the subject is implied. The right side shows the positions where the understood subject logically occurs.

Imperative Sentences	With Understood *You* Added
<u>Wait</u> for the delivery person, please.	(<u>You</u>) <u>wait</u> for the delivery person, please.
In an earthquake, <u>crawl</u> under a sturdy table.	In an earthquake, (<u>you</u>) <u>crawl</u> under a sturdy table.
Carolyn, <u>turn</u> down that stereo!	Carolyn, (<u>you</u>) <u>turn</u> down that stereo!

In the last example in the chart, the person to whom the sentence is addressed is named; however, *Carolyn,* a noun of direct address, does not function as the subject of the sentence. The subject is still understood to be *you.*

Subjects in Exclamatory Sentences.   Some exclamatory sentences share the same patterns as interrogative and imperative sentences.

In an exclamatory sentence, the subject may come after the verb or may be understood to be *you.*

The same technique employed to find subjects in interrogative and imperative sentences should be used to find the subject in an exclamatory sentence.

REVERSED ORDER: What else <u>could</u> I <u>have done</u>! (I <u>could have done</u> what else.)

UNDERSTOOD YOU: <u>Sit</u> down! ((<u>You</u>) <u>sit</u> down!)

Some exclamatory sentences may be so elliptical that both the subject *and* the verb are implied. For such sentences as these, common sense and context serve as your best guides for determining the unstated subject and verb.

Exclamatory Sentences with Understood Subjects and Verbs	With Understood Parts Added
Quick!	(You) come here quick!
Air!	I need air!

EXERCISE C: Locating Hard-to-Find Subjects. Each of the following sentences contains a subject that either follows its verb or is understood. Copy each sentence onto your paper, adding words or rephrasing it to make the subject come before its verb. Then underline the subject once and the verb twice.

1. On the table lay the unopened letter.
2. Did the first Macy's Thanksgiving Day Parade occur in 1926?
3. Through the speakers came the wonderful sound of blues artist B.B. King.
4. There are thousands of foster children in America ready for adoption.
5. Does John Denver typify a country singer or a ballad singer?
6. More benefits?
7. Where did you buy that granola?
8. Here are some tips on fly casting.
9. Don't forget to call me.
10. Was Henry Hudson Dutch or British?
11. Help!
12. Lead us in the Pledge of Allegiance, please.
13. There is his social security check.
14. Where was I to go!
15. Are teenagers adequately preparing themselves to become leaders of society?
16. Over the mountains trudged the weary but hardy pioneers.
17. After dinner, finish your homework.
18. There are real rattlesnake roundups in Texas.
19. Fire!
20. How much will the first space shuttles cost?

APPLICATION: Writing Different Kinds of Sentences with Hard-to-Find Subjects. The following outline lists the types of sentences that contain hard-to-find subjects. For each item construct a sentence using a topic of your own choosing.

1. Declarative sentences:
   a. Beginning with *there* or *here* used as an adverb.

b. Beginning with *there* as an expletive.
c. With inverted order.
2. Interrogative sentences:
    a. Beginning with a verb.
    b. Beginning with a helping verb.
    c. Beginning with *what, which, whose, who, when, why, where,* or *how.*
3. Imperative sentence with an understood *you.*
4. Exclamatory sentences:
    a. With an inverted order.
    b. With an understood *you.*
    c. With both the subject and the verb implied.

2.3 Complements

Some sentences are complete with just a subject and a verb or with a subject, verb, and modifiers, as in *The ointment stung* or *The burn ointment stung momentarily*.

The meaning of many sentences, however, depends on additional words to finish the idea begun by the subject and verb. For example, *Mr. Potter continuously mislays . . .* or *My novelette is . . .* remain confusing and incomplete even though each has a subject and verb. To complete the meaning of the predicate parts of those sentences, complements need to be added: for example, *Mr. Potter continuously mislays his glasses*; *My novelette is a satire*.

> A **complement** is a word or group of words that completes the meaning of the predicate of a sentence.

There are five different kinds of complements in English: *direct objects, indirect objects, objective complements, predicate nominatives,* and *predicate adjectives*. The first three occur in sentences with transitive action verbs, while the last two, often grouped together as *subject complements,* are found only with linking verbs. (For more information about action and linking verbs, see Section 1.2.)

■ Direct Objects

Direct objects, the most common of the five types of complements, complete the meaning of action verbs by telling who or what receives the action.

A **direct object** is a noun, pronoun, or group of words acting as a noun that receives the action of a transitive verb.

EXAMPLES: I <u>leased</u> a small beach bungalow.

<u>Mud</u> and <u>leaves</u> <u>clogged</u> the gutters.

To determine the direct object of a sentence, ask *What?* or *Whom?* after an action verb. If the sentence offers no answer, the action verb is intransitive and has no direct object.

EXAMPLES: The <u>curator</u> of the museum <u>led</u> the tour. (Led *what?* Answer: *tour.*)

The <u>employer</u> <u>reprimanded</u> her secretary. (Reprimanded *whom?* Answer: *secretary.*)

Her <u>voice</u> <u>echoed</u> in the halls. (Echoed *what?* Answer: none; the verb is intransitive.)

In the last example, *halls* is the object of the preposition *in*, not the direct object. An object of the preposition will never function as a direct object.

Keep alert for sentences with more than one direct object, called a *compound direct object.* If a sentence contains a compound direct object, asking *What?* or *Whom?* after the action verb will yield two or more answers.

EXAMPLES: The <u>mannequin</u> <u>wore</u> brown pants and a tweed blazer.

On the first Thanksgiving, the <u>Pilgrims</u> <u>ate</u> wild turkey, nuts, and corn.

EXERCISE A: Recognizing Direct Objects.

Some of the following sentences contain direct objects and some do not. For those sentences containing a direct object, write the verb and the direct object on your paper. For those that do not contain direct objects, write only the verb. Some sentences have compound direct objects.

1. I tipped the bellhop generously.
2. Before our winter vacation, we put antifreeze into the car.
3. Our overzealous watchdog bit the unsuspecting guest.
4. A devastating fire swept through the Las Vegas hotel.
5. I bought a pair of shoes and three sweaters.

6. Our Personnel Department carefully screened each of the applicants.
7. The countryside glistened with early morning dew.
8. From its lonely perch, a cormorant methodically surveyed its ocean paradise.
9. A new teakwood coffee table sat in my living room.
10. The dessert contained chocolate, egg white, and whipped cream.

■ Indirect Objects

Indirect objects are usually found only in sentences already containing a direct object.

An **indirect object** is a noun or pronoun that comes after an action verb and before a direct object. Its purpose is to name the person or thing that something is given to or done for.

Indirect objects are common with such verbs as *ask, bring, buy, give, lend, make, promise, show, teach, tell,* and *write.*

EXAMPLES:
$$\text{I } \underline{\text{promised}} \overset{\text{IO}}{\text{Kelly}} \overset{\text{DO}}{\text{a bicycle}} \text{ on his birthday.}$$

The <u>judge</u> <u>gave</u> the jury instructions.

Like direct objects, indirect objects can be compound.

EXAMPLE:
I <u>showed</u> my father and mother my poem.

When locating the indirect object in a sentence, first make sure the sentence contains a direct object. Then ask yourself one of these questions after the verb and direct object: *To or for whom?* or *To or for what?*

EXAMPLES:
The <u>teacher</u> <u>taught</u> our class public speaking. (Taught speaking *to whom?* Answer: *class.*)

We <u>made</u> the couch a slipcover. (Made a slipcover *for what?* Answer: *couch.*)

To avoid confusing an indirect object with a direct object, always remember to ask the right questions in the correct order. First, ask *What?* or *Whom?* after the verb to find the direct object. If the sentence contains a direct object, then ask *To or for whom?* or *To or for what?* after the verb and direct object.

EXAMPLE: Pat told Doug the solution.

Remember also that an indirect object always sits squarely between the verb and direct object. It will never follow the direct object nor will it ever be the object of the preposition *to* or *for*.

EXAMPLES: Shannon sent her picture to me.

Shannon sent me her picture.

In the first sentence, *to me* is a prepositional phrase following the direct object. Only when the preposition is dropped and the *me* precedes the direct object does *me* function as an indirect object.

EXERCISE B: **Recognizing Indirect Objects.** Two words in each of the following sentences are underlined. Write each word on a separate line next to the appropriate number on your paper. After each word, identify it as a *direct object, indirect object,* or *object of a preposition.*

EXAMPLE: Frank gave his friends vegetables from his garden.

friends   indirect object

vegetables   direct object

1. We bought the condominium for our daughter.
2. The university granted the incoming freshman a four-year scholarship.
3. The builder showed the prospective owners some special additions to the house.
4. Beverly Sills sang an aria at the charity gala.
5. Mrs. Phelps taught piano in her home.
6. Erik told his young campers a harrowing bedtime tale.
7. Aunt Harriet described our complete family tree to me.
8. When did they deliver the dining room set to you?
9. Our club made ice cream for the old-fashioned picnic.
10. I ordered you a sweater from the catalog.

■ Objective Complements

While an indirect object must precede a direct object, an *objective complement* can only follow one. As its name implies, the objective complement "complements" or adds to the meaning of the direct object.

> An **objective complement** is an adjective, noun, or group of words that follows a direct object and describes or renames it.

A sentence containing an objective complement may at first glance seem to have two direct objects. Identifying an objective complement is simplified when you know they occur only with such verbs as *appoint, call, consider, declare, elect, judge, label, make, name, select,* or *think.*

EXAMPLES: The <u>President</u> <u>appointed</u> him Secretary of Defense.

The <u>producers</u> of the drug <u>labeled</u> it Keflex.

<u>History</u> <u>judged</u> Abraham Lincoln a fine president.

Like other sentence parts, objective complements can be compound.

EXAMPLE: <u>I</u> <u>think</u> Dave a most talented swimmer and a brilliant lawyer.

To determine whether a word is an objective complement, say the verb and direct object, and then ask *What?*

EXAMPLE: The <u>committee</u> <u>declared</u> the chairman incompetent. (Declared the chairman *what?*   Answer: *incompetent.*)

EXERCISE C: **Using Objective Complements.** The following sentences are missing objective complements. Copy each sentence onto your paper, adding an appropriate objective complement of the type indicated.

1. We named our new sailboat (noun) .
2. The board considered the company's new president (adjective) .
3. Unanimously, my friends appointed me (noun) .
4. The editor of the magazine appointed Janet (noun) .

5. The neighborhood children think my yard _(noun)_ .
6. Our organization elected Terry _(noun)_ .
7. The new living room curtains make the room _(adjective)_
   and _(adjective)_ .
8. The jars were labeled _(noun)_ and _(noun)_ .
9. The builders named the housing development _(noun)_ .
10. A court judged the defendant _(adjective)_ .

■ Subject Complements

Many action verbs need direct objects, indirect objects, and objective complements to help them complete their meaning. Linking verbs, on the other hand, require *subject complements*.

> A **subject complement** is a noun, pronoun, or adjective that follows a linking verb and tells something about the subject of the sentence.

Subject complements are divided into two categories: *predicate nominatives* and *predicate adjectives*.

Predicate Nominatives.   Predicate nominatives refer to those "naming" parts of speech: nouns and pronouns.

> A **predicate nominative** is a noun or pronoun that follows a linking verb and renames, identifies, or explains the subject of a sentence.

As the following examples show, the subject and the predicate nominative are merely different words for the same person, place, or thing. Notice the compound predicate nominative in the last example.

EXAMPLES: Joan Roshon <u>became</u> a geologist for an oil company.

The <u>winner</u> <u>is</u> you.

<u>Fran Tarkenton</u> <u>is</u> a TV commentator and former football player.

Predicate Adjectives.   As the label indicates, a predicate adjective is not a noun or a pronoun, but an adjective.

A **predicate adjective** is an adjective that follows a linking verb and describes the subject of the sentence.

A predicate adjective refers to the subject by describing it in much the same way that any adjective modifies a noun or pronoun.

EXAMPLES: Your reasoning seems logical.

The melody sounded light and cheerful.

EXERCISE D: Identifying Subject Complements. Each of the following sentences contains a subject complement. Some are compound. Write each complement on your paper and identify it as a *predicate nominative* or *predicate adjective*.

1. The rainclouds appeared distant, yet forbidding.
2. After my course in astronomy, I became an avid stargazer.
3. The unruly child grew belligerent, then sullen.
4. Those plants to the left are hybrid sweet peas.
5. Paul Revere was a silversmith and a maker of dentures.
6. My quilted comforter felt warm and soft against my skin.
7. The air was sweet with the scent of apple blossoms.
8. She is both a competent nurse and a devoted mother.
9. The juice tasted bitter and warm.
10. The expansive lawns of the country estate looked perfectly green.

APPLICATION: Using Complements in Your Own Writing. Write two sentences to illustrate each of the four complements introduced in this section: *direct objects, indirect objects, objective complements,* and *subject complements.* Underline each subject once and each verb twice. Then identify the complements.

2.4 Basic Sentence Patterns

The simplest sentence in English has a verb and a subject that is either expressed or implied. Subjects, verbs, and the different kinds of complements form five other basic sentence patterns from which more complicated structures can be built. This section will review these basic patterns, which were introduced in the earlier sections of this chapter, to help you increase your awareness of the range of expression available.

■ Five Basic Patterns

Sentences with complements follow set patterns.

In the English language, subjects, verbs, and complements follow five **basic sentence patterns.**

Except as predicate adjectives or objective complements, adjectives are never part of a sentence's basic pattern. Nor are adverbs, conjunctions, interjections, or prepositional phrases, which primarily add details to or connections between the various sentence parts. As you study the examples in each of the following charts, mentally eliminate all of these additional words. The skeleton of the sentences will then become more visible to you.

The Basic Pattern Without Complements.   The simplest pattern for an English sentence is a subject followed by a verb. In such a pattern, the verbs are intransitive.

SENTENCE PATTERNS WITHOUT COMPLEMENTS	
Pattern	**Examples**
S–V	Donkeys bray.
	The duck waddled into the water.
	The limousine is here.

The Three Patterns with Transitive Verbs.   A sentence with a transitive action verb includes at least one complement: a direct object. A sentence with a direct object may also contain an indirect object or an objective complement.

SENTENCE PATTERNS WITH TRANSITIVE VERBS	
Pattern	**Examples**
S-AV-DO	She recklessly hit the brakes. [DO]
	Voraciously, Edgar ate the fresh salmon. [DO]
S-AV-IO-DO	I tipped the waiter [IO] five dollars. [DO]
	We bought our boat [IO] a new tachometer. [DO]

	DO OC
S-AV-DO-OC	We <u>named</u> our dog Major.
	The <u>censor</u> <u>judged</u> the movie appropriate for children.

In the first example the labels DO and OC appear above "dog" and "Major." In the second, DO and OC appear above "movie" and "appropriate."

The Two Patterns with Linking Verbs.   A linking verb will always link the subject of the sentence with a subject complement. The subject complement will be either a predicate nominative or a predicate adjective.

SENTENCE PATTERNS WITH LINKING VERBS	
Pattern	**Examples**
S-LV-PN	That <u>gentleman</u> <u>is</u> a foreign diplomat. [PN]
	<u>Success</u> in business <u>was</u> her goal. [PN]
S-LV-PA	My gas <u>bill</u> <u>was</u> outrageous. [PA]
	The <u>field</u> <u>grew</u> barren from overuse. [PA]

Patterns with Compound Sentence Parts.   Any of these basic sentence patterns can be expanded by making one or more of its parts compound. Such simple expansions can add variety and style to your writing.

SOME BASIC SENTENCE PATTERNS WITH COMPOUND PARTS	
Pattern	**Examples**
S-S-V	The <u>timekeeper</u> and <u>referee</u> <u>talked</u> on the sideline.
S-V-DO-DO	Our taxi <u>driver</u> <u>ran</u> a stop sign and a red light. [DO] [DO]
S-LV-LV-PN	My <u>aunt</u> <u>was</u> and still <u>is</u> a fine seamstress. [PN]
S-AV-DO-AV-DO-OC	The <u>storekeeper</u> <u>left</u> the shop and <u>appointed</u> me manager in her absence. [DO] [DO] [OC]

EXERCISE A: Identifying Basic Sentence Patterns. Copy the following sentences onto your paper. Underline the subjects once, the verbs twice, and circle the complements. Then, using the abbreviations introduced in the preceding charts, identify the sentence patterns. Be alert for compounds.

1. Resoundingly, I hit the blacktop and skinned my knees on the rough surface.
2. The retired couple made gardening their full-time occupation.
3. We conversed far into the night.
4. For such a small restaurant, the menu appeared extensive.
5. The loan officer and a secretary embezzled eighty thousand dollars from their company.
6. A strong drum beat and a fine brass section won the band first place.
7. He dived into the water and emerged two minutes later.
8. The actress flashed her smile and waved a gloved hand at the admiring crowd.
9. The picture on the rubber stamp became my trademark for all my correspondence.
10. After questioning, the suspect no longer seemed defensive and evasive.

APPLICATION: Writing Sentences in a Variety of Patterns. Write a paragraph about one of the following topics or think of a topic of your own. In your paragraph, include at least four of the sentence patterns shown in the charts on pages 77 and 78. Underline your subjects once, underline your verbs twice, and label your complements.

Wrapping a present
Scoring a goal (home run, basket)
Eating at a restaurant
Getting a haircut
Shopping for new clothes

Diagraming Basic Parts of Sentences   2.5

   A pictorial representation of a sentence is called a diagram. Just as a map can help a driver understand directions, so a diagram can help you visualize a sentence's structure. This section will explain the traditional rules for diagraming the basic sentence patterns that were covered in this chapter.

■ Subject, Verbs, and Modifiers

To diagram any sentence, begin with the subject and verb and then branch out to include modifiers of the subject and verb.

Subjects and Verbs.   To diagram a subject and a verb, draw a horizontal line, place the subject on the left and the verb on the right. Separate the two with a vertical line.

EXAMPLE: Malcolm should have volunteered.

| Malcolm | should have volunteered |

Adjectives and Adverbs.   Adjectives and adverbs sit on slanted lines beneath the words they modify.

EXAMPLE: The black smoke drifted up.

Articles (*a, an, the*), pronouns used as adjectives (*his, her, our,* and so on), and possessive nouns (such as *Howard's*) are all diagramed on slanted lines.

For adverbs that modify adjectives and other adverbs, place the word on a line below the word it modifies. Connect the two with a perpendicular line.

EXAMPLE: The extremely large bird glided surprisingly gracefully.

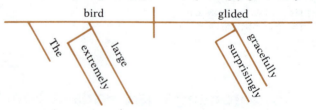

EXERCISE A: Diagraming Subjects, Verbs, and Modifiers.
Diagram each of the following sentences on your paper.

1. The giant python slithered silently.
2. Our silly scarecrow hung askew.
3. Her extremely high fever finally dropped.

4. Our gate swung wide open.
5. Every dedicated marathon runner must train continuously.

■ Compound Sentence Parts

Joining compound parts in sentences usually requires a conjunction, generally shown in a diagram on a dotted line between the words being connected.

Compound Subjects and Verbs. To diagram compound subjects and verbs, divide the horizontal line into as many parts as needed. Then on a dotted line joining the parts, write the conjunction that connects them.

For the positioning of correlative conjunctions and the placement of helping verbs in a sentence diagram, study the following example.

EXAMPLE: Both you and I must pack today and move out tomorrow.

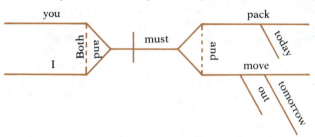

As the preceding example shows, modifiers in sentences containing compound parts are carefully positioned with the individual words they modify. If a word modifies an entire compound element, as illustrated in the following sentence, the modifier is positioned beneath the stem of the baseline.

EXAMPLE: Yesterday, the campers and counselors swam and fished.

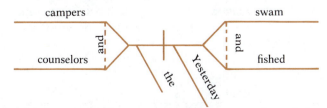

Compound Adjectives and Adverbs. A dotted line also joins compound adjectives and adverbs.

EXAMPLE: The long and complicated report was read quickly but not easily.

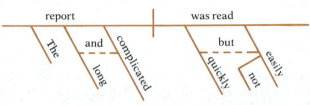

EXERCISE B: Diagraming Compound Parts of Speech. The following sentences contain compounds. Diagram each sentence on your paper.

1. Today, both Darrin and Peter memorized and rehearsed continuously.
2. The tiny tugboat and the gigantic cruise ship sailed together.
3. The almost defenseless yet still courageous army marched forward.
4. The horses neighed nervously and shied away.
5. Her letter, scented and pink, arrived today.
6. The original sheet was reduced and then copied.
7. Fresh vegetables and fruits were proudly displayed.
8. The suspect responded quietly, but defiantly.
9. Yesterday, the boys and girls ate and played outdoors.
10. The humid, dark, and deserted tunnel turned and twisted endlessly.

■ Sentences with Hard-to-Find Subjects

Imperative and interrogative sentences and sentences that begin with *there* or *here* have subjects that are often somewhat difficult to locate. Consequently, these sentences are sometimes more difficult to diagram than the sentences in Exercise A.

Imperative Sentences. When the subject of an imperative sentence is understood to be *you*, place it in parentheses on the baseline.

EXAMPLE: Call home immediately.

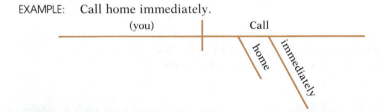

Interrogative Sentences. Interrogative sentences in which the subject follows the verb are diagramed in the regular subject-verb order.

EXAMPLE: Has Regina telephoned yet?

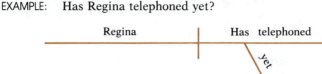

Sentences Beginning with *There* or *Here*. Rearrange a sentence beginning with *there* or *here* so that the subject comes first. Then, if *there* or *here* functions as an adverb, diagram it below the verb.

EXAMPLE: Here comes the parade.

If *there* functions as an expletive, place it on a horizontal line above the subject.

EXAMPLE: There are three strangers outside.

NOTE ABOUT EXPLETIVE STYLE: Use the position of an expletive for interjections and nouns of direct address.

EXAMPLE: Goodness, Diana, hurry up!

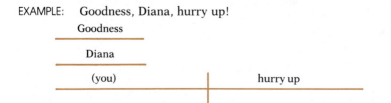

EXERCISE C: Diagraming Sentences with Hard-to-Find Subjects. Diagram each of the following sentences on your paper.

1. My, there goes one expensive automobile.
2. Here is my missing suitcase.
3. Leslie, do not dawdle so long.
4. When does the plane leave?
5. There was a spectacular sunset yesterday.

■ Complements

Since complements complete the meaning of a verb, they are appropriately diagramed on the predicate side of the sentence.

Direct Objects.   Direct objects sit on the same baseline as the subject and verb, and are separated from the verb by a short vertical line.

EXAMPLE: I sliced the cheese.

Compound direct objects are diagramed like compound subjects and verbs.

EXAMPLE: I handwashed your sweaters and silk blouses.

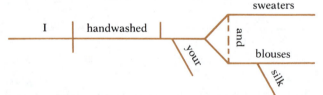

Indirect Objects.   An indirect object is located on a line below the verb as shown in the following example.

EXAMPLE: Dick bought us an electric skillet.

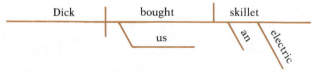

For compound indirect objects, split the line on which they sit into as many parts as required.

EXAMPLE: The owner leased Rita, Melanie, and me the largest apartment.

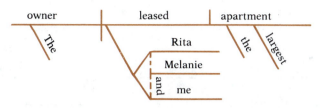

Objective Complements. Objective complements follow the direct object both in the actual sentence and in a diagram of the sentence. A short slanted line pointing toward the direct object separates it from the rest of the sentence as shown in the following example.

EXAMPLE: The supervisor named Wayne division manager.

If the objective complement is compound, diagram it as demonstrated in the following example.

EXAMPLE: She considered the applicant extremely mature and trustworthy.

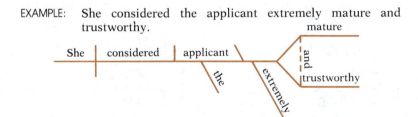

Subject Complements. In a diagram of a sentence, subject complements are placed on the baseline. Subject complements are separated from the linking verb by a line that slants back toward the subject and verb.

EXAMPLE: The unpaved road was bumpy.

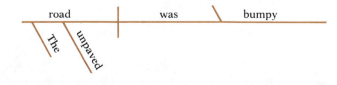

Compound subject complements are diagramed on a split line; as are other compound sentence parts.

EXAMPLE: The child's tonsils looked very red and swollen.

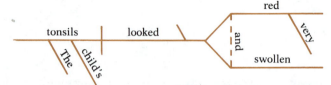

EXERCISE D: Diagraming Complements.

The following sentences contain complements. Diagram each sentence on your paper.

1. My old scrapbook held old snapshots and mementos.
2. The group gave Kirk and Nat a detailed map and some instructions.
3. His monthly salary was meager and inadequate.
4. My parents consider me an excellent driver.
5. Tanya is my sister and a good friend.

APPLICATION: Diagraming Different Kinds of Sentences.

Write a sentence that fits each of the following patterns on your paper. Include appropriate adjectives and adverbs and compound adjectives and adverbs. Then diagram the sentences you have written.

1. S-V
2. S-V-V
3. S-V-DO
4. S-V-DO-DO
5. S-V-IO-DO
6. S-V-IO-IO-DO
7. S-V-DO-OC
8. S-V-DO-OC-OC
9. S-S-V-PA-PA
10. S-V-PN

Phrases and Clauses

A proficient writer approaches language in much the same way that a sculptor approaches clay. Using their skills and imagination, they interact with the formless material to try to shape it into a work that will express their thoughts and personality. The previous chapters in this unit have discussed the essential materials at a writer's command: the parts of speech and the basic English sentence patterns. This chapter will describe the other elements that writers can use to expand the basic patterns and to achieve a greater range of expression.

Prepositional and Appositive Phrases 3.1

When one-word adjectives and adverbs cannot convey all of the details and relationships that a writer needs to express, the writer can often use a structure known as a *phrase* to express the precise idea.

> A **phrase** is a group of words, without a subject and verb, that functions in a sentence as one part of speech.

Two common types of phrases that are used to expand sentences are *prepositional phrases* and *appositive phrases.*

■ Prepositional Phrases

As described in Section 1.4, prepositional phrases begin with a preposition and end with a noun or pronoun called the object of the preposition. The object may have modifiers and may be compound.

EXAMPLES:
    Prep   Obj of Prep
on the freshly pressed white dinner jacket

    Prep   Obj of Prep   Obj of Prep
beside the driftwood and seaweed

Like one-word adjectives and adverbs, prepositional phrases are modifiers. Depending on the words they modify, they are called either *adjectival phrases* or *adverbial phrases.*

Adjectival Phrases. Like adjectives, adjectival phrases modify nouns and pronouns.

> An **adjectival phrase** is a prepositional phrase that modifies a noun or pronoun by telling what kind or which one.

Adjectival phrases can modify any sentence part occupied by a noun or pronoun.

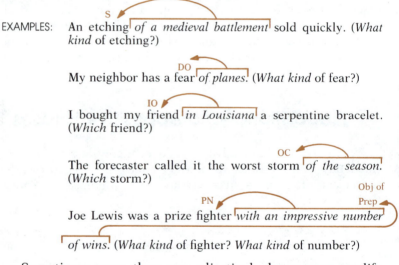

EXAMPLES: An etching *of a medieval battlement* sold quickly. (*What kind* of etching?)

My neighbor has a fear *of planes.* (*What kind* of fear?)

I bought my friend *in Louisiana* a serpentine bracelet. (*Which* friend?)

The forecaster called it the worst storm *of the season.* (*Which* storm?)

Joe Lewis was a prize fighter *with an impressive number of wins.* (*What kind* of fighter? *What kind* of number?)

Sometimes more than one adjectival phrase may modify the same word.

EXAMPLE: Water the plants *in the living room near the fireplace.*

Adverbial Phrases. Like adverbs, adverbial phrases modify verbs, adjectives, and other adverbs.

> An **adverbial phrase** is a prepositional phrase that modifies a verb, adjective, or adverb by pointing out where, when, in what manner, or to what extent.

When modifying a verb, an adverbial phrase will often precede the modified word.

MODIFYING A VERB: *In Central Park,* you can ride horse-drawn carriages. (Can ride *where?*)

The volcano rumbled *in the early morning hours.* (Rumbled *when?*)

I consumed the sundae *in short order.* (Consumed *in what manner?*)

Except for a small section, the lawn was mowed. (Was mowed *to what extent?*)

MODIFYING AN ADJECTIVE: I am angry *with you.* (Angry *in what manner?*)

MODIFYING AN ADVERB: The shovel bit deep *into the earth.* (Deep *where?*)

As with adjectival phrases, more than one adverbial phrase can modify the same word.

EXAMPLE: *Before breakfast,* the smell of bacon drifted *into my bedroom.* (Drifted *when?* Drifted *where?*)

EXERCISE A: Identifying Adjectival and Adverbial Phrases. The sentences in the following paragraph include prepositional phrases. Next to the appropriate number on your paper, write the prepositional phrases contained in each sentence. After each phrase write *adj* if it is adjectival or *adv* if it is adverbial. Be prepared to identify the words the phrases modify.

(1) Cultures around the world have different conceptions of physical beauty. (2) In China, for example, young girls once had their feet bound so that they measured only three or four inches. (3) In some societies today, pins and plugs inserted through the nose, lips, and ears are considered alluring. (4) Some Eskimos of North America wear bones in their lips whereas Australian aborigines prefer them through the septum of the nose. (5) Another body decoration involves creating lace-

like patterned bumps on the body. (6) The Nuba of Sudan rub mud into small incisions, and the resulting scars produce the desired patterns just underneath the skin's surface. (7) In parts of Burma, women with long, slender necks are deemed highly attractive. (8) The women, therefore, wear increasing numbers of brass spirals about their necks. (9) In several Asian societies, people stain their teeth with betel juice because white teeth are thought ugly. (10) Apart from these, Western culture has also had its share of unusual beauty habits: Corsets, hair dyeing, tattooing, and earpiercing are just a few.

■ Appositives and Appositive Phrases

To appose means "to place near or next to." Appositives and appositive phrases are words placed next to nouns and pronouns to provide additional information.

Appositives.   When you name something and then immediately rename it to give further information, you are using an appositive.

> An **appositive** is a noun or pronoun placed after another noun or pronoun to identify, rename, or explain it.

EXAMPLES: My dog, *a pointer*, stood silently alert in the brush.

We sailed aboard a small yacht, *the Truth*.

These examples show the appositives set off by commas. Commas are used only when the appositive contains *nonessential* (or *nonrestrictive*) material—that is, material that can be removed from the sentence without altering its meaning. If the material is *essential* (or *restrictive*), no commas are used.

EXAMPLES: My friend *Marilyn* broke her collarbone.

I initially thought the novel *The Promise* was depressing.

See Section 12.2 for more about punctuating appositives.

Appositive Phrases.   When an appositive is accompanied by one or more modifiers it becomes a phrase.

> An **appositive phrase** is a noun or pronoun with modifiers, placed next to a noun or pronoun to add information and details.

One-word adjectives, adjectival phrases, or other groups of words acting as adjectives can modify an appositive.

EXAMPLES: The linebacker, *a quick, strong senior from Notre Dame,* tackled the quarterback.

I lost my camera, *an Instamatic with an electronic flash.*

Appositives and appositive phrases can accompany nouns and pronouns occupying any part within a sentence.

WITH A SUBJECT:

My footgear, *sturdy hiking boots,* served me well during the long trek.

WITH A DIRECT OBJECT:

I bought a collector's ornament, *a delicate Norman Rockwell figurine.*

WITH AN INDIRECT OBJECT:

The man gave his wife, *his partner for twenty years,* a beautiful opal pendant.

WITH AN OBJECTIVE COMPLEMENT:

We called the puppy Boatswain, *the name of Lord Byron's favorite dog.*

WITH A PREDICATE NOMINATIVE:

Our new home was a lovely condominum, *an apartment conversion in a parklike setting.*

WITH THE OBJECT OF A PREPOSITION:

The ball flew into a nearby wooded area, *a copse of cottonwood and spruce.*

To set up contrasts, appositives and appositive phrases may begin with the word *not.*

EXAMPLE: You were supposed to pick me up at 7:00 p.m.—*not 8:00 p.m.*

Appositives and appositive phrases, like other sentence parts, can be compound.

EXAMPLE: The family singing group—*Mr. von Trapp, his wife, and children*—managed to escape from Austria during World War II.

In your own writing, use appositives and appositive phrases to tighten your sentences. Often, two sentences can be combined by reducing the information in one sentence into an appositive construction.

TWO SENTENCES: The fruit waited for the harvest. The fruit was sun-ripened peaches.

SENTENCE WITH APPOSITIVE PHRASE: The fruit, *sun-ripened peaches*, waited for the harvest.

EXERCISE B: Identifying Appositives and Appositive Phrases.

Write the appositive or appositive phrase from each of the following sentences.

1. We watched the holiday ballet *The Nutcracker Suite.*
2. Mae West's trademark, her hourglass figure, eventually became a symbol of Hollywood glamour.
3. The stockholders elected him chairman of the board, the company's most prestigious position.
4. The boy proudly blew his trumpet, his most treasured possession.
5. Our trip ended at the boardwalk, a mile stretch of flashing lights and wild rides.
6. I gave my great-uncle—a cantankerous yet lovable old man—a present on his eightieth birthday.
7. Letters during the Gold Rush era were sent by the fastest overland carrier then known, the Pony Express.
8. Our only means of transportation, a four-wheel drive truck, sat mired in the sand.
9. Our friends took their motor home, a deluxe vehicle with television and showers, on a camping trip.
10. I brought my secretary Pat Schubert the papers that needed typing.

EXERCISE C: Using Appositives and Appositive Phrases in Sentences.

Combine the following pairs of sentences by turning

the information from one into an appositive or appositive phrase.

1. The city of Washington, D.C., was designed by Major Pierre Charles L'Enfant. He was a famous French architect and engineer.
2. Georgetown is one of the most fashionable parts of Washington, D.C. Many government officials have residences there.
3. The Jefferson Memorial is a replica of the Pantheon in Rome. This memorial overlooks the Potomac River.
4. Each September, the President's Cup Regatta is held on the Potomac River. It is an annual motorboat racing contest.
5. The National Gallery houses many art treasures. It is one of the largest marble buildings in the world.

APPLICATION: **Using Prepositional and Appositive Phrases in Sentences.** Write sentences of your own using the following directions. Underline the prepositional and appositive phrases in your sentences.

1. Write a sentence about *wages*, using a prepositional phrase.
2. Write a sentence about *George Washington*, using an appositive phrase.
3. Write a sentence about *calculators*, using two prepositional phrases.
4. Write a sentence about *whales*, using an appositive phrase.
5. Write a sentence about *Mars*, using a prepositional phrase and an appositive phrase.

Verbal Phrases 3.2

The word *verb*, which is part of the grammatical term *verbal*, holds the clue to the meaning of the second word.

> A **verbal** is a word derived from a verb but used as a noun, adjective, or adverb.

Like verbs, verbals may be modified by adverbs and adverbial phrases or have complements. A verbal with modifiers or a complement is called a *verbal phrase*. This section will introduce the three kinds of verbals—participles, gerunds, and infinitives—and the phrases that can be formed around them.

■ Participles and Participial Phrases

Many adjectives you customarily use are actually verbals known as *participles*.

A **participle** is a form of a verb that acts as an adjective.

EXAMPLES: A *killing* frost swept through the valley.

A *frightened* doe froze in the glare of the headlights.

Forms of Participles.   Participles come in three forms: *present participles, past participles,* and *perfect participles.* The following chart shows how each of these participles is formed.

Kind of Participle	Form	Examples
Present participle	Ends in *-ing*	His *fascinating* responses convinced us. The water shone with *glimmering* phosphorescence.
Past participle	Usually ends in *-ed*, sometimes *-t, -en,* or another irregular ending	The *extended* table accommodated more people. The *engrossed* secretary didn't hear the phone.
Perfect participle	Includes *having* or *having been* before a past participle	*Having exercised,* I rested. *Having been challenged,* he produced the necessary proof.

Participles may either precede or follow the words they modify, answering *Which one?* or *What kind?* as do one-word adjectives.

Always be careful to differentiate between a verb in a sentence and a participle. A verb will have a subject and express the sentence's main action; a participle will describe a noun or pronoun.

Functioning as a Verb	Functioning as a Participle
Her muscles *are aching.*	She rubbed her *aching* muscles.
The employees *respected* their boss.	The *respected* boss had the employees' support.

Participial Phrases. The addition of modifiers and complements to a participle produces a *participial phrase.*

> A **participial phrase** is a participle that is modified by an adverb or adverbial phrase, or that has a complement. The entire phrase acts as an adjective in a sentence.

Look at the following sentences which show the different modifiers and complements that can occur in a participial phrase.

WITH AN ADVERB:

Burning brightly, the fire cast light into the room.

WITH AN ADVERBIAL PHRASE:

The bone *broken in three places* took months to heal.

WITH A DIRECT OBJECT:

Holding the snake, I felt its cool, scaly skin.

A participial phrase at the beginning of a sentence is commonly set off by a comma. The punctuation, however, varies for participial phrases found within the sentence. If the phrase is *nonessential* to the sentence, commas are placed around it. If, on the other hand, the phrase is *essential* to the meaning of the sentence, no commas are needed.

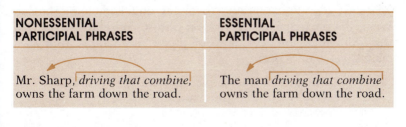

NONESSENTIAL PARTICIPIAL PHRASES	ESSENTIAL PARTICIPIAL PHRASES
Mr. Sharp, *driving that combine,* owns the farm down the road.	The man *driving that combine* owns the farm down the road.

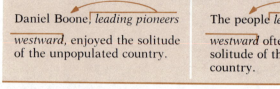

Daniel Boone, *leading pioneers westward*, enjoyed the solitude of the unpopulated country.

The people *leading pioneers westward* often enjoyed the solitude of the unpopulated country.

For more information about punctuating participial phrases, see Section 12.2.

Nominative Absolutes.   Sometimes, participles occur in phrases that are grammatically separate from the rest of the sentence. These phrases, called *nominative absolutes*, can show time, reason, or circumstance.

> A **nominative absolute** is a noun or pronoun followed by a participle or participial phrase. It functions independently of the rest of the sentence.

TIME: *Three hours having passed*, I decided to wait no longer.

REASON: *My stomach growling with hunger*, I made a sandwich.

CIRCUMSTANCE: Many students missed important exams, *the flu epidemic having struck at the end of the semester.*

The participle *being* is sometimes understood rather than expressed in some nominative absolutes.

EXAMPLES: *The camera (being) out of film*, we had to stop taking pictures.

I wrapped all the presents, *each (being) unique and colorful.*

Do not mistake a nominative absolute for the main subject and verb in a sentence. As a phrase a nominative absolute cannot stand independently as a complete sentence.

EXERCISE A: Recognizing Participles and Participial Phrases.
Write the participle or participial phrase contained in each of the following sentences on your paper. Then indicate if it is *present*, *past*, or *perfect*.

1. A scathing attack was delivered by the politician.
2. The wheat swaying in the wind was like waves.

3. The houses ruined by the fire smoldered until the next morning.
4. A giant balloon billowing forth with hot air rose slowly into the sky.
5. At the dance, the reserved girl sat in the shadow behind a large philodendron.
6. The dignitary following the President will address the Security Council today.
7. Having interviewed several people, the reporter felt ready to write the article.
8. I listened to the crows cawing continuously as they settled by the hundreds in the treetops.
9. Having been warned, I approached the guard dog with caution.
10. The document, yellowed with age, contained the information we needed.

EXERCISE B: **Writing Participial Phrases.** A verb is underlined in each of the following sentences. Change the verb into a participle, add modifiers or a complement, and use the phrase in a similar sentence of your own.

EXAMPLE: The town of 20,000 inhabitants <u>elected</u> a police chief last month.

The police chief <u>elected last month</u> will serve the town of 20,000 inhabitants.

1. The plane will be <u>delayed</u> for another hour.
2. The marathon runner <u>tired</u> too quickly and dropped out of the race.
3. The district attorney's persistent questions <u>badgered</u> the nervous witness.
4. We are carefully <u>planning</u> the reception so that it will run smoothly.
5. The students have <u>collected</u> clothing for the refugees.
6. Someone had <u>abused</u> the puppy, and it was now afraid of people.
7. The young woman was <u>satisfying</u> her thirst for knowledge with a tour around the world.
8. We <u>greased</u> the ball bearings with a good lubricant, and the skate wheels worked perfectly.
9. When the fielder <u>overthrew</u> the ball, the runner on third scored.
10. With precision, the company <u>patched</u> the down jacket so that the tear was hardly noticeable.

EXERCISE C: **Recognizing Nominative Absolutes.** The following sentences contain nominative absolutes. Copy each sentence onto your paper. Underline the subject once, the verb twice, and put a box around the nominative absolute.

1. The critics having given the movie a good review, we were eager to see it.
2. I read all the travel literature on Canada, my enthusiasm mounting with each brochure.
3. A month having passed with no news, I called our relatives on the phone.
4. The case having been settled, the attorneys did not spend long in court.
5. Temperatures over 100° for almost a month, the livestock began dying by the thousands.

■ Gerunds and Gerund Phrases

Verbs ending in *-ing* can sometimes be used as nouns called *gerunds*.

A gerund is a form of a verb that acts as a noun.

EXAMPLES: *Vaulting* is my best event in gymnastics.

Swallowing hurt my sore throat.

The Function of Gerunds in Sentences. By themselves gerunds function in sentences no differently than any other nouns.

SOME USES OF GERUNDS IN SENTENCES	
As a subject	*Striking* is considered a revolutionary tactic in some countries.
As a direct object	A chef must enjoy *cooking*.
As an indirect object	He gives *gardening* all of his attention.
As an object of a preposition	Lock the doors before *leaving*.
As a predicate nominative	Her worst fault is *lying*.
As an appositive	One field, *engineering*, has an open job market.

To avoid confusing verbs, participles, and gerunds—all of which can end in *-ing*—check the word's use within the sentence.

AS PART OF A VERB PHRASE: My friends *are traveling* across the country.

AS A PARTICIPLE: A *traveling* salesman came to the door.

AS A GERUND: *Traveling* tires me out.

NOTE ABOUT GERUNDS AND POSSESSIVE PRONOUNS: Only the possessive form of a personal pronoun is appropriate before a gerund.

INCORRECT: We were intrigued by *them pantomiming.*

CORRECT: We were intrigued by *their pantomiming.*

Gerund Phrases.   A gerund with modifiers or a complement is called a *gerund phrase.*

A gerund phrase is a gerund with modifiers or a complement, all acting together as a noun.

In the following chart, note the great variety of different kinds of modifiers and complements that a gerund phrase can contain.

GERUND PHRASES	
Gerund with adjectives	*His loud, persistent yawning* disrupted the meeting.
Gerund with adjectival phrase	*Worrying about the deadline* prevented the writer from sleeping.
Gerund with adverb	I estimated the cost by *calculating quickly.*
Gerund with adverbial phrase	*Fishing from the pier* is permitted.
Gerund with direct object	*Reproducing copies* grows more expensive each year.
Gerund with indirect and direct objects	Mr. Roberts suggested *writing the firm a letter.*

EXERCISE D: **Identifying Gerunds and Gerund Phrases.** Each of the following sentences contains a gerund or gerund phrase. Locate it and write it on your paper. Then identify its function in the sentence.

1. He left almost immediately after a day of teaching.
2. His newest hobby, arranging flowers, results in many beautiful centerpieces.
3. The U.S. Olympic hockey team gave playing hockey new glamour.
4. The librarian began cataloguing the newest books.
5. A necessary qualification for all applicants is possessing a business degree.
6. He likes spending his weekends in the country.
7. Talking during an examination is strictly forbidden in this class.
8. A substantial prize made winning the contest more important.
9. Raking leaves in the fall fills many of my afternoons.
10. A national baseball tradition, eating hot dogs at the game, brings in a tidy income to the concessionaires.
11. His special talent is reading people's minds.
12. She trembled at the thought of getting married.
13. Our club proposed giving the senior citizens a Halloween party.
14. I abhorred repairing the leaky roof.
15. A new art form being shown in restaurants is ice-sculpting.
16. I suggested dismissing her.
17. The space capsule completed its landing on the moon.
18. Her responsibility, handling all incoming calls and correspondence, took a good portion of each working day.
19. Solving the calculus problem left me in an exhilarated mood.
20. By gathering nuts throughout the fall, the squirrel was ready for a long winter.

■ Infinitives and Infinitive Phrases

Infinitives, the third type of verbal, can function as three parts of speech.

An infinitive is a form of a verb that comes after the word *to* and acts as a noun, adjective, or adverb.

EXAMPLES: I would like *to sleep.*

Our instructor taught us *to meditate.*

Forms of Infinitives.   There are two kinds of infinitives—*present infinitives* and *perfect infinitives*. The following chart shows how each kind is formed.

Kind of Infinitive	Form	Examples
Present infinitive	*To* plus the base form of a verb	I like *to debate.* *To concede* was cowardly.
Perfect infinitive	*To have* or *to have been* plus a past participle	I would have liked *to have gone.* *To have been praised* would have been delightful.

Do not mistake a prepositional phrase beginning with *to* for an infinitive. An infinitive will always be followed by a verb. A prepositional phrase beginning with *to* will be followed by a noun or pronoun.

INFINITIVES: to boast, to have excelled

PREPOSITIONAL PHRASES: to them, to a friend

Sometimes, infinitives do not include the word *to*. After the verbs *dare, hear, help, let, make, please, see,* and *watch,* the *to* will usually be understood rather than stated.

EXAMPLES: The student helped *teach.*

We watched the team *play.*

The Function of Infinitives in Sentences.   The flexibility of the infinitive enables it to be used in almost any capacity.

INFINITIVES USED AS NOUNS	
As a subject	*To have cheated* was immoral.
As a direct object	Barbara decided *to leave.*
As a predicate nominative	Our best protection was *to have been inoculated.*
As an object of a preposition	I was about *to speak.*
As an appositive	Our good intention, *to diet,* disappeared quickly.
INFINITIVES USED AS MODIFIERS	
As an adjective	The doctor gave me some pills *to take.*
As an adverb	The ice cream was easy *to freeze.*

Infinitive Phrases. An infinitive becomes an infinitive phrase with the addition of modifiers, complements, or subjects.

> An **infinitive phrase** is an infinitive with modifiers, a complement, or a subject, all acting together as a single part of speech.

Study the following examples to see some of the ways infinitives can be expanded into phrases.

INFINITIVE PHRASES	
Infinitive with adverb	The baby wanted *to wiggle continuously.*
Infinitive with adverbial phrases	I plan *to visit during the afternoon.*
Infinitive with direct object	The foghorn helped *warn the incoming ships.*
Infinitive with indirect and direct objects	The bank decided *to lend the family the money.*
Infinitive with subject and complement	The student requested *the college to send a catalog.*

EXERCISE E: Identifying Infinitives and Infinitive Phrases. Each of the following sentences contains an infinitive or infinitive phrase. Write each infinitive or infinitive phrase and after it, identify its part of speech as a *noun, adjective,* or *adverb.* If the infinitive or infinitive phrase is used as a noun, further identify its function as a *subject, direct object, predicate nominative, object of a preposition,* or *appositive.*

1. To embalm the dead quickly was a necessity in the heat of Egypt.
2. He loves to practice contract law.
3. The decision, to try for the two-point conversion, became the turning point in the game.
4. The young man had money to burn.
5. We heard the bells ring out the hour.
6. His financial goal was to earn one million dollars by age thirty-two.
7. Dirk was next to bat.
8. To capture the splendor of the scene on film required all her photographic skill.
9. His vacation plans were to shoot the Colorado rapids.

10. The boy planned to stay for a few weeks in Tokyo.
11. To learn about new inventions can be exciting.
12. You should remember to balance your checkbook monthly.
13. We watched Julia Child carve the leg of lamb.
14. You must use a stamp to mail a letter.
15. The city's plans are to build a large convention center and hotel complex.
16. The teacher helped the students understand the value of a thesaurus.
17. To research the subject adequately will involve much time.
18. One of my greatest thrills was to sky-dive from ten thousand feet.
19. We wanted it to snow during the winter holidays.
20. She wanted nothing except to be admired for her considerable talents.

APPLICATION: **Writing Sentences Using Verbals.** Change each of the following verbs into the two kinds of verbals indicated in the chart. Then use each one as a verbal phrase in a sentence of your own. Underline the verbal phrases in your sentences.

	Participle	Gerund	Infinitive
1. confuse	x		x
2. dress		x	x
3. achieve	x		x
4. spend	x	x	
5. yearn		x	x
6. blush	x		x
7. sail	x	x	
8. undertake		x	x
9. rule	x	x	
10. precede	x		x

Subordinate Clauses 3.3

Clauses, like the different types of phrases, are groups of related words, but unlike phrases, have a subject and a verb.

A **clause** is a group of words with its own subject and verb.

There are two kinds of clauses: *independent* and *subordinate* clauses.

An **independent clause** has a subject and a verb and can stand by itself as a complete sentence.

All complete sentences must contain at least one independent clause; additional independent or subordinate clauses may be added.

ONE INDEPENDENT CLAUSE:

The <u>school</u> <u>will perform</u> the musical *My Fair Lady*.

TWO INDEPENDENT CLAUSES:

<u>I</u> <u>ate</u> some crackers, but <u>I</u> <u>was</u> still hungry.

INDEPENDENT AND SUBORDINATE CLAUSES:

The <u>house</u> <u>was</u> quiet after the <u>children</u> <u>left</u> for school.

The last sentence in the preceding set of examples contains an example of the second kind of clause—the *subordinate clause*. Though *after the children left for school* contains a subject (*children*) and a verb (*left*), the clause cannot stand alone. It becomes meaningful only when joined to the independent clause *the house was quiet*.

A **subordinate clause,** although it has a subject and a verb, cannot stand by itself as a sentence; it is only part of a sentence.

Subordinate clauses provide the writer with an important tool since they can add important information and details to sentences and show relationships between separate ideas. Within sentences, subordinate clauses act as either adjectives, adverbs, or nouns.

■ Adjective Clauses

Adjective clauses describe, limit, or qualify nouns or pronouns in ways often not possible with one-word adjectives or adjectival phrases.

An **adjective clause** is a subordinate clause that modifies a noun or pronoun by telling what kind or which one.

An adjective clause appears after the noun or pronoun it modifies and usually begins with a relative pronoun (*who, whom, whose, which,* or *that*) or sometimes with a relative adverb (such as *when, where, why, before,* or *since*).

EXAMPLES: The rug, *which I bought recently,* will be delivered tomorrow.

I still remember the time *when you broke your arm.*

Essential and Nonessential Adjective Clauses.   Like participial and appositive phrases, adjective clauses are punctuated according to whether they add *essential* or *nonessential* information to the sentence.

An adjective clause that is not essential to the basic meaning of a sentence is set off by commas. An essential clause is not set off.

The following chart demonstrates the difference between nonessential and essential clauses. (For more information about punctuating adjective clauses, see Section 12.2.)

NONESSENTIAL ADJECTIVE CLAUSES	ESSENTIAL ADJECTIVE CLAUSES
We visited the observation deck of the Empire State Building, *which is one of the highest in the world.*	We visited the observation deck of the building *that until recently was the tallest in the world.*
Mira, who is a character in *The Women's Room*, represents the trapped housewife of the fifties.	The woman *who is the main character in The Women's Room* represents the trapped housewife in the fifties.

Introductory Words in Adjective Clauses.   Relative pronouns and relative adverbs not only begin adjective clauses but also function within the subordinate clause.

A relative pronoun or relative adverb functions (1) within the sentence to connect the adjective clause to the modified word and (2) within the clause as a subject, direct object, or other sentence part.

Relative pronouns act, first, as an introduction to the clause, and, second, as a subject, direct object, object of a preposition, or adjective *within* the clause. The role of the relative pronoun can be determined by isolating the adjective clause from the rest of the sentence and then by identifying its subject and verb. Since adjective clauses are sometimes in inverted order, you may need to rearrange the words mentally.

THE USES OF RELATIVE PRONOUNS WITHIN ADJECTIVE CLAUSES	
As a subject	*Sentence:* The fish *that was just reeled in* set a record. *Clause:* that was just reeled in
As a direct object	*Sentence:* Someone broke the window *that I recently fixed.* DO *Reworded clause:* I recently fixed that
As an object of a preposition	*Sentence:* This is my aunt *of whom I have spoken highly.* *Reworded clause:* I have spoken highly of Obj of Prep whom
As an adjective	*Sentence:* I have a friend *whose witty remarks amuse me.* *Clause:* whose witty remarks amuse me

NOTE ABOUT UNDERSTOOD RELATIVE PRONOUNS: In some adjective clauses, the relative pronoun may be understood rather than specifically stated.

EXAMPLE: The job *(that) I am applying for* pays well.

Relative adverbs do not possess the flexibility of relative pronouns; these words function only as adverbs within the clause.

THE USE OF RELATIVE ADVERBS WITHIN ADJECTIVE CLAUSES	
As an adverb	*Sentence:* The name of the inn *where we stayed* was the Benbow Inn. Adv *Reworded clause:* we stayed where

EXERCISE A: Identifying Adjective Clauses. The following sentences contain adjective clauses. Write each adjective clause on your paper, underlining its subject once and verb twice. Finally, circle the relative pronoun or relative adverb and identify its function in the clause. Be prepared to identify the noun or pronoun that each adjective clause modifies.

1. We visited the Canadian Rockies, which have spectacular scenery.
2. The statement I made earlier still reflects my position.
3. The woman whose shopping bag I mistakenly picked up seemed overly upset.
4. Luciano Pavarotti, who sings tenor at the Metropolitan Opera, will perform at the gala.
5. We confirmed our reservations at the hotel where we plan to stay.
6. The plane which I will take from Atlanta will stop in Dallas.
7. We had six inches of snow the day before you arrived.
8. The couch that I bought converts into a comfortable bed.
9. *The Miracle Worker*, which was written as a television drama in 1957, was produced again for television in 1979.
10. The oil on which our economy depends will be depleted in the next century.

EXERCISE B: Punctuating Adjective Clauses. The following sentences contain adjective clauses without punctuation. Copy each sentence onto your paper, underlining the adjective clause and adding commas if necessary.

1. Amazingly, model trains that can carry people have been built.
2. Arthur Ashe who is a successful tennis star has appeared on talk shows.
3. I devoured the fruit cake the day it arrived.
4. An organization called Compassionate Friends which helps parents deal with the death of a child provides a greatly needed service.
5. People who have grown up wealthy sometimes do not realize the value of money.

■ Adverb Clauses

An *adverb clause* functions in a sentence in much the same way one-word adverbs and adverbial phrases do.

An **adverb clause** is a subordinate clause that modifies a verb, adjective, adverb, or verbal. It does this by pointing out where, when, in what manner, to what extent, under what condition, or why.

An adverb clause contains a subject and a verb, though not the main subject and verb in the sentence, and begins with a subordinating conjunction such as *although, because, if, than, where,* or *while.* (For a more complete list of subordinating conjunctions, see Section 1.4.) This kind of subordinate clause may modify any word an adverb can.

ADVERB CLAUSES	
Modified Word	**Examples**
Verb	We called *because we were worried about you.*
Adjective	The graduate student appeared confident *as she took her oral exams.*
Adverb	The movie ended sooner *than we expected.*
Participle	The radio, blaring *as I attempted to do my studies,* made concentration impossible.
Gerund	Proofreading *before I hand in my papers* helps improve my grades.
Infinitive	I wanted to forage for wild blackberries *while the summer season lasted.*

Sometimes adverb clauses beginning with *as* or *than* are elliptical—that is, the verb or both the subject and the verb are understood but not stated.

VERB UNDERSTOOD: I ate as much dessert *as he (ate).*

SUBJECT AND VERB UNDERSTOOD: The hotel manager had more business *than (he had) rooms.*

For rules about the correct use of pronouns in elliptical clauses, see Section 6.2.

EXERCISE C: Identifying Adverb Clauses. Each of the following sentences contains an adverb clause. Write each clause on your paper and indicate whether it modifies a verb, adjective, adverb, or verbal.

1. She developed laryngitis whenever she caught even a mild cold.
2. Hobbling on crutches while my foot was sprained made life difficult.
3. Our crew rowed faster than our competition did.
4. We checked the stock report when the newspaper came.
5. The wheels of the train, clanging as they moved, occasionally emitted sparks.
6. We hoped to dig the well where the water table was high.
7. The oily streets are as slippery as butter is.
8. The coffee, gurgling as it perked, filled the room with a delicious aroma.
9. Because the deadline had passed, I had to pay twice the entry fee.
10. The class went to the library since they needed to complete some research.

EXERCISE D: Recognizing Elliptical Clauses. The following sentences contain elliptical adverb clauses. Write each clause on your paper, and in parentheses, add the understood words.

1. This haircut looks better than the last.
2. Karen Hinton is not as responsible as Millicent Ramat.
3. My brother has fewer blond streaks in his hair than red.
4. The doctor sees you more than me.
5. The child for whom I babysat was as good as gold.

■ Noun Clauses

The *noun clause* is the last of the three kinds of subordinate clauses.

A noun clause is a subordinate clause that acts as a noun in a sentence.

As the following chart shows, a noun clause can perform any function in a sentence that any other kind of noun can.

USES OF NOUN CLAUSES IN SENTENCES	
Function in Sentence	**Examples**
Subject	*Whatever tools you need* can be found at Ames Hardware.
Direct object	The dentist treated *whichever patient arrived first.*

Indirect object	The group sent *whoever requested information* a brochure about harp seals.
Object of a preposition	I will cut the board to *whatever length you desire.*
Predicate nominative	To get rid of this cold is *what I would like.*
Appositive	The students made their request, *that the due date for research papers be extended.*

Noun clauses frequently begin with *who, whom, whose, which,* or *that,* the same words that can begin adjective clauses. Some other words that can begin noun clauses are *whoever, whomever, whichever, what, whatever, where, how, when, if,* and *whether.* Besides serving to introduce a noun clause, these words sometimes function within the clause as adjectives, subjects, direct objects, or some other sentence part.

SOME USES OF INTRODUCTORY WORDS IN NOUN CLAUSES	
Function in Clause	**Examples**
Adjective	The child could not choose *which flavor of ice cream she wanted.*
Adverb	We read the can to find out *when the paint would dry.*
Subject	*Whoever understands this* should help those who do not.
Direct object	*Whatever my supervisor advises* I will do.
Introductory word only	The gardener said *that we should plant the bulbs now.*

When *that* functions merely as an introductory word, it may be omitted.

EXAMPLE: We remembered *(that) you wanted to go.*

Since some of the words that introduce noun clauses also introduce adjective and adverb clauses, do not let the introductory word be your only guide to determining the type of clause. Always check the function of the clause in the sentence. With noun clauses, you can also try substituting the words *it, you, fact,* or *thing* for the clause. If the sentence retains its smoothness, the clause is probably a noun clause.

NOUN CLAUSE: I knew *that you would volunteer.* (I knew *it.*)

EXERCISE E: **Identifying Noun Clauses.** Locate the noun clause in each of the following sentences and write it on your paper. Then indicate whether it is functioning as a *subject, direct object, indirect object, object of a preposition, predicate nominative,* or *appositive.* Be prepared to identify the function of the introductory word within the noun clause.

1. The system stifled whatever creativity I might have had.
2. We gave whoever ate at our restaurant an after-dinner mint.
3. Our five year goal—that we expand facilities—meant a huge capital outlay.
4. We found that her loquacity was difficult to bear.
5. Whoever signs this form must sign all other transactions.
6. The tourist inquired about what time the sightseeing bus was leaving.
7. The store sent whoever had charge accounts a monthly statement.
8. Her fear is that she will be caught in an elevator.
9. Whatever time the baby falls asleep will be his bedtime.
10. Give this verification slip to whoever is at the desk.

EXERCISE F: **Identifying Subordinate Clauses.** A clause is underlined in each of the following quotations. On your paper, identify the clause as *adjective, adverb,* or *noun.*

1. I have never been hurt by <u>what I have not said.</u> —Calvin Coolidge
2. Nothing is enough for the man <u>to whom enough is too little.</u> —Epicurus
3. You can't depend on your judgment <u>when your imagination is out of focus.</u> —Mark Twain
4. Those <u>who do not complain</u> are never pitied. —Jane Austen
5. <u>Whoever seeks to set one race against another</u> seeks to enslave all races. —Franklin D. Roosevelt
6. There are things <u>that are important</u> beyond all this fiddle. —Marianne Moore

7. <u>Whenever I prepare for a journey</u> I prepare as though for death. —Katherine Mansfield
8. Life leaps like a geyser for those <u>who drill through the rock of inertia.</u> —Dr. Alexis Carrel
9. <u>If a man does not know what port he is steering for,</u> no wind is favorable to him. —Seneca
10. The world stands out on either side no wider <u>than the heart is wide.</u> —Edna St. Vincent Millay
11. Wealth is not his that has it, but his <u>that enjoys it.</u> —Benjamin Franklin
12. <u>Though we travel the world over to find the beautiful,</u> we must carry it with us or we find it not. —Ralph Waldo Emerson
13. I beheld the wretch—the miserable monster <u>whom I had created.</u> —Mary Wollstonecraft Shelley
14. Vote for the man <u>who promises least;</u> he'll be the least disappointing. —Bernard M. Baruch
15. The zeal <u>which begins with hypocrisy</u> must conclude in treachery. —Francis Bacon
16. It is better to know some of the questions <u>than all of the answers.</u> —James Thurber
17. When I write, I am re-creating <u>what was created for me.</u> —Elizabeth Bowen
18. I have more memories <u>than if I were a thousand years old.</u> —Charles Baudelaire
19. Be charitable <u>before wealth makes thee covetous.</u> —Sir Thomas Browne
20. Never stand begging for that <u>which you have the power to earn.</u> —Miguel de Cervantes

APPLICATION: **Using Subordinate Clauses to Expand Sentences.** Complete each of the following sentences on your paper, filling in the blank with the kind of clause indicated.

1. Our Spanish club wanted to collect newspapers <u>(adverb clause)</u>.
2. The high school band <u>(adjective clause)</u> performed at a recent concert.
3. Here is the valuable antique <u>(adjective clause)</u>.
4. We went to the discount store <u>(adverb clause)</u>.
5. <u>(noun clause)</u> is not very important.
6. Her beautiful smile is <u>(noun clause)</u>.
7. <u>(adverb clause)</u>, I plan my wardrobe carefully.
8. Our family will eat <u>(noun clause)</u>.
9. We purchased some land <u>(adjective clause)</u>.
10. The fumes increasing <u>(adverb clause)</u>, I finally gave up my attempt.

Sentences Classified by Structure 3.4

A sentence can be classified according to the kind and number of clauses it contains. Different combinations of independent and subordinate clauses form four basic sentence structures: *simple, compound, complex,* and *compound-complex.* Being able to analyze these structures will help you check the logic and completeness of your own sentences.

A **simple sentence** consists of a single independent clause.

A **compound sentence** consists of two or more independent clauses joined by a comma and a coordinating conjunction (and, but, for, nor, or, so, yet) or by a semicolon.

A **complex sentence** consists of one independent clause and one or more subordinate clauses.

A **compound-complex sentence** consists of two or more independent clauses and one or more subordinate clauses.

As you study the examples of each structure in the following chart, notice that simple sentences can contain compound subjects, compound verbs, or both.

FOUR STRUCTURES OF SENTENCES	
Simple sentences	I received your letter last week.
	Either Fran or Dave will sell the tickets.
	Frightened by the thunder, the dog ran and hid under the bed.
Compound sentences	Our group addressed the envelopes, and another sorted them by ZIP code.
	Spring was arriving; buds were swelling on the trees.
Complex sentences	*Subordinate Clause* *Main Clause* Although the photograph had faded we could still make out many details.
	Main Clause *Subordinate Clause* The book, which recounts the history of South Africa, is banned in the very nation that it describes.

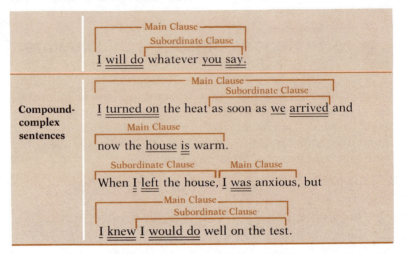

Notice in the preceding examples that in complex and compound-complex sentences the independent clauses are called *main clauses* to distinguish them from subordinate clauses. The subject and verb of a main clause, in turn, are usually called the *subject of the sentence* and the *main verb* to distinguish them from the other subjects and verbs. You should also note that sometimes in a complex or compound-complex sentence a noun clause may be an integral part of the main clause, as it is in the third example under complex sentences.

EXERCISE A: Identifying the Four Structures of Sentences. Read the following sentences and determine their structure. On your paper, identify them as *simple, compound, complex,* or *compound-complex.*

1. Neither did the winds die, nor did the heat subside.
2. The clerk rang up the sale and wrapped our purchases.
3. Though the detectives worked diligently, they could not unravel the mystery.
4. When the network produced the special *Shōgun,* the critics gave it mixed reviews.
5. The peninsula—a long, pencil-like projection—was covered with thick vegetation.
6. People who continually complain rarely have many friends.
7. We found the turnpike quickly, but then we ran out of gas.
8. The session was for whatever complaints people wanted to air, and the supervisors heard quite an assortment.
9. Leaving the safety of the harbor, we ventured out to sea.
10. The room was stuffy, so I opened the window nearest the chair where I sat.

APPLICATION: **Writing Sentences with Different Structures.** Write a sentence of your own that corresponds to each of the following structures. Underline each independent clause.

1. Simple sentence
2. Simple sentence with compound subject
3. Simple sentence containing an appositive phrase
4. Compound sentence with a verbal phrase
5. Compound sentence joined by a semicolon
6. Complex sentence with an adverb clause
7. Complex sentence with a noun clause
8. Complex sentence with an adjective and adverb clause
9. Compound-complex sentence
10. Compound-complex sentence with a noun clause and an adverb clause

Diagraming Sentences with Phrases and Clauses | 3.5

Phrases and clauses are each diagramed in a different way to set them apart visually. This section will teach you to diagram these elements and show you how these skills are used to diagram compound, complex, and compound-complex sentences.

■ Prepositional Phrases

A prepositional phrase is diagramed beneath the word it modifies. The preposition is placed on a slanted line and its object on a horizontal line. Modifers of the object are placed beneath it on slanted lines. Compound objects of the preposition are diagramed just like other compound parts.

EXAMPLE: The desk with the faulty leg is located in the first row or the second one.

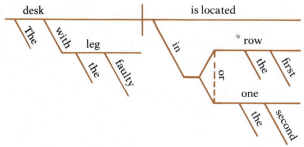

The following chart shows the technique for diagraming a prepositional phrase that modifies an adjective or adverb, the object of another prepositional phrase, or the same word that another prepositional phrase modifies.

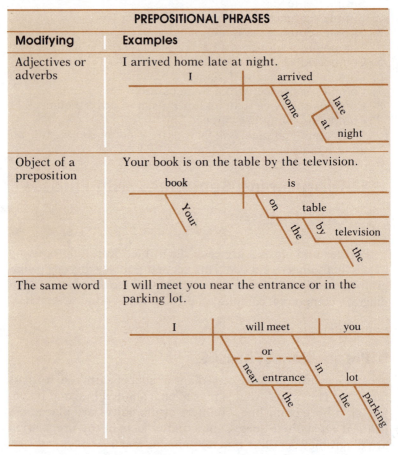

PREPOSITIONAL PHRASES	
Modifying	**Examples**
Adjectives or adverbs	I arrived home late at night.
Object of a preposition	Your book is on the table by the television.
The same word	I will meet you near the entrance or in the parking lot.

EXERCISE A: **Diagraming Prepositional Phrases.** Diagram each of the following sentences on your paper.

1. On the walls, the store had hung kites of every size and shape.
2. Sleepily, he pressed down the alarm button on his clock.
3. Our family piled into the station wagon and headed for the freeway.
4. My friend was sensitive to my needs and fears.
5. With dexterity, the mechanic changed the flat tire on our car.

■ Appositive Phrases

Diagram an appositive by placing it in parentheses following the noun or pronoun it renames. Position any of its modifiers directly beneath it.

EXAMPLE: Mrs. Rebholtz, a friend of the family, will visit next week.

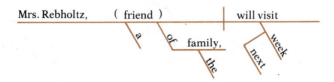

EXERCISE B: **Diagraming Appositive Phrases.** Using the techniques you have just learned, diagram each of the following sentences on your paper.

1. My home, a small, two-bedroom apartment, will be converted into a condominium.
2. I gave the bride, a young woman of twenty, some crystal candlesticks.
3. The organization, all two hundred members, wrote letters of protest.
4. We visited Columbia, a restored town of the Gold Rush days.
5. Jurors should report to Judge Bean, a strict but fair guardian of the law.

■ Verbal Phrases

Verbal phrases, which are constructed around participles, gerunds, and infinitives, are slightly more difficult to diagram than prepositional or appositive phrases. As you go through the following explanations, remember that verbals are never diagramed on a straight line and that they may have complements.

Participles and Participial Phrases. Participles that function as adjectives are placed on slanted lines beneath the noun or pronoun they modify. The participle is written so that it begins on a slanted line and ends on a horizontal line. Any modifiers or complements in a participial phrase are diagramed in the usual way.

EXAMPLE: A child selling candy door-to-door came to our house.

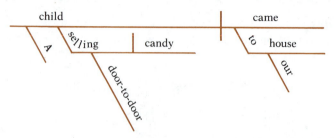

Since it is grammatically separate from the rest of the sentence, a nominative absolute is placed by itself above the baseline.

EXAMPLE: The business concluded for the year, the stockholders headed home.

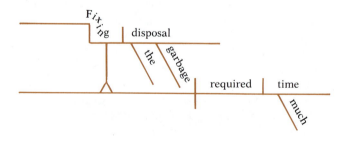

Gerunds and Gerund Phrases.   Gerunds can occupy any position in a diagram that a noun can. When they function as subjects, appositives, direct objects, or predicate nominatives, gerunds sit atop a pedestal on a stepped line. Any modifiers or complements are diagramed in the usual manner.

EXAMPLE: Fixing the garbage disposal required much time.

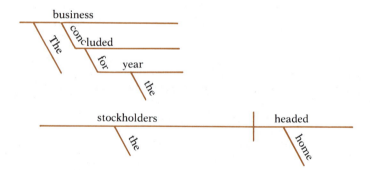

A gerund or gerund phrase functioning as an indirect object or as the object of a preposition goes on a stepped line extending from a slanted line.

EXAMPLE: We bought a small car for driving around town.

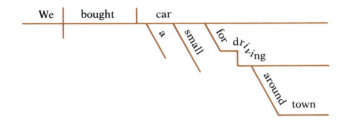

Infinitives and Infinitive Phrases.   Since infinitives can be used as nouns, adverbs, or adjectives, there are a variety of ways to diagram them. An infinitive used as a noun sits on a pedestal on a line similar to yet less complex than the line used for a gerund. Its modifiers and complements are diagramed in the usual manner. The following example shows an infinitive used as a predicate nominative.

EXAMPLE: My resolution for the new year is to exercise daily.

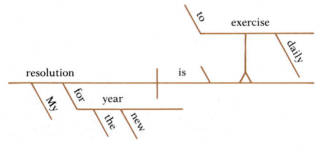

The diagram of an infinitive used as an adjective or adverb looks like the diagram of a prepositional phrase.

EXAMPLE: World War I was supposedly the war to end all war.

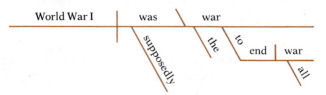

When an infinitive has an understood *to,* indicate the implied word in parentheses. If the infinitive has a subject, extend the left side of the infinitive line and place the subject there.

EXAMPLE: We heard thunder rumble during the night.

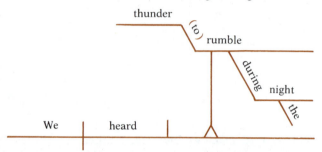

EXERCISE C: Diagraming Verbal Phrases. Diagram each of the following sentences on your paper.

1. The students writing feverishly in blue books are working on an examination.
2. Training for a major competitive event leaves an athlete little time for other activities.
3. They were requested to start the game with the national anthem.
4. Capitalizing on his good fortune, the man bought some real estate in the area.
5. The tea tasting of herbal spices felt good against my sore throat.
6. Help me tie this bow securely.
7. Six in the morning is too early to rise and shine.
8. Furnishing oranges and sodas for half time was the responsibility of the team manager.
9. Learning to diagram sentences develops both manual and mental skills.
10. Her worst habit, trailing into class late, led to her suspension.

■ Compound, Complex, and Compound-Complex Sentences

All the sentences you have diagramed up to this point have been simple sentences. However, diagraming the other three sentence structures—compound, complex, and compound-

complex—involves most of the same rules. The primary difference is in the addition of another baseline for each additional
clause.

Compound Sentences. Each of the independent clauses in
a compound sentence is diagramed separately. They are then
joined together at the verbs by a dotted step line. The conjunction or semicolon is written on this step line.

EXAMPLE: I drove and he slept.

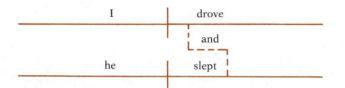

Complex Sentences. Diagraming complex sentences involves knowing how to position each of the three kinds of subordinate clauses in relation to the independent clause. An *adjective clause* is diagramed below the main clause as if it were
a separate sentence. A slanted dotted line going from the relative pronoun or relative adverb in the adjective clause to the
word the clause modifies joins the two. In the following example, the relative pronoun functions within the subordinate
clause as a subject.

EXAMPLE: The car that sped around the corner had no headlights.

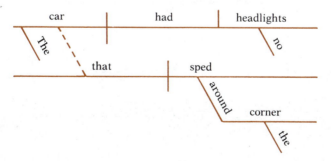

Since a relative pronoun can serve other functions in an adjective clause, be careful to place it in the diagram according
to its use. The following chart shows some of the other positions relative pronouns can occupy depending on their function in various adjective clauses.

DIFFERENT FUNCTIONS OF THE RELATIVE PRONOUN IN ADJECTIVE CLAUSES

Function of Relative Pronoun	Examples

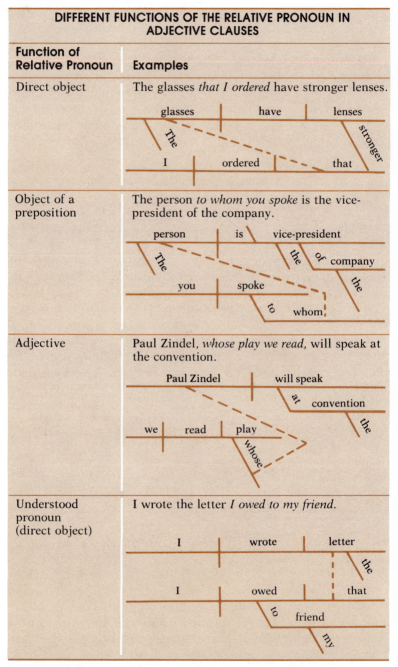

Direct object

The glasses *that I ordered* have stronger lenses.

Object of a preposition

The person *to whom you spoke* is the vice-president of the company.

Adjective

Paul Zindel, *whose play we read,* will speak at the convention.

Understood pronoun (direct object)

I wrote the letter *I owed to my friend.*

Unlike a relative pronoun in an adjective clause, a *relative adverb* functions in only one capacity in a subordinate clause: as an adverb.

EXAMPLE: The girl sat on the stool *where Lana Turner was discovered.*

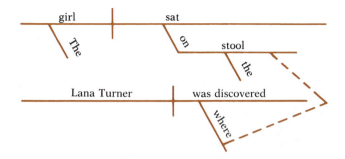

An *adverb clause* is diagramed like an adjective clause, but with one modification: The subordinating conjunction is written on the connecting line. This line should join the verb in the adverb clause to the modified verb, adjective, adverb, or verbal in the main clause. The following chart demonstrates this.

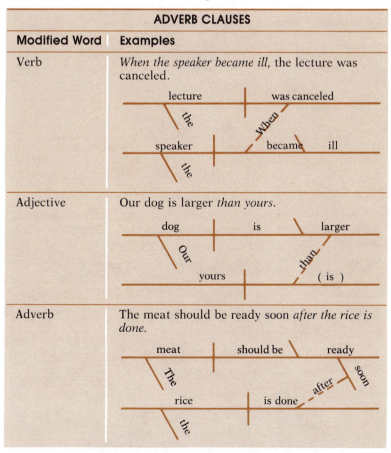

	ADVERB CLAUSES
Modified Word	**Examples**
Verb	*When the speaker became ill,* the lecture was canceled.
Adjective	Our dog is larger *than yours.*
Adverb	The meat should be ready soon *after the rice is done.*

Verbal	I want you to stop talking *when I am speaking.*

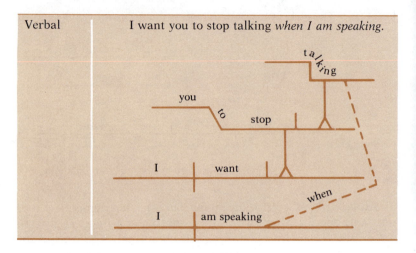

A *noun clause* is diagramed differently: It is placed on a pedestal in the position it occupies within the sentence. The first example shows the noun clause serving as a direct object.

EXAMPLE: I will wear *whatever is clean.*

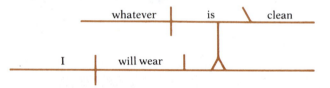

Noun clauses can also function in other ways—as subjects, indirect objects, objects of a preposition, to name just a few. As with adjective clauses, the introductory word in a noun clause can have different functions within the clause. Some of these variations are depicted in the following chart.

SOME DIFFERENT FUNCTIONS OF NOUN CLAUSES	
Function	**Examples**
Subject	*Whoever tries my sister's cookies is very brave.* 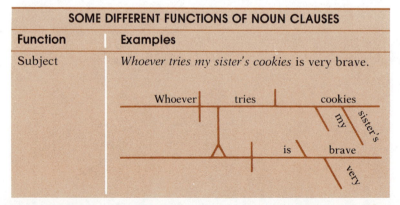

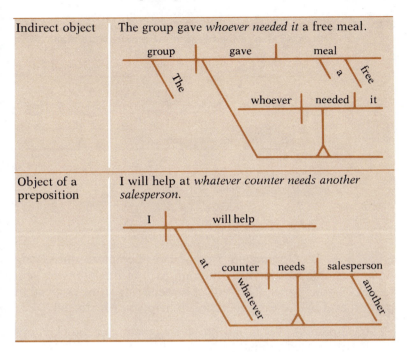

Indirect object	The group gave *whoever needed it* a free meal.

Object of a preposition	I will help at *whatever counter needs another salesperson.*

If a noun clause's introductory word has no other function than to introduce the clause, it is diagramed on the pedestal. In the following example, the word *that* is used simply to introduce the clause.

EXAMPLE: Earl said *that you had a birthday.*

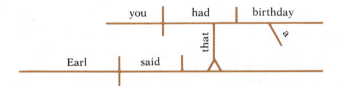

Compound-Complex Sentences.   To diagram these sentences, simply combine the skills you learned for diagraming compound and complex sentences. Begin by planning the diagram in your mind so that it will fit neatly on your paper. Then draw the separate clauses and connect them with the appropriate dotted lines. To diagram the following example, you would start with diagrams for the two independent clauses, being sure to leave enough space between and around them to diagram the subordinate clauses neatly.

EXAMPLE: The man who owned the shop fixed my typewriter, but he refused to charge me because the repairs were minor.

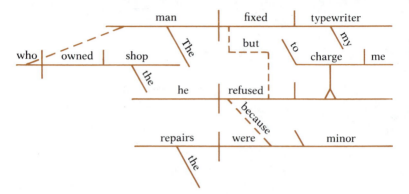

EXERCISE D: Diagraming Compound, Complex, and Compound-Complex Sentences. Diagram each of the following sentences on your paper. The type of sentence structure is given in parentheses before each sentence to help you get started.

1. (Compound) I was eating the ice cream cone quickly, but it still started to melt.
2. (Complex) After we finished our errands, we stopped for lunch.
3. (Compound) We must mail this today or it will not arrive on time.
4. (Complex) Salmon that are spawning know the exact river to which they must return.
5. (Compound-Complex) We should stay at whatever place is cheapest; money is scarce this month.
6. (Compound) Tracy had a serious automobile accident within the last year, but she still does not wear a seat belt in the car.
7. (Complex) We celebrated on the day when the project was complete.
8. (Complex) The couple sat drinking hot chocolate while a fire blazed before them.
9. (Compound-Complex) When he noticed a spot on his coat, he took it to the cleaners, but they were unable to remove the spot.
10. (Compound-Complex) The bus that was scheduled to take us had engine problems, so the company sent us another.

APPLICATION: Diagraming All Sentence Types. Select a short passage from a book written by an author you admire, or use

a paragraph from a composition that you have written recently. Copy each sentence onto your paper and draw its diagram underneath. Be prepared to discuss in class what the diagrams reveal about the passage's overall structure. For example, are the sentences varied or monotonously alike? Are subordinate clauses used effectively to show relationships between ideas, or are the ideas merely strung together in compound sentences?

Chapter 4

Correcting Sentence Faults

Proofreading your work takes additional time, but in the end, it usually results in a finer, more error-free product. If you know something about the most common errors in writing, you can more effectively eliminate them from your own work as you proofread. In this chapter you will examine the most prevalent sentence faults and be given guidelines for repairing them.

4.1 Fragments and Run-ons

Hasty writers sometimes omit crucial words, punctuate awkwardly, or leave their thoughts unfinished. All these mistakes contribute to two of the most common sentence errors: fragments and run-on sentences.

■ Fragments

Though established writers may use fragments purposefully for a stylistic effect, fragments are generally considered a writing error. This is especially true when fragments are used unintentionally. Most fragments in writing are phrases, subordinate clauses, or words in a series punctuated as if they were complete sentences.

> Do not unintentionally capitalize and punctuate phrases, subordinate clauses, or words in a series as if they were complete sentences.

If you have a problem with fragments, reading your work aloud will help you hear where your sentences actually begin and end. By listening to the natural pauses and stops, you should easily be able to identify awkward passages that need revision.

Sometimes, repairing a fragment will merely involve connecting it to words that come before or after it. Other fragments may require more work, such as rearranging, adding, or omitting words. The following chart shows some of the types of fragments you may encounter (italicized in the second column), as well as different methods for correcting them.

PHRASE FRAGMENTS		
Type	**Example**	**Correction**
Prepositional phrase	*With his hand in the cookie jar.* The four-year-old culprit was caught.	The four-year-old culprit was caught *with his hand in the cookie jar.*
Appositive phrase	The boat sank during the storm. *A hurricane with fierce winds and rains.*	The boat sank during the storm, *a hurricane with fierce winds and rains.*
Participial phrase with pronoun	The class boarded the bus. *The one waiting at the corner.*	The class boarded the bus *waiting at the corner.*
Gerund phrase	*Living in the computer age.* Our lives are made easier.	*Living in the computer age* makes our lives easier.
Infinitive phrase	This is all I expect. *To see the job done well.*	All I expect is *to see the job done well.*
CLAUSE FRAGMENTS		
Adjective clause	I read *War and Peace. Which was a condensed version.*	I read a condensed version of *War and Peace.*
Adverb clause	We quickly caught our limit. *After the fish finally tasted our new bait.*	*After the fish finally tasted our new bait,* we quickly caught our limit.
Noun clause	We will eat it. *Whatever our hostess serves us.*	We will eat *whatever our hostess serves us.*

If a series of words seems long enough to constitute a sentence, check it to make sure that it contains a subject and a verb *and* expresses a complete thought. It may be a long fragment masquerading as a complete sentence.

SERIES FRAGMENTS	
Fragment	**Sentence**
John Steinbeck's novel, *The Pearl,* with its sensitive, yet probing look at poverty and greed in the writing style so typical of this master storyteller.	John Steinbeck's no̲v̲e̲l, *The Pearl,* with its sensitive yet probing look at poverty and greed, i̲s̲ w̲r̲i̲t̲t̲e̲n̲ in the style so typical of this master storyteller.

EXERCISE A: Identifying and Correcting Fragments. Read each of the following items. If the words form one or more complete sentences, write *complete* on your paper. If the item contains a fragment, rewrite it to make one or more complete sentences. (Some items contain both a complete sentence and a fragment.)

1. Their faces shining with delight at seeing the popular star.
2. I wanted one thing. To take a long nap.
3. The committee was impressed by this application. Which we received just yesterday.
4. I enjoy working with my hands.
5. Traffic lights flashing erratically as the cars jammed in the intersection, unsure whose turn it was to proceed.
6. The apples cooked. With their sweet juices bubbling away.
7. Just as Mr. Chao said goodbye.
8. Classified ads filling the pages of the newspaper.
9. A report to write and math homework to do before tomorrow.
10. The stark silhouettes of the trees against the light of the moon.

■ Run-on Sentences

A run-on sentence, often simply called a *run-on,* is two or more sentences that are capitalized and punctuated as if they were one.

Use punctuation, conjunctions, or other means to join or separate the parts of a run-on sentence correctly.

There are two kinds of run-ons: *fused sentences*, which are two or more sentences joined with no punctuation, and *comma splices*, which have two or more sentences separated *only* by commas rather than by commas and conjunctions.

FUSED SENTENCE: The team pushed forward for the last yard they were inches short.

COMMA SPLICE: Only one package arrived in the mail, the other items never came.

As with fragments, proofreading or reading your work aloud will usually help you find any run-on sentences in your writing. Once found, they can be corrected by adding punctuation and conjunctions or by rewording the sentence. The following chart demonstrates the various methods for correcting run-ons.

FOUR WAYS TO CORRECT RUN-ONS	
With End Marks and Capitals	
Run-on: The sale was in full swing in the store people crowded the aisles.	*Sentence*: The sale was in full swing. In the store, people crowded the aisles.
With Commas and Conjunctions	
Run-on: The wrapping paper needed cutting we could not locate the scissors.	*Sentence*: The wrapping paper needed cutting, but we could not locate the scissors.
With Semicolons	
Run-on: Our zoo has acquired many rare animals, for example it now has a pair of pandas.	*Sentence*: Our zoo has acquired many rare animals; for example, it now has a pair of pandas.
By Rewriting	
Run-on: The horse show began late, someone had misplaced the registration forms.	*Sentence*: The horse show began late because someone had misplaced the registration forms. (Revised into a complex sentence.)
Run-on: We replaced the sparkplugs, the filter was also bad.	*Sentence*: We replaced the bad sparkplugs and filter. (Revised into a simple sentence with a compound direct object.)

EXERCISE B: Identifying and Correcting Run-on Sentences. Some of the following sentences are correct; others are run-ons. Write *complete* on your paper if the sentence is correct as written. If it is a run-on, correct it. Use each of the four methods for correcting run-ons at least twice.

1. I looked down the well was apparently dry.
2. We read the Preamble to the Constitution, our group felt anew the power of those words.
3. What a beautiful garden on the right the hedge has been shaped into mythical creatures.
4. During my free period I wanted to rest my busy schedule would not give me time later.
5. I mislaid my car keys, my house keys were also gone.
6. We admired the Wedgwood its delicate motifs on the blue background made it a beautiful ornament.
7. Talia threw away the check, but she eventually recovered it.
8. I generally liked the climate of the area where I lived I did not enjoy the subfreezing temperatures of winter.
9. Everyone should know simple courtesies, however the number of rude people proves that many do not.
10. I concocted my own spicy chili to eat it one needs an iron stomach.
11. The boy had trouble with the decimal point when multiplying a problem he always put it in the wrong place.
12. A furrier in New York was robbed; the alarm system had been professionally deactivated.
13. During natural disasters, the Red Cross provides aid, it gives food, blankets, and emergency care to the victims.
14. The thermometer broke, the mercury spilled onto the floor.
15. The fortress had stood impregnable for decades no marauding forces had broken through its walls.
16. It is expressly forbidden by law to litter freeways, nevertheless, they are covered by paper.
17. The peacock spread his feathers, and with pride he paraded in front of the hen.
18. Overalls have been popular recently many high school and college students wear them.
19. My cousin has bowled a perfect game once in his life; his teammate has also.
20. Riding a rickshaw in the Orient was more frightening than driving a car, we careened around corners and wound our way through the rush of traffic.

APPLICATION: Locating and Correcting Fragments and Run-ons. The following selection contains some fragments and run-ons. Write *correct* on your paper if the numbered sequence contains no errors. If it does contain an error, correct the sentence.

(1) Mosquitoes, those nasty little insects whose bites cause our skin to swell and itch. (2) They inhabit every state in the Union and most areas of the world. (3) Actually the bites should not be considered mere irritants they lead to many deaths every year. (4) These insects transmit many ailments. (5) Temporary insanity, filariasis, and many types of viral and bacterial infections. (6) Of course, mosquitoes must bite to survive, the females need the protein from the blood to produce their eggs. (7) The females weighing one ten-thousandth of an ounce when unfed and tripling that after a single bite. (8) One of nature's greatest achievements, the two intricate pumps inside the female's head. (9) They draw the blood to produce seventy-five eggs, only one bite is necessary. (10) Much has been done to halt the growth of mosquitoes, nothing, however, has been discovered that completely eradicates these insects.

Misplaced and Dangling Modifiers   4.2

To insure logical sentence construction and clear writing, careful writers put modifiers as close as possible to the words they modify. When modifiers are misplaced or left dangling, the result is often ludicrous or hopelessly confusing. This section will show you methods for correcting these errors.

■ Misplaced Modifiers

Misplaced modifiers occur when the modifer is placed too far from the word it should modify.

A **misplaced modifier** seems to modify the wrong word in the sentence.

Any phrase or clause that acts as an adjective or adverb can unintentionally be misplaced in a sentence.

MISPLACED MODIFIERS: A bicyclist ran into a fence *riding in the race*.

We heard the telephone ring *while watching TV*.

To correct the type of error shown in the preceding examples, move the phrase or clause so that it is closer to the word it actually modifies.

CORRECTED SENTENCES: A bicyclist *riding in the race* ran into a fence.

While watching TV, we heard the telephone ring.

One variation of the misplaced modifier is the *squinting modifier*—a phrase or clause that appears to modify two words at once.

SQUINTING MODIFIER: He heard *after he was married* that things would change.

The clause *after he was married* could modify either the verb *heard* or the verb phrase *would change*. To clarify the sentence, simply move the clause so that it clearly modifies one part of the sentence or the other.

CORRECTED SENTENCES: *After he was married*, he heard that things would change.

He heard that things would change *after he was married*.

EXERCISE A: Identifying and Correcting Misplaced Modifiers.

Each of the following sentences contains a misplaced modifer. Find it and rewrite the sentence correctly.

1. We saw the seagulls sitting at the sidewalk cafe.
2. Our friends called the pizza parlor to have a pizza made by phone.
3. Whirling round and round, we saw our clothes in the drier.
4. The grandfather clock awoke me, chiming out the hour.
5. He jumped to his feet and went out the door remembering the laundry.
6. Under the couch, he found the dollar.
7. The young girl ran toward her horse crying with joy.
8. The spaghetti sauce was served to the man smelling strongly of garlic.

9. The apartment buildings on the ground from the airplane looked small.
10. Covered with mold, he threw out the cheese.

■ Dangling Modifiers

With misplaced modifiers, the word that needs to be modified can be found within the sentence; with *dangling modifiers,* however, the word that should be modified is missing completely from the sentence.

> A **dangling modifier** seems to modify the wrong word or no word at all because the word it should modify has been omitted from the sentence.

Dangling modifiers are corrected by either adding the missing word to the main clause or rephrasing the modifier to include the missing word. The following examples show the most common kinds of dangling modifiers and the methods for correcting them.

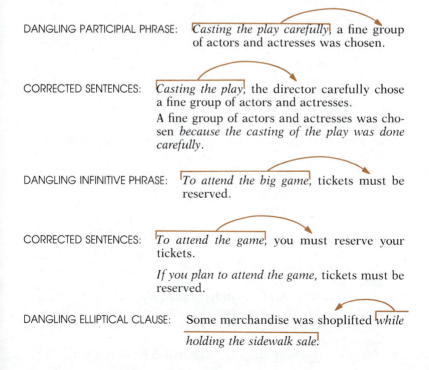

DANGLING PARTICIPIAL PHRASE: *Casting the play carefully,* a fine group of actors and actresses was chosen.

CORRECTED SENTENCES: *Casting the play,* the director carefully chose a fine group of actors and actresses.

A fine group of actors and actresses was chosen *because the casting of the play was done carefully.*

DANGLING INFINITIVE PHRASE: *To attend the big game,* tickets must be reserved.

CORRECTED SENTENCES: *To attend the game,* you must reserve your tickets.

If you plan to attend the game, tickets must be reserved.

DANGLING ELLIPTICAL CLAUSE: Some merchandise was shoplifted *while holding the sidewalk sale.*

CORRECTED SENTENCES: *While holding a sidewalk sale*, the store had some merchandise shoplifted.

Some merchandise was shoplifted *while the store was holding a sidewalk sale*.

EXERCISE B: **Identifying and Correcting Dangling Modifiers.** Read the following sentences. If the sentence is correct, write *correct* on your paper. If the sentence contains a dangling modifier, rewrite it using one of the techniques described in this section.

1. To eat before the game, dinner must be ready within fifteen minutes.
2. The chicken bone stuck in her throat while laughing.
3. Checking all the stations, the assembly line was running smoothly.
4. Having lost my hat in the wind, I unfortunately missed the trolley I wanted.
5. Falling on the asphalt, my knees were badly skinned.
6. To find our way to camp, the compass pointed out the direction.
7. To pursue the problem logically, a solution could easily be reached.
8. Dinner looked unappetizing after eating snacks all day.
9. You must rehearse a speech thoroughly before presenting it before a group.
10. Having decorated the cake with flowers, it looked like a work of art.

APPLICATION: **Avoiding Misplaced and Dangling Modifiers.** Complete each of the following sentences on your paper, filling in the blank with the kind of clause or phrase indicated. Make sure that you do not use any misplaced or dangling modifiers.

1. When carving the turkey,   __(independent clause)__ .
2. She devoured the meal   __(elliptical clause)__ .
3. __(participial phrase)__ , the jockey rode the horse to victory.
4. To remark on such a trivial matter, __(independent clause)__.
5. __(participial phrase)__ , the huge rock threatened the boats in the area.
6. Standing speechless before the group,   __(independent clause)__ .
7. Beautiful to look at,   __(independent clause)__ .
8. __(adverb clause)__ , the companies were merged.
9. __(participial phrase)__ , the family explained their destitute circumstances.
10. Before   __(gerund phrase)__ , he asked for a receipt.

Faulty Parallelism 4.3

Two parallel lines will run smoothly side by side—never colliding. Writers try to achieve a similar effect by writing a series of ideas in similar grammatical structures so that they will read smoothly—never colliding. If one element in a series is not parallel with the others, the sentence may be jarring and its meaning may be altered. This section will show you how to correct this sentence error, called *faulty parallelism*.

■ Correct Parallelism in Sentences

To express a comparison or a series of ideas of equal importance, careful writers use parallel grammatical structures.

Parallelism is the placement of equal ideas in words, phrases, or clauses of similar types.

A parallel grammatical structure can be two or more words of the same part of speech, two or more phrases of the same type, two or more clauses of the same type, and sometimes, for emphasis, two or more sentences of the same type.

PARALLEL WORDS: The boxer looked *strong, fit,* and *agile* as he entered the ring.

PARALLEL PHRASES: The greatest pleasure I know is *to do a good action by stealth,* and *to have it found out by accident.* —Charles Lamb

PARALLEL CLAUSES: The professor *whom I have met* and *whom you currently have in class* will be on television next week.

PARALLEL SENTENCES: *It couldn't be, of course. It could never, never be.* —Dorothy Parker

Now examine the following passage that begins *A Tale of Two Cities* by Charles Dickens, a novel about the French Revolution. Notice how the parallel structures set up vivid contrasts and end with the ironic sentence hinting at the political conflict to come.

EXAMPLE: It was the best of times, it was the worst of times, it was the age of wisdom, it was the age of foolishness, it was the epoch of belief, it was the epoch of incredulity, it was the season of Light, it was the season of Darkness, it was the spring of hope, it was the winter of despair, we had everything before us, we had nothing before us, we were all going direct to Heaven, we were all going direct the other way—in short, the period was so far like the present period, that some of its noisiest authorities insisted on its being received, for good or for evil, in the superlative degree of comparison only.

There were a king with a large jaw and a queen with a plain face, on the throne of England; there were a king with a large jaw and a queen with a fair face, on the throne of France. In both countries it was clearer than crystal to the lords of the State preserves of loaves and fishes, that things in general were settled for ever. —Charles Dickens

EXERCISE A: **Recognizing Parallel Structures.** Find the parallel structures in the following quotations and write them on your paper. Then identify what each is composed of: words, phrases, clauses, or whole sentences.

1. The earth belongs to the living, not to the dead.
   —Thomas Jefferson
2. Great men never feel great; small men never feel small.
3. Earth to earth, ashes to ashes, dust to dust, in sure and certain hope of the resurrection. —Book of Common Prayer
4. I love thee freely, as men strive for Right; I love thee purely, as they turn from Praise.
   —Elizabeth Barrett Browning
5. Communism possesses a language which every people can understand—its elements are hunger, envy, and death.
   —Heinrich Heine
6. Pleasures are transient; honors are immortal.
   —Greek Proverb
7. The less we know the more we suspect. —H.W. Shaw
8. We are born for cooperation, as are the feet, the hands, the eyelids, and the upper and lower jaws. —Marcus Aurelius
9. When I did well, I heard it never; when I did ill, I heard it ever. —English Proverb
10. I lingered round them, under that benign sky: watched the moths fluttering among the heath and harebells; listened to the soft wind breathing through the grass; and wondered how anyone could ever imagine unquiet slumbers for the sleepers in that quiet earth. —Emily Brontë

■ Faulty Parallel Structures

Faulty parallelism occurs when a writer uses unequal grammatical structures to express related ideas.

Correct a sentence containing faulty parallelism by rewriting it so that each parallel idea is expressed in the same grammatical structure.

Faulty parallelism can involve words, phrases, and clauses in series or in comparisons.

Nonparallel Words, Phrases, and Clauses in Series. Always check a series of ideas in your writing for parallelism. If, for example, you begin a series with prepositional phrases, make certain you maintain consistency by making all the items in the series prepositional phrases.

The following chart presents some nonparallel structures and shows how they can be repaired to restore the smoothness and clarity to the sentence. Notice how coordinating conjunctions (*and, but, or,* and so forth) often join series and can serve as a signal for you to check the items they connect for parallelism.

CORRECTING FAULTY PARALLELISM IN SERIES	
Nonparallel Structures	**Corrected Sentences**
Thinking, outlining, drafting, (Gerund Gerund Gerund) and *revision* (Noun) are four steps in the writing process.	*Thinking, outlining, drafting,* (Gerund Gerund Gerund) and *revising* (Gerund) are four steps in the writing process.
I was appalled *to see her* (Infin) *manners, to hear her bad* (Phrase, Infin) *language,* and *feeling her* (Phrase, Part) *intense animosity.* (Phrase)	I was appalled *to see her* (Infin) *manners, to hear her bad* (Phrase, Infin) *language,* and *to feel her intense* (Phrase, Infin) *animosity.* (Phrase)
Some experts feel *that our* (Noun) *population is too large,* but *it* (Clause, Indep) *will diminish.* (Clause)	Some experts feel *that our* (Noun) *population is too large* but *that it will diminish.* (Clause, Noun Clause)

Though correlative conjunctions, such as *both . . . and* or *not only . . . but also,* connect just two related items, writers often mistakenly include more words than are necessary under the umbrella of the first part of the conjunction. The result is faulty parallelism

NONPARALLEL: The student not only *won a National Merit scholarship* but also *a National Honor Society scholarship.*

CORRECTED: The student won not only *a National Merit scholarship* but also *a National Honor Society scholarship.*

Nonparallel Words, Phrases, and Clauses in Comparisons.   As the old saying goes, you cannot compare apples with oranges. In writing comparisons, you usually should not compare a phrase with a clause or with a different type of phrase. Furthermore, you should make sure your ideas themselves, as well as the structures you use to express them, are logically parallel.

CORRECTING FAULTY PARALLELISM IN COMPARISONS	
Nonparallel Structures	**Corrected Sentences**
Most people prefer *corn* to *eating* Brussels sprouts. *(Noun, Gerund, Phrase)*	Most people prefer *corn* to Brussels sprouts. *(Noun, Noun)*
I left my job *at 7:00 p.m.* rather than *stopping work at 5:00 p.m.* *(Prep Phrase, Part Phrase)*	I left my job *at 7:00 p.m.* rather than *at the usual 5:00 p.m.* *(Prep Phrase, Prep Phrase)*
I delight in foggy *days* as much as sunny *days* delight other people. *(S, DO, S, DO)*	I delight in foggy *days* as much as other people delight in sunny *days.* *(S, DO, S, DO)*

EXERCISE B: Correcting Faulty Parallelism. Each of the following sentences contains faulty parallelism. Rewrite each sentence so that it is in proper parallel form.

1. The new employee was lazy, insolent, and came tardy.
2. I think the plants did well because of the fertilizer rather than that I talked to them each day.
3. Karl either will go to the demolition derby or to the Egyptian museum.
4. I hate writing papers as much as having shots upsets me.
5. My father both wanted to keep his job at the bank and to move our family to the country.
6. Vincent van Gogh was a brilliant painter but unbalanced in the mind.
7. I would choose reading a book over a television show.

8. His old tennis shoes were dirty, smelly, and had many large holes.
9. The coach tells me that I bat well, but I field poorly.
10. Laughing together, sharing one another's close times, and to overlook faults—these are the things that make .true friends.

APPLICATION: **Writing Sentences Containing Parallel Structures.** Follow the instructions in parentheses to revise each of the following sentences. Make sure your revised sentences contain parallel structures.

1. Gathering honey, the bees work diligently.   (Add another participial phrase.)
2. I listened to the melody floating through the air.   (Add another independent clause.)
3. The writer published a novel.   (Add three adjectives.)
4. I love weeding in the garden.   (Compare weeding to something else.)
5. I will participate in the log rolling contest.   (Add two more prepositional phrases.)
6. The parade route headed down Main Street.   (Add two more verbs with prepositional phrases.)
7. The knight had to slay the dragon.   (Add two more infinitive phrases.)
8. I was pleased by the game we played.   (Add another prepositional phrase that is modified by an adjective clause.)
9. Whoever keeps the thermostat at 68° helps conserve energy.   (Add another noun clause.)
10. I prepared the canapés.   (Add two more direct objects.)

Faulty Coordination   4.4

And is a useful word for joining ideas, but when two or more independent clauses of unequal importance are joined by *and*, the result is *faulty coordination*. This section will help you recognize faulty coordination and show you how to correct it.

■ The Use of *And* in Compound Sentences

To coordinate means "to place side by side in equal rank." Two independent clauses that are joined by the coordinating conjunction *and*, therefore, should have equal rank. One idea should not be less important than the other.

Use *and* or other coordinating conjunctions only to connect ideas of equal importance.

CORRECT COORDINATION: John dusted the furniture, *and* I vacuumed the carpet.

Sometimes, however, writers carelessly use *and* to join independent clauses that either should not be joined or should be joined in another way so that the real relationship between the clauses will be clear. Then the faulty coordination puts all the ideas on the same level of importance whether or not they logically deserve to be. The precise relationship between the ideas is left haphazard and vague. (For more information about connecting your ideas logically, see Section 20.1.)

FAULTY COORDINATION: My tooth cracked, *and* I desperately needed to see the dentist.

I lost *and* the race was easy.

Occasionally, writers will string together so many ideas with *and*'s that the reader is left breathless.

STRINGY SENTENCE: The man who entered the restaurant wore a sportshirt and gray slacks *and* he asked for a table *and* the maitre d' apologetically said the man had to have a tie and jacket *and* the man became furious and left.

EXERCISE A: **Identifying Correct and Faulty Coordination.** Each of the following compound sentences is joined by *and*. For the four sentences in which *and* is properly used, write *correct* on your paper. For the other six, write *faulty*.

1. The spaniel has been snapping and barking at approaching strangers, and her puppies were born last night.
2. Willow trees lined the main street, and it was called Grand Avenue.
3. The children jumped into the unheated pool and squealed as they hit the water, and immediately they hopped out and dried themselves off and decided to forgo the swim.
4. The outside of my house wears a fresh coat of paint, and the inside has been newly redecorated.

5. I remembered that I had read the book a long time ago, and I saw the movie last night.
6. My throat felt parched, and the cool drink soothed it.
7. The covered wagon pulled its load over the plains and its wheel became mired in the mud and four oxen and five able bodies were needed to free it.
8. You will come, and our family will show you around our part of the country.
9. I relaxed while basking in the warm sun, and soon I fell fast asleep.
10. I could hardly get the key in the lock, and my fingers were numb from the cold.

■ Revising Sentences with Faulty Coordination

Faulty coordination can be corrected in several ways.

Revise sentences with faulty coordination by (1) putting unrelated ideas into separate sentences, (2) putting a less important or dependent idea into a subordinate clause, or (3) reducing an unimportant idea into a phrase.

When faulty coordination occurs in a sentence in which the independent clauses are not closely related, separate the clauses and omit the coordinating conjunction.

FAULTY COORDINATION: Steam was pouring forth from my car, *and* the gas station attendant said my radiator was cracked.

CORRECTION: Steam was pouring forth from my car. The gas station attendant said my radiator was cracked.

The second method for correcting faulty coordination takes a bit more thought. You will have to examine each independent clause and determine if one is less important or dependent on the other. If so, turn it into a subordinate clause.

FAULTY COORDINATION: My tooth cracked, *and* I desperately needed to see a dentist.

CORRECTED SENTENCE: When my tooth cracked, I desperately needed to see a dentist.

FAULTY COORDINATION: I lost *and* the race was easy.

CORRECTED SENTENCE: I lost, even though the race was easy.

The third method involves reducing an unimportant idea to a phrase—that is, changing the compound sentence into a simple sentence. An independent clause that can be reduced to a phrase will often begin with a pronoun and a linking verb, such as *he is* or *it was*. In the following example, notice that the second clause has been turned into a participial phrase and made part of the first clause.

FAULTY COORDINATION: The dog looked ferocious, and it was snarling and snapping at me.

CORRECTED SENTENCE: Snarling and snapping at me, the dog looked ferocious.

Stringy sentences should be broken up and revised using any of the three methods just described. Often, there will be several ways to regroup the ideas logically. Experiment with a few possibilities before making a choice. Following is one way that the stringy sentence on page 142 can be revised.

REVISION OF STRINGY SENTENCE: The man who entered the restaurant wore a sportshirt and slacks. When he asked for a table, the maitre d' apologetically said the man had to have a tie and jacket. At that, the man became furious and left.

EXERCISE B: **Correcting Faulty Coordination.** Each of the following sentences contains faulty coordination. Rewrite the sentences correctly, using each method of correction at least twice.

1. I slowly climbed to the lookout point and reaching the top provided me with a spectacular view.
2. The car is dented and it has room for six.
3. We watched a special on naturalist John James Audubon and the organization dedicated to birds is named after him.
4. The diesel truck had a full load and it slowed down going up the grade.
5. We turned on the television and a commerical promptly showed up and I turned the channel looking for something better and commercials were on wherever I turned.
6. Evan has a new wool pullover and he plans to wear it to the beach where the wind can turn very cold.
7. Tammy walked on her sprained ankle and the ankle started to swell again.

8. Rocky Bleir received a serious injury in Vietnam and he came back to play football for the Pittsburgh Steelers.
9. Some terminally ill people wish to be frozen, and this is the science of cryogenics.
10. The crowds to see the movie were enormous and we even ordered tickets prior to going, and unfortunately, we still sat near the screen and came away with kinks in our necks.

APPLICATION: **Avoiding Faulty Coordination in Sentences.** Combine each of the following sets of sentences, using coordination or subordination wherever appropriate. Check each of your combined sentences for faulty coordination.

1. I lost the gold charm. It had been a gift from my father.
2. Daydreams invade the waking hours. Nightmares haunt the darkness.
3. Millions of bats inhabit one particular cave. Each night, they journey to a lake over a hundred miles away.
4. I enjoy thumbing through encyclopedias. They contain fascinating articles.
5. The ice was inadvertently left out. It melted all over the countertop.
6. The handbook had a soft cloth cover. Inside, it was filled with clever ideas and shortcuts for household tasks.
7. The shepherds huddled near the fire, the only source of warmth on the lonely hill. Their dogs lay snuggled against their masters' legs.
8. I use a knapsack for a daylong hike. I switch to a backpack for longer excursions.
9. Prehistoric beasts once walked this land. Today, we study fossils from that time period.
10. I told the obnoxious man to stop talking during the movie. Next, I asked the management to remove him. They obliged me. The man was escorted from the theater, still talking loudly.

Review Exercises: Grammar

REVIEW EXERCISE 1: **Identifying the Parts of Speech**

On your paper, identify the part of speech—noun, pronoun, verb, adjective, adverb, preposition, conjunction, or interjection—of each of the following underlined words.

In 1962, (1) <u>Rachel Carson</u> wrote *Silent Spring*, a book (2) <u>which</u> opened the eyes of the public to the (3) <u>possibly</u> devastating effects of (4) <u>pesticides</u>. Since that time, researchers (5) <u>have produced</u> a significant amount of material on (6) <u>both</u> the beneficial and the debilitating effects of these chemicals. (7) <u>Presently</u>, (8) <u>over</u> 35,000 chemicals (9) <u>are sprayed</u> on fields to produce (10) <u>higher</u> yields. Many farmers are now able to produce double the harvest of the 1945 farmer, thanks to pesticides. (11) <u>Unhappily</u>, opponents report that pesticides have led (12) <u>directly</u> to at least (13) <u>fifty-two</u> deaths. (14) <u>Ominously</u>, (15) <u>they</u> point to findings that show pesticides and herbicides (16) <u>alter</u> brain activity and cause irritability, (17) <u>insomnia</u>, and reduced concentration. (18) <u>Alas</u>, each (19) <u>year</u>, more insects (20) <u>develop</u> a resistance to these dangerous sprays. Realizing the need (21) <u>for</u> methods to stop (22) <u>crop</u> destruction (23) <u>by</u> insects while still protecting the health of the (24) <u>population</u>, researchers are (25) <u>busy</u> looking for a safer alternative to insect sprays.

REVIEW EXERCISE 2: Using Basic Sentence Patterns

Write simple sentences using the following directions. Then, indicate the pattern of each of your sentences (for example, S-S-AV-DO). Finally, diagram each sentence on your paper.

1. Write a simple sentence with a compound direct object.
2. Write a simple sentence with a linking verb.
3. Write a simple sentence with an indirect object.
4. Write a simple sentence with a predicate adjective.
5. Write a simple sentence with a compound predicate adjective.
6. Write a simple sentence beginning with *here* or *there*.
7. Write a simple sentence with a compound subject and verb.
8. Write a simple question.
9. Write a simple command.
10. Write a simple exclamatory sentence.

REVIEW EXERCISE 3: Expanding Sentences with Phrases

On your paper, identify the underlined phrases as *prepositional, appositive,* or *verbal* phrases. Then identify the verbals as *gerund, participle,* or *infinitive.*

1. <u>To run the word processor correctly</u> will require some training <u>from the company</u>.

2. My eye problem, <u>severe astigmatism</u>, has forced me <u>to wear glasses</u>.
3. <u>Along the freeway</u>, huge pieces of asphalt had broken away <u>in the rain</u>.
4. The little girl, her pigtails <u>flying in the wind</u>, continued <u>to swing on the bars</u>.
5. <u>Running a business successfully</u> is impossible <u>during an office party</u>.
6. My friend <u>from the country</u> has a real fear of <u>running out of gas at night on a deserted road</u>.
7. I turned <u>on the heat</u> <u>to warm the house</u>.
8. The driver <u>racing in the red car</u> took that corner, <u>the dangerous Devil's Twist</u>, a little too fast.
9. <u>Having just been promoted</u>, I celebrated by <u>going out to dinner</u>.
10. Our two household pets—a fantail goldfish and a spotted turtle—do not eat us out <u>of house and home</u>.

REVIEW EXERCISE 4: Expanding Sentences with Clauses

Complete each of the following sentences, filling in the blank with the kind of clause indicated.

1. Bill Gittleson,   (adjective clause)   , showed up at the class reunion.
2. (noun clause)   will need to pay the damage.
3. (adverb clause)   , we relaxed on the beach.
4. (adverb clause)   , the athletes were chosen for the Olympic team.
5. I was first in line at the theater   (adjective clause)   .
6. We must surprise Kelly with   (noun clause)   .
7. The dentist pulled my wisdom teeth   (adjective clause)   .
8. We were parked next to the skating rink   (adverb clause)   .
9. No one suspected   (noun clause)   .
10. Tom was smarter   (adverb clause)   .

REVIEW EXERCISE 5: Diagraming Expanded Sentences

Identify each of the following sentences as *compound, complex,* or *compound-complex.* Then diagram each sentence on your paper.

1. The package which arrived in the mail contained homemade cookies from my mother.
2. After I had put the rolls in the oven, I started to make some fresh coffee.

3. I must take a business trip down South, but this week is a most incovenient time to do it.
4. The cat owner, who looked pleased by the Blue Ribbon on her cat, said whoever wanted to take a picture of her winner could.
5. While I waited for the train, I read a book; I, unfortunately, became so absorbed that I missed my connection.

REVIEW EXERCISE 6: Recognizing Sentence Faults

Each of the following sentences contains a sentence fault. On your paper, identify the kind of error it is—fragment, run-on, misplaced or dangling modifier, faulty parallelism, or faulty coordination—and then rewrite the sentence correctly.

1. I both handed in my essay and the homework today.
2. I tossed the salad listening to the news.
3. After rehearsing continuously, a long break was needed.
4. I like music and I bought an expensive stereo system.
5. The goat looked speculatively around his pen yielded nothing of interest.
6. The boat was due to sail at 9:00 a.m. and I arrived only seconds before and got a porter to unload my luggage and he helped me with it on to the ship.
7. The housewife pushing her cart expertly down the grocery aisle.
8. I washed the dishes wearing my best dress.
9. I enjoy the fresh smells, the bright colors, and feeling the warm sun as spring approaches.
10. When all had been said and done.

Chapter 5

Verb Usage

Like trees that grow almost imperceptibly, losing old branches and putting forth new buds, a living language slowly loses outmoded words and expressions and grows with new words and expressions. You will observe some of the minor changes in your own generation; major changes, however, can be detected only over the course of centuries.

This unit will give you guidelines for the correct use of standard English, which is simply the form of English considered acceptable by the majority of educated Americans today.

Standard English can be divided into two categories: formal and informal. Formal English is usually the better method of expression for structured situations, such as those in school or business. For example, formal English is used for writing theses, for completing job applications, and for presenting business reports to an audience. Informal English, on the other hand, is used in most nonacademic, casual situations, such as writing letters to friends or relaxed conversations. In order to use formal and informal English correctly, you need to know the rules that govern standard English usage. You will need to employ both your memory and your ability to choose language that suits the time, the place, and the occasion.

In this chapter you will study how verbs are formed and how they show time. The chapter will also explain how verbs express facts, commands, and wishes or possibilities, and how verbs indicate whether subjects perform or receive action.

5.1 Verb Tenses

Besides expressing actions or conditions, verbs have different *tenses* to indicate when the action or condition in the sentence occurred.

A **tense** is a form of a verb that shows time of action or state of being.

The following examples show how different forms of the same verb indicate changes in time.

EXAMPLES: Often I *laugh* at the wrong time.

A few days ago, I *laughed* loudly during a concert.

Today I probably *will laugh* at another inappropriate moment.

I *have laughed* joyfully at a friend's wedding.

I *had laughed* at his engagement party also.

Someday I *will have laughed* once too often.

■ The Six Tenses of Verbs

There are six tenses that indicate when the action or condition of a verb is, was, or will be in effect. Many of these tenses can take any of three forms: *basic, progressive,* or *emphatic.* Basic verb forms are used for most situations. Progressive verb forms are used to express a continuing action or state of being. Emphatic verb forms are used for emphasis, for questions, and for negative sentences. Notice in the following chart that emphatic forms are restricted to just two tenses: the present and past tenses.

BASIC, PROGRESSIVE, AND EMPHATIC FORMS OF THE SIX TENSES			
Tense	Basic Form	Progressive Form	Emphatic Form
Present	draw	am (*or* are, is) drawing	do draw
Past	drew	was (*or* were) drawing	did draw
Future	will draw	will be drawing	
Present Perfect	have (*or* has) drawn	have (*or* has) been drawing	
Past Perfect	had drawn	had been drawing	
Future Perfect	will have drawn	will have been drawing	

The name assigned to a verb is a combination of its tense and its form: *did draw* is called the past emphatic of the verb *draw*, and *had been drawing* is called the past perfect progressive of the verb *draw*. The basic forms, however, are described only by their tense names. Thus, *draw* is called the present of the verb *draw* and *will have drawn* is called the future perfect. Sometimes the basic forms of the present, past, and future tenses are called the simple tenses.

EXERCISE A: Recognizing Tenses. Copy the following names of the tense forms from Column A onto your paper. Then next to each, write the corresponding verbs from Column B. Note that some of the forms in Column A may have more than one verb in Column B.

Column A	*Column B*
1. Present	a. had been delivering
2. Past	b. are ringing
3. Future	c. do imagine
4. Present Perfect	d. had warped
5. Past Perfect	e. blend
6. Future Perfect	f. will have betrayed
7. Present Progressive	g. disintegrated
8. Past Progressive	h. will decide
9. Future Progressive	i. has blossomed
10. Present Perfect	j. was limping
Progressive	k. has been avoiding
11. Past Perfect Progressive	l. will be forming
12. Future Perfect	m. did investigate
Progressive	n. will have been studying
13. Present Emphatic	o. is singing
14. Past Emphatic	p. did arrive
	q. had cried
	r. will have been running

■ The Four Principal Parts of Verbs

Each verb in the English language has four principal parts from which all of the tenses are formed.

A verb has four principal parts: the **present** (base form), the **present participle**, the **past**, and the **past participle**.

The four principal parts of the verb *draw* are shown in the following chart.

PRINCIPAL PARTS OF *DRAW*			
Present	**Present Participle**	**Past**	**Past Participle**
draw	drawing	drew	drawn

The next chart shows which basic, progressive, and emphatic forms are derived from each of these four principal parts.

THE VERB FORMS OF *DRAW* DEVELOPED FROM PRINCIPAL PARTS
The Present: *draw*
Present: I *draw* Future: I *will draw* Present Emphatic: I *do draw* Past Emphatic: I *did draw*
The Present Participle: *drawing*
Present Progressive: I *am drawing* Past Progressive: I *was drawing* Future Progressive: I *will be drawing* Present Perfect Progressive: I *have been drawing* Past Perfect Progressive: I *had been drawing* Future Perfect Progressive: I *will have been drawing*
The Past: *drew*
Past: I *drew*
The Past Participle: *drawn*
Present Perfect: I *have drawn* Past Perfect: I *had drawn* Future Perfect: I *will have drawn*

You can see that helping verbs must be added to the principal parts to express certain verb forms. The future, for example, needs *will*; the future progressive needs *will be*; and the future perfect needs *will have*. Except in the simple present and past tense, every verb requires at least one helping verb to express time.

EXERCISE B: Identifying Principal Parts. Divide your paper into three columns and label them *Verb, Form,* and *Principal Part.* Then write in the appropriate column the verb from each of the following sentences, its form, and the principal part from which it was constructed.

EXAMPLE: I am working with everyone's cooperation.

Verb	Form	Principal Part
am working	present progressive	present participle

1. Fay will have written to every restaurant owner on Cape Cod.
2. He did moderate his strict code of behavior with understanding.
3. By Sunday I will have finished the assignment.
4. Thomas Hobbes, an English materialist, expressed his theory of human government in *Leviathan*.
5. He worked for many years as a plumber.
6. We had been considering a move to the Southeast.
7. A sheepdog brings in the stray ewes.
8. This photograph will capture the attention of everyone.
9. Donald was dreading his speech before the assembly.
10. I have revealed your plan to a few close friends.

■ Regular and Irregular Verbs

The way a verb forms its past and past participle determines whether it is classified as *regular* or *irregular*.

Regular Verbs. The majority of verbs are regular; their past and past participles are formed according to a predictable pattern.

The past and past participle of a **regular verb** are formed by adding *-ed* or *-d* to the present form.

The following chart shows regular verbs. The helping verb *have* has been added in parentheses to the past participle to serve as a reminder that *have* (or *has*) is needed to form any of the perfect tenses.

PRINCIPAL PARTS OF REGULAR VERBS			
Present	**Present Participle**	**Past**	**Past Participle**
listen	listening	listened	(have) listened
glimpse	glimpsing	glimpsed	(have) glimpsed
manage	managing	managed	(have) managed
contend	contending	contended	(have) contended

Irregular Verbs.   Although most verbs are regular, many of the most common verbs are irregular.

The past and past participle of an irregular verb are *not* formed by adding *-ed* or *-d.*

The following charts help to simplify the study of irregular verbs by grouping them according to common characteristics. For example, the first chart shows verbs with the same past and past participle. Study the charts carefully, giving special attention to those verbs that are troublesome to you. Notice the changes in spelling. Some of the present participles drop the final *-e* before adding *-ing* (*arising, driving,* and so on), and some of the past participles double the final consonant before adding *-en* (*gotten, stridden, bitten,* and so on). (Similar spelling changes may be found in some regular verbs as well.)

IRREGULAR VERBS WITH THE SAME PAST AND PAST PARTICIPLE			
Present	**Present Participle**	**Past**	**Past Participle**
bind	binding	bound	(have) bound
bring	bringing	brought	(have) brought
build	building	built	(have) built
buy	buying	bought	(have) bought
catch	catching	caught	(have) caught
cling	clinging	clung	(have) clung
creep	creeping	crept	(have) crept
fight	fighting	fought	(have) fought
find	finding	found	(have) found
fling	flinging	flung	(have) flung
forget	forgetting	forgot	(have) forgotten *or* (have) forgot
get	getting	got	(have) got *or* (have) gotten
grind	grinding	ground	(have) ground
hang	hanging	hung	(have) hung
hold	holding	held	(have) held
keep	keeping	kept	(have) kept
lay	laying	laid	(have) laid
lead	leading	led	(have) led
leave	leaving	left	(have) left
lend	lending	lent	(have) lent

lose	losing	lost	(have) lost
pay	paying	paid	(have) paid
say	saying	said	(have) said
seek	seeking	sought	(have) sought
send	sending	sent	(have) sent
shine	shining	shone *or* shined	(have) shone *or* (have) shined
show	showing	showed	(have) shown *or* (have) showed
sit	sitting	sat	(have) sat
sleep	sleeping	slept	(have) slept
spend	spending	spent	(have) spent
spin	spinning	spun	(have) spun
stand	standing	stood	(have) stood
stick	sticking	stuck	(have) stuck
sting	stinging	stung	(have) stung
strike	striking	struck	(have) struck
swing	swinging	swung	(have) swung
teach	teaching	taught	(have) taught
win	winning	won	(have) won
wind	winding	wound	(have) wound
wring	wringing	wrung	(have) wrung

IRREGULAR VERBS WITH THE SAME PRESENT, PAST, AND PAST PARTICIPLE

Present	Present Participle	Past	Past Participle
bid	bidding	bid	(have) bid
burst	bursting	burst	(have) burst
cost	costing	cost	(have) cost
cut	cutting	cut	(have) cut
hit	hitting	hit	(have) hit
hurt	hurting	hurt	(have) hurt
let	letting	let	(have) let
put	putting	put	(have) put
set	setting	set	(have) set
shut	shutting	shut	(have) shut
split	splitting	split	(have) split
spread	spreading	spread	(have) spread
thrust	thrusting	thrust	(have) thrust

IRREGULAR VERBS THAT CHANGE IN OTHER WAYS

Present	Present Participle	Past	Past Participle
arise	arising	arose	(have) arisen
be (am, is, are)	being	was (were)	(have) been
bear	bearing	bore	(have) borne
beat	beating	beat	(have) beaten *or* (have) beat
become	becoming	became	(have) become
begin	beginning	began	(have) begun
bite	biting	bit	(have) bitten
blow	blowing	blew	(have) blown
break	breaking	broke	(have) broken
choose	choosing	chose	(have) chosen
come	coming	came	(have) come
do	doing	did	(have) done
draw	drawing	drew	(have) drawn
drink	drinking	drank	(have) drunk
drive	driving	drove	(have) driven
eat	eating	ate	(have) eaten
fall	falling	fell	(have) fallen
fly	flying	flew	(have) flown
freeze	freezing	froze	(have) frozen
give	giving	gave	(have) given
go	going	went	(have) gone
grow	growing	grew	(have) grown
know	knowing	knew	(have) known
lie	lying	lay	(have) lain
ride	riding	rode	(have) ridden
ring	ringing	rang	(have) rung
rise	rising	rose	(have) risen
run	running	ran	(have) run
see	seeing	saw	(have) seen
shake	shaking	shook	(have) shaken
shrink	shrinking	shrank	(have) shrunk
sing	singing	sang	(have) sung
sink	sinking	sank	(have) sunk
slay	slaying	slew	(have) slain
speak	speaking	spoke	(have) spoken
spring	springing	sprang	(have) sprung

steal	stealing	stole	(have) stolen
stride	striding	strode	(have) stridden
strive	striving	strove	(have) striven
swear	swearing	swore	(have) sworn
swim	swimming	swam	(have) swum
take	taking	took	(have) taken
tear	tearing	tore	(have) torn
throw	throwing	threw	(have) thrown
wear	wearing	wore	(have) worn
weave	weaving	wove	(have) woven *or* (have) wove
write	writing	wrote	(have) written

When you have a question about the correct form of an irregular verb, you can either refer to one of these charts or consult a dictionary, which will list irregular verb forms.

EXERCISE C: Completing the Principal Parts of Regular and Irregular Verbs. Copy the following headings onto your paper, and write the given words in the appropriate columns, as shown. Then complete each line by filling in the three missing principal parts.

Present	Present Participle	Past	Past Participle
1. become	_____	_____	_____
2. _____	_____	crept	_____
3. _____	_____	approved	_____
4. lay	_____	_____	_____
5. experience	_____	_____	_____
6. _____	_____	_____	put
7. _____	lingering	_____	_____
8. _____	spreading	_____	_____
9. _____	_____	_____	advised
10. arise	_____	_____	_____
11. _____	directing	_____	_____
12. erase	_____	_____	_____
13. _____	_____	swung	_____
14. _____	grinding	_____	_____
15. _____	_____	imprisoned	_____
16. bite	_____	_____	_____
17. _____	_____	_____	shaken

18. _____	_____	shone	_____
19. _____	choosing	_____	_____
20. _____	_____	burned	_____

EXERCISE D: Choosing the Correct Forms of Irregular Verbs.
Choose the correct verb from the two choices in parentheses in each of the following sentences. Write the verb next to the appropriate number on your paper.

1. We were assailed by the stench of fish rotting on the shore where they had been (flinged, flung) by the explosion.
2. They must have (creeped, crept) into the house while we were out.
3. Bob is so excessively sentimental that I have (written, wrote) him a note of condolence on the death of his canary.
4. A sleek dalmation (sprang, sprung) into the limousine and the chauffeur closed the door.
5. The apparition supposedly had (ridden, rode) a black horse up to the door of the castle.
6. I have only (came, come) to deliver a message.
7. Carol had (broke, broken) her promise again.
8. He has always (throwed, thrown) salt over his shoulder to ward off bad luck.
9. Halfway through the race the horse had stumbled, (fallen, fell), and then thrown its rider to the ground.
10. I have never (blowed, blown) out all the candles with one breath.
11. His subtle sense of humor must have (gone, went) unnoticed most of the time.
12. She had (ate, eaten) lobster for the first time and thought it was delicious.
13. As the heat intensified in the burning building, the windows (busted, burst).
14. You have (wore, worn) those jeans until they are beyond repair.
15. She should have (brung, brought) lighter clothes for her vacation in a tropical climate.
16. I (bid, bidded) on several items at the auction but went home with nothing.
17. The concert (began, begun) before half the people had arrived.
18. His wife had (tore, torn) a strip of clothing and wrapped his lacerated hand.
19. Christina (sang, sung) alto in the church choir.
20. He had (bore, borne) the excruciating pain without a murmur.
21. The icy rain (freezed, froze) on the Eskimos' parkas.

22. Uncle Marty had (gave, given) all of his major assets to various charities.
23. She had (ran, run) in the relay race until she twisted her ankle.
24. As the merry-go-round circled around, Karen (catched, caught) the gold ring.
25. He had (taken, took) a compass but had neglected to consult it.
26. Closing her eyes, Gwen (drank, drunk) the bitter tonic.
27. Until he lost his self-assurance, Carl had (striven, strove) to be the company's best salesperson.
28. The chimpanzees (swinged, swung) from the topmost branches and threw banana peels to the ground.
29. Susan (grew, growed) a pumpkin so large it required two people to lift it.
30. In the past they had (spoke, spoken) with hostility to each other.
31. If I had (knew, known) the meeting would be this disorganized, I wouldn't have come.
32. She (saw, seen) something that made her shiver with dread.
33. He had already (bit, bitten) into the baked Alaska before he realized it was made with shaving cream.
34. In *Les Miserables* the major character was sent to prison because he had (stole, stolen) a loaf of bread.
35. Margaret vehemently (shaked, shook) the stick in the air to emphasize her point.
36. As soon as he had heard the bad news, Pat's father had (flew, flown) home to be with his daughter.
37. Ted was perturbed by his inability to have (growed, grown) a full beard by the week's end.
38. He has (swore, sworn) never to return to the home of his youth.
39. Helen (winded, wound) a sheet around herself and went to the costume party as a mummy.
40. She had (risen, rose) to accuse the white-haired man seated in the courtroom.
41. I (did, done) exactly what I was asked to do.
42. The survivors of the shipwreck (clinged, clung) to the rubber rafts.
43. Her wool sweater had (shrank, shrunk) after repeated washings.
44. In *Beowulf* the hideous monster Grendel sneaked into the hall and (slayed, slew) the sleeping warriors.
45. All the cars on this lot have been (driven, drove) less than fifty thousand miles.
46. He (swam, swum) ten laps before climbing out of the pool.

47. She (wrang, wrung) the truth from the suspect by making every imaginable threat.
48. The butler (rang, rung) a tiny crystal dinner bell to announce dinner.
49. A monarch butterfly had (flew, flown) too near the spider's web and was caught by sticky threads.
50. Mr. Vance (taught, teached) a health course that included lessons on life-saving techniques.

EXERCISE E: Writing the Correct Form of Irregular Verbs. Each of the following sentences contains two different verbs in parentheses. Divide your paper into two columns. In the first column, write the appropriate past or past participle form for the first verb in parentheses; in the second column, write the appropriate past or past participle for the second.

1. Our neighbors had (build) a kennel too close to our property and my father had (stride) over to demand an explanation.
2. Fay (grind) her teeth in her sleep, but eventually her bunkmates (grow) accustomed to the noise.
3. They had (spend) all their money and had (buy) nothing of any consequence.
4. He had (seek) his enemy and (fight) him fairly.
5. I have frequently (lend) Cindy money but she never has (pay) me back.
6. She (bind) her waist with a belt she had (weave) herself.
7. Without a captive audience Frank would never have (get) such an opportunity to have (spin) one of his lengthy yarns.
8. Mrs. Watkins (wring) her hands in despair because she had (break) her mother-in-law's wedding present.
9. The fox (creep) along the fence and suddenly (burst) into the chicken coop.
10. We (find) the small boy with his foot (stick) between the bars of the gate.
11. He (swing) the flag that he had (steal) high above the soldiers' heads.
12. Mrs. Whitman has (teach) for several years and her previous principal has (write) a good recommendation for her.
13. I should have (know) you would have (shrink) from doing your share of the work.
14. The horse had (split) his hoof on the blacktop and his trainer sadly (lead) it away.
15. Last night as I (sleep), I dreamed that I (swim) the English Channel.
16. Previously Jeff had (beat) all his opponents, but now he has (fall) into disgrace.

17. He (go) to Europe after he (lose) his wife and child.
18. The wounded deer had (lie) under the trees after it had (spend) itself by running.
19. After days without water, the rescued survivors (drink) until their stomachs (hurt).
20. Ocean spray (sting) their faces as they (hang) over the edge of the boat.

■ Verb Conjugation

The conjugation of a verb presents all its different forms.

A **conjugation** is a list of the singular and plural forms of a verb in a particular tense.

To conjugate a verb, such as the verb *draw*, first review its principal parts.

PRINCIPAL PARTS OF *DRAW*			
Present	Present Participle	Past	Past Participle
draw	drawing	drew	drawn

Next, match the singular personal pronouns *(I, you, he, she, it)* and the plural personal pronouns *(we, you, they)* with the correct singular and plural verb forms for each of the different tenses.

Three of the principal parts are used for the basic verb forms: the present to form the present and future tenses; the past to form the past tense; and the past participle to form the three perfect tenses.

CONJUGATION OF THE BASIC FORMS OF *DRAW*		
Present	**Singular**	**Plural**
First Person	I draw	we draw
Second Person	you draw	you draw
Third Person	he, she, it draws	they draw
Past		
First Person	I drew	we drew
Second Person	you drew	you drew
Third Person	he, she, it drew	they drew

Future		
First Person	I will draw	we will draw
Second Person	you will draw	you will draw
Third Person	he, she, it will draw	they will draw
Present Perfect		
First Person	I have drawn	we have drawn
Second Person	you have drawn	you have drawn
Third Person	he, she, it has drawn	they have drawn
Past Perfect		
First Person	I had drawn	we had drawn
Second Person	you had drawn	you had drawn
Third Person	he, she, it had drawn	they had drawn
Future Perfect		
First Person	I will have drawn	we will have drawn
Second Person	you will have drawn	you will have drawn
Third Person	he, she, it will have drawn	they will have drawn

A complete conjugation of the basic forms includes the two infinitives: the *present infinitive* consists of *to* before the present; the *perfect infinitive* consists of *to have* before the past participle.

INFINITIVE FORMS OF *DRAW*	
Present Infinitive	to draw
Perfect Infinitive	to have drawn

Only the present participle is used to form the six progressive forms. The following chart shows the formation of the progressive forms of the verb *draw*.

CONJUGATION OF THE PROGRESSIVE FORMS OF *DRAW*		
Present Progressive	**Singular**	**Plural**
First Person	I am drawing	we are drawing
Second Person	you are drawing	you are drawing
Third Person	he, she, it is drawing	they are drawing

Past Progressive		
First Person	I was drawing	we were drawing
Second Person	you were drawing	you were drawing
Third Person	he, she, it was drawing	they were drawing

Future Progressive		
First Person	I will be drawing	we will be drawing
Second Person	you will be drawing	you will be drawing
Third Person	he, she, it will be drawing	they will be drawing

Present Perfect Progressive		
First Person	I have been drawing	we have been drawing
Second Person	you have been drawing	you have been drawing
Third Person	he, she, it has been drawing	they have been drawing

Past Perfect Progressive		
First Person	I had been drawing	we had been drawing
Second Person	you had been drawing	you had been drawing
Third Person	he, she, it had been drawing	they had been drawing

Future Perfect Progressive		
First Person	I will have been drawing	we will have been drawing
Second Person	you will have been drawing	you will have been drawing
Third Person	he, she, it will have been drawing	they will have been drawing

As you can see in the preceding chart, when you conjugate the progressive forms of a verb, you are actually conjugating the basic forms of *be* followed by a present participle. In this case the present participle is *drawing:* I *am drawing*, I *was drawing*, I *will be drawing*, and so on.

The emphatic forms use just one principal part: the present, which is preceded by either *do* or *did* to indicate present emphatic or past emphatic.

CONJUGATION OF THE EMPHATIC FORMS OF *DRAW*		
Present Emphatic	**Singular**	**Plural**
First Person	I do draw	we do draw
Second Person	you do draw	you do draw
Third Person	he, she, it does draw	they do draw
Past Emphatic		
First Person	I did draw	we did draw
Second Person	you did draw	you did draw
Third Person	he, she, it did draw	they did draw

EXERCISE F: Conjugating Verbs. Using the preceding charts for the conjugation of *draw* as a model, conjugate the verbs *plan* and *break* in their basic, progressive, and emphatic forms. Then conjugate the verb *be*.

APPLICATION: Writing Sentences Using Basic, Progressive, and Emphatic Verb Forms. Write an original sentence for each of the following verbs, using the form indicated.

1. Past perfect of *borrow*
2. Present progressive of *land*
3. Future perfect of *spring*
4. Future perfect progressive of *fly*
5. Present of *communicate*
6. Present perfect progressive of *live*
7. Future progressive of *fling*
8. Present of *arm*
9. Future of *pierce*
10. Present of *burst*
11. Past progressive of *intend*
12. Present emphatic of *wear*
13. Perfect infinitive of *freeze*
14. Past of *lose*
15. Present emphatic of *surrender*
16. Future perfect progressive of *halt*
17. Past perfect progressive of *drop*
18. Present perfect of *preserve*
19. Future perfect of *spend*
20. Past emphatic of *build*
21. Present infinitive of *drive*
22. Present perfect of *swim*
23. Past emphatic of *discover*
24. Present perfect progressive of *sing*
25. Past perfect progressive of *go*

The Correct Use of Tenses

5.2

The basic, progressive, and emphatic forms of the six tenses show time within the three general categories of present, past, and future. The seven past verb forms show time occurring before the present. The four future forms show time occurring after the present.

THREE CATEGORIES OF TIME		
Past	**Present**	**Future**
◄————————— (now) —————————►		
Past	Present	Future
Past Emphatic	Present Emphatic	Future Perfect
Present Perfect		
Past Perfect		
Past Progressive	Present Progressive	Future Progressive
Present Perfect Progressive		Future Perfect Progressive
Past Perfect Progressive		

This section will explain how each verb form has a specific use that distinguishes it from the other forms.

■ Present, Past, and Future Time

Even if you are able to conjugate verbs in all of their forms, good usage depends on an understanding of how each form works within its general category of time to express meaning.

Uses of Tense in Present Time. As shown in the preceding chart, three forms indicate present time: the present *(I draw)*, the present emphatic *(I do draw)*, and the present progressive *(I am drawing)*.

Three forms of the present can be used to show present actions or conditions as well as various continuous actions or conditions.

The three basic uses of the present are shown in the following chart.

BASIC USES OF THE PRESENT

Present action: The vendor *shouts* to a potential customer.
Present condition: My cold *is* contagious.
Regularly occurring action: On weekends they *drive* to the country.
Regularly occurring condition: This mountain path *is* dangerous in winter.
Constant action: The moon *reflects* the sun's light.
Constant condition: Human beings *are* primates.

The present may also be used to express historical events. This use of the present, called the *historical present,* is occasionally used in narration to make past actions or conditions come to life in the present.

THE HISTORICAL PRESENT

Past action expressed in historical present: The events of July 4, 1776, *bring* to fulfillment for the first time the political ideals of the Enlightenment.
Past condition expressed in historical present: After the defeat of Antony and Cleopatra at Actium, Octavian *is* the undisputed master of the Roman Empire.

Another similar use of the present is called the *critical present.* It is most often used to discuss deceased authors and their literary achievements.

THE CRITICAL PRESENT

Action expressed in critical present: Sir Arthur Conan Doyle *writes* with a skill that *makes* his stories classics.
Condition expressed in critical present: In addition to his novels, Thomas Hardy *is* the author of eight volumes of poetry.

The present emphatic is used in four ways: for emphasis, for denying contrary assertions, for asking questions, and for negative sentences.

USES OF THE PRESENT EMPHATIC

For emphasis: I *did forget* to mail in the car's registration fee.
For denying a contrary assertion: I disagree. He *does listen*, but without seeming to.

For a question: Do you *supply* the equipment?

For a negative sentence: Estelle *does* not *mind* watching the children.

The present progressive, like all other progressive forms, is used to show a continuing action or condition.

USES OF THE PRESENT PROGRESSIVE

Continuing action: I *am recording* the notes from the meeting.

Continuing condition: Meg *is being* very careful about her choice of college.

Uses of Tenses in Past Time. There are seven verb forms within past time: the past *(I drew)*, the past emphatic *(I did draw)*, the present perfect *(I have drawn)*, the past perfect *(I had drawn)*, the past progressive *(I was drawing)*, the present perfect progressive *(I have been drawing)*, and the past perfect progressive *(I had been drawing)*. Each is used differently.

The seven forms of the past can be used to show a variety of actions and conditions that began in the past.

Notice in the first of the following charts, which illustrates the uses of the simple past, that the addition of such words as *two days ago* or *last week* changes the time expressed by the past from indefinite to definite. Observe also that the actions and conditions expressed by the simple past both begin and end at some time in the past.

USES OF THE PAST

Completed action (indefinite time): They *halted* work on the suspension bridge.

Completed condition (indefinite time): Several furnished apartments *were* available.

Completed action (definite time): They *halted* work on the suspension bridge two days ago.

Completed condition (definite time): Last week several furnished apartments *were* available.

The uses of the past emphatic are the same as those of the present emphatic: for emphasis, for denying a contrary assertion, for asking questions, and for negative sentences.

USES OF THE PAST EMPHATIC

For emphasis: The cactus *did grow* without any water.
For denying a contrary assertion: But I *did leave* a message for you!
For a question: When *did* the United States *recognize* China?
For a negative sentence: He *did* not *read* the memorandum.

The present perfect, the uses of which are illustrated in the next chart, is interchangeable with the past when it is used to express actions that began and ended at some indefinite time in the past. The present perfect, however, differs from the past in two important ways: (1) The present perfect always expresses indefinite time; such words as *two days ago* or *last week* cannot be added to a verb in the present perfect to make it definite. (2) The present perfect can be used to show actions and conditions continuing from the past to the present.

USES OF THE PRESENT PERFECT

Completed action (indefinite time): They *have antagonized* everyone.
Completed condition (indefinite time): They *have been* there twice.
Action continuing to present: It *has rained* intermittently.
Condition continuing to present: I *have felt* fatigued all day.

The past perfect expresses a past action or condition that took place before another.

USES OF THE PAST PERFECT

Action completed before another past action: Perhaps the nomadic hunters *had drawn* in the dirt before they drew on cave walls.
Condition completed before another past action: Rhoda *had been* a photographer until she studied law.

The three progressive forms in past time express different kinds of continuous actions or conditions, beginning and sometimes ending in the past.

USES OF THE PAST PROGRESSIVE

Continuous action completed in the past: I *was waiting* for my luggage.
Continuous condition completed in the past: I *was being* honest when I told him he has no talent as a magician.

USE OF THE PRESENT PERFECT PROGRESSIVE
Past action continuing to present: Edith *has been adding* more rocks and minerals to her collection.

USE OF THE PAST PERFECT PROGRESSIVE
Past action continuing from indefinite to definite time: He *had been dreaming* of victory until reality became inescapable.

As the preceding chart indicates, only the past progressive can express continuous conditions in past time. The use of *be* in the present perfect progressive *(has been being)* or the past perfect progressive *(had been being)* is nonstandard. The present perfect *(has been)* or the past perfect *(had been)* is used instead.

Uses of Tenses in Future Time.   Four forms are included in the future: the basic form of the future *(I will draw)*, the future perfect *(I will have drawn)*, the future progressive *(I will be drawing)*, and the future perfect progressive *(I will have been drawing)*.

The four forms of the future can be used to show various actions or conditions that will occur in the future.

The following chart shows two of the ways to express future time.

USES OF THE FUTURE
Future action: This favorable review *will establish* her as a talented new novelist.
Future condition: The comet *will look* like a star with a tail.

USES OF THE FUTURE PERFECT
Future action completed before another: By the time he is twenty-two, he *will have squandered* his inheritance.
Future condition completed before another: The orchestra *will have been* on tour for three months before the new concert season begins.

Notice in the next chart that the future progressive and the future perfect progressive are not used to express conditions: The forms *will be being* and *will have been being* are nonstandard English. In their place, the future *(will be)* and the future perfect *(will have been)* are used.

USE OF THE FUTURE PROGRESSIVE

Continuous action in the future: This device *will be saving* us gallons of heating oil during the winter months.

USE OF THE FUTURE PERFECT PROGRESSIVE

Continuous future action completed before another: Sharon *will have been sculpturing* for over ten years before she gives her first exhibit next spring.

NOTE ABOUT OTHER WAYS OF EXPRESSING FUTURE TIME: Certain adverbs and phrases can help the present and the present progressive express future time. In the first of the following sentences, *opens* is present, but *this weekend* helps it suggest the future. In the second sentence, *is sailing* is present progressive, but *tomorrow* helps it suggest the future progressive.

PRESENT SUGGESTING FUTURE TIME: A new Mexican restaurant *opens* in town this weekend.

PRESENT PROGRESSIVE SUGGESTING FUTURE TIME: That ship *is sailing* tomorrow for a cruise to the Bahamas.

EXERCISE A: **Recognizing the Uses of Verbs in Present Time.** All the verbs in the following sentences are in the present. Read each sentence carefully and decide which use of the present is intended. Then write the letter of the choice that best indicates the use of the verb on your paper.

   A. Present action or condition
   B. Regularly occurring action or condition
   C. Constant action or condition
   D. Historical or critical present
   E. Emphatic use
   F. Continuing action or condition

1. I *hope* you will like the meal that I have prepared.
2. These tight shoes *hurt* my feet.
3. Diane *is doing* remarkably well on her diet.
4. Tolstoy *is* the author of many thought-provoking short stories.

5. The sky *is becoming* overcast.
6. Halley's comet *returns* every seventy-six years.
7. I *am* sometimes forgetful.
8. Truth *is* Beauty.
9. Richard Wright *borrows* from his own experiences in *Native Sun*.
10. A flight from Chicago *does arrive* this afternoon.

EXERCISE B: Using the Past, the Past Emphatic, the Present Perfect, and the Past Perfect Forms. Complete each of the following sentences with a verb of the kind and form indicated in parentheses. Be prepared to explain why the indicated verb form is appropriate.

1. More than an hour ago I (action—past emphatic) you to deliver these packages.
2. The editor (action—past) an essay condemning racism.
3. Alexander Dumas (action—past perfect) plays before he began writing *The Three Musketeers*.
4. Our school (action—present perfect) the honor system.
5. I (action—past emphatic) for the leading role in the play.
6. The flag (action—present perfect) at half-mast all day.
7. There (condition—past) a shortage of rainfall in our area last summer.
8. My grandparents (condition—past perfect) in vaudeville until they grew tired of performing.
9. His hair (condition—present perfect) white since his childhood.
10. Yesterday someone (action—past) a car over the narrow bridge.

EXERCISE C: Using the Progressive Forms of the Past. Write five sentences of your own using each of the following verbs in the indicated progressive form. Be prepared to explain why the indicated verb forms are appropriate for your sentences.

1. taste—past perfect progressive
2. polish—past perfect progressive
3. gather—present perfect progressive
4. be—past progressive
5. discuss—present perfect progressive

EXERCISE D: Using the Future Tenses. Choose the correct verb form from the two future forms in parentheses in each of the following sentences. Write the verb next to the appropriate number on your paper. Be prepared to identify the form and explain what kind of action it indicates.

1. By nightfall I (will have planted, will have been planting) over a hundred disease-resistant elms.
2. I (will be, will have been) disappointed if all my friends are away for the summer.
3. If Ms. Ramon teaches this class, her enthusiasm (will motivate, will have motivated) the students.
4. Soon they (will be exploring, will have been exploring) the coast of Antarctica for nearly a month.
5. No pets (will have been allowed, will be allowed) in this new condominium.

■ Sequence of Tenses

In a complex or compound-complex sentence, the tense of the verb in the main clause often determines the tense that needs to be used for the verb in the subordinate clause. Moreover, the form of a participle or infinitive often depends on the tense of the main verb in the sentence.

Verbs in Subordinate Clauses. Frequently it is necessary to look at the tense of the main verb in a sentence before deciding the tense for the verb in a subordinate clause.

The tense of a verb in a subordinate clause should follow logically from the tense of the main verb.

As you study the combinations of tenses in the following charts, notice that the choice of tenses affects the logical relationship between the events that are being expressed. Some combinations make the events *simultaneous*—meaning that they occur at the same time. Other combinations make the events *sequential*—meaning that one event occurs before or after the other. By checking the sequence of tenses in your writing, you can be sure that your meaning is clear and logical.

SEQUENCE OF TENSES		
Main Verb in Present		
Main Verb	**Subordinate Verb**	**Meaning**
We *understand* . . .	Present that he *writes* novels.	Simultaneous events in present time.

	Pres Emph that he *does write* novels.	
	Present Prog that he *is writing* a novel.	
We *understand* . . .	*Past* that he *wrote* a novel.	Sequential events: the writing comes before the understanding.
	Past Emph that he *did write* a novel.	
	Present Perf that he *has written* a novel.	
	Past Prog that he *was writing* a novel.	
	Present Perf Prog that he *has been writing* a novel.	
We *understand* . . .	*Past Perf* that he *had written* a novel and *Past* *published* it last year.	Sequential events: the writing comes before the publishing, both of which come before the understanding.
	Past Perf Prog that he *had been writing* a novel, *Past* which he *published* last year.	
We *understand* . . .	*Future* that he *will write* a novel.	Sequential events: the understanding comes before the writing.
	Future Prog that he *will be writing* a novel.	

| We *understand* . . . | Future Perf
that he *will have written* a novel
Present
before he *graduates* next spring.

Future Perf Prog
that he *will have been writing* a novel
Present
before he *graduates* next spring. | Sequential events: the understanding comes before the writing, which comes before the graduating. |

Main Verb in Past

| We *understood* . . . | Past
that he *wrote* a novel.

Past Emph
that he *did write* a novel.

Past Prog
that he *was writing* a novel. | Simultaneous events in past time. |
| We *understood* . . . | Past Perf
that he *had written* a novel when we
Past
saw it in print.

Past Perf Prog
that he *had been writing* a novel
Past
when we *saw* it in print. | Sequential and simultaneous events: The writing comes before the understanding and the seeing—two simultaneous events in past time. |

Main Verb in Future

| We *will understand* . . . | Present
if he *writes* a novel. | Simultaneous events in future time. |

	Present Emph if he *does write* a novel. *Present Prog* if he *is writing* a novel.	
We *will understand* . . .	*Past* if he *wrote* a novel. *Past Emph* if he *did write* a novel. *Present Perf* if he *has written* a novel. *Present Perf Prog* if he *has been writing* a novel.	Sequential events: the writing comes before the understanding.

If a main verb is in one of the perfect or progressive forms, a subordinate verb is likely to be in either the present or past, depending on the meaning of the sentence.

If the Main Verb Is . . .	Then the Subordinate Verb Should Usually Be . . .
Present Progressive Present Perfect Progressive Future Perfect Future Progressive Future Perfect Progressive	Present
Present Perfect Past Progressive Past Perfect Past Perfect Progressive	Past

EXAMPLES: *Present Prog* — They *are stocking* their camper before they *hitch* it to the car. — *Present*

Present Perf Prog — We *have been rehearsing* daily because the play *opens* tomorrow night. — *Present*

Future Perf
The temperature *will have risen* by the time the sun

reaches its zenith.

Future Prog   Present
She *will be wearing* a cast until the fracture *heals.*

Future Perf Prog
My term paper *will have been lying* on his desk for weeks
Present
before he *reads* it.

Present Perf   Past
He *has cashed* the check that he *received* for his birthday.

Past Prog   Past
She *was dressing* inappropriately wherever she *went.*

Past Perf
The cattle *had sensed* the impending eruption minutes be-
Past
fore it actually *happened.*

Past Perf Prog   Past
Our neighbor *had been watering* our plants when we *were*
away.

Rather than memorizing rules for the sequence of tenses, learn to rely on logic as you construct your own sentences. If you first decide whether the events you wish to relate are simultaneous, sequential, or combinations of both, you should have little difficulty choosing the correct tenses to convey your intended meaning.

NOTE ABOUT *WOULD HAVE:* In a subordinate clause beginning with *if*, do not repeat the helping verbs *would have* when the main verb also contains *would have*. Instead, make the subordinate verb past perfect.

INCORRECT: If he *would have cooked* the leg of lamb properly, it *would have been* pink and juicy rather than black and dry.

CORRECT: If he *had cooked* the leg of lamb properly, it *would have been* pink and juicy rather than black and dry.

Time Sequence with Participles and Infinitives. Frequently the form of a participle or infinitive determines whether the event it expresses is simultaneous with another event or is sequential to another event. Participles can be present *(seeing)*, past *(seen)*, or perfect *(having seen)*. Infinitives can be either present *(to see)* or perfect *(to have seen)*.

The form of a participle or infinitive should set up a logical time sequence in relation to a verb in the same clause or sentence.

The time sequence between a verb and a present or past form of a verb is rarely a usage problem when the events they express are simultaneous.

SIMULTANEOUS EVENTS	
In Present Time	Present Present *Seeing* the results, she *laughs* whole-heartedly. Present Present He *needs to confirm* the results.
In Past Time	Present Past *Seeing* the results, she *laughed* whole-heartedly. Past Past *Seen* by thousands, the eclipse *lasted* only a few minutes. Past Present He *needed to confirm* the results.
In Future Time	Present Future *Seeing* the results, she *will laugh* whole-heartedly. Future Present He *will need to confirm* the results.

Sequential events can be expressed by the relationship of a perfect participle or perfect infinitive to a verb. The event expressed by the verbal should always logically come before the event expressed by the verb.

SEQUENTIAL EVENTS	
In Present Time	Perf Present Prog *Having seen* the results, she *is laughing* whole-heartedly. (The seeing comes before the laughing.)

	Present Perf He *is* fortunate *to have worked* with you. (The working comes before the being fortunate.)
In Past Time	Perf Past *Having seen* the results, she *laughed* whole-heartedly. (The seeing comes before the laughing.) Past Perf He *was* fortunate *to have worked* with you before Past you *resigned*. (The working comes before the being fortunate and the resigning.)
Spanning Past and Future Time	Perf Future *Having seen* her craftsmanship, I *will recommend* her work. (The seeing—a past event—affects the recommending, a future event.) Future By the end of the week he *will be* fortunate *to* Perf *have worked* with you. (The working comes before the being fortunate.)

EXERCISE E: Recognizing the Correct Forms of Verbs in Subordinate Clauses and of Participles and Infinitives. In each of the following sentences, the main verb has been underlined. Rewrite each sentence to include the construction indicated in parentheses. Remember that the main verb should determine the form of a verb in a subordinate clause, the form of a participle, or the form of an infinitive.

EXAMPLE: We <u>noticed</u> our neighbor's lights. (Add a phrase containing the present participle of <u>flash</u>.)

We noticed our neighbor's lights <u>flashing</u> a signal of distress.

1. Our captain <u>chose</u> John for the team. (Add a phrase containing the past participle of <u>know</u>.)
2. Eventually he <u>wrote</u> to his congresswoman. (Add a subordinate clause containing the past perfect of <u>try</u>.)
3. My plan <u>is</u> that I will leave before the evening train departs. (Change <u>will leave</u> to a perfect infinitive.)

4. She <u>is</u> afraid. (Add a subordinate clause containing the present perfect of <u>hear</u>.)
5. Joel <u>liked</u> watching the storm clouds gather. (Change <u>watching</u> to a present infinitive.)
6. A weathervane <u>spun</u> in the wind. (Add a phrase containing the past participle of <u>perch</u>.)
7. Lisa <u>is working</u> industriously at her new job. (Add a subordinate clause containing the present of <u>earn</u>.)
8. She <u>was</u> glad she had gained experience in the field of electronics. (Change <u>gained</u> to a perfect infinitive.)
9. The conductor <u>listened</u> to the cacophony in angry silence. (Add a phrase containing the perfect participle of <u>expect</u>.)
10. You <u>will notice</u> the difference. (Add a subordinate clause containing the present perfect of <u>observe</u>.)

APPLICATION: **Correcting Errors in Tense.** The following paragraph has errors in tense. Rewrite it, making necessary corrections. Circle verbs you have corrected on your paper.

(1) General Custer was not quite the honorable soldier that some historical accounts would have us believe. (2) Shortly after he returned to duty after years of suspension from the army—Custer was being found guilty at a court martial for, among other things, abandoning his men and having deserters shot without trials—he and General Elliott lead their troops against a Cheyenne village. (3) When it has become clear that the warriors would retaliate, Custer retreated, not waiting for Elliott and Elliott's soldiers, who will all be killed. (4) Just before the end of his military career and his life, Custer was receiving permission to ride into the Black Hills to gather "information" about the land and to explore the possibility of locating a military post in the area. (5) The Black Hills, a territory that was being owned by the Northern Plains tribes in perpetuity, has been rumored to be rich in gold. (6) With him Custer takes geologists who did find this precious metal. (7) As a result, hordes of prospectors have invaded the land, violating the treaty. (8) The Indians had objected and the government was sending soldiers, supposedly to force the miners' departure. (9) However, both miners and soldiers remained on the land. (10) In 1876 Custer is disobeying two orders by taking the Seventh Cavalry, which is under the command of another general, and by taking along a reporter who was supposed to be making Custer a newspaper hero. (11) The rest is common knowledge. (12) Custer has led them to a bloody defeat in the battle of Little Big Horn.

The Subjunctive Mood 5.3

In today's English there are three *moods,* or ways in which a verb can express an action or condition: indicative, imperative, and subjunctive. The *indicative mood,* the most common of the three, is used to make factual statements and to ask questions. The *imperative mood* is limited to sentences that give orders or directions.

INDICATIVE: He *is* always helpful.

IMPERATIVE: *Be* helpful.

The third mood, the *subjunctive,* is used less frequently than either of the other moods. The subjunctive mood is used less often partly because some of its uses have been taken over by other words in modern English and partly because many people forget that the subjunctive mood still fulfills an important function that the other two moods cannot.

There are only two important differences between verbs in the subjunctive mood and those in the indicative mood. (1) In the present tense, third-person singular verbs in the subjunctive mood do not have the usual -*s* or -*es* ending. (2) The subjunctive mood of *be* in the present tense is *be,* and in the past tense it is *were,* regardless of which personal pronoun or noun the verb follows.

Indicative Mood	Subjunctive Mood
He *listens* to my arguments.	I suggest that he *listen* to my arguments.
The paramedics *are* ready for emergencies.	The doctor insists that the paramedics *be* ready for emergencies.
She *was* impatient.	If she *were* impatient, she would not be suited for this work.

Knowing when and how to use these subjunctive verb forms will enable you to express certain ideas more clearly and accurately.

■ The Correct Use of the Subjunctive Mood

There are two general uses of the subjunctive mood in modern English.

> Use the **subjunctive mood** (1) in clauses beginning with *if*, *as if*, *as though*, or *that* to express an idea that is contrary to fact or (2) in clauses beginning with *that* to express a request, a demand, or a proposal.

You should not have any problem using the subjunctive mood correctly if you remember the two ways subjunctive verbs differ from indicative verbs and if you take notice of clauses that either express ideas contrary to fact or express requests, demands, or proposals.

Expressing Ideas Contrary to Fact.   Ideas contrary to fact are most commonly expressed as wishes or conditions. Using the subjunctive mood in these situations helps to show that the idea expressed is not now true and may never be true.

EXAMPLES: He wishes that he *were* more likable. (He is not now likable—and may never be likable.)

One impossible condition of employment was that she *be* ready to travel at any time. (She is not now ready to travel freely.)

He talks about art as though he *were* an expert. (However, he is not an expert.)

Expressing Requests, Demands, and Proposals.   Even though this use of the subjunctive mood also suggests that the ideas expressed are not now true, it indicates that they could or should be true in the future. Most verbs that make a request, a demand, or a proposal are usually followed by a *that*-clause, which will generally contain a verb in the subjunctive mood.

VERBS USUALLY FOLLOWED BY *THAT*-CLAUSES AND SUBJUNCTIVE VERBS		
request	demand	propose
ask	insist	recommend
prefer	order	suggest
	determine	move
	require	

REQUEST: The proctor requests that we *be* on time for the examination.

DEMAND: This school requires that each student *wear* a uniform.

PROPOSAL: He proposed that a motion *be* made to adjourn the meeting.

EXERCISE A: **Using the Subjunctive Mood.** Each of the following sentences contains a verb in the indicative mood that should be subjunctive. Rewrite each sentence, making the appropriate verb subjunctive.

1. He wishes that he was a few inches taller than his brother George.
2. The judge insisted that the reporter leaves the camera outside the courtroom.
3. I prefer that she waits in the lobby until I am ready to leave.
4. They stared at me as if I was a ghost.
5. If I was offended, I would certainly not be smiling.
6. On the contrary, he does not merely ask that a student attends his class.
7. Adam reacted as though he was being paid a compliment.
8. Every blouse on the rack looked as if it was second-hand.
9. I move that the minutes from yesterday's meeting are read.
10. It is necessary that you are more patient.

■ Auxiliary Verbs That Help Express the Subjunctive Mood

Since certain helping verbs suggest conditions contrary to fact, they can often be used in place of the usual subjunctive mood.

Could, would, or *should* can be used to help a verb express the subjunctive mood.

The following chart contrasts two ways of expressing the subjunctive mood. The sentences on the left contain the usual subjunctive form of the verb *be*: *were*. The sentences on the right have been reworded with *could*, *would*, and *should*.

THE SUBJUNCTIVE MOOD EXPRESSED THROUGH AUXILIARY VERBS	
If the future *were* clear, we'd act decisively.	If the future *could* be clear, we'd act decisively.
If someone *were* to excort her, she would go to the play.	If someone *would escort* her, she would go to the play.
If you *were* to move, would you write to me?	If you *should move*, would you write to me?

EXERCISE B: **Using Auxiliary Verbs to Express the Subjunctive Mood.** Each of the following sentences uses a subjunctive verb correctly. Rewrite each sentence, using an auxiliary verb to express the subjunctive mood.

1. If you were less messy, I would not have to pick up after you.
2. This meeting would run more smoothly if he were to leave.
3. She wishes that Kate were relaxed and comfortable.
4. If Noreen were to invite you, would you attend?
5. The house would be warmer if everyone were to keep the windows closed.

APPLICATION: **Writing Sentences Using the Subjunctive Mood.** Use each of the following words or phrases in a sentence of your own that contains the subjunctive mood. Underline the subjunctive verbs in your sentence.

1. require that
2. I suggest
3. that she be
4. as if
5. could be more enjoyable

5.4 Voice

If you studied the preceding sections, you know that verbs change form according to tense and mood. This section shows that verbs also have *voice*—the ability to indicate whether the subject performs the action or has the action performed on it.

Voice is the form of a verb that shows whether or not the subject is performing the action.

Only action verbs can indicate voice; linking verbs cannot. In English there are two voices: *active* and *passive*.

■ Active and Passive Voice

When the subject of a verb performs the action, the verb is active; when the subject receives the action, the verb is passive.

Active Voice.   Any action verb, regardless of whether it is transitive (with a direct object) or intransitive (without a direct object) can be in the active voice. (See Section 1.2 for more about transitive and intransitive verbs.)

> A transitive or intransitive verb is **active** when its subject performs the action.

In both of the following examples, the subjects perform the action. In the first example, the verb is transitive and, therefore, has a direct object, which receives the action of the verb. In the second example, the verb is intransitive; it has no direct object.

	S	DO
ACTIVE VERBS:	The puppeteer *manipulated* the strings.	

Leaves *gathered* in the corner of the garden.

Passive Voice.   Most action verbs can be passive as well as active.

> A verb is **passive** when its action is performed upon the subject. A passive verb almost never has a direct object and is always a verb phrase made from a form of *be* plus the past participle of a transitive verb.

In the following examples, the subjects are the receivers of the action. Instead of being responsible for the action, they are affected by the action. The first example names the performer, the puppeteer, but *puppeteer* is now the object of the preposition *by* instead of the subject. In the second example, no performer of the action is mentioned. Notice that neither example has a direct object.

PASSIVE VERBS: S   V   Obj of Prep
The strings *were manipulated* by the puppeteer.

S   V
The leaves *were gathered* into large plastic bags.

The tense of the helping verb *be* determines the tense of a passive verb. If, for example, the form of *be* is in the present tense, the passive verb is in the present tense, and so on. The past participle does not change. Here is a short conjugation in the passive voice of the verb *believe* in the three moods. Notice that there are only two progressive forms in the passive voice and no emphatic forms.

SHORT CONJUGATION OF *BELIEVE* IN THE PASSIVE VOICE	
Tense and Mood	Passive Form
Present Indicative	he is believed
Past Indicative	he was believed
Future Indicative	he will be believed
Present Perfect Indicative	he has been believed
Past Perfect Indicative	he had been believed
Future Perfect Indicative	he will have been believed
Present Progressive Indicative	he is being believed
Past Progressive Indicative	he was being believed
Present Imperative	(you) be believed
Present Subjunctive	(if) he be believed
Past Subjunctive	(if) he were believed

EXERCISE A: Distinguishing Between Active and Passive Voice. Write the verb from each of the following sentences on you paper. Then label it *active* or *passive*.

1. These essays were selected for their originality.
2. Our bread truck delivers as quickly as possible.
3. Murphy had been chosen for the task.
4. Carefully he removed the glass from the picture window.
5. They prepared for any eventuality.
6. Fry the eggs on one side only.
7. The last sentence in the contract has been reworded to eliminate its vagueness.
8. A fruit punch will be served at the dance.
9. My reflection stared back at me from the mirror.
10. The dog was being rewarded for his quick response.
11. She threw a handful of herbs into the pot.
12. Hundreds of applications were received at the personnel office.
13. His numerous complaints are being ignored.

14. These pants have shrunk at least two sizes.
15. A single guppy energetically swam around the large tank.
16. Pools of stagnant water were lying beneath the broken spouts.
17. The tigers will have been fed by the time we arrive at the zoo.
18. Wilma's seeming indifference is misconstrued by her acquaintances.
19. They discussed their views with the President.
20. A cold compress was quickly applied to the wound.

EXERCISE B: Conjugating Verbs in the Passive Voice. Conjugate each of the following four verbs in the passive voice. Conjugate using only the personal pronoun indicated in parentheses. Use the chart on page 186 as your guide.

1. deliver (with *it*)
2. praise (with *you*)
3. nominate (with *I*)
4. alert (with *they*)

■ Using Active and Passive Voice

As soon as you can distinguish between active and passive voice, you can use this knowledge to improve your own writing. Most accomplished writers prefer the active voice to the passive voice.

Use the active voice whenever possible.

Usually a verb can convey the same information in either the active or the passive voice. The active voice, however, is more direct and economical. Unless you have a definite reason for choosing the passive voice, use the active voice instead. Notice, for example, that the first sentence that follows is shorter and more direct than the other one is.

ACTIVE VOICE: Debbie *repaired* the dripping faucet.

PASSIVE VOICE: The dripping faucet *was repaired* by Debbie.

The passive voice does, however, have two important uses.

Use the passive voice (1) to emphasize the receiver rather than the performer of an action or (2) to point out the receiver when the performer is unknown or unimportant and not named in the sentence.

RECEIVER EMPHASIZED: Only Laurel *was mystified* by the message.

PERFORMER UNKNOWN: A ransom note *was tacked* to the door.

PERFORMER UNIMPORTANT: The article stated that a fence *will be erected* immediately around the abandoned mine shaft.

EXERCISE C: Using the Active Voice. Ten sentences in Exercise A contain verbs in the passive voice. Rewrite each of these sentences in the active voice, changing or adding words as necessary. Be prepared to explain which voice is better.

EXERCISE D: Correcting Unnecessary Use of the Passive Voice. Most of the verbs in the following paragraph are in the passive voice. Rewrite the paragraph, changing as many of the underlined passive verbs into active ones as you think necessary to improve the paragraph. It is not necessary to change every passive verb.

(1) He had no time left to wonder why he had forced himself to take a course in public speaking. (2) The summation of the student whose name alphabetically preceded his own was listened to by Ben, standing in the wings of the brightly lit auditorium. (3) The necessary organizational skills had been given to Ben by three months of practice in the classroom. (4) But today the old symptoms of fear were being returned. (5) Now, without waiting for his name to be called, Ben walked mechanically onto the stage. (6) The neatly written index cards were carefully placed on the podium's solid wooden surface, the microphone was adjusted, and he looked out at the impersonal, waiting sea of faces. (7) A few minutes later, when his speech was concluded, the notes were gathered by Ben and he prepared to walk from the stage. (8) He thought he was being reproached by the audience through their absolute silence. (9) Then the clapping was begun by one person, and suddenly he was washed by waves of applause. (10) Lingering at the podium for a moment, Ben allowed himself to receive their recognition.

APPLICATION: Using Voice Correctly in Writing. Describe an incident, like the one in Exercise D, in which you forced yourself to do something that you were afraid to do. Include two appropriate uses of the passive voice: one that emphasizes the receiver rather than the performer of an action and another in which the performer is not named. Make sure all of the other verbs in your description are active.

Chapter 6

Pronoun Usage

At one time in the English language, both nouns and pronouns changed their form according to their use in a sentence. For example, the form that a noun would have as a subject was different from the form it would have as a direct object. Today, English relies more on syntax (the order of words in a sentence) than on changes in form, or *case,* to indicate a word's use. Nevertheless, this old characteristic of English has not entirely disappeared. Nouns still change form when they are used to show possession. An apostrophe and an *s* (*today's* weather) or just an apostrophe (the *bees'* hive) is added to the usual form of the noun. Some pronouns change form even more noticeably. *We,* for example, which is used for subjects (*We* are leaving), becomes *us* for objects (Jan gave *us* another chance) and *our* for possession (Where are *our* overcoats?).

This chapter will explain the relation between a pronoun's form and its use in a sentence and will show you how to use the various case forms of pronouns correctly in sentences.

Case 6.1

In the English language, only nouns and pronouns have *case.*

Case is the form of a noun or pronoun that indicates how it is used in a sentence.

The following chart lists the three cases—*nominative, objective,* and *possessive*—and shows the uses of each in a sentence. Notice that the nominative has three uses and the objective has five uses, while the possessive has only a single use: to show ownership.

189

Case	Use in a Sentence
Nominative	subject of a verb predicate nominative nominative absolute
Objective	direct object indirect object object of a verbal object of a preposition subject of an infinitive
Possessive	to show ownership

Nouns generally pose no difficulty since they change form only to show possession. Most possessive singular nouns add *'s,* and most plural nouns add just an apostrophe. (See Section 12.6 for a complete explanation of the way in which the possessive case of nouns is formed.) Personal pronouns, however, have several different forms to indicate how they are being used in a sentence.

■ The Cases of Personal Pronouns

The following chart shows the personal pronouns grouped according to the three cases. Since *you* and *it* have the same forms for both the nominative and objective cases, neither pronoun presents a usage problem.

Nominative	Objective	Possessive
	Singular	
I	me	my, mine
you	you	your, yours
he, she, it	him, her, it	his, her, hers, its
	Plural	
we	us	our, ours
you	you	your, yours
they	them	their, theirs

Study the two preceding charts. Learn both to recognize each pronoun by case and to recognize the uses of each case in sentences. For example, *I* is a nominative pronoun; it can be used as a subject but not as the object of a preposition, and so on.

NOTE ABOUT POSSESSIVE PRONOUNS: The possessive pronouns *my, your, his, her, its, our,* and *their* are used before nouns to show ownership; they function as adjectives. The other possessive pronouns shown in the preceding chart are used by themselves and can fill any position in a sentence that a noun can. *His* and *its* can also be used by themselves strictly as pronouns.

EXAMPLES: *His* essay won. (adjective)

His won. (subject)

The judges chose *his.* (direct object)

EXERCISE A: **Identifying Case.** Divide your paper into two columns, labeling the first column *Case* and the second *Use.* For each of the following sentences, write the case of the underlined pronoun and its use.

1. <u>My</u> parents are strict and never waver in their decisions.
2. My friends and I gave <u>him</u> a pet snake.
3. His most receptive listeners were <u>we</u> and they.
4. Mrs. Stapleton's displeasure with <u>us</u> is caused by her insistence upon perfection.
5. If a recording company will give <u>us</u> an audition, our group may yet be famous.
6. Visiting the botanical gardens was <u>his</u> idea.
7. Their excellent credit references establish <u>them</u> as good potential buyers.
8. The caretaker and his wife's cottage was empty, <u>they</u> apparently having departed without notice.
9. I will send <u>them</u> a map to our new house.
10. This restaurant will not let <u>us</u> in without jackets.
11. The prettiest garden is <u>theirs</u>.
12. The apothecary jars now had an assortment of penny candies in <u>them</u>.
13. <u>Yours</u> is not the best answer nor is it the worst.
14. Instead of restoring the old battleship, they were considering sinking <u>her</u> at sea.
15. The only student who qualified for the scholarship was <u>she</u>.

16. <u>Their</u> assimilation into the new culture was remarkably quick.
17. As though to prove her lack of imagination, <u>she</u> answered with a cliché.
18. A rapid ascent in the elevator left <u>me</u> with an unsettled stomach.
19. <u>He</u> dazzled the audience with his magical feats.
20. After helping Jackie regain consciousness, <u>they</u> raised her to her feet.

■ The Nominative Case

The nominative case is used when a personal pronoun acts in one of three ways.

> Use the **nominative case** for the subject of a verb, for a predicate nominative, or for the pronoun in a nominative absolute construction.

NOMINATIVE PRONOUNS	
As subjects	*I* will paint the ceiling while *she* sands the woodwork.
As predicate nominatives	The award-winning scientists were *he* and *she*.
In a nominative absolute	*They* having meticulously groomed themselves, their neat appearance was not a surprise.

Informal Use of the Predicate Nominative.   Though formal usage requires that a nominative pronoun follow a linking verb, the objective case is often used instead in conversation and other informal situations.

FORMAL: It was *I* who requested the explanation.
            The driver of the car was *he*.

INFORMAL: It was *me* who requested the explanation.
               The driver of the car was *him*.

Remember, however, that the formal usage is generally preferred in academic and business situations.

Nominative Pronouns in Compounds. Be sure that a pronoun used as part of a compound subject or compound predicate nominative is in the nominative case.

COMPOUND SUBJECT: The electrician and *we* will make a thorough inspection. (*Not* "The electrician and us . . .")

Her brother and *she* cannot speak civilly to each other. (*Not* "Her brother and her . . .")

COMPOUND PREDICATE NOMINATIVE: The club's most devoted members were Rudy and *he*.
(*Not* ". . . Rudy and him.")

Most damaged by the slander were Frannie and *I*.
(*Not* ". . . Frannie and me.")

You can check whether the pronoun you have chosen for a compound construction is correct by mentally skipping the noun and using the pronoun alone in the sentence.

Nominative Pronouns with Appositives. When a pronoun used as a subject or predicate nominative is followed by a noun in apposition, make sure the pronoun is in the nominative case, just as though it were used by itself.

EXAMPLES:
                S   Appos
We environmentalists regard heavy reliance on coal with skepticism. (*Not* "Us . . . regard . . .")

                                              PN
The strongest supporters of the bill were *they* the
    Appos
students. (*Not* "The . . . supporters . . . were . . . them . . .")

EXERCISE B: Using Pronouns in the Nominative Case. Complete each of the following sentences with an appropriate nominative pronoun: *I, we, he, she,* or *they.* Write the pronoun on your paper.

1. Their usual laughter announced that Reggie and _____ had arrived.
2. _____ himself should be the best judge.
3. Her complexion shone with good health, _____ having thrived in the cold climate.
4. With furtive glances in his direction, Grace and _____ crossed the street.
5. History will prove that the best president of the century was _____.

6. _____ the taxpayers will be the ones to pay for this expensive project.
7. _____, the well-known international banker, having made millions, left the world of finance for a life of privacy.
8. Never was there a better gymnast than _____.
9. Kevin and _____ are still considered the favorites in the competition.
10. _____ entrepreneurs appreciate the risks involved in this venture.
11. People knew J. P. Morgan was a philanthropist, _____ having endowed the Pierpont Morgan Library.
12. The unifying members of the family were the grandfather and _____.
13. Did Francisco and _____ organize the block party?
14. Unquestionably _____ are the leading publishers of children's literature.
15. Pat and _____ shoveled the snow from the sidewalk.
16. Before signing the document _____ read the small print carefully.
17. The worst archers at the field trials were Gary and _____.
18. Late for a meeting, _____ quickly hailed a taxi.
19. The most enterprising exhibitors at the science fair were Edith and _____.
20. Jacques serves braised veal that _____ gourmets never fail to appreciate.

■ The Objective Case

Objective pronouns are used for any kind of object in a sentence, as well as for subjects of infinitives.

Use the **objective case** for the object of any verb, verbal, or preposition, or for the subject of an infinitive.

OBJECTIVE PRONOUNS	
As a direct object	A piece of plaster hit *him* on the head.
As an indirect object	My uncle sent *me* a lace fan from Spain.
As the object of a participle	The sharks following *them* were menacing.

As the object of a gerund	Answering *you* will be difficult.
As the object of an infinitive	I am obligated to help *her*.
As the object of a preposition	The helmeted guard stood before *us*.
As the subject of an infinitive	Several firms wanted *him* to audit their records.

Objective Pronouns in Compounds.   As with the nominative case, errors involving objective pronouns most often occur in compound constructions. When in doubt about which case to use, mentally use the pronoun in question by itself. In the following examples, the underlined objective pronouns are correct.

COMPOUND DIRECT OBJECT: Cracking ice floes warned (Burt and) him. (*Not* ". . . warned . . . he.")

COMPOUND INDIRECT OBJECT: Sally told (my cousin and) me everything. (*Not* ". . . told . . . I everything.")

COMPOUND OBJECT OF PREPOSITION: What was the cause of the argument between (you and) them? (*Not* ". . . between . . . they?")

Objective Pronouns with Appositives.   When a pronoun used as an object or as the subject of an infinitive is followed by a noun in apposition, remember to use the objective case as if the pronoun were by itself.

EXAMPLES: The final examination intimidated *us* students. (*Not* ". . . intimidated we . . .")

Aunt Gertrude bought *us* amazed nieces and nephews a boa constrictor. (*Not* ". . . bought we . . .")

The exploration of the planets will be a great challenge for *us* astronauts. (*Not* ". . . for we . . .")

EXERCISE C: Using Pronouns in the Objective Case. Complete each sentence with an appropriate objective pronoun: *me, him, her, us,* or *them*. Write the pronoun on your paper.

1. Telling _____ that his car needs a new transmission will not be easy.
2. Africa's diamond mines provide work for _____.
3. This restaurant makes _____ waiters and waitresses wear uniforms.
4. Joe fled to the farthest corners of the world, but the guilt haunting _____ still remained.
5. In the huge library an information assistant gave _____ boys invaluable help.
6. I forgot to inform _____ of his right to legal counsel.
7. A forbiddingly rocky landscape challenged _____ determined back-packers.
8. While we explored the old barn, a low flying bat gave Lynn and _____ a moment of panic.
9. Our younger sister always wanted _____ to take her wherever we went.
10. The fear paralyzing Marion and _____ was irrational.
11. Through the early morning haze the ferry took my friends and _____ across the water.
12. We have to show _____ that we are eager to cooperate.
13. The airport near _____ was closed during the storm.
14. Stop persecuting _____ because their ways are not yours.
15. The personnel manager told _____ to complete an application.
16. The difficulties troubling Daniel and _____ can be gradually eliminated.
17. John's rapid calculations left _____ perplexed.
18. You cannot obtain pedigree papers for your dogs without registering _____.
19. I bought this book for you and _____ to read.
20. The camp director told Terry and _____ to give the girls their swimming lessons.

■ Two Errors to Avoid in Using Possessive Pronouns

Although errors are less common in the possessive case than they are in the other two cases, there are two mistakes involving possessive pronouns that you should learn to avoid. The first involves gerunds.

Use a possessive pronoun before a gerund.

Do not be tempted to use an objective pronoun before a gerund.

EXAMPLES: *Your* meandering about the topic is confusing. (*Not* "You meandering . . .")

We objected to *his* insinuating that our motives were corrupt. (*Not* ". . . him insinuating . . .")

Ms. Malin insists on *our* attending every class. (*Not* ". . . us attending . . .")

Another mistake to avoid is using an apostrophe with a possessive pronoun.

Do not use an apostrophe with any possessive pronoun.

Forms such as *yours, hers, ours,* and *theirs* are already possessive; the use of an apostrophe with any of these forms is always incorrect. Remember also that *its, your,* and *their* are possessive pronouns whereas "it is," "you are," and "they are" are contractions meaning *it is, you are,* and *they are.*

POSSESSIVE PRONOUNS: The angry notes in the suggestion box are *hers.*

Its appeal is to all age groups.

They left *their* past behind.

CONTRACTIONS: *It's* not likely that he will return.

We're not selling and *they're* not buying.

EXERCISE D: Using Possessive Pronouns. Choose the correct form of the pronoun in each of the following sentences from the choices in parentheses. Be prepared to explain the reason for your choice.

1. The car's dragging tailpipe made (its, it's) approach easy to detect.
2. (Their, They're) experience in aerodynamics makes them valuable in the control room.
3. This house has been well-maintained and (its, it's) in a desirable location.
4. (Your, You're) light tap on the door wasn't heard by any of us.
5. Diminishing profits and general dissatisfaction precipitated (me, my) selling the business.

6. The winning ticket is (yours, your's)!
7. Frightened by (him, his) raving, I edged toward the door.
8. (Hers, Her's) is a radically new approach to the interpretation of dreams.
9. They dislike (your, you) meddling in these confidential matters.
10. (Your, You're) invited to attend the premier.

APPLICATION: Writing Sentences with Nominative, Objective, and Possessive Pronouns. Write five sentences of your own using the following pronouns as indicated. Then label the case of each pronoun *nominative, objective,* or *possessive.*

1. Use *he and I* as a compound predicate nominative.
2. Use *my* before a gerund.
3. Use *yours and ours* as the compound subject of a verb.
4. Use *she* as part of a nominative absolute construction.
5. Use *us* as the subject of an infinitive.

6.2 Special Problems Involving Case

Choosing the correct case of the pronoun *who* and its relative *whoever* is a problem for many people. Those who do not understand the distinction between *who* and *whom*, for example, tend to use *who* all the time. Those who do understand the difference may nevertheless be heard to say, "*Whom* may I say is calling?" Such usage is wrong.

Another perennial problem involves personal pronouns in elliptical clauses. Although "John is stronger than *me*" may sound correct, it is not formal English. The pronoun should be *I*. This section will focus on these two problems involving case and will help you understand how syntax determines which pronoun should be used.

■ The Correct Uses of *Who* and *Whoever*

Who and its various forms are used as interrogative pronouns in questions and as relative pronouns or introductory words in complex sentences. *Whoever* usually acts as a relative pronoun or as the introductory word in a noun clause.

> Learn to recognize the various cases of *who* and *whoever* and to use them correctly in sentences.

The following chart shows the three case forms of these pronouns and their uses.

THE FORMS AND USES OF *WHO* AND *WHOEVER*		
Case	Form	Use
Nominative	who, whoever	subject of a verb predicate nominative
Objective	whom, whomever	direct object object of a preposition subject of an infinitive
Possessive	whose, whosever	to show ownership

The possessive forms are seldom misused. *Whosever* is used only in such rare constructions as "Take *whosever* umbrella is in the hallway." *Whose,* however, should not be confused with the contraction *who's,* which means "who is" or "who has."

POSSESSIVE CASE: *Whose* umbrella is this?

CONTRACTION: *Who's* taken my umbrella?

The nominative and objective cases are the real source of problems. To avoid errors, get into the habit of analyzing the structure of your sentences whenever you need to use *who* or *whoever.* Use the nominative forms for subjects and predicate nominatives; use the objective forms for direct objects, objects of prepositions, and subjects of infinitives.

SUBJECT: *Who* asked the question?

PREDICATE NOMINATIVE: The questioner is *who?*

DIRECT OBJECT: *Whom* did you ask?

OBJECT OF PREPOSITION: From *whom* can I expect an answer?

SUBJECT OF INFINITIVE: I did not know *whom* to ask.

Now study the two kinds of sentences in which these pronouns can appear.

In Direct Questions. *Who* is the correct form when the pronoun is the subject of a simple question; *whom,* when the pronoun is the direct object or the object of a preposition. A question in the normal subject-verb order will always correctly begin with *who*.

EXAMPLE:
$$\overset{S}{Who} \overset{V}{wants}$$
Who wants a free ticket to the game?

A question in inverted order, on the other hand, will never correctly begin with *who*. To check whether you should be using *whom* instead of *who*, try rewording the question as a statement. If you find yourself changing the order of the words, you will often find that you need to use *whom*.

EXAMPLES: *Whom* were you discussing?

S   V   DO
You were discussing *whom*.

Whom did you receive a letter from?

S   V   Obj of Prep
You did receive a letter from *whom*.

NOTE ABOUT THE INFORMAL USE OF *WHO:*   In conversation, *who* is generally used instead of *whom* whenever the pronoun is the first word in a question. Most people use *whom* only when it directly follows a preposition or when *who* would sound awkward.

INFORMAL: *Who* were you discussing?

Who did you receive a letter from?

FORMAL AND INFORMAL: To *whom* did you send that letter?

In Complex Sentences.   Choosing the correct case of *who* or *whoever* in a complex sentence will be easier if you remember that the pronoun's use within the subordinate clause determines its case. (See Section 3.3 for more information about subordinate clauses.)

EXAMPLE: They carefully screened *whoever* applied for the scholarship.

In the preceding example, the pronoun appears to be the direct object of *screened*, in which position the correct pronoun would be *whomever*. A closer look at the pronoun's position, however, reveals that it is the subject of the subordinate clause *whoever applied for the scholarship.* Thus the nominative form *whoever* is correct. The entire subordinate clause is the direct object of the sentence.

Follow these steps to check whether the case of a pronoun in a subordinate clause is correct. (1) Isolate the subordinate clause. (If the complex sentence is a question, you may first need to rearrange it in normal subject-verb order.) (2) If the subordinate clause itself is inverted, rearrange the words in their usual order. (3) Determine the pronoun's use within the subordinate clause.

EXAMPLE: *Who* may I say is calling?

　　　　　Reworded sentence: I may say *who* is calling.

　　　　　Subordinate clause: who is calling

　　　　　Use of pronoun: subject of verb *is calling*

　　　　　Case for subject: nominative—*who* is correct

EXAMPLE: Is the man with the long sideburns the person *whom* they suspect?

　　　　　Subordinate clause: whom they suspect

　　　　　Reworded clause: they suspect *whom*

　　　　　Use of pronoun: direct object of *suspect*

　　　　　Case for direct object: objective—*whom* is correct

EXAMPLE: The old recluse chased away *whomever* his dog barked at.

　　　　　Subordinate clause: whomever his dog barked at

　　　　　Reworded clause: his dog barked at *whomever*

　　　　　Use of pronoun: object of preposition *at*

　　　　　Case for object of preposition: objective—*whomever* is
　　　　　　　　　　　　　　　　　　correct

Sometimes subordinate clauses are interrupted by parenthetical expressions, such as *I think, we believe,* or *they say.* These extra words have no effect on the syntax of the rest of the clause. Thus, you should mentally eliminate them when choosing the case of *who* or *whoever.* In the following examples, the parenthetical expressions have been set off in parentheses.

EXAMPLES: The independent candidate is the one *who* (experts predict) will win the election.

The independent candidate is the one *whom* (experts predict) the voters will elect.

EXERCISE A: Using the Forms of *Who* and *Whoever*. Complete each of the following sentences with the correct form of *who* or *whoever*. After each answer, identify the pronoun's use in the clause in which it appears.

1. You should respond to _____ challenges your honesty.
2. _____ did Elizabeth Bennett ultimately marry?
3. His harmless pranks are only played on people _____ he likes.
4. Anyone _____ likes tennis will also like this game.
5. Actually, my brother, _____ you seem to think is perfect, does have a few faults.
6. Write a personal narrative about someone _____ earned your respect.
7. Is it Matthew _____ plays lead guitar in the band?
8. This gentle mare will adopt any colt _____ mother has died.
9. Claude Monet, _____ advanced the technique of impressionism, was a French painter.
10. Mercury was the Roman god _____, I think, was similar to the Greeks' Hermes.
11. On _____ did you place the blame?
12. His biggest worry is _____ to invite to the prom.
13. I would like to thank _____ sent me this anonymous letter.
14. _____ did you say was invited?
15. Ask to speak with _____ is in charge.
16. The astronauts _____ explored the moon were my heroes.
17. We wondered _____ initials were carved on the apple tree.
18. That young man is a talented gymnast _____ I admire.
19. Maggie is the girl _____, it seems, always gets the most awards.
20. Your brusque manner annoys _____ you approach.

EXERCISE B: Writing Sentences with Forms of *Who* and *Whoever*. For each of the following items, write a sentence using the form of the pronoun indicated in parentheses.

EXAMPLE: *Who* (as the subject of a subordinate clause)

Rembrandt is just one of many brilliant artists <u>who</u> died bankrupt and lonely.

1. *Who* (as a subject of a question)
2. *Whomever* (as the direct object in a subordinate clause)
3. *Whom* (as the direct object of a question)
4. *Whoever* (as the subject in a subordinate clause)
5. *Whom* (as the object of a preposition in a question)

■ The Correct Use of Pronouns in Elliptical Clauses

An elliptical clause is one in which some words are omitted but still understood; the word *are*, for example, is omitted in the elliptical clause *than you* at the end of the sentence "I am older than you." Errors in pronoun usage can easily be made when an elliptical clause is used in making a comparison. In such a sentence, either the subject, verb, or both can be understood. You will have to fill in the missing words of the clause to determine what pronoun to use.

In elliptical clauses beginning with *than* or *as*, use the form of the pronoun that you would use if the clause were fully stated.

The following two models can help you visualize the structure of complex sentences with elliptical clauses. The boxes on the right show how the position of the pronoun in relationship to the omitted words determines whether the pronoun should be nominative or objective.

Words Left Out After Pronoun

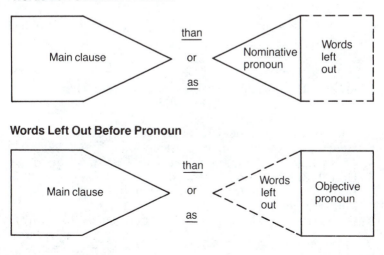

Words Left Out Before Pronoun

The following examples fit the models; the understood words have been included in parentheses.

WORDS LEFT OUT AFTER PRONOUN: Beverly is as dedicated as *he* (is dedicated).

WORDS LEFT OUT BEFORE PRONOUN: You gave Lewis more than (you gave) *me*.

To determine the correct pronoun for an elliptical clause, first mentally add the missing words. If the understood words come after the pronoun, choose a nominative form (*I, we, he, she, they*). If the understood words come before the pronoun, choose an objective form (*me, us, him, her, them*).

As you can see in the next set of examples, the case of the pronoun can sometimes change the entire meaning of the sentence.

NOMINATIVE PRONOUN: They thought more highly of her than *I* (did).

OBJECTIVE PRONOUN: They thought more highly of her than (they did of) *me*.

EXERCISE C: Choosing the Correct Pronoun in Elliptical Clauses. Complete the elliptical clause in each of the following sentences. Then choose the correct pronoun from the choices in the parentheses and cross out the incorrect pronoun. You may be able to complete some sentences with either choice.

EXAMPLE: He does more for the senior class than (I, me).

He does more for the senior class than he does for (I, me).

He does more for the senior class than (I, me) do.

1. My friend enjoyed your company more than (I, me).
2. You are less skilled in gymnastics than (she, her).
3. Carla works as hard as (we, us).
4. These allergies bother me more than (he, him).
5. Henry gave Dorothy more presents than (I, me).
6. This wholesale company is as reliable as (they, them).
7. He values his job more than (she, her).
8. Bob Dylan is a better performer than (he, him).
9. I encouraged him more than (she, her).
10. Grace was as awkward in social situations as (he, him).

EXERCISE D: **Writing Sentences with Elliptical Clauses.** Use each of the following groups of words to write sentences of your own containing elliptical clauses. After writing your sentences, check to see that the pronouns are used correctly by mentally completing the elliptical clauses.

EXAMPLE: as likable as she

Her elder sister is as likable as she (is likable).

1. more than me
2. as happy as he
3. better than she
4. less than he
5. as wise as they
6. as pretty as I
7. less successful than she
8. more than us
9. as mistrustful as we
10. as well as them

APPLICATION: **Correcting Errors in Pronoun Usage.** Seven of the following sentences contain an error in formal usage. Rewrite each incorrect sentence to eliminate the error. For each correct sentence, write *correct*. Be prepared to explain why the correct sentences need no changes.

1. Whom do you think will be victorious?
2. Our Brazilian guest knew more about the local customs than us.
3. Whoever Joe threw the ball to caught it and passed it to whoever was standing out of bounds.
4. Who's billfold is that?
5. Alfred is as interested in astronomy as they.
6. The person who receives this prize will be whomever guessed the correct number of beans.
7. I will vote for whomever they chose as a candidate.
8. No one was happier at the news of the birth than us.
9. Who do you think I should choose to be my manager?
10. The next dictator will be someone whom the experts say will be even more inflexible.

Agreement

If you play a musical instrument, you know how one sour note can ruin an entire performance. Success depends on making all the notes flow harmoniously. The same principle applies to the sentences you write. All the parts of a sentence should work together in harmony. One ungrammatical or illogical word can sound like a sour note and jar a reader or listener. The term *agreement* describes two kinds of harmony that sentences must have: (1) Subjects and verbs must agree in number. (2) Pronouns must agree with their antecedents. This chapter will explain the many rules that apply in these two areas of agreement.

7.1 Subject and Verb Agreement

If you are an experienced speaker of English, you automatically make most subjects and verbs agree as you form your sentences. The process is usually quick and simple. First, you mentally identify a word as a subject. Next, you determine whether the word is singular or plural. Finally, you match the subject with a singular or plural form of a verb. Sometimes, however, the nature of the subject or the pattern of the sentence can cause you to make a mistake. When this happens, you need to slow down your mental process and consciously analyze the steps. You must also consider the *number* of the subjects and verbs you use.

■ The Number of Nouns, Pronouns, and Verbs

In English only three parts of speech can indicate number: nouns, pronouns, and verbs.

Number refers to the two forms of a word: singular and plural. Singular words indicate one; plural words indicate more than one.

Recognizing most nouns and pronouns as either singular or plural is seldom a problem. Most nouns form their plurals simply by adding -s or -es. Some, such as *mouse* or *ox*, form their plurals irregularly: *mice, oxen*. The singular and plural forms of pronouns are listed in Section 1.1. *I*, for example, is singular; *we* is plural.

The number of verbs affects agreement only in two areas: in the present tense and in tenses using the helping verb *be*. The following chart covers the first of these areas. Notice that the only change in form occurs in the third-person singular column, where an -s or -es is added to the base form of the verb.

SINGULAR AND PLURAL VERBS IN THE PRESENT TENSE		
Singular		**Plural**
First and Second Person	**Third Person**	**First, Second, and Third Person**
(I, you) behave	(he, she, it) behaves	(we, you, they) behave
(I, you) try	(he, she, it) tries	(we, you, they) try

The next chart illustrates those forms of the helping verb *be* that change form depending on whether they are singular or plural. The other forms of *be* rarely cause problems.

THE HELPING VERB *BE*	
Singular	**Plural**
(I) am	(we) are
(he, she, it) is	(they) are
(I, he, she, it) was	(we, they) were
(he, she, it) has been	(they) have been

Distinguishing between the singular and plural forms of nouns, pronouns, and verbs is the first step in avoiding errors in agreement.

EXERCISE A: Determining the Number of Nouns, Pronouns, and Verbs. For each of the following items, write whether the noun or pronoun is singular or plural. Then choose the verb from the choices in parentheses that agrees in number with the noun or pronoun.

EXAMPLE: meat (roasts, roast)

            singular   roasts

1. volcano (explodes, explode)
2. hands (shakes, shake)
3. ivy (grows, grow)
4. walls (is crumbling, are crumbling)
5. meteorite (flashes, flash)
6. harmonica (plays, play)
7. vitamins (fortifies, fortify)
8. memories (was rushing, were rushing)
9. puddles (is, are)
10. we (laughs, laugh)

■ Agreement with Singular and Plural Subjects

Two general rules of subject and verb agreement cover all of the more specific rules.

A singular subject must have a singular verb.

A plural subject must have a plural verb.

In the following examples, subjects are underlined once, verbs twice.

SINGULAR SUBJECT AND VERB: Jeremy craves affection.

                                She was being coy.

PLURAL SUBJECT AND VERB: These boys crave affection.

                                They were being coy.

Intervening Phrases and Clauses.   When a sentence contains a phrase or clause that separates the subject from its verb, simply ignore the intervening group of words when you check for agreement.

A phrase or clause that comes between a subject and its verb does *not* affect subject-verb agreement.

Notice in the following examples that the intervening words have no effect on the subject-verb agreement. In the first, the singular subject, *decision,* agrees with a singular verb, *is,* despite the intervening phrase. In the second, the plural subject agrees with a plural verb despite the intervening clause.

EXAMPLES: The <u>decision</u> of the legislators <u>is</u> final.

The <u>families</u> whose town was flooded during the hurricane <u>require</u> temporary shelter.

Intervening parenthetical expressions, such as those beginning with *as well as, in addition to, in spite of,* or *including,* also have no effect on subject-verb agreement. Such expressions are usually set off by commas or other punctuation.

EXAMPLE: Your <u>information</u>, in addition to the data gathered by the computer, <u>is helping</u> to solve the problem.

Relative Pronouns as Subjects. When *who, which,* or *that* acts as the subject in a subordinate clause, its verb will be singular or plural depending on the number of the pronoun's antecedent.

The antecedent of a relative pronoun affects the pronoun's number and determines its agreement with a verb.

In the first of the following examples, the antecedent for *who* is *one;* therefore, the verb, *has,* is singular because *one* is singular. In the second example, the antecedent of *who* is *candidates;* the verb *have* is plural because *candidates* is plural.

EXAMPLES: Chuck is the only one of those candidates <u>who</u> <u>has</u> prior experience in government.

Chuck is just one of several candidates <u>who</u> <u>have</u> prior experience in government.

Study these two examples carefully, noting the distinction in meaning. In the first example, Chuck ("the one") stands out from the larger group of candidates; the basic meaning of the sentence is "Chuck is the only one who *has* experience." In the second example, however, the subordinate clause refers to the group, not to the individual: All of the candidates *have* experience.

EXERCISE B: **Making Singular and Plural Subjects Agree with Their Verbs.** Write the subject from each of the following sentences and then choose the correct verb from the choices in parentheses. Write *S* if the subject is singular and *P* if it is plural.

1. Her powerful grip (results, result) from lifting and carrying.
2. A gravel driveway (provides, provide) better traction.
3. Dark blue (goes, go) well with most other colors.
4. Seen through a microscope, the snowflake's lacy pattern (fills, fill) us with wonder.
5. They sometimes (provokes, provoke) me to anger.
6. Minor headaches (indicates, indicate) stress.
7. His cellar (hides, hide) a dreadful secret.
8. Most kitchen countertops (is, are) laminated plastic.
9. These wallpaper designs (is, are) reproduced in miniature.
10. Australia (was, were) the original home of this wombat.

EXERCISE C: **Making Subjects and Verbs Separated by Phrases and Clauses Agree.** Write the subject from each of the following sentences and then choose the correct verb from the choices in parentheses.

1. Acupuncture, a medical procedure that comes to us from the Chinese, (is, are) receiving greater attention.
2. In the park a crumbling pavilion used for concerts (evokes, evoke) memories of the past.
3. Turpentine, derived from coniferous trees, (is, are) used to clean messy paint spills.
4. This casserole, which is made with beef and various vegetables, (serves, serve) six people.
5. Her only piece of jewelry, an unusual pendant made with tiny seashells, (is, are) hanging from her neck.
6. This daguerreotype, as well as those on the far wall, (was, were) among the first ever made.
7. These easy exercises, along with the one described in that book, (is, are) designed to relax you.
8. During this crisis, his ability to deal with problems (seems, seem) to be crumbling.
9. The houses built on the beach (needs, need) firmer foundations.
10. Dairy products, such as cream or butter, (causes, cause) food to spoil quickly in warm weather.
11. Senior citizens from all over the county (has, have) come here to protest the rising cost of living.

12. The wax pears, arranged in a bowl, (fools, fool) people every time.
13. Ants carrying tiny burdens on their backs (struggles, struggle) back to the colony.
14. My uncle, who is as eccentric as anyone you might know, (talks, talk) incessantly.
15. A fledgling with two anxious parents (has, have) been trying to return to the nest all morning.
16. The debate to be shown on several television stations this evening (is, are) worth seeing.
17. The total, equaling the money in the cash register plus the credit slips, (is, are) two thousand dollars exactly.
18. Walter's mule, a mean animal that bites anyone who comes too close, always (brays, bray) a warning.
19. This slice of bread with mold growing on its sides (was, were) lying in the bottom of the bread drawer.
20. A bear with two cubs (has, have) been seen near the mouth of the river.

EXERCISE D: Making Relative Pronouns Agree with Their Verbs. Divide your paper into four columns and label them *Relative Pronoun, Antecedent, Number,* and *Verb.* Then fill in the information from each of the following sentences, choosing the correct verb from the choices in parentheses.

1. These games of chance, which often (costs, cost) naive players a fortune, will be investigated by the district attorney.
2. Brandy is the only one out of the twenty dogs in the obedience class that (ignores, ignore) every command.
3. The orchestra will play a medley of songs that (appeals, appeal) to most audiences.
4. Jeanette is the strongest of the survivors who (was, were) trapped in the cave.
5. This is one of those practical jokes that (hurts, hurt) everyone involved.
6. Buy some outfits, whatever you like, that (makes, make) you look slim.
7. Only a basic understanding of the sciences that (is, are) taught in junior high school is needed for this course.
8. One of the chemicals that (was, were) found in the river comes from two different sources.
9. Dr. Cooper is one of those rare general practitioners who willingly (makes, make) house calls.
10. The collection of poems, which (was, were) not favorably reviewed in many literary journals, won two awards nevertheless.

■ Compound Subjects

Different rules of agreement apply when the words *or, nor,* or *and* are used to join two or more subjects.

Singular Subjects Joined by *Or* or *Nor.* Both *or* and *nor* require a singular verb when each part of a compound subject is singular.

Two or more singular subjects joined by *or* or *nor* must have a singular verb.

In the following example, the conjunction *or* joins two singular subjects and indicates a singular compound subject.

EXAMPLE: Either <u>green</u> or <u>blue</u> <u>is</u> a suitable color for the background.

Plural Subjects Joined by *Or* or *Nor.* Of course, a plural counterpart to the preceding rule is necessary.

Two or more plural subjects joined by *or* or *nor* must have a plural verb.

EXAMPLE: Neither the <u>paints</u> nor the <u>brushes</u> <u>are</u> in the studio.

Subjects of Mixed Number Joined by *Or* or *Nor.* When the subjects joined by *or* or *nor* are mixed in number, determining the number of the verb is slightly more difficult.

If one or more subjects are singular and the others are plural and they are joined by *or* or *nor*, the subject closest to the verb determines the agreement.

In the first of the following examples, the subject nearest the verb, *candles*, is plural and, therefore, requires a plural verb: *were used*. In the next example, the order of the subjects is changed. Now the singular subject *lamp* is nearest the verb; therefore, a singular verb, *was used*, is necessary.

EXAMPLES: At one time either a whale-oil <u>lantern</u>, a kerosene <u>lamp</u>, or <u>candles</u> <u>were used</u> to light the front hall.

At one time either <u>candles</u>, a whale-oil <u>lantern</u>, or a kerosene <u>lamp</u> <u>was used</u> to light the front hall.

Compound Subjects Joined by *And.* A single rule applies to most situations in which *and* joins two or more subjects.

A compound subject joined by *and* is generally plural and must have a plural verb.

Regardless of whether the parts of the compound subject are all singular, all plural, or mixed in number, the conjunction *and* usually signals the need for a plural verb.

EXAMPLES: At one time a whale-oil <u>lantern</u> and a kerosene <u>lamp</u> <u>were used</u> to light the front hall.

At one time kerosene <u>lamps</u> and candles <u>were used</u> to light the front hall.

At one time <u>candles</u> and a kerosene <u>lamp</u> <u>were used</u> to light the front hall.

Exceptions occur (1) when the parts of the compound subject equal one thing and (2) when the word *each* or *every* is used before a compound subject. Either of these situations requires a singular verb.

SINGULAR COMPOUND SUBJECTS: <u>Bread</u> and <u>butter</u> <u>was</u> all that they offered us.

Every <u>chart</u> and <u>diagram</u> <u>was drawn</u> with precision.

EXERCISE E: Making Compound Subjects Agree with Their Verbs. Write the compound subject from each of the following sentences on your paper. Then choose the correct verb from the choices in parentheses. Be prepared to tell which rule applies.

1. Each crack and crevice in the sidewalk (was, were) filled with cement.
2. The many days of waiting and weeks of uncertainty (has, have) kept Miriam in an anxious state.
3. Several dented helmets and a few shattered swords (was, were) found strewn across the ancient battlefield.
4. Glass, wood, tile, or other materials (is, are) used to create beautiful mosaics.
5. Coal or wood (is, are) burned in this stove.
6. Probably neither Jupiter, Saturn, nor the other outer planets (is, are) capable of sustaining life.
7. A hammer and a screwdriver (is, are) all that you will need.
8. Thrilling rides and an exciting midway (draws, draw) people to the annual fair.

9. Neither threats nor coaxing (causes, cause) Art to be swayed from a decision.
10. Ham and eggs (is, are) my favorite breakfast.
11. Several household utensils and a bronze cauldron (has, have) been recovered from the burial mound.
12. Neither redwoods nor giant sequoias (grows, grow) in this part of the country.
13. The cost of the eye examination and the price for new glasses (was, were) paid for by my parents.
14. Leather coats or vinyl jackets (is, are) being worn this year.
15. Every table and chair in this house (was, were) built by my great-grandfather.
16. A book or a magazine (helps, help) to pass the time spent on the bus.
17. Either expertly applied paint or varnish (has, have) given a professional look to these wooden dressers.
18. Either the elevator or the escalators (takes, take) you to the housewares department.
19. The antique cup and saucer (was, were) neatly displayed on a wooden stand.
20. Beside the fireplace two calico cats and a spotted dog (was, were) waiting for our return.

■ Agreement with Other Kinds of Subjects

The rules covered thus far in this section are the ones that most often apply to subject-verb agreement. However, some subjects, because of their position within a sentence or because of their form, can be confusing. The rest of this section will explain how verbs must agree with these potentially confusing subjects.

Subjects in Inverted Sentences.   In a sentence where the usual subject-verb order is reversed, it is easy to make an error in agreement.

A verb that comes before its subject must still agree with it in number.

Sentences are inverted for several different reasons. In the first of the following examples, the sentence pattern is inverted for emphasis. The singular subject *chick* agrees with the singular verb *was*. The subject-verb agreement is unaffected by the prepositional phrase at the beginning of the sentence. In the second example, *there* signals a verb-subject pattern. The last sentence is an inverted question.

EXAMPLES: Under the hen's wings <u>was</u> a tiny <u>chick</u>.

There <u>are</u> your <u>coat</u> and <u>gloves</u>.

<u>Aren't</u> those frayed <u>ropes</u> dangerous?

One exception to this rule occurs when the expletive *it* begins a sentence. Then, the verb is always singular, even if the subject is plural.

EXAMPLES: It <u>was</u> <u>they</u> whose lives were threatened.

It <u>was</u> my <u>friends</u> and <u>I</u> who made the noise.

NOTE ABOUT *THERE'S* AND *HERE'S:*   A common mistake is the misuse of *there's* and *here's*, contractions for *there is* and *here is*. As singular constructions, they cannot agree with plural subjects.

INCORRECT: Here<u>'s</u> <u>Ann</u> and <u>Tanya</u> now.

CORRECT: Here <u>are</u> <u>Ann</u> and <u>Tanya</u> now.

Subjects of Linking Verbs.   Another agreement problem involves linking verbs and predicate nominatives.

A linking verb must always agree with its subject, regardless of the number of its predicate nominative.

If, for example, the subject of a linking verb is plural and the predicate nominative is singular, remember that it is always the subject that determines the verb's number.

EXAMPLES: <u>Rockets</u> <u>were</u> the ^PN^ signal to begin the battle.

The <u>signal</u> to begin the battle <u>was</u> ^PN^ rockets.

Collective Nouns.   Collective nouns—words such as *jury, family,* or *committee*—name groups of persons or things. They may be either singular or plural depending on the meaning you assign to them.

A collective noun is singular and agrees with a singular verb when the group it names is considered to be a single unit.

A collective noun is plural and agrees with a plural verb when the group it names is considered to be individuals with different feelings or points of view.

SINGULAR: The <u>team</u> <u>has won</u> every game.

A <u>flock</u> of starlings <u>is flying</u> overhead.

PLURAL: The <u>team</u> <u>are quarreling</u> in the locker room.

The <u>flock</u> of starlings <u>jostle</u> one another as they race for the pieces of bread.

One collective noun, *number,* deserves special attention: When used with *the, number* is always singular; when used with *a, number* is always plural.

SINGULAR: The <u>number</u> of whooping cranes <u>has been increasing</u> steadily.

PLURAL: A <u>number</u> of whooping cranes <u>have been reared</u> successfully by sandhill cranes, an unendangered species.

Singular Nouns with Plural Forms.   Nouns that look plural but are actually singular can also cause agreement problems.

Nouns that are plural in form but singular in meaning agree with singular verbs.

Some of these nouns name branches of knowledge: *acoustics, aesthetics, civics, economics, gymnastics, mathematics, physics, politics,* and *social studies.* Others are singular in meaning because, like collective nouns, they name single units: *macaroni* (one dish consisting of many pieces of pasta); *measles, mumps,* and *rickets* (one disease); and so on.

SINGULAR: <u>Mathematics</u> <u>is</u> my most difficult subject.

<u>Measles</u> <u>threatens</u> unborn babies.

Some of these words are especially tricky. When *ethics* and *politics,* for example, name characteristics or qualities rather than branches of knowledge, their meanings are plural. Similarly such words as *data, eyeglasses, media, pliers, scissors,* and *trousers* generally take plural verbs although they name single items or collective ideas.

PLURAL: Nina's <u>ethics</u> <u>are adjusted</u> to fit any occasion.

Jack's <u>politics</u> <u>were</u> not our concern.

The <u>media</u> <u>have been accused</u> of causing the politician's defeat.

Indefinite Pronouns.　Indefinite pronouns used as subjects are often a source of confusion.

Depending on its form and meaning, an indefinite pronoun can agree with either a singular or a plural verb.

Refer to the list of indefinite pronouns in Section 1.1. Notice that some are always singular. Included here are those ending in *-one (anyone, everyone, someone),* those ending in *-body (anybody, everybody, somebody),* and those that imply one *(each, either).* Others are always plural: *both, few, many, others,* and *several.* A few can be either singular or plural: *all, any, more, most, none,* and *some.* Review the list until you can recognize the number of any indefinite pronoun.

Following are examples from each category.

ALWAYS SINGULAR:　Almost <u>everyone</u> <u>likes</u> his music.

<u>Everybody</u> <u>is expected</u> to be here tomorrow.

<u>Neither</u> of the dresses <u>looks</u> good on you.

ALWAYS PLURAL:　<u>Both</u> of these shoes <u>squeak</u>.

<u>Many</u> in the class <u>excel</u> in writing.

<u>Others</u> <u>overlook</u> the difficulties.

EITHER SINGULAR OR PLURAL:　<u>Most</u> of the pie <u>was eaten</u>.

<u>Most</u> of the hinges <u>have been oiled</u>.

When the indefinite pronoun is one that can be either singular or plural, the pronoun's antecedent determines the pronoun's number. In the first of the preceding examples, the antecedent of *most* is *pie,* a singular noun; therefore, *most* is singular. In the second example, the antecedent of *most* is *hinges,* a plural noun; therefore, *most* is also plural.

NOTE ABOUT *MANY A, NONE,* AND *ANY:*　*Many a* always precedes a singular subject. A singular subject must agree with a singular verb.

EXAMPLE:　Many a vegetable <u>dish</u> <u>has been ruined</u> by over-cooking.

None and *any* occasionally are singular even when they have plural antecedents. In this situation, *none* means "not one" and *any* means "any one."

EXAMPLES: **None** of their friends <u>is attending</u> the party.

Hasn't <u>any</u> of my relatives <u>sent</u> me a birthday card?

Titles.   The titles of books and other works of art can be misleading if they sound plural or consist of many words.

A title is singular and must have a singular verb.

EXAMPLES: <u>Dr. Jekyll and Mr. Hyde</u> <u>is</u> a psychological thriller.

<u>The Gleaners</u> by Jean François Millet <u>depicts</u> peasant women working in a field.

Amounts and Measurements.   Other kinds of subjects that sound plural but can actually be singular are amounts and measurements.

A noun expressing an amount or measurement is usually singular and must usually have a singular verb.

In the first three of the following examples, the subjects agree with singular verbs: *Twenty-five cents* is a single sum of money; *four tablespoons*, a single measurement; and *three fourths*, one part of a whole. In the last example, however, *half* refers to many individual items and is therefore plural.

EXAMPLES: <u>Twenty-five cents</u> <u>starts</u> the dryer in the laundromat.

<u>Four tablespoons</u> of salt <u>has made</u> the soup inedible.

<u>Three fourths</u> of that nation <u>is</u> impoverished.

<u>Half</u> of the leaflets <u>were</u> carelessly scattered over the parking lot.

EXERCISE F: Making Confusing Subjects Agree with Their Verbs. Divide your paper into three columns, labeling them *Subject, Singular or Plural,* and *Verb.* For each of the following sentences, find the subject and write it in the first column. Then decide whether its meaning is singular or plural and write your answer in the second column. Finally, choose the correct verb from the choices in parentheses and write it in the third column.

1. As usual our swimming team (is, are) trying to recover from its latest defeat.
2. Here (is, are) the different options for your consideration.

3. Written by the British author Thackeray, *The Virginians* (is, are) set in colonial America.
4. His tactics at first (seems, seem) to be self-serving.
5. The herd of bewildered cattle (is, are) milling about aimlessly inside the enclosure.
6. His mumbled apology and its obvious insincerity (was, were) my reason for disliking him.
7. Two gallons of whitewash (is, are) all that we need for these basement walls.
8. The newspaper media (covers, cover) both national and international events.
9. Thermodynamics (is, are) concerned with the relations between heat and mechanical energy.
10. Her broken eyeglasses (was, were) lying on the ground.
11. Franz Liszt's *Les Préludes* (is, are) a symphonic poem written for orchestra.
12. A swarm of killer bees (is, are) slowly advancing northward.
13. A good idea for raising money (is, are) having everyone demonstrate a craft and having people sign up for lessons.
14. Twenty dollars (includes, include) the price of the room and a continental breakfast.
15. At the beginning of the play, a group of girls, some walking, others skipping, (enters, enter) singing.
16. To and fro in their narrow cage (paces, pace) the tawny lions.
17. All of his change (was, were) tossed onto the table.
18. At this moment few (remains, remain) in the room.
19. The clergy (is, are) divided over minor issues in doctrine.
20. Mumps (is, are) a dangerous disease in adults.
21. Eugene's faltering steps (was, were) the first sign of his recovery from a long period of illness.
22. *Giovanni Arnolfini and His Wife* (was, were) painted by Jan Van Eyck.
23. Nearly half of the hamsters (was, were) rejected by their mother.
24. Any of these furnaces (does, do) a good job of heating a house.
25. A number of quails (is, are) hiding in the underbrush.

APPLICATION: **Applying the Rules of Subject and Verb Agreement.** Complete each of the following sentences with an appropriate present-tense form of a verb. Be prepared to cite which rule of subject-verb agreement you used to complete each sentence.

1. The receptive audience _____ even the worst of the acting.

2. Biogenetics _____ by Professor Randolph, an inspired teacher.
3. Those plants and flowers whose leaves are brown _____ in need of care.
4. Blurred vision and headaches _____ the first indication of his illness.
5. Kathy is one of the few students in her class who _____ all of the assignments.
6. None of the radishes or cucumbers _____ ready to be picked.
7. "Calloused" or "insensitive" best _____ her character.
8. Here _____ five dollars, which is all I am able to contribute.
9. Pelting rains or strong winds _____ the bare soil.
10. Spaghetti and meatballs _____ here for lunch every Wednesday.
11. The clown with the orange nose and over-sized shoes _____ funny.
12. Churchill, together with Roosevelt and Stalin, _____ the Yalta Conference.
13. The confetti _____ in small cardboard boxes.
14. Once again our family _____ turns doing the more objectionable household tasks.
15. Neither water nor chemicals effectively _____ a fire like this one.

7.2 Pronoun and Antecedent Agreement

Like a subject and its verb, a pronoun and its antecedent must agree. An antecedent is the word or group of words for which the pronoun stands. (See Section 1.1 for a more detailed definition of the term *antecedent*.)

■ Agreement Between Personal Pronouns and Antecedents

While a subject and verb must agree simply in number, a personal pronoun and its antecedent must agree in three ways.

A personal pronoun must agree with its antecedent in number, person, and gender.

Number, as you may already know, refers to a word's being either singular or plural. *Person* refers to a pronoun's ability to indicate either the person speaking (first person); the person spoken to (second person); or the person, place, or thing spoken about (third person). *Gender* is the characteristic of nouns and pronouns that indicates whether the word is *masculine* (referring to males), *feminine* (referring to females), or *neuter* (referring to neither males nor females).

The only personal pronouns that, in themselves, indicate gender are third person and singular. The following chart lists these personal pronouns and some nouns according to gender.

GENDER OF NOUNS AND PERSONAL PRONOUNS					
Masuline		**Feminine**		**Neuter**	
Noun	**Pronoun**	**Noun**	**Pronoun**	**Noun**	**Pronoun**
father	he	sister	she	road	it
nephew	him	daughter	her	pain	its
steward	his	stewardess	hers	Seattle	

The following example illustrates the way in which a pronoun and its antecedent must agree in the three areas of number, person, and gender. The antecedent *stewardess* is singular in number, is in the third person, and is feminine in gender. *Her* agrees with the antecedent since it too is singular, third-person, and feminine.

EXAMPLE: The *stewardess* disregarded *her* own safety to help the passengers escape the burning plane.

Agreement in Number Between Personal Pronouns and Compound Antecedents.   When an antecedent is compound, making the pronoun agree can be a problem. Keep the following three rules in mind when determining the number of compound antecedents.

In general use a plural personal pronoun with two or more antecedents joined by *and.*

PLURAL: *Melissa* and *I* are studying for *our* exams.

In general use a singular personal pronoun with two or more singular antecedents joined by *or* or *nor.*

SINGULAR: Either *Craig* or *Todd* will bring *his* stereo to the dance.

One exception to the first two rules occurs when a distinction must be made between individual and joint ownership. If individual ownership is intended, then a singular pronoun is used to refer to a compound antecedent. If joint ownership is intended, a plural pronoun is used.

SINGULAR (individual ownership):   Both *Nat* and *Cecily* were reluctant to take along *her* dog. (Cecily owns the dog.)

PLURAL (joint ownership):   Both *Nat* and *Cecily* were reluctant to take along *their* dog. (Both Nat and Cecily own the dog.)

SINGULAR (individual ownership):   Neither my *brother* nor my *father* would allow me to use *his* car. (The brother and the father each own a car.)

PLURAL (joint ownership):   Neither my *brother* nor my *father* would allow me to use *their* car. (The brother and father own the same car.)

The third rule applies to compound antecedents whose parts are mixed in number.

Use a plural personal pronoun if any part of a compound antecedent joined by *or* or *nor* is plural.

PLURAL: When the *boys* or their *sister* comes home, give *them* this message.

Shifts in Person and Gender.   Unnecessary shifts in either person or gender spoil agreement between pronouns and their antecedents.

Do not shift person or gender between a pronoun and its antecedent.

A shift in person or gender can be corrected by simply replacing the incorrect pronoun with one that agrees.

SHIFT IN PERSON: *Mike* is attending the state university because *you* pay less tuition there.

CORRECT: *Mike* is attending the state university because *he* pays less tuition there.

SHIFT IN GENDER: The *horse* threw *its* head back and stood on *his* hind legs.

CORRECT: The *horse* threw *its* head back and stood on *its* hind legs.

Generic Masculine Pronouns.   A masculine pronoun that is used to refer to a singular antecedent whose gender is unknown is said to be *generic,* meaning that it applies to both masculine and feminine genders in general.

> Use a masculine pronoun (*he, him,* or *his*) with a singular antecedent whose gender may be either masculine or feminine.

EXAMPLE: Any *person* can learn to ski if *he* tries.

Although the generic masculine pronoun is the traditional standard usage, many people avoid it because it inadvertently excludes females. Rephrasing to avoid gender entirely is usually the equitable solution.

EXAMPLES: Any *person* who tries can learn to ski.

People can learn to ski if *they* try.

In rephrasing sentences to eliminate generic masculine pronouns, you should generally avoid resorting to the use of two pronouns: "Any person can learn to ski if *he or she* tries." Such usage can easily become awkward when a passage contains many pronouns. Moreover, you should also avoid a generic feminine pronoun: "Any person can learn to ski if *she* tries." Such usage is not standard English and tends to create more problems than it solves.

EXERCISE A: Making Personal Pronouns Agree with Their Antecedents. Complete each of the following sentences with a suitable personal pronoun. Be sure each pronoun agrees with its antecedent.

1. Boris and Leo improved _____ act by constant practice.
2. If the dark blue paint or the pale yellow is not oil-based, don't use _____.

3. Neither the furniture nor the rugs retained _____ new appearance for long.
4. Every participant in the games showed _____ appreciation for the host country's warm welcome.
5. If you use either upholstery tacks or a stapler, _____ will secure the material only temporarily.
6. Andy and Lois Anderson sold several acres of _____ property to a large corporation.
7. Lincoln is Nebraska's capital and Omaha is _____ largest city.
8. Neither Mark nor Sam could find _____ keys to the car.
9. Any adult familiar with hospital procedures knows _____ should not bring small children during visiting hours.
10. Both Nick and his dog Mutt know _____ routine.

EXERCISE B: **Correcting Shifts in Person and Gender.** Eight of the following sentences contain unnecessary shifts in person or gender. Rewrite any faulty sentences. For those sentences that need no revision, write *correct*.

1. A person should check their diving equipment before descending.
2. Those hikers will soon realize that you cannot walk for miles in shoes meant for dress wear.
3. Try to be just since you expect justice in return.
4. Ms. Michaels is teaching a course in linguistics to the seniors, a subject that they find difficult.
5. Easily swayed by shifts in public opinion, the committee have not yet finished its debates.
6. The welders wear goggles so that your eyes will be shielded from the sparks.
7. Trying to protect her calf, the cow disregarded its own safety as the coyotes approached.
8. We learned from experience in the chemistry laboratory that you should often try a second experiment if the first fails.
9. Next Friday our classes will be shortened so that they can go to an important assembly.
10. As hurricane Donna swept along the predicted path, it left destruction in her wake.

EXERCISE C: **Revising Sentences with Generic Masculine Pronouns.** Two sentences in Exercise A call for the use of a generic masculine pronoun. Identify these two sentences and rewrite them to eliminate the generic pronoun.

■ Personal Pronoun and Indefinite Pronoun Agreement

When an indefinite pronoun such as *each, one,* or *several* is the antecedent of a personal pronoun, errors in agreement may sometimes occur. (See Section 1.1 for a complete list of indefinite pronouns.) In these cases, the following rule should help.

Use a singular personal pronoun when the antecedent is a singular indefinite pronoun.

An intervening phrase or clause does not affect agreement in number between a personal pronoun and its antecedent. Notice in the first of the following examples that the antecedent of *its* is *either* (a singular pronoun), not *bears.* In the next two examples, notice that while the *gender* of the personal pronouns *(her, his)* is determined by other words in the sentences *(women, men),* the *number* of the personal pronouns is determined by the singular antecedents *(one, each).*

EXAMPLES: *Either* of these bears will perform for *its* trainer. (*Not* "... *their* trainer.")

One of the women seemed reluctant to volunteer more of *her* time. (*Not* " ... *their* time.")

Each of the men in the brigade was responsible for *his* buddy. (*Not* "... *their* buddy.")

Sometimes strict adherence to the preceding rule may result in an illogical sentence. Then let common sense determine the number of the personal pronoun. In the following sentence, for example, *neither* is a singular antecedent in agreement with *it;* logic, however, calls for a plural personal pronoun.

ILLOGICAL: Because *neither* of the windows would budge, we had to leave *it* open.

CORRECT: Because *neither* of the windows would budge, we have to leave *them* open.

NOTE ABOUT AGREEMENT WITH SINGULAR INDEFINITE PRONOUNS: In informal situations, the plural personal pronoun *their* is often used to refer to singular indefinite pronouns such as *anybody, everybody, no one,* and *somebody.* In formal writing, however, the generic *his*, or a rephrasing of the sentence, is still considered more appropriate.

INFORMAL: *Anybody* can contribute *their* ideas for the blueprint.

FORMAL: *Anybody* can contribute *his* ideas for the blueprint.

FORMAL AND INFORMAL: *Anybody* can contribute ideas for the blueprint.

EXERCISE D: Making Personal Pronouns Agree with Indefinite Pronouns. Choose the correct pronoun from the choices in parentheses in each of the following sentences. Be prepared to explain the reason for your choices.

1. Each of the aerialists finished performing and then raised (his, their) arms to the crowd.
2. Any one of these paints will retain (its, their) color for many years.
3. Both of these workers will complete (his, their) assignments on time.
4. If everybody rushes through the doors together, avoid (him, them) by stepping aside.
5. Everybody who helped clean up the neighborhood is invited to come to the block party and bring (his, their) friends.
6. No one employed in this office should bring (his, their) personal problems to work.
7. Since one of the passengers in the overturned vehicle seemed dazed, the ambulance took (him, them) to the hospital.
8. No one in the summer workshop felt (he, they) had profited from the experience.
9. While neither of the apples looked ripe, we had no choice but to eat (it, them).
10. Nobody driving across the bridge at 1:05 P.M. realized that (he, they) had narrowly escaped death.
11. When each of the children seemed irritable, Miriam realized it was time for (his, their) nap.
12. Surprisingly, neither of these wigs, with (its, their) unnatural colors, looked strange on Phil.
13. Everyone who spoke appeared unwilling to state (his, their) opinion.
14. Many who heard the small-craft warning thought (he, they) could outwit the storm.
15. Before either of the honored guests left, we asked (him, them) for a second appearance.

16. Anyone who walked down the foggy, deserted street would have thought (he, they) had entered an alien world.
17. Prior to living in the dormitory, each of the girls had tried living in (her, their) own apartment.
18. Several of the photographs taken of her had lost (its, their) finish.
19. Few of the items in the store seemed worth (its, their) price.
20. Everybody who listened to the soothing music felt (his, their) muscles gradually relax.

■ Agreement Between Reflexive Pronouns and Antecedents

Reflexive pronouns—those ending in *-self* or *-selves*—should be used only to refer to a word appearing earlier in the sentence, as in "Our parents treated themselves to a vacation."

A reflexive pronoun must agree with an antecedent that is clearly stated.

Do not use a reflexive pronoun if a personal pronoun can logically be used instead. In the first of the following sentences, *herself* has no antecedent. The personal pronoun *her* should be used in its place.

POOR: The hard work was done by Leslie and *herself*.

CORRECT: The hard work was done by Leslie and *her*.

EXERCISE E: Using Reflexive Pronouns Correctly. Two of the following sentences are correct; the others have agreement problems involving reflexive pronouns. For each correct sentence, write the reflexive pronoun and its antecedent. Rewrite each faulty sentence to correct the usage problem.

1. Mr. Cole and his son cleared the land by themselves.
2. To whom other than herself should the award be given?
3. The dog dug up the bone and gave itself a well-seasoned treat.
4. In their haste Mary and Jean forgot to invite John and myself.
5. Andrea and himself were the most popular couple at the prom.

APPLICATION: **Demonstrating the Rules of Pronoun and Antecedent Agreement.** Use each of the following antecedents and a meaningful personal pronoun in a sentence of your own. Make sure that the pronoun and its antecedent agree in person, number, and gender.

1. flavor
2. neither
3. nation
4. guests and we
5. Heather or Claire

6. few
7. Jacob and his brothers
8. actress
9. most
10. pilot

7.3 Special Problems with Pronoun Agreement

Pronouns whose antecedents are too general, ambiguous, or too distant can cloud the meaning of a sentence. This section will show you how to correct these special problems if they should arise in your own writing.

■ Vague, Overly General Pronoun References

A pronoun's antecedent should always be stated or clearly understood. If the reference to the antecedent is vague or overly general, confusion may arise.

Antecedents for *Which, This, That,* and *These.* The pronouns *which, this, that,* and *these* are often used incorrectly to refer to a vague or overly general idea.

The pronouns *which, this, that,* and *these* should not be used to refer to a vague or overly general idea.

In the following sentence it is impossible to point to exactly what *this* stands for.

VAGUE REFERENCE: Mr. Winter, our host, insisted his wife did nothing well. Mrs. Winter contended she was one of a long line of excellent equestrians. *This* ruined the meal for all of us.

"This what?" a reader might ask. The answer is not stated nor is it clearly understood. You can correct such vague, overly general references in either of two ways. (1) Turn the pronoun into an adjective that modifies a specific noun. (2) Revise the sentence to eliminate *which, this, that,* or *these.*

CORRECT: Mr. Winter, our host, insisted his wife did nothing well. Mrs. Winter contended she was one of a long line of excellent equestrians. *This argument* ruined the meal for all of us.

CORRECT: Mr. Winter's insistence that his wife did nothing well and Mrs. Winter's contention that she was one of a long line of excellent equestrians ruined the meal for all of us.

Antecedents for *It, They,* and *You.*   The personal pronouns *it, they,* and *you* must also have clearly stated antecedents.

The personal pronouns *it, they,* and *you* should not be used with vague, implied, or illogical antecedents.

The best way to correct such errors is generally to replace the personal pronoun with a specific noun.

In the first of the following sentences, *it* has no clear antecedent. In the second sentence, *they* has no antecedent at all.

VAGUE REFERENCE: I need to have a tooth extracted. After having a local anesthetic, I will hardly feel *it.*

CORRECT: I need to have a tooth extracted. After having a local anesthetic, I will hardly feel the *extraction.*

IMPLIED ANTECEDENT: I was an avid fan of Brenda Starr for years before *they* revealed the identity of her mystery man.

CORRECT: I was an avid fan of Brenda Starr for years before the *cartoonist* revealed the identity of her mystery man.

A somewhat different problem occurs when the personal pronoun *you* is misused. The use of *you* is valid only when it refers directly to the reader or listener.

In the first of the following sentences, *you* is vague and should be replaced with another pronoun, such as *one* or *I.* In the second sentence, *you* is not appropriate unless the reader or speaker lived in the time described. *You* needs to be replaced with a specific noun.

VAGUE REFERENCE: The gathering was so somber that *you* hardly dared break the silence.

CORRECT: The gathering was so somber that *one* (or *I*) hardly dared break the silence.

ILLOGICAL REFERENCE: Before homes had modern plumbing, *you* had to pump water from a well.

CORRECT: Before homes had modern plumbing, *people* had to pump water from a well.

NOTE ABOUT *IT*:   In a number of idiomatic expressions, *it* is used correctly without an antecedent. In phrases such as *"It is dark," "It is time,"* and *"It is raining,"* the idiomatic use of *it* is accepted as formal standard English.

EXERCISE A: Correcting Vague, Overly General Pronouns.

Rewrite each of the following sentences to correct the faulty pronoun agreement.

1. For a settler to stake a claim, you first had to live on the land.
2. We grumbled about the work done on the house because they left the roof open and the floors warped.
3. Cal always wore a neatly press handkerchief in his vest pocket and a diamond pin on his lapel. That made him feel rich.
4. During the weather forecast they predicted sunny skies and cool temperatures for the rest of the week.
5. I quickly shifted to a more neutral topic and this prevented the inevitable argument over politics.
6. She wore a sweater over her blouse and a vest over the sweater. That was too bulky.
7. Valery is self-disciplined and energetic. These will be useful throughout life.
8. Ross writes articles for the sports section of our school newspaper, and this makes him well-known at the games.
9. We are building an extension onto our small ranch, and it should help everyone to feel less cramped.
10. After washing and waxing his new car, Jack polished the chrome and cleaned the interior. This was a monthly project.
11. Nellie has always been slightly aloof and quiet. These have alienated her from her peers.
12. When my father spoke angrily, you listened.
13. Near the East River in New York City you can see the United Nations Headquarters.
14. George was too busy and involved with his own work, which was his way of ignoring people.

15. When we stayed in Massachusetts, they told us to visit Walden's Pond.
16. As an Egyptian priest, you probably were taught to write hieroglyphics.
17. Unless a translator is familiar with different dialects, you cannot expertly render current South American literature into English.
18. As gusts blew the tumbleweeds across the prairie, it seemed playful.
19. Two of my brothers run for the track team, which is a sport that teaches discipline.
20. Our tour guide gave us background information on Rainier National Park and the Grand Coulee Dam. That impressed us.

■ Ambiguous Pronoun References

The word *ambiguous* comes from a Latin verb meaning "to wander." Sometimes writers inadvertently let their pronoun references wander in such a way that a pronoun seems to have more than one possible antecedent. Such ambiguous references are confusing and need to be corrected.

Personal Pronouns with Two or More Antecedents.   A personal pronoun's antecedent should always be unmistakable.

A personal pronoun should always refer to a single, obvious antecedent.

In the following sentence *he* is confusing because the pronoun can refer either to *Sam* or *Steve:* Who needs the vacation? The sentence needs to be rephrased to eliminate the confusion caused by the ambiguous pronoun.

AMBIGUOUS REFERENCE: Sam told Steve that *he* needed a vacation.

CORRECT: Sam said that Steve needed a vacation.

CORRECT: While talking to Steve, Sam said that he himself needed a vacation.

Ambiguous Repetition of Personal Pronouns.   Sometimes repetition of the same pronoun within a sentence can create confusion.

> Do not repeat a personal pronoun in a sentence if it can refer each time to a different antecedent.

AMBIGUOUS REPETITION: Janet shouted to Kelly when *she* saw that *she* was about to be splashed by a passing bus.

To whom does the second *she* refer: To Janet or to Kelly? The sentence needs rephrasing to clarify the meaning.

CORRECT: Janet shouted to Kelly when *she* saw that *Kelly* was about to be splashed by a passing bus.

CORRECT: Janet shouted to Kelly when *Janet* saw that *she herself* was about to be splashed by a passing bus.

In the last sentence, notice that the intensive pronoun *herself* makes it clear that the personal pronoun refers to Janet.

EXERCISE B: **Correcting Ambiguous Pronoun References.** Rewrite each of the following sentences to correct the ambiguous pronoun references.

1. The stewardess assured the woman that the plane would be landing soon and that she would have someone to help her find the missing luggage.
2. This bonsai is growing in a container that discourages root growth, but it still seems too small.
3. While Barney wheeled his small son around the park, he was very contented.
4. Jon was forced to take a detour onto a country road, and it seemed to lead nowhere.
5. The woman entering the subway collided with another woman who was just exiting. After regathering her parcels, she seemed unruffled.
6. You would never have known that Suzanne, who was so unassuming, had inherited a vast fortune from her mother. She was a very shrewd woman.
7. The visitors wandering through the rooms filled with priceless Oriental carpets and beautiful furnishings gaped in wonder at them.
8. Our weekend guests promised to return to our lodge next summer and bring additional vacationers, but they never came.
9. The waitress served us slices of warm bread and gave us the menus. We buttered and ate them immediately.
10. This recipe for spinach quiche is my favorite. It is easy to follow and it tastes best soon after it is removed from the oven.

■ Avoiding Distant Pronoun References

A final rule for pronoun references applies to situations in which the pronoun's antecedent is too remote.

A personal pronoun should always be close enough to its antecedent to prevent confusion.

There are two ways to correct a distant pronoun reference. (1) Move the pronoun closer to its antecedent. (2) Eliminate the pronoun through revision.

DISTANT REFERENCE: Two chickens moved about in the doorway. On the porch, an old rocker creaked slightly back and forth. *They* pecked aimlessly at the floor.

CORRECT: As the two chickens moved about in the doorway, *they* pecked aimlessly at the floor. On the porch . . .

CORRECT: Pecking aimlessly at the floor, the two chickens moved about in the doorway. On the porch . . .

EXERCISE C: Correcting Distant Pronoun References. Each of the following groups of sentences has at least one pronoun located too far from its antecedent. Rewrite each group to correct the distant references.

1. Nick let his finger trace the almost obscured letters on the marker. For over a hundred years the tall grasses and weeds had grown over these graves in what was now a meadow where he and Tim, his Irish setter, had gone today for a walk. He mused over the patience and perhaps grief of the person who had painstakingly carved them, without benefit of modern tools.
2. A sharp-eyed barker, his voice rising above the clamor, begged the passing crowds to see the marvelous tattooed man for themselves. Tommy felt for his last crumpled dollar and hesitated only briefly. Drawn by his promise of a once-in-a-lifetime, never-to-be-forgotten thrill, Tommy held out the money.
3. In many stories by Ray Bradbury, the Martians are described as gentle, highly intelligent creatures who are destroyed by people from earth. They are written so skillfully that readers truly feel they have entered another world.
4. Not far from the shore, a small sailboat seemed motionless, its mast like a needle. Red and white buoys dotted the horizon. Gulls spiraled over the whitecaps, darting down now

and then to snatch their food. There was no one on it to un-
furl the sails.

5. We plunged our hands into cardboard boxes, bringing out
handfuls of salty popcorn. Before us on the screen were the
actual faces of the men, women, and children who formed
the bread lines during the Great Depression. Once it was
gone, we guiltily felt for the snacks that would last us until
the movie ended.

APPLICATION: **Correcting Special Problems with Pronoun
Agreement.** Rewrite each of the following sentences to correct
the errors in pronoun agreement. Be prepared to cite the rule
that applies to each of your corrections.

1. We told them to follow us and bring their children. But
when we turned around, they weren't there.
2. Muffins fresh from the oven filled wicker baskets. Jars of
homemade jam, the fruit glistening along the glass sides,
made our mouths water. Coffee, still slowly perking, sat
ready on the stove. They were golden brown and drenched
with butter.
3. The wall paneling is mahogany and the rug is brown. It is
very dark.
4. Frank peeled the potatoes while Anna sliced the onions
and Casey chopped the celery. All of them were needed for
the stew.
5. The representatives told the managers that they should try
a more modern approach to selling.
6. Remember that gasoline fumes are explosive. Special care
should be taken in filling stations. Under the right conditions, all it takes to ignite them is the light from a match
or the spark from a car's engine.
7. I told my brother about the four-leaf clover I found pressed
in the old book, but then I forgot where it was.
8. The meeting had gone badly, Mr. Snelling reflected, as he
loosened his tie. He had forgotten to bring the recommendation that his latest boss had written for him, and he
thought he was not dressed appropriately. It had been
given to him by his daughter and was a conservative
brown.
9. Respect yourself and the rest will follow. That is necessary.
10. His lungs ached from holding his breath. Thick smoke
poured under the door as he irrationally groped for his
glasses. Soon they would involuntarily expand, seeking air.
11. When my mother was a child, they were not permitted to
wear jeans to school.

12. Swimming helplessly in the old cistern, a mouse searched for a means to escape. Finally, its back legs skittering on the cement wall, the mouse climbed out. Located in the basement, it had been built to hold water for use during the dry season.
13. The air in an improperly ventilated room soon becomes stuffy, which can be corrected easily.
14. We were shocked when everyone came to our house and offered their views. They were not expected.
15. First he glared at the man who had knocked his packages on the ground, and then he demanded an apology. Surprised at this anger, he stopped to pick them up.
16. Gerald has never learned the basics of rhetoric. This makes him uncomfortable before a large audience.
17. As Jasper looked down from the helicopter, he could see the villages he had known most of his life and their tiny houses. His excitement over his return faded and was replaced by a feeling, almost physical, of his own smallness. Then it circled several times and began the descent. As the details below him grew clearer, he suddenly remembered them as they were.
18. I plastered the ceiling while Tom held the ladder, which was not too difficult.
19. During the Olympics in Russia, you were only permitted to stay at certain hotels.
20. When Jennifer's mother said she couldn't leave before she finished her work, she was relieved.

8

Adjective and Adverb Usage

You have probably noticed that adjectives and adverbs change form, especially in comparisons. The sentence "Our city's mass transportation system is *cleaner* and *more efficient* than theirs" compares the qualities of one city's transportation system to another's. In a slightly different sentence, however, "Our city's mass transportation system is the *cleanest* and *most efficient*," the qualities of one system are compared to those of all others. The change in the forms of the adjectives alters the meaning of the sentence.

This chapter will explain first how various adjectives and adverbs are formed. Then it will show you how to eliminate specific errors that often occur in comparisons. If you need to begin by reviewing adjectives and adverbs, refer to Section 1.3.

8.1 Degrees of Comparison

Most adjectives and adverbs in English have three forms, two of which are used in making comparisons.

Adjectives and adverbs have different forms to show **degrees of comparison.**

The three degrees are called *positive, comparative,* and *superlative*. The *positive* degree is the form of an adjective or adverb when it is not being used in a comparison. This is the basic form of the adjective or adverb that you will find listed in a dictionary. The *comparative* degree is the form used to compare *two* things. The *superlative* degree is the form used to compare *three or more* things.

■ The Degrees of Comparison

In the following chart both kinds of modifiers are shown in each of the three degrees. Notice the three different ways that the words change form in the comparative and superlative degrees: (1) with -*er* and -*est*, (2) with *more* and *most*, and (3) with entirely different words.

Positive	Comparative	Superlative
Adjectives		
slow	slower	slowest
disagreeable	more disagreeable	most disagreeable
good	better	best
Adverbs		
slowly	more slowly	most slowly
disagreeably	more disagreeably	most disagreeably
well	better	best

EXERCISE A: **Recognizing Positive, Comparative, and Superlative Degrees.** Each of the following sentences has an adjective or adverb in the positive, comparative, or superlative degree. Write each modifier on your paper and identify its part of speech and degree.

1. This chair is more comfortable than that one.
2. Andrew wore his good suit to the celebration.
3. His was the most concerned voice she had heard.
4. Jan deftly flipped the pancake in the air.
5. Your best decision should be made after you rest.
6. Max is more determined when the odds are against him.
7. These pears will ripen more quickly if the sun reaches them.
8. The cat's claws were swiftly unsheathed.
9. Please let me try on the smallest size.
10. They were more disappointed by his attitude than by his failure.

■ Regular Forms

Just as there are both regular and irregular verbs, adjectives and adverbs can be either regular or irregular. Most, however, are regular. The number of syllables in regular modifiers determines how they form their degrees.

Modifiers of One and Two Syllables.   The first of two rules applies to modifiers with one or two syllables.

> Use *-er* or *more* to form the comparative degree and *-est* or *most* to form the superlative degree of most one- and two-syllable modifiers.

The more common method for forming the comparative and superlative degrees of one- and two-syllable modifiers is with *-er* and *-est* rather than with *more* and *most*.

EXAMPLES:

tiny	tinier	tiniest
blue	bluer	bluest
smart	smarter	smartest
funny	funnier	funniest

An exception occurs with adverbs ending in *-ly*. Regardless of the number of syllables, they always use *more* and *most* to form their comparative and superlative degrees.

EXAMPLES:

curtly	more curtly	most curtly
shrewdly	more shrewdly	most shrewdly

More and *most* are also used with certain adjectives of one- or two-syllables when *-er* and *-est* would sound awkward.

EXAMPLES:

brisk	more brisk	most brisk
spiteful	more spiteful	most spiteful
charming	more charming	most charming

Modifiers of More Than Two Syllables.   For modifiers of three or more syllables, forming the comparative and superlative degrees is easy.

> Use *more* and *most* to form the comparative and superlative degrees of all modifiers of three or more syllables.

EXAMPLES:

beautiful	more beautiful	most beautiful
superfluous	more superfluous	most superfluous
experimental	more experimental	most experimental

NOTE ABOUT COMPARISONS WITH *LESS* AND *LEAST:* Meaning the opposite of *more* and *most*, *less* and *least* can be used to form another version of the comparative and superlative degrees of most modifiers.

EXAMPLES:

appetizing	less appetizing	least appetizing
discordantly	less discordantly	least discordantly

EXERCISE B: Forming the Comparative and Superlative Degrees of Regular Modifiers. Each of the following sentences contains the positive degree of a regular modifier. For each sentence write two sentences of your own—one using the comparative degree of the modifier and the other using the superlative degree. Underline your comparative and superlative forms.

EXAMPLE: Johnny's condition is reported to be <u>stable</u>.

Our economy is <u>more stable</u> than it was.

This chair is the <u>most stable</u> one that I have ever built.

1. You were <u>lucky</u> to have lived through the experience.
2. We thought his manner was <u>pretentious</u>.
3. Her chicken soup is utterly <u>tasteless</u>.
4. I <u>rapidly</u> removed my hand from the grill.
5. A <u>threatening</u> gesture made John flinch.
6. Bob's increasingly <u>depressed</u> behavior worries me.
7. The mare, due to foal, moved <u>heavily</u> across the pasture.
8. A freckled face grinned <u>mischievously</u> up at me from under the table.
9. She responded <u>coldly</u> and with the deliberate intention of rudeness.
10. Their <u>patronizing</u> insult was disregarded by those who had heard it.

■ Irregular Forms

Because several adjectives and adverbs form their comparative and superlative degrees in unpredictable ways, it is necessary to memorize them.

The irregular comparative and superlative forms of certain adjectives and adverbs must be memorized.

As you read the following chart, separate the irregular modifiers that cause problems for you from the ones you already use correctly. Then study and memorize them.

IRREGULAR FORMS OF MODIFIERS		
Positive	**Comparative**	**Superlative**
bad	worse	worst
badly	worse	worst
far	farther	farthest
far	further	furthest
good	better	best
ill	worse	worst
late	later	last *or* latest
little (amount)	less	least
many	more	most
much	more	most
well	better	best

Two pairs of these irregular modifiers deserve special study because their positive forms are often confused. The two pairs are *bad* and *badly,* and *good* and *well.* First, keep in mind their parts of speech: *Bad* and *good* are adjectives, *badly* is an adverb, and *well* can be either an adjective or an adverb, depending on its meaning in a sentence. Next, remember (1) that linking verbs (*is, appear, become, feel, look, sound,* and so on) are often followed by predicate adjectives that modify the subject and (2) that action verbs (*act, do, go, perform,* and so on) are often followed by adverbs that modify the verb. The following two patterns visually demonstrate this information. (See Section 1.2 for a more thorough explanation of action and linking verbs.)

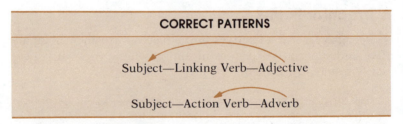

CORRECT PATTERNS

Subject—Linking Verb—Adjective

Subject—Action Verb—Adverb

If you remember these two patterns, you should not make the mistake of placing an adverb, such as *badly,* after a linking verb or of allowing an adjective, such as *good*, to follow an action verb. Such sentence patterns are incorrect because they force one part of speech to do the job of another.

S LV Adv
INCORRECT PATTERN: The room looks *badly* without any curtains.

CORRECT: The room looks *bad* without any curtains.

S AV Adj
INCORRECT PATTERNS: Betty plays the piano *good*.

S AV Adj
My little sister behaves *bad* during meals.

CORRECT: Betty plays the piano *well*.

My little sister behaves *badly* during meals.

NOTE ABOUT *GOOD* AND *WELL:*   As adjectives, *good* and *well* have slightly different meanings. *Good* usually refers to quality or appearance. It can also refer to a general state of well-being.

QUALITY: This steak is *good.*

APPEARANCE: The new furniture looks *good* in this room.

WELL-BEING: I felt *good* after discussing my problem with you.

Well usually refers to satisfactory conditions or to a person's health.

CONDITION: All is *well* at home.

HEALTH: The long rest made him *well* again.

EXERCISE C: Forming the Comparative and Superlative Degrees of Irregular Modifiers.

This exercise is similar to Exercise B except that now the modifiers are irregular. Follow the directions for Exercise B.

1. Robert Burns, the Scottish poet, became <u>ill</u> and died of leprosy.
2. Our new line of cosmetics is selling <u>well</u>.
3. We walked <u>far</u> before we saw a gas station.

4. Cranking the handle of the ice-cream freezer is a <u>good</u> way to increase your appetite.
5. Vincent grabbed for the cup of coffee, but it was too <u>late</u>.
6. There is too <u>little</u> flour left to make a pie.
7. This self-cleaning oven uses <u>much</u> electricity.
8. Holidays are <u>bad</u> times for some people.
9. <u>Many</u> sleighs were driven over this snowy road.
10. She went <u>far</u> in her studies of wolf behavior.

EXERCISE D: Distinguishing Between *Bad, Badly, Good*, and *Well*. Complete each of the following sentences with the appropriate positive form of *bad, badly, good,* and *well.*

1. A little salt in a person's food is especially _____ in very hot weather.
2. Becky wrote _____ until she began to work on improving her handwriting.
3. Your new trenchcoat looks _____ on you.
4. The canned food on the top shelf has turned _____.
5. He should do _____ in college.
6. Cedar chips tossed on a fire make the air smell _____.
7. The old cat can no longer defend itself _____.
8. He always performs _____ when no one is listening.
9. People who listen _____ can actually learn to improve their attentiveness.
10. Raw shrimp quickly becomes _____ if it is not iced.

■ Double Comparisons

Double comparisons are a usage error that results when both methods for forming a comparative or superlative degree are used.

> Do not add both *-er* and *more* (or *less*) or both *-est* and *most* (or *least*) to a regular modifier. Furthermore, never add these endings or words to any irregular comparative or superlative form.

Double comparisons are unnecessarily repetitious and sound awkward.

INCORRECT: The food served in the hospital is *more blander* than home-cooking.

CORRECT: The food served in the hospital is *blander* than home-cooking.

INCORRECT: That is the *least likeliest* possibility of all.

CORRECT: That is the *least likely* possibility of all.

INCORRECT: We will have *lesser* money this year after taxes.

CORRECT: We will have *less* money this year after taxes.

INCORRECT: This is the *most happiest* day of my life.

CORRECT: This is the *happiest* day of my life.

EXERCISE E: **Correcting Errors with Modifiers.** Seven of the following sentences have double comparisons. Three are correct. If the sentence has a double comparison, rewrite the sentence correctly. If the sentence is correct, write *correct* on your paper.

1. Further cooking of this meat will only make it more tougher.
2. The mare's eyes are the most deepest brown.
3. Hers was the more masterly presentation of that challenging subject.
4. Jed's home on wheels was the brightest and most mobilest any wanderer could hope for.
5. My cold was less worse yesterday than it is today.
6. The tiger kitten is the least tamest of the litter.
7. I think Uriah Heep was more obsequious than all other characters.
8. Ms. Burns' and her husband's tempers are the most volatilest combination.
9. If it rains during the night, these icy roads will only become worse.
10. A more politer way of telling them the truth should certainly be found.

APPLICATION: **Using the Degrees of Comparison in Sentences.** Write sentences of your own using each of the following words in the degree indicated.

1. sure—superlative
2. trustworthy—comparative
3. alert—positive
4. good—superlative
5. bad—positive
6. badly—superlative
7. far—positive
8. malicious—comparative
9. windy—comparative
10. well—positive
11. good—comparative
12. far—superlative
13. likely—superlative
14. late—comparative
15. much—comparative

8.2 Clear Comparisons

Once you know how to form regular and irregular adjectives and adverbs in the three degrees, you can work on eliminating problems with comparisons. There are four common problems involving comparisons: (1) using the wrong degree, (2) mistakenly comparing unrelated things, (3) illogically comparing related things, and (4) using absolute modifiers illogically.

■ Using Comparative and Superlative Forms

One basic rule with two parts covers the correct use of comparative and superlative forms.

Use the comparative degree to compare *two* persons, places, things, or ideas. Use the superlative degree to compare *three or more* persons, places, things, or ideas.

As the following examples illustrate, there need not be any obvious reference to specific numbers when you make a comparison. The number of items being compared is often indicated in the context of the sentence.

COMPARATIVE: Orange paint will be *more conspicuous* than yellow.

I am *less talented* than Sheila.

This weekend was *more hectic* than the last.

SUPERLATIVE: Orange is the *most conspicuous* color of all.

I am the *least talented* person for this type of work.

This was the *most hectic* weekend we have had.

NOTE ABOUT THE SUPERLATIVE DEGREE FOR EMPHASIS: The superlative degree can also be used solely for emphasis, without indicating any specific comparison.

EXAMPLES: The movie is *most exciting*.

Our decision is *most definitely* final.

EXERCISE A: Using the Comparative and Superlative Degrees Correctly. For each of the following sentences write the suitable comparative or superlative form of the modifier in parentheses.

1. This road will be (muddy) after the snow melts.
2. He has the (good) record on the team.
3. Your reasoning would be (clear) if you would think through the problem slowly.
4. My grades in art history were (good) this semester than last.
5. Wear a (warm) coat and leave the other in the closet.
6. His parents had three boys; Randy is the (old).
7. Brad is (much) eager to learn the decision of the scholarship committee.
8. Snow is (heavy) than usual after a rainfall.
9. Josh is (susceptible) to respiratory diseases than his twin brother.
10. I have always thought that her eyes are (much) beguiling than anyone else's.

■ Balanced Comparisons

Unbalanced comparisons are illogical and sometimes unintentionally ludicrous.

Make sure that your sentences compare only items of a similar kind.

In the following unbalanced examples, the sentences illogically compare dissimilar things: *Message* cannot be compared to *postcard;* an *idea* cannot be compared to *Monica; plants* in a greenhouse cannot be compared to an entire *greenhouse.*

UNBALANCED: A *message* conveyed by telephone is more private than a *postcard.*

CORRECT: A *message* conveyed by telephone is more private than *one* written on a postcard.

UNBALANCED: Bud's *idea* is less original than *Monica.*

CORRECT: Bud's *idea* is less original than *Monica's.*

UNBALANCED: The *plants* in this greenhouse are lusher than the *greenhouse* down the road.

CORRECT: The *plants* in this greenhouse are lusher than *those* in the greenhouse down the road.

EXERCISE B: Making Balanced Comparisons. Rewrite each of the following sentences to correct the poorly balanced comparison.

1. Duane's work on the blackboard is more legible than Linda.
2. The conditions in the eye of a hurricane are calmer than the perimeter.
3. Vacuuming the floors is less objectionable than the trash.
4. A moose's antlers are bigger than a deer.
5. The spots on a serval, an African cat, are similar to a bobcat.
6. In this part of the country, discomfort caused by contact with poison ivy is more likely than poison oak.
7. There are fewer calories in a small tossed salad than a hamburger.
8. The floats in this year's parade are fewer than the one last year.
9. I think listening to music is more relaxing than a television program.
10. The water in the Great Lakes is purer than they were a decade ago.

■ *Other* and *Else* in Comparisons

Another kind of illogical comparison results when something is unintentionally compared to itself.

When comparing one of a group with the rest of the group, make sure that your sentence contains the word *other* or the word *else*.

In the first of the following examples, *the Grand Canyon*, which is one of the national parks, cannot reasonably be compared to all national parks. Adding *other* excludes the Grand Canyon from the rest of the national parks. In the second set of examples, *the new member* cannot be compared to all the members in the band because the new member is one of those people. Adding *else* excludes the new member from the rest of the group.

ILLOGICAL: We thought the Grand Canyon was *more beautiful than any* national park we visited.

CORRECT: We thought the Grand Canyon was *more beautiful than any other* national park we visited.

ILLOGICAL: The new member plays jazz *better than anyone* in the band.

CORRECT: The new member plays jazz *better than anyone else* in the band.

EXERCISE C: **Using *Other* and *Else* in Comparisons.** Rewrite each of the following sentences to correct the illogical comparison.

1. Arnold's report on the history of humanism was more fascinating than anyone's.
2. The village parson was more respected than any person who lived there.
3. Dora steered her canoe through the rapids with a skill greater than the contestants'.
4. Ask Marge to check the records because she is more thorough than anyone.
5. Rosalie, the winner of five consecutive magic contests, could perform more tricks than anyone we ever saw.

■ Absolute Modifiers

A few modifiers cannot be used in comparisons because they are *absolute* in meaning—that is, their meanings are entirely contained in the positive degree. If, for example, one vase is *priceless*, another vase cannot be *more priceless*. Since *priceless* means "of limitless monetary value," another item cannot possibly be more valuable than something that is already beyond value.

Avoid using absolute modifiers illogically in comparisons.

Among the most common absolute modifiers are the words *dead, entirely, eternal, fatal, final, identical, infinite, mortal, opposite, perfect,* and *unique.* Rather than use words such as these in comparisons, you should try to find similar words whose meanings are not absolute.

ILLOGICAL: This truth is *more eternal* than any other.

BETTER: This truth is *more enduring* than any other.

ILLOGICAL: Your thesis is *more unique* than anyone else's.

BETTER: Your thesis is *more original* than anyone else's.

Many idiomatic expressions, however, use absolute modifiers correctly in comparisons.

EXAMPLES: You couldn't be *more right.*

The *squarer* compartment accommodates more luggage.

Expressions of this sort are accepted as standard English, but you can usually find a word that better expresses you precise meaning.

EXERCISE D: Avoiding Absolute Modifiers in Comparisons.
Rewrite any of the following sentences in which the absolute modifier is used illogically. For any sentence in which you think the modifier is used idiomatically and clearly, write *correct*.

1. We were more completely at home in the rambling old house than we would have thought possible.
2. Of these two antique rocking chairs, I am offering you the more perfect one.
3. Unfortunately, his choice was the most irrevocable one.
4. I couldn't have been more utterly overwhelmed.
5. A more rectangular painting will look better over the fireplace.
6. The main road is straighter than this dirt path.
7. He felt more mortal after his fiftieth birthday.
8. After the operation on her retina, Holly was less blind.
9. A coral snake's venom is more fatal than that of a rattlesnake.
10. The flowers planted in the shade are more nearly dead than the ones planted in the sunshine.

APPLICATION: Writing Clear Comparisons.
For each of the following, write a clear, effective comparison in one sentence. Make sure both parts of the comparison are balanced.

EXAMPLE: Compare the difference between two woodwind instruments.

An oboe is somewhat longer and thinner than a clarinet.

1. Compare three units of measurement.
2. Compare the differences between two domestic animals.
3. Compare one profession with another.
4. Compare three actors or actresses.
5. Compare a contemporary author's novel with a deceased author's novel.

Miscellaneous Usage Problems

Many small problems that can spoil the clarity of your speaking or writing do not fall into any of the broad categories of usage that were covered in preceding chapters. Some of these problems involve customary distinctions between standard and nonstandard usage. Others have to do with the less discernable differences between acceptable and less preferred usage. Still other words can cause problems merely because they share similar meanings or spellings. The next two sections are intended to help you improve your mastery of the small details that contribute to effective speaking and writing.

Double Negatives 9.1

In today's English a clause usually needs just one negative word—such as *never, no, nobody, none, nothing, nowhere, not,* or the contraction *n't*—to convey a negative idea. More than one negative word can be redundant and confusing.

■ Using Negative Words Correctly

A clause containing two negative words when only one is needed is said to contain a *double negative.*

Do not write sentences with **double negatives.**

The following sets of examples show that double negatives can be corrected by eliminating one negative word or the other.

DOUBLE NEGATIVE: Janet *wouldn't* do *nothing* to help herself.

CORRECT: Janet *wouldn't* do anything to help herself.

Janet would do *nothing* to help herself.

DOUBLE NEGATIVE: *Nobody* here wants *no* trouble.

CORRECT: *Nobody* here wants any trouble.

Everybody here wants *no* trouble.

DOUBLE NEGATIVE: I *couldn't never* understand him.

CORRECT: I *couldn't* ever understand him.

I could *never* understand him.

Using Negatives in Clauses.   Sentences containing more than one clause can correctly contain more than one negative word. Each clause, however, usually contains no more than one negative word.

SUBORDINATE CLAUSE   MAIN

EXAMPLE: Since we did*n't* remember to mail the invitations, *nobody*

CLAUSE

came to the party.

Using *But* Negatively.   When *but* is used as an adverb, it will often have a negative sense. If so, it should not be accompanied by another negative word.

DOUBLE NEGATIVE: He *wasn't but* a child at the time.

CORRECT: He was *but* a child at the time.

He was *only* a child at the time.

Other Negative Words.   In addition to the negative words already mentioned, there are *barely*, *hardly*, and *scarcely*. None of these words should be used with other negative words.

DOUBLE NEGATIVE: He *wasn't barely* able to talk when he began to read.

CORRECT: He was *barely* able to talk when he began to read.

He *wasn't* yet talking well when he began to read.

DOUBLE NEGATIVE: I *couldn't hardly* endure the pain.

CORRECT: I could *hardly* endure the pain.

I nearly *couldn't* endure the pain.

DOUBLE NEGATIVE: She *didn't scarcely* have time to comb her hair.

CORRECT: She *scarcely* had time to comb her hair.

She almost *didn't* have time to comb her hair.

EXERCISE A: **Avoiding Double Negatives.** Rewrite each of the following sentences to eliminate the double negatives.

1. Philip Nolan never did nothing to antagonize the men aboard the ship.
2. You should not drive that car nowhere without snow tires.
3. Nobody knew none of the answers on the exam.
4. I can't find my address book nowhere.
5. No one never saw the bear tracking us.
6. Never mix no chlorine bleach with ammonia.
7. Norman won't repeat nothing told to him confidentially.
8. She didn't tell nobody about her disappointing visit to the city.
9. Nobody in our community never realized water was a precious resource until there wasn't enough.
10. None of us never forgot an important date in our family.

EXERCISE B: **Correcting Double Negatives.** The following phrases contain double negatives. Eliminate each error and expand the phrase into a sentence of your own.

1. wouldn't hardly try
2. wasn't nobody there
3. couldn't scarcely walk
4. shouldn't never impose
5. weren't but a few
6. isn't barely tolerable
7. nothing won't hurt
8. didn't want no pity
9. hadn't none left
10. not asked nobody

■ Understatement

Occasionally a speaker or writer may want to imply a positive idea without actually stating it. This indirect method is called *understatement.* Understatement may be used to minimize the importance of an idea, or, conversely, to emphasize its importance. Regardless of the motive, understatement is usually achieved by combining a word with a negative prefix, such as *in-*, *un-*, or *non-*, with a negative word.

EXAMPLES:　Such accidents are *scarcely unavoidable.*

This phenomenon *isn't* entirely *inexplicable.*

EXERCISE C: **Writing Understatements.** Rewrite each of the following sentences as an understatement. Underline the negative word and the negative prefix in your sentence. Be prepared to explain the difference between the direct statements and the understatements.

1. The price for this dimestore trinket is estimable.
2. Tad is certainly a conformist.
3. I am impressed by your fluency in Russian.
4. During the sale, all items are refundable.
5. Taking some time for yourself is essential.
6. Jill acts decisively on crucial matters.
7. Interruptions from inquisitive children were frequent.
8. Our company is managed for profit.
9. Their militant code was violent.
10. Considering the barbaric manners of his guests, I think Bob's conduct was quite honorable.

APPLICATION: **Writing Negative Sentences.** None of the following sentences contains negative words. Rewrite each sentence to express a negative idea.

1. Any other person could have written such a scathing letter to the editor.
2. Something I carelessly said must have aroused their suspicion.
3. Their actions are consistent with the tenets of their faith.
4. This salad made from the dandelion greens could taste better.
5. Each one of the team's members showed good sportsmanship.

9.2　One Hundred Common Usage Problems

To make the best possible use of this gathering of usage problems, first read each problem. As you read, note the items that need your special attention. Then use the exercises at the end to test your understanding. After you have completed the exercises, you should continue to refer to the section whenever you are preparing formal written or spoken material.

To use this section as a reference tool, remember that the usage problems are listed in alphabetical order. When there are two or more words or phrases included within a problem, they too will generally be in alphabetical order. If you cannot find what you are looking for, check the index located at the back of the book.

(1) *A* and *An*. The article *a* is used before consonant sounds; *an*, before vowel sounds. When using *a* and *an* before words beginning with *h*, *o*, or *u*, make sure that you have chosen the correct article. Sometimes these three letters have consonant sounds; at other times they have vowel sounds.

CONSONANT SOUNDS: a *h*istorical document (*h*-sound)

a *o*ne-way street (*w*-sound)

a *u*niversal human right (*y*-sound)

VOWEL SOUNDS: an *h*onest day's work (no *h*-sound)

an *o*pen door (*o*-sound)

an *u*nearthly howl (*u*-sound)

(2) *Accept* and *Except*. *Accept*, a verb, means "to receive." *Except*, a preposition, means "leaving out" or "other than."

VERB: I *accept* your challenge to a debate.

PREPOSITION: Everyone came to the picnic *except* her.

(3) *Accuse* and *Allege*. Notice the distinction in the meanings of these two verbs. *Accuse* means "to blame" or "to bring a charge against." *Allege* means "to claim something that has not been proved."

EXAMPLES: We mistakenly *accused* an innocent bystander.

The employees *allege* that their employer ignored safety regulations.

(4) *Adapt* and *Adopt*. *Adapt*, a verb, means "to change." *Adopt*, also a verb, means "to take as one's own."

EXAMPLES: We *adapted* our sleeping habits to the long Arctic summer days.

They *adopted* the homeless waif.

(5) Advice and Advise. Notice the difference in meaning between these related words. *Advice* is the noun, meaning "an opinion." *Advise* is the verb, meaning "to give an opinion to."

NOUN: I need your *advice*.

VERB: Hikers are *advised* to take along a canteen of water.

(6) Affect and Effect. *Affect* is almost always a verb meaning "to influence" or "to bring about a change in." *Effect*, usually a noun, means "result." Occasionally, *effect* is a verb; then it means "to bring about" or "to cause."

VERB: The years spent in the mines *affected* his lungs.

NOUN: One *effect* of her travels was a new open-mindedness.

VERB: The new administration *effected* many changes in foreign policy.

(7) Aggravate. Aggravate means "to make worse." Avoid using this word to mean "to annoy."

PREFERRED: Scratching will only *aggravate* the mosquito bite.

LESS ACCEPTABLE: He was *aggravated* by their lack of comprehension.

(8) Ain't. *Ain't*, originally a contraction of *am not*, is not considered acceptable standard English. Avoid using it in all writing.

NONSTANDARD: He *ain't* come home yet.

CORRECT: He *hasn't* come home yet.

(9) All Ready and Already. *All ready*, two separate words, is an expression meaning "ready." The expression functions as an adjective. *Already* is an adverb meaning "by or before this time" or "even now."

ADJECTIVE: I am *all ready* to listen to your report.

ADVERB: I have *already* made a decision.

(10) All Right and Alright. *Alright,* though it is more and more frequently seen in print, is not considered a correct spelling. Always use the two-word form in your writing.

PREFERRED: My sprained wrist is *all right* now.

LESS ACCEPTABLE: Whatever you decide is *alright* with me.

(11) All Together and Altogether. These two adverbs have different meanings. *All together* means "all at once." *Altogether* means "completely" or "in all."

EXAMPLES: We will march *all together* in the rally.

    You are *altogether* mistaken about my brother's character.

(12) A Lot, Alot, and Allot. *A lot* is an informal expression meaning "a great many" or "a great amount." Avoid using it in formal writing. *Alot* is nonstandard and should never be used. *Allot,* a verb, means "to divide in parts" or "to give out in shares."

NONSTANDARD: She had *alot* of relatives.

CORRECT: She has *a lot* of relatives.

BETTER: She has *many* relatives.

VERB: The government *allotted* the funds equally among the researchers.

(13) A.M. and P.M. *A.M.* refers to hours before noon; *P.M.* to hours after noon. Never spell out numbers when you use these abbreviations. In addition, never use such phrases as "in the morning" or "in the afternoon" with them.

INCORRECT: The train arrives at *eleven A.M. in the morning* and departs at *one P.M.*

CORRECT: The train arrives at *11:00 A.M.* and departs at *1:00 P.M.*

(14) Among and Between. *Among* and *between* are both prepositions. *Among* always implies three or more. *Between* is generally used with just two things.

EXAMPLES: There is a feeling of discontent *among* the citizens.

    Juan got *between* Carlos and me.

(15) *Amount* and *Number*. Use *amount* with qualities and quantities that cannot be counted. Use *number* with things that can be counted.

EXAMPLES: a small *amount* of cream, a large *amount* of profit

a *number* of empty bottles, a *number* of books

(16) *Anxious*. *Anxious* means "worried," "uneasy," or "fearful." Do not use it as a substitute for *eager*.

AMBIGUOUS: I am *anxious* to meet new people.

CLEAR: I am always *eager* to meet new people.

CLEAR: I am always *anxious* about meeting people for the first time.

(17) *Anyone*, *Everyone*, *Any One*, and *Every One*. Learn to distinguish between these one-word and two-word forms. *Anyone* and *everyone* mean "any person" and "every person." *Any one* means "any single person (or thing)," and *every one* means "every single person (or thing)."

EXAMPLES: *Anyone* who is interested in joining the debate team should attend the meeting after school.

Everyone complained about the service.

Any one of these students could be elected class president.

Every one of the dishes was broken.

(18) *Anyway*, *Anywhere*, *Everywhere*, *Nowhere*, and *Somewhere*. These adverbs should never end in -*s*.

NONSTANDARD: The weather may be inclement, but we will go hiking *anyways*.

CORRECT: The weather may be inclement, but we will go hiking *anyway*.

(19) *As*. Do not use the conjunction *as* to mean "because" or "since."

PREFERRED: We stayed home, since our mother was sick, and helped prepare dinner.

LESS ACCEPTABLE: We stayed home, as our mother was sick, and helped prepare dinner.

(20) *As To.* *As to* is considered awkward. Replace it with a single preposition such as *about, for,* or *of.*

NONSTANDARD: Scientists have several theories *as to* how the continents were formed.

CORRECT: Scientists have several theories *about* how the continents were formed.

(21) *At.* Do not use *at* after *where.* Simply eliminate the word *at.*

NONSTANDARD: Do you know where the bus station is *at?*

CORRECT: Do you know where the bus station is?

(22) *At About.* Avoid using *at* with *about.* Simply eliminate either the word *at* or the word *about.*

PREFERRED: We arrived at lunch time.

We arrived *about* lunch time.

LESS ACCEPTABLE: We arrived *at about* lunch time.

(23) *Awful* and *Awfully.* *Awful* is used informally to mean "extremely bad." *Awfully* is used informally to mean "very." Both modifiers are overused and should be replaced with more descriptive words. In formal writing, use *awful* only to mean "inspiring fear."

INFORMAL: He looked *awful* after the operation.

BETTER: He looked *pale and defeated* after the operation.

INFORMAL: I am *awfully* tired.

BETTER: I am *exhausted.*

FORMAL: The man fell on his knees in the *awful* presence of the king.

(24) *A While* and *Awhile.* *A while* is an article and a noun and is usually used after the preposition *for.* *Awhile* is an adverb, which in itself means "for a while."

NOUN: Stay for *a while* and keep me company.

ADVERB: Rest *awhile* before you leave.

(25) *Beat* and *Win*. *Beat* means "to overcome (an opponent)." *Win* means "to achieve victory in." Do not use *win* in place of *beat*.

INCORRECT: The Dodgers *won* the Yankees in the World Series.

CORRECT: The Dodgers *beat* the Yankees in the World Series.

(26) *Because*. Do not use *because* after *the reason*. Rephrase the sentence using one or the other.

NONSTANDARD: *The reason* we are late is *because* our car broke down.

CORRECT: We are late *because* our car broke down.

CORRECT: *The reason* we are late is that our car broke down.

(27) *Being That* and *Being As*. Avoid using either expression. Use *since* or *because* instead.

NONSTANDARD: *Being that* (or *as*) the tide was coming in, we left.

CORRECT: *Since* (or *Because*) the tide was coming in, we left.

(28) *Beside* and *Besides*. As prepositions, these two words have different meanings and cannot be interchanged. *Beside* means "at the side of" or "close to." *Besides* means "in addition to."

EXAMPLES: The athletic field is *beside* the school.

Who *besides* you will come to the play?

(29) *Blond* and *Blonde*. These two words originally came from French, in which *blond* refers to males and *blonde* to females. Although many writers continue to make this distinction in English, *blond* may correctly be used to refer to either gender.

INCORRECT: My brother is a *blonde*.

CORRECT: My brother is a *blond*.

CORRECT: Harriet is the *blond* (or *blonde*) standing at the top of the stairs.

(30) ***Bring*** **and** ***Take.*** *Bring* means "to carry from a distant place to a nearer one." *Take* means the opposite: "to carry from a near place to a more distant place."

EXAMPLES: Please *bring* your paper to me here.

Will you *take* the dog to the veterinarian?

(31) ***Bunch.*** *Bunch* means "a number of things of the same kind." Avoid using this word to mean "group."

PREFERRED: She bought a *bunch* of grapes.

LESS ACCEPTABLE: A *bunch* of us went downtown.

BETTER: A group of us went downtown.

(32) ***Burst,*** ***Bust,*** **and** ***Busted.*** *Burst* is the standard present, past, and past participle of the verb *burst*. *Bust* and *busted* are nonstandard forms.

NONSTANDARD: I will *bust* if I take one more bite.

He shouldn't have *busted* the blister.

CORRECT: I will *burst* if I take one more bite.

He shouldn't have *burst* the blister.

(33) ***But What.*** Do not use *but what*. Instead, use *that*.

NONSTANDARD: I don't doubt *but what* I will win.

CORRECT: I don't doubt *that* I will win.

(34) ***Can*** **and** ***May.*** Use *can* to mean "to have the ability to." Use *may* to mean "to have permission to" or "to be possible or likely to."

ABILITY: This scale *can* register up to five hundred pounds.

PERMISSION: Yes, you *may* leave.

POSSIBILITY: It *may* rain today.

(35) ***Can't Help But.*** This is a nonstandard expression. Use *can't help* plus a gerund instead.

NONSTANDARD: I *can't help but* wonder where you have been.

CORRECT: I *can't help wondering* where you have been.

(36) *Clipped Words.* Avoid using clipped or shortened words such as *gym, phone,* and *photo,* in formal writing.

FORMAL: The plans for a new *gymnasium* will be presented at the meeting.

INFORMAL: The plans for a new *gym* will be presented at the meeting.

(37) *Condemn* and *Condone.* Notice the difference in the meanings of these two verbs. *Condemn* means "to express strong disapproval of." *Condone* means "to pardon or overlook."

EXAMPLES: They *condemned* him for his indifference to the suffering of others.

I cannot *condone* such cruelty.

(38) *Continual* and *Continuous.* Notice the difference in the meanings of these related adjectives. *Continual* means "occurring again and again in succession." *Continuous* means "occurring without interruption."

EXAMPLES: His *continual* coffee breaks caused the manager to fire him.

His *continuous* absence from work caused the manager to fire him.

(39) *Different From* and *Different Than.* Though the distinction is beginning to disappear, *different from* is preferred to *different than.*

PREFERRED: Your concept of fun is *different from* mine.

LESS ACCEPTABLE: Your concept of fun is *different than* mine.

(40) *Doesn't* and *Don't.* Do not use *don't* with third-person singular pronouns and nouns. Use *doesn't* instead.

NONSTANDARD: He *don't* like heights.

My watch *don't* keep accurate time.

CORRECT: He *doesn't* like heights.

My watch *doesn't* keep accurate time.

(41) Done. *Done* is the past participle of the verb *do*. It should always follow a helping verb.

NONSTANDARD: She always *done* more than what was expected of her.

CORRECT: She *has* always *done* more than what was expected of her.

(42) Dove. *Dove*, a past tense of *dive*, is considered unacceptable by many speakers and writers. Use *dived* instead.

PREFERRED: He *dived* into the ice-cold water.

LESS ACCEPTABLE: He *dove* into the ice-cold water.

(43) Due To. *Due to* means "caused by." It should only be used to begin a phrase that clearly and logically modifies a noun. When in doubt try replacing *due to* with another expression, such as *because of*.

NONSTANDARD: She became blind *due to* a freak accident.

CORRECT: Her blindness was *due to* a freak accident.

(44) Due To The Fact That. All of these words are unnecessary. Use *since* or *because* instead.

PREFERRED: *Since* he was undernourished, he easily became sick.

LESS ACCEPTABLE: *Due to the fact that* he was undernourished, he easily became sick.

(45) Each Other and One Another. *Each other* and *one another* are usually interchangeable. At times, however, *each other* is more logically used in reference to only two; *one another*, in reference to more than two.

EXAMPLES: People should be kind to *each other* (or *one another*).

As the couple walked, they held *each other's* hand.

In our large family, we make every effort to be considerate of *one another's* privacy.

(46) *Emigrate* **and** *Immigrate.* Notice the difference in the meanings of these two verbs. *Emigrate* means "to leave a country for a new residency." *Immigrate* means "to enter a country to establish residency."

EXAMPLES: During the Potato Famine, many Irish people *emigrated* from Ireland.

Many Irish people *immigrated* to the United States.

(47) *Enthusiastic* **and** *Enthused.* *Enthusiastic* is the standard form. Avoid using *enthused.*

NONSTANDARD: All of us are *enthused* about the community project.

CORRECT: All of us are *enthusiastic* about the community project.

(48) *Etc.* *Etc.* is an abbreviation of the Latin phrase *et cetera,* meaning "and so on." Thus, it is wrong to write *and etc.* In formal writing it is best to avoid using this abbreviation altogether.

INCORRECT: From the Salvation Army you can buy shirts, slacks, jackets, *and etc.*

CORRECT: From the Salvation Army you can buy shirts, slacks, jackets, *etc.*

FORMAL: From the Salvation Army you can buy shirts, slacks, jackets, and other articles of clothing.

(49) *Farther* **and** *Further.* *Farther* refers to distance. *Further* means "additional" or "to a greater degree or extent."

EXAMPLES: The sun is much *farther* from us than the moon.

We want *further* information from the planning committee.

Further enlightenment on the causes of cancer is needed.

(50) *Fewer* **and** *Less.* Use *fewer* with things that can be counted. Use *less* with qualities and quantities that cannot be counted.

EXAMPLES: *fewer* complaints, *fewer* problems, *fewer* diseases

less coffee, *less* incentive, *less* trouble

(51) *Former* **and** *Latter.* *Former* refers to the first of two previously mentioned items. *Latter* refers to the second of the two.

EXAMPLE: The box contained hollyhocks and sweet williams. The *former* we planted along the wall; the *latter* we thought would be more suited for the rock garden.

(52) *Get, Got,* and *Gotten.* All forms of the verb *get* are acceptable in standard usage, but it is best to avoid using *get, got,* and *gotten* in formal writing.

INFORMAL: All residents will *get* a form in the mail.

FORMAL: All residents will *receive* a form in the mail.

Whenever possible, try to use a more specific word in place of *get.*

ACCEPTABLE: *get* a license, *got* wealthier, to have *gotten* recognition

BETTER: *obtain* a license, *acquired* greater wealth, to have *earned* recognition

(53) *Good, Lovely,* and *Nice.* These three adjectives are weak and overused. Whenever possible, substitute a more specific adjective.

WEAK: *good* description, *lovely* vacation, *nice* taste

BETTER: *clear* description, *exotic* vacation, *refined* taste

(54) *Hanged* and *Hung.* Use *hanged* to mean "executed." Use *hung* to mean "suspended."

EXAMPLES: The revolutionary council *hanged* the ministers of the former government.

A spider plant *hung* from the ceiling.

(55) *Healthy* and *Healthful.* People are *healthy;* things are *healthful.*

PREFERRED: Bean sprouts are *healthful* in any diet.

LESS ACCEPTABLE: Bean sprouts are *healthy* in any diet.

(56) *If* and *Whether.* These two subordinate conjunctions are interchangeable. When using *whether,* it is not necessary to include *or not* after it.

EXAMPLE: We wonder *if* (or *whether*) Joe will meet us here.

(57) *In* and *Into*. *In* refers to position. *Into* suggests motion.

POSITION: Each piece of silverware is *in* the correct place.

MOTION: Put all of the silverware *into* (not *in*) the drawer.

(58) *Irregardless*. Avoid using this word. Use *regardless* instead.

NONSTANDARD: Choose the most experienced applicant *irregardless* of personality.

CORRECT: Choose the most experienced applicant *regardless* of personality.

(59) *Its* and *It's*. *Its* is a possessive personal pronoun; *it's* is a contraction for *it is*.

PRONOUN: Her shoe had lost *its* heel.

CONTRACTION: Act quickly before *it's* too late.

(60) *Judicial* and *Judicious*. Do not confuse the meaning of these adjectives. *Judicial* means "relating to the administration of justice." *Judicious* means "showing wisdom."

EXAMPLES: The Supreme Court is our highest *judicial* tribunal.

King Solomon's *judicious* decision revealed the child's true mother.

(61) *Kind Of* and *Sort Of*. Do not use *kind of* and *sort of* to mean "rather" or "somewhat."

NONSTANDARD: You look *kind of* pale.

CORRECT: You look *somewhat* pale.

(62) *Kind Of A* and *Sort Of A*. Do not use *a* after *kind of* and *sort of*.

NONSTANDARD: Which *kind of a* dressing do you want on your salad?

CORRECT: Which *kind of* dressing do you want on your salad?

In addition, avoid such expressions as "this kind of books" or "these sorts of examination." If *kind* or *sort* is singular, the object of the preposition *of* should also be singular. If *kind* or *sort* is plural, make sure the object is plural too.

NONSTANDARD: this *kind* of book*s*

                 these *sorts* of examination

CORRECT: this *kind* of book

             these *sorts* of examination*s*

(63) ***Learn* and *Teach*.** *Learn* means "to acquire knowledge." *Teach* means "to give knowledge to."

EXAMPLES: Helen Keller *learned* the word "water."

             Anne Sullivan taught (not *learned*) Helen the word "water."

(64) ***Leave* and *Let*.** *Leave* means "to allow to remain." *Let* means "to permit." Do not reverse the meanings.

NONSTANDARD: *Let* me alone!

CORRECT: *Leave* me alone!

NONSTANDARD: *Leave* me do this by myself.

CORRECT: *Let* me do this by myself.

(65) ***Lie* and *Lay*.** Notice the different in the meanings and uses of these two verbs. *Lie* means "to recline." Its principal parts are *lie, lying, lay,* and *lain*. As an intransitive verb, it does not take an object. *Lay* means "to put or set down." Its principal parts are *lay, laying, laid,* and *laid*. As a transitive verb, it usually does take an object.

LIE: *Lie* down for an hour and rest.

     After I became tired, I *lay* down and rested.

     The dog has *lain* there all afternoon.

LAY: *Lay* your books on the desk.

     He gently *laid* the eggs in the basket.

     She has *laid* forty slate slabs to form a walkway through the garden.

(66) ***Like, As,* and *As If*.** *Like* is a preposition meaning "similar to." *As* and *as if* are conjunctions. *As* means "in the same way that." *As if* means "that" or "as it (or someone) would if."

NONSTANDARD: He is crafty *like* a fox is crafty.

CORRECT: He is crafty *as* a fox is crafty.

CORRECT: He is crafty *like* a fox.

NONSTANDARD: It seems *like* we will be good friends.

CORRECT: It seems *as if* we will be good friends.

(67) *Lose* and *Loose*. *Lose* is always a verb, generally meaning "to miss from one's possession." *Loose* is usually an adjective or part of such idioms as *cut loose, turn loose,* or *break loose*.

VERB: Don't *lose* this telephone number.

ADJECTIVE: The door hinge was *loose*.

IDIOM: The goat broke *loose* from the pen.

(68) *Mad*. In formal usage, the adjective *mad* means "insane." Used informally, *mad* means "angry."

FORMAL: Jane Eyre soon learned that Mr. Rochester's wife was quite *mad*.

INFORMAL: I am *mad* at you for ignoring me.

(69) *May Be* and *Maybe*. *May be* is a helping verb and verb. *Maybe* is an adverb meaning "perhaps."

VERB: You *may be* right.

ADVERB: *Maybe* I can investigate this matter myself.

(70) *Of*. Do not write *of* after a helping verb such as *should, would, could,* or *must*. Use *have* instead. Moreover, do not use *of* after *outside, inside, off,* and *atop*. Simply eliminate it.

NONSTANDARD: He *must of* remembered he had a commitment elsewhere.

CORRECT: He *must have* remembered he had a commitment elsewhere.

PREFERRED: He fell *off* the stool.

LESS ACCEPTABLE: He fell *off of* the stool.

(71) *OK, O.K.,* and *Okay.* In informal writing, *OK, O.K.,* and *okay* are acceptably used to mean "all right." Do not use either the abbreviations or *okay* in formal writing, however.

FORMAL: This architect's blueprint looks flawless.

INFORMAL: This architect's blueprint looks *okay*.

(72) *Ought.* Never use *ought* with *have* or *had*. Simply eliminate *have* or *had*.

NONSTANDARD: After being repaired this washing machine *had ought* to work.

CORRECT: After being repaired this washing machine *ought* to work.

(73) *Outside Of.* Do not use this expression to mean "besides" or "except."

NONSTANDARD: No one came to the party *outside of* Dinah.

CORRECT: No one came to the party *except* Dinah.

(74) *Parameter.* This word is correctly used only in mathetmatical contexts, in which it designates a variable. Do not use *parameter* to mean "boundary," "limit," "scope," "detail," and so on.

NONSTANDARD: The purpose of this meeting is to determine the *parameters* of the problem.

CORRECT: The purpose of this meeting is to determine the *limits* of the problem.

(75) *Persecute* and *Prosecute.* Do not confuse the meaning or spelling of these words. *Persecute* means "to subject to ill treatment." *Prosecute* means "to bring a lawsuit against."

EXAMPLES: He was *persecuted* for his religious beliefs.

Jack is being *prosecuted* for libel.

(76) *Plenty.* *Plenty,* a noun, does not mean "very." It is usually correctly followed by *of,* as in "plenty of food."

NONSTANDARD: Liz is *plenty* angry about your forgetting to invite her.

CORRECT: Liz is *very* angry about your forgetting to invite her.

(77) *Plurals That Do Not End in -s.* The plurals of certain nouns from Greek and Latin are formed as they were in their original languages. Words such as *criteria, media,* and *phenomena* are plural and should not be treated as if they were singular *(criterion, medium, phenomenon).*

INCORRECT: I do not agree with *that criteria* for selecting a winner.

CORRECT: I do not agree with *those criteria* for selecting a winner.

INCORRECT: The mass *media is* responsible for the fast and accurate distribution of information.

CORRECT: The mass *media are* responsible for the fast and accurate distribution of information.

(78) *Poorly.* *Poorly* is used in an informal way to mean "ill." Avoid this use in formal situations.

INFORMAL: Grandmother is feeling *poorly.*

FORMAL: Grandmother is feeling *ill.*

(79) *Precede* and *Proceed.* *Precede* means "to go before." *Proceed* means "to move or go forward."

EXAMPLES: The *preceding* paragraph introduced the topic.

Proceed to the next step.

(80) *Principal* and *Principle.* As an adjective, *principal* means "most important" or "chief"; as a noun, it means "a person who has controlling authority." *Principle,* always a noun, means "a fundamental law."

ADJECTIVE: The *principal* reason for evacuating the town was the danger of thyphoid fever.

NOUN: Mr. Clark is the school's *principal.*

NOUN: "Thou shalt not kill" is a *principle* of many religions.

(81) *Raise* and *Rise.* *Raise,* a transitive verb that generally takes an object, means "to lift," "to increase," or "to grow." *Rise,* an intransitive verb that does not take an object, means "to move upward" or "to be increased."

EXAMPLES: Platform heels *raised* him to average height.

Smoke *rises* from the chimneys every morning.

(82) *Real.* *Real* means "authentic." The use of *real* to mean "very" or "really" should be avoided in formal writing.

FORMAL: This painting with Picasso's signature is *real*.

INFORMAL: Dwight was *real* discouraged.

BETTER: Dwight was *very* discouraged.

(83) *Says.* *Says* should not be used as a substitute for *said*.

NONSTANDARD: Then she *says* to me, "Be quiet!"

CORRECT: Then she *said* to me, "Be quiet!"

(84) *Set* and *Sit.* *Set*, a transitive verb that generally takes an object, means "to put (something) in a certain place." *Sit*, an intransitive verb that does not take an object, means "to be seated."

EXAMPLES: *Set* the chair in this corner.

Sit in a chair before you buy it.

(85) *Shall* and *Will.* These helping verbs are interchangeable in most instances. Except in questions asking for permission or agreement, however, *will* is the more commonly used.

EXAMPLES: *Shall* we go out for Chinese food?

We *will* go.

(86) *Shape.* The standard meaning for the noun *shape* is "spatial form." Do not use *shape* to mean "condition."

STANDARD: The *shape* of this lens is convex.

INFORMAL: The driver of the demolished car is in serious *shape*.

BETTER: The driver of the demolished car is in serious *condition*.

(87) *Slow* and *Slowly.* Although *slow* can now be used as either an adjective or an adverb, careful writers still use it as an adjective. *Slowly* is preferred as the adverb.

CORRECT: Turtles are *slow*.

PREFERRED: Crawl *slowly* along this ledge.

LESS ACCEPTABLE: Move *slow*.

(88) *So.* *So* is acceptable as a conjunction. It should not be used, however, to begin a sentence.

STANDARD: Move over *so* I can sit down.

NONSTANDARD: *So* she vanished without leaving a trace.

CORRECT: She vanished without leaving a trace.

(89) *Take And.* This is a nonstandard expression. Eliminate it entirely.

NONSTANDARD: *Take and* put these flowers in a vase.

CORRECT: Put these flowers in a vase.

(90) *Than* and *Then.* *Than* is used in comparisons. Do not confuse it with the adverb *then*, which usually refers to time.

EXAMPLES: A pig is smarter *than* most dogs.

   Wait until the sun begins to shine throught the rain and *then* look for a rainbow.

(91) *That, Which,* and *Who.* Be sure to use these relative pronouns correctly. *That* refers to people or things; *which* refers only to things; *who* refers only to people.

PEOPLE: She reminds me of someone *that* (or *whom*) I used to know.

THINGS: I forgot the key *that* (or *which*) opens this door.

(92) *Their, There,* and *They're.* Do not confuse the spellings of these three words. *Their*, a possessive pronoun, always modifies a noun. *There* can be used either as an expletive at the beginning of a sentence or as an adverb. *They're* is a contraction for *they are*.

PRONOUN: The frightened cattle milled around *their* pen.

EXPLETIVE: *There* can be no room for error.

ADVERB: *There* are the recently excavated artifacts.

CONTRACTION: I hope *they're* leaving soon.

(93) Them, Them There, These Here, This Here, and That There. *Them* is always a personal pronoun, never an adjective. When a sentence calls for an adjective, use *these* or *those* in place of either *them* or *them there*. To correct a sentence containing *these here, this here,* and *that there,* simply leave out *here* and *there*.

NONSTANDARD: *Them* flowers certainly look pretty.

CORRECT: *These* flowers certainly look pretty.

NONSTANDARD: *This here* knife needs sharpening.

CORRECT: *This* knife needs sharpening.

(94) Till and Until. These words are interchangeable. Be careful, however, of spelling. *Till* should not be spelled *til* or *'til*; *until* always ends in one *l*.

EXAMPLE: The children played *till* (or *until*) it was dark.

(95) To, Too, and Two. Do not confuse the spellings of these three words. *To,* a preposition, begins a prepositional phrase or an infinitive. *Too,* an adverb, modifies adjectives and other adverbs. Do not forget the second *o*. *Two* is a number.

PREPOSITION: *to* a concert

INFINITIVE: *to* think

ADVERB: *too* quiet, *too* awkwardly

NUMBER: *two* cents, *two* umbrellas

(96) Unique. *Unique* means "one of a kind." It should not be used to mean *odd, interesting,* or *unusual*. Since the word means "one of a kind," such expressions as *most unique, very unique,* and *extremely unique* are illogical and should not be used.

NONSTANDARD: He enjoys the *most unique* life style.

CORRECT: He enjoys a *unique* life style.

(97) *Want In* and *Want Out*. These are nonstandard expressions for "want to come in" or "want to enter," and "want to leave" or "want to get out."

NONSTANDARD:　The dog is scratching at the door because he *wants in*.

CORRECT:　The dog is scratching at the door because he *wants to come in*.

Moreover, do not use *want* before such prepositions as *down*, *off*, or *up*.

NONSTANDARD:　I *want down* from this horse.

CORRECT:　I *want to get down* from this horse.

(98) *Ways*. *Ways* is plural. Do not use it after the article *a*. Use instead the singular form *way*.

NONSTANDARD:　I have *a* considerable *ways* to go before I reach Connecticut.

CORRECT:　I have *a* considerable *way* to go before I reach Connecticut.

(99) *When* and *Where*. Do not use *when* or *where* directly after a linking verb.

NONSTANDARD:　My best childhood memory *was when* my parents gave me a pony.

　An automat *is where* food is dispensed by machines.

CORRECT:　My best childhood memory is of being given a pony by my parents.

　An automat is a cafeteria *where* food is dispensed by machines.

In addition, do not use *where* as a substitute for *that*.

NONSTANDARD:　I read in a magazine *where* ancient coins are a good investment.

CORRECT:　I read in a magazine *that* ancient coins are a good investment.

(100) *-wise*. Avoid using this suffix to create new words for a particular situation.

PREFERRED: This freezer is very energy-efficient.

LESS ACCEPTABLE: *Energywise*, this freezer is very efficient.

EXERCISE A: **Avoiding Usage Problems (1–10).** Choose the correct expression from the choices in parentheses in each of the following sentences. Try to complete the exercise without looking back in the book.

1. They should have (all ready, already) left by now.
2. Did your broken ankle (affect, effect) your vacation plans?
3. Jem (ain't, isn't) capable of performing before an audience.
4. Everyone (accept, except) me was dressed in black.
5. You look (all right, alright) without any mascara.
6. A speck of dust can (aggravate, annoy) an inflamed eye.
7. His (advice, advise) should be ignored.
8. "But Brutus says he was ambitious; And Brutus is (a, an) honorable man."
9. He tried to (adapt, adopt) a philosophy of nonviolence.
10. The teacher was (aggravated, annoyed) by my total disinterest.
11. One (affect, effect) of the radiation was a change in chromosomes.
12. The ice cream is (all ready, already) to be served.
13. I (accept, except) your proposal.
14. The report (accuses, alleges) negligence by the manufacturer.
15. It is not (all right, alright) for you to barge in uninvited.
16. She (accused, alleged) him of trying to evade the issue.
17. An injection of insulin (affected, effected) an immediate improvement in his condition.
18. This pamphlet (advices, advises) pregnant women not to take aspirin or to smoke.
19. The pioneers (adapted, adopted) to a hostile environment.
20. We heard (a, an) hysterical, ghostly laugh.

EXERCISE B: **Avoiding Usage Problems (11–20).** Follow the directions for Exercise A.

1. My car keys must be (somewhere, somewheres) in my pocketbook.
2. We should shout the cheer (all together, altogether).
3. You can do (alot, much) to improve yourself.
4. One black orchid grew (among, between) the many white ones.
5. The trainer feels very (anxious, eager) about the colt's injured leg.
6. Despite economic predictions, I remain an optimist (anyway, anyways).

7. School is dismissed at three (P.M., P.M. in the afternoon).
8. (Any one, Anyone) of these television sets works equally well.
9. I haven't seen Jenny (anywhere, anywheres).
10. An enormous (amount, number) of garbage was piled in a heap.
11. Becky and Jim were (all together, altogether) exhausted after the marathon dance.
12. He gave no explanation (as to, for) his strange behavior.
13. She tripped on the rug (as, because) she walked toward us.
14. Ask (anyone, any one) for assistance.
15. Willy was (anxious, eager) to help his neighbors.
16. How should the committee (a lot, alot, allot) the money?
17. Be at the door by 10:00 (A.M., A.M. in the morning).
18. We left all the windows open (as, since) no rain was forecast.
19. There should be no strife (among, between) you and me.
20. A large (amount, number) of complaints were registered.

EXERCISE C: Avoiding Usage Problems (21–30). Follow the directions for Exercise A.

1. She becomes (awfully, very) afraid in crowded elevators.
2. When he was a young man, my grandfather was a (blond, blonde).
3. Listen to this record for (a while, awhile) and tell me if you like it.
4. After dark they should know where their children (are, are at).
5. The reason the flowers died is (because, that) no one watered them.
6. I (beat, won) her at a game of handball.
7. (Being that, Since) they expected death at the hands of the Romans, the people of Masada killed themselves.
8. Please (bring, take) that hammer here.
9. Be at the house (at about, at) five o'clock.
10. (The reason my grandmother lives with us now is, My grandmother lives with us now) because she was lonely.
11. (Beside, Besides) Japan and Germany, what other countries made up the Axis Powers?
12. I look (bad, awful) in shades of purple.
13. (Bring, Take) these overdue books back to the library.
14. The telegram arrived (at about, about) noon.
15. Marlene always keeps a kerosene lamp (beside, besides) the door.
16. Karen and Eric are (blonds, blondes).
17. He drove down the wrong street and now doesn't know where he (is, is at).

18. Try to (beat, win) the other team if you can.
19. Stay (a while, awhile) and tell us about your new job.
20. Let's go to the movies (being as, since) there is little else to do.

EXERCISE D: Avoiding Usage Problems (31–40). Follow the directions for Exercise A.

1. Her new car (can, may) hold more people than mine.
2. We (can't help but admire, can't help admiring) Faye's courage.
3. The soap bubbles will (burst, bust) upon contact.
4. Gentlemen, I take umbrage at your offensive (ad, advertisement) in yesterday's newspaper.
5. The (continual, continuous) noise of trains rumbling past his house every half hour kept him awake.
6. Join our (bunch, group) if you enjoy friendship and good conversation.
7. The courts cannot (condemn, condone) his brutality.
8. She has little doubt (but what, that) her son is most qualified.
9. In my previous letter to your firm, I requested that the (phones, telephones) be repaired promptly.
10. The American Standard System is (different from, different than) the Metric System.
11. Calypso music (doesn't, don't) receive much attention in this country.
12. I don't know (but what, that) Barbara is correct in her assumption.
13. Without plasma this accident victim (doesn't, don't) have a chance for survival.
14. Paris was (different from, different than) what she expected.
15. I (can't help but regret, can't help regretting) my insensitivity to your misery.
16. The flower girl carried a (bunch, group) of daisies.
17. After seeing how much I wanted to ride the tractor, he said that I (can, may) learn how to drive it.
18. The dictator was universally (condemned, condoned) for his ruthless treatment of dissidents.
19. Olivia (burst, busted) the balloon with a tack.
20. (Continual, Continuous) walking from dawn until dusk raised blisters on their feet.

EXERCISE E: Avoiding Usage Problems (41–50). Follow the directions for Exercise A.

1. Lance fractured his skull when he (dived, dove) into a shallow pond.

2. Thousands of Cubans have (emigrated, immigrated) to the United States.
3. She became more and more (enthused, enthusiastic) as the day of her departure approached.
4. (Due to, Because of) an unavoidable delay, the results of the poll can't be given until next week.
5. The man had swallowed coins, nuts, bolts, (and etc., etc.).
6. He sometimes (done, has done) work for us in the past.
7. (Farther, Further) suggestions will be appreciated.
8. (Because of, Due to) a heavy rainfall, this expressway has been temporarily closed.
9. I (did, done) better in this class because I cared.
10. Put (fewer, less) water in the soup for a thicker consistency.
11. Drive a little (farther, further) and you will see the castle high on a hill.
12. (Due to the fact that, Since) the air conditioner isn't working properly, everyone should wear light clothing.
13. I propose to you, the committee, a thorough plan for revitalizing subways, buses, (and other means of mass transportation, etc.).
14. (Fewer, Less) nails are needed for this type of paneling.
15. Squealing gleefully, the children (dived, dove) into the pile of leaves.
16. Without any help from her family, Abigail (done, has done) well to finish college.
17. The starving victims of political revolution (emigrated, immigrated) from Cambodia.
18. I will be forced to buy a new car (because, due to the fact that) my old car's transmission is beyond repair.
19. We (dived, dove) head-first into the inviting water.
20. An (enthusiastic, enthused) concern for the environment will benefit all of us.

EXERCISE F: Avoiding Usage Problems (51–60). Follow the directions for Exercise A.

1. Eugene is a (nice, friendly) person.
2. Colorful lanterns were (hanged, hung) from the beams.
3. Sandra (got, earned) the respect of the class.
4. (Irregardless, Regardless) of the choppy water, Matt guided the boat beyond the buoys.
5. Put these figurines back (in, into) that curio cabinet.
6. Toward the end of our vacation we visited New York and Washington. What impressed me most in the (former, latter) city was the Lincoln Memorial.
7. Sunshine is (healthy, healthful) because it is a source of vitamin D.

8. Neither parent will (get, obtain) custody of the children.
9. Let's go (in, into) this famous international restaurant.
10. We were confident that the administrator would make a (judicial, judicious) decision.
11. They have a (lovely, close) relationship after thirty years of marriage.
12. Near Charlottesville, Virginia, are two presidential homes: Jefferson's Monticello and Monroe's Ash Lawn. The (former, latter) is pictured on the back of a nickel, along with Jefferson's portrait on the front.
13. (Its, It's) the house with the gabled roof that attracts notice.
14. Mary's shiny hair and clear skin indicated that she was (healthy, healthful).
15. The boy had (gotten, climbed) to the topmost branches of the tree.
16. He gave a (good, detailed) account of his expenditures.
17. The husky held (its, it's) head high as Jim placed the dog at the head of the team.
18. He (hanged, hung) his coat on the peg in the hall.
19. What are the responsibilities of the (judicial, judicious) branch of the government?
20. Tell them the truth (irregardless, regardless) of their reaction.

EXERCISE G: Avoiding Usage Problems (61–70). Follow the directions for Exercise A.

1. (Lie, Lay) the baby on the scales.
2. He (learned, taught) us how to check the oil in the crankcase.
3. There (may be, maybe) a hidden clause in the contract.
4. The sun looks (kind of, somewhat) reddish as it sets.
5. A (lose, loose) knot was tied around his wrists.
6. She preened herself (as, like) a peacock would.
7. What (kind of, kinds of) insects are these?
8. A remnant of the tribe must (of, have) settled in this valley.
9. (Leave, Let) us alone!
10. Let me (lose, loose) from these shackles.
11. (Lie, Lay) down on the couch until your dizziness passes.
12. If I could (of, have) removed this splinter sooner, it would have been less painful.
13. I hope I don't (lose, loose) my job in the warehouse.
14. What (sort of, sort of a) jacket do you want to buy?
15. I'm (sort of, rather) reluctant to criticize Paul's work.
16. (May be, Maybe) you will listen to me now.
17. Please (leave, let) me stay as your apprentice.

18. The teacher (learned, taught) the class phonics.
19. His lunatic ravings convinced everyone that he was (angry, mad).
20. You look (as if, like) someone who has just had a harrowing experience.

EXERCISE H: Avoiding Usage Problems (71–80). Follow the directions for Exercise A.

1. There (had ought, ought) to be a law against this.
2. Carl is (plenty, very) lame after hiking all day.
3. Many strange phenomena (has, have) been reported at the house.
4. The developers discussed the (parameters, details) of the new housing project.
5. Tell the reporters that the mayor has resigned because he has been feeling (ill, poorly).
6. Mr. President, will the hostages at the embassy be (okay, safe)?
7. Everyone (outside of, except) Geoffrey wore a heavy coat.
8. She (hadn't ought, ought not) to talk loudly.
9. It is against my (principals, principles) to destroy these documents.
10. The Puritans had been (persecuted, prosecuted) for their supposedly heretical beliefs.
11. (Besides, Outside of) the excellent service, there is nothing to recommend this hotel.
12. The landscaper's plan showed the (parameters, boundaries) of the garden.
13. It is time to announce that the queen is feeling (ill, poorly).
14. (Plenty, Very) exasperated, Connie righteously insisted upon an explanation.
15. Scrutinize the (preceding, proceeding) paragraph for errors.
16. The (principal, principle) actor in this film is Humphrey Bogart.
17. Book publishing in many ways is the least modernized (media, medium).
18. Excuse me, Sir Robert, is everything (satisfactory, okay)?
19. Shall we (precede, proceed) to examine the evidence?
20. He will be (persecuted, prosecuted) for forgery.

EXERCISE I: Avoiding Usage Problems (81–90). Follow the directions for Exercise A.

1. (Set, Sit) here where we can talk undisturbed.
2. He is in poor (shape, condition) after weeks of lying in bed.
3. A frog is larger (than, then) a toad.

4. Prolonged contact with sugar is (real, very) bad for the enamel on your teeth.
5. I jumped when she (says, said) to me, "There's a spider on your shoulder."
6. We walked (slow, slowly) along the avenue.
7. Rodney promised to apologize but then he (says, said) he wouldn't.
8. (Take and leave, Leave) these folders on John's desk.
9. With many hands to help, the pioneers (raised, rised) the log cabin in less than a week.
10. (So, Then) the boomerang began to return.
11. There was a flash of lightning and (than, then) a clap of thunder.
12. (Set, Sit) this heavy trunk somewhere in the hall.
13. Stand in the light (because, so) I can take your picture.
14. The plastic flowers surprisingly looked (real, very) pretty.
15. (Raise, Rise) yourself to your feet.
16. Virgil laughed and (said, says), "Impossible!"
17. (Slow, Slowly) the wind and rain eroded the soil.
18. The (condition, shape) of the box is rectangular.
19. The bread will continue to (raise, rise) as the yeast ferments.
20. She (took and handed, handed) the money to the cashier.

EXERCISE J: Avoiding Usage Problems (91–100). Follow the directions for Exercise A.

1. (Their, They're) version of handball is jai alai.
2. I still have a long (way, ways) to walk before I reach home.
3. The beggar (which, who) always stood at the gate was not there today.
4. A trash can is (the place where, where) your refuse belongs.
5. I just (want out, want to get out) of this difficult situation.
6. (Moneywise, In financial matters), she is very shrewd.
7. These roses won't grow well (til, till) they've been pruned.
8. Sarah's approach to a potential customer is (more unique, unique).
9. (There, They're) the best acrobatic team in the world.
10. Use (too, two) cloths—one for waxing, and one for polishing.
11. Ronda drove a great (way, ways) just to see you.
12. He (wants in, wants to come in) to escape the furious mob.
13. (Them there, Those) hairless dogs won't live for a week in this subzero climate.
14. We want (to, two) perfect our system of gathering information.
15. This apartment will not be available (till, untill) next month.

16. Some people think that the third time a person goes under the water is (the time, when) he will sink.
17. A clown's (absolutely unique, unique) face helps to establish her qualities as a performer.
18. There were (to, too) many bystanders for the police to apprehend the robbers.
19. Jocelyn is very active (sportswise, in sports).
20. (Their, There) are no two fingerprints alike.

EXERCISE K: Correcting Usage Problems. Forty-two of the following fifty sentences contain one error or problem in usage. Rewrite each incorrect sentence, correcting the mistake. If the sentence is correct, write *correct*.

1. Everything is alright now that your father is home.
2. Outside of Ginny, everyone was interested in the poetry reading.
3. The skeleton of a reptile is different from the skeleton of a mammal.
4. Merv should be finished painting at about the same time I am.
5. Ted says, "I don't have any time to waste."
6. Let us all be considerate of one another.
7. Will looks like he just saw a ghost.
8. When I give the signal, sing all together.
9. The pond should of been stocked with fish.
10. Being that everyone had finished eating, we went out on the veranda.
11. Shall I open a joint account in our name?
12. Relax for a while and your headache will disappear.
13. Take and deliver these newspapers to your customers.
14. Anyone of these tablecloths will look equally good.
15. His flight was delayed due to thick fog.
16. There just ain't any way he can earn that much money.
17. As your physician, I must tell you that you need to get the diagnosis of a specialist.
18. In the small shop they could see numerous clocks everywheres they looked.
19. Throw your quarter in the basket of the toll booth.
20. The children were anxious to open their presents.
21. Try to bust the balloon with a pin.
22. A startled bullfrog dove off the lily pad.
23. Stir the soup with that there wooden spoon.
24. It was okay for the reporters to go along with the President.
25. Our team has several ideas as to how we can improve our playing.

26. At a pharmacy one can buy cosmetics, drugs, and etc.
27. Her singing was effected by a sinus condition.
28. People that need assistance will be waiting in line.
29. Please take your own ice skates when you come.
30. Clarence can't help but speak slowly and carefully.
31. Foodwise, this meat is one of the best buys.
32. Your statement don't answer my question.
33. Who beside Maurice will volunteer for this unpleasant job?
34. Amnesty International condemned the maltreatment of the hostages.
35. Even if it does look cloudy, let's go to the zoo anyways.
36. Melanie slipped and fell off of the step.
37. I don't wonder but what Kim is always arguing with her sister.
38. The kitten wants under the fence.
39. The boys worked slow building their fort.
40. Some of us need farther explanation.
41. Due to the fact that the ceiling is so low, the canopy bed will have to go elsewhere.
42. The insurance company alleged someone of being an arsonist.
43. She is trying to sew a kind of a flounce on the hem.
44. Where are the tools I left on the counter?
45. In this damp weather Dad's arthritis makes him feel poorly.
46. Baked potatoes contain less calories than french fries.
47. We saw a bunch of pelicans diving for their food.
48. Irregardless of his bad disposition, he is still a competent teacher.
49. Bill seems sort of tired and listless.
50. The fall is when all the tourists come to see the leaves change color.

APPLICATION: **Using Expressions Correctly.** Write a sentence of your own for each of the following expressions. Proofread your sentences carefully after you finish writing.

1. condone
2. principle
3. let
4. raise
5. bunch
6. former . . . latter
7. further
8. its
9. ought
10. accept
11. prosecute
12. mad
13. done
14. set
15. immigrate
16. lie
17. all ready
18. adapt
19. lay
20. except

Chapter 10

Levels of Language

In the English language, there are two broad categories of usage: standard and nonstandard. Standard English, used by the majority of Americans, is the more uniform of the two. There is little variation in the grammar of standard English between one region of the United States and another, or even between one English-speaking country and another. Differences in the meanings of words are also slight. All that may vary significantly is the way the language is pronounced. Nonstandard English, however, is characterized by many variations from what is considered the norm. Within certain areas, social or ethnic groups, or professions, there may be many words or expressions or pronunciations that are not part of the language of the general population.

Each of the two broad categories of standard and nonstandard English consists of different levels of usage. Standard English includes formal and informal language, whereas nonstandard English includes many kinds of dialects, slang, and overly technical language.

LEVELS OF LANGUAGE	
Standard	Nonstandard
Formal	Dialect
Informal	Slang
	Overly Technical Language

Each of these levels of language serves a purpose and contributes to the overall richness of the English language. It is logical, however, that your teachers should expect you to use formal and informal English in the classroom since these are the levels of language considered most appropriate for communicating in the worlds of business and government and the arts. Within your community, at home, or among your friends, other levels of language may at times be more appropriate.

As a student, you should work to acquire a thorough understanding of standard English since mastery of this kind of language will enable you to communicate effectively and comfortably in many academic and professional situations. In addition, you should learn to recognize the other levels of language and to know when each is appropriate or inappropriate.

The Varieties of English   10.1

English is spoken by over six hundred million people around the world—either as a first language or as a second language. It is the primary language not only of Britain and Ireland but also of Australia, Jamaica, New Zealand, and, of course, the United States and most of Canada. English is also spoken as a second language in many parts of Africa, Asia, and the South Pacific. It is the language of diplomats and international airline pilots. Geography and cultural differences have brought about many variations in the way English is spoken in different parts of the world. Even within one nation, English may vary from one region to another. It is remarkable, then, that in spite of the many variations within the same language most speakers of English from diverse parts of the globe can still communicate with one another without too much difficulty.

■ Standard English

In the United States, the language used by most educated people is called standard English. It is spoken and written somewhat differently in formal and informal situations. The distinction between formal and informal English may be as simple as whether a person says "Please be seated" to an honored guest or "Grab a chair" to a good friend.

Formal English.   Serious speaking and writing, such as that found in a President's State of the Union Message or a scholarly analysis, usually requires the use of formal English. This is the language of the schools and universities, of government, and of most businesses. At its best it is never stilted or unnecessarily difficult to comprehend.

Formal English is the manner of spoken and written English that adheres to traditional standards of correctness. It is characterized by an extensive vocabulary, complete grammatical constructions, and elaborate sentence structures. It avoids contractions, casual expressions, and colloquialisms.

The following excerpt from *A Distant Mirror*, a book about European society in the 1300's, illustrates formal English. Notice the elaborate and varied sentence patterns and the absence of contractions, casual expressions, or colloquialisms.

EXAMPLE:

Formidable and grand on a hilltop in Picardy, the five-towered castle of Coucy dominated the approach to Paris from the north, but whether as guardian or as challenger of the monarchy in the capital was an open question. Thrusting up from the castle's center, a gigantic cylinder rose to twice the height of the four corner towers. This was the *donjon* or central citadel, the largest in Europe, the mightiest of its kind ever built in the Middle Ages or thereafter. Ninety feet in diameter, 180 feet high, capable of housing a thousand men in a siege, it dwarfed and protected the castle at its base, the clustered roofs of the town, the bell tower of the church, and the thirty turrets of the massive wall enclosing the whole complex on the hill. Travelers coming from any direction could see this colossus of baronial power from miles away and, on approaching it, feel the awe of the traveler in infidel lands at first sight of the pyramids. —Barbara W. Tuchman

Informal English.   Although you will often need to express your ideas in formal English, especially when writing, the level of language you are most likely to encounter and be expected to use in everyday situations is informal English. This is the language of newspapers, advertisements, television, personal letters, and polite conversation.

Informal English is the manner of spoken and written English that is colloquial, or conversational. Its vocabulary is somewhat less extensive than that of formal English; it permits looser grammatical constructions and uses shorter sentence structures.

The following is a personal letter written by Flannery O'Connor, a famous Southern writer. Although the letter contains a few humorous, nonstandard passages, especially at the beginning, the writing is for the most part casual, conversational informal English.

EXAMPLE:

8 March 64

Cain't you and Benny pay us a visit Easter, especially if you are taking Agnes to St. Petersburg, you would naturally be moving in the right direction. We can send Joe to Atlanta to meet you if you let us know in time to run him down. We hope you can.

Me, I just got out of the hospital where I had my middle entered by the surgeons. It was all a howling success from their point of view and one of them is going to write it up for a doctor magazine as you usually don't cut folks with lupus. But the trip in was necessary though nothing turned out malignant and I will soon be restored on turnip green potlicker. Right now I am just killing time and would be mighty proud to see you & Benedict. It's a good time of year to see these parts. Everything is in bloom . . .

R. says this is a joint invitation. I am the scribe around here, even in extremis. —Flannery O'Connor

EXERCISE A: **Identifying Formal and Informal English.** Read each of the following quotations carefully. If the quotation is an example of formal English, write *formal* on your paper. If it is an example of informal English, write *informal*. Be prepared to explain the reasons for your decisions.

1. Like it or not, you know, Dinah, you can't leave all that junk you've collected in there to rot. It was sent to you for a specific purpose. And—judging at least by my own experience—quite a bit of trouble was gone to hunting it out. —Elizabeth Bowen.

2. How was it you happened to get sent up on that Springfield job? Was it because you wouldn't prove an alibi for fear of compromising somebody in extremely high-toned society? Or was it simply a case of a mean old jury that had it in for you? It's always one or the other with you innocent victims. —O. Henry

3. Given the country's enormous transformation through industrial growth and communications mobility, its federal arrangements have become increasingly devoid of economic and geographic substance. —Zbigniew Brzezinski

4. But there's one thing I would give anything for. And that's a piano. If we had a piano I'd practice every single night and learn every piece in the world. That's the thing I want more than anything else. —Carson McCullers

5. "If you're right, then I'm wrong and we can all forget it," said Hazel. "But I'm going to get to the bottom of this.

Someone must go and see. I'd go myself, but I've got no speed with this leg." —Richard Adams

6. I often hear from people who have been stricken with some kind of overwhelming tragedy, and at the time that they write they are often very close to desolation. Naturally, I feel very strongly for such people, and I try to console them as best I can, although this is difficult when one knows them only by the few words of a broken-hearted letter. —Rose Kennedy

7. They were married. The wedding march pealed out. The pigeons fluttered. Small boys in Eton jackets threw rice; a fox terrier sauntered across the path; and Ernest Thorburn led his bride to the car through that small inquisitive crowd of complete strangers which always collects in London to enjoy other people's happiness or unhappiness. —Virginia Woolf

8. The garden was quiet. Beyond its walls no echo of footsteps could be heard above the soft incessant splash of the waterfall. The silence was planned, as everything in the garden was planned, though all seemed nature itself. —Pearl S. Buck

9. The last light of the sun was streaming over the rampart of green hills to the west, brimming the leafy valleys with liquid gold, then emptying itself in a sort of abandonment of glory into the vast domed space of sky and sea beyond. —Elizabeth Goudge

10. The living room in the Twilly's house was so damp that thick, soppy moss grew all over the walls. It dripped on the picture of Grandfather Twilly that hung over the melodeon, making streaks down the dirty glass like sweat on the old man's face. —Nathaniel Benchley

■ Nonstandard English

The line that divides nonstandard English from informal standard English is a thin one. It is not, however, impossible to tell the difference in most situations. Three categories of nonstandard English that are relatively easy to distinguish from informal English are *dialect, slang,* and *overly technical language.*

Dialect. A dialect is any distinctive pattern of speech within a language whose use is restricted to a specific geographical location or to a specific social or ethnic group. A dialect is considered nonstandard because its use is not widespread.

Dialect is a nonstandard form of English that is confined to a particular geographical area or social group. It is characterized by words, expressions, pronunciations, and grammatical constructions that are not commonly found in standard English.

Dialects develop within a language when people live in isolation. The more isolated the people are, the more their dialect will vary from the standard form. As geographical, social, and ethnic barriers disappear between separate peoples, their dialects tend to merge. In the twentieth century, the mass media and the ease with which people can travel have blurred many of the distinctions between dialects. American television programs, for example, are now regularly broadcast in England. Through them many distinctly American words, expressions, and pronunciations have become part of British English.

The following stanza from the poem "To a Mouse" by Robert Burns is an example of the Scottish dialect of English. Although many of the words and pronunciations are not part of your everyday speech, you should still be able to understand the meaning.

EXAMPLE: Wee, sleekit, cow'rin', tim'rous beastie,
O what a panic's in thy breastie!
Thou need na start awa sae hasty,
        Wi' bickering brattle!
I wad be laith to rin an' chase thee
Wi' murd'ring pattle! —Robert Burns

Slang.   Slang is made up of words such as "neat" and phrases such as "hang out" that enjoy a usually short-term popularity. Slang generally originates among small groups sharing a common social bond or activity, as among students or rock musicians.

Slang is a nonstandard form of English containing words and expressions that are generally colorful and expressive but short-lived.

The larger the group and the more closely they are associated with the mainstream of society, the more likely it is that their slang will become part of the standard vocabulary. Most Americans, for example, would recognize a used car dealer's use of the term *cream puff* to mean "a car in excellent condition" and might even use it themselves in a classified ad. On the other hand, the slang words that a group of smugglers might use, almost like secret code words, to shield their activities from the outside world have little chance of becoming standard vocabulary. In the following, note such slang words as "pad," "C-note," and "ace."

EXAMPLE:

> Bosie and Jan left Sam's pad in a real hurry once he began to spill his gut. It seems Sam needed a C-note to bribe some prof into changing a flunking grade into an ace. —Rosemary Frost

Overly Technical Language.   Based on formal standard English, technical language has an important function for people who need to communicate about specific areas of knowledge, such as nuclear physics, linguistics, psychiatry, or even sports. When used accurately, technical language can effectively convey complicated ideas to anyone who has mastered the necessary vocabulary. Technical language can be considered nonstandard, however, when it clouds rather than illuminates ideas. It is then sometimes called *jargon*.

Overly technical language is a nonstandard form of English that is limited in its use to specific areas of knowledge.

The following excerpt is an example of overly technical language from the medical profession. Unless you have studied medicine, this passage will probably overwhelm you.

EXAMPLE:

> The most dramatic instance of the dietary management of a genetic defect is in the case of phenylketonuria (PKU). In this disease the amino acid phenylalanine and some of its metabolites accumlate because of a defect in the hydroxylation of phenylalanine to tyrosine. —James Bordley

EXERCISE B: Identifying Dialect, Slang, and Overly Technical Language. Read each of the following passages carefully. Label each quotation *Dialect, Slang,* or *Overly Technical Language.* Be prepared to explain the reasons for your decisions.

1. "How your husband does spoil that child, Bessy!" said Mrs. Glegg in a loud "aside" to Mrs. Tulliver. "It'll be the ruin of her, if you don't take care. *My* father niver brought his family up so, else we should ha' been a different sort o' family to what we are." —George Eliot
2. Now over here we have the freezer. Looks sorta like a coffin, doesn't it? Maybe now you can see why it gives me the

creeps. Can't tell what might be in there, but I've got this terrible compulsion to find out! —Patrick F. McManus

3. The Yankees are going for the kill. Randolph leads off the game with a double against Steven Renko and, two outs later, Jackson knocks Randolph home for a 1–0 lead. Rudy May has not given up a hit in the fourth inning when Dave Stapleton lashes a low line drive toward rightfield. Willie Randolph doesn't have time to run—just time to dive. He catches the ball inches off the ground before making a four-point landing—elbows and knees. Then May goes on to pitch a six-hit shutout. —George Vecsey

4. In a direct-entry key-to-disk system, a single magnetic disk or disk pack can be connected simultaneously to dozens of "key stations" with operators keying in data at each station. A small-size computer is also connected to the disk, for the purpose of editing data from the key stations before they are recorded on the disk. —Judith B. Edwards

5. "Aye-yuh," the foresighted backwoodsman is thinking, "summah's about petered out, and then we got six–seven months uh wintah, guess we'll make it, just barely, and then after the black flies we got summah again for a couple uh weeks, and then we got wintah . . . I don't know if I'm up to it." —John Skow

6. Trying to act like a big shot, he'd already shown himself up for a dope. No wonder thay were laughing at him, the way he had let Merle cheat him. —Henry Gregor Felsen

7. It was nigh to midnight, and it had set into rain when he woke us. It had been a misdoubtful night, with the storm making; a night when a fellow looks for most anything to happen before he can get the stock fed and himself to the house and supper et and in bed with the rain starting . . . —William Faulkner

8. And this 'oss is as wick as an eel. Could kick a fly's eye out. Ah can't get near 'im nohow. Goes straight up wall when he sees anybody . . . I tell you I had 'im to t'blacksmith t'other day and feller was dead scared of 'im. Twiltin' gurt 'oss 'e is. —James Herriot

9. Through hypnotic age progression, Dr. Wilbur had metamorphosed what had been fixations in the past into viable aparts of the present. The hope was that this would become the bedrock on which to erect the superstructure of integration, a way to open the pathways to the original Sybil—and restore her. —Flora Reta Schreiber

10. The cutting stylus is installed in the cutter head by fastening the rear of the cantilever to the head assembly through a compliant rubbery mounting, much in the fashion of most moving-coil and some moving-iron phono cartridges. —Gary Stock

■ American English

The way English is used in the United States reflects the history of the nation. From the time the Puritans settled in New England to the present, American English has grown and changed and developed a character all its own. Each new wave of immigrants has contributed not only to the life of the nation but also to the vitality of its language. Two ways these contributions can be seen are in what linguists and lexicographers call Americanisms and regionalisms.

Americanisms.   In the 1600's, when the Europeans were colonizing the areas that today comprise the United States, English was but one of many languages spoken in America. In addition, there were the many different languages of the Native American groups, of the Dutch, French, and Spanish settlers, and of the African slaves. As the English colonists prospered, so did their language. Within two centuries, English became the dominant language. As it spread it picked up useful words and phrases from the languages it replaced. The colonists also invented many new expressions themselves. These many additions to the language are know as Americanisms.

An **Americanism** is a word, expression, or meaning that first came into the English language in the area now known as the United States.

The following chart lists just a few of the many thousands of Americanisms that have become part of American English since the early 1600's. The list is constantly growing with new words such as *quadrophonic, quasar,* and *blastoff.* As you read the chart, note the dates. These indicate when the words first appeared in *written* English. It can be presumed that the words had already become part of the spoken language before these dates.

SOME AMERICANISMS		
Source	**Word**	**Date**
Native American	raccoon	1608
	moccasin	1612
	persimmon	1612
	moose	1613
	hickory	1618
	skunk	1634

English Colonists	hummingbird	1632
	snowshoe	1666
	bullfrog	1698
	colonist	1701
	western frontier	1721
	corn bread	1775
	Indian summer	1778
Dutch	boss	1653
	scow	1669
	sleigh	1696
French	levee	1719
	prairie	1770
	picayune	1805
Spanish	adobe	1759
	coyote	1759
	mustang	1808
	pueblo	1808
	canyon	1834
	avocado	1838
	rodeo	1844
African	banjo	1774
	jumbo	1808

Regionalisms. People who wish to hide their regional origins should never talk with a dialectologist, for these careful observers of language can tell where a person was born and raised simply by listening to the way the person uses certain words and expressions.

A **regionalism** is a word, expression, or pronunciation that is characteristic of a certain area of a country.

If, for example, you call a dragonfly a *darning needle,* a dialectologist would guess that you or your ancestors came from New England or New York. Similarly, if you call this insect a *snake doctor,* your roots are probably in Appalachia. If you are a Southerner, you might call a dragonfly a *mosquito hawk.*

Many expressions and speech patterns are characteristic of certain regions. Often the speech patterns show the influence of the grammatical structure of a foreign language that was once spoken in the region, such as German among the Pennsylvania Dutch or French in Louisiana. When the speech patterns vary significantly from standard English patterns, the regionalisms are usually considered dialect.

SOME REGIONAL EXPRESSIONS	
Source	**Expression**
Pennsylvania Dutch	Throw the cow over the fence some hay.
	It's going to give a storm.
	He don't know what for.
Louisiana French	I don't got but five cents, me.
	What you do now?
	You been try make me mad.
Appalachia	Hit's acomin' on to rain.
	Hain't never heared no such thing.
New England	How be you?
	Can't rightly know for sure.
Tidewater (Eastern Virginia)	Gotta study on it first.
	I'm plum beat out.

Many special pronunciations of words are also regionalisms. In Brooklyn, for example, *girl* might be pronounced to rhyme with *soil*. In Boston, *car* and other words ending with *r* are usually pronounced without the final letter. In Charleston, South Carolina, *I am* sounds like *arm*.

Many words and expressions that began as regionalisms have spread so far across the country that they are now part of the general vocabulary of other regions. Dialectologists have traced the movement of the word *pail*, for example, from the North to the South and the word *bucket* from the South to the North. Television and movies have done much to spread regionalisms across the country. By being aware of the words, expressions, and pronunciations that are used around you, you can tap the richness and variety of American English and use it judiciously and expressively.

EXERCISE C: **Discovering Americanisms.** Many American place names originally came from Native American words. For example, *Mississippi* originally meant "big river." Using a detailed map of your state or one of the entire United States, find ten place names that you suspect might be of Native American origin. Then, using the resources in your library, try to discover the original meanings of the words. Consider looking in dictionaries, encyclopedias, and history books for the answers you need.

EXERCISE D: **Exploring Regionalisms.** Read the following sentences and choose the word from the choices in parentheses that you would normally use in your everyday speech. There are no wrong answers. Next, compare your choices with those of your classmates. Keep a tally of your findings and try to discover any regional similarities based on the regional backgrounds of the students in your class.

1. Open the (shades, blinds).
2. The children were playing on a (seesaw, teeter-totter, tilt, tippity-bounce).
3. It is five minutes (of, to, till) two.
4. If the room is cold, you may need a (comforter, comfort, quilt) on the bed.
5. A hundred people were standing (in, on) line.
6. Put the dishes in the (cupboard, cabinet, closet).
7. The fruit salad was made with (cottage cheese, pot cheese, smearcase).
8. On hot summer nights, my parents sit on the front (steps, porch, stoop).
9. My favorite vegetable is (string beans, snap beans, green beans).
10. It's easy to cross the (brook, creek, run, branch, stream) if you know where the stones are.

APPLICATION: **Researching the Varieties of English.** Research one of the following topics in your library and prepare a short written or oral report on your findings. Use not only encyclopedias but also individual books about language. Include in your report a general description of your subject (origins, history, characteristics) and several examples of interesting words, expressions, and pronunciations.

1. Australian English
2. Scottish

3. Appalachian Regionalisms
4. Pennsylvania Dutch
5. Gullah
6. Black English
7. Cajun
8. Creole
9. Hawaiian Regionalisms
10. Regional Pronunciations in Urban Areas (such as Boston, Pittsburgh, New York City, Baltimore, Charleston, Davenport)

Review Exercises: Usage

REVIEW EXERCISE 1: A Review of Terms

This unit has covered many terms and definitions. As a review, answer each of the following questions as clearly as possible.

1. What are the six basic tenses? What do these tenses indicate?
2. How are the basic, progressive, and emphatic forms developed from principal parts?
3. How do you determine whether a verb is regular or irregular?
4. What is a conjugation?
5. What are perfect infinitives?
6. What are the three categories of time?
7. What is the use of historical present? Of the critical present?
8. What is meant by the term "sequence of tenses"?
9. What is subjunctive mood? In what two ways do verbs in the subjunctive mood differ from those in the indicative mood?
10. How can auxiliary verbs be used to express the subjunctive mood?
11. What is the active voice? The passive voice? Which voice is usually preferred? Why?
12. What are the three cases? What are the various uses of each case?
13. How do you determine the correct case of a pronoun that begins a subordinate clause?
14. How do you determine which pronoun case is correct within an elliptical clause?
15. How must a subject and verb agree?

16. What is an antecedent? In what three ways must a pronoun agree with its antecedent?
17. What is the use of each of the three degrees of comparison? In what ways do regular adjectives and adverbs form their comparative and superlative degrees? What is a double comparison?
18. What is a balanced comparison? How do you avoid comparing something with itself? What is an absolute modifier?
19. What is the difference between standard and nonstandard English? In what types of situations is each appropriate? What are the differences between dialect, slang, and technical language?
20. What are Americanisms? What are regionalisms?

REVIEW EXERCISE 2: The Principal Parts and Conjugation of Verbs

Divide your paper into four columns. Label the first *Present,* the second *Present Participle,* the third *Past,* and the fourth *Past Participle.* In these columns, list the principal parts for each of the following verbs. Then conjugate the six basic forms, the six progressive forms, and the two emphatic forms of each verb.

1. promote (with *they*)   2. drive (with *he*)

REVIEW EXERCISE 3: Tenses

Write a sentence of your own for each of the following verbs, using the form of the verb indicated in parentheses. Underline the verb in each sentence.

1. listen (future perfect progressive)
2. order (simple present)
3. proceed (critical present)
4. decide (past perfect progressive)
5. slay (past emphatic)
6. catch (historical present)
7. hang (present progressive)
8. mark (future)
9. place (past progressive)
10. break (historical present)
11. beware (present emphatic)
12. grind (future progressive)
13. teach (critical present)
14. be (past perfect)
15. give (past progressive)
16. understand (past perfect)
17. do (present perfect progressive)
18. delay (simple past)
19. shove (present progressive)
20. swing (future perfect)

REVIEW EXERCISE 4:   Sequence of Tenses

Write sentences of your own that include each of the following verbs or verbals. (For the first four items, you will need to write complex sentences.) Be sure that the form of the verb in the subordinate clause, the form of the infinitive, or the participle is logically determined by the main verb. Then underline the main verb in each sentence.

Verb in Subordinate Clause	*Infinitive*	*Participle*
1. realize	5. to derive	8. planning
2. shut	6. to have	9. amusing
3. had been	encouraged	10. having
instructed	7. to have	waited
4. has predicted	believed	

REVIEW EXERCISE 5:   Mood

Identify the mood of each underlined verb in the following sentences as *indicative, imperative,* or *subjunctive.*

1. We prefer that you <u>remain</u> where you are.
2. <u>Watch</u> where you are placing your feet as you dance.
3. If there <u>were</u> any reason to doubt you, I might be skeptical of your story.
4. Around the bend we <u>could see</u> our new home.
5. <u>Try</u> to believe what I am telling you.
6. This job requires that everyone <u>be</u> able to do the work efficiently and thoroughly.
7. When <u>has</u> there ever <u>been</u> a better day for sailing?
8. The equator <u>is</u> equidistant from the North and South poles.
9. She insists that he <u>report</u> any dissatisfaction among the staff.
10. <u>Write</u> about an historical event that helped to shape the present.

REVIEW EXERCISE 6:   Voice

Identify the voice in each of the following sentences as *active* or *passive.* Rewrite each passive sentence in the active voice.

1. The food was left untouched on everyone's plates.
2. Several people sought shelter under the pavilion.

3. Streamers were hung for the festivities.
4. Ms. Baxter favorably impressed each one of us.
5. We radioed the Coast Guard for help.
6. We were shocked by his impropriety.
7. His head lowered, the angry moose charged at his tormentors.
8. Many trees had been cut down in the depleted forest.
9. The walls had been painted bright orange.
10. Her garage door was shattered by the impact of the car.

REVIEW EXERCISE 7: Pronoun Usage

Choose the correct pronoun from the choices in parentheses in each of the following sentences.

1. The best golfers on the green were (us, we) women.
2. We heartily supported (him, his) determination to succeed in athletics.
3. They want their guest and (I, me) to take our shoes off at the door.
4. Jack was the culprit (who, whom) I think took the last of the chocolate-chip cookies.
5. A strong current pulled John and (he, him) under the water.
6. Patricia and (I, me) decided that our experience had been valuable.
7. She will give a reward to (whoever, whomever) returns her billfold.
8. (You, Your) driving from Kentucky to New York doesn't seem like a good idea.
9. (He, Him) having issued an ultimatum, we felt reluctant to do his bidding.
10. (Who's, Whose) the man standing in the back of the auditorium?
11. The most involved people in the discussion were Rebecca and (I, me).
12. Despite (its, it's) difficulty, I enjoyed reading Conrad's *Lord Jim*.
13. Anne and her brother are better musicians than (us, we).
14. Detailed maps of the city were distributed among the tourists and (them, they).
15. The investigators were (who, whom)?
16. Warnings about the difficulty of the exam made (us, we) nervous students apprehensive.
17. We are eager to meet you (who, whom) we have always admired.
18. (Who's, Whose) name will be first to be called?

19. Give these to (whoever, whomever) is sitting at the front desk.
20. Eileen is far more patient than (I, me).

REVIEW EXERCISE 8: Agreement

Each of the following sentences contains an error in agreement either between a subject and its verb or between a pronoun and its antecedent. Rewrite each sentence to correct the error. Be prepared to explain the reason for the correction.

1. We mowed the lawn, trimmed the hedges, and polished the car; these made us tired.
2. *Stories for Late at Night,* by Alfred Hitchcock, are too disturbing to read before bedtime.
3. Social studies are a course I always do well in.
4. It isn't too late for us to do the assignment and it isn't complicated, so let's get it done.
5. Simon is just one of the many talented people who has created the scenery for our play.
6. Ramon told Peter that he should have brought something to read.
7. As children, Bennie and myself were always the ones who tagged along with the older boys.
8. Most of the fragments from the broken glass has been swept off the floor.
9. Neither Kay nor Barbara is willing to do their share.
10. Anybody can request that they be transferred to a different department.

REVIEW EXERCISE 9: Comparisons

Each of the following sentences contains an incorrect comparison. Rewrite each sentence to correct the error.

1. Abe is far more nicer than his friend Hal.
2. A cool drink tastes well on a hot day.
3. Your ability to make rapid calculations without pen or paper is greater than Helen.
4. Although we enjoyed the hike, Marion said it was the most worst ordeal he had ever experienced.
5. Her lemon soufflé is the most lightest dessert.
6. The noise in our classroom was louder than the one next to us.
7. Jo did so good during the year that she was not required to take the final exam.

8. If Nan becomes any iller, she will have to be hospitalized.
9. This reproduction of a still life by Gauguin is the most identical to the original.
10. His was the most likeliest explanation.

REVIEW EXERCISE 10: Special Problems of Usage

Each of the following sentences contains two or more errors in usage. Rewrite each sentence to correct the errors.

1. I couldn't hardly dare raise my eyes to the principle.
2. Gentlemen, the newspaper media is plenty anxious to report with accuracy.
3. Tom was so enthused when he won us at the game.
4. A bunch of my friends were standing there, but they never saw nothing happen.
5. Jim hadn't done anything accept an honest day's work.
6. They looked everywheres, but they couldn't find where her engagement ring was at.
7. Due to the fact that he was ignorant moneywise, he lost his savings to a swindler.
8. There was a long ways between us and our too pursuers.
9. The reason our friends had to wait for awhile was because there car had a flat tire.
10. It seems like we maybe lost in our own neighborhood.

REVIEW EXERCISE 11: Identifying Different Levels of Language.

Identify each of the following sentences as *standard* or *nonstandard* English. If the sentence is standard, further identify it as *formal* or *informal*. If the sentence is nonstandard, identify it as *dialect*, *slang*, or *overly technical language*.

1. She made a fuss over the kids and they made a fuss over her. There was a lot of chatter and I noticed Rory looking at Francie, a frown puckering his forehead. He tilted his head a little to one side as if listening. I could almost see the wheels churning inside his head. He was trying to figure something out. —Marie Killilea
2. I never stop worrying, I'm so good at it. And the lessons I learned were drawn into my brain like hieroglyphics pressed in by a stick. I am used to danger. I can't understand a life without it. That was one of the hieroglyphics of suffering, the nonsense syllables. If suffering isn't there, I have to find it. —Susan Fromberg Schaeffer

3. Well, if you truly wanta know, I'm a fella that's asked questions an' give her some thought. She's a nice country. But she was stole a long time ago. You git acrost the desert an' come into the country aroun' Bakersfield. An' you never seen such purty country—all orchards an' grapes, purtiest country you ever seen. —John Steinbeck

4. I had forgotten to draw my curtain, which I usually did; and also to let down my window-blind. The consequence was, that when the moon, which was full and bright (for the night was fine), came in her course to that space in the sky opposite my casement, and looked in at me through the unveiled panes, her glorious gaze roused me. —Charlotte Brontë

5. They'd be so tickled when they got to South Bend that you'd never hear them razz the old burg again. —Ring Lardner

6. I am not afraid of adversity, having suffered setbacks and bounced back. I think that my character has been improved by my difficult childhood. I have gained resilience, will power, determination, and appreciation for what I have, not regret for what I lack. —Susan Massie

7. The explication of media's most essential attributes is needed for two major reasons. First, media as a special case of instructional means consist essentially of contents compounded with structural elements such as codes, formats, and methods. Structure is based on symbolic codes both in nontechnological media (e.g., languages) and in technological media (e.g., television and maps).—Gavriel Salomon and Akiba A. Cohen

8. In the same drawer there was a leather case with a broken thingamajig to close it, and it had jewelry in it—a lot of junky women's jewelry that looked like it was made out of paste and stuff. —Paul Zindel

9. In December the first frosts came with the full moon, and then my nights of vigil held a quality harder to bear. There was a sort of beauty to them, cold and clear, that caught at the heart and made me stare in wonder. From my windows the long lawns dipped to the meadows, and the meadows to the sea, and all of them were white with frost, and white too under the moon. —Daphne du Maurier

10. Sweeter, you air a hard hearted man. You've kilt a lot of snakes and hung 'em on the fence to make it rain. They air still hangin' there. I ain't heard a rain-crow croakin' yet ner felt a drap of rain. —Jesse Stuart

UNIT **III**

Mechanics

Chapter 11

Capitalization and Abbreviation

The goal of every writer is to write clearly and to develop a style that is both personal and effective. Before being able to achieve this goal, however, a writer must master the mechanics of writing. The word *mechanics* refers to the technical part of constructing sentences. A writer who has mastered the mechanics of writing uses capital letters properly, writes abbreviations in their correct forms, and punctuates many different kinds of sentences correctly.

This chapter presents rules for the use of capital letters and abbreviations. The rules for capitalization and abbreviation have developed gradually over the years to help people write material so that others can readily understand their meaning. You are probably already familiar with the restricted use of capital letters to signal only certain important words. You may also already use abbreviations in certain situations to save time and space. Studying or reviewing the rules in this chapter can help you perfect your writing skill.

11.1 Capitalization

Capitalization signals the beginning of a sentence or points out certain words within a sentence.

To **capitalize** means to begin a word with a capital letter.

■ Signaling First Words

You should always signal the start of a new idea by capitalizing the first word in all types of sentences.

Capitalize the first words in declarative, interrogative, imperative, and exclamatory sentences.

DECLARATIVE: A piece of art often reflects the times in which an artist lives.

INTERROGATIVE: Do you find contemporary art difficult to interpret at times?

IMPERATIVE: Look around you, for art is everywhere.

EXCLAMATORY: That Van Gogh painting was magnificent!

If a quotation is a complete sentence, it should also begin with a capital.

Capitalize the first word in a quotation if the quotation is a complete sentence.

EXAMPLES: The instructor began by saying, "Music is a way of painting a picture with melodies."

"To play effectively, you must truly understand the piece you are playing," the professor continued.

"You must practice every day," he emphatically stated. "Nothing is more important than practice."

"If one hears bad music," Oscar Wilde once observed, "it is one's duty to drown it by one's conversation."

The first two of the preceding examples show quotations that consist of one sentence each. The third example shows a quotation that consists of two sentences. Notice that the first word of each sentence is capitalized. The last example consists of one sentence that is interrupted by a "he said/she said" phrase. Only the first word of one sentence that has been interrupted is capitalized.

When only a portion of a sentence is quoted, do not capitalize the first word unless it is the first word in the sentence in which it is included.

EXAMPLE: As Dostoyevsky advocated, an artist needs to paint what exists around him or her, for art should always be a means of "responding to human needs."

If a sentence follows a colon, it should also be capitalized. The first word of a list of words or phrases following a colon, however, should not be capitalized.

Capitalize the first word after a colon if the word begins a complete sentence.

COMPLETE SENTENCE: He made one point over and over: The painting is more lasting than the person who paints it.

LIST OF WORDS OR PHRASES: I saw some famous art work at the Dresden exhibit: lovely ivory carvings, Rembrandt paintings, and a magnificent armor display.

Interjections and question fragments are also capitalized.

Capitalize the first word in interjections and question fragments.

INTERJECTIONS: Oh, yes! Awful!

QUESTION FRAGMENTS: Why not? When?

Poetry should always be written as the poet intended it to be. In most poetry the first word in each line is capitalized even if it does not begin a new sentence.

Capitalize the first word in each line of most poetry.

EXAMPLE: I mind where we parted in yon shady glen,
On the steep, steep side of Ben Lomond,
Where in the deep purple hue the Highland hills we view,
And the moon coming out in the gloamy —Lady John Scott

NOTE ABOUT *I* AND *O*:   You should always capitalize the pronoun *I* and the interjection *O*, even when they appear in the middle of a sentence.

EXAMPLES: Father and I agreed on a plan.

"Long fed on boundless hopes, O race of man,
How angrily thou spurn'st all simpler fare!"
—Matthew Arnold

Do not capitalize the interjection *oh* unless it occurs at the beginning of a sentence. The interjection *O*, used almost exclusively in poetry, should always be capitalized, no matter where it appears in a sentence.

Colons and capitals are also used in formal resolutions that state the subjects of debates and legislative decisions and acts.

Capitalize the first word after a colon in a formal resolution.

EXAMPLE: Resolved: That the Senior Class hold a car wash next Saturday to raise money for new band uniforms.

EXERCISE A: **Capitalizing First Words.** Copy each of the following items, capitalizing the appropriate words.

1. "your explanation," said the teacher, "is difficult to accept."
2. i lived with visions for my company,
   instead of men and women, years ago,
   and found them gentle mates, nor thought to know
   a sweeter music than they played to me.
   —Elizabeth Barrett Browning
3. resolved: that the state legislature increase the school year by three days.
4. the candidate expressed his anger: he could not believe the allegations of the opposing party.
5. remember the line, "o blithe spirit!"
6. i wonder, oh, i wonder, how she will ever get over her grief.
7. how much?
8. how many times have you visited Texas and New Mexico?
9. the mayor said, "we are honored to have you visit our city."
10. oh, no!

■ Capitalizing Proper Nouns

Nouns, as you know, name persons, places, and things. They are classified as either common or proper. Proper nouns, which name specific examples of people, places, or things, require capitalization.

Capitalize all proper nouns.

COMMON NOUNS: judge, town, clock, sister, ship, violin, sailors, states, apples

PROPER NOUNS: Judge Alexander P. Stevens, Patricia Davis, Cape Cod, Broadway, Denmark, Mississippi Valley, *Newsweek*, *Air Force I*, *Still Life with Apples*

As you can see from the preceding examples, there are several categories of proper nouns. One category is names.

Capitalize each part of a person's full name.

EXAMPLES: Felicia A. Burton, G. T. Schmidt, Luis Teresina

Surnames sometimes consist of several parts. Capitalize both parts of surnames beginning with *Mc, O', or St.*

EXAMPLES: McNamara, O'Sullivan, St. John

If, however, surnames begin with *de, D', la, le, Mac, van,* or *von,* spelling may differ. To ensure accuracy, ask for the correct spelling.

EXAMPLES: D'Ambrosio or de Ambrosio or Dambrosio

Van Fleet or van Fleet or Vanfleet

The proper names of animals should also be capitalized.

EXAMPLES: Lad, a dog   Flicka, a horse

Proper nouns referring to particular places must also be capitalized. Many of them consist of more than one word and a few contain articles, prepositions, and conjunctions. Articles, prepositions, and conjunctions are not usually capitalized.

Capitalize geographical and place names.

The following chart provides a variety of examples of geographical terms and place names.

GEOGRAPHICAL AND PLACE NAMES	
Streets:	Fulton Street, Linden Boulevard
Boroughs, Towns, and Cities:	Brooklyn, Wilmette, Houston, Los Angeles
Counties, States, and Provinces:	Orange County, Arizona, British Columbia
Nations and Continents:	Zimbabwe, the United States of America, Europe, South America
Mountains:	Mount McKinley, Atlas Mountains
Valleys and Deserts:	Shenandoah Valley, Sahara Desert
Islands and Peninsulas:	Canary Islands, Molokai, Sinai Peninsula

Sections of a Country:	the Southwest, New England, the Great Plains
Scenic Spots:	Olympic National Park, the Colosseum, the Continental Divide
Rivers and Falls:	Amazon River, Bridalveil Falls
Lakes and Bays:	Lake Huron, Wilson Lake, San Francisco Bay
Seas and Oceans:	Adriatic Sea, Pacific Ocean
Celestial Bodies:	Saturn, the North Star, Haley's Comet
Monuments and Memorials:	Washington Monument, Arlington National Cemetery, the Alamo
Buildings:	Carnegie Hall, San Francisco City Hall
School and Meeting Rooms:	Laboratory C, Room 14, the Oval Office

NOTE ABOUT CAPITALIZING DIRECTIONS: Words indicating direction can be used in two ways: to name a section of a country and to give travel directions. These words are capitalized only when they refer to a section of a country.

EXAMPLES: The older urban areas of the industrial Northeast suffer from many problems.

They have been accepted at Sam Houston State College.

To reach the county fair, travel two miles west and one mile south.

NOTE ABOUT CELESTIAL BODIES: Do not capitalize *moon* and *sun*, as you do the names of other celestial bodies. Capitalize *earth* only when you refer to it as one of the planets. Do not capitalize earth when it is preceded by the word *the*.

EXAMPLE: The moon is in orbit around the earth, and the earth is in orbit around the sun.

NOTE ABOUT CAPITALIZING *THEATER, HOTEL, COLLEGE,* AND SIMILAR WORDS: Words such as *theater, hotel, college, room,* and so forth are not capitalized unless the word is part of the proper name.

EXAMPLES: They plan to attend college next fall.

They have been accepted at Sam Houston State College.

Capitals are also used with words referring to historical periods, events, documents, dates, and holidays.

Capitalize the names of specific events and periods of time.

SPECIFIC EVENTS AND TIMES	
Historical Periods:	the Renaissance, the Mesozoic Era
Historical Events:	World War II, the Russian Revolution, Battle of King's Mountain, Rio de Janeiro Conference, Trail of Tears
Documents:	the Magna Charta, Declaration of Independence
Days and Months:	Tuesday, Fridays, July 20, the third week in April
Holidays and Religious Days:	Easter, Father's Day, Martin Luther King Day, Hanukkah, St. Valentine's Day
Special Events:	Berkshire Music Festival, the Rose Bowl, Eastern States Exhibition

NOTE ABOUT THE SEASONS: Do not capitalize any reference you make to the seasons.

EXAMPLE: In late spring we plant tomatoes in our garden.

References to groups of all kinds are also capitalized. These include references to organizations, government bodies, races, nationalities, languages spoken by different nationalities, and religions.

Capitalize the names of various organizations, government bodies, political parties, races, nationalities, and the languages spoken by different groups as well as references to the religions of various groups.

VARIOUS GROUPS	
Clubs:	Kennedy High School Stamp Club, Rotary, New York Athletic Club, Knights of Columbus
Organizations:	the Salvation Army, American Medical Association, Veterans of Foreign Wars
Institutions:	National Museum of Art, the Boston Symphony, Johns Hopkins Hospital
Schools:	Adlai E. Stevenson High School, Stanford University, The College of St. Catherine, Rensselaer Polytechnic Institute
Businesses:	Allied Chemical Corporation, International Coins and Currency, Inc., Prentice-Hall of Canada, Ltd.

Government Bodies:	the Senate, House of Lords, Nuclear Regulatory Commission, Federal Deposit Insurance Corporation, Army of the Potomac
Political Parties:	Republican Party, Liberal Party, the Democrats
Races:	Mongoloid, Negro, Caucasian
Nationalities:	American, Canadian, Mexican, German, Israeli, Japanese, Iranian, Swiss, Congolese
Languages:	English, French, Spanish, Italian, Polish, Swahili, Hindi
Religious References:	*Christianity:* God, the Lord, the Father, the Holy Spirit, the Bible, the New Testament, the Holy Father *Judaism:* God, the Lord, the Prophets, the Torah, the Talmud *Islam:* Allah, the Prophets, the Koran, Mohammed, Muslims *Hinduism:* Brahma, the Bhagavad Gita, the Vedas *Buddhism:* the Buddha, Mahayana, Hinayana

NOTE ABOUT PRONOUN REFERENCES: When you use pronouns to refer to the Judeo-Christian deity they should always be capitalized.

EXAMPLE: I prayed for *His* help.

When referring to ancient mythology, you should *not* capitalize the word *god* or *goddess*. The names of the gods and goddesses, however, are capitalized.

EXAMPLES: the *gods* of ancient Greece

the Roman *god* Mars

Finally, three more categories of proper nouns also require capitalization. Study the rule and the examples in the following chart.

Capitalize the names of awards, the names of specific types of air, sea, space, and land craft, and brand names.

OTHER IMPORTANT PROPER NOUNS	
Awards:	Nobel Peace Prize, Father of the Year, Pulitzer Prize, Stanley Cup, Oscar, Arista
Specific Air, Sea, Space, and Land Craft:	a Boeing 727, *S.S. Columbia*, *Viking 1*, Metroliner
Brand Names:	Kellogg's Special K, Zenith televisions

EXERCISE B: **Using Capitals for Proper Nouns.** Proper nouns have not been capitalized in the following sentences. Copy the sentences onto your paper, capitalizing the proper nouns correctly. If a sentence requires no further capitalization, write *correct*.

1. The army of the cumberland operated mainly in the states of georgia, tennessee, and kentucky during the civil war.
2. My friend speaks a number of languages: spanish, french, german, and italian.
3. In the course on comparative religions, we studied the old testament, the new testament, and the koran.
4. My teacher insists that we read the declaration of independence, the constitution, and the bill of rights.
5. Our trip to the washington area included visits to the lincoln memorial and the tomb of the unknown soldier.
6. Bolivia, located in the central part of south america, is separated from the pacific coast by chile and peru.
7. My sister received a new york state regents scholarship and a westinghouse science award.
8. Of all the methods of travel, I prefer flying on a lockheed tristar.
9. For science I prepared a chart illustrating the different positions of the big dipper.
10. The culver city art league meets the second monday of every month.
11. The prom at longfellow high school will be on friday night, june 17.
12. School begins the day after labor day, and our first holiday is rosh hashana in late september.
13. Much to our surprise, there was no national book award for poetry this year.
14. Now that we have learned so much about the moon, I wonder how long it will take to get new information about the sun.
15. Marie, who was the leader of arista in high school, was recently elected to phi beta kappa in college.

16. If you have a complaint about your mercury cougar, I suggest you write to the customer relations department of ford motor company in dearborn, michigan.
17. One meeting will be held in conference room b, and the other will be held in conference room 5 in the basement.
18. My family saw the picasso paintings at the museum of modern art.
19. Several of my classmates are sending college applications to northwestern university and to the university of chicago.
20. President during the era of good feelings was james monroe.

■ Capitalizing Proper Adjectives

A proper adjective is an adjective formed from a proper noun or a proper noun used as an adjective. Most proper adjectives require capitalization.

Capitalize most proper adjectives.

PROPER ADJECTIVES FORMED FROM PROPER NOUNS:

American, Wilsonian, Biblical, Chinese

PROPER NOUNS USED AS ADJECTIVES:

a Chicago accent   a Eugene O'Neill play   Bible study

Some proper adjectives are no longer capitalized, however.

Do not capitalize certain frequently used proper adjectives.

EXAMPLES: pasteurized, turkish towel, french toast, herculean, venetian blinds, quixotic

Brand names used with common nouns are capitalized according to the following rule.

Capitalize a brand name used as an adjective, but do not capitalize the common noun it modifies.

EXAMPLES: Westinghouse refrigerator, Levi jeans

When two proper adjectives are used with one common noun, be guided by the following rule.

Do not capitalize a common noun used with two proper adjectives.

Compare the examples in the following chart. Notice in each case that a common noun used with two or more proper adjectives is not capitalized.

One Proper Adjective	Two or More Proper Adjectives
Conservative Party	Conservative and Liberal parties
Main Street	Main, Welch, and Macopin streets
Mississippi River	Mississippi and Missouri rivers

The last two rules governing the use of capitalization with proper adjectives concern proper adjectives to which prefixes have been attached and proper adjectives hyphenated in other ways.

Do not capitalize prefixes attached to proper adjectives unless the prefix refers to a nationality.

EXAMPLES: pro-English

all-American

Franco-Prussian

Anglo-American

Notice that the prefixes in the first two examples are not capitalized. The second two are capitalized because they refer to nationalities.

Occasionally, you will come across a proper adjective hyphenated in another way.

In a hyphenated adjective, capitalize only the proper adjective.

EXAMPLE: Swedish-speaking immigrant

EXERCISE C: **Using Capitals for Proper Adjectives.** The following items contain proper adjectives. Copy each item onto your paper, correcting any adjective that is improperly capitalized. If an item is already capitalized properly, write *correct*.

1. french fries
2. Biblical

3. First and Second Avenues
4. Japanese

5. Anglo-American
6. lake Erie
7. pasteurized
8. Congressional
9. Ford Automobile
10. a herculean task
11. pro-american
12. Lake placid

13. a William Shakespeare Play
14. Greek-Speaking
15. an Anglo-french treaty
16. singapore monsoon
17. Spanish-speaking
18. a Canadian Gold coin
19. a boeing 747
20. A Persian Rug

■ Capitalizing the Titles of People and Things

The titles of people and things must also be capitalized correctly. The following rules will guide you in the correct use of capitals for titles.

Capitalize titles of people and titles of works.

Titles of People. Various types of titles are used to refer to people.

Capitalize a person's title when it is followed by the person's name or when it is used in direct address.

PRECEDING A PROPER NAME: Governor Wilson addressed the state legislature.

IN DIRECT ADDRESS: Doctor, will you discuss my symptoms again?

IN A GENERAL REFERENCE: Have you ever met the mayor of our city?

The following chart illustrates the capitalization of a number of different titles. Notice the treatment of prefixes and suffixes in particular.

TITLES OF PEOPLE	
Commonly Used Titles:	Sir, Madam, Doctor, Professor, Father, Reverend, Rabbi, Sister, Archbishop, Sergeant, Ensign, Governor, Senator, Ambassador
Abbreviated Titles:	(Before names) Mr., Mrs., Dr., Prof., Gen. (After names) Jr., Sr., Ph.D., Esq.

Compound Titles:	Commander in Chief, Secretary of Defense, Vice President, Lieutenant Governor
Titles with Prefixes or Suffixes:	Mayor-elect Ross ex-Senator Norman

Titles for certain extremely high-ranking officials are always capitalized.

Capitalize the titles of certain high government officials even when the titles are not followed by a proper name or used in direct address.

Titles that are always capitalized include those of the President, Vice President, and Chief Justice of the United States, as well as that of the Queen of England.

EXAMPLE: The Chief Justice was pleased when the President appointed him.

As a sign of respect, when you refer to a specific person whose name is not used, you may capitalize the person's title just as you would the title President.

EXAMPLE: The General has served the country well.

Frequently, people refer to their relatives by their titles. These references follow the next rule.

Capitalize titles showing family relationships when the title is used with the person's name or in direct address. The title may also be capitalized when it refers to a specific person, except when the title comes after a possessive noun or pronoun.

WITH THE PERSON'S NAME: Aunt Nancy speaks several languages.

IN DIRECT ADDRESS: I'm glad you're coming for dinner, Grandmother.

REFERRING TO A SPECIFIC PERSON: Will Father fix it for me?

WITH A POSSESSIVE NOUN: George's mother will meet us.

WITH A POSSESSIVE PRONOUN: His cousin Leslie goes to my school.

Capitalizing Things.   You should also capitalize the titles and subtitles of various works.

Capitalize the first word and all other important words in the titles of books, periodicals, poems, stories, plays, paintings, and other works of art.

Notice in the following chart that none of the articles (*a*, *an*, and *the*) is capitalized unless it is the first word of a title. Because conjunctions and prepositions are not considered important words, they are not capitalized unless they are the first word of the title or contain more than four letters.

	TITLES OF WORKS
Books:	*Profiles in Courage* *The United States: A History of the Republic*
Periodicals:	*The Wall Street Journal* *Newsweek*
Poems:	"To a Prize Bird" "The Rime of the Ancient Mariner"
Stories:	"The Red-Headed League" "The Two Bottles of Relish"
Plays:	*On Borrowed Time* *Joan of Lorraine*
Paintings:	*Woman with the Blue Veil* *Still Life with Basket of Apples*
Music:	"This Land Is Your Land" *Carmen*

When the title of a course of study is a language or is followed by a number, it requires capitalization also.

Capitalize titles of couses when the courses are language courses or when the courses are followed by a number.

WITH CAPITALS: Spanish, Sociology I, English 2

WITHOUT CAPITALS: biology, algebra, homemaking

EXERCISE D: **Using Capitals with Titles of People and Things.** Titles of people and things have not been capitalized in the following sentences. Copy the sentences onto your paper, capitalizing the titles correctly.

1. Phillip Whitney, m.d., and professor Raul Alvarado are the featured speakers at this evening's meeting.
2. Yesterday captain Stanzione reprimanded the private.
3. Our guest was mayor-elect Sanderson.
4. I registered for psychology 1, french, and geology.

5. May I tell grandfather about our plans now, mother?
6. We have been informed that governor Brandon will arrive at noon to meet with the president.
7. Have you read the book *lee's lieutenants* by Douglas Southall Freeman?
8. Two of Diego Rivera's finest paintings are *man and machinery* and *betrayal of cuernavaca.*
9. My aunt Margaret and I enjoy the poetry of Emily Dickinson, especially "success is counted sweetest."
10. I often find myself humming the tune of the song "you are the sunshine of my life," which was written by Stevie Wonder.

■ Capitalizing Parts of Social and Business Letters

Capital letters are also required in parts of social and business letters. Review the format for both types of letters in Section 26.1, and study the following chart as a guide for proper capitalization.

Social Letters	
Heading:	422 Brook Boulevard Escondido, California 92027 January 10, 1981
Salutation:	Dear Eric, Dear Aunt Emily,
Closing:	With love, Your cousin,
Business Letters	
Heading:	421 Vandemark Road Sidney, Ohio 45367 February 11, 1981
Inside Address:	Office of Naval Research 800 North Quincy Street Arlington, Virginia 22217
Salutation:	Gentlemen: Dear Sirs: Dear Mrs. Williams:
Closing:	Yours truly, Sincerely yours, Very truly yours,

EXERCISE E: **Using Capitals in a Business Letter.** All of the capital letters have been left out of the following letter. Copy it onto your paper, including all the necessary capitals.

43 berry hill lane
cornwall, new york 12518
november 5, 19_____

director of admissions
fairleigh dickinson university
1000 river road
teaneck, new jersey 07666

dear sir:

after speaking with my college adviser, i may be interested in enrolling in the college of business administration at fairleigh dickinson university in september of next year.

would you please send me your catalog for the college of business administration? i am also interested in your admission requirements and details of the financial aid package provided by the university.

since i live some distance from the college, i would also like information about on-campus housing or housing in the teaneck area.

thank you very much for your assistance.

yours truly,

_____
(sign your name)

APPLICATION: **Using Capitalization Rules in Original Sentences.** Use each of the following directions to write sentences of your own, using capitals wherever necessary.

1. Write a sentence in which you name the title of a book and its author.
2. Write a sentence in which you mention the name of the governor of your state.
3. Write a sentence in which you give someone directions. Use words such as *east, northwest, south,* and so on.

4. Name a favorite professional team and write a sentence about it.
5. Write a sentence about a person who speaks two or more languages. Name the languages.
6. Write a sentence about a famous historic site that you have visited or would like to visit.
7. Write a sentence about the two oceans that border the United States.
8. Write a sentence naming one of your favorite record albums.
9. Write a sentence in which you mention both your junior and senior high school by name.
10. Write a sentence that includes a direct quotation.
11. Write a sentence about a famous battle or treaty.
12. Write a sentence in which you mention a theater, museum, or other cultural building by name.
13. Write a sentence naming a special sports event.
14. Write a sentence in which you mention three different states you have visited or would like to visit.
15. Write a sentence in which you give the date of your birth.
16. Write a question about a product. Use the brand name in your question.
17. Write two sentences. Have the second sentence explain the first one. Join the two sentences with a colon.
18. Write a sentence describing a characteristic you particularly like in a relative. Use both the relative's name and a title indicating his or her relationship to you in the sentence.
19. Write a sentence naming a book you have read recently.
20. Write a sentence naming your three favorite courses.

11.2 Abbreviation

Abbreviations have been around a long time. They can be traced back to the time when artisans chiseled messages on stone tablets and scribes wrote religious texts on parchment. Using abbreviations helped these people save both time and space.

To **abbreviate** means to shorten an existing word or phrase.

Today, thousands of abbreviations exist in the English language. This section presents the conventions governing the use of many abbreviations you may want to use in your writing.

Study and review the rules in the section carefully so you will know which abbreviations can be used in formal writing and which should be reserved for informal situations such as writing addresses, lists, and notes. The rules, examples, and charts in this section will also guide you in forming different types of abbreviations correctly.

■ Abbreviations of Names and Titles of People

A number of rules govern the use of abbreviations for names and titles. The first concerns the abbreviation of a person's name.

People's Names. The first time you use a person's name in formal writing, it should be written out in full. In addresses or lists, initials may be used in place of the given name.

Use a person's full given name in formal writing, unless the person uses initials as part of his or her formal name.

EXAMPLE: Alice Higgins is a well-known newspaper columnist.

Additional references to the same person may be made in different ways. Sometimes, you may wish to use only the last name with a title. At other times, you may decide to use the last name alone.

FIRST REFERENCE: Alice Higgins, the well-known newpaper columnist, will address the twelfth grade.

LATER REFERENCES: Miss Higgins will speak about preparing for a career in journalism.

Higgins will respond to questions after her address.

People's Titles. The titles of people are often abbreviated. First, consider the category of social titles that appear before the proper names of people.

Abbreviations of social titles before a proper name begin with a capital letter and end with a period. They can be used in any type of writing.

SOCIAL TITLES: Mr., Messrs. (plural of Mr.), Mrs., Mme. (Madame or Madam), Mmes. (plural of Mrs. or Mme.)

Social titles are usually abbreviated. There are, however, two exceptions. *Miss* is not an abbreviation, so it does not end with a period. *Ms.* is written as if it were an abbreviation for a word, but it is not. It may be used before a proper name to refer to either a single or a married woman.

Remember to use abbreviations of social titles only when they are followed by proper names.

USED INCORRECTLY: The Mrs. is not at home.

USED CORRECTLY: Mrs. Connolly and Mr. Irving were our class advisors.

Mmes. Johnson and Stack worked long hours to make the book sale a success.

Sometimes you may wish to use professional, religious, political, or military titles in your writing.

Abbreviations of other titles used before proper names also begin with a capital letter and end with a period. They are used less often in formal writing.

The abbreviations for some common titles of position and rank appear below. Others may be found in a dictionary.

ABBREVIATIONS OF COMMON TITLES	
Professional	**Religious**
Dr. Doctor	Rev. Reverend
Atty. Attorney	Fr. Father
Prof. Professor	Sr. Sister
Hon. Honorable	Br. Brother
Political	**Military**
Pres. President	Pvt. Private
Sen. Senator	Sgt. Sergeant
Rep. Representative	Capt. Captain
Gov. Governor	Lt. Col. Lieutenant Colonel
Amb. Ambassador	Maj. Gen. Major General
Sec. Secretary	Ens. Ensign
Treas. Treasurer	Cmdr. Commander
Supt. Superintendent	Vice Adm. Vice Admiral
Com. Commissioner	Adm. Admiral

When you use the *full* name of an individual, you may abbreviate the titles that appear in the chart.

EXAMPLES: Sen. Max Willis is running for reelection.

Supt. of Schools Lisa Baxter met with the Board of Education.

Do not abbreviate the titles in the preceding chart, however, when they are used only with a person's surname.

INCORRECT: Gov. Barrett proposed this piece of legislation.

CORRECT: Governor Barrett proposed this piece of legislation.

INCORRECT: I told Prof. Willard about the experiment.

CORRECT: I told Professor Willard about the experiment.

The abbreviation *Dr.* is an exception. It is often used in front of only a surname.

EXAMPLE: Dr. Rinehart works at the clinic on Thursday.

When you wish to establish the educational qualifications of a person in your writing, you may use an abbreviation of an academic degree. Abbreviations of academic degree generally follow people's names.

Abbreviations of titles after a name start with a capital letter and end with a period. They are set off with commas from the rest of the sentence and can be used in any type of writing.

The following chart presents the most common abbreviations of academic degrees.

ABBREVIATIONS OF ACADEMIC DEGREES	
B.A. (or A.B.) Bachelor of Arts	R.N. Registered Nurse
B.S. (or S.B.) Bachelor of Science	M.D. Doctor of Medicine
M.A. (or A.M.) Master of Arts	D.D.S. Doctor of Dental Surgery
M.S. (or S.M.) Master of Science	
M.B.A. Master of Business Administration	Esq. Esquire (lawyer)
	LL.D. Doctor of Laws
M.F.A. Master of Fine Arts	D.D. Doctor of Divinity
M.S.W. Master of Social Work	Ed.D. Doctor of Education
L.P.N. Licensed Practical Nurse	Ph.D. Doctor of Philosophy

EXAMPLES: I suggested Steven R. Gregg, Ed.D., as a consultant.

Lucy Gordon, M.B.A., was appointed to the committee.

Never use both a title before a person's name and an academic degree after the person's name.

INCORRECT: Prof. Charles Stevenson, Ph.D., recently retired.

CORRECT: Prof. Charles Stevenson recently retired.

Charles Stevenson, Ph.D., recently retired.

Two other common titles, *Jr.* and *Sr.*, are also placed after the full name of a person and set off with commas.

EXAMPLES: John R. Wiggins, Sr., is now over ninety years of age.

Andrew Baretta, Jr., will graduate next month.

EXERCISE A: **Using Titles Correctly in Sentences.** Rewrite each of the following sentences, correcting the error in the use of an abbreviated title.

1. Will you ask Lt. Green to check the roster?
2. Miss. Fern Ralston has enrolled in Wheatley College.
3. Arthur Stevens Jr. hopes to succeed his father.
4. I know that Dr. Homenick, M.D., is fully qualified to perform the operation.
5. B.A. Linda Wong chose to continue until she received her masters degree.
6. Mr and Mrs Rinaldo volunteered to organize the awards ceremony.
7. Will you ask Sec. Maxwell to join us?
8. Mary Montini, our Rep., introduced an important resolution.
9. Has M.D. Boris Knopf been named director of the hospital?
10. I spoke to Arnold Webber, d.d.s., only yesterday on the phone.

EXERCISE B: **Using Abbreviated Titles in Original Sentences.** Write formal sentences of your own using each of the following abbreviated titles.

1. Messrs.
2. Ph.D.
3. Sr.
4. R.N.
5. Maj. Gen.
6. Gov.
7. Dr.
8. Mme.
9. Ens.
10. M.D.

■ Abbreviations of Time and Geographical References

In your writing you will sometimes need to refer to time or to a geographical location. The following rules will help you decide whether or not to use abbreviations for these references.

Time References. The abbreviations for common time spans are not used in formal writing, but you will find them useful in informal situations.

Abbreviations for clocked time begin with a small letter and end with a period. Abbreviations for days of the week or months of the year begin with a capital letter and end with a period. These abbreviations are not used in formal writing.

CLOCKED TIME:	sec.	second(s)	hr.	hour(s)
	min.	minute(s)	yr.	year(s)

DAYS OF THE WEEK:	Mon.	Monday	Fri.	Friday
	Tues.	Tuesday	Sat.	Saturday
	Wed.	Wednesday	Sun.	Sunday
	Thurs.	Thursday		

MONTHS OF THE YEAR:	Jan.	January	July	July
	Feb.	February	Aug.	August
	Mar.	March	Sept.	September
	Apr.	April	Oct.	October
	May	May	Nov.	November
	June	June	Dec.	December

Unlike the preceding abbreviations, A.M. and P.M. and B.C. and A.D. may be used in both formal and informal writing. First, consider A.M. and P.M.

For abbreviations of time before noon and after noon, either capital letters followed by periods or small letters followed by periods are acceptable. They can be used in any type of writing.

EXAMPLES: A.M. or a.m. (ante meridiem, before noon)

P.M. or p.m. (post meridiem, after noon)

Use **A.M.** or **P.M.** in your writing only when you use numerals to refer to the time of day.

EXAMPLES: We started climbing the mountain at 5:30 a.m.

We reached the summit at four in the afternoon.

Avoid using words such as *morning* or *evening* with the abbreviations **A.M.** or **P.M.** Using both the words and the abbreviations results in a redundant expression.

REDUNDANT EXPRESSION: At 3:30 p.m. this afternoon, we had a severe thunderstorm.

BETTER: At 3:30 p.m. we had a severe thunderstorm.

At 3:30 this afternoon, we had a severe thunderstorm.

Next, consider the abbreviations B.C. and A.D., which are used with historical dates. The abbreviation B.C. means before Christ. The abbreviation A.D. means *anno Domini,* "in the year of the Lord." These abbreviations are used with numerals to refer to dates. The letters B.C. always follow the numerals; A.D. may either follow or precede the numerals.

> **Abbreviations for historical dates before and after the birth of Christ require capital letters followed by periods. They can be used in any type of writing.**

EXAMPLES: The archaeological relics were reliably dated at about 50 B.C.

In A.D. 110, barbarian hordes began crossing the mountains and invading the small settlements.

When a writer uses neither B.C. nor A.D. with a historical date, the reader may assume that A.D. is intended.

EXAMPLE: A severe drought struck the region in the middle of the sixth century. (meaning 550 A.D.)

If a writer wished to use A.D. in the preceding example, the abbreviation would be placed after the word *century.*

Geographical References.   Almost all abbreviations for geographical locations should be reserved for informal writing situations.

Abbreviations for geographical terms before or after a proper noun begin with a capital letter and end with a period. They are seldom used in formal writing. *

The following chart lists some common geographical terms and their abbreviations. They should be used primarily in addresses, lists, and note-taking situations. Avoid them in formal writing.

COMMON GEOGRAPHICAL ABBREVIATIONS	
Apt. Apartment	Natl. National
Ave. Avenue	Pen. Peninsula
Bldg. Building	Pk. Park, Peak
Blk. Block	Prov. Province
Blvd. Boulevard	Pt. Point
Co. County	Rd. Road
Dist. District	Rte. Route
Dr. Drive	Sq. Square
Ft. Fort	St. Street
Is. Island	Terr. Territory
Mt. Mountain	

There are two sets of abbreviations for states. The traditional form of abbreviation is a shortening of the state name, capitalized at the beginning and ending with a period. This form, incidentally, does not have abbreviations for Alaska, Hawaii, Iowa, and Utah.

The United States Postal Service has instituted a new system of abbreviations for states. Each abbreviation consists of two capital letters, and no period is required after the abbreviation. The Postal Service wants you to use them when you address mail. Include the postal ZIP number immediately after the abbreviation.

Traditional abbreviations for states begin with a capital letter and end with a period. They are seldom used in formal writing. The official Postal Service abbreviations for states require capital letters with no periods. They also are not generally used in formal writing.

The following chart shows both types of state abbreviations.

STATE ABBREVIATIONS

State	Traditional	Postal Service	State	Traditional	Postal Service
Alabama	Ala.	AL	Montana	Mont.	MT
Alaska	Alaska	AK	Nebraska	Nebr.	NB
Arizona	Ariz.	AZ	Nevada	Nev.	NV
Arkansas	Ark.	AR	New Hampshire	N.H.	NH
California	Calif.	CA	New Jersey	N.J.	NJ
Colorado	Colo.	CO	New Mexico	N. Mex.	NM
Connecticut	Conn.	CT	New York	N.Y.	NY
Delaware	Del.	DE	North Carolina	N.C.	NC
Florida	Fla.	FL	North Dakota	N. Dak.	ND
Georgia	Ga.	GA	Ohio	O.	OH
Hawaii	Hawaii	HI	Oklahoma	Okla.	OK
Idaho	Ida.	ID	Oregon	Ore.	OR
Illinois	Ill.	IL	Pennsylvania	Pa.	PA
Indiana	Ind.	IN	Rhode Island	R.I.	RI
Iowa	Iowa	IA	South Carolina	S.C.	SC
Kansas	Kans.	KS	South Dakota	S. Dak.	SD
Kentucky	Ky.	KY	Tennessee	Tenn.	TN
Louisiana	La.	LA	Texas	Tex.	TX
Maine	Me.	ME	Utah	Utah	UT
Maryland	Md.	MD	Vermont	Vt.	VT
Massachusetts	Mass.	MA	Virginia	Va.	VA
Michigan	Mich.	MI	Washington	Wash.	WA
Minnesota	Minn.	MN	West Virginia	W. Va.	WV
Mississippi	Miss.	MS	Wisconsin	Wis.	WI
Missouri	Mo.	MO	Wyoming	Wyo.	WY

NOTE ABOUT D.C.: The traditional abbreviation for the District of Columbia is D.C.; the Postal Service abbreviation is DC. Use the traditional abbreviation in formal writing whenever it follows the word *Washington.*

EXAMPLE: Have you visited Washington, D.C.?

EXERCISE C: Identifying Time and Geographical Abbreviations. Copy each of the following abbreviations onto your paper, and write its meaning next to it.

1. TX	6. Apt.	11. a.m.	16. N.C.
2. Mt.	7. P.M.	12. CA	17. B.C.
3. A.D.	8. Natl.	13. Co.	18. Conn.
4. Ave.	9. Fri.	14. Del.	19. Pk.
5. MI	10. WI	15. Oct.	20. hr.

■ Abbreviations of Latin Phrases, Measurements, and Numbers

Knowing abbreviations for Latin phrases, measurements, and numbers will help you both in writing and in your reading.

Latin Phrases.   Writers often use Latin abbreviations in footnotes and bibliographic references. You may also have occasion to use them in your note-taking.

Use small letters and periods for most abbreviations of Latin expressions. These abbreviations are not used in formal writing.

The following chart offers a selection of frequently used Latin phrases and their abbreviations.

ABBREVIATIONS FROM LATIN		
Abbreviation	**Latin Phrase**	**Meaning**
ad inf.	ad infinitum	to infinity
c., ca., *or* circ.	circa	about (used with dates)
e.g.	exempli gratia	for example
et al.	et alii	and others
etc.	et cetera	and so forth
ex lib.	ex libris	from the books (of)
ex off.	ex officio	officially; by the virtue of one's office
f.		and the following (page or line)
ff.		and the following (pages or lines)
ib. *or* ibid.	ibidem	in the same place
i.e.	id est	that is
in loc. cit.	in loco citato	in the place cited
n.b. *or* N.B.	nota bene	note well; take notice
non seq.	non sequitur	it does not follow
per an.	per annum	by the year

pro tem.	pro tempore	for the time; temporarily
viz.	videlicet	to wit; namely
vs.	versus	against
v.v.	vice versa	the order being changed

Most of these Latin abbreviations are set off with commas in sentences.

EXAMPLES: Grandfather rambled on about many of his interests, e.g., politics, cattle raising, bronco busting, and fishing.

Marie is now considering several professions, viz., medicine, law, and public relations.

Measurements.   You will find abbreviations for measurements used often in fields such as science, mathematics, homemaking, and industrial arts.

With traditional measurements use small letters and periods to form the abbreviations. With metric measurements use small letters and no periods to form the abbreviations. These abbreviations are not used in formal writing except with numerals.

The following chart presents some of the most commonly used traditional measurements and their abbreviations. You are probably already familiar with most of them.

ABBREVIATIONS OF TRADITIONAL MEASUREMENTS					
in.	inch(es)	tsp.	teaspoon(s)	pt.	pint(s)
ft.	foot, feet	tbsp.	tablespoon(s)	qt.	quart(s)
yd.	yard(s)	oz.	ounce(s)	gal.	gallon(s)
mi.	mile(s)	lb.	pound(s)	F.	Fahrenheit

Notice that the abbreviation *F.* for Fahrenheit is an exception to the rule. It is capitalized.

Metric measurements are used extensively throughout the world. You will benefit by learning the most frequently used measurements and their abbreviations. Then, you can consult dictionaries or other references, which contain complete lists of metric measurements, for any others you may need to know.

ABBREVIATIONS OF METRIC MEASUREMENTS			
mm	millimeter(s)	g	gram(s)
cm	centimeter(s)	kg	kilogram(s)
m	meter(s)	L	liter(s)
km	kilometer(s)	C	Celsius

Notice that the abbreviations for both liter and Celsius are exceptions to the rule. They are both capitalized.

Numbers.   In your writing, you will often have to decide whether to spell out numbers or to use numerals.

In formal writing spell out most numbers or amounts less than one hundred and any other numbers that can be written in two words or less.

EXAMPLES: We counted twenty-three squirrels in the park yesterday.

The band has 137 members.

Whenever a number appears at the beginning of a sentence, it should be spelled out. Often, it is better to reword the sentence so the number appears in some other position.

Spell out all numbers found at the beginning of the sentence.

ACCEPTABLE: Three hundred forty people gave the actors a standing ovation.

BETTER: The audience of 340 people gave the actors a standing ovation.

Certain types of numbers, on the other hand, are almost always written in numerals.

Use numerals when referring to fractions, decimals, and percentages, as well as for dates and addresses.

Remember to place these figures within a sentence to avoid having to write them out at the beginning of a sentence.

FRACTION: The new baby weighted 7½ pounds.

DECIMAL: An inch is approximately equal to 2.54 centimeters.

PERCENTAGE: They estimated that Australia has 26 percent of the world's aluminum reserves.

DATE: The meeting will be held on March 25.

ADDRESS: The office is located at 46 Union Street.

EXERCISE D: Identifying Latin Phrases. Copy each of the following abbreviations of Latin phrases onto your paper, and write its meaning in English next to it.

1. e.g.
2. f.
3. viz.
4. i.e.
5. pro tem.

6. n.b.
7. ibid.
8. non seq.
9. etc.
10. et al.

EXERCISE E: Abbreviating Measurements. Copy each of the following items onto your paper. Then rewrite each item using numerals and abbreviations correctly.

1. six grams
2. eight millimeters
3. two tablespoons
4. three and a half miles
5. four-and-one-tenth ounces

6. six feet
7. two inches
8. fifty kilometers
9. two pints
10. The address is fifty-three Main Street.

■ Abbreviations of Business and Government Groups

Some businesses abbreviate the final word in their titles.

An abbreviated word in a business name begins with a capital letter and ends with a period. Most of these abbreviations are not used in formal writing.

BUSINESS ABBREVIATIONS: Co. (Company); Inc. (Incorporated)

Bros. (Brothers); Ltd. (Limited)

In formal writing only *Inc.* and *Ltd.* are generally abbreviated. Sometimes organizations, especially large ones, are referred to by abbreviations formed from the first letter of each word in the organization's name. Businesses, labor unions, and other groups may abbreviate their names in this manner.

Use all capital letters and no periods to abbreviate the names of familiar organizations, large business firms, labor unions, government agencies, and other things whose abbreviated names are pronounced letter by letter as if they were words. These abbreviations are often used in formal writing.

The following chart lists some of the organizations that use this type of abbreviation. Notice in the last category that some familiar things are also abbreviated in this way.

ABBREVIATION FOR ORGANIZATIONS		
Business Firms:	CBS	Columbia Broadcasting System
	UPI	United Press International
	RCA	Radio Corporation of America
Labor Unions:	ILGWU	International Ladies Garment Workers Union
	AFL-CIO	American Federation of Labor and Congress of Industrial Organizations
	UMW	United Mine Workers of America
Government Agencies:	FDA	Food and Drug Administration
	IRS	Internal Revenue Service
	VA	Veterans Administration
Other Groups and Things:	NAACP	National Association for the Advancement of Colored People
	AAUW	American Association of University Women
	TV	Television
	CPR	Coronary Pulmonary Resuscitation

These abbreviations may be used in all types of writing. It is best, however, to give the complete names of less familiar items first and enclose the abbreviation in parentheses following the name. After that, the reader will know what the abbreviation means, and the abbreviation may be used alone.

EXAMPLE: The Nuclear Regulatory Commission (NRC) is responsible for licensing nuclear power plants in the United States. The NRC is also responsible for setting safety standards for the nuclear power industry.

An acronym is a word formed from the first letter or letters of a group of words and then pronounced as a word. Some organizations use acronyms to abbreviate their names.

Use all capital letters and no periods for acronyms that form the names of organizations. These acronyms are often used in formal writing.

ACRONYMS: VISTA   Volunteers in Service to America

OPEC   Organization of Petroleum Exporting Countries

Acronyms that may not be recognized by your audience are usually used only after the complete name of the organization has been used once followed by the acronym in parentheses.

EXAMPLE: The North Atlantic Treaty Organization (NATO) was organized in 1949. The members of NATO agreed to settle disputes among themselves by peaceful means, to develop their capacity to resist an armed attack by others, and to consider an armed attack upon any one of the members as an attack upon them all.

EXERCISE F: **Abbreviating Names of Organizations.** Copy each of the following items onto your paper. Then write the abbreviation for each.

1. Food and Drug Administration
2. Smith Brothers
3. United Press International
4. United Nations
5. Television
6. Internal Revenue Service
7. Federal Bureau of Investigation
8. Volunteers in Service to America
9. North Atlantic Treaty Organization
10. Nuclear Regulatory Commission

■ A List of Other Commonly Used Abbreviations

You will probably see many of the abbreviations in the chart on the following pages in your reading and in the business world.

OTHER COMMONLY USED ABBREVIATIONS

anon.	anonymous	G.P.O.	General Post Office
approx.	approximately	Gr.	Greek, Grecian
assoc.	associate or association	grad.	graduate, graduated
assn.	association	grat.	gratis (free of charge)
aux. or auxil.	auxiliary	hdqrs.	headquarters
A.W.O.L.	absent without leave	hi-fi	high fidelity
bibliog.	bibliography	hosp.	hospital
bkt.	basket	ht.	height
bu.	bushel	ill. or illus.	illustrated
bull.	bulletin	incl.	including, inclusive
b.v.	book value	intro.	introductory, introduction
bx(s).	box(es)	ital.	italics
cap.	capital letter	j.g.	junior grade
CB	citizens band	k. or kt.	karat or carat
ch. or chap.	chapter	L.	left
C.O.D.	cash on delivery	mdse.	merchandise
dept.	department	meas.	measure
disc.	discount	mfg.	manufacture
doz.	dozen(s)	mgr.	manager
ea.	each	misc.	miscellaneous
ed.	edition, editor, edited	mkt.	market
EDT	Eastern Daylight Time	M.O.	money order
equiv.	equivalent	m.p.h.	miles per hour
est.	established	mtge.	mortgage
EST	Eastern Standard Time	Myth. or mythol.	mythology or mythological
ext.	extra, exterior	No.	number
fac.	facsimile	P. and L. or P. & L.	profit and loss
fict.	fiction	paren.	parenthesis
FM	frequency modulation	Pat. Off.	Patent Office
fwd.	forward	pc(s).	piece(s)
gloss.	glossary	pg.	page
gov. or govt.	government		

pkg.	package	rm(s).	ream(s)
poet.	poetical, poetry	r.p.m.	revolutions per minute
POW	prisoner of war	R.S.V.P.	please reply
pp.	pages	sc.	scene
prop.	proprietor	sp.	spelling, species, specimen
pr(s).	pair(s)	spec.	special, specific
pseud.	pseudonym		
pub.	published, publisher	SRO	standing room only
pvt.	private	SST	supersonic transport
R.	right		
recd.	received	treas.	treasury, treasurer
ref.	reference, referee	vol.	volume
rhet.	rhetorical, rhetoric	wkly.	weekly
		wt.	weight

EXERCISE G: **Identifying Some Common Abbreviations.** Copy the following abbreviations onto your paper. Then write the meaning of each abbreviation.

1. bxs.
2. cap.
3. C.O.D.
4. ea.
5. hosp.
6. ht.
7. m.p.h.
8. pp.
9. pseud.
10. sp.

APPLICATION: **Using Abbreviations in Sentences.** Following the rules in this section for using abbreviations, write ten sentences of your own. Include an example of each of the following types of abbreviation in each sentence.

1. a social title
2. a military title
3. an academic degree
4. time after noon
5. year before the birth of Christ
6. an address
7. a percent
8. a Latin phrase
9. a government agency
10. an acronym

Punctuation

Commas, quotation marks, parentheses, and periods—all these punctuation marks are visual signs, signals that help a reader understand an author's intentions. Why has an author used an exclamation mark instead of a period? Why are certain words in a passage underlined or italicized? Why has a writer enclosed a particular word in brackets? The reader who understands the rules of punctuation will know.

To understand the rules of punctuation and to punctuate correctly yourself it is necessary to have a thorough knowledge of the elements of sentence structure. You should be able to recognize an appositive, a list of items in a series, a coordinate adjective, a participial phrase, and a complex or compound sentence. Each of these elements—and many others—is punctuated in a specific way.

Once you have mastered the basic principles of punctuation, you can use punctuation marks dramatically. A dash, a colon, or an exclamation mark in the right place calls attention to or highlights an idea. You have probably noticed in your reading how effectively some writers use punctuation marks to help them communicate with their readers.

This chapter presents the major rules of punctuation. Studying and reviewing each section can help you master these rules that are so important to effective writing.

End Marks 12.1

End marks include the period, the question mark, and the exclamation mark. They are used to conclude sentences and phrases. The period and question mark are also used in several special situations.

335

■ End Marks with Sentences and Phrases

To conclude sentences and phrases correctly you must know whether to use a period, a question mark, or an exclamation mark. First, look at the rules governing the use of the period.

The Period. The period is the most frequently used end mark.

> Use a period to end a declarative sentence, a mild imperative, and an indirect question.

A declarative sentence is a statement of fact or opinion. An imperative sentence gives a command or a direction. Imperative sentences often begin with a verb. An indirect question restates a question within a declarative sentence.

STATEMENT OF FACT: Richard Wright wrote *Native Son* and *Black Boy.*

STATEMENT OF OPINION: I believe we did the right thing.

COMMAND: Finish your homework before you go out.

DIRECTION: Turn left at the second traffic light.

INDIRECT QUESTION: We asked her how she was able to complete her project so rapidly.

The Question Mark. Direct questions, often in inverted word order, require a question mark at the end.

> Use a question mark to end an interrogative sentence, an incomplete question, or a statement intended as a question.

INTERROGATIVE SENTENCES: Have you changed your opinion about the cause of your problem?

Which country do you expect to visit next?

QUESTION FRAGMENTS: Why? How much?

STATEMENTS INTENDED AS QUESTIONS: This clock runs on batteries?

We're going to have spaghetti for dinner?

Statements intended as questions should not be used too often. It is often better to rephrase them as direct questions.

STATEMENT INTENDED AS A QUESTION: You agree?

REPHRASED AS A DIRECT QUESTION: Do you agree?

The Exclamation Mark.   An exclamation mark is intended for emphasis. It calls attention to an exclamatory sentence, an imperative sentence, or an interjection. Exclamation marks should be used sparingly. They should be reserved for those occasions when you want to indicate strong emotion in a dramatic way.

> Use an exclamation mark to end an exclamatory sentence, a forceful imperative, or an interjection expressing strong emotion.

EXCLAMATORY SENTENCES: His admission of guilt shocked us all!

That sunset is magnificent!

IMPERATIVE SENTENCES: Never try that trick again!

Come here quickly!

An interjection can be used with either a comma or an exclamation mark. Using an exclamation mark increases the emphasis you give the interjection.

WITH A COMMA: Oh, she is usually on time.

WITH AN EXCLAMATION MARK: Oh! What an amazing turn of events!

EXERCISE A: **Using End Marks with Sentences and Phrases.** The end marks have been left out of the following items. Number your paper from 1 to 10. Copy each item onto your paper, and punctuate it properly.

1. Be careful   These steps are slippery
2. How many times have you tried to win a race
3. Fowler's *Modern English Usage* is an extremely useful reference book
4. This new model runs on diesel fuel
5. Well   This is more than we expected
6. She asked if I had achieved my goal
7. He took that course last year
8. Benjamin Franklin, an American Renaissance man, was a statesman, scientist, inventor, and author
9. What   You expect this panel to believe that
10. Choose the building materials for the fence carefully

■ Other Situations Requiring a Period or a Question Mark

Most abbreviations end with a period.

Use a period to end most abbreviations.

If you do not know whether a period is required after a particular abbreviation, refer to Section 11.2 on abbreviations.

ABBREVIATIONS WITH PERIODS: in. Dr. etc. Sr. C.O.D. a.m.
D.D.S. Ave. Mrs. Tex. Co. B.C.

ABBREVIATIONS WITHOUT PERIODS: FBI   mm   NASA   TX

When an abbreviation ending with a period is found at the end of a sentence, do not add another period as an end mark.

INCORRECT: The speaker will be Adam Martin, Jr..

CORRECT: The speaker will be Adam Martin, Jr.

If an end mark other than a period is required, however, add the end mark.

EXAMPLE: Is the speaker Adam Martin, Jr.?

Periods are also used after numbers and letters in outlines.

Use a period after numbers and letters in outlines.

EXAMPLE: I. Maintaining your pet's health
A. Diet
1. For a puppy
2. For a mature dog
B. Exercise
C. Cleanliness
D. Preventing accidents

Occasionally you may wish to use a fact in your writing that you cannot verify. A question mark within parentheses can be used to show uncertainty in such cases. It should only be used, however, when the fact cannot be verified.

Use a question mark in parentheses (?) after a fact or statistic to show its uncertainty.

EXAMPLE: Mohammed was born in 570 (?) A.D.

EXERCISE B: Using Periods and Question Marks in Other Situations.
Copy the following items onto your paper, adding the necessary end marks. Indicate uncertainty about any years included in the items. If an item does not need any additional periods or question marks within parentheses, write *correct*.

1. The tiny toad was 15 mm long.
2. Are more space flights by astronauts being planned by NASA?
3. Confucius, who died in 479 B.C., was a Chinese philosopher and teacher.
4. The calendar page gave the following date: Oct. 26.
5. The package was addressed to Mr Luis Ramirez, 23 Grove St , St Paul, Minn.
6. At 10:30 P M the baby finally fell asleep.
7. I Vitamin A
   - A. Sources
     - 1. Milk, butter, eggs
     - 2. Green and yellow vegetables
   - B. Value
     - 1. Preserves health of skin
     - 2. Preserves health of mucous membranes
8. The date for the marathon for the benefit of the March of Dimes was listed as Sat , Apr 17 at 8 a m.
9. Jeanette Rankin was the first woman elected to the U S Congress.
10. The book was written by the well-known historian Arthur Schlesigner, Jr.

APPLICATION: Using End Marks Correctly in Your Own Writing.
Choose a topic and write a paragraph about it in which you use each of the end marks appropriately at least once.

Commas 12.2

This section presents the rules governing the use of commas. To use commas correctly, you must have a thorough knowledge of sentence structure. Studying this section can help you master the conventions governing the use of commas and, at the same time, serve as a review of some basic elements of sentence structure.

■ Commas to Separate Basic Elements in Sentences

Commas are used to separate certain basic elements in sentences. These include independent clauses in compound sentences, items in a series, and coordinate adjectives. First, consider commas used to separate the independent clauses in a compound sentence.

Compound Sentences.   Two or more independent clauses properly joined and punctuated form a compound sentence. The independent clauses are often joined by coordinate conjunctions: *and, but, for, nor, or, so,* and *yet.* Commas are then used to separate the independent clauses.

> **Use a comma before the conjunction to separate two or more independent clauses in a compound sentence.**

EXAMPLES: My cousin travels all over the United States each summer, but my brother prefers to stay at home near his friends.

The baseball team has played well so far, and the team hopes to win the remaining three games of the season.

Remember to use both a comma and a coordinate conjunction in a compound sentence. Using only a comma would result in a run-on sentence.

Notice also that the ideas in both of the independent clauses in each of the preceding examples are related. You should never construct a compound sentence from two unrelated clauses.

Finally, take care not to confuse a compound sentence with a simple sentence containing a compound verb. Compare the following examples.

SIMPLE SENTENCE WITH A COMPOUND VERB: David brought his car in for repairs and waited for it for three hours.

COMPOUND SENTENCE: David brought his car in for repairs, and he waited for it for three hours.

Items in a Series.   Next, look at the rule governing items in a series. A series consists of three or more words, phrases, or subordinate clauses of a similar kind.

Use commas to separate three or more words, phrases, or clauses in a series.

WORDS IN A SERIES: Flounder, scrod, bluefish, and mackerel are all in season.

Her performance was flawless, exciting, and inspiring.

PHRASES IN A SERIES: Running at first, walking part way, and limping the final steps, I reached the railroad station as the train pulled in.

To check the accuracy of the experiment, we took four readings: at dawn, at noon, at dusk, and at midnight.

SUBORDINATE CLAUSES IN A SERIES: The Labor Department's report stressed that workers were excessively crowded, that the machines lacked safety guards, and that the ventilation system was inadequate.

Notice that the number of commas in each of the preceding series is one less than the number of items in the series. If there are three items in a series, two commas are used. If there are four items in a series, three commas are used.

It would also be correct to omit the last comma before the conjunction. If you use this alternative style, be sure to use it consistently, unless a comma is needed before the conjunction to avoid confusion.

CORRECT: We enjoyed the sparkling waves, sunshine and cool ocean breezes.

CONFUSING: We enjoyed the sparkling waves, cool ocean breezes and sunshine.

ALWAYS CLEAR: We enjoyed the sparkling waves, cool ocean breezes, and sunshine.

When conjunctions are used to separate all the items in a series, no commas are needed.

EXAMPLE: We ate hot dogs and baked beans and potato salad at the picnic.

Avoid commas also between items such as *salt and pepper* that are paired so often that they are thought of as one item.

EXAMPLE: Please put the silverware, salt and pepper, and napkins on the table.

Coordinate Adjectives.   Sometimes two or more adjectives are used together. *Coordinate adjectives*, adjectives equal in rank, are separated by commas.

Use commas to separate adjectives of equal rank.

COORDINATE ADJECTIVES: a dark, dismal hallway

a tall, attractive, young woman

An adjective is equal in rank to another if the word *and* can be inserted between them without changing the meaning of the sentence. Another way to test whether or not adjectives are coordinate is to reverse their order. If the sentence still sounds correct, the adjectives are of equal rank. Test the preceding examples using these two methods, and you will see that the adjectives are indeed coordinate.

If you cannot place the word *and* between adjectives or reverse their order without changing the meaning of the sentence, they are called *cumulative adjectives*. Do not use a comma between cumulative adjectives.

Do not use commas to separate adjectives that must stay in a specific order.

CUMULATIVE ADJECTIVES: a new winter coat

many successful people

EXERCISE A: Punctuating Simple and Compound Sentences. Some of the following sentences are compound and need a comma to separate the independent clauses. Copy only the compound sentences onto your paper, adding the necessary commas. If a sentence is not compound, write *correct*.

1. My mother and father arrived on time but we had to wait for the other relatives.
2. Our family traveled to Canada last summer and hopes to visit parts of Europe next year.
3. Leslie will graduate from high school this June and several of her other friends will graduate with her but her best friend will not graduate until next year.

4. These customers want their merchandise delivered today or they plan to cancel their orders.
5. We want to do some shopping at the mall and then go to a movie.
6. Our car needs a complete tuneup for it has been over six months since it has had one.
7. We neither wanted their assistance now nor would we accept it at some future time.
8. Mother baked three peach pies and froze them for the picnic.
9. Join us at the meeting this evening for it promises to be dramatic and exciting.
10. The sun rose early and shone until the afternoon shower.
11. Max will study art in Paris this summer and hopes to get a scholarship to the Sorbonne for next year.
12. Slim has excellent manners and he always impresses parents.
13. For my report I finished reading *Movies and Methods* and I am about to start *How to Read a Film.*
14. This sentence has two full independent clauses but the other has a compound verb.
15. The ambassador will arrive on the last flight tonight or he will be on an early flight tomorrow morning.
16. Our hockey team arrived early in Greenvale and waited for more than an hour for its bus.
17. I called my parents and told them I would be late.
18. We will take the exam on Friday and should have our grades next week.
19. Ann and Dorothy have been accepted at the same college and plan to be roommates next year.
20. Will you work this summer or vacation with your parents?

EXERCISE B: **Punctuating Items in a Series and Coordinate and Cumulative Adjectives.** Copy the following sentences onto your paper, adding the necessary commas to separate items in a series or coordinate adjectives. For any sentences that do not require commas, write *correct.*

1. The leader of the rock group was a thin blond youth.
2. Fresh fruit green vegetables lean meat and grain products were part of her diet.
3. She wore her new blue jeans.
4. Our advisor planned the trip chartered the bus and arranged the hotel reservations.
5. A well-planned thoughtful speech followed the brief introduction.

6. Battles were fought in New Jersey New York Pennsylvania Delaware and Virginia during the Revolutionary War.
7. These hardy plants grow equally well in window boxes in home gardens and in open fields.
8. The survey of the city showed that many buildings were abandoned that many small businesses had closed and that the streets needed repair.
9. For Christmas we bought Father a pair of soft pigskin gloves.
10. The vessel slipped into port on a rainy moonless night.

■ Commas to Set Off Added Elements in Sentences

Many individual words, phrases, and clauses also need to be set off with commas. These include introductory material, parenthetical expressions, and nonessential material. First, consider introductory material.

Introductory Material.   This type of material consists of words, phrases, or clauses that appear at the beginning of a sentence.

Use a comma after an introductory word, phrase, or clause.

The following examples show what types of introductory material should be set off with commas.

INTRODUCTORY WORDS:	Yes, we do expect to hear from them soon.
	No, there has been no response.
	Well, I was definitely surprised by her question.
NOUNS OF DIRECT ADDRESS:	Barry, will you be able to come to the meeting?
COMMON EXPRESSIONS:	Of course, you may go to the game with us.
INTRODUCTORY ADVERBS:	Hurriedly, they gathered up their books and papers.
	Patiently, the children's mother explained it to them again.
PREPOSITIONAL PHRASES: (of four or more words)	In the shade of the maple tree, a family of racoons lived.
	After the difficult exam, we were all exhausted.

In the beginning he was afraid.
In the very beginning, he was afraid.

PARTICIPIAL PHRASES: Moving slowly, she approached the injured puppy.

Seated next to each other in the auditorium, we introduced ourselves and started to chat.

INFINITIVE PHRASES: To choose the right book, I consulted the card catalog.

To finish my work on time, I will have to work through lunch.

ADVERBIAL CLAUSES: When she asked for permission to go, she was sure it would be denied.

If you collect coins, you may be interested in this one.

Only one comma should be used after a prepositional, participial, or infinitive phrase that is compound.

EXAMPLES: In the front pocket of his old jeans, he found the key.

Lost in the woods and frightened by the darkness, the campers huddled together near the fire.

To choose the correct word and to spell correctly, I often consult the dictionary.

Occasionally, you may also need to use a comma to prevent confusion with a prepositional phrase of less than four words.

CLEAR: In the morning we ate breakfast at a diner.

CONFUSING: In the rain drops seeped through the window frame.

CLEAR: In the rain, drops seeped through the window frame.

Parenthetical Expressions.   The second type of material that needs to be set off with commas is made up of parenthetical expressions. Parenthetical expressions are words or phrases that interrupt the flow of a sentence.

Use commas to set off parenthetical expressions.

The following examples show various types of parenthetical expressions. Notice that they may come at the end of a sentence or in the middle. When a parenthetical expression appears in the middle of a sentence, two commas are needed to set it off from the rest of the sentence.

NOUNS OF DIRECT ADDRESS: Will you have lunch with us today, Ted?

I wonder, Dr. Green, if I have any cavities?

CERTAIN ADVERBS: The tickets were all sold a week before the concert, however.

We were not able, therefore, to buy one.

COMMON EXPRESSIONS: I listened to the teacher's explanation as carefully as anyone in the room, I think.

He gave us, in fact, all the information we required.

CONTRASTING EXPRESSIONS: Tom is seventeen, not eighteen.

Lisa's acting ability, not her attractiveness, got her the lead in the school play.

Nonessential Material.   Finally, consider the need for commas with nonessential material. Appositives, participial phrases, and adjective clauses can be either essential or nonessential. (The terms *restrictive* and *nonrestrictive* are also used to refer to these two kinds of materials.) Essential material, which is necessary to the meaning of a sentence, is not set off with commas.

ESSENTIAL APPOSITIVE: The singer *Diana Ross* is also a talented actress.

ESSENTIAL PARTICIPIAL PHRASE: The woman *buying the tomatoes* is my mother.

ESSENTIAL ADJECTIVE CLAUSE: The report *that the committee will consider today* was prepared by members of the first aid squad.

The preceding examples illustrate three kinds of essential elements. In the first example, the appositive *Diana Ross* identifies one singer from all others. In the next example, the participial phrase *buying the tomatoes* identifies a specific woman. In the last example, the adjective clause *that the committee will consider today* identifies a specific report. Because they limit or restrict identification to the person or thing described in the appositive, participial phrase, or adjective clause, these items are all essential. They cannot be removed without changing the meaning of the sentences, so they require no commas.

Nonessential elements also provide information, but that information is not essential to the meaning of the sentence. Because nonessential elements do not alter the meaning of the rest of the sentence and are not necessary for purpose of identification, they require commas to set them off.

Use commas to set off nonessential expressions.

NONESSENTIAL APPOSITIVE: Diana Ross, the singer, is also a talented actress.

NONESSENTIAL PARTICIPIAL PHRASE: My mother, buying the tomatoes, is a marvelous cook.

NONESSENTIAL ADJECTIVE CLAUSE: The first aid squad's report, which the committee will consider today, took six months to prepare.

The nonessential elements in the preceding examples are interesting, but they are not necessary to the main ideas in the sentences. *Diana Ross, my mother,* and *the first aid squad's report* clearly identify the items under discussion. The nonessential elements, therefore, are set off with commas.

EXERCISE C: **Setting off Introductory Material.** Copy the following sentences onto your paper, adding the necessary commas. If a sentence requires no commas, write *correct*.

1. To practice my speech I rehearsed it in front of a mirror.
2. Cautioned by her mother and warned by her friends Betsy drove slowly through the busy intersection.
3. At the supermarket checkout counters always seem to have long lines.
4. In the kitchen we packed provisions for our camping trip.
5. If the weather is pleasant we hope to attend a concert in the park tonight.
6. George will you help at the bazaar on Saturday?
7. Of course the judge will punish the offenders.
8. Weakened by the storm the battered merchant ship limped into port two weeks late.
9. Delightedly Steve opened the door and greeted his cousins.
10. No I never thought we would have a chance to win the first prize.

EXERCISE D: **Setting Off Parenthetical Expressions.** Copy the following sentences onto your paper, inserting any commas needed to set off parenthetical expressions.

1. There are five houses on that street now not the two you remember.

2. You are responsible nevertheless for doing all the assignments.
3. Professor Watkins is I believe one of the top economic experts in the country.
4. Have you been able to find the information Miss Regan?
5. Most of us were surprised in fact by his unusual frankness.
6. His irresponsible behavior not his lack of ability caused his problems.
7. It seems to me however that she should have consulted you first.
8. The results we hope will be beneficial to everyone.
9. You know Mrs. Bennett we will do everything we can to help.
10. Please be ready therefore to present your report about space exploration on Friday.

EXERCISE E: **Distinguishing Between Essential and Nonessential Material.** Copy the following sentences onto your paper, inserting any commas needed to set off nonessential material. If a sentence contains essential material, which does not require commas, write *correct*.

1. The surf cresting against the sea wall damaged a number of summer cottages.
2. O'Hare Airport which is one of the busiest airports in the world has severe traffic problems.
3. The building chosen for demolition was in the center of the block.
4. This is Dr. Stevenson whom you heard lecture about conserving our resources last week.
5. Heinrich Schliemann who unearthed the ruins at Troy and Mycenae wanted to excavate the Minoan ruins on Crete.
6. I quickly recognized the road that you described in your letter.
7. The three little boys playing near the fence all live on the next street.
8. The Interstate Commerce Commission which was authorized by Congress in 1887 has the power to regulate commerce among the states.
9. The original Fort Laramie built by fur traders William Sublette and Robert Campbell was established in 1834 near the junction of the North Platte and Laramie rivers in what is now the state of Wyoming.
10. The two books recommended by our science teacher are available in the library.

■ Commas in Other Situations

You will also need to use commas in your writing in other situations.

Dates.   When you write dates made up of several parts, use commas to avoid confusion.

> When a date is made up of two or more parts, use a comma after each item except in the case of a month followed by a day.

EXAMPLES: My sister graduated from high school on June 16, 1980, and my brother graduated from college on June 16, 1981.

Friday, August 23, was the day we met.

If dates contain only months and years, you may omit the commas if you wish.

EXAMPLES: In July, 1981, I started my part-time job.

In July 1981 I started my part-time job.

Geographical Names.   Geographical names also may have several parts.

> When a geographical name is made up of two or more parts, use a comma after each item.

EXAMPLES: My aunt who lives in Houston, Texas, is coming to visit.

Vancouver, British Columbia, Canada, is a beautiful city.

Titles After a Name.   Whenever you use a title after the name of a person or a company, you will have to add commas.

> When a name is followed by one or more titles, use a comma after the name and after each title.

EXAMPLES: Susan Martini, Ph.D., teaches chemistry.

Charles W. Higgins, Jr., M.D., is an anesthesiologist.

Addresses.   Commas are also necessary when you write addresses.

Use a comma after each item in an address made up of two or more parts.

EXAMPLES: Send a copy of the report to Mrs. Robert Brooks, 145 River Road, Jacksonville, Florida   32211.

Commas are placed after the name, street, and city in the preceding example. Instead of inserting a comma between the state and the ZIP code, extra space is left between them.

Most commas are unnecessary when an address is included in a letter or on an envelope or package. You still need a comma, however, between the city and the state.

EXAMPLE: Mrs. Robert Brooks
145 River Road
Jacksonville, Florida   32211

Salutations and Closings.   Conventions also govern the use of commas in other parts of letters.

Use a comma after the salutation in a social letter and after the closing in all letters.

SALUTATIONS: Dear Emily,   Dear Uncle Frank,   My dear Friend,

CLOSINGS: Yours truly,   Sincerely,   Your friend,

Large Numbers.   Using commas makes large numbers easier to read.

With numbers of more than three digits, use a comma after every third digit counting from the right.

EXAMPLES: 3,823 students

205,000 gallons

2,674,970 tons

You should not, however, use commas with ZIP codes, telephone numbers, page numbers, or serial numbers.

ZIP CODE: 07632

TELEPHONE NUMBER: 805-555-6224

Elliptical Sentences.   In elliptical sentences words that are understood are left out. Inserting commas in elliptical sentences makes them easier to read.

Use a comma to indicate the words left out of an elliptical sentence.

EXAMPLE: Alan did his homework slowly and carefully; Fred, quickly and carelessly.

The words *did his homework* have been omitted from the second clause of the elliptical sentence. The comma has been inserted in their place, however, so the meaning is still clear.

Direct Quotations.   Another use of commas is to indicate where direct quotations begin and end.

Use commas to set off a direct quotation from the rest of a sentence.

EXAMPLES: "You left for school early this morning," commented Ann's father.

She responded, "I had choir practice before school."

"I hope," Ann's father said, "that the audience will realize how hard you have all worked to make the concert a success."

For Clarity.   Finally, you may need to use commas to prevent readers from misunderstanding a sentence.

Use a comma to prevent a sentence from being misunderstood.

UNCLEAR: In the reservoir water is stored.

CLEAR: In the reservoir, water is stored.

NOTE ABOUT THE CARELESS USE OF COMMAS: You have now seen many rules governing the use of commas. Studying these rules will help you use commas correctly in your writing. Knowing the rules will also help you avoid using unnecessary commas. Because commas appear so frequently in writing, some people are tempted to use them where no commas are required. Be sure you know why you are inserting commas each time you use them.

The following examples illustrate some ways commas may be misused. Avoid making these mistakes in your own writing.

MISUSED WITH AN ADJECTIVE AND NOUN: After our long hike, we enjoyed the cool, refreshing, breeze.

CORRECT: After our long hike, we enjoyed the cool, refreshing breeze.

MISUSED WITH A COMPOUND SUBJECT: During the subway strike, my friend Nancy, and her sister Julia, walked to school every day.

CORRECT: During the subway strike, my friend Nancy and her sister Julia walked to school every day.

MISUSED WITH A COMPOUND VERB: The center fielder leaped as high as he could, and caught the ball.

CORRECT: The center fielder leaped as high as he could and caught the ball.

MISUSED WITH A COMPOUND OBJECT: She bought a quilted jacket with knitted cuffs, and a hood.

CORRECT: She bought a quilted jacket with knitted cuffs and a hood.

MISUSED WITH PHRASES: Reading the letter, and thinking of how he would answer it, Brian never heard his mother call him for dinner.

CORRECT: Reading the letter and thinking of how he would answer it, Brian never heard his mother call him for dinner.

MISUSED WITH CLAUSES: He discussed what nutrients are essential to good health, and which foods will best supply them.

CORRECT: He discussed what nutrients are essential to good health and which foods will best supply them.

EXERCISE F: Using Commas in Other Situations. Copy the following sentences onto your paper, inserting the necessary commas.

1. The contestants must send their entries before May 30 1982 to Contest Box 16 Chicago Illinois   60607.
2. Harold Andre Sr. lives in Santa Barbara California.
3. In 1978 the United States imported 8230000 barrels of oil.
4. In one day 5675 people called the toll-free phone number 800-555-0220 to pledge money for the charity drive.
5. Jim spent his savings on a new bicycle; Pat on a typewriter.
6. "We'll be late" Virginia worried "unless we hurry."
7. In the dark stairways can prove hazardous.
8. Karen Wilson D.D.S. will open an office in this building.
9. Paul said "On Saturday I will mow the lawn."
10. Montreal Quebec Canada has a population of approximately 1214300 people.

APPLICATION 1:Using Commas in a Social Letter. Copy the following friendly letter onto your paper, inserting the necessary commas.

> 736 Williams Avenue
> Dayton Ohio   45402
> August 5 1981

Dear Margaret
　　Well after almost six weeks of travel my family and I have returned from our exciting trip to Egypt. Returning to the United States we were struck by the difference in cultures. It felt I think like going from an old world to a new.
　　Naturally we saw all the famous sights: the pyramids and sphinx at Giza the temples of Karnak and Luxor the Aswan Dam and of course Cairo. Much to my surprise I was fascinated by Cairo the capital city of Egypt. I visited the Zoological Garden the Egyptian Museum the Cairo Tower Mohammed Ali Mosque and many other interesting places.
　　My mother bought an antique gold bracelet. As if that weren't enough she also invested in a caftan called a galabias and a small brass tray.
　　I'm looking forward to your visit next week and I'll tell you about the rest of my experiences then.

> Affectionately
> Brad

APPLICATION 2: Using Commas Correctly in Your Own Writing. Construct ten original sentences according to the following directions.

1. Write a compound sentence joined by the conjunction *but*.
2. Write a sentence containing a series of three phrases.
3. Write a sentence containing two coordinate adjectives.
4. Write a sentence containing two cumulative adjectives.
5. Write a sentence beginning with a participial phrase.
6. Write a sentence containing a parenthetical expression.
7. Write a sentence containing a nonessential appositive.
8. Write a sentence that includes a direct quotation.
9. Write an elliptical sentence.
10. Write a sentence that requires a comma to prevent mis-understanding.

12.3   Semicolons and Colons

This section presents the rules governing the use of semicolons (;) and colons (:). Knowing how to use a semicolon correctly in your writing can help you handle situations in which you need to establish a relationship between independent clauses. Using semicolons can also help you avoid confusion in sentences that contain other internal punctuation. Knowing the rules governing the use of colons can help you use colons correctly as introductory devices to point ahead to additional information as well as in other special situations.

■ The Semicolon

A semicolon establishes a relationship between two or more independent clauses in a compound sentence. It should be used only when the two independent clauses are closely related in both thought and structure.

> **Use a semicolon to join independent clauses that are not already joined by the conjunctions *and, or, nor, for, but, so,* or *yet.***

The most common way for writers to join independent clauses is by using one of the coordinate conjunctions mentioned in the preceding rule. The clauses are then separated with a comma.

EXAMPLE: We explored the attic together, and we were amazed at all the useless junk we found there.

When no coordinate conjunction is used, however, independent clauses should be joined with a semicolon.

EXAMPLE: We explored the attic together; we were amazed at all the useless junk we found there.

Sometimes, the second independent clause may begin with a conjunctive adverb or a transitional expression. Conjunctive adverbs include such words as *also, furthermore, accordingly, besides, consequently, however, instead, namely, nevertheless, otherwise, similarly, therefore, indeed,* and *thus.* Transitional expressions include *as a result, first, second, at this time, for instance, for example, in fact, on the other hand, that is, in conclusion,* and *finally.*

Use a semicolon to join independent clauses separated by either a conjunctive adverb or a transitional expression.

CONJUNCTIVE ADVERB: We visited seven countries in only two weeks; consequently, we missed many interesting historical sites.

TRANSITIONAL EXPRESSION: She never knew his name; in fact, she really had no interest in meeting him.

In both examples the conjunctive adverb or transitional expression is separated from the rest of the second independent clause by a comma. A comma is used because the conjunctive adverb or transitional expression serves as an introductory expression in the second independent clause.

A semicolon is also used to avoid confusion when independent clauses or items in a series already contain a number of commas.

Consider the use of a semicolon to avoid confusion when independent clauses or items in a series already contain commas.

INDEPENDENT CLAUSES: The forest, filled with thick underbrush, seemed impassable; and the hungry, tired pioneer family slumped to the ground in despair.

ITEMS IN A SERIES: I was convinced that we had won when I heard the music of the band, playing our victory march; the jubilant players, clapping and shouting; and the roar of spectators, rising to their feet.

In the last example, semicolons are used instead of commas to separate the three major parts of the series. Commas are used within each of the major parts to set off the modifying participial phrases. When items in a series contain nonessential appositives or adjective phrases, you will also need to use semicolons to separate the major parts of the series.

EXERCISE A: Punctuating Compound Sentences and Items in a Series. Some of the following sentences need semicolons to join independent clauses or to separate items in a series. Other sentences require commas. Copy the sentences onto your paper, inserting the necessary semicolons or commas.

1. The committee was unhappy with the decision nevertheless, they understood why it had been made.
2. Jean wanted the position in the firm but she was disturbed about some of the working conditions.
3. Ben struggled up the steep, rocky hill and when he reached the top, Ben collapsed in a heap on the ground.
4. The clipper, battered by the vicious storm, fought a losing battle the main mast, weakened by the winds, crashed to the deck.
5. My cousin Hank, who is an attorney in Atlanta my friend Betty, who lives next door and Betty's brother, who is home from college for the weekend, are coming for dinner tonight.
6. I plan to serve spaghetti and meat balls salad and garlic bread.
7. The storm washed out the road therefore, it took us an additional hour to reach the cabin.
8. Bran contains large amounts of fiber and nutritionists recommend adding it to our diets.
9. The children had looked forward eagerly to moving however, they were disappointed when they learned that few children lived in their new neighborhood.
10. After studying every night for a week, I felt confident that I would do well on the test yet I still felt slightly nervous as I took my seat in class.

■ The Colon

Colons are used in several situations. Primarily, colons serve as introductory devices.

Use a colon before a list of items following an independent clause.

EXAMPLES: As part of our assignment, we had to interview a group of experts: an economist, a political scientist, a business manager, and a consumer advocate.

His travels took him to a number of continents: Africa, Australia, Asia, and South America.

Notice that each list in these examples follows an independent clause. If general terms such as *a group of experts* or *a number of continents* were not used, colons would not be appropriate since you would no longer have independent clauses preceding the lists.

EXAMPLES: As part of our assignment, we had to interview an economist, a political scientist, a business manager, and a consumer advocate.

His travels took him to Africa, Australia, Asia, and South America.

Sometimes an independent clause preceding a list ends in a phrase such as *the following* or *the following items*. These phrases should signal you to use a colon to introduce the list that follows.

Colons are also used to introduce certain kinds of quotations.

Use a colon to introduce a quotation that is formal or lengthy or a quotation that does not contain a "he said/she said" phrase.

EXAMPLES: Chief Justice Holmes wrote: "It is only through free debate and free exchange of ideas that government remains responsive to the will of the people and peaceful change is effected."

The poem by Elizabeth Barrett Browning began: "How do I love thee? Let me count the ways."

Dialogue or a casual remark should be introduced by a comma, even if the quotation is lengthy. Use the colon for more formal quotations or for those which do not contain a "he said/she said" phrase.

A colon may also be used to introduce a sentence that explains the sentence that precedes it.

Use a colon to introduce a sentence that summarizes or explains the sentence before it.

EXAMPLE: His explanation for being late was believable: He had had a flat tire on the way.

When a colon introduces a complete sentence, as in this example, notice that the sentence introduced by the colon starts with a capital letter.

Another item introduced by a colon is a formal appositive that follows an independent clause.

Use a colon to introduce a formal appositive that follows an independent clause.

EXAMPLE: I had finally decided on a career: nursing.

Because the colon is a stronger punctuation mark than a comma, using the colon gives more emphasis to the appositive it introduces than a comma does.

Colons are also used in a variety of other situations.

Use a colon in a number of special writing situations.

The following chart presents examples of colons used in special writing situations. Study the examples carefully, so you will be able to use colons correctly when these situations arise.

SPECIAL SITUATIONS REQUIRING COLONS	
Numerals Giving the Time:	1:30 A.M. 9:15 P.M.
References to Periodicals: (Volume Number: Page Number)	*Scientific American* 74:12 *Sports Illustrated* 53:15
Biblical References: (Chapter Number:Verse Number)	I Corinthians 13:13 Exodus 14:21
Subtitles of Books and Magazines:	*A Field Guide to the Birds: Eastern Land and Water Birds*
Salutations in Business Letters:	Dear Mrs. Gordon: Dear Sir:
Labels Used to Signal Important Ideas:	Danger: High voltage
References to Publishers in One Style of Bibliography:	New York: Alfred A. Knopf

EXERCISE B: Using Colons. Copy each of the following sentences onto your paper, inserting the necessary colons.

1. The office manager gave us a list of needed supplies paper clips, correction fluid, rubber bands, and brass fasteners.
2. School was closed because of the bad weather a raging blizzard.
3. Warning This product is for external use only.
4. The Boeing 727 taxied to a landing at exactly 7 05 A.M.
5. The full title of Jozef Garlinski's book is *The Enigma The Inside Story of the German Enigma Codes and How the Allies Broke Them.*
6. Historian Samuel Eliot Morison describes the simultaneous deaths of Jefferson and Adams on July 4, 1826 "The lives of Thomas Jefferson and John Adams, the one eighty-three and the other ninety years old, were flickering to a close. Could they live until the Fourth, the fiftieth anniversary of the adoption of that great Declaration for which they were jointly responsible? All America was praying that they would."
7. She recited Matthew 6 14 and 6 15.
8. The coach's explanation was simple and direct The team, as a result of last year's record, had decided to go with the younger players in an effort to rebuild.
9. His historical research took him to a number of countries England, Belgium, France, Austria, and Germany.
10. The book you need is called *The Revolution Remembered Eyewitness Accounts of the War for Independence* edited by John C. Dann.

APPLICATION 1: Using Semicolons and Colons Correctly. Copy each of the following sentences onto your paper, inserting the necessary semicolons or colons.

1. Joanne purchased all the picnic supplies soda, potato chips, frankfurters, chopped meat, rolls, and fresh fruit.
2. The family agreed with the doctor's prognosis nevertheless, they decided to get another doctor's opinion.
3. The United States Postal Service issued an unusually attractive commemorative stamp It depicts General Bernardo de Galvez at the Battle of Mobile in 1780.
4. The first record contains selections from the group's latest concert the second record is a compilation of old hits.
5. The narrator was a well-known scientist and author Carl Sagan.
6. The President welcomed the foreign dignitary "The people of the United States welcome you and hope that your visit will be a pleasant and productive one."

7. This is her plan She wants to spend two days in Milan and a week in Florence.
8. Mary Ellen invited Bill, who enjoyed playing cards Sarah, who loved to dance and Glen, who didn't enjoy parties at all.
9. There are two direct flights to Ireland, one leaving at 1130 p.m. and the other at 2 05 a.m.
10. Six pupils took the state scholarship examination this morning the rest of the group decided to wait for the next test.

APPLICATION 2: Using Semicolons and Colons in Your Own Writing. Write a paragraph about one of the following topics: a favorite relative, your plans for next year, an interesting place to visit, a hobby. Include in your paragraph semicolons used in two different ways and colons used in three different ways.

12.4 Quotation Marks and Underlining

You will often wish to use direct quotations in your writing, for they can greatly enliven short stories and other works of fiction. Direct quotations provide the reader with the actual words of a character. Readers learn much about the character, both from what he or she says and from the way he or she speaks. Is the character truthful? Are the character's words the opposite of his or her actions? The reader learns to judge.

Direct quotations can also be used to support or refute ideas and arguments in nonfiction. When you quote directly from an expert in a particular field, you help to prove the point you are trying to make.

This section illustrates different ways to write and punctuate direct quotations. It also explains the use of underlining and quotation marks to indicate different types of titles, names, and words. Studying the rules and examples in this section can help you improve any kind of writing you do.

■ Using Quotation Marks with Direct Quotations

There are two ways in which you can quote another person's words. One way is to reproduce the person's exact words or thoughts. This is called a direct quotation. When you give the general meaning of another person's words or thoughts but use your own words, it is called an indirect quotation.

> A **direct quotation** represents a person's exact speech or thoughts and is enclosed in quotation marks (" "). An **indirect quotation** reports the general meaning of what a person said or thought and does not require quotation marks.

DIRECT QUOTATION: "If I am elected," said the candidate, "I will sponsor a bill to improve local public transportation."

INDIRECT QUOTATION: The candidate said that she wanted to see an improvement in local transportation.

Both types of quotations, direct and indirect, are acceptable when you write. Using a direct quotation when it is possible to do so, however, results in more interesting and convincing writing.

The rule for an uninterrupted direct quotation is a simple one.

> Use quotation marks before and after an uninterrupted direct quotation.

EXAMPLE: "I may not be true to my ideals always, but I believe in the law of love, and I believe you can do nothing with hatred."
—Clarence Darrow

Notice that this quotation begins with a capital letter. The same is true of every complete sentence of quoted material.

Many direct quotations contain not only the actual words of the speaker but also words identifying the speaker. These identifying words or phrases are called "he said/she said" phrases or conversational tags.

CONVERSATIONAL TAGS: she asked   he agreed   they replied

my father explained   Jenny shrieked

the President announced   I whispered

The possibilities for conversational tags are limitless and depend solely upon the writer's inventiveness. All conversational tags, however, have one common characteristic: They are never enclosed in quotation marks.

Conversational tags may appear in various positions in relation to direct quotations. First, consider a conversational tag used as an introductory expression.

When an introductory expression precedes a direct quotation, place a comma or colon after the introductory expression and write the quotation as a full sentence.

EXAMPLE: My mother warned, "You're now an adult and must be responsible for your own actions."

If you use something other than a conversational tag as your introductory expression or if the introductory conversational tag is more formal in tone, use a colon instead of a comma to set it off.

EXAMPLE: Bert rose to his feet: "I nominate Marge Wheatley for class president."

At the end of the meeting, Marge spoke of her willingness to serve: "I hope to lead this class in carrying out many exciting activities."

Sometimes a conversational tag may appear as a concluding expression.

When a concluding expression follows a direct quotation, write the quotation as a full sentence ending with a comma, question mark, or exclamation mark inside the quotation mark, and then write the concluding expression.

EXAMPLE: "You're now an adult and must be responsible for your own actions," my mother warned.

Notice in this example that a comma comes before the closing quotation mark and a period follows the conversational tag.

Finally, you may use a conversational tag to interrupt the words of a direct quotation.

When a direct quotation of one sentence is interrupted, end the first part of the direct quotation with a comma and a quotation mark, place a comma after the interrupting expression, and then proceed with a new quotation mark and the rest of the quotation.

EXAMPLE: "You are now an adult," my mother warned, "and must be
responsible for your own actions."

You will notice in this example that, when a quotation is
interrupted by a conversational tag, two sets of quotation
marks are used to enclose the quotation and two commas are
used to set off the conversational tag.

Sometimes a conversational tag interrupts a quotation several sentences in length.

**When two sentences in a direct quotation are separated by an
interrupting expression, end the first quoted sentence with a
comma, question mark, or exclamation mark and a quotation
mark; place a period after the interrupter; and then write the
second quoted sentence as a full quotation.**

EXAMPLE: "You are now an adult," warned my mother. "You must
be responsible for your own actions."

Writers usually make use of all three positions in which
conversational tags may be placed. Using different positions
for these expressions helps to add variety to a writer's sentence
structure.

It is also possible, of course, to quote just part of a sentence
directly.

**When a quoted fragment is included in a sentence, enclose
the quoted fragment in quotation marks, but do not use commas to set the fragment off from the rest of the sentence. Capitalize the first word of the fragment only when it falls at the beginning of the sentence or when it is a proper noun or a proper
adjective.**

EXAMPLE: In an essay "The Town Dump," Wallace Stegner calls the
town dump of Whitemud, Saskatchewan, near his home
"our poetry and our history."

If a phrase or portion of a sentence is quoted at the beginning of a sentence, it would, of course, be capitalized.

EXAMPLE: "Our poetry and our history" is how Wallace Stegner refers to the town dump of Whitemud, Saskatchewan, in an
essay "The Town Dump."

EXERCISE A: **Enclosing Direct Quotations in Quotation Marks.** Copy each of the following sentences onto your paper, inserting the necessary quotation marks. If a sentence does not need any quotation marks, write *correct*. Remember that indirect quotations are not enclosed in quotation marks. The one quoted fragment has been underlined so you can tell where the quoted part begins and ends.

1. I am going to take my driver's test today, said Gloria.
2. My father replied, I will be happy to support you in your efforts.
3. Tell me what happened, I pleaded. I can't bear to be in suspense any longer.
4. The principal asked us if we were on our way to the band concert.
5. The bus driver sighed, Why don't you have the correct change?
6. The salesclerk told us the price of the piano.
7. I know, she answered. I just heard the news on the radio.
8. My little brother says I am <u>the world's bossiest sister</u>.
9. The judge rapped the gavel sharply on the bench: This courtroom will come to order.
10. I am so pleased you can visit us, wrote Joyce. We have all missed you since you moved away.

■ Using Other Punctuation Marks Correctly with Quotation Marks

Quotation marks are used with commas, semicolons, colons, and all the end marks. The location of the quotation marks in relation to the different punctuation marks varies, depending upon which punctuation mark is used. It is important, therefore, for you to know the following rules in order to place the punctuation marks correctly in your writing.

Always place a comma or a period inside the final quotation mark.

EXAMPLES: Marge said, "We're all ready to leave now."

"Give us just another minute," called Mother.

The rule for the use of semicolons and colons with quotation marks is just the opposite.

Always place a semicolon or colon outside the final quotation mark.

EXAMPLES: We were just informed about his "willingness to serve"; we are all pleased.

The convention gave her ideas its "strong endorsement": Most of the delegates promised to work for their adoption.

The use of question marks and exclamation marks with quotation marks requires a more complicated rule. Study the following rule and examples carefully.

Place a question mark or exclamation mark inside the final quotation mark if the end mark is part of the quotation and outside the final quotation mark if the end mark is not part of the quotation.

EXAMPLES: Larry shouted, "Where is my report?"

My sister retorted, "I will not be insulted!"

The question mark and exclamation mark in these examples are placed inside the final quotation mark because they apply only to the quoted portion of each sentence and not to the entire sentence. Now, compare these examples with the following.

EXAMPLES: Did the officer ask, "Where were you this morning"?

We were shocked when he cried, "Foul"!

In the first example, the question mark applies to the entire sentence. In the second example, the exclamation mark dramatizes the entire sentence.

EXERCISE B: Placing Other Punctuation Marks Correctly with Quotations. Copy the following sentences onto your paper, adding quotation marks and any other punctuation marks that are necessary. The quoted material is underlined so you can tell where it begins and ends.

1. H. L. Mencken called William Jennings Bryant the national tear duct
2. Did they ask What can we do to help
3. Father agreed I think you can be whatever you want to be

4. Winston Churchill described his Labor Party opponent as <u>a sheep in sheep's clothing</u>
5. She agreed to <u>work day and night</u> I never saw her so sincere   (Use a semicolon.)
6. <u>Hooray</u> she shouted <u>We won the game</u>
7. Oscar Wilde commented about a famous contemporary <u>Mr. Henry James writes fiction as if it were a painful duty</u>
8. <u>Is that clear</u> she asked
9. He said <u>You are the winner of the first prize</u> First prize was the camera I had always wanted   (Use a colon.)
10. Gertrude Stein gave the following advice to Ernest Hemingway <u>Remarks are not literature</u>

■ Using Quotation Marks in Special Situations

Special situations requiring quotation marks include dialogues or quotations of more than one paragraph. Sometimes, you may also wish to include only a portion of a person's words in a quotation, or you may need to include one quotation within another. Studying the following rules and examples will guide you in these special situations.

Dialogues and Long Quotations.   One of the best ways to move the action forward in a short story or novel is by using dialogue, the words of the characters themselves.

There are many ways to write dialogue. All writers, however, must follow the conventions for writing quotations so that their readers will be able to keep track of who is speaking.

When writing dialogue, begin a new paragraph with each change of speaker. Use quotation marks at the beginning and at the end of each speaker's words.

The following selection from *The Pearl* by John Steinbeck illustrates this rule. Read the passage through for meaning. Then go back and analyze it line by line.

EXAMPLE: The wind drove off the clouds and skimmed the sky clean and drifted the sand of the country like snow.
    Then Juan Tomas, when the evening approached, talked long with his brother. "Where will you go?"
    "To the north," said Kino. "I have heard that there are cities in the north."
    "Avoid the shore," said Juan Tomas. "They are making a party to search the shore. The men in the city will look for you. Do you still have the pearl?"

"I have it," said Kino. "And I will keep it. I might have given it as a gift, but now it is my misfortune and my life and I will keep it." His eyes were hard and cruel and bitter.

Coyotito whimpered and Juana muttered little magic words over him to make him silent.

"The wind is good," said Juan Tomas. "There will be no tracks."

They left quietly in the dark before the moon had risen.

As you can see, Steinbeck uses both dialogue and description to move the story forward. He also uses quotation marks according to the rules you have just learned.

In your reading of fiction, you will find many different styles of writing dialogue. Stop occasionally to analyze what you read. You can improve your own style of writing by analyzing the styles of others.

A different rule is followed when a writer uses several consecutive paragraphs of material quoted from the same person.

For quotations longer than a paragraph, put quotation marks at the beginning of each paragraph and at the end of the final paragraph.

EXAMPLE: John McPhee in his book *Giving Good Weight* has written an essay about a canoe trip down the St. John River in northern Maine. He introduces his readers to the river in the following way.

"We have been out here four days now and rain has been falling three. The rain appears to be ending. Breaks of blue are opening in the sky. Sunlight is coming through, and a wind is rising.

"I was not prepared for the St. John River, did not anticipate its size. I saw it as a narrow trail flowing north, twisting through the balsam and spruce—a small and intimate forest river, something like the Allagash, which is not many miles away. The river I imagined would have been river enough, but the real one, the actual St. John, is awesome and surprising. How could it, unaltered, be here still in the northeastern United States? There is nothing intimate about it. Cities could be standing beside it. It's a big river."

Notice in the preceding example that each paragraph of quoted material has quotation marks at its beginning. Only the last paragraph of quoted material, however, has quotation marks at the end.

Ellipsis Marks and Single Quotation Marks.   Sometimes a writer wants to present only a portion of a direct quotation. This special situation requires the use of ellipsis marks (. . .) to indicate that some of the words in the quotation are being omitted.

Use three ellipsis marks in a quotation to indicate that words have been omitted.

The following examples show a complete quotation and then ellipsis marks used at the beginning, in the middle, and at the end of a quotation.

AN ENTIRE QUOTATION: "The Black River, which cuts a winding course through southern Missouri's rugged Ozark highlands, lends its name to an area of great natural beauty. Within this expanse are old mines and quarries to explore, fast-running waters to canoe, and wooded trails to ride." —Suzanne Charlé

ELLIPSIS AT THE BEGINNING: Suzanne Charlé describes the Black River area in Missouri as having " . . . old mines and quarries to explore, fast-running waters to canoe, and wooded trails to ride."

ELLIPSIS IN THE MIDDLE: Suzanne Charlé wrote, "The Black River . . . lends its name to an area of great natural beauty. Within this expanse are old mines and quarries to explore, fast-running waters to canoe, and wooded trails to ride."

ELLIPSIS AT THE END: Suzanne Charlé wrote, "The Black River, which cuts a winding course through southern Missouri's rugged Ozark highlands, lends its name to an area of great natural beauty. . . . "

Notice in the last example that when a period is part of the omitted portion of the quotation, it is added along with the ellipsis marks to conclude the sentence.

Another special situation involving quotation marks occurs when a writer wishes to include one quotation within another.

Use single quotation marks for a quotation within a quotation.

EXAMPLES: "I will always remember my grandmother quoting Shelley, 'If winter comes, can spring be far behind?' "

"The doctor said, 'Good News!' and broke into a smile."

Writers often rephrase sentences in order to avoid using a quotation within a quotation. The same information can usually be presented in a less complicated way.

EXERCISE C: **Writing Original Dialogue.** Develop and write approximately one page of original dialogue. Use two or three different characters and include a few lines of description wherever necessary. Enclose the lines of dialogue in quotation marks. Include enough conversational tags so that there will be no confusion about who is speaking.

EXERCISE D: **Punctuating with Ellipsis Marks and Single Quotation Marks.** Copy each of the following sentences onto your paper, inserting double quotation marks or single quotation marks as required.

1. "Then the president turned to us and said, I'm afraid I must decline, and walked from the room."
2. Robert Benchley once jested, I haven't been abroad in so long that I almost speak English without an accent.
3. Katherine Mansfield begins the quotation with I want, by understanding myself, to understand others. . . .
4. "Later they studied Hamlet's famous soliloquy, which begins, To be, or not to be, that is the question."
5. Mark Twain ends his criticism of Sir Walter Scott: . . . He did measureless harm; more real and lasting harm, perhaps, than any other individual that ever wrote.
6. My mother said, I always wanted to sing at the Metropolitan Opera.
7. William Peden's review of *The Magic Barrel* reads, Bernard Malamud is completely himself, Malamud, and nobody else. . . . He possesses a gift for characterization that is often breathtaking.
8. "She asked, How did it happen? and burst into tears."
9. Writing about Bernard Shaw, Oscar Wilde quipped that he . . . hasn't an enemy in the world, and none of his friends like him.
10. "What do you think she meant when she said, You'll soon learn something surprising?"

■ Distinguishing Between the Uses of Underlining and Quotation Marks

Several methods are used to indicate different types of titles in various situations. These methods include italics, underlining, and quotation marks. Books, magazines, and other printed material use *italics,* a slanted type face, to indicate some types of titles. In handwritten or typed material, underlining would be used for the same titles. Other titles require the use of quotation marks. The following examples illustrate these methods of indicating titles.

PRINTED: I finally located Vachel Lindsay's poem "Abraham Lincoln Walks at Midnight" in *A Little Treasury of American Poetry.*

TYPEWRITTEN: I finally located Vachel Lindsay's poem "Abraham Lincoln Walks at Midnight" in <u>A Little Treasury of American Poetry</u>.

The following rules and examples will guide you in indicating titles correctly.

Underlining.   In your writing you will always need to underline certain titles.

Underline the titles of long written works, the titles of publications that are published as a single work, the titles of shows, and the titles of works of art.

BOOK: <u>To Kill a Mockingbird</u> is a modern classic.

PLAY: Did you see that performance of <u>Long Day's Journey into Night</u>?

MAGAZINE: I read <u>Time</u> and <u>Newsweek</u> to keep up with current events.

NEWSPAPER: She agreed with the story in the Los Angeles <u>Times</u>.

MUSICAL: She took her sister and brother to see <u>Peter Pan</u> and enjoyed it as much as they did.

PAINTING: Marc Chagall's painting <u>The Green Violinist</u> is one of my favorites.

NOTE ABOUT NEWSPAPER TITLES: The portion of the title that should be underlined will vary from newspaper to newspaper. <u>The New York Times</u> should always be fully capitalized and underlined. Other papers, however, can usually be treated in one of two ways: the Los Angeles <u>Times</u> or the <u>Los Angeles Times.</u> Unless you know the true name of a paper, choose one of these two forms and use it consistently.

Several other types of titles should also be underlined in handwritten or typed material.

Underline the names of individual air, sea, space, and land craft.

EXAMPLE: My brother served on the aircraft carrier <u>Kitty Hawk</u>.

Underlining is also used for foreign words.

Underline foreign words or phrases not yet accepted into English.

EXAMPLES: The voyage was so rough that they suffered from <u>mal de mer</u> constantly.

We put on our coats, said <u>auf Wiedersehen</u>, and hurried away.

Many foreign words and phrases are used so often by English-speaking people that they are now considered to be part of our language. Although these words may often retain their foreign pronunciation, they are no longer underlined or italicized.

NOT UNDERLINED: chili, amour, milieu, lasagna, plaza, gestalt, raconteur, teriyaki, andante, sauna

Consult a dictionary that contains foreign words and phrases if you are in doubt about whether a particular word or phrase should be underlined in your writing.

Letters, numbers, and words used as names for themselves are also underlined or italicized.

Underline letters, numbers, or words used as names for themselves.

EXAMPLES: I cannot tell the difference between her <u>i</u>'s and her <u>l</u>'s.

Is that an <u>8</u> or a <u>6</u>?

Avoid sprinkling your speech with <u>you know</u>.

In addition, you may occasionally wish to use underlining to emphasize a particular word or phrase in your writing.

Underline words that you wish to stress.

EXAMPLE: What a <u>ridiculous</u> situation!

In most cases, you should indicate emphasis not by underlining but by choosing and arranging your words with care. Reserve underlining for use only in special instances.

Quotation Marks.   Quotation marks are used to indicate other types of titles.

> Use quotation marks around the titles of short written works, episodes in a series, songs, parts of a long musical composition, or a work that is mentioned as part of a collection.

EXAMPLES: "Edward, Edward" and "Lord Randal" are two of my favorite English ballads.

Winifred Welles' essay "The Attics" describes the impression she received as a child exploring her grandfather's attic.

Read Chapter 1, "Dialogue and Action," in Understanding Drama.

"The Tell-Tale Heart" is a horror tale that made me shiver.

One of the most loved songs of the American people is Woody Guthrie's "This Land Is Your Land."

Titles Without Underlining or Quotation Marks.   There are two types of titles that require neither underlining nor quotation marks. One of these is made up of religious works.

> Do not underline or place in quotation marks mentions of the Bible, its books, divisions, or versions, or other holy scriptures, such as the Koran.

EXAMPLE: Her recitation of the Twenty-Third Psalm made us all feel better.

The second category of titles that requires neither underlining nor quotation marks is made up of various kinds of government documents.

> Do not underline or place in quotation marks the titles of government charters, alliances, treaties, acts, statutes, or reports.

EXAMPLES: Have you ever read the Declaration of Independence?

The Versailles Treaty was signed in 1919 and officially ended World War I.

EXERCISE E: Using Underlining and Quotations Marks in Sentences. Copy the following sentences onto your paper, underlining or enclosing in quotation marks those titles and other words that require such treatment. For those items that require neither, write *correct*.

1. For years Americans have quoted maxims from Franklin's Poor Richard's Almanac.
2. The French expression le style c'est l'homme was one of her favorite sayings.
3. The Twentieth Century Limited traveled between New York and Chicago.
4. I'm Nobody! Who Are You? is one of Emily Dickinson's best known poems.
5. The opening song in the musical Cabaret, Willkommen, has been called one of the most effective opening numbers of all time.
6. The Christian Science Monitor is a newspaper with a nationwide readership.
7. I just finished reading Edwin Arlington Robinson's poem Luke Havergal.
8. Don't use too many and's in your writing.
9. Air Force II is the plane used by the Vice President and other dignitaries.
10. The New York Times has great political influence.
11. Patti Page and Anne Murray both recorded the song Tennessee Waltz.
12. Shelley's poem To a Skylark begins with the famous line "Hail to thee, blithe Spirit!"
13. Thomas Paine's Common Sense was one of the most influential pamphlets ever written.
14. Chrome Yellow and Point Counter Point are two Huxley novels reflecting the author's disillusionment after World War I.
15. The Dictionary of Literary Terms is a useful reference work for the student of literature.
16. The One Hundredth Psalm was read during the service.
17. Macbeth and Hamlet are included in the curriculum.
18. Beethoven's Symphony No. 1 in C Major, Op. 21, has many of the characteristics of a Mozart symphony.
19. The North Atlantic Treaty Organization is an alliance of European countries that includes the United States.
20. The Seeds of Content in Sports Illustrated is an article describing why baseball players chew sunflower seeds.

APPLICATION 1: Applying the Rules Governing the Use of Quotation Marks and Underlining. Copy the following sentences onto your paper, using quotation marks or underlining as necessary.

1. My father insisted, I expect each of you to obey the safety rules.
2. Two of romantic painter John Constable's works are Salisbury Cathedral and Haystacks.
3. The Prologue to The Canterbury Tales begins with the following words: When in April the sweet showers fall. . . .
4. I cannot condone, said the principal, your behavior.
5. Thomas Henry Huxley wrote, I had two years of pandemonium of a school . . . and after that neither help nor sympathy in any intellectual direction till I reached manhood.
6. When will you remember to phone if you are going to be late? asked my mother.
7. In his essay Dunkirk, Winston Churchill describes the most famous retreat in history.
8. I particularly enjoyed Emily Brontë's novel Wuthering Heights.
9. "Then my sister said, I am going to enlist! and my mother began to cry."
10. Herbert Bookbinder is the memorable hero of Herman Wouk's novel The City Boy.
11. What factors led you to that conclusion? she asked.
12. Two of Rodgers and Hammerstein's best musicals are The King and I and Oklahoma.
13. I believe that the New York Daily News has the largest morning circulation of any American newspaper.
14. In Sonnet 29 Shakespeare argues that love brings such wealth . . . That then I scorn to change my state with kings.
15. This trust, said the lawyer, will provide for you until you are eighteen.
16. That's my final offer, she blurted. Take it or leave it.
17. What did she mean when she said, We are happy now? Jill wondered.
18. Mutatis mutandis is a technical expression that comes from Latin.
19. Remember to cross your t's and dot your i's.
20. Charles Lindbergh made the first nonstop solo flight from New York to Paris in The Spirit of St. Louis in 1927.

APPLICATION 2: **Using Quotation Marks and Underlining Correctly in Your Own Writing.** Write ten original sentences according to the following directions.

1. Write a sentence that contains the name of a movie you have seen recently.

2. Write as a direct quotation some advice you plan to give any grandchildren you may have. Include a conversational tag in your sentence.
3. Write a sentence containing the name of a song or a poem associated with a particular holiday or special event.
4. Write a sentence containing the name of a local newspaper.
5. Write a sentence containing a foreign word or phrase not yet accepted as part of the English language.
6. Write a sentence containing the title and description of a piece of sculpture you might create.
7. Write a sentence containing the name of an individual air, sea, space, or land craft.
8. Write a sentence containing the name of a short story or poem you might read to a young child.
9. Write a sentence containing the name of a government document.
10. Write a sentence in which you use a word as a name for itself.

Dashes, Parentheses, and Brackets 12.5

Three additional punctuation marks are less frequently used than others but are important in certain writing situations. You should be familiar with the uses of dashes (—), parentheses (( )), and brackets ([ ]) and be able to use them when they are required.

■ Using Dashes

The dash is a strong, dramatic punctuation mark. It has specific uses and should not be used as a substitute for the comma, semicolon, or parentheses. Overuse of the dash is a poor practice and diminishes its effectiveness.

Now that you have been forewarned, consider the proper uses of the dash.

Use dashes to indicate an abrupt change of thought.

EXAMPLES: The decrepit truck shook and rumbled its way slowly up the hill—it must have been at least thirty years old.

The hurricane struck at dawn—to this day survivors gasp as they retell the story.

A dash can also be used to set off interrupting ideas.

Use dashes to set off interrupting ideas in a dramatic fashion.

EXAMPLE: It was a desperate gamble—she stood little chance of winning—but she took it anyway.

Another dramatic use of the dash is to summarize a group of items in a series.

Use a dash to set off a summary statement.

EXAMPLE: The Browns, the Whittiers, and the Santinos—these fine neighbors brought food and warm clothing to us during the flood.

Appositives may also be punctuated with dashes in certain circumstances.

Use dashes to set off a nonessential appositive in the middle of a sentence (1) when the appositive is long; (2) when it is already punctuated; (3) when it is introduced by words such as _for example_ or _that is;_ and (4) when you want to be especially dramatic.

EXAMPLES: The cause of her illness—a strange virus affecting the nervous system—troubled her doctors.

Some of my friends—for example, Bill, Frannie, and Tracey—waste a great deal of time watching television.

In addition, you may use dashes to punctuate nonessential modifiers that contain internal punctuation or that you wish to emphasize strongly.

Use dashes to set off nonessential modifiers (1) when the modifier is already punctuated and (2) when you want to be especially dramatic.

EXAMPLE: We are going to Yellowstone National Park—which has spectacular geysers, waterfalls, and wild animals—for our vacation.

Finally, you may use dashes to set off certain parenthetical expressions.

Use dashes to set off a parenthetical expression (1) when the expression is long; (2) when it is already punctuated; and (3) when you want to be especially dramatic.

EXAMPLE: Last Saturday night at the party—have you ever seen so much food?—I danced all evening long.

EXERCISE A: **Understanding the Use of the Dash.** The following sentences, written by professional writers, contain dashes used properly. Read each sentence carefully and then write the rule that governs the use of each dash or pair of dashes.

1. Neither of the pair immediately spoke—they only prolonged the preliminary gaze suggesting that each wished to give the other a chance. —Henry James
2. The excessive slaughter in this war was caused by an enhancement of what we had observed in the Civil War—the increased lethal power of explosives. —Samuel Eliot Morison
3. Bobby and Harry Jones and Dickie Delacroix—the villagers pronounced this name "Dellacroy"—eventually made a great pile of stones in one corner of the square and guarded it against the raids of the other boys. —Shirley Jackson
4. Nonetheless, the force of the modern pattern of infection was clearly evident by 1700, or by 1750 at the latest—and not only in Europe, but throughout the world. —William E. McNeill
5. She had bought a new dress for the occasion—a long black crepe dinner dress with a rhinestone buckle and a bolero—and a pair of silver slippers to wear with it, because she was supposed to go up on the stage with him to keep him from falling. —Flannery O'Connor

■ Using Parentheses

Parentheses are generally used to set off material within a sentence. Commas may also be used for this purpose. In fact, commas are the appropriate punctuation marks to use for this purpose in most cases, especially when the material is short and closely related in meaning to the rest of the sentence. Parentheses, on the other hand, are appropriate in some circumstances.

Use parentheses to set off asides and explanations only when the material is not essential to the meaning of the sentence or when the aside or explanation consists of one or more sentences.

EXAMPLES: Her job responsibilities (as she learned within the month) were far greater than she had been told.

Documentary novels (two of the most successful are Dreiser's *An American Tragedy* and Capote's *In Cold Blood*) are fictionalized accounts of events based upon newspaper reports or other documentary evidence.

Parentheses are the strongest separators that writers can use. Notice in the preceding examples that, although the material enclosed in parentheses is not essential to the meaning of the sentences, the writers have indicated that they consider the material important by using parentheses. The use of parentheses calls attention to the material they enclose.

Special Uses of Parentheses.   Parentheses are also used to enclose numerical information.

Use parentheses to set off the dates of a person's birth and death or other explanations involving numerals.

EXAMPLES: John Dryden (1631–1700) wrote *All for Love,* the best of many Restoration dramas.

Her Portland phone number is (303) 555-4211.

In addition, parentheses may be used to indicate items in a series.

Use parentheses around numbers and letters marking items in a series.

EXAMPLES: In the next three years, his research will take him to (1) Lisbon, Portugal; (2) Montreal, Canada; (3) Bucharest, Romania; and (4) New Delhi, India.

The sports activities include (a) tennis, (b) golf, (c) swimming, (d) gymnastics, and (e) track.

Using Other Punctuation Marks with Parentheses.   Parentheses are often used in conjunction with other punctuation marks. Several rules govern these situations.

When a parenthetical phrase or declarative sentence interrupts another sentence, do not capitalize the initial word or use any end mark inside the parentheses.

EXAMPLE: My grandfather's car (he used to take us riding in it on Sunday afternoons) was finally sold to an antique car dealer.

Follow the next rule when you interrupt a sentence with a question or exclamatory sentence in parentheses.

When a parenthetical question or exclamatory sentence interrupts another sentence, use both an initial capital and an end mark inside the parentheses.

EXAMPLES: Alan Alda (Doesn't he play Hawkeye in *Mash?*) was an intelligent and articulate guest on the talk show last night.

Aunt Louise (She is the best cook!) invited us for Thanksgiving dinner.

When you place a sentence in parentheses between two other sentences, the following rule will guide you in punctuating it correctly.

When a parenthetical sentence falls between two complete sentences, use both an initial capital and an end mark inside the parentheses.

EXAMPLE: Robert Browning often displayed modern psychological insights. (See "My Last Duchess" as an example.) This tends to be true of great writers no matter how long ago they may have lived.

The final rule will guide you in punctuating parenthetical phrases.

In a sentence with a parenthetical phrase, place any punctuation belonging to the main sentence after the second parenthesis.

EXAMPLE: The union committee agreed to the terms (after some deliberation), and they explained the contract to the members (with some doubts about their reaction).

EXERCISE B: **Enclosing Material in Parentheses.** Copy the following sentences onto your paper, inserting the appropriate parentheses. Remember to follow the rules governing the use of other punctuation marks with parentheses also.

1. Florence Nightingale 1820–1910 is regarded as the founder of modern nursing.
2. She served as a nurse during the Crimean War 1854–1856.
3. For dinner we had steak, baked potatoes, and broccoli. I have always disliked broccoli. A homemade apple pie was served for dessert.
4. Built in 1826, the stone barn a Hancock Shaker Village landmark housed fifty-two cows.
5. Estoril we drove there from Lisbon is a popular tourist attraction in Portugal.
6. Mystic Village in Connecticut and Sturbridge Village in Massachusetts Have you ever visited either of them? recreate life of an earlier period.
7. Her plan is to create a garden of 1 lilacs, 2 roses, 3 tulips, and 4 daffodils.
8. The firm's New Jersey phone number is 201 555–4678.
9. Because of last night's snowstorm What a blizzard!, school was cancelled today.
10. When you apply to a college, be sure you send a the completed application, b your high school transcript, c your SAT scores, d several references, and e the registration fee.

■ Using Brackets

Brackets are used to enclose a word or phrase added by a writer to the words of another.

Use brackets to enclose a word or words inserted in a quotation by a writer who is quoting someone else.

EXAMPLES: Bosley Crowther concluded his review of *Bonnie and Clyde:* "And it leaves an astonished critic wondering just what purpose Mr. Penn and Mr. Beatty think they serve with this strangely antique, sentimental claptrap, which opened yesterday [August 13, 1967] at the Forum and the Murray Hill."

Critic Louis Untermeyer wrote: "Alexander Pope has in our own times been rehabilitated [by whom?] and raised to glory."

The Latin expression *sic* (meaning *thus*) is sometimes enclosed in brackets to show that the author of the material being quoted has misspelled or mispronounced a word or phrase.

EXAMPLE: To quote poor Dogberry, "Be vigitant [sic], I beseech you."

EXERCISE C: **Enclosing Material in Brackets.** Copy the following items onto your paper, inserting the necessary brackets.

1. "We the people of the United States, in order to form a more perfect Union of the thirteen former colonies, establish justice, insure domestic tranquility, provide for the common defense. . . . "
2. Archie Bunker's "ground rules and priororities sic" are always unreasonable.
3. "Fourscore and seven years ago 87 years, our fathers brought forth on this continent a new nation. . . . "
4. "Me and Harry sic was promoted," boasted the little girl.
5. "I pledge allegiance to the flag of the United States of America and to the republic for which it stands, one nation, under God added in 1954, indivisible, with liberty and justice for all."

APPLICATION: **Using Dashes, Parentheses, and Brackets in Your Own Writing.** Write ten sentences of your own. Each one should illustrate a different rule governing the use of dashes, parentheses, and brackets. Remember to follow the rules governing the use of other punctuation marks with parentheses when you write the sentences that illustrate the correct use of parentheses.

Hyphens and Apostrophes 12.6

As a writer you must know the rules governing the use of hyphens and apostrophes. Although the rules are not difficult, you must study them and the examples that illustrate them carefully to avoid making mistakes.

■ Hyphens

Hyphens are used to join some words and to divide others. The hyphen (-) resembles the dash (—) but is shorter. In your handwriting be sure to make your hyphens half the length of your dashes. In typewriting, one hyphen mark is used for a hyphen, while two hyphen marks are used for a dash.

Writers use hyphens with numbers, word parts, and words. First, consider the use of hyphens with numbers.

With Numbers. Hyphens are used to join compound numbers.

> Use a hyphen when writing out the numbers *twenty-one* through *ninety-nine.*

EXAMPLES: twenty-eight ounces   fifty-five apartments

Fractions used as adjectives are also hyphenated.

> Use a hyphen when writing fractions that are used as adjectives or adverbs.

EXAMPLES: seven-tenths inch   three-quarters finished

A fraction used as a noun is not hyphenated, however.

EXAMPLE: Two thirds of the voters favored the bill.

With Word Parts. In some circumstances a hyphen is used following a prefix.

> Use a hyphen after a prefix that is followed by a proper noun or adjective.

EXAMPLES: pre-Civil War   mid-February   un-American

Some of the prefixes often found before proper nouns or proper adjectives are *ante-, anti-, mid-, post-, pre-, pro-,* and *un-.* Remember to hyphenate them when they are followed by proper nouns or proper adjectives.

Hyphens are always used with three particular prefixes and one suffix.

> Use a hyphen in words with the prefixes *all-, ex-, self-* and words with the suffix *-elect.*

EXAMPLES: all-powerful   ex-jockey   self-made   mayor-elect

With Compound Words. Some compound words are also joined with hyphens.

Use a hyphen to connect two or more words that are used as one word, unless the dictionary gives a contrary spelling.

Although some compound words are written as one word and others are written as two words, some compound words are joined with a hyphen. Always consult your dictionary if you are in doubt about the spelling of a compound word.

EXAMPLES: sister-in-law   secretary-treasurer   six-year-olds

In addition, you will need to use a hyphen with some compound modifiers.

Use a hyphen to connect most compound modifiers that come before nouns. Do not use a hyphen when the modifier includes a word ending in -*ly*, or in a compound proper adjective or a compound proper noun acting as an adjective.

EXAMPLES WITH HYPHENS: a well-made pair of jeans

the bright-eyed children

an up-to-date decision

EXAMPLES WITHOUT HYPHENS: widely distributed information

East European languages

Red River Valley

When compound modifiers follow a noun, they generally do not require the use of hyphens.

EXAMPLE: The jeans were well made.

If your dictionary lists a word as hyphenated, however, it should always be hyphenated.

EXAMPLE: The news was up-to-date.

For Clarity.   Sometimes a word or group of words might be misread if a hyphen were not used.

Use a hyphen within a word when a combination of letters might otherwise be confusing.

EXAMPLES: semi-illiterate   re-press (to press again)

              ball-like bounce   re-serve (to serve again)

You should also use a hyphen to prevent confusion when words may be combined incorrectly.

Use a hyphen between words to keep the reader from combining them erroneously.

EXAMPLES: ten foot-soldiers   the special-delivery man

To Divide Words at the End of a Line. Four rules govern the use of hyphens to divide words at the end of a line. Although writers try to avoid dividing a word at the end of a line, sometimes they must, and hyphens are used for this purpose.

The first rule to remember if you must divide a word is to divide it between syllables.

If a word must be divided, always divide it between syllables.

Needless to say, this rule tells you that you may never divide a one-syllable word at the end of a line. When you must divide a word of more than one syllable, place the hyphen at the end of the first line as shown in the following example.

EXAMPLE: For some time now, the children had been sending letters describing their adventures at camp.

The second rule governing the use of hyphens to divide words deals with single letters.

Do not divide a word so that a single letter stands alone.

INCORRECT: a-bout   i-deal   toast-y

CORRECT: about   ideal   toasty

In addition, proper nouns and proper adjectives should never be divided.

Do not divide proper nouns or proper adjectives.

INCORRECT: Fe-licia   Amer-ican

CORRECT: Felicia   American

Finally, a rule governs the use of hyphens with words that are already hyphenated.

Divide a hyphenated word only after the hyphen.

INCORRECT: We are going to the circus with my sister and my brother-in-law.

CORRECT: We are going to the circus with my sister and my brother-
in-law.

EXERCISE A: **Using Hyphens to Join and Divide Words.** Some of the following items have been hyphenated incorrectly or lack necessary hyphens. Rewrite the incorrect items following the rules you have just studied. If an item is already correct, write *correct* on your paper. Note that some of the items show a division at the end of a line.

1. Span-ish
2. up-to-date report
3. sis-ter in law
4. thirty first floor
5. semiinvalid
6. self adjusting
7. ex-Senator
8. bell-like
9. proAmerican
10. well intentioned advice
11. secretary-treasurer
12. Repress your shirt.
13. two thirds cup
14. all around athlete
15. president elect
16. greatly-exaggerated story
17. South-American history
18. Sierra Nevada Mountains
19. frisk-y
20. excitem-ent

■ Apostrophes

Apostrophes are used (1) to form possessives with nouns and some types of pronouns, (2) to form contractions, and (3) to form plurals in several special situations. First, consider the use of apostrophes to show possession.

Forming Possessives.   The following rule tells you how to show possession with singular nouns.

Add an apostrophe and -s to show the possessive case of most singular nouns.

EXAMPLES: the wallet of the woman   the woman's wallet

the collar of the dog   the dog's collar

the jacket of the boy   the boy's jacket

the brakes of the bike	the bike's brakes
the lines of the actress	the actress's lines

Notice in the last example that even when a noun ends in -*s* the possessive is usually formed by adding an apostrophe and an -*s*. When the resulting word would be hard to pronounce, however, only an apostrophe is added.

AWKWARD: Charles's parents left yesterday for Idaho.

BETTER: Charles' parents left yesterday for Idaho.

In forming the possessive case of plural nouns, two rules should be followed. The first rule deals with most plural nouns.

Add an apostrophe to show the possessive case of plural nouns ending in -*s* or -*es*.

EXAMPLES: the barking of the dogs   the dogs' barking

the color of the leaves   the leaves' color

The other rule to follow when forming the possessive case of plural nouns govens nouns that do not end in -*s* or -*es*.

Add an apostrophe and -*s* to show the possessive case of plural nouns that do not end in -*s* or -*es*.

EXAMPLES: the books of the women   the women's books

the grazing lands of the oxen   the oxen's grazing lands

When you wish to form the possessive case of a compound noun, follow the next rule.

Add an apostrophe and an -*s* (or just an apostrophe if the word is a plural ending in -*s*) to the last word of a compound noun to form the possessive.

NAMES OF BUSINESSES AND ORGANIZATIONS:

the Salvation Army's headquarters

the Department of the Interior's budget

the Johnson Associates' clients

TITLES OF RULERS AND LEADERS:

Peter the Great's army

Louis XVI's palace

the chairman of the board's advice

HYPHENATED COMPOUND NOUNS USED TO DESCRIBE PEOPLE:

my sister-in-law's car

the secretary-treasurer's idea

Possessive expressions involving time, amounts, and the word *sake* are formed by following the next rule.

To form possessives involving time, amounts, or the word *sake*, use an apostrophe and -*s* or just an apostrophe, depending on whether the possessive is singular or plural.

TIME: a month's pay   three days' vacation

AMOUNT: one dollar's worth   two cents' worth

SAKE: for Heaven's sake   for goodness' sake

Note in the last example that the final -*s* is often dropped in expressions involving the word *sake.*

Sometimes people share ownership, and sometimes several people each claim individual ownership. The particular circumstances you are writing about will affect the use of the apostrophe.

To show individual ownership, add an apostrophe and -*s* at the end of each noun in a series. To show joint ownership, add an apostrophe and -*s* to the last noun in the series.

INDIVIDUAL POSSESSION: Janet's and Grace's coats are hanging in my locker.

JOINT POSSESSION: I always enjoyed Bob and Ray's radio show.

Be sure each time you form the possessive case of any noun, whether individual or joint ownership is involved, that the owner's complete name appears before the apostrophe. By checking in this way, you can avoid many problems.

INCORRECT SINGULAR: Jame's skates

CORRECT SINGULAR: James's skates

INCORRECT PLURAL: two girl's books

CORRECT PLURAL: two girls' books

Forming the possessive case of pronouns requires two other rules.

Use an apostrophe and -s with indefinite pronouns to show possession.

EXAMPLES: everyone's time   one another's friends

somebody's umbrella   each other's homework

Notice in two of the examples that you add an apostrophe and -s only to the last word of a two-word indefinite pronoun to form the possessive.

A different rule applies when you want to form the possessive of personal pronouns.

Do not use an apostrophe with the possessive forms of personal pronouns.

The possessive form of personal pronouns already shows ownership. Pronouns in this form should be left just as they are to show possession.

EXAMPLES: his jazz records   our house

her blue sweater   its tires

their party   whose paper

Be careful not to confuse the contractions *who's, it's,* and *they're* with possessive pronouns. They are contractions for *who is, it is,* and *they are.* Remember also that *whose, its,* and *their* show possession.

PRONOUNS: Whose homework is this?

Its tires were all flat.

Their dinner is ready.

CONTRACTIONS: Who's at the door?

It's going to rain.

They're going to the beach.

Forming Contractions.   Another important use of the apostrophe is in forming contractions. One general rule covers all the different types of contractions.

Use an apostrophe in a contraction to indicate the position of the missing letter or letters.

VERB AND *NOT:*	cannot	can't
	could not	couldn't
	are not	aren't
	will not	won't

PRONOUN AND *WILL:*	he will	he'll
	you will	you'll
	I will	I'll

PRONOUN AND *WOULD:*	she would	she'd
	we would	they'd
	I would	I'd

PRONOUN AND *HAVE:*	they have	they've
	we have	we've
	I have	I've

PRONOUN OR NOUN AND A *TO BE* VERB:	you are	you're
	she is	she's
	they are	they're
	Jane is	Jane's
	where is	where's

Notice in the preceding examples that one contraction changes letters as well as drops them: *Will not* becomes *won't* in contracted form.

Contractions of this sort should be used sparingly in formal writing. Their use should be reserved mainly for dialogue. Otherwise, write out the words.

Another type of contraction is often found in informal writing. Study the following examples of contractions for years.

EXAMPLES: the class of '84   the depression of '29

Still another type of contraction is occasionally found in poetry.

EXAMPLES: e'en (for *even*)   o'er (for *over*)

Other contractions represent the abbreviated form of the longer phrase *of the* as it is written in several different languages.

EXAMPLES: O'Hare   o'clock

d'Lorenzo   l'Abbe

These letters are most often combined with surnames.

As noted on page 389, when you write dialogue, you will sometimes want to keep the flavor of the speaker's individual speaking style. This is an excellent place in which to use any contractions the speaker might use. You may also want to approximate in your writing a regional dialect or a foreign accent. Often dialects or foreign accents include unusual pronunciations or omitted letters.

EXAMPLES: Hi, ol' buddy. How you been feelin'?

Waal, mebe you're right.

Avoid overusing the apostrophe with contractions even in dialogue. As with other punctuation marks, overuse reduces effectiveness and impact.

Using Apostrophes in Special Situations.   The following rule presents four other situations where you will need to use apostrophes.

Use an apostrophe and -s to write the plurals of numbers, symbols, letters, and words used to name themselves.

EXAMPLES: during the *1860's*

your *2's* and *3's*

three *?'s* in a row

m's and *n's*

no *if's* or *maybe's*

EXERCISE B: **Using Apostrophes.** Rewrite each of the following items, following the instructions in parentheses.

1. the typewriter of the man (Put in the possessive case.)
2. two of the clock (Write the contracted form.)
3. the book of James (Put in the possessive case.)
4. 1984 (Write the contracted form.)
5. the house of the Joneses (Put in the possessive case.)
6. the cribs of the babies (Put in the possessive case.)
7. the sports of the women (Put in the possessive case.)
8. the stories of each other (Put in the possessive case.)
9. 12 (Write the plural form.)
10. who is (Write the contracted form.)
11. will not (Write the contracted form.)
12. The sandwich belongs to whom? (Reword, substituting a possessive pronoun for *to whom.*)
13. the advice of the Department of Defense (Put in the possessive case.)
14. the comedy act of Martin and Lewis (Put in the possessive case.)
15. they are (Write the contracted form.)
16. the report of someone (Put in the possessive case.)
17. the son of Queen Elizabeth II (Put in the possessive case.)
18. a vacation of two weeks (Put in the possessive case.)
19. the bicycles of Jane and Mike (Put in the possessive case.)
20. the horse's mane (Reword, substituting a possessive pronoun for *horse's.*)

APPLICATION: **Using the Rules for Hyphens and Apostrophes in Original Sentences.** Choose ten different rules from this section. Then write sentences of your own that illustrate each of the rules you have chosen.

Review Exercises: Mechanics

REVIEW EXERCISE 1: Reviewing Terms

How many of the new terms and definitions you have learned in this section do you remember? Answer each of the following questions as clearly as possible.

1. In identifying sections of the country, the words *North*, South, East, and West are capitalized. When are these words not capitalized? Give an example.
2. What is an abbreviation? Give three types of abbreviations that are always acceptable in formal writing.
3. What do the abbreviations B.C. and A.D. stand for? Does the phrase "during the 1770's" refer to B.C. or A.D.? How can you tell?
4. Where would you check to see whether the abbreviation for the title Sergeant is Sgt. or Sarge.?
5. What common characteristics do the official United States Postal Service abbreviations for the states have?
6. What is an acronym? Give two examples of acronyms.
7. What does the abbreviation *ibid.* mean?
8. What three punctuation marks are called end marks? When should each be used?
9. What is the difference between a semicolon and a colon? Give an example of an instance when each should be used.
10. What is the difference between a direct and indirect quotation? Which type requires the use of quotation marks?
11. What is a noun of direct address? How should it be punctuated?
12. What are the seven coordinating conjunctions? With what must a coordinating conjunction be used in order to punctuate most compound sentences correctly?
13. What is an appositive? How should an appositive be punctuated?
14. What is the difference between an essential and nonessential clause? How is each punctuated?
15. What is an ellipsis mark? When should it be used?
16. Which kinds of titles are enclosed in quotation marks? Which are underlined?
17. How does the use of brackets differ from the use of parentheses? What does the abbreviation *sic* mean in brackets?
18. What are two uses of the dash? When should dashes not be used?
19. What is a hyphen? Give three uses of the hyphen.
20. Besides showing possession, what are two other uses of the apostrophe?

REVIEW EXERCISE 2: Using Capitalization and Abbreviation

Each of the following items contains two versions of the same word or phrase. One version is correct and the other is incorrect. Use each correct word or phrase in a sentence of your own.

1. the Greek goddess Athena *or* the Greek Goddess Athena
2. French-Speaking Canadians *or* French-speaking Canadians
3. Pleasant Valley High School *or* Pleasant Valley high school
4. the Cleveland browns *or* the Cleveland Browns
5. FDIC *or* F.D.I.C.
6. mt. Washington *or* Mt. Washington
7. Nurse Betty Olsen, R.N. *or* Betty Olsen, R.N.
8. natl. *or* natal.
9. the World Trade Center *or* the World trade center
10. Ariz. *or* Az.
11. 711 River Road *or* 711 River Ro.
12. Secretary of Defense Marshall *or* Secretary of defense Marshall
13. kg *or* Kg.
14. Dear miss Wilson *or* Dear Miss Wilson
15. 3 qt. oil *or* 3 qts. oil
16. Senator-elect Brown *or* Senator-Elect Brown
17. e.g. *or* eg.
18. Kennebec and Penobscot rivers *or* Kennebec and Penobscot Rivers
19. Anglo-French *or* anglo-French
20. the bill of Rights *or* the Bill of Rights

REVIEW EXERCISE 3: Using Punctuation Marks Correctly

Write a sentence of your own for each of the following instructions. Be sure to punctuate each sentence correctly.

1. A sentence with a direct quotation and a conversational tag
2. A sentence with an appositive following the subject
3. A compound sentence punctuated with a semicolon
4. A compound sentence punctuated with a comma and the coordinating conjunction *but*
5. A sentence beginning with *well*
6. A sentence using a colon in front of a list of five items
7. A sentence punctuated with an exclamation mark
8. A complex sentence beginning with an introductory adverbial clause (Use the subordinate conjunction *although.)*
9. A complex sentence with an essential clause
10. A complex sentence with a nonessential clause
11. A sentence containing an indirect question
12. A question ending with a noun of direct address
13. A sentence beginning with a present participial phrase
14. A sentence containing a subject of three words in a series
15. A sentence containing the title and author of a book

16. A compound sentence punctuated with a semicolon (Begin the second independent clause with *however*.)
17. A sentence beginning with an infinitive phrase and containing the title of a book
18. A sentence containing the title of a poem
19. A sentence containing a noun in the possessive case
20. A sentence in which some explanatory material is enclosed in parentheses

IV

Vocabulary and Spelling

Chapter 13

Vocabulary Building

You are probably aware of how important a good vocabulary is to success in school. At your present stage in life, a good vocabulary is an important asset outside of school as well, since job, college, or vocational school interviews are in your near future. With a good vocabulary at your command, you can express yourself clearly and communicate exactly the meaning you intend.

The techniques discussed in this chapter should help you expand your vocabulary. Section 13.1 presents methods you can use to fix the meaning of new words in your mind. The second and third sections explain at greater length how to use two of these methods. Section 13.2 discusses examining phrases and sentences in which a word occurs in order to determine the meaning of the word. Section 13.3 discusses how to determine the meaning of words by analyzing their parts.

13.1 Techniques for Building Vocabulary

Building a vocabulary is not just a question of acquiring a collection of long, impressive-sounding words. The keys to real vocabulary development are extensive reading and the use of the dictionary, plus whatever memory techniques suit you best. This section will present some of these memory techniques.

■ Ways to Learn New Words

A good way to begin expanding your vocabulary is to gather a list of words. These may be words you find in your textbooks or in your general reading.

Set aside a special section in your notebook for each of your courses where you can enter new words and their definitions. Then use one or more of the following techniques to study and review the words.

Grouping Words.   One memory technique that can be used with the words in your notebooks is to break up the material to be learned into smaller units. For example, it is easier to memorize a ten-digit number such as 2035552527 if you separate it, as you would a telephone number, into 203-555-2527. The same trick works for vocabulary study. Group a list of twenty words into five sets of four words each and study each group separately.

Using Folded Paper.   In recording new words in a notebook, it may also be helpful to divide each page into three columns. List the new words in Column 1. Write the definitions in Column 3. In Column 2 enter any bridge words, or hints, that will remind you of the word's meaning. For the word *dichotomy*, you might, for example, use a bridge word such as *divide*. To review your entries, simply fold the paper to cover either the definitions or the words.

Using Flash Cards.   Since carrying your notebooks with you everywhere might not be practical, you may want to use index cards with the words listed on one side and the definitions on the other. You can carry a few of these cards with you at all times so that when you have a few spare minutes you can flip through them. This kind of frequent review is essential if you are to learn a number of new words.

Using a Tape Recorder.   Some people learn best through their eyes, others through their ears. If you are one of the latter, a tape recorder might help you learn new words. If you have access to a tape recorder, you can read onto the tape a group of words you want to learn. After each word, pause for about ten seconds and then read its definition. Replay the tape, trying to insert the definition into the ten-second pause, until you know all of the definitions by heart.

EXERCISE A: Evaluating Techniques. Select five words from the vocabulary section of each of your course notebooks. After studying these words for a week, test yourself by using each word in a sentence that shows you know the meaning of the word. Then write a short paragraph explaining which of the preceding methods—grouping words, folded paper, flash cards, or tape recorder—was most useful to you.

■ More Ways to Expand Your Vocabulary

The introduction to this section mentioned that the keys to vocabulary development are extensive reading and the regular use of the dictionary. It is almost inevitable that the more you read, the more your vocabulary will grow. It is also true that the more your vocabulary grows, the more enjoyable your reading will be.

Increase your reading and make use of special reading skills to increase your vocabulary.

Increasing Your Reading.   It is quite easy to enlarge the scope of your reading. Visit the library and look at some books in areas that are new to you. If you usually read science fiction, try a historical novel. Or you may want to read further on a subject that interests you now. If you are an avid reader of the sports pages in the newspaper, look for a biography of an athlete you admire.

When you read, you will probably meet unfamiliar words. You may not want to interrupt your reading, but make a mental note of the words and look them up in a dictionary when you have finished the passage or the chapter. Then write each word, with its definition, on a piece of paper. You might want to keep a list of new words you come across in your reading. Think about these words and their meanings. Visualize them. Try to use them in conversation or in your writing. Soon they will be a part of your vocabulary.

Using Context.   Often you may come upon an unfamiliar term in the midst of a very interesting passage. Since you will generally not want to interrupt your train of thought by looking the word up in a dictionary, you may find yourself guessing at its meaning using the clues offered by the words surrounding it. This process is called "using context clues."

EXAMPLE: Richard was so eager to know the value of the old coin that he took it to a numismatist.

Even if you never saw the word before, you could guess that a numismatist is a specialist in coins. You would be wise, of course, to check your guess in a dictionary. Not only would you verify the definition of the word, but you would also learn something of its history. You would learn, for example, that the word *numismatist* is derived from the Greek word for *coin*, which itself came from the word for *law*.

Using Structure.   You probably know the meaning of quite a few prefixes, roots, and suffixes. When you analyze these parts of a word, you are using the word's structure to determine its meaning.

EXAMPLE: *intervention* is made up of *inter-* (between) + *-ven-* (to come) + *-tion* (the act of)

Therefore, *intervention* means "the act of coming between." When you use structure, it is still a good idea to check your guess in a dictionary. Words may acquire meanings beyond the literal meanings of their parts.

In the next two sections, you will be able to practice using context clues and structure to determine the meanings of words.

EXERCISE B: **Determining the Meanings of Words.** Try to guess the meaning of each of the following underlined words. Write down your guesses and then check each one in a dictionary. Next to each guess, write the correct definition and the method you used to make your guess.

1. The philatelist was determined to add the rare stamp to her collection.
2. The name on the envelope looked so beautiful it must have been written by a calligrapher.
3. The dermatologist was able to cure the rash in a short time.
4. To conceal his identity, Boris signed the petition with a pseudonym.
5. Kim's illness was diagnosed as psychosomatic.

APPLICATION: **Using New Vocabulary Words.** From the vocabulary sections of your course notebooks or from your personal vocabulary list, select five words. Use each in an original sentence in such a way that a person unfamiliar with the word could guess its meaning through the use of context.

Using Context 13.2

This section will show you how to use a number of different types of context clues to determine the meaning of new words. As mentioned in Section 13.1, the information in the sentence in which the word occurs gives a clue to its meaning.

Use context clues in all of your reading to improve both your vocabulary and your general reading comprehension.

Sometimes writers deliberately supply clues to help the reader understand the thought. The following chart gives examples of the types of context clues writers use. You may find it useful whenever you come across a new word in your reading.

TYPES OF CONTEXT CLUES

Clue	Example	Method
Formal definition	Many plant *rhizomes*, underground stems or root systems, offer an excellent source of nutritious food.	The reader is given a definition of the word *rhizome*, which means "an underground stem."
Familiar words	The loud, shrill cries of the bluejays broke the early morning silence as they *raucously* called other jays to the bird feeder.	The use of the familiar words *loud* and *shrill* coupled with *cries* alerts the reader to the meaning of *raucously*: "loudly," or "rough-sounding."
Comparison	The *monsignor*, like a village priest, blessed the pilgrims at the shrine with gentleness and compassion.	The comparison of the *monsignor* with a village *priest* shows the reader that the former is connected in some way with the Catholic Church. *Monsignor* is a title of honor given to certain priests.
Contrast	His English students were more *tractable* than he had anticipated; in fact, only his obstinate fifth period class resisted an appeal to participate in some choral reading.	*Only* used with the words *obstinate* and *resisted* indicates contrast. *Tractable* means "easily led."
Synonyms	Jack's *ignominious* behavior was shameful and disgraceful.	*Shameful* and *disgraceful* are synonyms for *ignominious*.
Antonyms	His sisters reacted to Jack's behavior differently. Angie spoke of Jack with *acerbity* and anger, while Jessica spoke with sweetness and love.	*Acerbity* and *anger* contrasted with *sweetness* and *love* indicate that *acerbity* is an antonym of *sweetness*. *Acerbity* means "bitterness."

Summary	Shane was completely *distraught*. She couldn't find her glasses; her papers were all over; she didn't know how to get to the vet's office; but she had to get the injured puppy to the doctor.	The actions described in the second sentence are summed up in the word *distraught*, which means "mentally confused" or "extremely troubled."
Previous knowledge of an associated word	San Francisco, California, is located in an active *seismic* area.	Previous contact with the word *seismograph* (an instrument that records the severity of the earth's tremors) coupled with an awareness of the famous San Francisco earthquake should alert the reader to the meaning of the word *seismic*, which means "of or having to do with or caused by earthquakes."

In addition to recognizing certain types of context clues, it also helps to have an orderly way of using them. The following chart lists the steps to take in using context clues effectively.

STEPS FOR USING CONTEXT CLUES

1. Read the sentence, leaving out the unfamiliar word.
2. Examine the surrounding words and note the type of clues they provide.
3. Guess at the meaning of the word.
4. Read the sentence again, substituting your guess for the unfamiliar word.
5. Check your guess in the dictionary; write the word and the definition in the vocabulary section of your notebook or include it in your personal vocabulary list.

■ Using Context Clues When Reading About Careers

Try your context skills on the following paragraph. It represents the type of material you might find in a book or article describing the work of a young woman who has a job in the legal field. Read the whole paragraph to get the overall meaning. Then use the steps in the preceding chart to help you to determine the meaning of each underlined word. Jot your guesses on a sheet of paper.

EXAMPLE: Lynda Work, a young attorney well-trained in <u>juris-prudence</u>, announced that contrary to early, <u>spurious</u> reports Ramsey Franklin had not died <u>intestate</u>. She never <u>vacillated</u> in her <u>unfeigned</u> intent to fulfill every detail of the will, and she proceeded to clarify the terms of the will for the benefactors, refusing to <u>obfuscate</u> the terms through the use of legal terminology. She assured the benefactors that Franklin, not a <u>penurious</u> man, had left generous bequests to his heirs in a complete and detailed <u>codicil</u> attached to the will. She recommended that all financial obligations in <u>arrears</u> at the time of Franklin's death be paid quickly so that the estate would not be tied up in unnecessary <u>litigation</u> with any creditors.

EXERCISE A: Choosing Meanings. Use your list of guesses from the preceding paragraph for this exercise. For each of the following words, choose the definition that most closely matches the meaning of the word as it was used in the paragraph. Then check your answer in a dictionary.

1. litigation
   a. division of the law
   b. confusion
   c. lawsuit
   d. counterfeit

2. penurious
   a. thoughtful
   b. stingy
   c. genuine
   d. false

3. arrears
   a. overdue bills
   b. waver in mind
   c. uprisings
   d. toward the back

4. jurisprudence
   a. impartiality
   b. legal power
   c. science of law
   d. legal rights

5. codicil
   a. having no will
   b. addition to a will
   c. lawsuit
   d. systematic arrangement

6. spurious
   a. false
   b. irregular
   c. real
   d. supplement

7. intestate
   a. addition to a will
   b. without an estate
   c. between or among states
   d. having made no will

8. obfuscate
   a. to waver
   b. to confuse
   c. to flee from
   d. to part with money

9. unfeigned
   a. pretended
   b. inexhaustible
   c. false
   d. genuine

10. vacillate
    a. inoculate
    b. unoccupied
    c. waver in mind
    d. waiver

■ Using Context Clues When Reading for Pleasure

Articles about food and its preparation often include words borrowed from other languages. The following paragraph has a number of words borrowed from French. Through the use of context clues, try to guess the meaning of the underlined words. Jot your guesses down on a piece of paper.

EXAMPLE: Jon, who regarded himself as a <u>perspicacious</u> <u>gourmet</u>, read the menu carefully before placing an order with the hovering waiter. He decided to begin with a small cup of <u>consommé</u>. He wavered between the chicken milanese and the lobster. After deciding on the chicken, he ordered <u>lyonnaise</u> potatoes, mushrooms <u>sautéed</u> in butter, carrots <u>julienne</u>, and the spinach <u>soufflé</u> served in an individual <u>ramekin</u>. He selected chocolate <u>mousse</u> and <u>espresso</u> to complete the meal.

EXERCISE B: **Using Context Clues to Complete Sentences.** Use your list of guesses from the preceding paragraph for this exercise. For each of the following sentences, choose the word from the paragraph that best completes each sentence. Then check your answer in a dictionary.

1. The true _____ selects food carefully and eats sparingly but with much pleasure.

   a. gourmet   b. julienne   c. soufflé

2. The cook must be careful not to jar the container when removing a(n) _____ from the oven.

   a. espresso   b. gourmet   c. soufflé

3. The chef will _____ the mushrooms very quickly in a special pan.

   a. soufflé   b. sauté   c. julienne

4. The homemaker must be a _____ shopper in these days of high food prices.

   a. soufflé   b. lyonnaise   c. perspicacious

5. Italian coffee, called _____, is a fullbodied, strong drink.

   a. mousse   b. espresso   c. ramekin

6. The doctor recommended that Sarah have a small cup of _____ before trying to eat any solid food.

   a. julienne   b. consommé   c. sauté

7. Many brides consider themselves lucky if they receive a set of _____ for a wedding present.

   a. gourmets   b. espressos   c. ramekins

8. Food processors make preparing vegetables _____ extremely simple.

   a. julienne   b. ramekin   c. gourmet

9. French cooks prepare a delicious dessert called _____ using egg whites, whipped cream, and often, chocolate.

   a. ramekin   b. gourmet   c. mousse

10. _____ potatoes please those people who like the flavor of fried onions.

   a. perspicacious   b. lyonnaise   c. julienne

EXERCISE C: Defining Words. Now that you have checked the meanings of the words in Column A in a dictionary, you can select the words from Column B that correctly define the words in Column A.

Column A	*Column B*
1. soufflé	a. Italian-style coffee
2. julienne	b. small baking dish
3. gourmet	c. baked dish made fluffy by the addition of egg whites
4. ramekin	
5. perspicacious	d. having keen judgment
6. mousse	e. prepared with onions
7. espresso	f. clear soup
8. consommé	g. to fry quickly in butter
9. lyonnaise	h. light, chilled dessert
10. sauté	i. cut into strips
	j. excellent judge of good food

■ Using Context Clues When Reading for Information

Newspaper and magazine articles about developments in the field of medicine often require knowledge of some rather difficult terms. As you read the following paragraphs, use your context skills to guess at the meaning of the underlined words. You might find it helpful to refer to the charts on pages 400 and 401. Jot down your guesses on a piece of paper.

EXAMPLE: Dr. Rosalyn Yalow received the Nobel Prize in Medicine in 1977. The fifty-nine-year-old <u>laureate</u> works at the Bronx Veterans Administration Hospital in New York, where she has been chief of <u>nuclear</u> medicine since 1970.

      The test for which Dr. Yalow received the Nobel Prize is used to measure the <u>concentrations</u> of various substances in the blood to determine changes that take place in diseased bodies. Her work in this area began when she and her <u>colleague</u> used the test to measure the amount of <u>insulin</u> in the blood of diabetes patients. The scientists discovered that when diabetics were injected with insulin, their blood produced <u>antibodies</u> against the insulin. These antibodies acted as <u>foreign</u> proteins in the body.

      The test developed by Dr. Yalow and her colleague is being used today by blood banks to detect the presence of the <u>hepatitis</u> virus in blood intended for use in transfusions. Dr. Yalow predicts that her work will have as great an <u>impact</u> on <u>infectious</u> disease control as it has had on the treatment of hormonal disorders.

EXERCISE D: Choosing Meanings.

Use your list of guesses from the preceding paragraphs for this exercise. For each of the following words, choose the definition that most closely matches the meaning of the word as it was used in the paragraphs. Then check your answer in a dictionary.

1. colleague
   - a. inventor
   - b. scientist
   - c. fellow worker
   - d. college graduate

2. hepatitis
   - a. seven-sided figure
   - b. infection of the hip
   - c. inflammation of the joints
   - d. inflammation of the liver

3. laureate
   - a. girl's name
   - b. evergreen shrub
   - c. honored person
   - d. rope for a horse

4. concentration
   - a. strength
   - b. meeting
   - c. meditate
   - d. granting an argument

5. nuclear
   - a. relating to atomic nuclei
   - b. hard to understand
   - c. energy
   - d. physics

6. foreign
   - a. not domestic
   - b. imported
   - c. outside the country
   - d. not natural to the body

7. infectious
   a. tending to spread
   b. tender and loving
   c. of a lower order
   d. without end

8. insulin
   a. to keep heat or cold out
   b. like an island
   c. hormone that helps the body use sugar
   d. isolated

9. impact
   a. lodged in the jaw
   b. power to produce change
   c. agreement
   d. taking little space

10. antibody
    a. penicillin
    b. puritanical
    c. political group
    d. a protein produced in the body

APPLICATION: Using New Words in Context. Choose any one of the following activities.

1. Imagine that you are either a very wealthy person or a person with just a few precious possessions. Write a short will in which you leave your possessions to family members or friends. Use at least five of the vocabulary words from this section. Try to use them in such a way that someone who is not a lawyer would be able to understand your will.
2. Write a short letter to a friend describing a delicious meal you just enjoyed. Use at least five of the words from this section in such a way that your friend would know exactly what you had to eat.
3. Imagine you are a newspaper reporter. Write a few paragraphs as if they were part of a longer article describing an achievement in the field of medicine. Use at least five of the words from this section in such a way that the average reader would be able to understand your article.

13.3 | Using Structure

The context in which you find a word provides external clues to its meaning. This section discusses internal clues to the meaning of words. The internal clues are the parts of words —prefixes, roots, and suffixes.

The main part of a word, the part that carries its basic meaning, is the root. Roots can sometimes stand alone (for example, the root *act*). Often, however, they must be completed with a prefix or a suffix (for example, the root *-ven-*). A prefix is a word part added at the beginning of a word that changes its meaning (happy/*un*happy). A suffix is a word part added at the end of a word that changes the meaning or part of speech of the word (act/act*or*).

Learn the meanings of common prefixes, roots, and suffixes to improve your vocabulary and your reading comprehension.

If you master the prefixes, roots, and suffixes in the charts in this section, you should be able to determine the meanings of hundreds of words simply by analyzing them in terms of their structure. Of course, a dictionary check is indispensable, especially since many words acquire special meanings over the years. These meanings are not always evident from the combined meanings of the parts of the word.

■ Prefixes

The following chart lists thirty prefixes with their origins. (The abbreviations L., Gr., and O.E. stand for Latin, Greek, and Old English.) The additional forms of prefixes whose spelling varies according to the root word to which they are added are listed in parentheses. (For example, the prefix *in-* changes to *im-* in the word *immortal*.)

THIRTY COMMON PREFIXES		
Prefix	**Meaning**	**Examples**
ab- (a-, abs-) [L.]	away, from	abrasive, amorphous, absent
ad- (ac-, af-, al-, ap-, as-, at-) [L.]	to, toward	adhere, accede, affect, alloy, apply, aspect, attend
anti- [Gr.]	against	antiwar
circum- [L.]	around, about, surrounding, on all sides	circumvent
com- (co-, col-, con-, cor-) [L.]	with, together	comrade, coordinate, collapse, confer, correlate

de- [L.]	away from, off, down	decentralize
dis- (di-, dif-) [L.]	away, apart, cause to be opposite of	discomfort, divide, differ
epi- [Gr.]	upon, over, on the outside	epidemic
ex- (e-, ec-, ef-) [L.]	forth, from, out	express, eject, ecstatic, effort
extra- [L.]	outside, beyond	extraterritorial
hyper- [Gr.]	over, above, excessive	hyperbole
in- (il-, im-, ir-) [L.]	not, "un"	ineffectual, illimitable, immaculate, irregular
in- (il-, im-, ir-) [L.]	in, into, within, on, toward	intrude, illustrate, impress, irradiate
inter- [L.]	between	interfere
mal- [L.]	bad, wrongful, ill	malfunction
mis- [O.E.]	wrong	mistrial
mono- [Gr.]	alone, one	monotone
non- [L.]	not	nonprofit
ob- (o-, oc-, of-, op-) [L.]	toward, against	observe, omission, occupy, offend, oppose
over- [O.E.]	above, over the limit, in excess	overload
post- [L.]	after	postscript
pre- [L.]	before	predate
pro- [L.]	forward, forth, favoring, in place of	provide
re- [L.]	back, again	review
semi- [L.]	half, partly	semifinal
sub- (suc-, suf-, sup-) [L.]	beneath, under, below	subconscious, succession, suffer, support
super- [L.]	above, beyond, on top	superhuman
syn- (syl-, sym-, sys-) [Gr.]	with, together with, at the same time	synthesis, syllable, sympathy, system
trans- [L.]	across	transfer
un- [O.E.]	not	ungrateful

EXERCISE A: **Defining Words with Prefixes.** For each of the following words, select the definition that most closely matches the meaning of the word. Be sure to check your guesses in a dictionary.

1. supervise   a. overcome   b. oversee
                    c. overhaul   d. succeed

2. hypercritical   a. imaginary   b. extremely active
                 illness
                 c. hard to   d. excessive publicity
                 please

3. malice   a. active ill will   b. hateful
           c. harmful   d. long-handled
                            hammer

4. extraneous   a. extraordinary   b. not essential
              c. an outgoing   d. costing or
                 person   spending too much

5. synchronize   a. sympathize   b. be a symbol
               c. rhythmic   d. cause to move or
                            occur at the same
                            time

6. avert   a. turn away   b. return
         c. eliminate   d. straight

7. discern   a. divide   b. perceive
           c. throw away   clearly
                          d. dissect

8. proficient   a. professed   b. recipient
            c. lacking   d. skilled

9. defraud   a. distort   b. cheat
          c. put off   d. disagree

10. semiconscious   a. ill at ease   b. half awake
                c. fully awake   d. inattentive

■ Roots

The root carries the basic meaning of the word and is, therefore, the most significant of the three word parts. By adding various prefixes and suffixes to a particular root, you can form whole families of related words. For example, the root *-puls-* (also spelled *-pel-*) is the base for *impulse, repel, propeller, expel, appellate, repulsion,* and many other words. The spelling of a root word can change depending on the letters surrounding it. For example, if your wrote the sentence *I need a powerful motor to move my mobile home,* you would have used the same root three times. Can you find the three words that have the same root?

The chart that follows lists thirty roots, their origins, and their meanings. The chart also lists the different forms for each root included as well as words containing each root.

THIRTY COMMON ROOTS

Root	Meaning	Examples
-ama- (-ami-) [L.]	to love	amiable
-cap- (-capt-, -cept-, -ceipt-, ceive-, -cip-) [L.]	to take, seize	capacity, captive, receptive, receipt, deceive, incipient
-ced- (-ceed-, -cess-) [L.]	to go, yield	intercede, proceed, process
-dic- (-dict-) [L.]	to say, point out in words	predicate, dictatorial
-duc- (-duce-, -duct-) [L.]	to lead	introduce, abduct
-fac- (-fact-, -fec-, -fect-) [L.]	to do, make	faculty, factory, confection, perfect
-fer- [L.]	to bring, carry	conference
-graph- [Gr.]	to write	biography
-ject- [L.]	to throw	eject
-leg- (-log-) [Gr.]	to say, speak, reason	legible, logical
-manu- [L.]	hand	manuscript
-mit- (-mis-) [L.]	to send	transmit, permission
-mov- (-mob-, -mot-) [L.]	to move	movable, mobile, motor
-plic- (-pli-, -ploy-, -ply-) [L.]	to fold	explicate, pliant, employer, reply
-pon- (-pos-) [L.]	to put, place	postpone, impose
-port- [L.]	to carry	transport
-puls- (-pel-) [L.]	to drive	impulse, expel
-quir- (-ques-, -quis-) [L.]	to ask, say	require, request, inquisition
-sci- [L.]	to know	conscience
-scrib- (-script-) [L.]	to write	inscribe, postscript
-sens- (-sent-, -senti-) [L.]	to feel	sensible, sentiment
-sist- [L.]	to stand	persist
-spec- (-spect-) [L.]	to see	speculate, respect
-string- (-strict-) [L.]	to bind, tighten	stringency, restrict
-ten- (-tain-, -tin-) [L.]	to hold, contain	tenement, retain, pertinent
-tend- (-tens-, -tent-) [L.]	to stretch	pretend, tense, extent

-vad- (-vas-) [L.]	to go	pervade, evasive
-ven- (-vent-) [L.]	to come	intervene, prevent
-vert- (-vers-) [L.]	to turn	convert, diversion
-vid- (-vis-) [L.]	to see	evidence, visual

EXERCISE B: **Using Roots to Define Words.** Copy each of the words in the first column onto your paper and underline the root in it. Then find the meaning of the word in the second column and write it next to the word.

1. conscience
2. portable
3. facilitate
4. consensus
5. complicate
6. manual
7. inducement
8. amicable
9. constriction
10. tenet

a. an opinion held by all or most people
b. operated by hand, pertaining to the hand
c. friendly, showing good will
d. motive, incentive
e. a tightness or inward pressure
f. a sense of what is right or wrong
g. to make easier
h. capable of being carried
i. a doctrine or opinion held as true
j. to make difficult or involved

■ Suffixes

The third and last word part to be considered is the suffix. A suffix is a syllable or group of syllables added to the end of a word to form a new word. Some suffixes, called inflectional suffixes, have a number of functions. They can be used to make nouns plural (doughnut, doughnut*s*), show degrees of comparison in modifiers (sleepy, sleepi*er*, sleepi*est*), or show changes in verb form (skate, skat*ed*, skat*ing*).

The suffixes presented in this section, however, are those that change the meaning and, often, the part of speech of a word. For example, if you add the suffix *-tion* to the verb *predict*, you will have the noun *prediction*. If you add the suffix *-able*, you will have the adjective *predictable*. If you add the suffix *-ly* to the adjective *predictable*, you will have the adverb predictably. The chart that follows lists twenty-five suffixes with their various forms and their origins. It also shows the part of speech that results when a particular suffix is added to a word.

TWENTY-FIVE COMMON SUFFIXES

Suffix	Meaning	Examples	Part of Speech
-able (-ible) [L.]	capable of being; tending to	believable, divisible	adjective
-ac (-ic) [Gr.]	characteristic of; relating to	hypochondriac, prosaic	noun or adjective
-al [L.]	like; suitable for	comical	adjective
-ance (-ence) [L.]	the act of; the quality or state of being	defiance, diffidence	noun
-ant (-ent) [L.]	that shows, has, or does; a person or thing that shows, has, or does	compliant, occupant, inherent, superintendent	adjective or noun
-ary (-ery) [L.]	pertaining to; connected with	honorary, surgery	adjective or noun
-ate [L.]	making, applying, or operating on	animate	verb
-cy (-acy) [Gr.]	quality; condition; state	hesitancy, fallacy	noun
-esque [L.]	in the manner or style of	picturesque	adjective
-ful [O.E.]	full of; characterized by; having the ability or tendency to	spoonful, beautiful	noun or adjective
-fy [L.]	to make; to cause to become; to cause to have	magnify	verb
-ish [O.E.]	of or belonging to; rather; tending to	stylish	adjective
-ism [Gr.]	the act, practice, or result of; characteristic of the theory of	pacifism	noun
-ist [Gr.]	a person who does or makes; a person skilled in; a believer in	pianist	noun
-ity [L.]	state of being; character; condition of	charity	noun

-ive [L.]	tending to; a person who	declarative, detective	adjective or noun
-ize (-ise) [Gr.]	to make	characterize, improvise	verb
-less [O.E.]	without; lacking	humorless	adjective
-ly [O.E.]	in a certain way	deliberately, locally	adjective or adverb
-ment [L.]	result or product of	statement	noun
-ness [O.E.]	state of being	promptness	noun
-or [L.]	a person or thing that; a quality or conditon that	inventor, horror	noun
-ous (-ious) [L.]	marked by; given to	dangerous, gracious	adjective
-tion (-ion, -sion, -ation, -ition) [L.]	the action of; the state of being	friction, invasion, preparation, condition	noun
-ure [L.]	act or result of; instrument of; state of being	tenure, pleasure	noun

EXERCISE C: **Using Suffixes to Form New Words.** Add a suffix to each of the following roots to form a word that fits the definition given at the right. Write each new word and its part of speech on your paper. Then check your answers in a dictionary.

1. graph-
2. amic-
3. mot-
4. vent-
5. puls-

a. relating to handwriting
b. tending to be friendly
c. a reason for tending to
d. a risky or dangerous undertaking
e. to beat rhythmically

APPLICATION: **Using Structure to Determine Meaning.** Use your knowledge of the meanings of word parts in analyzing the following words. First, write each word on your paper and circle the root. Then underline any prefix once and any suffix twice. Jot down what you think the word means and then check your guess in a dictionary. Finally, use each word in a sentence.

1. requisition
2. conjecture
3. malediction
4. deductive
5. inversion

6. precedence
7. contentious
8. supplication
9. deference
10. sufferance

Chapter 14

Spelling Improvement

One of the reasons spelling is an important skill is that the lack of it is so noticeable. A reader's response to your writing, whether in school or out, will be affected by spelling errors. People often feel that poor spelling is a sign of carelessness and will judge a writer who makes spelling errors accordingly.

If you have problems with spelling, it is encouraging to know that the great majority of words in the English language are spelled in a regular manner according to a few definite rules. A knowledge of these rules, then, will give you the key to the correct spelling of most words. It is even more encouraging to know that there are proven techniques to help overcome spelling problems. The first section of this chapter will supply you with some of these and give you an opportunity to practice them. The second section will summarize the basic rules.

14.1 Techniques for Improving Spelling

Whether your spelling skills are excellent, adequate, or in need of improvement, a dictionary is a big help. When you proofread written work, use a dictionary to check a doubtful spelling or to learn the spelling of a difficult word. If you find that you are consistently misspelling certain words, the techniques in this section will be especially helpful.

■ Some Basic Methods for Spelling Improvement

When you write the first draft of a composition or of an important letter, you may be thinking of content rather than of spelling. Consequently, you might misspell words that you actually know how to spell. Since you know the correct spelling, these errors can easily be corrected through proofreading. However, there may be other words that really are spelling problems. Words that often cause problems include words that have confusing endings, words that sound like other words, and the inevitable demons. In addition, there may be words that are new to you or words that you have heard but have never written. You can, of course, solve these spelling problems immediately by referring to the dictionary. For long-term spelling improvement, however, you may want to create a personal spelling list in a special section of your notebook. You may also find it useful to hold regular practice sessions, create special memory aids, and study lists of spelling demons.

Recording Problem Words.   Perhaps the most important technique for improving your spelling is recording in a special section of your notebook the correct spelling of any words that you find difficult.

> Use a dictionary to correct spelling errors and record problem words in a personal spelling list.

Whenever a teacher returns a corrected composition or test, check it for spelling errors. In a dictionary, look up the correct spelling of those words. Then set up a personal spelling list in any way that is helpful for you. You may, for example, choose to divide a page into two columns, labeling the first, "Misspelled Words." Here you can enter the words exactly as you have misspelled them. This column will enable you to analyze your errors. The second column can be headed "Correct Spelling." Fill it in after you have looked up the word in a dictionary. Some students also find it helpful to record in a third column hints for remembering correct spellings.

Practicing Problem Words.   For some people, writing the correct spelling of a word once is sufficient to fix it in their memory. For most people, however, it is necessary to practice the correct spelling.

> Set up regular practice sessions to study problem words.

The chart that follows explains an efficient way to commit the spelling of your problem words to memory.

MEMORIZING THE SPELLING OF PROBLEM WORDS

1. Observe each word on your list carefully, noticing the arrangement of letters. Try to visualize the word. For example, observe the word *accommodate*, noticing that there are two *c*'s and two *m*'s.

2. Pronounce the word to yourself in syllables. For example, if you remember that *lightning* has only two syllables, you will have no trouble with the spelling. (If you mispronounce it as *light-en-ing*, you will probably misspell it.)

3. Write the correct spelling of the word on a separate piece of paper and then check to see if you have spelled it correctly.

4. Review your list until you have mastered each word.

Using Mnemonics to Improve Spelling.   The word *mnemonics* is derived from a Greek word meaning "to remember." A mnemonic device, then, is a trick to help you remember something.

Use memory aids to improve your spelling.

One trick is to look for one or more familiar words within a problem word.

EXAMPLES: earnest   Put your *ear* to the *nest* for *earnest*.

nuclear   Are the arguments concerning nu*clear* plants *clear?*

prairie   Is there still fresh *air* on the pr*air*ie?

Another spelling mnemonic device is to associate the spelling of a problem word with a related idea.

EXAMPLES: parallel   Think of the two *l*'s as parallel lines.

separate   To separate something you break it apart. Both *separate* and *apart* have two *a*'s.

Try to make up your own memory aids, add them to your spelling list, and you will probably see an improvement in your spelling skills.

Memorizing Spelling Demons.   You are probably familiar with the lists of words commonly referred to as spelling demons. Some of these words follow the basic rules. Others follow no rule. All may be words that will cause problems for you now or in the future.

Check lists of spelling demons to identify additional problem words.

Look over the following list and check yourself. Add to your personal spelling list any words you are not absolutely sure of and practice them regularly, using any mnemonic devices you can think of.

COMMON SPELLING DEMONS

abbreviate	conscience	handkerchief	possession
absence	conscientious	height	prairie
accidentally	conscious	hygiene	precede
achieve	contemporary	hypnotic	precision
acquaintance	continuous	immigrant	preferable
accommodate	controversial	immobile	prejudice
accumulate	convenience	incorrigible	preparation
adjective	coolly	independence	principal
admittance	cordially	indigestion	principle
adolescence	correspondence	infinite	privilege
advertisement	counterfeit	inflammable	probably
aerial	courageous	initial	procedure
aerosol	courtesy	inoculate	proceed
aggravate	criticism	interfere	prompt
aggressive	criticize	irrelevant	pronunciation
aisle	curiosity	journal	protein
allowance	curious	judicial	pseudonym
all right	cylinder	knowledge	psychology
amateur	deceive	laboratory	punctuation
ambassador	decision	labyrinth	really
analysis	defendant	lawyer	recede
analyze	defiance	legitimate	receipt
anecdote	deficient	library	recognize
anniversary	delinquent	license	recommend
annual	descendant	lieutenant	reference
anonymous	description	lightning	rehearse
anxiety	desert	loneliness	reliance
apostrophe	despair	maintenance	religious
apparatus	desperate	mathematics	repetition
apparent	dessert	meanness	restaurant
appearance	development	mediocre	rhythm
apprentice	dining	merchandise	ridiculous
appropriate	disappear	meteor	schedule
argument	disappoint	mileage	scissors
ascend	disastrous	millionaire	secretary
assassinate	discern	miniature	separate
association	disciple	mischievous	sergeant
athletic	dissatisfied	misspell	similar
attendance	distinction	mortgage	sincerely
audience	distinguish	museum	sophomore

awkward	doubt	naturally	souvenir
banquet	earnest	necessary	spaghetti
barrel	economical	neighbor	spiritual
behavior	efficient	nickel	straight
believe	eighth	ninety	substitute
beneficial	eligible	nuclear	succeed
benefit	embarrass	nuisance	superintendent
bicycle	emergency	obsolete	supersede
bookkeeper	eminent	obstacle	surprise
bulletin	enemy	occasion	suspicious
bureau	envelope	occasionally	syllable
business	environment	occur	symmetrical
cafeteria	equipped	occurred	technique
calendar	equivalent	odyssey	technology
cancel	erroneous	omitted	temperament
capital	essential	opinion	temperature
capitol	exaggerate	optimistic	temporary
captain	exceed	outrageous	tenant
career	exercise	pamphlet	thorough
carriage	exhaust	parallel	tomatoes
category	exhibit	paralyze	tomorrow
cemetery	exhilarate	particularly	tragedy
census	existence	pastime	truly
cereal	explanation	permanent	twelfth
changeable	extension	permissible	unanimous
chauffeur	extraordinary	personally	unforgettable
clothes	familiar	perspiration	unnecessary
colonel	fantasy	persuasive	vaccine
column	fascinate	phantom	vacuum
committee	February	physician	vegetable
comparative	financial	pigeon	villain
competitor	foreign	pneumonia	vitamin
concede	grammar	political	Wednesday
condemn	guarantee	pollution	weird
congratulate	guidance	possess	whether

EXERCISE A: Proofreading, Recording, and Practicing Problem Words. The following paragraph contains ten spelling errors. Find the misspelled words and write them correctly on your paper. Check each one in a dictionary. If you find that you have made errors, record the words in your spelling list. Then practice the words using the steps given in the chart on page 416.

(1) The skilful asking of questions is an esential part of the repetoire of the efective teacher. (2) Since it is practicaly imposible to conceive of teaching without the asking of questions, successfull teaching strategys will include analizing all aspects of the question-asking procedure.

EXERCISE B: Using Mnemonics to Master Spelling Demons. Write the following words on your paper, filling in the missing letters. Then check each word in a dictionary and record any words you missed in your spelling list. Finally, try to devise a mnemonic device for the spelling of each missed word.

1. fanta___y
2. congra___ulate
3. gramm___r
4. acquaint___nce
5. exten___ion

6. audi___nce
7. od___ssey
8. caf___teria
9. absen___e
10. opt___mistic

■ Diagnosing Your Spelling Errors

In working with spelling demons, you may have noticed that many of them do not follow any specific rule. They must simply be memorized. Other hard-to-spell words, such as those in the following test, are spelled according to definite rules. After taking this test, correcting it, and analyzing your errors, you should be able to zero in on the rules you need to study. You may, for example, have no difficulty spelling the plural forms of words and yet have trouble with the *ie/ei* words.

Analyze your spelling errors to determine your areas of weakness and then study the rules that will help you.

To take the following diagnostic test, read each sentence and then jot down the word that correctly completes the sentence. Exercise C will show you how to analyze your errors.

1. Is your new jacket _____? (Special Rules for Confusing Suffixes)

    (a) reversable   (b) reversible   (c) reservable

2. I consulted a _____ book in the library. (Special Rules for Confusing Suffixes)

    (a) reference   (b) referance   (c) referrence

3. We are _____ a letter to the mayor today. (Basic Rules for Suffixes)

    (a) writting   (b) writing   (c) writeing

4. We put plenty of _____ in the stew. (Basic Rules for Plurals)

    (a) tomatoes   (b) tomatos   (c) tomato's

5. I was _____ in the election results.   (Basic Rules for Prefixes)

   (a) disappointed   (b) dissappointed   (c) disapointed

6. The _____ train blocked the crossing.   (Basic *ie/ei* Rule)

   (a) fraight   (b) frieght   (c) freight

7. We are _____ our papers before handing them in.   (Basic Rules for Suffixes)

   (a) editting   (b) edditing   (c) editing

8. If you have no errors on this test, you are an _____ speller.   (Special Rules for Confusing Suffixes)

   (a) excellent   (b) excelant   (c) excellant

9. The color of the _____ is beautiful in the autumn.   (Basic Rules for Plurals)

   (a) leafs   (b) leaves   (c) leavs

10. Because he had _____ his return address, Ed received no response to his letter.   (Basic Rules for Suffixes)

    (a) omitted   (b) ommitted   (c) omited

EXERCISE C: **Analyzing Your Spelling Errors.** After your test has been corrected, look at each of your errors and note the item in parentheses after each sentence. Then look up the rules in Section 14.2 and study the examples, exceptions, and any charts provided. Finally, record the words you misspelled in your spelling list. Review them periodically, as suggested in the chart on page 416.

APPLICATION: **Mastering Your Problem Words.** Choose ten words from your personal spelling list. Use them in a paragraph describing your reaction to a book you have read recently or to a sports event you have read about or attended.

14.2 A Catalog of Spelling Rules

This section catalogs the basic rules governing the spelling of most of the words in the English language. If you spend some time studying these rules, you should be able to spell many words almost automatically. You might want to concentrate on the rules that you diagnosed in the previous section as being problem areas for you.

■ The *ie* and *ei* Rule

If you were to ask a group of people, young, old, and in-between, what spelling rule stands out in their mind, they would probably give the following rule.

Write *i* before *e*
Except after *c*,
Or when sounded like *a*
As in *neighbor* and *weigh.*

Helpful as this rule is for many words, such as *chief, ceiling, reindeer,* and *freight,* it has exceptions. For example, the following words do not have a *c,* nor do they have the long *a* sound, yet they use the *ei* spelling.

EXCEPTIONS:

either	leisure	sheik
foreign	neither	their
height	seize	weird

For another group of *ie/ei* words, another rule may be used.

When *c* is pronounced *sh,* write *i* before *e.*

EXAMPLES:

ancient	efficient
conscience	sufficient

EXERCISE A: **Spelling** *ie* and *ei* **Words.** Copy the following *ie/ei* words, filling in the missing letters in the correct order.

Conscious of the fact that I had studied my (1) anc____nt history assignment very (2) br____fly, I was understandably nervous when I took the exam. When I (3) rec____ved the corrected test the next day, I was afraid to look at it. When I finally looked, I couldn't (4) bel____ve my eyes! I had (5) n____ther failed nor squeaked by with a C. At the top of the paper was a beautiful A! I almost (6) shr____ked with joy. However, my (7) ch____f emotion was not (8) conc____t but sheer (9) rel____f. Next week, I'll plan to set aside (10) suffic____nt time to study instead of trusting to luck.

■ Spelling Plural Forms

The plurals of most nouns are formed by the addition of -*s* or -*es*.

Add -*s* or -*es* to form the plural of most nouns.

The addition is determined by the noun ending. For these additions and for spelling changes that result, consult the following chart.

ADDITIONS AND SPELLING CHANGES WHEN FORMING PLURALS			
Noun Ending	**Rule**	**Examples**	**Exceptions**
s, x, z, sh, ch	Add -*es*.	businesses, boxes, waltzes, dishes, churches	
o preceded by a consonant	Add -*es*.	heroes, potatoes	Musical terms: pianos, sopranos
o preceded by a vowel	Just add -*s*.	patios, rodeos	
y preceded by a consonant	Change *y* to *i* and add -*es*.	colonies, cities	
y preceded by a vowel	Just add -*s*.	journeys, holidays	
f, ff, fe	Add -*s*.	proofs, cliffs	Change -*f* to -*v* and add -*s* or -*es*: wives, loaves

The plurals of some nouns are formed in irregular ways. In addition to the familiar change from *mouse* to *mice* and from *goose* to *geese*, there are nouns such as *datum*, which becomes *data*, *medium*, which becomes *media*, and *radius*, which becomes *radii*. In addition, the singular forms of some nouns are used to denote the plural (*sheep, moose*) while there are only plural forms (*politics, mathematics*) for some other nouns.

Compound nouns may also cause problems. To form the plurals of compound nouns written as separate or hyphenated words, make the modified nouns plural.

EXAMPLES: passer-by   passers-by

bucket seat   bucket seats

If you are unsure of how to form a plural, check a dictionary. If no plural form is given, simply add *-s* or *-es* to the singular form.

NOTE ABOUT OTHER SPECIAL PLURALS: As explained in Section 12.6, an apostrophe is used to form the plurals of letters (*a's, b's,* and *c's*), numbers *(the 1950's)*, symbols *(&'s)*, and words used as words *(and's)*.

EXERCISE B: Forming Plurals. Write the plural form of each of the following words. Check your answers in a dictionary.

1. leaf
2. tomato
3. circus
4. fly
5. pen pal
6. roof
7. crisis
8. lunch
9. radio
10. salmon

■ Adding Prefixes to Roots

The addition of a prefix does not affect the spelling of the root.

When a prefix is added to a word, the spelling of the root word remains the same.

EXAMPLES: dis + satisy = dissatisfy

mis + spell = misspell

re + consider = reconsider

un + polluted = unpolluted

For more examples of roots with prefixes added, you can refer to the chart that begins on page 407. The chart also indicates the way the spelling of certain prefixes is changed when the prefixes are joined to certain roots. Notice, however, that the rule still applies—the spelling of the root word remains the same. The reason the spelling of the prefix is changed is for ease of pronunciation.

EXAMPLES: *ad-* becomes *ap-* before *prove: approve*

in- becomes *ir-* before *reverent: irreverent*

sub- becomes *sup-* before *press: suppress*

EXERCISE C: Spelling Words with Prefixes. Form new words by adding one of the following seven prefixes to each of the numbered roots. You will have to use some of the prefixes more than once. You may also have to change the form of the prefix.

com-, de-, dis-, ex-, in-, mis-, sub-

1. -pose
2. -interpret
3. -pound
4. -respond
5. -marine

6. -appear
7. -literate
8. -migrate
9. -appropriate
10. -press

■ Adding Suffixes to Roots

When spelling a word to which a suffix has been added, there are two things you should look at: (1) the ending of the root word and (2) the beginning letter of the suffix.

Before adding a suffix, notice the last letters of the root word and the first letter of the suffix.

The following chart details the spelling changes that are necessary when suffixes are added to roots.

SPELLING CHANGES BEFORE SUFFIXES			
Word Ending	Suffix Added	Rule	Exceptions
consonant + y (mercy, defy)	most suffixes (ful, ance)	Change *y* to *i*. merciful, defiance	Most suffixes beginning with *i*: hurry becomes hurrying defy becomes defying
vowel + y (convey, employ)	most suffixes (or, ment)	Make no change. conveyor, employment	A few short words: day becomes daily gay becomes gaiety
any word ending in e (prove, strive)	suffix beginning with a vowel (able, ing)	Drop the final *e*. provable, striving	1. Words ending in *ce* or *ge* with suffixes beginning in *a* or *o*: notice becomes noticeable courage becomes courageous

			2. Words ending in *ee* or *oe*: see becomes seeing toe becomes toeing
			3. A few special words: dye becomes dyeing be becomes being
any word ending in e (care, love)	suffix beginning with a consonant (ful, ly)	Make no change. careful, lovely	A few special words: true becomes truly argue becomes argument judge becomes judgment
consonant + vowel + consonant and a stressed syllable (forbid', permit')	suffix beginning with a vowel (en, ed)	Double the final consonant. forbid'den, permit'ted	1. Words ending in *w* or *x*: draw becomes drawing box becomes boxed 2. Words in which the stress changes after the suffix is added: prefer' + ing becomes prefer'ring BUT prefer' + ence becomes pref'erence
consonant + vowel + consonant and an unstressed syllable (budg'et, depos'it)	suffix beginning with a vowel (ed, or)	Make no change. budg'eted, depos'itor	No major exceptions
1 vowel + consonant in one-syllable word (step, run)	suffix beginning with a vowel (ing, er)	Double the final consonant. stepping, runner	Words ending in *w* or *x*: draw becomes drawing box becomes boxed
2 vowels + consonant in one-syllable word (pour, heat)	suffix beginning with a vowel (ed, ing)	Make no change. poured, heating	No major exceptions

EXERCISE D: Spelling Words with Suffixes. Spell each of the following items correctly.

1. propel + -er
2. wrap + -ing
3. peace + -ful
4. arrive + -ing
5. extreme + -ity

6. tour + -ing
7. request + -ed
8. final + -ist
9. annoy + -ance
10. happy + -ness

■ Spelling Words with Confusing Suffixes

Although the rules in the preceding chart can help you add most suffixes, you should also become familiar with certain groups of suffixes that are often confused with one another.

Learn to distinguish between confusing groups of suffixes.

-able, -ible.   The rules governing the use of this pair of suffixes depend on a knowledge of Latin verbs. You can learn the spelling of some words with these endings, however, by studying the following chart. For words not included, check a dictionary.

Common Words Ending in -*able*		Common Words Ending in -*ible*	
acceptable	imaginable	accessible	irresistible
advisable	irritable	convertible	permissible
available	memorable	digestible	possible
believable	peaceable	edible	responsible
comfortable	predictable	eligible	reversible
considerable	reasonable	flexible	sensible
durable	taxable	horrible	terrible

-ance (-ancy, -ant) and -ence (-ency, -ent).   If a noun takes the *a* spelling of this suffix (*defiance*) the corresponding adjective will also take the *a* spelling (*defiant*). The same applies to the *e* spelling (*eloquence, eloquent*). It is not easy to determine which spelling to use, but there is one rule that helps. Words with a hard *c* or *g* sound usually take the *a* spelling (*significance, arrogant*). Those with a soft *c* or *g* sound usually take the *e* spelling (*deficiency, efficient*). There are many -*ance* and

-ence words, however, without *c* or *g* sounds. To learn the spelling of some of the most common of these words, study the following chart.

Common Words Ending in -ance		Common Words Ending in -ence	
abundance	entrance	absence	experience
acquaintance	guidance	coherence	independence
appearance	importance	coincidence	lenience
assistance	maintenance	conference	opulence
brilliance	radiance	consequence	patience
clearance	tolerance	convenience	presence
		correspondence	residence
		excellence	violence

-ary, -ery. People are often confused about whether to end a word with *-ary* or *-ery*. Fortunately, very few words end in *-ery*. Once you learn these words, you will know that most other words with an ending that sounds similar will take the *-ary* spelling. The following chart will help you decide, in most cases, whether to use *-ary* or *-ery*.

Common Words Ending in -ary		Common Words Ending in -ery	
auxiliary	necessary	cemetery	nursery
boundary	secretary	distillery	scenery
elementary	secondary	millinery	stationery
February	stationary	monastery	(note paper)
honorary	(not moving)		winery
imaginary			
library	temporary		
military	vocabulary		
momentary	voluntary		

-cy, -sy. Another confusing pair of suffixes is *-cy* and *-sy*. Again, only a few words end in *-sy*. If you learn the words in the following chart, you can be fairly sure that other words end in *-cy*. If you are not sure of a spelling, always consult a dictionary.

COMMON WORDS ENDING IN *-sy*

autopsy	epilepsy
biopsy	fantasy
courtesy	heresy
curtsy	hypocrisy
ecstasy	idiosyncrasy
embassy	pleurisy

-eous, -ious, -ous, -uous.   Confusion may also arise over the spelling of words ending in *-eous, -ious, -ous,* and *-uous.* Some of this confusion can be resolved by paying strict attention to the pronunciation of the word. The words ending in *-uous,* for example, can be easily distinguished from the others if they are pronounced carefully. The following are the most common of these words.

COMMON WORDS ENDING IN *-uous*

ambiguous	ingenuous
conspicuous	strenuous
continuous	sumptuous
fatuous	

Deciding whether to use *-eous* or *-ious* is more difficult, since pronunciation does not help you. With these endings, it may be more helpful to memorize the spelling of the most common words in these two groups. Fortunately, the lists are not too long.

Common Words Ending in *-eous*		Common Words Ending in *-ious*	
advantageous	gorgeous	anxious	harmonious
beauteous	miscellaneous	atrocious	ingenious
courageous	outrageous	cautious	laborious
courteous	righteous	conscientious	officious
erroneous	simultaneous	conscious	precious
		contagious	rebellious
		curious	religious

delicious	repetitious
fictitious	superstitious
furious	suspicious
gracious	

Careful pronunciation is the key to the correct spelling of words ending in *-ous*. Since there are so many *-ous* words, your best bet is to learn the words in the preceding lists. If a word does *not* appear in one of the lists, it probably takes the *-ous* ending.

-ify and -efy. Here again your choices are simplified because one of this pair is rarely used. Of common English words, only the words in the following chart end in *-efy*.

Words Ending in *-efy*	
liquefy	rarefy
putrefy	stupefy

-sion, -tion. Some of the confusion over the use of this pair of suffixes can be resolved by using the following chart to learn the spelling of some of the most commonly used words that have these suffixes. However, the chart includes just a sampling. If you are not sure of a word that does not appear in the following chart, look it up in a dictionary. It may help you to remember that if a word has the *zh* sound, *as in confusion*, the suffix is *-sion*.

Common Words Ending in *-sion*		Common Words Ending in *-tion*	
abrasion	extension	affirmation	contradiction
aggression	fission	alteration	corruption
allusion	fusion	appreciation	distraction
apprehension	illusion	civilization	flirtation
confusion	immersion	competition	gratification
conversion	intercession	completion	justification
discussion	intrusion	connection	multiplication
dissension	mission	constriction	portion
	version	contention	satisfaction

EXERCISE E: Spelling Words with Confusing Suffixes. Choose the correctly spelled word from each of the following pairs and write it on your paper.

1. Do not include any (miscellaneous, miscellanious) information.
2. They're building an (extention, extension) on the old factory.
3. The physics test was (impossibly, impossably) difficult.
4. Only a student with a (brillient, brilliant) mind could hope to pass it.
5. Coming late to rehearsal is (unacceptible, unacceptable).
6. She had an (excellent, excellant) chance of making the team.
7. Have you ever visited a (monastery, monastary)?
8. At least he had the (courtecy, courtesy) to return my call.
9. What (elementery, elementary) school did you attend?
10. The doctor thought it (advisible, advisable) to exercise the injured arm.

APPLICATION: Using Spelling Rules in Writing Sentences.

1. Write five original sentences, each containing a word spelled with *ei* or *ie*. Three of these sentences should also contain plural nouns.
2. Write five original sentences, each containing a word with a prefix. Two of these sentences should also contain plural nouns.
3. Write four original sentences, each containing one of the following:
   (a) a word ending in *y* with a suffix added
   (b) a word ending in *e* with a suffix added
   (c) a one-syllable word ending in a consonant with a suffix added
   (d) a multisyllable word ending in a consonant with a suffix added
4. Write six original sentences, each containing a word ending in one of the confusing groups of suffixes.

V

Study Skills

Basic Study Skills

After high school, you may never again be asked to identify the tone of a newspaper editorial or the propaganda devices used in a television commercial. You may never be asked to give a five-minute informational speech or to write a précis of a chapter of a novel. However, the skills that you use to perform these tasks are skills that you will continue to draw on throughout your life.

Presumably, you will continue to read, write, listen, and speak, whether you continue your education or go immediately into the job market. You will read job-related as well as personal material; you will write either in carrying out personal correspondence or as part of your job. You will be continually listening to others—both in conversation and in job-related matters. Finally, the way you express yourself in speaking will often give others their first impression of you.

This chapter will discuss ways in which you can improve your skills in all of these areas. It will also offer pointers on organizing information and getting a job.

15.1 Setting Goals for School and Life

Acquiring and practicing reading, writing, listening, and speaking skills can help you become a more effective, active learner in school and out of school. These four skills lead naturally from one to another, each relying on the others for growth and reinforcement. You can increase your abilities in all of these areas by setting goals for yourself and by following certain suggestions offered later in this section

The best place to begin, however, is not with these particular skills, but with an even more basic element—the issue of time.

■ Organizing Your Schedule

Your last year in high school is a transitional year—probably a very busy one. It is a year in which you will prepare yourself for work, additional schooling, or both; and it is a year in which many students have numerous leisure-time activities as well. With so many things going on, this is also an important year for learning to organize your time.

> Each week, plan a work, study, and leisure-time activity schedule on an hour-by-hour basis.

Your first consideration in planning your schedule should be your school courses. This year offers you a last chance to maintain or improve the grades that will be sent to other schools or employers. An after-school job or the lead in the senior play is no excuse for letting your grades slip and may suggest to someone examining your record that you are unable to manage your time efficiently. When planning your weekly schedule, keep the following guidelines in mind.

SUGGESTIONS FOR PLANNING A WEEKLY SCHEDULE

1. Budget at least 45 minutes each day for each major subject you are taking.
2. Use weekends to work on long-term research and writing assignments. (Do not use them to catch up on daily assignments.)
3. Schedule your study time for periods when you will be alert and relaxed—generally not late at night or early in the morning.
4. Use study halls effectively—for reviewing and reorganizing class notes, completing exercise assignments, doing library research, and so on.

Reviewing your schedule each week will enable you to accommodate special situations as they occur—a change in your working hours, extra rehearsals or sports practice, a special social event, an announced test, a new long-term research project, and so on. Your teachers may not be willing to accept an extra shift at work, a four-page application form that was due, a late dress rehearsal, or a date you could not pass up as an excuse for an incomplete assignment.

Anyone can find time for the things they want to do. The successful people are the ones who first accomplish what they must do and then—because they have scheduled their time well—are still able to do the things they want to do.

EXERCISE A: **Preparing Your Own Schedule.** Write the days of the week across the top of your paper. Down the side of the paper, record each hour of the day from 7:00 A.M. to 10:00 P.M. Then follow these steps to plan your personal schedule for the week.

1. List your class schedule.
2. List any work hours and the hours of any clubs or school activities to which you are committed. (Since these hours are usually determined by someone else, they are often inflexible.)
3. If you have any responsibilities at home with fixed hours (preparing dinner, for example), record these at the appropriate times.
4. Go over your list of assignments for the week and record the times each day when you will work on them. Do not overlook study hall periods, and be sure to include extra time if you have a test to review for or a long-range assignment to work on.
5. If you cannot find at least 45 minutes for each major subject, look over the second and third steps to see where you can find some extra time. If you must use the last time slot in a day for study, schedule it for the subject or assignment you find least demanding.

■ Setting Goals

Basic skills in reading, writing, listening, and speaking are among the survival skills you will need throughout your life to increase your learning and problem-solving abilities. These skills correlate highly with success.

> Improve your basic skills in reading, writing, listening, and speaking to improve your chances for success.

The basic skills involved in academic success and the skills needed for success in employment are much the same. Employers in one community listed the skills in the following chart as the most desirable traits in potential employees in order of importance. A college or vocational school admissions officer would undoubtedly list many of the same traits. Notice how many of them relate to reading, writing, listening, and speaking.

SUCCESS-RELATED SKILLS

1. A positive attitude toward one's work (or study)
2. Ability to follow directions
3. Ability to listen
4. Good reading comprehension
5. Legible handwriting
6. Accuracy with figures
7. Good writing ability
8. Effective speaking ability
9. Accurate spelling
10. Neatness and common sense

As you can see, the list stresses skills that most people should be able to acquire with practice. Whether you are in the top half of your class or the bottom half, you *can* acquire these basic skills. If you truly want to succeed in further education, on the job, and in life in general, the effort needed to acquire these skills will be worth your time.

On the following pages, you will find ideas for working on your listening and speaking skills, as well as suggestions for expanding your personal reading program. Unit VI is devoted to increasing your writing skills.

EXERCISE B: **Setting Personal Goals.** Identify the three traits in the preceding chart in which you are weakest, and write these traits in the front of your notebook. Review the list each morning and make an effort in each class to improve these skills. When you have finished this section, reevaluate your list and try to determine the progress you have made.

■ Listening to and Following Directions

Whether you are in the classroom or on the job, listening to and following directions is of major importance. You may be perfectly capable of handling the material or the task at hand, but if you fail to follow the specific directions given, you may fail to achieve the desired result.

One basic rule should help you improve your listening skills greatly.

Recall directions immediately after they are given to you.

The suggestions in the following chart should also prove useful.

SUGGESTIONS FOR IMPROVING YOUR ABILITY TO LISTEN
1. If you are uncertain about the directions you are to follow, ask to have the directions repeated.
2. Try to recall the directions mentally once again before actually beginning the task.
3. Mentally link directions together in a series of visual images for better retention.
4. Write down any directions you feel you may have trouble remembering.
5. After completing a task, check to see that you have followed all directions completely.

EXERCISE C: **Correcting Faulty Listening Skills.** For one week make a note of each error you make because you failed to listen well to directions. Try to classify the source of each problem, keeping a tally of each problem that falls into one of the following categories. When you have isolated the causes of your listening problems, make an effort to correct these specific types of errors.

1. Missing the main idea of the instructions
2. Missing an important detail in the instructions
3. Missing one or two key words in the instructions
4. Jumping to a faulty or hasty conclusion
5. Failing to complete all aspects of the instructions

■ Speaking in Discussions

Active participation in classroom discussions, club meetings, and job-related meetings demands an ability to combine speaking and listening skills. If you have not first listened closely to the announced topic and the comments and contributions of other speakers, you will not be able to form your own opinion or make a meaningful contribution to the discussion.

Prepare to contribute to discussions by first listening attentively and then following certain guidelines to make your contribution as useful as possible.

There are few things more annoying than taking part in a discussion or meeting dominated by one person who does not really listen to what others are saying. To avoid being this kind of participant—or the nonparticipant who sits back and offers nothing—begin by trying to sharpen your listening skills. A good system for directing your thinking in a discussion and for following its contours and content intelligently is called linked thinking. To use this method, follow the chart below.

QUESTIONS TO ANSWER WHEN USING LINKED THINKING

1. What is the topic of the discussion?
2. What did the first speaker add to the discussion?
3. What was your personal reaction to the first speaker's comments?
   a. If the person offered an opinion, do you agree or disagree?
   b. Do you have anything of value to add in either instance?
4. What did the next speaker add to the discussion?
5. What was your reaction to the second speaker's comments?
6. What did the third speaker add to the discussion?
7. What was your personal reaction?

The linked-thinking process should be carried out quickly in your head. You should also learn to disregard certain types of information. Information that is repetitive, that strays too far from the topic under discussion, or that is of little value need not be included in your linked thinking.

To make a decision about orally responding to a particular point made in the discussion, evaluate the response section of the linked-thinking pattern. If you can answer yes to "Do I agree with the prior speaker?" or "Do I disagree with the prior speaker?" and yes to "Do I have anything of value to add?" make an immediate response. Keep the following suggestions in mind when you make your response.

GUIDELINES FOR RESPONDING IN A DISCUSSION

1. Keep to the main topic; do not go off into a minor related area.
2. Make your point as clearly and quickly as possible.
3. If you are expressing the same point of view as another person, acknowledge this agreement and immediately add the new information or ideas that support your viewpoint.
4. If you are disagreeing strongly with another person, do so as courteously as possible, backing up your own opinion and avoiding personal remarks.

5. Learn to enter a discussion by listening carefully for a speaker's concluding statement and being ready to start immediately with your own response.

Like any other skill, speaking in discussions takes practice. Your timing will not always be exact when you start out, but the more you practice, the better you will get.

EXERCISE D: **Speaking in Discussions.** For each discussion you attend in the next week, make a chart like the partially completed one that follows. Fill in the chart for each discussion or meeting in which you are involved. Record your own opinions and responses and try to improve the number and quality of your responses in each succeeding discussion.

TOPIC: CLASS TRIP				
Speaker	Speaker's Opinion	Own Opinion Agree	Disagree	Own Response
Speaker 1	charge $25.00 per student		√	—
Speaker 2	hold a bake sale	√		—
Speaker 3	have a talent show	—	—	—
Speaker 4	hold a raffle		√	last raffle failed
Speaker 5	cancel the trip		√	—

■ Developing the Pleasure-Reading Habit

What you read will greatly influence not only your knowledge but also your ability to express yourself. Research has shown that people who read widely have better vocabularies, express themselves better in speaking and writing, and in general possess better verbal and reasoning skills than those who do not.

During your school years, you have probably been required to read a certain number of novels, biographies, essays, and short stories for class each year. This transitional year—after which you may not have such readings assigned—is an ideal time to ask yourself this question: "What will I read when I can choose my reading matter for myself?" It is also a time in which you can begin to build the pleasure-reading habit, not just for enjoyment but also for the added benefits mentioned in the preceding paragraph.

If you have not yet acquired the habit of reading for pleasure, begin with a half hour of reading daily.

In making the transition from required reading to pleasure reading, you should try to do more reading rather than less. The best way to do this is to keep yourself constantly surrounded by a variety of reading materials that you may find particularly interesting. Books and other reading materials may seem expensive, but libraries contain more books, magazines, and newspapers than most people could read in a lifetime.

The following chart offers suggestions that can be followed with materials you either buy or borrow from the library.

SUGGESTIONS FOR DEVELOPING THE PLEASURE-READING HABIT
1. Get into the habit of reading the newspaper on a daily basis.
2. Regularly read several of your favorite magazines.
3. Always keep a book or magazine handy in your desk, book bag, or the place where you relax to encourage reading in your free time.
4. Discuss what you are reading with your friends.
5. Read the book review sections of newspapers and magazines to keep abreast of new material that may interest you.

If you are not in the habit of reading for pleasure, now is the time to begin acquiring the habit. The first step is to convince yourself of the value of reading for your personal growth and satisfaction as well as for your own success in life. Next, you will need to locate reading material that appeals to you. Finally, at least until you have developed the habit, you will need to set aside a special time each day for personal reading.

The following chart suggests a wide range of plays and novels that have remained popular for many years. Pleasure reading, however, is not confined to these categories. A short time spent browsing through specific subject cards in your library card catalog will suggest a host of titles in nonfiction areas. (See Section 17.1 for more details about the use of the card catalog.)

READING SUGGESTIONS

Austen, Jane   *Pride and Prejudice*

Bowen, Elizabeth   *The House in Paris*

Brontë, Charlotte   *Jane Eyre*

Brontë, Emily   *Wuthering Heights*

Carroll, Lewis   *Alice in Wonderland*

Conrad, Joseph   *Heart of Darkness* and *Lord Jim*

Dickens, Charles *A Tale of Two Cities, David Copperfield, Great Expectations, Bleak House,* and *Pickwick Papers*

Dostoevsky, Fyodor   *The Brothers Karamazov* and *Crime and Punishment*

Doyle, Arthur Conan   *The Hound of the Baskervilles*

Eliot, George   *Adam Bede*

Faulkner, William   *The Bear*

Fitzgerald, F. Scott   *The Great Gatsby*

Fitzgerald, Robert (translator)   *The Odyssey*

Forster, E. M.   *A Passage to India*

Gaines, Ernest   *The Autobiography of Miss Jane Pittman*

Golding, William   *Lord of the Flies*

Hansberry, Lorraine   *A Raisin in the Sun*

Hardy, Thomas   *Far from the Madding Crowd*

Hawthorne, Nathaniel   *The Scarlet Letter*

Hemingway, Ernest   *The Old Man and the Sea*

Ibsen, Henrik   *A Doll's House*

Lattimore, Richmond (translator)   *The Iliad*

Lee, Harper   *To Kill a Mockingbird*

Lewis, Sinclair   *Main Street*

Miller, Arthur   *Death of a Salesman*

O'Neill, Eugene   *Ah! Wilderness*

Orwell, George   *Animal Farm*

Paton, Alan   *Cry, the Beloved Country*

Renault, Mary   *The Last of the Wine*

Sayers, Dorothy L.   *The Nine Tailors*

Scott, Walter   *Ivanhoe, The Heart of Midlothian,* and *Kenilworth*

Shaw, George Bernard   *Androcles and the Lion, Major Barbara, Pygmalion,* and *Saint Joan*

Sophocles   *Oedipus Rex*

Steinbeck, John   *The Pearl*

Tennyson, Alfred Lord   *Idylls of the King*

Thackeray, William   *Vanity Fair*

Tolstoy, Leo *War and Peace*
Wharton, Edith *The House of Mirth*
White, T. H. *The Once and Future King*
Wilder, Thornton *Our Town* and *The Skin of Our Teeth*

Reading can bring you more pleasure than almost any other habit you can acquire. Rather than stop reading after high school, you should try to increase the amount of reading you do. It is never too late to become a reader.

EXERCISE E: **Developing a Personal Reading List.** Make a list of five things that you will read during the coming month. You may include books from the preceding chart or required reading from earlier years that you never got around to. Include at least one magazine and one work of nonfiction.

APPLICATION: **Examining Your Goals.** Answer the following questions to examine the progress you have made while working on this section. Answer the questions again at the end of each of the next three weeks to see if you continue to improve.

1. Have you made weekly hour-by-hour schedules?
2. Have you been able to follow the schedules or do you need to be more realistic in making them up?
3. Have you revised your schedules to add at least a half hour a day for pleasure reading?
4. Have you identified the skills you most need to improve?
5. Have you worked conscientiously to improve those skills?
6. Have you identified any problems in listening to directions?
7. Has your ability to follow oral directions improved?
8. Have you increased the number of times you contribute to group discussions?
9. Have you been faithfully reading the selections on your personal reading list?
10. Have you increased both your interest in pleasure reading and the amount of time you spend doing it?

Organizing Information 15.2

By the twelfth grade, your teachers will seldom tell you when to take notes. In fact, they will generally assume that you can decide for yourself not only when to take notes, but also how thorough the notes should be and what form the notes should take. Such decisions, however, are not always easy to make and come only through experience, practice, and refinement.

Although it may often be easier to decide simply to read carefully at home or to listen closely in class instead of taking notes, such a decision may sometimes be shortsighted. Since you may be tested weeks later on your reading assignments and class lectures, good notes will often make it much easier to review the material thoroughly and systematically.

■ Knowing When to Take Notes

Efficient note-taking is difficult and involves several skills: reading, listening, writing, organizing, and making decisions. In addition, it frequently involves a revision stage in which an original set of notes is reworked to make the notes better organized and more useful later on. The first step in note-taking, however, is to recognize when you should take notes.

Recognize situations in which note-taking will be helpful and then get into the habit of taking notes automatically.

In trying to decide whether to take notes in a particular situation, ask yourself the five questions in the following chart. If the answer to at least two of the questions is yes, you should take notes on the reading or lecture.

QUESTIONS TO ASK WHEN DECIDING WHETHER TO TAKE NOTES
1. Will you be tested on the material?
2. Will notes be the only reliable source of material for review?
3. Can you reinforce your reading or listening on this topic by taking notes?
4. Is the material being covered applicable to other situations?
5. Can you benefit from practice in note-taking?

Once you have made the decision to take notes, you must decide what to write down. You will not want to rewrite in note form either an entire reading or an entire class lecture. In addition, you should be paying attention to the reading or the instructor while you are taking notes, and you should not be so busy writing that you miss important information. When taking notes, it is best to confine what you write to main ideas and *major* supporting details. Often this will be only 10 to 15 percent of what you read or hear. Later, preferably the same day, you should review your notes to reorganize, summarize, annotate, or supply additional details.

EXERCISE A: **Deciding When to Take Notes.** List five situations you generally encounter each week in which it is important to take notes. Tell which of the questions in the preceding chart helped you decide that note-taking would be valuable in each situation.

■ Knowing What Form of Note-Taking to Use

Although the form of note-taking you decide to use will depend on the type of material you are working with, you will find that almost all notes are organized around main ideas. Whatever form you decide to use, it is always helpful to organize the main ideas in such a way that they are easy to find when you are revising or reviewing. In addition, it is usually a good idea to leave space around main ideas so that you can easily supply additional information at a later time. Finally, you will find it a good practice to put the date and topic at the top of all notes you take.

Because different situations lend themselves to different types of note-taking, you should practice each type so that it will be easy for you to use when you need it.

The Modified Outline. The modified outline is the simplest kind of note-taking and the one you will most commonly use for class notes. It groups information on a particular topic under major category headings and has a somewhat informal organization.

Use a modified outline when taking notes from a class lecture, audiovisual material, and printed material, especially when it has very few organizational headings.

One great advantage of the modified outline is that it is easier to use than the more highly structured forms. It is easy to take notes in this form while you are listening and then later restructure the modified outline in another form. Simply record each major topic as a heading when it is introduced; then list related facts under the heading, using dashes, numbers, or letters.

MODIFIED OUTLINES:

Major Heading	Major Heading
—Related fact	1. Related fact
—Related fact	2. Related fact
—Related fact	3. Related fact

Major Heading	Major Heading
—Related fact	1. Related fact
—Related fact	2. Related fact

The Formal Outline.   A formal outline not only places information under major headings, but it also shows the relative importance of the information and its relation to other information. Formal outlining is best suited to note-taking from readings that are highly structured and contain a number of headings. It is also very useful for preparing to write an essay or to give a speech.

Use a formal outline when you are taking notes from a text, especially one with a series of headings, or when you are preparing to write an essay or to give a speech.

Because the format of a formal outline is quite specific and highly structured, you will sometimes have to prepare a rough draft first. One strategy might be to begin with a modified outline and then reorganize the information in it into a formal outline. This process will help you determine the relative importance of each piece of information. You can use the following model as a guide. It shows how to rank information based on relative importance.

FORMAL OUTLINE:

I. First main idea
  A.
  B. } Major details explaining I.
  C.
    1.
    2. } Minor details explaining C.
      a.
      b. } Sub-details about 2.
        (1)
        (2) } Additional sub-details about b.
          (a)
          (b) } Minor details about (2).
            i.
            ii. } Minor details about (b).

II. Second main idea
(and so on)

Notice the alternation of numerals and letters and the use of indentation in the model. Notice, too, that a formal outline never includes a single item by itself; if there are not at least two details to be added under each larger heading, do not break the entry down into subcategories.

Most of the formal outlining you do will take the form of a *topic outline*, with words and phrases used to convey the information. Read the following passage and then study the topic outline based upon it.

PASSAGE:

Modern magic did not really start until the 1880's. Its father is considered to be Jean Houdin, a Frenchman, who developed rules for conjuring. Houdin was also a highly skilled mechanic and watchmaker. Today modern magicians can perform feats of magic that would have been impossible years ago because they now have better mechanical equipment and greater knowledge of audience psychology.

Today's magician usually depends on his skill with his hands, on his knowledge of psychology, and sometimes, on mechanical devices. Since magic tricks are meant to fool people, the use of psychology is important. The magician must keep people from noticing all the movements of his hands and from thinking about the secret parts of his equipment. He must also lead the audience to draw false conclusions. The magician's success depends on the fact that many things seen by the eye do not register on the mind. —Edward B. Fry

OUTLINE:　I. Development of modern magic
　　　A. Jean Houdin in 1880's
　　　　1. Father of modern magic
　　　　　a. Frenchman
　　　　　b. Mechanic and watchmaker
　　　　2. Developed rules for conjuring
　　　B. Modern magicians
　　　　1. Better equipment
　　　　2. Greater knowledge of psychology
　　II. Tools of modern magicians
　　　A. Physical skill (rapid hand movements)
　　　B. Psychology
　　　　1. Distract audience from movements and equipment
　　　　2. Encourage false conclusions
　　　C. Mechanical devices

Occasionally, your teacher may ask you to prepare a *sentence outline*, particularly when you are preparing for a speech or for a long, formal paper. A sentence outline follows the rules and format of the topic outline but uses sentences rather than words or phrases in listing the information. It is most useful when you want to give a speech or write a paper directly from your outline.

The Free-Form Outline. Unlike other outline forms, the free-form outline is not written and organized from top to bottom. Instead, the main idea is placed in the center, with related information branching off from it. It is most useful when you are taking notes from loosely structured material in which only the highlights are important.

> Use a free-form outline when taking notes from loosely organized material or when you need to recall only highlights.

As you can see from the following diagram of a free-form outline, the format is relatively unimportant and only very brief notes need be taken. The visual impact of the notes makes information in this form relatively easy for many people to recall.

EXAMPLE:

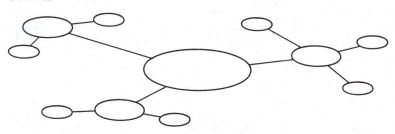

Summaries. Regardless of the form of note-taking you use, a two- or three-sentence summary of the notes can provide a valuable additional step in the note-taking process. In writing such a summary, include only the main ideas from the notes you have taken, and write these ideas in your own words.

> Use a summary to record main ideas in your own words.

Preparing a brief formal summary encourages you to review the notes you have taken, to determine the major ideas, and to internalize these ideas by writing them in your own words. In later reviews for tests, you can use the summaries to recall the most important information and to see how many details you can remember about the topic. If you cannot fill in details from memory, you can then review the more detailed notes from which each summary was written.

EXERCISE B: **Making a Modified Outline.** Reread the passage about modern magic on page 445. Then write a modified outline of the material using at least two headings.

EXERCISE C: **Making a Topic Outline.** Read the following passage. Then write a topic outline that contains at least three major headings.

Two basic magic tricks are making objects seem to appear and making objects seem to disappear. A combination of the two makes for some interesting effects. For example, the magician puts a small ball under one of several cups. The ball then seems to jump from one cup to another or to change color. What actually happens is that the magician, employing quick hand movements or a mechnical device, hides one ball. While doing so, the magician talks to the audience and waves a bright cloth with one hand. The audience is too busy watching the cloth and listening to the patter to notice that the other hand is hiding the ball.

Another favorite trick is to cut or burn something and then make it appear whole again. What actually happens is that the magician makes the damaged object disappear by quickly hiding it while the audience watches something else. The magician then makes the object appear whole again by displaying an identical object that has not been damaged.

There are a number of so-called mind-reading tricks in which the magician purports to tell a person what he or she is thinking. For some of these tricks, the magician has the person write down the thoughts and then secretly obtains the paper. Another technique is to have a trained helper blindfold the magician and ask the audience to hold up various objects. The helper tells the magician what the objects are, without mentioning their names, by using key words or code words while talking to the magician. This trick may take the magician and helper many months to learn.

Tricks in which a magician apparently cuts people in half or makes them disappear are called illusions. The word *illusion* is used because mirrors are often used to perform such tricks. The most famous illusion trick is that of sawing a person in half. A person is put into a long box with his or her head sticking out one end and feet sticking out the other. The magician takes an ordinary saw and cuts the box in two. The audience is shocked, thinking perhaps that the person is dead. A few minutes later, however, the magician puts a "magic" cape over the box and the person comes out. The person the audience saw being cut in two was only an image in a mirror—an illusion. —Edward B. Fry

EXERCISE D: **Making a Free-Form Outline.** Write a free-form outline for the following passage. Place the main idea in the center, with related information branching off from it.

> Magic is as popular today as it was in ancient times. Records show that over 2,000 years ago magic performances were being given in ancient Egypt, India, Rome, China, and Greece. These early magicians only performed for small groups of people on a street corner or for a king and his friends. The magicians in those days used only small objects that they could carry with them or borrow, such as cups, pebbles, knives, and string.
>
> Early magicians frequently wore a large apron with many pockets in which they could carry their props. The big apron served as identification and as a place to hide things while performing. Magicians also carried a small folding table on which to perform their tricks.
>
> About 1400, more elaborate tricks were invented which used larger equipment, such as boxes and barrels with false bottoms. Under these false bottoms the magician could hide a bird, rabbit, plant, or whatever he wanted to make appear suddenly. From one barrel he could make several different liquids pour forth while he told the audience that he was changing the entire contents of the barrel by magic. People of that time knew very little about mechanical devices, so it was easier for the magician to deceive them. —Edward B. Fry

EXERCISE E: **Writing Summaries.** Below each of the three outlines you have made in Exercises B, C, and D, write a two- or three-sentence summary of the information in the outline.

■ Developing Your Own Personal Shorthand

A knowledge of formal shorthand, designed for taking down every word spoken, can actually be a handicap in taking good notes because it may encourage you to take more notes than you need. However, a system that allows you to abbreviate some words and use symbols for certain other words in order to record important information more quickly can make your note-taking much more efficient.

Create your own shorthand for note-taking purposes.

Creating your own shorthand is not difficult if you are aware of common abbreviations and know how to cut down on the number of letters in a word. Even abbreviating one out of every four or five words can reduce your writing time by over 20 percent.

When using your own shorthand, use abbreviations for common words and spell out other words. Except when you are preparing a sentence outline, use only phrases to take down information. Make certain, however, that your abbreviations and phrases can be expanded mentally to make sense. Otherwise their whole purpose has been lost.

There are a number of ways to develop your own personal form of shorthand. The suggestions in the following chart should be especially helpful in forming shorthand abbreviations.

SUGGESTIONS FOR CREATING YOUR OWN SHORTHAND	
Suggestions	**Examples**
1. Eliminate vowels from words.	lk (like), lrn (learn), wrt (write)
2. Use capital letters to designate some words and small letters to designate others.	P (paragraph), Q (question), p (page), w (with)
3. Use slashes, letters, and symbols for certain words.	b/4 (before), b/c (because), w/o (without)
4. Use only the first and second or first, second, and third letters of a word.	ch (chapter), ex (example), dif (different), ref (reference)
5. Use only the first and last letters of a word.	rt (right), wd (word), vs (versus)
6. Use symbols and numbers to designate words.	# (number), ∴ (therefore), 2 (two, too, to)
7. Use standard abbreviation symbols.	@ (at), i.e. (that is), etc. (and so on), & (and)

EXERCISE F: **Using Your Own Shorthand for Taking Notes.** Take the topic outline you completed in Exercise C and see if you can abbreviate some of the words in the outline using the suggestions in the preceding chart.

APPLICATION: **Evaluating Your Note-Taking Skills.** After taking notes over a period of two weeks, answer the following questions.

1. Do you have a system for deciding when and what type of notes to take?
2. Do you limit your note-taking to approximately 10 to 15 percent of the material?

3. Do you know how to construct modified and free-form outlines?
4. Do you know how to construct a formal outline for an essay or speech?
5. Do you regularly summarize the main ideas from your notes in your own words?
6. Do you attempt to create your own shorthand for note-taking?

15.3 Getting a Job

A potential employer has only a limited knowledge of your qualifications for a particular job. A decision about which applicant to hire will generally be based on résumés, job applications, interviews, and references submitted by a number of applicants. Because a potential employer's access to you and to competing applicants is so limited, it is important for you to be able to make the most of each step in getting a job so that you can convince the potential employer that you should be hired.

■ Reading Classified Want Ads

The first step in getting a job is to analyze your skills, interests, and goals. The next step is to find out what jobs are available that might be suitable for you. Frequently people hear about jobs through friends. Often people go to an employment agency for help. However, reading the want ads in newspapers or those in professional publications is probably the most common way of learning about job opportunities.

Learn to read and understand classified want ads.

Because advertising space is limited and costs money, classified ads use a fairly standard set of abbreviations for terms that occur frequently. Once you become familiar with the terms and abbreviations given in the following chart, you should have little difficulty interpreting standard classified want ads.

COMMONLY ABBREVIATED WORDS IN CLASSIFIED WANT ADS

acctg.	accounting		H.S.G.	high school graduate
admin.	administration, administrative		incl.	includes
ass't.	assistant		int'l.	international
bkkp.	bookkeeper, bookkeeping		med.	medical
			mfr.	manufacturer
bnfts.	benefits		mgmt.	management
clk.	clerk		m/f	male or female
coll. grad.	college graduate		nec.	necessary
			ops.	operators
comm'l.	commercial		O.T.	overtime
corp.	corporate, coporation		pref'd.	preferred
			prsn.	person
dept.	department		req'd.	required
dir.	director		secy.	secretary
exec.	executive		skls.	skills
exp.	experience		sten.	stenography
f/pd	fee paid		trnee.	trainee
f/pt	full or part time		wpm	words per minute
grwth pot'l.	growth potential		w/wo	with or without

After a little practice, you should be able to fill in the missing words and begin to read classified ads without stopping to think about their peculiar style. The following comparison of a classified ad and a translation of the ad may give you a better idea of what to expect.

INTERPRETING A CLASSIFIED WANT AD

Wanted Secy. to assist VP/ investment. M/F. min. 55 wpm w/wo steno. Will consider H.S.G.'s, secy. school grads, secy. with any exp. Bnfts. include med., dental, tuition. E.O.E.	Wanted: A Secretary to assist the Vice President of investment. Male or female. Minimum 55 words per minute in typing, with or without stenography. Will consider high school graduates, secretarial school graduates, or secretary with any experience. Benefits include medical, dental, and free tuition. We are an equal opportunity employer.

In addition to learning how to read a want ad, you should learn to check regularly to see what new jobs are available. Many local papers carry more employment ads on certain days of the week, and most Sunday papers have a special section of employment ads. If you get into the habit of checking the wants ads at regular intervals, you will be less likely to miss the job that is just right for you.

EXERCISE A: Examining Classified Want Ads. On a separate sheet of paper, write out the following classified ad for taxi cab drivers. Add any necessary words, and write out all abbreviations.

> Wanted taxi drivers—immed. hr. F/Pt and Wknds. AM/PM shfts. Know. N.Y.C. Trnee. prgm. unless you have Class 4 Lic. $400 wkly. plus lib. med. bnfts. F/Pd agency.

Then find want ads for two jobs that you would consider applying for. Write out the full ad for each job as you did above.

■ Writing a Résumé

The term *résumé* means "summary." The résumé that you prepare for potential employers is simply a formal summary of your background and interests as they relate to employment. A résumé serves two purposes, one for you and one for the employer. It helps you systematically sort out your experiences and organize those that make you a good job candidate, a step that can make you feel more confident in an interview. A résumé also helps a potential employer see at a glance the kinds of experience and interests you have and how your background fits a particular job opening.

Keep an updated résumé ready to send to potential employers.

Because your objective in preparing a résumé is to get a job, you should emphasize only the positive things in your background. However, it is important that the information you *do* include in the résumé be truthful. You need not mention a course that you failed to complete or your reasons for leaving a previous job. On the other hand, you should not make it sound as if your experience is more extensive than it really is. The following suggestions should help you prepare a good résumé.

SUGGESTIONS FOR WRITING A RÉSUMÉ

1. Keep the résumé short, possibly limited to one page.
2. Plan the spacing between items so that the résumé is easy to read.
3. Be sure that your résumé is neatly typed.
4. Include information that emphasizes your suitability for the kind of job you want.
5. Update your résumé every six months or each year.
6. Keep multiple copies of your résumé.

Frequently, job candidates have not seen a specific classified ad but would like to work for a particular company. In such cases, they may mail out their résumés in the hope that there is a job available. If you choose this method of seeking employment, be sure to accompany your résumé with a cover letter. (See Section 26.1 for suggestions for writing this kind of business letter.) In such a letter, you may want to ask the potential employer to keep your résumé on file for future openings if there is no job presently available.

One of several different forms that may be used for a résumé is shown on page 454. The most important consideration is that the information be well organized and assigned to labeled categories so that a potential employer can easily find the information he or she is looking for. The following paragraphs offer details about various elements you may want to include in your own résumé.

The Heading.   The heading at the top of the résumé should include your name, address, and phone number. If you are presently employed and can receive calls on the job, you may want to list both residence and business phone numbers.

Position Desired.   This category may include the specific title of a job you have seen advertised or a simple description of the type of work you would like. If you have a long-range career goal in mind at this point, your entry after this category might read something like this: "Entry level position as . . . with possibility for advancement leading to. . . ."

Education.   Begin with your most recent educational experience and work backwards. After each listing give the dates of attendance, as well as the city and state of each school. Do not overlook any special courses taken outside of school that are particularly relevant to the type of employment you are seeking: typing, music, auto mechanics, and so on.

```
                          LEE WILSON

                        10 Main Street
                       Middletown, NY 00000
                        (414) 555-5829

Position
Desired:        Assistant Interior Decorator

Education:      Middletown High School, Middletown, NY
                commercial art courses, will gradu-
                ate June 1982
Work
Experience:     Fashion Plate, Middletown, NY (pre-
                sent part-time employment); design-
                ing store window displays

                Middletown Barn Theater, Middletown,
                NY (apprentice, summer 1981); build-
                ing, painting, and decorating sets;
                acquiring props and furniture

Interests:      swimming, bicycling, reading, draw-
                ing

Activities:     Middletown swim team (1978-1979)

                Thespians (1980-1981), stage manager
                for class plays

                High School Gazette (1979 to present),
                lay-out, paste-up, some cartooning

References:     Ms. Mary Ellington (employer)
                Fashion Plate
                14 Pleasant Street
                Middletown, NY 00000
                (414) 555-4565

                Mr. Harold deWinter (employer)
                Stage Manager
                Middletown Barn Theater
                R.R. 3
                Middletown, NY 00000
                (414) 555-8972

                Ms. Isabelle Evans (art teacher)
                Middletown High School
                Middletown, NY 00000
                (414) 555-7906
```

Work Experience.   Begin with your most recent employment and again work backwards. Be sure that each entry includes the name of the employer (company or individual), the address, the dates of employment, and a brief description of your responsibilities. In this category you may want to include both paid and volunteer work.

Interests.   This category should describe briefly what you enjoy doing with your leisure time. Such information often provides an employer with topics for follow-up questions in an interview and may suggest how your outside interests may be compatible with certain aspects of the job.

Activities.   In this category you should describe clubs and organizations to which you belong, listing the roles you play in each. You should also mention any awards or honors you have received in connection with such activities.

References.   Before preparing your résumé, obtain permission from three responsible adults to use their names as references. The references you give may include former employers, teachers, guidance counselors, coaches, club advisors, religious leaders, or adult friends. Do not use relatives as references unless they have also been employers. Along with the name of each reference, include the person's relationship to you, the person's address, and the person's phone number.

EXERCISE B: Developing a Résumé. Using the format illustrated on page 454 or an adaptation of it, compose a résumé of your own. You may want to keep in mind one of the jobs from the want ads you found for Exercise A.

EXERCISE C: Finding References. Write a letter to one of the people you would like to list as a reference. Mention in the letter the job you are applying for and ask permission to use the person's name. Include a word of thanks. (See Section 26.1 for details on letter form.)

■ Filling Out a Job Application

Whether you are answering a classified ad or following up on a reply to an inquiry you have sent through the mail, your next step in getting a job will probably be filling out the company's application form. Since this part of the employment process is usually done in the personnel or employment office, you will not yet have met your potential employer. Your job application may, in fact, provide that person's first impression of you as a job candidate.

Fill out a job application form accurately, completely, and honestly.

Knowing in advance the types of information common to most application forms will make your task easier. You will need to include your social security number, jobs you have held and dates of employment, names and addresses of schools you have attended and dates of attendance, and the names and addresses of people who have agreed to give you a reference. You may find it helpful to write out this information in advance and bring it with you to the personnel or employment office. In addition, the following suggestions can be useful in filling out job applications.

SUGGESTIONS FOR FILLING OUT JOB APPLICATIONS

1. Type or neatly print all information.
2. Check your spelling carefully.
3. Leave no blanks, unless you have made a note of explanation.
4. Be truthful in answering all questions.
5. Use additional paper if you need it to answer some questions more fully.
6. Include any information that would be considered job-related.
7. Start with most recent job and school experiences and then work backwards.
8. Include a cover letter with applications that are mailed.

Job applications are not difficult to fill out if you are familiar with the questions and terms used on most applications. Some of the frequently used terms are given in the following chart.

WORDS COMMONLY USED ON JOB APPLICATIONS

Agency	A place that will try to locate a job for you
Benefits	Insurance, hospitalization, vacation pay, and so on
Career goals	The jobs you are aiming for now and in the future
Clerical	Office work
Citizenship	The country in which you were born in most cases
Compensation	The pay you receive on the job, as well as the pay you receive if you are out of work or injured
Convicted	Found guilty of a crime

Dependents	Children or adults that you support financially
Entry level	The job in which you started or will start
Former employer	The last person that you worked for
Handicap	A physical problem
Maiden name	A woman's last name at birth
Qualifications	Whatever shows that you can do the job
References	People who know you well enough to give an honest evaluation of your qualifications
Résumé	A description of yourself and your job qualifications
Social security	The money that you will receive after retirement in most cases
Salary	The pay for the job you do
Selective service classification	Draft board number, if you have one
Termination	The point at which you quit or leave a job
Veteran	A person who has served in the armed forces

The sample job application on page 458 is fairly typical of those you may encounter. Although job applications vary in length from one to four pages, those for beginning positions are usually only a page or two. As you fill out an application form, keep these two objectives in mind: (1) Gain the interest of the employer through the words you use to describe your qualifications, and (2) make the employer want to meet you. You are undoubtedly only one of several people applying for this job, and you want your application to stand out from the rest. (See Section 26.2 for information about the essay portion of applications if you expect to encounter this type of question.)

The first job application you fill out will be the most difficult. You may be unsure how much or how little information to include or whether the information you do give is appropriate to the question. However, as with any other skill, you will gain confidence and ease with repeated practice.

If you are giving your application directly to an employer, you will not need a cover letter. If you are sending your application through the mail, however, do enclose a cover letter with it. The cover letter should include information on the job opportunity you are applying for and times when you can be available for an interview. If you have not heard from the em-

Prentice-Hall, Inc.   AN EQUAL OPPORTUNITY EMPLOYER

EMPLOYMENT APPLICATION   *PLEASE PRINT.*

TODAY'S DATE	NAME (FIRST, MIDDLE, LAST)		SOCIAL SECURITY NO.

ADDRESS (NUMBER, STREET, CITY, STATE, AND ZIP) — AREA CODE – PHONE NO.

EDUCATION — HIGHEST GRADE COMPLETED — COURSE

DETAIL YOUR EDUCATIONAL BACKGROUND — DEGREE / CERTIFICATE

ARE YOU IN U.S.A. ON A TEMPORARY VISA? YES ☐ NO ☐   EVER APPLIED TO WORK AT PH BEFORE? WHEN?   WHO REFERRED YOU TO US?

HAVE YOU EVER BEEN CONVICTED OF A CRIME? IF YES, PLEASE EXPLAIN.

IN EMERGENCY, NOTIFY (NAME) — AREA CODE – PHONE NO. AT   HOME ☐   WORK ☐

COMPLETE ADDRESS WHERE THIS PERSON CAN BE CONTACTED

DO YOU HAVE ANY PHYSICAL CONDITION THAT MAY PREVENT YOU FROM SATISFACTORILY PERFORMING THE JOB FOR WHICH YOU ARE APPLYING?

WORK HISTORY - *Account for all employment, including periods of unemployment. Start with most recent.*

DATES FROM	THRU	COMPANY AND ADDRESS	SUPERVISOR'S NAME	FINAL POSITION & SALARY	REASON FOR LEAVING

MILITARY EXPERIENCE BRANCH	FROM	THRU	RANK ACHIEVED	SPECIAL SCHOOLS OR TRAINING

FOR WHAT JOB ARE YOU APPLYING?	FULL TIME ☐	PART TIME ☐	HOURS PREFERRED	WHAT ARE YOUR SALARY NEEDS?	DO YOU TYPE?	TAKE STENO?

OTHER SKILLS OR TALENTS YOU WOULD LIKE TO DEVELOP

Please read the following statement carefully, and add your signature in the space provided.

I understand that if I am employed and if any statement herein is not true or if my references are not entirely satisfactory to my Employer, I may be released immediately. If I am released for either of these reasons I will be paid only through the day of release. If I am employed, I further understand and agree that when my employment is terminated by retirement or otherwise, I must return all of Employer's property in my custody.

SIGNATURE OF APPLICANT _____ DATE_____

INTERVIEWER AND D.H. please complete other side.

ployer within two weeks, do not hesitate to write again or to telephone to ask whether or not your application was received. If you telephone, inquire courteously about the status of your application.

EXERCISE D: **Filling Out an Application.** Obtain an actual job application form from a local employer or from your school's guidance or placement office. For practice, fill it out neatly and carefully, just as if you were applying for a job.

■ Preparing for a Job Interview

If you get to the point of being interviewed for a job, your résumé and your application form have probably already made a favorable impression. The next step—the interview itself—is often the most difficult and frightening for many people. However, if you prepare your presentation and your follow-up for the interview in advance, not only will you not be overwhelmed but you will also improve your chances of getting the job.

Prepare for a job interview by learning about the job and by reviewing your résumé.

One of the best ways to prepare for an interview is to go through a mock job interview. Ask an adult you know who has experience in interviewing people for jobs or one who has been interviewed for jobs several times to go over your résumé and to play the interviewer by asking you questions a potential employer might ask. This mock interview will give you practice in answering questions fully and sensibly and will prepare you for possibly difficult questions that you may want to think over in advance. In addition to the mock interview, you might follow the additional suggestions presented in the following chart.

SUGGESTIONS FOR PREPARING FOR AN INTERVIEW
1. Learn something about the job and employer by either getting brochures from the company or talking with local residents who know something about the company.
2. Plan to wear clothing that is clean, neat, and suitable to the occasion.
3. Be prepared to follow up on information in your résumé or on the application form.
4. Prepare to ask questions about the job that may not arise in the course of the interview.
5. Be prepared to take an employment test or to be interviewed by more than one person.

EXERCISE E: **Preparing for an Interview.** Prepare a list of ten to twelve questions that you could ask the person who is interviewing you during a job interview. Include questions about such areas as job responsibility, employee benefits, and possible promotions.

■ Interviewing for a Job

If you have taken the time to prepare for the job interview, you should have more self-confidence, which your interviewer will sense. In addition to self-confidence, the interviewer will also be evaluating your poise, enthusiasm, and sincerity.

Present a positive image to a potential employer.

Allow plenty of time to get to the interview so that you are not frantic and breathless when you arrive. It is better to be a few minutes early than a few minutes late. In addition, coming late to an interview may suggest to the employer that you might be chronically tardy as an employee.

When you have been introduced, wait for the interviewer to shake your hand and invite you to be seated. Sit erect and try to maintain eye contact with the interviewer. Do not smoke, chew gum, twist your hair, swing your leg, or fiddle with something in your lap. Such habits suggest nervousness and may annoy or distract the interviewer. If you need to take any notes during the interview, try to do so as unobtrusively as possible. Always remember to be pleasant and polite and to answer all questions completely, honestly, and without the use of slang expressions.

The following chart lists some of the questions you may be asked during the interview.

COMMONLY ASKED QUESTIONS

1. Why are you interested in the job you are applying for?
2. What skills would you bring to this job?
3. Are there any areas in your personal life (health problems, continuing education, needs of a sick or disabled family member, transportation problems, and so on) that would conflict with the demands of the job?
4. What are your career goals?
5. What would you do if . . .? (In this type of question, the interviewer would give you a particular job-related problem to discuss.)
6. What were your responsibilities in your last job?
7. What are your greatest strengths?
8. How do you think other people would describe you?
9. What do you like to do in your spare time?
10. What are your reading habits? What are you reading now?

When you answer questions in an interview, avoid criticizing past employment situations or making excuses for past mistakes. Take time to answer the questions fully and be as honest as you can. Do not be afraid to show enthusiasm or to say that you would very much like a particular job.

After a job interview, follow up with a brief note to the interviewer. (You may confirm the correct spelling of the person's name and title with a secretary before you leave.) Send a note a few days after the interview and restate your interest in the job. In addition, thank the interviewer for taking the time to talk with you, as in the following sample letter.

```
              10 Main Street
              Middletown, NY 00000
              May 15, 1982

              Mr. Ian Hollister
              Dream House Interiors
              72 State Street
              Middletown, NY 00000

              Dear Mr. Hollister:

              Thank you so much for the time you spent with me
              last Monday afternoon. I enjoyed our talk and the
              tour of your premises, especially the display of
              antique candlesticks.

              If chosen to work as your assistant, I know I will
              enjoy the work and will certainly do my best to
              please you and your clients.

              Sincerely,

              Lee Wilson
              Lee Wilson
```

Some employers call selected job candidates back for a second interview after screening a larger number of applicants. Second interviews usually include more probing questions, may include a test or a trial assignment, and may be conducted by a different person. Even though you have passed one screening interview, you should prepare just as thoroughly for a call-back interview. Once again, a confident, relaxed, and capable attitude will give you an edge over other contenders.

EXERCISE F: **Answering an Interviewer's Questions.** Select a job that you would like to apply for. Then study the ten common interview questions listed on page 460. Respond to each of these questions in writing as if you were really talking to an interviewer.

APPLICATION: **Evaluating Your Skills in Getting a Job.** Answer the following questions to evaluate your skills in getting a job.

1. Do you check the classified ads on a regular basis?
2. Can you read a classified want ad without any difficulty?
3. Can you organize and write a résumé that will interest an employer?
4. Can you list three people who would agree to give a written or oral reference to a potential employer?
5. Do you recognize and understand most of the terms used on job application forms?
6. Can you answer the commonly asked interview questions?
7. Do you know the form for writing business letters, and can you write a good follow-up letter?

Test-Taking Skills

Taking tests does not end with school but occurs in many situations in later life as well. Sometimes the test may be as insignificant as a test for a driver's license (which can always be taken over at a later time). Sometimes it may be as crucial as an employment test for a job that you need. Such tests are generally standardized and consist of multiple-choice questions.

In educational and employment situations, the standardized tests you are most likely to encounter from now on will be one of three types. *Achievement tests,* such as the California Achievement Tests or the English Composition Test, are designed to determine the level of proficiency the test-taker has achieved in a given subject area. *Aptitude tests,* such as the SAT and ACT, are intended to compare one test-taker's skill in reading, writing, vocabulary, and mathematics with the skills of others across the country. *Employment tests* are designed to determine the test-taker's suitability for a particular career.

You cannot prepare for standardized tests by studying specific content. Instead, you must prepare by learning and practicing basic skills, techniques, and approaches to understanding and answering the types of questions generally included on such tests. The two sections that follow will prepare you to take the vocabulary and reading comprehension portions of standardized tests with a greater chance for success.

Vocabulary Questions on Standardized Tests

16.1

Most standardized tests for employment or college entrance include a separate and extensive section focusing exclusively on vocabulary. Employers and college admissions officers place a great deal of emphasis on such tests because research has shown a high correlation between vocabulary test results and the potential for success on the job and in school.

The vocabulary section of standardized tests usually follows a multiple-choice format. Typical questions call for the identification of synonyms and antonyms and the completion of sentences and analogies. Becoming familiar with the types of questions included in standardized vocabulary tests can greatly enhance your chances of success—both in achieving a good score on the tests and in reaching the goals that have led you to take the test.

■ Synonym and Antonym Questions

A *synonym* is a word with the same or nearly the same meaning as another; an *antonym* is a word with a meaning opposite that of another. The most common mistake students make in taking synonym and antonym tests is failing to look for the right relationship.

> Read directions carefully to see whether you are being asked to identify a synonym or an antonym for the given word. Then follow certain steps to find the correct answer.

After determining the nature of the question, you should pronounce the word carefully to yourself to make sure that you have the correct word in mind. Then use the steps in the following chart to eliminate most or all of the incorrect answers.

ELIMINATING INCORRECT ANSWERS ON SYNONYM AND ANTONYM TESTS	
Step 1:	If you are looking for a synonym, eliminate any antonyms. If you are looking for an antonym, eliminate any synonyms.
Step 2:	Eliminate words that merely look or sound like the given word.
Step 3:	Eliminate words that can be associated with the word but are not accurate definitions.
Step 4:	Eliminate words that are only partly the same or partly opposite in meaning.

EXAMPLE: Find the synonym for the given word.

officious   (1) official   (2) meddlesome   (3) busy
(4) withdrawn   (5) annoying

Step 1: (4) can be eliminated because it has the opposite meaning.

Step 2: (1) can be eliminated because it looks and sounds similar but is unrelated in meaning.

Step 3: (5) can be eliminated because it can be associated with the word but does not define it.

Step 4: (3) can be eliminated because it suggests only part of the meaning.

Answer: (2) meddlesome

EXAMPLE: Find the antonym for the given word.

> *exonerate* (1) onerous (2) acquit (3) arrest
> (4) condemn (5) accuse

Step 1: (2) is a synonym.

Step 2: (1) looks similar but is not opposite in meaning.

Step 3: (3) can be associated with the opposite but is not itself opposite in meaning.

Step 4: (5) suggests only part of the opposite meaning.

Answer: (4) condemn

EXERCISE A: Answering Synonym and Antonym Questions.

Choose the *synonym* for each of the following words.

1. *taciturn* (1) silent (2) calm (3) talkative
   (4) tactful (5) late
2. *ruddy* (1) healthy (2) rugged (3) rosy (4) colorful
   (5) round
3. *fortuitous* (1) incidentally (2) courageous (3) fortified
   (4) accidental (5) frank
4. *blandishment* (1) curse (2) mildness (3) flattery
   (4) blemish (5) blandness
5. *amorphous* (1) formless (2) simple (3) incoherent
   (4) rudimentary (5) well-developed

Choose the *antonym* for each of the following words.

6. *malign* (1) criticize (2) tumorous (3) attack (4) praise
   (5) assist
7. *indigenous* (1) indigent (2) native (3) alien (4) lazy
   (5) whole
8. *precipitous* (1) rainy (2) level (3) steep (4) dry
   (5) sloped
9. *secular* (1) clerical (2) tomb (3) laic (4) round
   (5) spiritual
10. *depravity* (1) loss (2) corruption (3) honor (4) innocence
    (5) mortality

■ Sentence Completion Questions

Because sentence completion questions ask you to select the best word to complete a given sentence, the context, or meaning of the surrounding words, can be a great help.

Use context clues to help find the right answer to sentence completion questions.

In the following example, two steps are shown for answering this type of question. The first involves finding context clues. The second involves testing words in the sentence itself.

EXAMPLE: Choose the word that best completes this sentence.

Unable to confirm any of his symptoms, Johnny's parents suspected that their shy son was only _____ illness to avoid performing in the school play.

(1) developing   (2) fainting   (3) feigning   (4) camouflaging
(5) having

Step 1:   Find key words in the sentence that provide clues.

Unable to confirm suggests pretending, and *avoiding* a dreaded situation suggests a reason for pretending.

Step 2:   Test the words in the sentence.

Words (1) and (5) suggest that Johnny actually *was* ill, rather than pretending. Word (4) has some suggestion of pretense but does not make sense in the sentence. (A shy child would not camouflage illness to avoid a public appearance.) Word (2) makes no sense in the context of the sentence, but it sounds like (3). Testing (3) in the sentence confirms that it is the correct choice.

Answer: (3) feigning

EXERCISE B: **Answering the Sentence Completion Questions.** Use context clues to find the word that best completes each of the following sentences.

1. After the bloody battle, the troops were _____ and retreated to their homeland.

(1) victorious   (2) vanquished   (3) cremated   (4) jubilant
(5) honored

2. The community objected that the proposed highway would be a _____ rather than a boon for the area.

   (1) favor   (2) panacea   (3) disaster   (4) help   (5) courtesy

3. The presence in the marketplace of rayon, nylon, and other _____ fabrics created a need for new laundry products.

   (1) magic   (2) delicate   (3) new   (4) natural   (5) synthetic

4. The suspect's alibi would not stand up in court because there was no one to _____ it.

   (1) challenge   (2) avow   (3) refute   (4) arrest
   (5) corroborate

5. The reporter's _____ hostility to the President's plan angered the White House staff.

   (1) overt   (2) occasional   (3) subtle   (4) covert   (5) tired

6. Each invitation was hand-lettered by a _____.

   (1) graphologist   (2) printing press   (3) calligrapher
   (4) colophon   (5) typist

7. Since neither side would concede on any issue, a federal _____ panel will attempt to avert a strike.

   (1) arbitration   (2) judiciary   (3) election   (4) injunction
   (5) social

8. The actor was completely _____ in his portrayal of Abraham Lincoln.

   (1) convinced   (2) obvious   (3) credulous   (4) identical
   (5) credible

9. A spoonerism is a _____ of the initial sounds of two words, as in "a weaky squeal" for a "squeaky wheel."

   (1) combination   (2) transposition   (3) confusion
   (4) omission   (5) change

10. Perkins accepted the loss as one of life's _____ and hoped for better luck tomorrow.

    (1) vicissitudes   (2) vestiges   (3) holidays   (4) outrages
    (5) whimsies

■ Analogy Questions

An analogy is an expression of a relationship between two ideas. In analogy questions the relationship between two words is established and you are asked to find or complete an additional pair of words that expresses the same relationship.

> To solve analogy questions, study the relationship between the terms and the order in which they are given and look for words that have the same relationship.

Identifying the relationship between the established pair is the most important part of solving analogy problems. The following chart lists the most common relationships. The form used in the examples is the typical form. The first one can be translated to read *calm is to tranquil as last is to final*. The relationship in each pair is that of synonyms.

COMMON ANALOGY PATTERNS	
Type of Pattern	**Examples**
Synonyms	calm:tranquil::last:final
Antonyms	quiet:noisy::innocent:guilty
Similar categories	carrot:potato::hemlock:spruce
Main and subcategories	tuber:potato::conifer:hemlock
Sub- and main categories	potato:tuber::hemlock:conifer
Whole and part	wheel:rim::tree:branch
Part and whole	rim:wheel::branch:tree
Product and substance	omelet:eggs::pottery:clay
Categories of use	surgeon:scalpel::photographer:camera
Different forms of the same word	ring:rung::choose:chosen
Grammatical combination	man:woman::masculine:feminine

In the first of the following examples, you will see the steps that can be used to complete any analogy questions.

EXAMPLE: Select the term that completes this analogy.
frame:picture::_____: water

(1) rain   (2) chlorine   (3) fluoride   (4) cistern   (5) ocean

Step 1: Read the analogy in sentence form, keeping all terms in the same order.

Frame is to picture as *what* is to water.

Step 2: Determine the relationship between the terms in the complete pair and look for a similar relationship in the incomplete pair.

A picture is contained in a frame. Water is contained in . . . .

Step 3: Eliminate any words that do not fit at all and test those that seem possible.

Answer: (4) cistern (frame:picture::cistern:water)

When both terms are missing on one side of the analogy, you still must begin by identifying the relationship between the words in the complete pair. Then you must check that the possible pairs follow the same order as the given terms.

EXAMPLE: Choose the terms that best complete this analogy.
apple:cider:: _____ : _____

(1) cheese:milk   (2) toast:bread   (3) juice:fruit
(4) solid:liquid   (5) meat:sausage

Step 1: Apple is to cider as *what* is to *what*.

Step 2: Cider is made from apples.

Step 3: Choice (4) does not fit at all. The terms in (1), (2), and (3) are in the wrong order.

Answer: (5) meat:sausage (apple:cider::meat:sausage)

EXERCISE C: Answering Analogy Questions. Select the terms that best complete each analogy.

1. archipelago:island::

   (1) lions:pride   (2) constellation:star   (3) mountain:hill
   (4) symphony:orchestra   (5) chapter:book

2. guitar:pick::

   (1) bow:violin   (2) keys:piano   (3) clarinet:reed
   (4) drum:drumsticks   (5) puck:hockey

3. impoverished:affluent::

   (1) wholesale:retail   (2) baker:millionaire
   (3) rich:wealth   (4) poverty:fluency   (5) indigent:needy

4. avarice:greed::

   (1) candor:honesty   (2) thrifty:frugal   (3) conduit:water
   (4) precaution:accident   (5) valor:cowardice

5. speech:introduction::

   (1) gun:race   (2) overture:act   (3) book:preface
   (4) preamble:Constitution   (5) speaker:audience

6. women:woman::

   (1) boys:men   (2) deer:deer   (3) mouse:mice   (4) oxen:ox
   (5) potatoes:potato

7. painter:studio::

   (1) attorney:court   (2) office:secretary   (3) sculptor:chisel
   (4) sculpture:museum   (5) teacher:chalkboard

8. pecan:nut::

   (1) apple:fruit   (2) house:domicile   (3) bean:coffee
   (4) clarinet:reed   (5) meat:sandwich

9. arrow:archer::

   (1) choir:organ   (2) sea:sailor   (3) needle:tailor
   (4) actor:stage   (5) song:singer

10. algebra:geometry::

   (1) school:subject   (2) shape:number   (3) botany:zoology
   (4) theorem:equation   (5) plane:solid

APPLICATION: **Evaluating Your Vocabulary Test Skills.** Make up twenty vocabulary questions following the models in this section. Include five questions and multiple-choice answers in each of the following categories: synonyms, antonyms, sentence completions, and analogies. Exchange tests with another student, and answer the questions on his or her test. Return the test and grade the other student's answers to your questions. Then check and correct any answers that were incorrect on the test that you took.

Reading Comprehension Questions on Standardized Tests

16.2

Most standardized tests include one or more sections on reading comprehension. The purpose is to test both your ability to read quickly enough to get through most of the material and your ability to understand what you have read. You can improve your performance on this kind of test if you know how to approach the test and what kinds of questions to expect.

The questions testing your understanding, or comprehension, generally include specific multiple-choice questions about the content of the paragraphs you have read as well as some questions testing your understanding of specific words used in the passage.

Another kind of reading test question has a somewhat different form. After reading a single paragraph with one word missing, you are asked to choose from the possibilities the best word for the blank. This type of question tests your understanding of the content of the paragraph, your ability to use context clues, and your knowledge of specific vocabulary words.

■ Basic Reading Comprehension Questions

Reading comprehension questions test how carefully you read and how well you interpret what you read. They test to see if you are merely reading words or if you are reading thoughtfully to determine the meaning of what you read. Such questions generally fall into one of five basic categories covered in the next few pages: main-idea questions, detail questions, inference questions, definition questions, and questions about tone, purpose, and form.

Become familiar with the basic types of reading comprehension questions and the techniques for answering them.

Before examining the specific types of questions found on reading tests, read the following passage carefully as if you were taking a test. You will use this passage in working with the comprehension questions.

PASSAGE:

Speed Skiing

Downhill skiing and speed skiing involve many of the same skills: balance, reflexes, a deft touch, and nerve. But downhill skiers make turns that keep their speed down to about 80 mph while speed skiers can attain speeds up to 124 mph. Since speed skiers just go straight down a mountain as fast as possible, speed skiing can certainly be considered one of the world's most thrilling sports.

The speed skier reaches high speeds quickly because of the pitch of the mountains being skied. However, to get to these speeds, the skier must be able to withstand vibrations that start in the tips of his skis. These vibrations grow more violent with acceleration, move back to the boots, and then up to the legs. Soon the skier's entire body is being severely rattled. The skis twist and bend insanely, and the air rips at the skier's arms. At about 110 mph, though, the vibration stops, and the howling moves behind the skier. It is as though he has broken the sound barrier.

After passing through a timing trap, where speed is measured, skiers must worry about slowing down at the end of the course. Gravitational forces on the body are enormous there, because the pitch of the course changes from steep to nearly flat in a short distance. The best speed skiers reach this so-called "transition" at about 110 mph, and they feel as though steel bands are strapped across their chests, trying to pull them down and back. To avoid falls in transition, skiers have to keep their skis as straight as possible and then do a situp when they slow down to about 100 mph. If they use too much pressure on the ski tips, they can go headfirst into the deadliest type of fall in speed skiing. A somersault at 100 mph can snap a spinal cord, or worse.

Because of the high speed being traveled by speed skiers, they need specially designed gear. The gear consists of an aerodynamic helmet and a slippery wet suit to cut wind resistance. The suit is sealed to the skier's boots and has airfoils from knee to heel. The suit is also nonporous and made with attached hand coverings. This suit would be illegal to wear in downhill skiing because it would have little braking effect on a downed skier who is sliding.

Since the present speed skiing record is 124 mph, several competitors are trying to break it by attaining speeds in the 130 mph range. —Adapted from Michael McRae

The key to finding the best answer to a question on a reading comprehension test is similar to the method of finding the correct answer on standardized vocabulary tests. Often the best procedure is to eliminate some answers by looking for answers that are clearly unrelated, illogical, or incorrect. A few other hints can also help you. When you examine the five basic types of questions, keep the following general principles in mind.

GENERAL STRATEGY FOR ANSWERING QUESTIONS	
Type of Answer	**Reason to Eliminate**
Too narrow	Answer covers too small a portion of the reading.
Too wide	Answer covers a wider area than the reading.
Irrelevant	Answer has nothing to do with the reading or is relevant to the reading but not to the particular question.
Incorrect	Answer distorts or disputes the facts in the reading.
Illogical	Answer is not backed up by the facts in the reading.
Similar form of answer	At a quick glance, the answer looks similar to the true answer.
Opposite form of answer	Through the use of such words as *not* or *untrue*, the answer is made the reverse of the true answer.

Main-Idea Questions.   A main-idea question is basically a question that asks you to tell what the selection is about. It will not ask you to list any of the specific details that were included but will instead ask you to determine the subject of the entire passage.

Choose the most inclusive answer to a main-idea question.

A main-idea question may require you to retitle the passage, to state the topic, to choose a topic sentence, or to select the sentence that best tells what the passage is about. You may find it helpful to skim the first and last paragraphs of the passage before answering this type of question since writers frequently state their topic at the beginning or at the end of a passage.

The following main-idea question is based on the reading on speed skiing. Answer the question yourself and then compare your answer with those that follow.

EXAMPLE: Another title for the article about speed skiing might be

(1) Types of Skiing
(2) The Dangers of Speed Skiing
(3) Survival of the Fastest in Winter Sports
(4) Training to Be a Speed Skier
(5) Winter Sports

Answers: (1) Too broad   (2) Too narrow   (3) Correct
(4) Irrelevant   (5) Too broad

Detail Questions.   These are usually the easiest questions to answer because you can look back at the passage to find the answer.

Scan the passage to find details that you cannot recall from your first reading.

Detail questions are ones that you can generally count on getting right because the answer is actually in the selection and does not involve a personal judgment. However, in order to answer a detail question, you may sometimes need to put together information from two different sentences, use comparison and contrast, or do some simple arithmetic.

The following detail question is based on the speed skiing selection. Look back at the passage if you need to in order to answer the question.

EXAMPLE: The difference in speeds obtained by an expert speed skier and an expert downhill skier is *approximately*

(1) 10 mph   (2) 20 mph   (3) 40 mph   (4) 80 mph
(5) 124 mph

Answer: (3) 40 mph (The difference between 80 mph and 124 mph = 44 mph.)

Inference Questions.   These are probably the most difficult questions to answer because you can never find the answer directly in the passage. Instead, you must piece together a number of facts and make a generalization based on these facts.

Find specific facts to support your answer to an inference question.

Most inference questions include one of these key words: *think, predict, indicate, feel, probably, seem, imply, suggest, as-*

sume, infer, and *most likely.* When you come upon a question that contains one of these words, look back at the selection to find the specific sentences that the question refers to. Then look there for factual clues that you can use to make a sound generalization. Remember, in answering an inference question you are really making a guess, but your guess *must* be based on facts from the reading, not on your own opinions.

The following inference question is based on the reading on speed skiing. Choose the best answer.

EXAMPLE: The author's view of speed skiers is that they seem to be

(1) angry at the world   (2) fearless   (3) foolish   (4) overly ambitious   (5) fearsome

Answer: (2) fearless

Definition Questions.   These are basically vocabulary questions about difficult words in a passage or about ordinary words that are used with a special meaning in the passage. Most often you will be able to arrive at the meaning of a word by examining its *context,* the words that surround it.

Use context clues to answer a definition question.

To answer a definition question, first locate the word to be defined in the passage. Reread the sentence in which the word appears carefully and try to determine its meaning. Then try substituting each of the possible answers in the sentence to see which is closest in meaning. Avoid choosing a word that looks or sounds like the word to be defined unless you have tested it in context.

The following definition question is based on the reading about speed skiing. Choose the best answer.

EXAMPLE: The word *nonporous* in the fourth paragraph means

(1) tight   (2) waterproof   (3) slippery   (4) green   (5) loose

Answer: (2) waterproof

Tone, Purpose, and Form Questions.   This last type of question, far less common than the other four types, involves a judgment about how and why the writer wrote the selection. The *tone* of a passage reflects the writer's attitude toward both the subject and the audience. The *purpose* defines the effect the writer wishes to have on the audience. The *form* is the organization the writer uses.

Few writers have a neutral attitude toward their subjects, and most will convey to the reader—through their choice of words and the impression they create—one or more of the following tones.

POSSIBLE TONES

indifference	disappointment	indignation
appreciation	respect	hostility
admiration	approval	doubt
adoration	surprise	suspicion
optimism	anger	rage
pride	regret	pessimism
contempt	restraint	rejection
objectivity	irony	amusement

The ability to recognize the type of writing involved in a passage will frequently help you answer questions about purpose. The following chart describes common types of writing and the author's probable purpose in using each.

TYPES OF WRITING

Type	Description	Purpose
Expository writing	Writing that backs up ideas with explanations	To explain ideas clearly through facts
Persuasive writing	Writing that supports opinions with facts and/or reasons	To convince the reader or urge the reader to action
Descriptive writing	Writing that paints pictures with words	To paint word pictures for the reader
Narrative	Writing that relates a story	To give an account in story form
Chronicle	Writing that presents a chronological progression of historic events	To sequence factual information

Propaganda	Persuasive writing used to convince or to mislead	To sway the reader to a particular point of view
Humor	Writing that makes something seem funny	To make the reader laugh
Satire	Writing that ridicules a person or situation	To make fun of something in order to inspire correction
Imagery	Writing that produces mental images	To give the reader images through the use of words

As you read a passage, you can also try to observe which of the following common patterns of organization the author has used. Some writers will use only one of the patterns, while others may use a combination.

COMMON ORGANIZATIONAL PATTERNS

Logical sequence of events	Cause and effect
Comparison and contrast	Series of examples
Problem and solution	Order of importance
	Spatial order

The following question is based on the speed skiing selection. Skim the selection again before choosing the best answer if you need to.

EXAMPLE: What type of writing has the author used?

(1) humor   (2) satire   (3) propaganda   (4) expository
(5) narrative

Answer: (4) expository

EXERCISE A: **Answering Reading Comprehension Questions.** Read the following selection. Then, for each question after the selection, determine (1) the type of question being asked and (2) the correct answer.

Learn how to cook! That's my invariable answer when I am asked to give forth with money-saving recipes, economy tips, budget gourmet dinner menus for six people under ten dollars, and the like. Learn how to cook! That's the way to save money.

You don't save it buying hamburger helpers and prepared foods; you save it buying fresh foods in season or in large supply, when they are cheapest and usually best, and you prepare them from scratch at home. Why pay for some one else's work, when if you know how to do it, you can save all that money for yourself? Knowing how to do it also means doing it fast and preparing parts of a dish or a meal whenever you have a spare moment in the kitchen. That way, cooking well doesn't take a great deal of time, and when you cook well, you'll be eating far better meals than you could buy from the freezer, or at a restaurant.

Cooking well, too, doesn't mean cooking fancy, it just means that anything you set your hand to makes good eating, be it mashed potatoes, chicken soup, meat balls, or a twelve-layer cake. French food, by the way, isn't fancy unless, like other cooking, it wants to be fancy; perhaps it sounds so because it is in a foreign language, but a *coq au vin* is a chicken stew, a *pot-au-feu* is a boiled dinner, a *mayonnaise de volaille* is a chicken salad, *soubise* is plain old rice cooked with onions, and there is nothing fancy about any of them.

But what is continually pleasing about the French way of cooking is that you *do* something with the food. You don't just boil it, butter it, and dish it out. Not usually. You arrange your cooked broccoli spears like the spokes of a wheel in a round shallow baking dish, you sprinkle them with cheese and butter, and you brown them lightly in the oven. Those very few minutes of effort turn them from a plain vegetable into "a dish." You don't serve your hamburgers plain. No! After sautéing them you swirl some wine and shallots into the pan, and perhaps a chopped tomato along with a good pinch of herbs. There—with a few seconds' rapid boil, a swirl, and a seasoning, you spoon the sauce over the meat, and they aren't just hamburgers any more, they have taken a far more serious and deliciously gastronomic significance.

Again, for a quick dessert, you gather a modest variety of canned fruits, boil them a few minutes in their own syrup with strips of lemon peel and a stick of cinnamon; then, while their syrup is boiling down to a glaze, you arrange the fruits beautifully in a serving dish, interspersing them, perhaps, with thinly sliced bananas and a sprinking of supermarket sliced almonds (always on hand in your freezer for such occasions). When you spoon the glaze over the fruits, you have a lovely looking dessert that, also, has a certain sophistication of taste. Yet how very simple it is.

These few examples are typical of the French approach, that of taking ordinary everyday ingredients, and with a little bit of love and imagination, turning them into something appealing, even exciting, and certainly fun to make as well as to serve and to eat. —Julia Child

1. The selection is mainly about
   (a) French cooking   (b) economizing on meals   (c) nutrition
   (d) cooking good food using everyday ingredients   (e) menu planning

2. The word *sautéing* in the third paragraph means
   (a) boiling   (b) baking   (c) grinding   (d) frying quickly
   (e) making a sauce
3. How do you think the author would rate a TV dinner?
   (a) poor quality for too much money   (b) poor quality but
   a fair price   (c) inferior value   (d) average value   (e) good
   to have on hand for an emergency
4. What pattern has the author used to organize her material?
   (a) comparison and contrast   (b) a series of examples
   (c) problem and solution   (d) cause and effect   (e) sequence
   of events
5. A *mayonnaise de volaille* is a
   (a) salad dressing   (b) chicken salad   (c) sandwich spread
   (d) dessert   (e) chicken stew

■ Cloze Reading Comprehension Questions

The purpose of cloze reading comprehension questions is to test both your ability to read carefully and your vocabulary. A cloze reading question consists of a paragraph with a blank in place of a missing word and a series of possible choices.

When answering cloze reading questions, base your answer on the entire paragraph.

The word that is missing is not always a difficult or unfamiliar word. However, it is always a key word—one that will show whether you have understood the entire passage.

EXAMPLE: Read the following paragraph. Then choose the word that best fits in the blank.

We must be careful not to confuse two types of development in the child. Physical development follows a definite and predictable path toward maturation. For example, a child who learns to crawl will certainly outgrow this mode of locomotion and proceed toward walking. This kind of maturation follows _____ tendencies in the human and has a certain degree of independence from teaching. But social development, the acquisition of standards of behavior, the restriction of impulses and urges, will not develop without teaching. . . .—Selma H. Fraiberg

(1) learned   (2) observed   (3) independent   (4) inherited
(5) regressive

Answer: (4) inherited

EXERCISE B: Answering Cloze Reading Comprehension Questions. Read each of the following passages. Then use the context of the entire passage to select the correct missing word for each.

1. We believe that people used cowries [shells] as currency in India, China and the Middle East for thousands of years before Christ and in later times they circulated in the greater parts of the continents of Africa and Asia and all through the Pacific Islands. Only a generation ago natives used cowries as money on the west coast of Africa, where 5,000 shells were worth one Indian rupee—then about a shilling. The cowrie is still not completely extinct. So important was it as a(n)_____ that, when the Japanese invaded New Guinea in 1942 and handed out cowrie shells so recklessly that their value fell sharply, it threatened to disrupt the financial stability of the island. —J. P. Jones

   (a) artifact   (b) weapon   (c) art object   (d) currency
   (e) curiosity

2. Cynthia was always the same with Molly: kind, sweet-tempered, ready to help, professing a great deal of love for her, and probably feeling as much as she did for anyone in the world. But Molly had reached to this superficial depth of affection and intimacy in the first few weeks of Cynthia's residence in her father's house; and if she had been of a nature prone to analyse the character of one whom she loved dearly, she might have perceived that, with all Cynthia's apparent _____, there were certain limits beyond which her confidence did not go; where her reserve began, and her real self was shrouded in mystery. —Elizabeth Gaskell

   (a) cheerfulness   (b) frankness   (c) beauty   (d) honesty
   (e) boldness

■ Preparing for Reading Tests on Your Own

Reading itself is the best preparation for reading tests. Read daily for pleasure, and read enough so that you feel comfortable with different types of writing, different writing styles, and different techniques for dealing with unfamiliar words.

Establish good daily reading habits to help prepare for reading comprehension tests.

Good daily reading habits include regular pleasure reading, reading with a purpose, continual questioning for comprehension, and some sort of reading summation. Reading comprehension is a thinking process. It requires organization, analysis, and application. It calls upon you to bring together the many reading skills that you have developed over the years and to use them to increase your understanding. The following chart offers a number of suggestions for ways you can improve the skills you already have by practicing them on a daily basis to prepare for reading tests.

PREPARING FOR READING TESTS

1. Increase the amount of pleasure reading you are presently doing.
2. Gradually increase your reading speed so that you can do more reading during the same period of time.
3. Learn to enjoy all types of reading matter—fiction, biography, criticism, technical material, and so on.
4. Refuse to be satisfied with surface reading. Probe for deeper meaning.
5. Get in the habit of looking for main ideas, important details, and inference clues as you read.
6. Always be on the look out for words in introductions, summaries, headings, and questions that will help you understand the main ideas in the material you are reading.
7. Pose questions as you read. Then read to answer your questions.

EXERCISE C: **Improving Your Reading Comprehension Skills.**
Make up a schedule for the next week to broaden the types of personal reading you do. Set aside a specific time each day, and list the type of material you will read. You may want to read some of each type each day or one type one day and another the next. Include in your schedule one selection from each of the following categories.

1. A discussion of a scientific discovery or process
2. A biography of someone from a different period
3. A review of a book, play, or movie
4. A news report or editorial on a current political issue
5. A work of general interest

APPLICATION: Evaluating Your Reading Comprehension Test **Skills.** Ask yourself the following questions to see how well you are likely to perform on the reading comprehension portion of a standardized test.

1. Are you able to identify the five types of questions commonly asked on reading comprehension tests?
2. Do you understand and apply the principles for eliminating incorrect multiple-choice answers?
3. Do you check the beginning and end of selections to see if the main idea is stated in either or both places?
4. Are you able to locate quickly specific facts in a selection you have just read?
5. Are you able to find facts to support your inferences?
6. Do you use context clues to define words?
7. Can you easily identify the type of selection you are reading and the author's purpose and organization?
8. Do you consider the entire passage in finding the answer to a cloze reading comprehension question?
9. Do you have a schedule for improving and broadening your reading?
10. Do you apply what you have learned in English literature classes to your personal reading?

Library and Reference Skills

What is a modern library? Librarians like to think of it as a culture, recreation, and information center—a place where the many different materials collected provide information and entertainment for the people who use the library. Although this chapter will be more concerned with the library as an information center, remember the other aspects.

What makes the library an information center? Books, pamphlets, periodicals, records, pictures, newspapers, and other materials have been chosen and arranged so that the users of the library will be able to find the information they need. The card catalog, special indexes, and other tools are provided as aids to finding such information. Finally, the librarians are there to help people use the material in the library and to direct them to sources of information beyond the library walls.

The purpose of the next two sections is to show you how to get the most out of the libraries you use. The first section will concentrate on ways of using the library's resources to find the books you need for research, study, and general reading. The second section will show you how to use the major reference tools in the library. The final section in the chapter is devoted to the dictionary, perhaps the most important reference tool of all.

Library Skills 17.1

In order to use the library to your best advantage, you must be able to use the card catalog efficiently and then quickly find the books on the shelves. You must also be able to plan any research you must do and know how to find apparently elusive information. These skills are the subject of this section.

■ Using the Card Catalog

When you first enter any new library, you might at first assume that it will be difficult to find the books you want. However, there will always be a card catalog there to help you.

Remember that the card catalog is the key to finding books in the library.

Your first step in learning to use any library is learning how to use the card catalog. You will have to learn what types of cards are found in the card catalog, what information they contain, and how they are arranged. Before you do that, however, there is one important thing for you to remember. The card catalog is primarily a tool for finding whole books. Although certain cards will list *parts* of books, your source for this type of information will generally be reference books.

Kinds of Catalog Cards.   The card catalog allows you to zero in on the books you need from many different directions. The route you follow depends on the information you have at the start. Every fiction book in the library has at least a title and an author card. Every nonfiction book has, in addition, at least one subject card.

Title, author, and subject cards will give you the information you need about almost every book in the library.

If you know the title of the book, go to the card catalog and look for the *title card.* In the following example, the title is *Computers and Their Uses.* The card is alphabetized under *Computers.* Note that the title is at the top of the card.

TITLE
CARD:

```
001.64    Computers and Their Uses
D         Desmonde, William Herbert, 1921-

              Computers and their uses / by
          William H. Desmonde. --Englewood
          Cliffs, N.J.: Prentice-Hall, Inc.,
          c 1971.
              xvi; 427 p.; illus.; 24 cm
              Includes bibliographical refer-
          ences.

              ISBN 0-13-165498-5

          1. Electronic digital computers.
          2. Electronic data processing.
          I. Title.
```

Perhaps you are not sure of the exact title of a book, but you do know the author. In such a case, go to the catalog and look at the books listed by that author. For the book on computers, you will find an *author card* like the one in the following example. It will be alphabetized by the last name of the author, *Desmonde*.

AUTHOR
CARD:

```
001.64    Desmonde, William Herbert, 1921-
D             Computers and their uses / by
          William H. Desmonde.--Englewood
          Cliffs, N.J.: Prentice-Hall, Inc.,
          c 1971.
              xvi; 427 p.; illus.; 24 cm
              Includes bibliographical refer-
          ences.

              ISBN 0-13-165498-5

          1. Electronic digital computers.
          2. Electronic data processing.
          I. Title.
                          O
```

When a book has more than one author, you should be able to find it by looking up either author. Do not give up, however, until you have checked under the name of each author.

Sometimes you may be searching for information about a certain subject. If you are using the library for research, this situation is common. In such a case, go to the card catalog and look for a *subject card*. It will be filed alphabetically according to the subject. As in the following example, the card will be similar to an author or title card; the major difference will be that the subject is written across the top of the card.

SUBJECT
CARD:

```
001.64    COMPUTERS
D
          Desmonde, William Herbert, 1921-
              Computers and their uses / by
          William H. Desmonde.--Englewood
          Cliffs, N.J.: Prentice-Hall, Inc.,
          c 1971.
              xvi; 427 p.; illus.; 24 cm
              Includes bibliographical refer-
          ences.

              ISBN 0-13-165498-5

          1. Electronic digital computers.
          2. Electronic data processing.
          I. Title.
                          O
```

While author, title, and subject cards are the most important cards in a catalog, they are not the only ones. There are a few other types of cards that can be very useful, among them *cross-reference cards.*

Cross-reference cards will refer you either to the specific subject heading used in the catalog or to related subjects.

Looking up subject cards for information you want to find is generally very easy. Sometimes, however, the books you want will not be found under the subject you have chosen. Since the library uses a standard list of headings, it is quite possible that the books may be found under a subject heading that has not occurred to you. Also, the list of standard headings changes over time, so the library may use different headings at different times for the same subject. In order to help you find the information you need, the catalog contains *see* and *see also* cross-reference cards.

A *see* card will refer you from a subject heading that is not used to a subject heading that is used. For example, if you look up the subject heading *Solar power,* you may see a card such as the following.

CROSS-REFERENCE CARD:

```
              SOLAR POWER

                  See

              Solar Energy




                   ◯
```

The information on this card tells you that to find books about solar power you must look under the subject heading *Solar energy.*

Another kind of cross-reference card is a *see also* card. This kind of card lists additional subject headings found in the card catalog and is meant to refer you to related subjects. If you are looking for books about American art, you may find the following card.

MORE DETAILED CROSS-REFERENCE CARD:

```
                        ART, AMERICAN

                          See also

              Afro-American Art
              Architecture, American
              Architecture, Colonial
              Painting, American




                              ◯
```

A final type of catalog card is called an *analytic card*. This card, however, refers you only to *parts* of books.

Analytic cards will tell you where you can find parts of books.

Useful information about Albert Einstein, for example, can be found in the book *Contemporary Immortals* by Archibald Henderson, as shown on the following analytic card.

ANALYTIC CARD:

```
    920      Albert Einstein, 1879-1955, in
    H
             Henderson, Archibald, 1877-
                Contemporary immortals / by Archibald
             Henderson.--New York, London: D. Appleton
             and Co., c 1930.
                xii; 208 p.; illus.; 21 cm

             Contents: Albert Einstein.--Mahatma
             Gandhi.--Thomas Alva Edison.--Benito Mus-
             solini.--George Bernard Shaw.--Guglielmo
             Marconi.--Jane Addams.--Orville Wright.--
             Ignace Jan Paderewski.--Marie Sklodowska
             Curie.--Henry Ford.--Rudyard Kipling.

                ISBN 0-8369-0533-4

             1. Biography.  I. Title.
                              ◯
```

Specific Information Found on the Cards.   Once you recognize the different kinds of cards found in the card catalog and the basic kinds of information they contain, you should look more closely at the additional details the cards present.

Become familiar with the types of information found on catalog cards.

The following example is labeled for easy analysis. The number in the upper left-hand corner of the card, the *call number,* will help you locate the book on the shelf. The card also lists the author's date of birth and the publication date of the book itself, two details that can help you decide if the book is current enough for your purpose. Some topics—medicine and science, for example—require the most up-to-date information you can find. The next line of the card tells you that the book has a preface and that the text is 154 pages long. Sometimes, because you have limited time for research, the length of a book is relevant. Notice also that the book is illustrated. The following line on the card tells you that the book has a bibliography but no index.

Finally, look at the tracings at the bottom of the card. They tell you that there are cards in the catalog for this book under two subject headings, *Listening and Communications.* At first this information may not seem to be of much use, since you already have the book's number. However, it can be very useful when you need additional information on the subject.

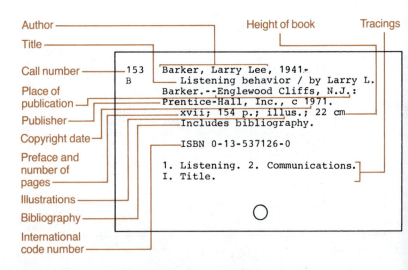

Arrangement of the Cards. In addition to knowing what kinds of catalog cards there are and what kinds of information you can find on them, you need to know something about the card catalog itself and how it is arranged. The first thing you should know is that there are two basic arrangements for card catalogs.

A card catalog may be a dictionary catalog or a divided catalog.

In a *dictionary catalog*, all of the cards are arranged continuously in alphabetical order. This arrangement is usually used in smaller libraries. A *divided catalog*, on the other hand, is divided into at least two separate sections. The most common division is to have one catalog in alphabetical order for subject cards and another one, also in alphabetical order, for author and title cards.

In some libraries there may also be other similar catalogs for non-book materials. In addition, some libraries may use a COM catalog, a computer-generated catalog with listings available on microfilm or microfiche. In some cases a COM catalog will include books that are not in that library but are in another library that is part of the same system.

Regardless of the type of catalog you are using, you will have difficulties if you fail to recognize the system of alphabetizing that is used. There are two different ways of alphabetizing: letter by letter and word by word. Library catalogs use the second system.

Use word-by-word alphabetizing to find cards in a card catalog.

Letter-by-letter alphabetizing is found in most dictionaries and in some encyclopedias. In letter-by-letter aphabetizing, the order of the entries is determined by the order of the letters in the entire entry, even if the entry consists of more than one word. In word-by-word alphabetizing, on the other hand, the order of the entries is determined by the order of letters in the first word and then by the order in the next word. Thus, in letter-by-letter alphabetizing, *Newfoundland* comes before *New York*. In word-by-word alphabetizing, *New York* comes before *Newfoundland*. The following chart lists some examples of a variety of terms alphabetized both letter by letter and word by word.

DICTIONARY AND LIBRARY ALPHABETIZING	
Letter by Letter	**Word by Word**
Newbery	New Deal
New Deal	New Jersey
newest	New Paltz
New Jersey	New York
New Paltz	Newbery
newspaper	newest
New York	newspaper

In addition to learning the general rule for alphabetizing in a card catalog, you should learn a few more specialized rules. The four rules that follow should help you find almost any listing quickly.

Ignore *a*, *an*, and *the* when they are the first words of a title.

Thus, *The Dred Scott Case* would be filed alphabetically under *D* for *Dred*, not *T* for *The*.

Treat *Mc* and *Mac* as if they were both *Mac* and alphabetize accordingly.

Thus, *McBrien, McCarthy, Macdonald,* and *machine* are in correct alphabetical order.

Treat abbreviations and numbers as if they were written out.

Thus, *20* is treated as if it were *twenty,* and *Dr.* as if it were *doctor.*

Books *by* an author are filed before books *about* an author.

Thus, *The House of Mirth* by Edith Wharton comes before a biography about Edith Wharton.

EXERCISE A: Recognizing Types of Catalog Cards. Study the following card. Then make title and subject cards for the same book.

```
391      Wilcox, Ruth Turner, 1888-
W             Folk and festival costume of the
         world / by R. Turner Wilcox.--New
         York: Scribner, c 1965.
              Unpaged; illus.; 28 cm

              ISBN 0-684-15379-3

         1. Costume.  I. Title.

                         O
```

EXERCISE B: **Understanding the Information on the Cards.** Study the following card. Then give the information requested after the card.

```
613.71   Kuntzleman, Beth A.
K             The complete guide to aerobic danc-
         ing / by Beth A. Kuntzleman and the
         Editors of Consumer guide.--Skokie,
         Ill.:Publications International, c 1979.
              96 p.; illus.; 28 cm

              ISBN 0-449-80001-6

         1. Aerobic exercises. 2. Dancing.
         I. Title.

                         O
```

 1. The call number
 2. The author
 3. The title
 4. The copyright date
 5. The publisher
 6. The place of publication
 7. The number of pages in the book
 8. Any information about pictures or photographs
 9. Any information about bibliography or index
10. The subject headings under which the book is also found

EXERCISE C: **Alphabetizing Cards.** Alphabetize the following sets of cards.

1. *New Year's Day, The Newest Idea, Newark's Future*
2. *The Creative Balance, Out of Chaos, 7 Ways to Win, An Empty Room, Machinery at Work, Macdonald's Farm*

■ Finding the Books

Once you have learned to use the card catalog quickly and efficiently, you should learn to use the call numbers and the location symbols on the cards to find the books you want with similar ease.

Finding Nonfiction.   A good way to start your search for a nonfiction book is to remember that the call number in the upper left-hand corner of the catalog card for a work of nonfiction also appears on the spine of the corresponding book. The books are arranged on the shelves in call-number order. Usually labels at the ends of the rows of shelves will tell you which call numbers (for example, 300–499) can be found in each row.

Nonfiction is arranged on the shelves in call-number order.

The call number is simply a way of classifying books according to one of two systems—the Dewey Decimal System or the Library of Congress System. The Dewey Decimal System is older and is the one used in most public and school libraries. The Library of Congress System was designed as a more precise way of classifying knowledge. It is used primarily in large college libraries, where the huge number of books demands greater precision. Although you do not need to know a great deal about either system in order to find the books on the shelves, understanding something about how each system works can be helpful, especially if you have difficulty finding information on a particular topic.

The Dewey Decimal System is a numerical system in which knowledge is classified hierarchically. All knowledge is divided into ten main classes, which are subdivided into one hundred divisions, which are subdivided into one thousand sections, which are subdivided into even more precise subcategories. It is possible to carry out the numbers to great lengths, thereby providing fairly precise breakdowns. In this section only the basic breakdowns will be considered.

The following chart shows how the Dewey Decimal System works.

THE DEWEY DECIMAL SYSTEM

Classes	Divisions	Sections	Further Categories
000 Generalities	300 Social sciences	320 Political science	324 The political process
100 Philosophy and related disciplines	310 Statistics	321 Kinds of governments and states	324.1 International organizations and activities
200 Religion	320 Political science		
300 Social sciences	330 Economics	322 Relation of state to social groups	324.2 Political parties
400 Language	340 Law		324.3 Auxiliary organizations
500 Pure science	350 Public administration	323 Relation of state to its residents	
600 Technology	360 Social problems and services		324.4 Special interests
700 The arts		324 The political process	324.5 Nomination of candidates
800 Literature	370 Education		
900 Geography and history	380 Commerce (Trade)	325 International migration	324.6 Elections
	390 Customs, etiquette, folklore	326 Slavery and emancipation	324.7–324.8 Practical politics
		327 International relations	324.9 Historical and geographical treatment of elections
		328–329 Legislation	

The first column in the chart lists the ten classes; the second lists the ten social science divisions as an example of the divisions; the third lists the political science sections of the social science division; and the last lists a further breakdown of the section on the political process. Thus, in the call number 324.2, the 3 designates a book concerned with a social science; the first 2 designates a book about political science; the 4 designates a book about the political process; and the 2 after the decimal point designates a book specifically concerned with political parties.

Each call number has, in addition to a number, a letter under the number. This letter normally stands for the first initial of the last name of the author. When books have the same number, the arrangement on the shelf is alphabetical by the letters under the numbers.

Because the Dewey Decimal System is revised periodically, you will not always find a consistent matching of subject to number. Thus, you should not be surprised to find occasionally two very similar books in different locations.

The Library of Congress System is an alphanumeric system. The call numbers begin with letters and continue with numbers, reversing the Dewey Decimal System. The main classes are designated by a single letter; combinations of two letters designate the subclasses. The letter designations are followed by a numerical notation, from 1 to 9999, which can be further subdivided to indicate divisions and subdivisions. As in the Dewey Decimal System, there is also a letter for the author. This letter is followed by a number that further breaks down the name. The following chart illustrates how the system works.

LIBRARY OF CONGRESS SYSTEM		
General Schedule	**Partial Schedule for H**	**Partial Schedule for HA**
A General works	H General works on social science	HA Statistics
B Philosophy and religion	HA Statistics	1–23 General books on statistics
C–F History	HB–HJ Economics	29–33 Theory and method
G Geography	HM–HX Sociology	35 Study and teaching
H Social sciences		36–40 Organization
J Political science		41–48 General works
K U.S. law		155–173
L Education		Universal statistics
M Music		175–4010
N Fine arts		By country
P Literature		
Q Science		
R Medicine		
S Agriculture		

T	Technology
U	Military science
V	Naval science
Z	Bibliography and library science

Using the information in the chart, you can see that the call number HA 35 contains an H for social science, followed by an A for statistics and a 35 for the study and teaching of statistics.

Although the Library of Congress System differs in many ways from the Dewey Decimal System, the method for finding books on the shelves is similar. With the Library of Congress System, simply start with letters rather than numbers.

Finding Fiction. Both the Dewey Decimal System and the Library of Congress System are designed to classify all of the books in a library. However, many libraries, especially the smaller ones, remove several types of books from the basic system. The type of book most often removed is fiction.

Fiction is generally arranged on the shelves alphabetically by the last name of the author, then by the title of the book.

The first thing you should notice about the following card for a work of fiction is that there is no call number in the upper left-hand corner. Instead, the letter F is generally used to show that the book is fiction, and the first letter of the author's last name is placed below it.

CARD FOR
FICTION:

```
F    Hawthorne, Nathaniel, 1804-1864.
H        The Blithedale romance / ed. by Arlin
     Turner.--New York: Norton, c 1958.

         ISBN 0-393-00164-4

     I. Title.
```

As you may have noticed, this is a much simpler system than that used for nonfiction. It is simple enough for even the youngest library user to follow. Simplicity is one of the basic reasons for classifying fiction in this manner.

Finding Other Special Materials.   Several other kinds of location symbols are used by libraries to group other materials that have been removed from the basic classification system.

Learn the location symbols for other materials that your library has removed from the basic classification system.

Reference books are commonly marked with the letter R in front of the call number to indicate that they are there mainly for reference purposes. This marking usually means that the books are shelved separately and may not be removed from the library.

Biographies are commonly marked B, Biog, or 92, which is short for 920, the Dewey Decimal number for general biography. In addition to the symbol for biography, the books are generally coded with either the first initial or the name of the subject of the biography. Thus $\frac{B}{N}$ and $\frac{B}{Nixon}$ can both mean that the book is a biography of Nixon. The books are then shelved in a separate section and alphabetized by the name of the subject of the biography, not by the name of the author. Many libraries have a separate biography section and still shelve some biographies in the Dewey Decimal System area. Usually even those in the second group are alphabetized by the subject, not by the author.

Many libraries use other location symbols as well. The people who set up a library have to decide which method of organizing the library's collection is best for the people using the books. In those libraries where the decision has been made to set up many small collections, you may find such symbols as M for mysteries, SF for science fiction, LP for books with large printing, YA for books meant for young adults, LH for a local history collection, and BA for a business alcove. The symbols may vary, but the idea is the same. When books have been pulled out of the basic classification system, a special location symbol is usually added to the card catalog to facilitate finding the book. Non-print items are also likely to carry special symbols that vary from library to library.

EXERCISE D: Finding Books on the Shelves.

1. Arrange each of the following groups of numbers in the order in which they would appear on the shelves.

   a. | 016 | 973.7 | 973.47 | 629.2 | 070 |
      | B | C | D | G | M |
      | 131.3 | 305.8 | 312.6 | 371.93 | 324.3 |
      | O | J | M | D | J |

   b. | 324.209 | 650.14 | 658.3 | 658.4 | 784.3 |
      | K | L | N | A | M |

   c. LD 5361.T4   AY 1185   H1   HD 8039   HD 8076

2. Alphabetize the following books of fiction.
   a. Ernest Hemingway, *The Old Man and the Sea*
   b. Ernest Hemingway, *For Whom the Bell Tolls*
   c. Kurt Vonnegut, *Jailbird*
   d. Kurt Vonnegut, *The Player Piano*
   e. Jane Austen, *Pride and Prejudice*
   f. Mildred Taylor, *Roll of Thunder, Hear My Cry*
   g. Elizabeth Pope, *The Perilous Guard*

3. Find biographies of a literary figure, a sports figure, and a political leader. Give the call number or location symbol of each book and the names of the books on either side of the books chosen.

■ Planning Research Work in the Library

Although the library has many uses, you may find it most useful at this point for research. Knowing how to find books and other materials quickly is essential to research. Knowing how to plan ahead is almost as important.

Begin your research work by gathering basic information about your topic.

In order to find information about anything, it is first necessary to know enough about your topic to be able to place it in some sort of context. To do this, you must know where to look for basic information. You must also know what kind of information will be useful when you start your actual research.

Sources of Basic Information.   There are several ways to find enough about a topic to be able to start exploring it in depth. Before you even go to the library, you have a two-fold job: (1) to pick a topic (unless the topic is assigned) and (2) to learn some basic information about the topic. The best place to start may be with your class notes and your textbook. If you do not have a topic, you can use your notes and textbook to help you focus on what you have learned and what has most interested you. If you do have a topic, you can use your notes and textbook to uncover basic information.

If you have difficulty choosing a topic or find that your topic is not clearly covered in your notes or textbook, the library should be your next stop. Libraries usually contain books with ideas for term papers on various subjects. If these do not help, you can go to an encyclopedia and read a general article covering the material in your course to find some ideas to pursue. The encyclopedia is also a good source of basic information.

Types of Basic Information.   The first thing you need to know in order to find further information on your topic is the general subject area under which your topic will be found. If you are doing research in science, for example, you will need to know if your general subject falls into the area of biology, chemistry, or biochemistry. If you are looking for information about an author, you will need to know if the writer is a novelist, an essayist, a poet, a dramatist, or a historian.

You may also find the following types of information helpful when you begin your actual research.

INFORMATION NEEDED FOR EFFICIENT RESEARCH WORK

1. What synonyms can be used to describe your topic?
2. What are some related subject areas?
3. What is the time period associated with your topic?
4. What is the geographical area associated with your topic?

Thinking along these lines can often lead to just the sources you are looking for.

EXERCISE E: Planning Your Research. Using your textbook, notes, or an encyclopedia, pick a topic and list the following information about it.

1. The correct name of your topic
2. The general subject or subjects it comes under
3. Some synonyms for the topic

4. Some related subjects
5. The time frame involved, if any
6. The geographical area involved, if any

■ Finding Other Sources

You may wonder why you cannot simply go to the card catalog and find the information you need just by looking up the correct name of your topic. Sometimes it is possible to do just that, but there are other times when it is not. The catalog may use different terms for your topic. There may not be much information on your topic in your library. There may be too many people looking for information about your topic or a similar topic so that all of the books that the library has on the topic are out. When these things happen, you need to use your imagination to find the information you need.

Use your imagination to find elusive information.

There are several ways to find information when the obvious ways do not work.

Checking More General Topics. If you have been looking up your topic directly and have found nothing, you should try synonyms for your topic. If this approach fails, you can try a more general topic. If you are trying to find information about the Industrial Revolution in England, for example, try English history, English economic history, European economic history, or European history in the eighteenth and nineteenth centuries.

Checking Related Topics. A similar approach is to look for books on related topics. If you are trying to find out about American relations with Russia, for example, try books about American foreign policy, American history, Russian history, or Russian foreign policy.

Making Your Own Connections. If you have a topic that requires you to compare two things and you can find nothing that makes the comparison, you may have to create your own connections. If you need to compare Eugene O'Neill's use of language with that of Tennessee Williams, for example, you may have to read books about each writer's use of language and make your own comparisons.

Using Biographies.   Suppose an assignment requires you to find information about a certain period in history. If, after consulting the history books, you need more details, it is often helpful to look up biographies of a famous person who lived at that time. For example if you cannot find enough information about sixteenth century England, try biographies of Queen Elizabeth. You may also find it helpful to read biographies of contemporaries. If you are doing a paper on Alexander Hamilton and need more information, you might consult a biography of Thomas Jefferson.

Using Other Types of Materials.   If you have difficulty finding printed material on your topic, you can check to see if the library has any films, records, or tapes containing the information you need.

Using Other Libraries.   If all of these suggestions fail, remember that there are other libraries. Most libraries can get you books from other libraries. If you know the book you need, ask the librarian if he or she can get it for you from another library. If you need the book rapidly, ask if the librarian can find out what other libraries have the book and then pick up the book yourself. Of course, you can also simply go to another library and start the process all over again.

EXERCISE F: **Using Other Sources.** Using the preceding suggestions, find information about the last years of Anne Boleyn's life without using a biography of Anne Boleyn. Tell what sources you chose and why you chose them.

APPLICATION: **Using Library Skills.** To evaluate your ability to use the card catalog, find books, do research, and locate hard-to-find material, complete each of the following steps.

1. Pick a topic.
2. Using the card catalog, find eight to ten books about your subject. Remember to use cross-reference cards and the tracings on the cards. Also, use any of the suggestions given in this section to find elusive material.
3. Go to the shelves and check to see if the materials are available and if they have the information you need.
4. Repeat the first three steps until you have found eight to ten books. If necessary, ask the librarian to help you find books in another library.
5. List the books and other materials you have chosen. If they are not directly related, explain why you chose them.

Reference Skills 17.2

Whether you are doing research for an assignment or to satisfy your own curiosity, a knowledge of how to use reference materials quickly and efficiently can be invaluable. You are probably already familiar with the way they are marked and arranged in a library.

Reference books are generally marked with an R in front of the call number and kept in a separate room or area, which may be further subdivided by type of material. The area will probably also include materials such as pamphlets and periodicals and, possibly, duplicate copies of heavily used circulating materials.

In addition to knowing where reference works are kept, you should be able to distinguish between different types of reference books. One of the most important distinctions is that between fact books and indexes. A fact book (for example, an almanac) contains a great deal of concrete information and is meant to be consulted for specific facts, not to be read through. An index (for example, *The Readers' Guide to Periodical Literature*) is used to locate information contained in other books, newspapers, or magazines.

Another way of distinguishing between reference books is to describe them as general or specialized. General reference books cover a great many subjects. Specialized reference books cover a single subject in greater depth. You are probably already using a number of the more general tools but may be missing the benefits of the more specialized works.

In this section you will have a chance to review the uses of general reference materials and learn more about specialized materials. Fact books and indexes will be discussed under each heading. This section will also discuss periodicals, show you how to find reference materials not contained in your library, and discuss ways of choosing the right reference materials for a particular assignment.

■ General Reference Books

General reference books are among the most useful books in a library. There are several types. Among them are dictionaries, encyclopedias, almanacs, atlases, and gazetteers. Because dictionaries will be discussed at length in Section 17.3, in this section the discussion will center on other types of general works.

Encyclopedias.   As noted in Section 17.1, general encyclopedias are very useful at the beginning of a research project. You can use them to find most or all of the basic information you need to know about your topic in order to begin your research. In addition, the bibliography at the end of an encyclopedia article can be a valuable source for further information. An encyclopedia is also a good source for finding many other kinds of information quickly. If you need to know the date Pearl Harbor was attacked by Japan, for example, you can find it in an encyclopedia.

Use encyclopedias to find basic facts and bibliographies.

A general encyclopedia is usually a multivolume set arranged alphabetically. One volume, usually the first or last, is an index, which will refer you both to subjects for which there are complete articles and to subjects that are contained within articles. In addition, many of the articles themselves will refer you to related articles found elsewhere in the encyclopedia. Any or all of these sources can be very useful in helping you find information that does not appear under the expected listing in the encyclopedia itself.

The following example is taken from the index to the *Encyclopedia Americana*. The first reference, to Volume 20, page 1, is a reference to the main article on the subject. The other references are to other articles that contain additional information about the same subject.

EXAMPLE: NAVAJO (Navaho) (Amerind)
            20–1; 15–6; 22–774; 27–690
            Arizona 2–306, 309
            Athapaskan Languages 2–603
            blankets 15–12
            dance 15–22
            diet 15–11
            Ghost 12–724
            homes 15–12
            Indian wars 15–30
            irrigation project 20–209
            Monument Valley Navajo Tribal Park 19–427
            Music 19–662; 15–24
            rugs 23–858
            Weaving 28–550
            Illus. 2–ARIZONA: 2–300; 15–INDIAN, AMERICAN; 15–12; rug 23–853; sand painting 24–221; swastika 26–91

In order to be useful, an encyclopedia must be current. There are several ways this is accomplished. One way is to publish a totally new edition. The more common method is to follow a policy of continuous revision. This means that each time a new edition of the encyclopedia is published some articles are revised, usually those on subjects in which the information has been most affected by the passage of time. In addition, many encyclopedias publish yearbooks. An encyclopedia yearbook has a two-fold purpose: It brings together information about the events of the year, often in a chronological arrangement, and it presents information about new or expanding areas of knowledge. Because of this, an encyclopedia yearbook can be a very useful tool when doing research.

Most libraries contain many different sets of encyclopedias. Among the most commonly found are *Encyclopedia Americana,* the *Encyclopaedia Britannica, Collier's Encyclopedia, The World Book Encyclopedia,* and the *Random House Encyclopedia.* They are all useful and, in many ways, similar. However, as you use them you will discover that they have different areas of strength. The *World Book,* for example, has excellent illustrations and is very good for simple, to-the-point explanations of basic material. The *Encyclopedia Americana* is especially good for information about American cities and states. The *Britannica* is an excellent, somewhat higher-level general encyclopedia with an unusual arrangement. Instead of having a single alphabetical arrangement with an index volume, it comes in two separately alphabetized sets. The main set, called the Macropaedia, includes long articles on a number of subjects. The other set, the Micropaedia, contains much shorter articles giving basic information about a large number of subjects. In many ways the Micropaedia serves as an index for the Macropaedia. When you use these encyclopedias and others, you will find other areas in which each tends to excel.

Almanacs. An almanac is one of the most basic tools in the library. It is a perfect example of a fact book and should often be the first book you turn to when you need small pieces of specific information.

Use almanacs for all kinds of miscellaneous information.

An almanac contains geographic, political, statistical, historical, and other miscellaneous information. If you want to know the date of an earthquake in Alaska or the winner of the

1954 World Series, you can find it easily in an almanac. However, unlike an encyclopedia, an almanac seldom provides useful background information. Nor is it arranged alphabetically. Because the arrangement of an almanac is by broad subject areas, the best way to find the information you need is through the index. The best known almanacs are the *World Almanac and Book of Facts* and the *Information Please Almanac.* When you use them, you will discover a number of slight differences in their coverage of material.

Atlases and Gazetteers.   Atlases and gazetteers are similar but not identical. The essential difference between the two is that gazetteers contain no maps.

> Use atlases primarily to obtain information from maps; use gazetteers to find other geographical information.

You probably have used the maps in atlases from time to time. You may not realize, however, how much information can be conveyed through maps. There are several different types of atlases, all of which have different uses.

The type of atlas you are probably most familiar with is a general atlas. A general atlas consists primarily of political maps showing the boundaries of countries and states and the locations of cities, towns, rivers, and oceans. A general atlas may also include topographic maps showing the physical characteristics of the land. In addition, some general atlases include maps covering such topics as industry, climate, and population density. A particularly good atlas, which contains a variety of maps, is the *National Atlas of the United States.* Others are the *World Book Atlas* and the *National Geographic Atlas of the World.*

The historical atlas is another important type of reference book. In a historical atlas, maps are arranged to show changes over time. Among the major historical atlases are *Shepherd's Historical Atlas,* which covers world history, *The Atlas of American History,* which covers American history, and the *West Point Atlas of American Wars,* which has excellent battle maps. These are just a few examples of a very wide-ranging type of reference work.

The economic atlas is a type of atlas with which you may not be familiar. It contains maps designed to give economic information: that is, information about energy, industry, population, agriculture, and so on. A good example is the *Oxford Economic Atlas of the World.*

Closely related to the atlas is the gazetteer, a reference work that gives geographical information without using maps. An excellent example is the *Times Atlas Gazetteer.* A geographical dictionary is similar to a gazetteer except that it includes fewer places and gives more information about each. A good example of this type of reference book is *Webster's New Geographical Dictionary.*

Other General Reference Tools.   Since it is impossible to fit every book into only a few small categories, these last few paragraphs on general reference tools will discuss a few miscellaneous books that can be useful for special assignments.

Check your own library to discover other useful general reference materials.

One type of miscellaneous material is local reference material. Most libraries, however small, make some effort to collect information of purely local concern. Reference materials may include a directory of local officials or the proceedings of your local legislative body.

Another area of particular interest to most people today is consumer information. Of course, "consumer information" is a very vague term, and it is often difficult to determine just what a library has in this area. However, there are several helpful tools that may be available in your own library. Among these are consumer directories such as *The Consumer Protection Guide* and *Help, the Useful Almanac,* which can give you ideas about how to remedy any problems you may have as well as a list of agencies that can assist you. In addition, directories that provide names of government officials or business firms and their addresses can be very useful. Be sure to ask your librarian to help you find any information you need in this area.

EXERCISE A: **Using Encyclopedias.** Find each of the following items of information and list the source of your information.

1. List two major events of the thirteenth century.
2. Give the date that Anchorage, Alaska, was founded.
3. List three books giving information about the economy of Libya.
4. List four major events of 1978.
5. Explain how the letter *K* is expressed in Morse code.

EXERCISE B: **Using Almanacs.** Find each of the following items of information and list the source of your information.

1. Who won the Pulitzer Prize for biography in 1939?
2. What is the wording of the Equal Rights Amendment proposed in the 1970's?
3. What is the largest island in the world?
4. What play has had the longest Broadway run?
5. Who was the first Secretary of Defense?

EXERCISE C: **Using Atlases and Gazetteers.** Find each of the following items of information and list the source of your information.

1. Tell what country Kofu is found in and give its latitude and longitude.
2. List the various peoples of Austria-Hungary in 1914.
3. List three tourist centers in Europe whose principal attraction is the sea.
4. Give two American and two Mexican cities bordering the Gulf of Mexico.
5. List the countries bordering Iran.

EXERCISE D: **Using Other Tools.** Find each of the following items of information and list the source of your information.

1. Draw up a list of your major local officials.
2. Find out who represents you in your state legislature and in Congress.
3. Find the address of the State Board of Medical Examiners in Kentucky.
4. List three states that have no-fault automobile insurance.
5. Find the name of the federal agency concerned with household moving.

■ Specialized Reference Books

Although general reference books have a wide variety of uses, specialized reference books may be more useful for certain assignments.

Use specialized reference books to find in-depth information about a particular field.

Many specialized reference works are similar to the more general reference works. There are a number of specialized dictionaries and encyclopedias, all of which go into more detail in their special areas than the more general reference works. In addition, there are a number of specialized fact books and indexes.

The treatment in the following paragraphs begins with three types of works that may be especially useful in English classes. These are followed by listings of works that may be useful in your other classes, as well as in research work you do for English.

Dictionary of Synonyms.   A dictionary of synonyms can help you make your writing more interesting and more precise. It can help you find a synonym to substitute for a word that you have used too often. It can also help you find a word that more clearly expresses exactly what you mean.

Two very good dictionaries of synonyms are *Roget's International Thesaurus* and *Funk and Wagnall's Modern Guide to Synonyms*. In its latest editions, *Roget's* is arranged in strict alphabetical order. The following example is taken, however, from one of the earlier editions, still found in many libraries. Words are arranged categorically and can be found most quickly through the alphabetical index. The first example, from the index, gives various references to different meanings of the word *peace*. The second example, from the main portion of the book, gives a list of synonyms for *peace* when the word is used in the sense of "truce."

INDEX
ENTRY:

> **peace**
> *n.* accord 794.1
>   agreement 26.1
>   comfortableness
>   887.2
>   order 59.1
>   peacefulness 803
>   quiescence 268.1
>   silence 451.1
>   truce 804.5
> *interj.* peace be with
>   you! 803.11
>   silence! 451.14

MAIN
ENTRY:

> .5 **truce, armistice, peace;** pacification, treaty of peace, suspension of hostilities, **cease-fire,** stand-down, breathing spell, cooling-off period; Truce *or* Peace of God, Pax Dei, Pax Romana; temporary arrangement, *modus vivendi* [L]; hollow truce, *pax in bello* [L]; demilitarized zone, buffer zone, neutral territory.

Biographical Information.   When you are doing research, you will often find that biographical information is essential. There are several reference books that can help you find this type of information. Some are general; some cover specific fields. Some cover the present; others cover the past. Some give a great deal of information; others, a bare minimum.

One of the most useful of the general tools is *Current Biography*, a work that is published each month and then bound annually. The series contains information about important people in all fields. The articles are long and include portraits and bibliographies. Except for the obituary listings, only people living at the time of publication are included.

A very different source of biographical information is found in the *Who's Who* series. The information in these books is obtained from the answers to questionnaires and consists of only basic facts such as occupation, date of birth, schools attended, jobs held, association memberships, and publications. There are several books in this series: *Who's Who in America, Who's Who* (British), *Who's Who in Finance and Industry, Who's Who in American Art,* and many others. *Who Was Who* and *Who Was Who in America* include significant people no longer living. The *Who's Who* books are more useful for the large number of people included than for the quantity of information about any one person.

Two other good sources, both international in scope, are *Webster's Biographical Dictionary*, which comes in one volume, and the *McGraw-Hill Encyclopedia of World Biography*, which comes in a multivolume set. Both have fairly short articles covering a wide range of people.

Good sources for people no longer living are the *Dictionary of American Biography* and the *Dictionary of National Biography* (British), both multivolume sets with long articles about the fairly prominent people they include. Another good source, devoted to Americans no longer living, is *The National Cyclopedia of American Biography*, which includes a slightly larger group of people than the *Dictionary of American Biography* does.

Many excellent biographical tools are limited to a single field. *Contemporary Authors*, a multivolume set covering both major and minor American authors, is especially useful. *Twentieth Century Authors* and *World Authors, 1950–1970* are two other good examples in the literary field. They are best for information on well-known authors.

If you need biographical information about scientists, an excellent source is *The Dictionary of Scientific Biographies*, a multivolume set with a separate index volume. It contains long articles with excellent coverage of both the lives and works of the scientists included. A similar tool is *Men of Mathematics*.

Two very good indexes round out the major biographical sources. The first, *Biography Index*, indexes material found in periodicals and books. The other, *The New York Times Obituary Index*, indexes obituaries in *The New York Times* from 1858 through 1968. This, together with the entries under the subject heading *Deaths* in the main index of *The New York Times*, can be an excellent source for information.

Literary Information.   In addition to biographical material about authors, you may sometimes need critical analyses of their works. The reference tools available in this area can be divided into two basic types, handbooks and indexes.

A literary *handbook* is a book that contains brief articles about authors and their works, as well as information about literary movements. Handbooks are useful primarily for gathering basic information. Two especially good series are *The Oxford Companion Series* and *The Penguin Companion Series*. Each series contains several volumes covering several different types of literature, including American, English, French, Spanish, Oriental, and African. Two other good handbooks are *The Cambridge History of English Literature* and the *McGraw-Hill Encyclopedia of World Drama*. A related tool is a dictionary of literary terms, a good example of which is the *Dictionary of World Literary Terms*.

An *index* is the tool you should use when you want to find a poem, a short story, or a play that has not been published separately. An index can also be useful when you need to locate the source of a quotation. When you are looking for a poem, you can use *Granger's Index to Poetry*, which allows you to trace poems by author, subject, title, or first line. When you are looking for a short story, you can use the *Short Story Index*. When you are looking for a play, either the *Play Index* or *Ottemiller's Index to Plays in Collections* can be used. When you are looking for the source of a quotation, you have several choices. Perhaps the best known is *Bartlett's Familiar Quotations*, which is arranged chronologically by author, with author and keyword indexes. *The Dictionary of Quotations*, by Bergen Evans, and the *Home Book of Quotations* are arranged by topic with author indexes.

Indexes of various kinds are also very helpful when your most pressing need is for a critical review of an author or for criticism of a specific work. An excellent source for this kind of information is the *Book Review Digest,* which will direct you to book reviews found in various magazines and journals. Published several times a year and then collected in an annual yearbook, the volumes in this series are arranged alphabetically by author, with subject and title indexes in each volume. The entries in each volume are made up of a series of summaries, or digests, of book reviews, with a reference to the periodical in which the full review appears. A similar publication, *Book Review Index,* is only an index. There are no summaries of the reviews, just references to the periodicals in which the reviews are found.

There are also several indexes that offer in-depth literary criticism. A particularly useful series is the *Library of Literary Criticism,* which contains volumes covering British, American, German, French, and Slavic literature. Each author entry consists of a digest of information about criticism of the author's works and a reference to original sources, which will be found either in books or in periodicals. Other useful series are *Twentieth Century Literary Criticism,* covering authors from 1900 to 1960, and *Contemporary Literary Criticism,* covering contemporary novelists since 1960. Once again, there are excerpts of criticism of a work and references to the sources of the criticism. In both of these series, the excerpts are long enough to be useful.

In addition, there are several indexes that are more specialized; examples are *Dramatic Literary Criticism* and *A Guide to Critical Reviews,* which covers American drama, musicals, and screenplays.

Finally, there is the *Essay and General Literature Index,* which can help you obtain information on a wide range of topics. In it you can find information about such varied topics as the Supreme Court and medical ethics, as well as information about various authors writing about these and other topics. Many of the indexes that have been mentioned so far have contained references only to articles in periodicals. The *Essay and General Literature Index* is different in that it is designed to help you find material in anthologies and collections of essays. Essentially, it is an index to parts of books. Each volume consists of a single alphabetical arrangement that covers authors, titles, and subjects. Each author entry is arranged in the same way—first it lists the author's own works published in a given year, then general studies about the author and the author's work, and finally discussions of the author's individual works. The following entry for Sinclair Lewis is taken from a 1978 volume. Since Lewis died in 1951, none of his own works are listed for the year 1978. Note, however, that there are entries in 1978 about his general work and about one of his individual works, *Main Street*. In the first entry, the essay is to be found in a book by S. E. Hyman entitled *The Critic's Credentials*. The second entry lists a book by P. D. Goist entitled *From Main Street to State Street*.

MAIN ENTRY: **Lewis, Sinclair**
                              About
     Hyman, S. E. Anthropologist of Gopher Prairie. *In* Hyman, S. E. The critic's credentials p97-101
     About individual works
     Main Street
     Goist, P. D. The ideal questioned but not abandoned: Sherwood Anderson, Sinclair Lewis, and Floyd Dell. *In* Goist, P. D. From Main Street to State Street p21-34
     Watkins, F. C. Main Street: culture through the periscope of ego. *In* Watkins, F. C. In time and place p193-213

Music and Art.   There are also several good sources of information in the areas of music and art. Among the most useful are several excellent encyclopedias and dictionaries. The one-volume *Harvard Dictionary of Music* and the multivolume *Grove's Dictionary of Music and Musicians* are useful for information about classical music. *Rock On: The Illustrated Encyclopedia of Rock 'N Roll* and *The Encyclopedia of Pop, Rock, and Soul* offer useful information about popular music.

The *McGraw-Hill Dictionary of Art* provides basic information about art and artists. The *McGraw-Hill Encyclopedia of Art* contains more comprehensive explanations of art movements, the art of individual artists, and the art of specific nations. It also has excellent illustrations. *The Oxford Companion to Art* is a good one-volume reference work. *The Art Index* is a good source for periodical information about art and related fields.

Science and Mathematics.   Another important area that has some excellent reference sources is that of science and mathematics. Two valuable scientific encyclopedias are the *McGraw-Hill Encyclopedia of Science and Technology* and the

Encyclopedia of Chemical Technology. The latter covers a broad range of topics, including such diverse topics as blood coagulants, bleaching agents, and water desalination. Two good dictionaries are the *McGraw-Hill Dictionary of Scientific Terms* and James' *Mathematical Dictionary.*

There are also some very useful handbooks covering science and mathematics. These usually include tables and other basic facts. Good examples are *The Handbook of Physics and Chemistry* and the *Handbook of Tables for Mathematics.*

Social Studies.   Social studies is an extremely large field with many different types of reference books. The most inclusive encyclopedia in this area is the *Encyclopedia of the Social Sciences*, which includes information about the entire field, broadly defined. In it you can find information about psychologists and psychology, ideologies, economics and economists, and politics and political philosophers. A similar encyclopedia with a narrower coverage is the *Encyclopedia of Philosophy*, which contains information on topics ranging from the ancient philosophers to the modern philosophical movements. It also includes a good deal of information about political philosophy.

A good multivolume reference work in the field of social studies is the *Dictionary of American History*, which is particularly useful for quickly finding basic information about topics related to American history. Other social studies dictionaries include *Safire's Political Dictionary* and the *Dictionary of the Social Sciences.*

Two excellent sources for information about foreign countries are the *Stateman's Yearbook* and *Europa Yearbook: A World Survey*. Both are published annually and give basic information about all of the countries in the world. Each work includes information about the history, area, population, governmental structure, and economy of the countries. *Europa* is more comprehensive, including information on such topics as the press and university systems. It also lists government officials as well as historical and statistical information and has a section about international organizations.

For quickly finding information about government personnel and organizations in the United States, you can use the *Congressional Directory* or the *United States Government Manual*. If you need more information about American politicians, the best source may be the *Almanac of American Politics*, which contains biographical information, information about key votes, and ratings by various organizations for each of the people covered. Once you have identified the people involved in the topics you are researching, you can go to one of the biographical reference works mentioned earlier. Most states publish similar directories. You can check with your library to see if it has any such directories for your state.

Another important group of social studies reference works deals with laws passed by Congress and cases heard by the United States Supreme Court. The best source on laws may be the *Congressional Quarterly*, which has information about all major bills being considered or passed, along with the congressional votes on the bills. The *Congressional Quarterly Almanac*, published once a year, has several appendices covering such subjects as votes, special reports, and presidential messages. If you need information about laws passed by year, you can go to the *Statutes at Large*. On the other hand, if you want information about laws codified by subject, you can go to the *United States Code*.

One of the best reference works for information about the Supreme Court is *Leading Constitutional Decisions*, which gives information about all major Supreme Court cases. Another useful work is *The Justices of the Supreme Court*, which focuses on the justices but also includes a case index.

There are also several useful indexes in the social studies area. The *Social Science Index* is a good index of periodical articles; *PAIS* indexes both periodicals and government documents. A related work, not quite an index, is the *Harvard Guide to American History*, which acts as a comprehensive bibliographical source to materials on American history. It comes in two volumes, the first arranged by subject and the second arranged in chronological order.

The most complete reference work for the kind of statistical information often needed in social studies is probably the *Statistical Abstract of the United States*. Especially useful are the footnotes that appear after each table to guide you to the original source of the information whenever you need greater detail. On the international level, the United Nations publishes two extremely useful statistical tools: (1) the *Demographic Yearbook*, which has statistics on population and mortality, and (2) the *Statistical Yearbook*, which has economic statistics. When you use either of these, you must remember that the statistics published by the United Nations are collected and provided by the various countries and, therefore, may vary somewhat in quality.

EXERCISE E: **Using Dictionaries of Synonyms.** Find each of the following items of information and list the source of your information.

1. List two words that mean "lack of unity" and two that mean "on a reduced scale."
2. List two antonyms for *modest*.

EXERCISE F: **Using Biographical Reference Tools.** Follow the instructions for Exercise E.

1. When and where was Linda Ronstadt born?
2. When did Emmeline Pankhurst live, and what was she famous for?
3. Bergen Evans died in 1978. What were his major accomplishments according to at least two of his obituaries?
4. What books did Belva Plain write?
5. Where was Bob S. Bergland born? What schools did he attend?

EXERCISE G: **Using Literary Reference Tools.** Follow the instructions for Exercise E.

1. List at least two books that contain the poem "La Belle Dame Sans Merci."
2. List the dates of birth and death for Sinclair Lewis as well as the titles of three of his books.
3. Define *high comedy*.
4. List four sources for reviews of Mary Gordon's novel *Final Payments*.
5. List two sources that deal with the novels of Saul Bellow and tell what novels they are concerned with.

EXERCISE H: **Using Music and Art Reference Tools.** Follow the instructions for Exercise E.

1. Who wrote the *Classical Symphony* and when?
2. What is Elton John's real name?
3. What are the generally accepted dates for romanticism in art?

EXERCISE I: **Using Science and Mathematical Reference Tools.** Follow the instructions for Exercise E.

1. What is an isotron?
2. What is the square root of 350?
3. What is a chameleon?

EXERCISE J: **Using Social Studies Reference Tools.** Follow the instructions for Exercise E.

1. What political parties exist today in Portugal?
2. How many bills did President Carter veto in 1978? What were they?
3. How did your own United States senators vote on a recent bill of interest to you? What was the bill?
4. What is the importance of the Supreme Court case of *Miranda vs. Arizona?* What did it decide?
5. How many telephones were there per every one hundred inhabitants of Romania in 1975?
6. What is the importance of Fort Sumter to American history?

■ Periodicals and Pamphlets

Along with the other types of material in the library's reference section, you are likely to find a number of periodicals and pamphlets. These can be very useful for finding some types of information.

Use periodicals and pamphlets to find current and concise information about a number of subjects.

Periodical is a general term for anything that is published at intervals during a year. The term is usually used to refer to magazines and journals, but it can also refer to newspapers.

Magazines and Journals. *Magazine* is the term generally used for the more popular weekly and monthly periodicals. *Journal* is the term used for the more scholarly monthly and quarterly periodicals. There are many periodicals of both types, some general and some very specialized. They all share the general characteristic of being good for current, concise information. Almost every library has some periodicals; larger libraries will usually have a good-sized collection.

In order to find information in periodicals, you need to use periodical indexes. There are many types of indexes, some for journals, some for magazines, some general, and some specialized. A number of specialized indexes to periodicals have already been mentioned. For everyday use, however, the most valuable is probably *The Readers' Guide to Periodical Literature,* an alphabetically arranged subject and author guide to articles in most of the more common periodicals. Another index, the

Popular Periodical Index, covers mainly popular magazines and is often the first index to pick up a new magazine. You may also find that your library subscribes to a new index called the *Magazine Index*, which is a computer-generated index to most of the periodicals in *The Readers' Guide* as well as several others. The references in the *Magazine Index* are displayed on a screen, and since the index is computer generated, entries are always found within a single alphabetical grouping, thereby eliminating the need to look through several volumes.

Although there are slight differences in format among the various indexes, they are sufficiently alike so that if you learn to use one of them, *The Readers' Guide*, you should be able to use any of them. The labels added to the following example from *The Readers' Guide* should help you interpret the various entries. The first full entry under the heading *Petroleum* (after the two "see also" references), for example, is for an article entitled "Oils and Rubber from Arid Land Plants" by J. D. Johnson and C. W. Hinman. The article includes bibliographical materials, footnotes, illustrations, and a map. It appeared in the magazine *Science*, Volume 208, on pages 460 to 464. The issue was dated May 2, 1980.

Subject heading — · · · — "See" reference

"See also" references ·

PETROLEO Brasileiro (firm) See Petroleum industry—Brazil

PETROLEUM

Title of article — *See also*
Fuel, Colloidal
Oil shales

Oils and rubber from arid land plants. J. D. Johnson and C. W. Hinman. bibl f il map — Authors — Illustration and map

Title of magazine — Science 208:460-4 My 2 '80

Osage oil cover-up. W. J. Broad. il Science 208: 32-5 Ap 4 '80 — Bibliography and footnotes

Volume and pages — Petroleum plantations for fuel and materials. M. Calvin. bibl il BioScience 29:533-8 S '79; Discussion. 30:221 Ap '80 — Date

Finance

Subheading — Oil's gusher. Time 115:88 My 5 '80

Newspapers.   Newspapers, like other periodicals, are good for finding current and concise information. However, except for a few special articles, the information tends to be limited. A newspaper generally gives only the basics of a news story, while a magazine or journal will usually give you additional explanation and background information. Although there are many newspapers, your library probably has very few, possibly only your local newspaper and *The New York Times*, which is considered a newspaper of record.

Although several newspapers have indexes, the index to *The New York Times* is one of the most complete, both in terms of time (it goes back to 1851) and in terms of general coverage. It is also found in most libraries. Thus, it is probably the most useful index to learn to use. This index, which is published annually, is arranged alphabetically by subject. Important article titles are printed in bold. Perhaps most important is the fact that each reference includes a good abstract of the basic facts in an article so that the index alone is often all you need. The following example from the 1979 volume, with labels for the various parts, should make the system clear.

Date, section, page, and column ─

Subject heading ─

"See also" references ─

Abstract on article ─

(M) for medium length;

(S) for short;

(L) for long

IRAQ. See also Arab League. Ethiopia. Ag 18. Iran, F 14. Je 4,7,16. Ag 26. N 24. D 15,16,18. Jordan, Jl 2.

Article on Iraq's shift to moderate posture in Arab and world affairs and its growing independence from USSR; most startling shift was rapprochement reached with Syria in Oct; drawing (M), Ja 7,IV,2:3

Efforts of Kurds to win autonomy revd; map (S), Ja 7,IV,2:4

Syrian Pres Assad and Iraqi Pres Bakr will meet in Damascus on Jan 20 to strengthn their renewed pol and mil alliance (S), Ja 10,2:3

King Hussein of Jordan meets with Syrian Pres Assad after plans are reptd for merger between Syria and Iraq (S). Ja 17,6:2; Iraqi Vice Pres Saddam Hussein and Assad discuss unification, Demascus (S). Ja 29,5:4; Syria and Iraq end high-level meeting; say more time is needed to arrange merger (S), Ja 31,5:6

Iraqi Information Min Saad Qasim Hammudi says revolution in Iran is internal affair and not gen Shiite uprising that will spread; says Khomeini's role is that of Iranian leader and not leader of Shiite sect (M), F 26,1:2

In addition to providing local papers and a paper such as *The New York Times,* many libraries subscribe to a service called *Newsbank. Newsbank* uses microfiche to reprint articles about urban and public affairs from many newspapers around the country. The service also provides paper indexes that act as guides to the information on the microfiche. Another very useful source for basic news items is *Facts on File,* a weekly digest of world news. It is particularly useful for finding current information about government leaders around the world.

Pamphlets.   Pamphlets, small paperbound texts issued by many groups from private agencies to government, are also useful for finding current information. Unlike periodicals, however, pamphlets do not assume any prior knowledge and always give a concise background for the subjects they cover. Thus, they may be especially useful for subjects that are new to you. They are usually arranged alphabetically by subject in what is called a vertical file. Because each library uses its own subject headings, you should consult a librarian if you have any trouble finding the pamphlets you need.

EXERCISE K: Using *The Readers' Guide.* Look up material about the American hostages in Iran in *The Readers' Guide to Periodical Literature*. Make a list of at least five articles on this subject. If there are any related "see also" headings, list them as well.

EXERCISE L: Using *The New York Times Index.* Follow the instructions for Exercise K, this time using *The New York Times Index*. Note any differences in the number and types of articles written in each index during the same period.

■ Other Ways of Obtaining Reference Materials

Although your library is likely to have most if not all of the reference works discussed in this section, you still may not always have everything you need. In such a case, there are a number of additional steps that you can take.

When you need information that is not in the library, consider writing to national and local organizations, whose addresses you may be able to obtain in the library.

If the library has a copy of Gale's *Directory of Associations*, you can use it to find the name and address of a national organization that is directly concerned with your topic. If you do not have time for a mailing, or if your library has no such directory, you might check with the librarian to see if there is a local organization that might be able to give you similar information or, possibly, an interview. You might also check to see if your library keeps any records of such local associations.

When you need information on a local topic, the information is much less likely to be in printed form. Once again, a local association may be willing to help you. If you need the latest population estimate for your city, you can call the local planning department. If you need information about the number of new houses built in a certain period, you can call the local building department. In such cases, however, your best bet may be to check first with the librarian to see if the library has records covering this information. If it does not, the librarian may be willing to help you find the necessary organization to contact.

EXERCISE M: Obtaining Additional Reference Materials. Follow these steps, listing the sources of your information.

1. Find the addresses of two national organizations concerned with mental health.
2. See if the library can supply you with a local address for such an organization.
3. See if the library has any records from the local health department. If not, obtain the telephone number of the health department.

■ Choosing the Right Material

Once you know how and where to find materials in and out of the library, you will probably be able to carry out any research you must do much more efficiently. Two additional guidelines can also be useful when you are choosing between different types of materials.

Card Catalog Versus Index.   The general rule for choosing between the card catalog and an index is a very simple one.

> Use the card catalog to find books and an index to find parts of books.

In many cases, however, you will need both. If you need criticism of a novel by Eudora Welty, for example, the best place to start may be with an index such as the *Essay and General Literature Index*. Once you have specific references to the novel, you can check the card catalog to see if the library has the books.

Different Types of Material.   A more difficult decision may be whether to use a book, a reference work, a magazine, a newspaper, a pamphlet, or a local agency.

> Think carefully about your needs before you choose the material you will consult.

Books will generally give you the most information and are often the best choice when there is little or no new information available on your topic. You would probably, for example, want to use books for information about Colonial furniture. On the other hand, books will seldom contain the latest information on a topic. Thus, if you are doing a long report on the history of furniture, you may want to go to books for the historical aspects and to newspapers and other periodicals for the latest information.

Reference materials are good for background information and often best for small bits of factual information. If you need to know the capital of North Dakota, for example, you will probably find the information most quickly in a reference book.

Periodicals are particularly good for finding current or contemporary information; followed over time, they can also give you a historical view. If you want to know the reactions to the Supreme Court decision on the desegregation of schools, you can go to the magazines and newspapers of the time. If you want to know the reaction ten years later, you can use articles written ten years later.

Pamphlets are also good for current, concise information and will give you a quick summary of any background material you need in order to understand a subject. If you need basic information about careers in government, for example, the best source may be a pamphlet.

If you need information of a local nature, you may be able to find it in local newspapers or local records. If not, you can call a local agency. You may need to go to a local agency, for example, to see how many houses have been sold in the last year in your town or what the latest crime figures are.

EXERCISE N: Choosing Between the Card Catalog and an Index. Decide whether you should use the card catalog, an index, or both for each of the following items. Then explain why and how you would use each source.

1. To find a short story
2. To find criticism of Jane Austen's *Pride and Prejudice*
3. To find out about foods mentioned in the Bible
4. To find criticism of a short story

EXERCISE O: Choosing a Source. Decide what type or types of material you would use to find each of the following kinds of information. Then explain why you chose each type of material.

1. A history of the Napoleonic wars
2. Enough information about capital punishment for a debate
3. The cost of living in 1978
4. The incidence of crime in your city
5. Contemporary reactions and later thoughts about the internment of Japanese-Americans during World War II

APPLICATION: **Using What You Have Learned.** Carry out the following steps to test your ability to use the library's many resources.

1. Pick a topic involving some current event.
2. Choose eight to ten sources for your topic. Explain why and how you chose each.
3. Check to see if they are available.
4. If not, try again and explain how you widened the search. If you are unable to find enough information in the library, explain how you propose to widen the search further.

Dictionary Skills 17.3

A good dictionary is a valuable resource. In addition to giving the meanings and spellings of words, a dictionary indicates how to break words into syllables and how to pronounce words correctly. It also gives a word's part of speech—that is, how it can be used in a sentence. Most dictionaries show the derivations of words as well, and a few even tell when a word first appeared in written English and what it meant at a particular time in history. Many dictionaries also contain essential facts about famous people, events, and places and explain the meanings of common abbreviations and foreign words. Some provide tips for correct usage. Although most of these features and others can be found in a typical dictionary, all dictionaries are not the same.

■ Kinds of General Dictionaries

Lexicographers, the people who make dictionaries, always have a particular audience in mind when they prepare a new edition of a dictionary. Thus, if you were to shop for a dictionary at your local bookstore, you would probably find several shelves of dictionaries representing the work of different teams of lexicographers and publishers. There would be picture-book dictionaries for children just learning to read and dictionaries for students to use in their studies or for adults to use at home or at work. You might even find large, unabridged dictionaries intended to help scholars in their research. With such a variety of dictionaries available, it is important that you use one that is right for you.

Use a dictionary that suits your needs at school or at a job.

The dictionary you use should be neither too easy nor too difficult for you. It should contain all of the words you are likely to encounter in your studies, on a job, or in your general reading. It should explain these words to your satisfaction in language you can understand. A picture-book dictionary that you may have had since you were a child will not help you understand all of the words in a physics text or in a trainee program to become, for example, a medical insurance claims adjuster. On the other hand, a scholarly dictionary containing thousands of pages would be both unwieldy and unnecessary for most of your needs. Nevertheless, you should be aware of how all of these different dictionaries are made so that you know what kind of information you can expect to find in each of them.

How Dictionaries Are Made.   To assemble a dictionary, lexicographers spend many years researching and writing. Modern methods have speeded up the process, but ten years ago it was reported that a team of lexicographers was working on a dictionary of the Welsh language. They had taken fifty years to reach the letter *H*. Professional readers help lexicographers keep track of new words and changes in the meanings of old words. They glean information from a variety of current fiction, nonfiction, newspapers, and professional and popular magazines. They examine works published not only in the United States but also in other English-speaking countries. The readers then record their findings on cards that are gathered and filed alphabetically for later reference. Some lexicographers have begun using computers to organize and store this information since their collections often contain more than three million cards. A typical card may look like the following example.

EXAMPLE:

```
backlist, adj.

                    Because our resources are
                    limited, we have to special-
                    ize, to make our imprint stand
                    for things that concern people
                    these days--career-changing,
                    parenting, health, solar hous-
                    ing and the like. Few of our
                    books are returned unsold by
                    bookstores, most become steady
                    backlist sellers. We've had to
                    let very few of our books go out
                    of print.
                       --from ''Paperback Talk'' by
                    Ray Walters. The New York Times
                    Book Review, November 9, 1980,
                    page 41.
```

These cards provide the evidence on which the lexicographers base their decisions about whether or not to include a particular word or meaning in a dictionary. If, for example, ten cards were found in the file for the word *backlist*—the cards coming from a variety of sources spanning several years—the lexicographers would probably decide to include this relatively new word in their dictionary.

Once the decision is made to include a new word in the dictionary, the next step is to fashion the definition from the information on the cards. Using the information shown above, a lexicographer might define *backlist* as "publishing from a list of books that were first published and offered for sale in previous years."

Many other decisions are made as the lexicographers and their staff sift through the card file. Some new words and some new meanings of old words may be intentionally excluded because the lexicographers cannot find enough evidence in the card file to warrant their inclusion in the dictionary. Other words may be excluded because they are no longer used or because they are considered foreign. As a matter of policy, most lexicographers do not include the new Latin names of plants and animals and the names of rare chemical compounds. Still other words or meanings may be unintentionally excluded because they entered the language while the dictionary was being assembled. Lexicographers do, however, attempt to include all of the words and meanings that their criteria allow, depending also on whether the dictionary is unabridged or abridged.

Unabridged Dictionaries. *Unabridged* means "not shortened." The word applies to any dictionary that is not a shortened version of some larger dictionary. It does *not* mean that the dictionary contains all of the words of a language. Unabridged dictionaries generally contain 250,000 to 500,000 words, while it is estimated that the English language contains at least 600,000 words.

Two well-known unabridged dictionaries found on special stands in most libraries are *Webster's Third New International Dictionary of the English Language* (published in 1966) and *The Random House Dictionary of the English Language, Unabridged Edition* (published in 1967). You should consult these books whenever you need very specific definitions and extremely detailed information about words, particularly obsolete words that you may find in old literature. Notice in the following example the detail and thoroughness of an unabridged dictionary's definitions.

UNABRIDGED: ¹**old-fashioned** \'ə¦əə\ *adj* **1 a :** of, relating to, or characteristic of a past era **:** ANCIENT, ANTIQUATED ⟨wears an *old-fashioned* black bow tie —Green Peyton⟩ ⟨*old-fashioned* houses, with their ornamental cornices and high gables —*Amer. Guide Series: Mich.*⟩ ⟨men with the *old-fashioned* hellfire in their sermons —*Atlantic*⟩ ⟨suggested reviving *old-fashioned* home and classroom discipline with physical punishment —*N.Y. Times*⟩ **b :** adhering to traditions or standards of a past era **:** CONSERVATIVE ⟨my mother's family . . . more *old-fashioned*, more pious, and in a word more Victorian even than the English county families of the time —Harold Nicolson⟩ **c :** reminiscent of the past **:** NOSTALGIC, QUAINT ⟨two editions, one of them bound in *old-fashioned* blue gingham —H.H.Reichard⟩ ⟨attendants carried *old-fashioned* bouquets —*Springfield (Mass.) Union*⟩ **2 :** out of date **:** supplanted by something more modern **:** OBSOLETE ⟨thirty *old-fashioned* propeller planes —J.A.Michener⟩ ⟨*old-fashioned* methods for making maple sugar —Murray Schumach⟩ ⟨propaganda — the *old-fashioned* name for psychological warfare —George Fischer⟩ **3** *dial chiefly Eng* **:** of a mature or intelligent nature **:** KNOWING ⟨the collie . . . had turned on him an *old-fashioned* eye —John Buchan⟩ **4 :** growing wild **:** of early hybrid origin — used esp. of a rose — **old-fash·ioned·ly** *adv*

Another well-known unabridged dictionary, the *Oxford English Dictionary* (commonly known as the O.E.D.), fills twelve volumes and several supplements. Probably the most ambitious dictionary ever produced, the O.E.D. differs from the two mentioned above in that it is a historical dictionary. It organizes a word's meanings by dates. This organization allows you to determine when a word first appeared in written English, what it meant at a particular time, and how its meanings have changed over the years. Each meaning is followed by dates and examples of the word in use. In the following excerpt from the

O.E.D.'s coverage for *eye-witness,* notice how the word was first used in the early sixteenth century. Compare this use with later meanings of the word.

O.E.D.:

Eye-witness. [f. Eye *sb.*[1] + Witness.]

† **1.** One who gives testimony to what he has seen with his own eyes. *Obs.*

1539 Taverner *Erasm. Prov.* (1552) 43 One Eye wytnesse, is of more value, than tenne eare wytnesses. **1591** Spenser *M. Hubberd* 1278 Which yet to prove more true, he meant to see, And an ey-witnes of each thing to bee.

2. One who can give testimony from his own observation; one who has seen a thing done or happen.

1590 Sir J. Smyth in *Lett. Lit. Men* (Camden) 57, I do not write the same of mine owne certaine knowledge, as a eye wittness. **1611** Bible 2 *Pet.* i. 16 Wee..were eye witnesses of his Maiestie. **1615** W. Hull *Mirrour of Maiestie* 89 The death of such a sonne .. whereof shee was an eyed witnesse. **1694** Ld. Molesworth *Acc. Denmark* 44 Received not only from eye-witnesses, but also from some of the principal..Actors. **1744** Berkeley *Siris* § 17 Leo Africanus ..describes, as an eye-witness, the making of tar in Mount Atlas. **1798** Ferriar *Illustr. Sterne* i. 17 Brantome, an eye-witness .. informs us. **1855** Macaulay *Hist. Eng.* IV. 93 Different estimates were formed even by eyewitnesses. **1878** *N. Amer. Rev.* CXXVI. 180 It is the narration, by an eye-witness, of the memorable *coup d'etat* of 1851.

† **3.** The result of actual observation; a report made by one who was present. *Obs.*

1627 Hakewill *Apol.* i. i. § 5. 9 By the eye-witnesse of Ioachimus Rheticus, and others, it hath been proved. **1671** Milton *Samson* 1594 Give us .. Eye-witness of what first or last was done.

Hence **Eyewitnessing** *vbl. sb.*

1857 H. Miller *Test. Rocks* iv. 154 Had they been revealed by vision as a piece of eye-witnessing.

Abridged Dictionaries. Several companies publish shorter dictionaries especially suited to the needs of the general public and of students in particular. Unless you want special information about a word or need the meaning of a rare word, chances are you will find all you need to know in an abridged dictionary. Often called college or school dictionaries, these books are designed for everyday use at home, in the office, and in the classroom.

SOME ABRIDGED DICTIONARIES FOR EVERYDAY USE

The American Heritage Dictionary of the English Language

The Oxford American Dictionary

Webster's New Collegiate Dictionary

Webster's New World Dictionary of the American Language, Second College Edition

---

Considerably smaller and less expensive than unabridged dictionaries, abridged dictionaries usually list between 150,000 and 200,000 words. In addition to containing fewer words, abridged dictionaries also usually list fewer definitions for a word than unabridged dictionaries do. Compare, for example, the following entry with the one from the unabridged dictionary shown on page 524.

ABRIDGED: ¹old–fash·ioned \-ˈfash-ənd\ *adj* **1 a :** of, relating to, or characteristic of a past era ⟨wears an ~ black bow tie —Green Peyton⟩ **b :** adhering to customs of a past era **2 :** out of date — **old–fash·ioned·ly** \-ən-dlē\ *adv*

EXERCISE A: **Comparing Unabridged and Abridged Dictionaries.** Compare an unabridged dictionary to an abridged dictionary by completing the following steps. Record your findings in two columns for easy comparison.

1. Write the full title and most recent publication date of each book.
2. Write the number of pages contained in each book.
3. Look up a common word in both dictionaries. How does the coverage differ? Be specific.
4. Find five words that are included in the unabridged dictionary but not in the other. Why, do you suspect, were they left out of the shorter book?

■ What General Dictionaries Contain

When you read and write, you should always have a good abridged dictionary within easy reach for quick reference. By consulting your dictionary often and by familiarizing yourself with its features, you can increase both your knowledge of words and the precision with which you use them. The rest of this section will describe the features found in most everyday dictionaries. As you read the following descriptions, keep in mind that all dictionaries are not the same. Apply what you learn here to your own dictionary.

Learn to recognize and use the various features of your dictionary.

If you are at all uncomfortable using your dictionary or if you have acquired a new dictionary, the place to begin learning about it is in the book's introduction.

Front Matter. A good dictionary contains an introduction that explains how to use it efficiently. Here, in addition to a description of all of the book's features, you will usually find instructions on how to look up a word, how to find words whose spelling you are unsure of, and how to interpret the pronunciation symbols. A complete pronunciation key and a list of all of the abbreviations used throughout the dictionary will also be found in this part of the book.

Back Matter. Many dictionaries contain helpful charts and lists at the back of the book. Look here for tables of weights and measures; metric conversion tables; guides to punctuation, manuscript form, and business-letter style; proofreaders' marks; explanations of special signs and symbols; and lists of colleges and universities. Some dictionaries also list foreign terms, biographical names, and geographical names separately at the back of the book rather than alphabetically within the main part of the dictionary.

Main Entries. Each word included in a dictionary, along with all of the information about it, is called a *main entry*. The word itself is called the *entry word*. All of the entry words are listed in strict alphabetical order, letter by letter, right to the end of the entry word.

EXAMPLE: lip
              lip-read
              lip service
              lipstick
              liquefy

An entry word may be a single word, a compound word (two or more words acting as a single word), an abbreviation, a prefix or suffix, or the name of a special event. Many dictionaries also include foreign terms and names of persons and places within the main part of the book.

KINDS OF ENTRY WORDS	
Single Word	dra·mat·ics
Compound Word	dram·a·tis per·so·nae
Abbreviation	dram. pers.
Prefix	dem·i-
Suffix	-dom

Event	Decoration Day
Foreign Term	do·lo·ro·so
Person	De·moc·ri·tus
Place	Dol·o·mites

Preferred and Variant Spellings.   A dictionary is an authority for the spelling of words. Most English words have only one correct spelling, as shown by the entry word. Some words, however, can be spelled in more than one way. The spelling most commonly used is called the *preferred spelling*. Less commonly used spellings are called *variant spellings*. If the form you are looking up is a variant spelling, the entry will refer you to the entry that begins with the preferred spelling. Here you will also find the definition of the word.

VARIANT SPELLING: **Doomsday Book** *same as* Domesday Book

PREFERRED SPELLING: **Domesday Book** [said to be so named because it judged all men without bias, like the Last Judgment] the record of a survey of England made under William the Conqueror in 1086, listing all landowners and showing the value and extent of their holdings

If a main entry shows two entry words, the form listed first is usually more commonly used and thus the preferred spelling.

ALTERNATE SPELLINGS: **dé·cor, de·cor** (dā kôr′, dā′kôr) *n.* [Fr. < L. *decor*, beauty, elegance < *decere*, to befit, be suitable: see ff.] **1.** decoration **2.** the decorative scheme of a room, stage set, etc.

Syllabification.   Centered dots, spaces, or slashes in an entry word indicate how words are divided into syllables. If words are already hyphenated, hyphens will take the place of these symbols. The word *short-tempered*, for example, has three syllables: short-tem·pered. Most, but not all, of these divisions can be used for word breaks at the end of a line of writing. (See Section 12.6 for specific rules about breaking words into syllables at the ends of lines of writing.)

Pronunciation.   Pronunciations appear after most entry words, usually in parentheses or between diagonal lines. Pronunciations usually do not accompany entries that are not full words, such as abbreviations, prefixes, and suffixes. Nor are they usually found for entries that are compound words when the individual words are main entries themselves.

The dictionary indicates how to pronounce words by re-spelling them using a *phonetic alphabet.* A phonetic alphabet is a set of letters and special symbols. Each letter and symbol is assigned one sound. Since phonetic alphabets vary somewhat from one dictionary to another, it is important that you become familiar with the one in the dictionary you use. A *pronunciation key* at the front or back of your dictionary lists and explains all of the pronunciation symbols used throughout that book. Study this key carefully. Most dictionaries also provide short pronunciation keys on every other page to help you pronounce the words.

Although the general system may vary from dictionary to dictionary, you should learn to recognize four particular pronunciation symbols that usually indicate the same kinds of vowel sounds in all general dictionaries. These are the macron (ˉ), the dieresis (¨), the circumflex (ˆ), and the schwa (ə). A knowledge of these symbols will help you interpret many pronunciations.

FOUR COMMON PRONUNCIATION SYMBOLS		
Symbol	**Sound**	**Example**
macron/ˉ	long vowels (ā, ē, ī, ō, ū)	(fāt) = fate (mēt) = meet (slī) = sly (lōm) = loam (fū) = few
dieresis/¨	open *a* (ä)	(bärk) = bark
circumflex/ˆ	open *o* (ô)	(pô) = paw
schwa/ə	any unstressed vowel	(bō′ə) = boa (shā′kən) = shaken (van′ə tē) = vanity (kə lekt′) = collect (fō′kəs) = focus

Short vowel sounds are easy to understand in pronunciations. Most general dictionaries do not mark them.

SHORT VOWELS: (mask) = mask
(rent) = rent
(sit) = sit
(plot) = plot
(kup) = cup

Dictionaries use different combinations of vowels and symbols to indicate other vowel sounds. Some examples are: oi, ou, o͞o, and u̇ or oo.

OTHER VOWEL SOUNDS: (boi) = boy
                                (loud) = loud
                                (po͞ol) = pool
                                (ku̇k) or (kook) = cook

Consonants seldom pose a problem. Most of them are pronounced as you would expect. Those, such as *g* in *gigantic,* that can have either a soft or a hard sound are simply assigned a second letter. *C, q,* and *x,* which can be represented by other consonants, are not used in the pronunciation key.

EXAMPLES: (jes′chər) = gesture (j = soft *g*)
               (gām) = game (g = hard *g*)
               (sent) = cent (s = soft *c*)
               (kär) = car (k = hard *c*)
               (kwit) = quit (kw = *q*)
               (aks) = ax (ks = *x*)

Finally, three other consonant sounds you should learn to recognize in pronunciations are *s* in *measure, th* as in *thin,* and *th* as in *then.* Most dictionaries represent the *s* in *measure* with zh, and the *th* in *thin* with th; the methods used to represent the *th* in *then,* however, vary.

EXAMPLES: (mezh′ər) = measure
               (thin) = thin

               (*th*en) = then
               (t̲h̲en) = then
               (ᴛʜen) = then

In addition to helping you pronounce the sounds correctly, the dictionary shows you which syllables are stressed. The syllable that gets the most emphasis has a *primary stress,* usually indicated by a heavy mark after the syllable (′). Words of more than one syllable may have a *secondary stress,* indicated by a shorter, lighter mark after the syllable (′). Unstressed syllables have no stress marks. Again, symbols may vary from one dictionary to another. For example, *Webster's New Collegiate Dictionary* places stress marks before the syllables to which they apply and uses a high-set mark (′) for primary stresses and a low-set mark (‚) for secondary stresses.

When two or more pronunciations for a word are shown, the preferred pronunciation is given first. Following are some entry words with their pronunciations. Notice not only the stress marks but also how additional pronunciations are indicated in abbreviated form.

PRIMARY STRESS ONLY: **drag·on** (drag′ən)

PRIMARY AND SECONDARY STRESSES: **drag·on·fly** (drag′ən flī′)

MORE THAN ONE PRONUNCIATION: **div·i·dend** (div′ə dend′, -dənd)

Part-of-Speech Labels and Inflected Forms.   The dictionary also indicates how a word can be used in a sentence—whether it functions as a noun, a verb, or some other part of speech. This information is given in abbreviated form, usually after the pronunciation of a word but sometimes at the end of the entry. Entries of two or more separate words, such as *kidney bean* or *islets of Langerhans,* have no part-of-speech labels because they are always nouns. Some dictionaries also omit part-of-speech labels for the names of people and places since these, too, are always nouns.

When necessary, the dictionary shows inflected forms after the part-of-speech label. An inflected form may be the plural form of a noun, the different forms of an adjective or adverb, or the principal parts of a verb. Notice in the following example that inflected forms are sometimes abbreviated.

Parts of speech labels ——
Inflections ——

que·ry (kwir′ē) *n.,* *pl.* **-ries** [< L. *quaere,* 2d pers. sing., imper., of *quaerere,* to ask, inquire] **1.** a question; inquiry **2.** a doubt **3.** a question mark (?), placed after a question or used to query written or printed matter —*vt.* **-ried, -ry·ing 1.** to call in question; ask about **2.** to question (a person) **3.** to question the accuracy of (some matter in a manuscript or printer's proof) by marking with a question mark —*vi.* to ask questions or express doubt —*SYN.* see ASK

Etymologies.   The origin and history of a word is called its *etymology* or *derivation.* In dictionaries the etymology of an entry word usually appears in brackets soon after the pronunciation or part-of-speech label. In some dictionaries, the etymology is placed at the end of a main entry.

The historical information in an etymology is arranged from the most recent to the least recent. This information is written in a code made up of symbols, abbreviations, and different kinds of type. One kind of type may indicate, for example, a cross-reference to another etymology. Since the codes for etymologies vary from one dictionary to another, it is best to study the introduction in your particular dictionary to understand the code. The following example, however, should give you the basic idea.

EXAMPLE: **al·pha·bet** (al′fə bet′) *n.* [LL. *alphabetum* < LGr. *alpha-bētos* < Gr. *alpha* + *bēta*, the first two letters of the Greek alphabet] **1.** the letters of a language, arranged in a traditional order **2.** a system of characters, signs, or symbols used to indicate letters or speech sounds **3.** the first elements or principles, as of a branch of knowledge —*vt.* **-bet′ed -bet′ing** to alphabetize

The etymology can be translated to read, "*Alphabet* comes from the Late Latin word *alphabetum,* which came from the Late Greek word *alphabētos,* which came from the two Greek words *alpha* and *bēta,* the first two letters of the Greek alphabet."

Definitions.   Many words in English have multiple meanings. These meanings, or senses, are called *definitions.* All meanings for the same part of speech are grouped together in the dictionary and numbered consecutively. Sometimes a definition will be broken into parts to show different shades of meaning. In such a case, the different parts will be arranged by letters: a, b, c, and so on. Most dictionaries help clarify the different meanings of an entry word with a phrase or sentence showing the word in use.

Definition with two parts ——

Examples of word in use ——

fi·ber, fi·bre (fī′bər) *n.* [Fr. *fibre* < L. *fibra,* ? akin to *filum,* thread: see FILE¹] **1.** *a)* a slender, threadlike structure that combines with others to form animal or vegetable tissue *b)* the tissue so formed [muscle *fiber*] **2.** a slender, threadlike structure made from a mineral or synthetically [rayon *fibers*] **3.** *a)* any substance that can be separated into threads or threadlike structures for spinning, weaving, etc. [cotton *fiber*] *b)* any such thread or structure [wool *fibers*] **4.** a threadlike root **5.** the texture of something [a fabric of coarse *fiber*] **6.** character or nature; quality [a man of strong moral *fiber*] —**fi′ber·like′** *adj.*

When you are checking a word that has more than one meaning, read each definition carefully to find the one that matches the context of the word in the sentence you are reading or writing. You should be able to substitute the correct definition for the word in the sentence. Which definition of *fiber,* for example, can be substituted for the word in the following sentence: "After several days a small *fiber* emerged from the seed"? Only the fourth definition makes sense when substituted: "After several days a small *threadlike root* emerged from the seed."

Usage and Field Labels.   Words and meanings that are considered acceptable in formal situations by most speakers and writers of a language are said to be standard usage. Dictionaries indicate informal and nonstandard words and meanings with *usage labels,* such as *Slang, Informal* (or *Colloquial*), *Dialect,* and *British.* The label lets you know that a particular word or meaning may be unsuitable or not understood in certain situations. (See Chapter 10 for more about levels of usage.) Sometimes usage labels are also used to indicate whether a word in a particular meaning is usually plural or capitalized.

Other words or meanings may be restricted to a particular occupation, activity, or branch of knowledge. Dictionaries indicate this restricted usage with *field labels* such as *Medicine, Soccer,* or *Mathematics.*

Both usage labels and field labels usually appear before the definitions to which they apply.

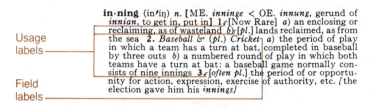

Usage labels ——

Field labels ——

in·ning (in′iŋ) *n.* [ME. *ininge* < OE. *innung,* gerund of *innian,* to get in, put in] **1** [Now Rare] *a)* an enclosing or reclaiming, as of wasteland *b)* [*pl.*] lands reclaimed, as from the sea **2.** *Baseball &* (*pl.*) *Cricket a)* the period of play in which a team has a turn at bat, completed in baseball by three outs *b)* a numbered round of play in which both teams have a turn at bat: a baseball game normally consists of nine innings **3** [*often pl.*] the period of or opportunity for action, expression, exercise of authority, etc. [the election gave him his *innings*]

Some dictionaries use field labels sparingly, relying instead on the definition to indicate the field.

EXAMPLE:
²**in·ning** \″\ *n* -s [in sense 1, fr. gerund of ³*in;* in sense 2, fr. ²*in* + -*ing*] **1 a :** the act of taking in, gathering, or enclosing; *specif* **:** the act of reclaiming land esp. from the sea or a marsh **b innings** *pl* **:** reclaimed lands **2 a innings** *pl but sing or pl in constr* **:** a division of a cricket match in which one side continues batting until ten players are retired or the side declares; *also* **:** the time a player stays as a batsman until he is out, until ten teammates are out, or until his side declares **b :** a team's turn at bat in baseball ending with the third out; *also* **:** a division consisting of a turn at bat for each team **c :** a division of a contest in other sports (as a turn at serving in badminton, two throws by one player or two throws by each contestant in horseshoes) or a player's turn in croquet) **d :** a chance or turn for action or accomplishment (as to display one's prowess, caliber, or ability) ⟨the factual . . . romance has had its ∼ —Parker Tyler⟩ ⟨the young conductor who is currently having his ∼s —Douglas Watt⟩ ⟨the opposition party now had its ∼s⟩ ⟨keep silent in order to give the adversary his ∼ —Edmond Taylor⟩

Idioms.   An *idiom* is an expression that has a meaning different from that which the words would literally suggest. Expressions such as *take stock in, cast the first stone,* and *up and around* are idioms.

Idioms are usually listed in alphabetical order near the end of a main entry or at the end of the definitions for a particular part of speech. The key word in the expression usually determines the main entry under which the idiom appears. If the idiom seems to have two or more key words, as in *take stock in,* you should generally look under the noun first (*stock*). If there are no nouns in the idiom, as in *up and around,* you should look under the first key word (*up*).

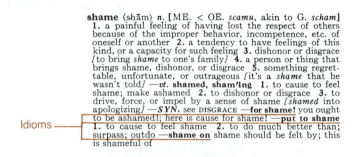

Idioms

shame (shām) *n.* [ME. < OE. *scamu,* akin to G. *scham*] **1.** a painful feeling of having lost the respect of others because of the improper behavior, incompetence, etc. of oneself or another **2.** a tendency to have feelings of this kind, or a capacity for such feeling **3.** dishonor or disgrace [to bring *shame* to one's family] **4.** a person or thing that brings shame, dishonor, or disgrace **5.** something regrettable, unfortunate, or outrageous [it's a *shame* that he wasn't told] —*vt.* **shamed, sham′ing 1.** to cause to feel shame; make ashamed **2.** to dishonor or disgrace **3.** to drive, force, or impel by a sense of shame [*shamed* into apologizing] —*SYN.* see DISGRACE —**for shame!** you ought to be ashamed!; here is cause for shame! —**put to shame 1.** to cause to feel shame **2.** to do much better than; surpass; outdo —**shame on** shame should be felt by; this is shameful of

Derived Words and Run-on Entries.   Words formed by the addition of a common suffix, such as *-ly* or *-ness,* to an entry word are called *derived words* or *run-on entries.* The suffixes are added to change words from one part of speech to another. Derived words are found at the end of a main entry and are not defined. They simply appear with their part-of-speech labels and sometimes with pronunciations. If you are not sure of the meaning of a derived word, look up the meaning of the suffix and combine that with the meaning of the entry word.

Derived words

shal·low (shal′ō) *adj.* [ME. *shalow* < OE. **scealw* < IE. base **(s)kel-,* to dry out, whence Gr. *skellein*] **1.** not deep [a *shallow* lake] **2.** lacking depth of character, intellect, or meaning; superficial —*n.* [*usually pl., often with sing. v.*] a shallow place in a body of water; shoal —*vt., vi.* to make or become shallow —*SYN.* see SUPERFICIAL —**shal′low·ly** *adv.* —**shal′low·ness** *n.*

Synonymies.   A *synonym* is a word closely related but not identical in meaning to another word. In some dictionaries you will see below the entry a block of words after the heading *SYN.* Here the differences in meaning among synonyms are explained. These explanations are called *synonymies.* Antonyms, or words opposite in meaning, are sometimes found here, too.

Synonymy

ex·cel (ik sel′) *vi., vt.* **-celled′, -cel′ling** [ME. *excellen* < OFr. *exceller* < L. *excellere,* to raise, surpass, excel < *ex-,* out of, from + *-cellere,* to rise, project < IE. base **kel-,* to project, whence HILL, Gr. *kolophōn*] to be better or greater than, or superior to (another or others)
SYN.—excel implies superiority in some quality, skill, achievement, etc. over all or over the one (or ones) specified [to *excel* at chess]; **surpass** implies a going beyond (someone or something specified) in degree, amount, or quality [no one *surpasses* him in generosity]; **transcend** suggests a surpassing to an extreme degree [it *transcends* all understanding]; **outdo** implies a going beyond someone else or a previous record in performance [he will not be *outdone* in bravery]

EXERCISE B: **Using Front and Back Matter.** Use the front and back matter of your dictionary to answer the following. Write the name of the dictionary and your answers.

1. On what page or pages of the front matter does a list appear showing all abbreviations used in the dictionary?
2. What are the meanings of the following: ME., OFr., pp., vt.?
3. Where is Wellesley College and when was it founded?
4. What are the meanings of the following symbols: ⊕ (in astronomy), ♂ and ♀ (in biology), ⇌ (in chemistry), ∞ (in mathematics), &c. (in miscellaneous situations)?

EXERCISE C: **Alphabetizing Entry Words.** Put the following words in letter-by-letter alphabetical order.

1. pitcher
2. pitchfork
3. pitch-dark
4. piteous
5. Pitcairn Island
6. pitch pine
7. pitfall
8. pitch
9. pitcher plant
10. pitchblende

EXERCISE D: **Determining Preferred Spellings.** Determine whether the following are preferred or variant spellings. If the spelling is preferred, write *preferred* on your paper; if it is variant, write the preferred spelling.

1. acknowledgement
2. lichee
3. towards
4. highjack
5. judgment

EXERCISE E: **Understanding Pronunciations.** Copy from your dictionary the preferred pronunciations for the following words. Be prepared to pronounce the words aloud in class.

1. beauteous
2. lissome
3. Upanishad
4. egalitarian
5. porphyry
6. expatiate
7. nucleic
8. cuneiform
9. incunabula
10. litotes

EXERCISE F: **Finding Part-of-Speech Labels.** Use your dictionary to determine the part-of-speech labels for each of the following entry words. After each label, record the number of definitions listed for that part of speech.

1. inside
2. catch

EXERCISE G: Interpreting Etymologies. Find the etymologies for the following words in your dictionary. Then write a sentence describing the origin and history of each.

1. catamaran
2. quark
3. valediction
4. caprice

EXERCISE H: Applying Definitions to Words in Context. Look up the word *credit* in your dictionary. Which definition fits each sentence. Write each definition on your paper.

1. We must give him *credit* for his honesty.
2. The couple applied for *credit* to buy a new sofa.
3. The overpayment has been *credited* to your account.
4. Her name was not listed in the film's *credits*.

EXERCISE I: Finding Usage Labels and Field Labels. Use the usage labels and field labels in your dictionary to help answer the following questions.

1. What meanings of *upon* are now obsolete?
2. Where in the United States might you hear the word *pung*?
3. What does *quotation* mean in business or commerce?
4. In what field does *spaghetti* have a special meaning?

EXERCISE J: Finding the Meaning of Idioms. Use your dictionary to find the meaning of each of the following idioms. Record each definition and the entry word you use.

1. send for
2. get off the ground
3. from the horse's mouth
4. burn the candle at both ends

EXERCISE K: Finding Derived Words. Write any derived words you find in your dictionary under the following words.

1. cannibal
2. jealous
3. spicy
4. consign

APPLICATION: Using Your Dictionary Efficiently. Use your dictionary to find the answers to the following questions. After each answer, record the time you spent finding it.

1. When was Martin Luther King, Jr., born?
2. What period in history is described by the word *baroque*?
3. What does the idiom *between Scylla and Charybdis* mean?
4. What is a *Gorgon*?
5. From what language did the word *average* originally come? What did the word originally mean?

UNIT VI

Composition

Chapter 18

Word Choices

Words build sentences; they also express ideas, reveal a writer's purpose and attitude, and create a mood for readers. When you first begin to write any sentence, your word choices may seem limitless. Quickly, however, you will generally see that to communicate your thoughts effectively you must avoid certain unnecessary or inaccurate words. This chapter points out some of the problems writers often encounter in choosing words and discusses a variety of methods to avoid these problems.

18.1 Identifying Problems in Wording

Wordiness can hide your ideas in a jungle of unnecessary language. Therefore, when you write, you should be concise so that a reader can easily understand the points you are making.

Another problem writers can have involves using words that do not belong with the rest of the words in a group of sentences. These inappropriate words can destroy the tone of the sentences. You should try to maintain a consistent tone in all your writing.

This section discusses removing unnecessary words from your sentences and avoiding inappropriate words.

■ Problems with Wordiness

Wordiness is one of the enemies of clear communication but too few words can fail to provide necessary information. Good writing uses the right number of words for the ideas being expressed.

Sparse sentences do not contain enough information, such as examples, facts, and other details. If too many details are missing, the reader might not grasp what you are trying to say, as in the following passage.

Passage with sparse sentences	The National League playoffs this year were exciting. There were numerous rallies throughout the series, which established a record.

On the other hand, too much material can be confusing and tedious. This version of the passage contains empty words, repetitions, and overly complicated constructions.

Passage with repetitious language and other wordiness	The playoff games for the National League pennant, which took place this fall at the end of this year's baseball season, were particularly thrilling, exciting, and impressive to those who watched. The strengths of the two opposing teams were evenly matched to a remarkably unusual degree and the fierce and intense competitiveness on the part of the players of both sides had the result of producing numerous comebacks, rallies, and upsets, particularly in the crucial seventh, eighth, and ninth innings at the end of the normal period of play. The series of games went to its full five games, and all these games were bitterly fought, to the extent that four of them went into extra innings in order to break a tie, thereby establishing a historical baseball record.

The best writing provides complete information without an overload of words, as in this improved version of the passage.

Complete and concise passage	The playoffs for the National League pennant were especially charged with excitement this year. The two opposing teams were unusually well-matched and the fierce competitiveness on both sides sparked numerous late-inning comebacks and upsets. The series went to its full five games and, remarkably, four of those five games were forced into tie-breaking extra innings.

Eliminating Deadwood.   Nonessential words are called *deadwood*. These words and phrases fill out sentences without adding meaning. Such padding only confuses and distracts a reader.

Once you are able to identify deadwood, you can easily eliminate it from your writing. Some deadwood consists of meaningless words. Hedging words, another form of deadwood, are unnecessary qualifiers. Although hedging words may seem safe to use because they are noncommittal, they can lengthen and weaken sentences. The following chart contains words and phrases that are usually deadwood.

DEADWOOD		
Empty Words		
there is (are)	the thing that	of the opinion that
the area of	to the extent that	what I mean is
by way of	it is a fact that	for the reason that
a great deal (of)	in the manner that	due to
the fact that	is the one who is	while at the same time
Hedging Words		
somewhat	it seems (that)	sort of
almost	tends to	kind of
rather	in a way	that might or might not

If you eliminate these expressions from your sentences, your ideas will stand out much more sharply. But you should make certain that the sentences still make sense. Occasionally qualifying words, such as *almost*, may be necessary for accuracy. If you take out deadwood, you may have to rephrase the sentence, as in some of the following examples.

WITH DEADWOOD: Rains continued for two more days *to the extent that* they caused major highways to be closed.

CONCISE: Rains continued for two more days causing major highways to be closed.

WITH DEADWOOD: *Due to the fact that* construction workers are on strike, building plans have halted.

CONCISE: Because construction workers are on strike, building plans have halted.

WITH DEADWOOD: I *tend to* be made angry when *there is* a train delay.

CONCISE: Train delays anger me.

Eliminating Redundancy.   Words that repeat ideas in a sentence are *redundant*. You can identify redundancy by looking for words or phrases that repeat the meaning of other words.

Write concisely by eliminating redundant words, phrases, and clauses.

Notice in the following sentences how redundancy can be eliminated.

REDUNDANT: He used a baseball slightly deformed *in shape* to create a curve in the pitch. (*Deformed* already refers to shape.)

CONCISE: He used a slightly deformed baseball to create a curve in the pitch.

REDUNDANT: Susan, who is just a beginning horseback rider, *over*-exaggerates the height of her jumps. (*Exaggerate* means "overstate.")

CONCISE: Susan, who is just a beginning horseback rider, exaggerates the height of her jumps.

REDUNDANT: My friend, *who loves to play musical instruments*, enjoys playing the guitar, the piano, and the trumpet. (*Enjoys playing* and the rest of the sentence convey a love of playing musical instruments.)

CONCISE: My friend enjoys playing the guitar, the piano, and the trumpet.

Eliminating Wordy Structures.   The extra words used to form phrases and clauses can often be eliminated to make sentences more concise. Whenever you can shorten a lengthy phrase or clause without changing the meaning of the sentence, take the opportunity to tighten the sentence.

When possible, reduce wordy phrases and clauses to shorter structures.

In the following chart, you will find examples of phrases and clauses that can be reduced.

REDUCING WORDY STRUCTURES	
Wordy Phrase:	He spoke *from an objective viewpoint*.
Concise:	He spoke objectively. (Phrase reduced to a single-word modifier.)

Wordy Phrase:	Mr. Bloom will send roses *to his wife*.
Concise:	Mr. Bloom will send his wife roses. (Phrase reduced to a noun and modifier.)
Wordy Clause:	Michael is an excellent singer, and *he is also a member of the orchestra*.
Concise:	Michael is both an excellent singer and a member of the orchestra. (Clause reduced to part of a compound complement.)
Wordy Clause:	At the door was a man *who was selling magazines for charity*.
Concise:	At the door was a man selling magazines for charity. (Clause reduced to a participial phrase.)
Wordy Clause:	Nicholas II, *who was the czar of Russia*, was overthrown during the revolution of 1917.
Concise:	Nicholas II, czar of Russia, was overthrown during the revolution of 1917. (Clause reduced to an appositive.)
Wordy Clause:	For biology experiments, we need specimens *that are fresh*.
Concise:	For biology experiments, we need fresh specimens. (Clause reduced to a single-word modifier.)

EXERCISE A: Eliminating Deadwood and Redundancy. Eliminate any deadwood and redundancy from the following sentences, and rewrite each sentence to make it concise. You may have to reorganize the words or rephrase the ideas in a sentence.

1. Wondering thoughtfully about possible punishments, Roberta decided to tell her parents about the fact that she had dented the car.
2. Dr. Sanders, being of the opinion that snakes are extremely dangerous, would rather view them through clear glass that is transparent.
3. Left alone in the vacant, empty classroom, Michele somewhat regretted following her adventurous friends.
4. A hurricane which may or may not move into our area is capable of causing extensive damage to our area.
5. Due to the fact that colleges often decide on applicants during the winter of the year, they ask for applications during the fall.
6. At that point in time, Janice thought to herself about dropping physics and adding calculus to her schedule.

7. Pressure will build beneath the pavement to the extent that it will crack the pavement unless a release valve is added to the existing pipes that are there.
8. A large black cloud enormous in size testified to the extent of how serious the explosion had been.
9. Rather furious that Ronald was the one who was laughing in class, Mr. Kelton insisted on an apology.
10. At the same time as cars lined up before the open bridge, a string of little tugboats proceeded one after another up the river.

EXERCISE B: **Reducing Wordy Constructions.** Shorten the wordy phrases or clauses in each of the following sentences to make each sentence concise. You may have to change the word order of some of the sentences when you rewrite them.

1. A dangerous reconnaissance mission that was completed by Division 6 earned every man who was participating a service medal.
2. *QB VII*, a novel that was written by Leon Uris, was made into a film.
3. Over the years, termites nested in the foundation, and they slowly ate away wooden supports.
4. Glen Richardson, who was running in the marathon, finished in a time that was respectable.
5. Fillmore's varsity basketball team, which was coached by Mr. Paul Johnson, enjoyed a season that was quite successful.
6. The beaches that are along the Magill south shore have slowly eroded, and this erosion has prompted property owners to demand government action.
7. On stage he wore a cape that was long and black and a mustache shaped like a handlebar.
8. He found his source information, which was in the vertical file and which was listed under the heading "Astronomy."
9. Anyone who is interested in part-time jobs should visit the Youth Employment Service, which is on the second floor.
10. A possum that was cornered in our basement glared at us in a threatening manner, and it was hissing as we moved closer.

■ Problems with Tone

Your word choices determine the *tone* of your sentences, which, like the tone of your voice when you speak, indicates your feelings about your subject and your audience. When you write, your language reveals whether you are approaching your topic seriously or lightly, enthusiastically or coolly. Your language also signals whether you intend to explain, instruct, persuade, or entertain your audience. Your reader interprets your attitude through the clues you offer in your word choices. Your words should sound as if they belong together, all of them accurately reflecting your attitude toward your subject and audience; that is, your words must be consistent throughout a passage.

A consistent tone, however, can be undermined by any of several problems. If your tone is interrupted by trite expressions, self-important words, or slang, readers may become confused or irritated. Therefore, you should learn to recognize these and other problems and avoid them in your writing.

Avoiding Clichés.   Clichés are worn-out expressions, such as *light as a feather* or *clean as a whistle*, that can deaden the tone of your sentences. Once these expressions were colorful, but they have faded through overuse. Because these expressions no longer create vivid images in readers' minds, they only weaken your writing, making it sound prefabricated and tired.

> Replace clichés with fresh, direct words and expressions.

As you see in the following examples, clichés sound dull. You should be able to recognize them easily, and you should choose fresher, more direct language instead.

CLICHÉ: Getting the lead in the play put Ricky *on cloud nine*.

REVISED: Getting the lead in the play *exhilarated* Ricky.

CLICHÉ: The President put his *John Hancock* on the bill.

REVISED: The President *signed* the bill.

Avoiding Euphemisms and Self-Important Language. Expressions that cushion the truth or that sound pompous and self-important distort the tone of your writing and mislead the reader. *Euphemisms* are overly polite sayings that soften reality: For example, *pass away* is a euphemism for *die*, and *detained* is a euphemism for *arrested*. *Self-important language* tries to impress the reader. It includes flowery expressions with too many modifiers. It can also consist of unnecessarily lengthy words and complicated structures, which sound pretentious.

All of these expressions introduce a falseness and emptiness into your writing and should be eliminated.

Replace euphemisms and self-important language with direct language.

In the following examples, you can see how euphemisms and self-important language have been replaced by direct, sincere language.

EUPHEMISM: The representatives of the countries had a *frank exchange of views*.

REVISED: The representatives of the countries had a *disagreement*.

SELF-IMPORTANT LANGUAGE: To *become competent* at their *chosen craft,* the *industrious fledgling artisans* worked *feverishly* seven days a week.

REVISED: To *improve their work,* the *young silversmiths labored* seven days a week.

Avoiding Slang, Jargon, and Foreign Terms. *Slang* is the informal language of a particular social group, while *jargon* is the specialized vocabulary of a profession or occupation. Both are forms of language with special meanings that may not be generally understood, and both can distort the tone of a passage. Similarly, unnecessary *foreign terms* can mystify readers who do not understand them. You should replace such language with expressions and explanations that are more widely understood.

Replace slang, jargon, and foreign terms with precise, understandable language.

Slang can vary from day to day, from place to place, and from group to group. Only a small portion of slang becomes a permanent part of the language. Slang appeals to a limited audience, and although it can sound colorful in speech when it is new, it often sounds obsolete and ridiculous in written communication. For these reasons, it is not effective or acceptable in most writing. In addition, slang gives your writing a careless, overly casual tone, as you can see in the following example.

SLANG: We decided to *beg off* from Mr. Lehman's invitation.

REVISED: We decided to *decline* Mr. Lehman's invitation.

Like slang, jargon is too specialized a language to be used in formal writing. Each occupation has its own jargon, which usually sounds overly technical to the outsider. If you *have* to use technical language in your writing, explain your terms carefully. In the following example, the jargon is easily replaced by a more generally understood expression.

JARGON: Cars whose engines are air-cooled do not require *water-retentant coolants*.

REVISED: Cars whose engines are air-cooled do not require *radiators*.

Foreign expressions can puzzle your readers even more than slang and jargon. They can be intimidating because they interject an inflated tone into your writing. Substitute English equivalents for such expressions, as in the following revision.

FOREIGN TERM: He had a gift for choosing the *mot juste*.

REVISED: He had a gift for choosing the *right word*.

Avoiding Overly Emotional Language. *Emotional language* consists of name-calling, extreme modifiers, and other expressions that arouse readers' fears, loves, and hates but do not appeal to their reason and understanding. Overly emotional statements will disrupt the rational tone you should be aiming for in your writing. In addition, they will make you seem untrustworthy to most readers and will arouse the hostility of those readers who disagree with you.

Replace overly emotional language with reasonable language.

In the following passage, the overly emotional statements sound angry and immature. Notice that the second passage says essentially the same thing but sounds more reasonable and worthy of the reader's serious attention.

Overly emotional language
: The City's most recent cutbacks in garbage removal are just another indication of the *idiocy* and *insensitivity* of the *demagogues* who run the government. Conspiring with the *tightwad plutocrats* who run the banks, these *party hacks obviously care nothing* about the health and comfort of the *beleaguered residents* of this city.

Revised   The City's most recent cutbacks in garbage re-
                 moval are evidence of what could be a *disturbing new
                 policy* in this *administration.* Those *responsible* for
                 such service cuts seem to be *more concerned* with sat-
                 isfying the *fiscally-conscious bankers* of this city than
                 with safeguarding the health and comfort of the *av-
                 erage taxpayer.*

EXERCISE C: Correcting Inconsistencies in Tone.

In each of the following sentences, you will find a word or expression that disrupts the tone of the sentence. Identify the type of problem in each sentence: cliché, euphemism, self-important language, slang, jargon, foreign term, or overly emotional language. Then, eliminate the weakness as you rewrite the sentence, underlining the words you use to replace the problem words.

1. Because the food in the school cafeteria was poisonously disgusting, most of the students began to bring their own lunches to school:
2. The police apprehended the alleged perpetrator in the act of robbing the jewelry store.
3. Because the Chairman was *in absentia*, the vote was postponed.
4. Firemen tried to calm poor old Mr. Davis, running around like a chicken with its head cut off, as flames engulfed his barn.
5. Customs officials stopped the car on the Canadian border because the driver had ripped off a tax-free gift shop in New York.
6. Aunt Lilly hired a new household domestic engineer to cook meals for the family and take care of the house.
7. Mr. Edgar Baines, President of the Tallyrand Corporation, elevated to prominence Carmen Miro to begin as Tallyrand's new Director of Corporate Planning.
8. I think the President was a total creep to contradict himself.
9. The lecture was so dull that I crashed right in the middle of it.
10. The airplane taxied down the runway and rose into the azure heavens as easily as a bird.

EXERCISE D: Improving Tone in a Passage.

Read the following passage and decide what tone you think it should have for a general audience unfamiliar with rock groups. Then, eliminate the words or phrases that make the tone disjointed and confusing. Finally, rewrite the passage maintaining a consistent tone.

(1) Popular since the mid-1960's, the rock band called *The Who* has wowed 'em from England to Woodstock with their incredibly magical and wondrous special effects and stage shows. (2) They have blasted away the pathetic fools who have tried to compete with them.

(3) *The Who* came to New York City in 1979 to give one of their finest shows ever. (4) Pete Townshend, lead guitarist, did some really cool jumps and splits. (5) Lead singer Roger Daltrey was at the top of his form as was bassist John Entwhistle. (6) The leading percussional figure of the band had been Keith Moon, but after he passed away in 1977, his duties fell to Kenny Jones, who did an outrageous job at the 1979 concert. (7) Dressed to kill, the band hung in there with the flavor of the old days and delivered their coup de grace with an electrifying version of "Won't Get Fooled Again."

(8) *Who* concerts are now established musical events, and people of all ages recognize this group. (9) Their popularity since the 1979 concert has not diminished.

APPLICATION: Choosing Your Words Carefully. Use one of the following suggested topics or think of one of your own to write a passage of about 150 to 200 words. As you choose words, concentrate on being concise, and avoid words or expressions that can undermine your tone. When you have written a first draft, use the rules in this section to double-check your writing. Make any necessary revisions and then write a good final copy.

A show (play, movie, television special) that impressed you
An unforgettable acquaintance you made while traveling
An insight you gained about a friend
The frustration of a boring task or job
Plans you once made for a special adventure (a trip, a prank, a tour)

18.2 Choosing Effective Words

The words you choose in your sentences should be both precise and concise in order to express your ideas forcefully.

This section offers suggestions for enlivening your writing by paying attention to your verbs, modifiers, nouns, and the variety of your words. It explains how to choose the most suitable synonyms to fit your meaning and context. It also explores other stylistic devices, such as figures of speech, sensory impressions, and symbols and encourages you to study professional writing to develop your own use of language.

■ Choosing Precise Words

Using weak verbs, passive constructions, and vague modifiers can weaken the impact of your writing. You can learn to recognize such colorless or ineffective words and replace them with vivid and specific language whenever possible.

Recognize the difference between bland or ineffective words and strong, colorful language. •

Notice how the following passage sounds weak even though it makes its points and provides ample information. Linking verbs and bland modifiers, in particular, rob the passage of vitality.

Bland and indirect language

The Wizard of Oz is a film classic. It was made in 1939 by an excellent cast headed by Judy Garland and is still very enjoyable to watch. One good scene is Dorothy's arrival in Munchkinland from Kansas. The Wicked Witch is killed by Dorothy's house, and hundreds of midgets, playing Munchkins, are happy about this event.

Vivid, precise modifiers and action verbs in the active voice make the following revised version much clearer and livelier.

Revised for more vivid and active language

The 1939 film classic, *The Wizard of Oz*, with Judy Garland, still charms audiences with its delightful silliness. Few people can forget Dorothy's trip from Kansas in her uprooted house and her crashlanding on the Wicked Witch in Munchkinland where hundreds of grateful Munchkin midgets sing and dance around Dorothy, their deliverer.

Action Words.   More than any other part of speech, verbs make the difference between forceful and weak writing. Action verbs in the active voice can enliven your sentences, whereas linking verbs and passive verbs can deaden them.

Use action verbs in the active voice whenever possible to make statements precise and lively.

While linking verbs such as *is, seem,* or *become* are occasionally necessary in sentences, they convey no action of their own, and therefore can weaken your statements, particularly when you use too many of them in a series. The following chart shows how action verbs can give new force to sentences.

USING ACTION VERBS INSTEAD OF LINKING VERBS	
Linking Verb:	Steve's costume *was* frightening to the little children.
Action Verb:	Steve's costume *frightened* the little children.
Linking Verbs:	The judges *were* certain that Alvin *was* the winner of the race.
Action Verbs:	The judges *declared* that Alvin *won* the race.
Linking Verbs:	Neighbors *became* irritated because music from our house *was* loud.
Action Verbs:	Neighbors *complained* because music *blasted* from our house.

You may also be able to strengthen sentences by making the verbs convey more of the action. For instance, in some noun/verb/noun constructions, the verb and the second noun can be replaced by a single more vivid verb, as in the following chart.

USING DIRECT VERBS INSTEAD OF NOUN/VERB/NOUN CONSTRUCTIONS	
Noun/Verb/Noun:	Baron Von Steuben *led* the Continental Army *in drills* at Valley Forge.
Revised:	Baron Von Steuben *drilled* the Continental Army at Valley Forge.
Noun/Verb/Noun:	Heavy rains *caused* a *flood* in our basement.
Revised:	Heavy rains *flooded* our basement.
Noun/Verb/Noun:	The newspaper *gave* its *endorsement* to the incumbent.
Revised:	The newspaper *endorsed* the incumbent.

Another method of making statements more vivid and forceful is to use verbs in the active rather than the passive voice. The active voice connects the performer and the action strongly and clearly, whereas the passive voice separates them and dilutes the force of the idea expressed. Although the passive voice can be useful to express certain ideas, you can often increase the impact and exactness of your sentences by changing from passive to active voice.

CHANGING PASSIVE VOICE TO ACTIVE VOICE	
Passive:	This driving test *was failed* nine times out of ten.
Active:	Nine out of every ten people *failed* this driving test.
Passive:	The sunshine *was filtered* by the fog.
Active:	The fog *filtered* the sunshine.
Passive:	Advanced Composition *was taught* by Ms. Wilson last term.
Active:	Ms. Wilson *taught* Advanced Composition last term.

Vivid and Specific Language.   Your language should be as vivid and specific as possible in order to sharpen your meaning and attract your reader's attention. Try to use graphic words with crisp, precise meanings rather than bland and general terms that can make your writing vague and can lose a reader's interest.

Use vivid, specific words to focus descriptions, relate actions, and convey meanings exactly.

Fuzzy descriptions result from vague modifiers. For example, words such as *good, impressive,* and *exciting* may indicate that something is worthy of notice but do not say *how* or *why.* The following chart demonstrates how vivid, specific word choices can clarify and freshen sentences.

USING VIVID MODIFIERS	
Vague:	Our old family doctor was *unforgettable.*
Vivid:	Our old family doctor was *compassionate* but *foolishly absentminded.*
Vague:	He made *pleasant* sounds on his guitar.
Vivid:	He made *soothing, liquid* sounds on his guitar.

Whenever you can, you should use specific, concrete words instead of overly general words. General or abstract nouns and verbs can leave a reader with indistinct ideas. Specific, concrete words, on the other hand, help to create a more detailed, well-focused picture. For example, *hamburger cookout, astronomer,* and *split-level house* are more vivid and precise than *meal, scientist,* and *family dwelling.* Similarly, *devoured, assem-*

bled, and *shouted* represent actions more clearly than *had, did,* and *spoke.* The following chart gives further examples of meaning improved by specific words.

USING SPECIFIC NOUNS AND VERBS	
General:	The batter *pleased* the *crowd* with a *hit* that won the game.
Specific:	The batter *lifted thousands from their seats* with a *game-winning double.*
General:	*People at the scene* were sure that Mike had *gone* to a phone.
Specific:	*Witnesses in the restaurant* were sure that Mike had *rushed* to a phone.
General:	The *leader* vowed to *win* against the enemy.
Specific:	The *admiral* vowed to *seize the enemy's flagship.*

Still another way to enliven your sentences is to use a variety of words instead of overusing any one word in a passage. If you get stuck repeating one word—for example, one adjective throughout a passage—a reader will become distracted by that word and miss your ideas. Notice how the repetition of the word *interesting* saps the meaning from the first of the following passages, while the varied, specific language in the second communicates more information.

FINDING PRECISE SUBSTITUTIONS FOR AN OVERUSED WORD

Passage with an Overused Word

The many *interesting* concepts in J.R.R. Tolkien's trilogy *The Lord of the Rings* captured my *interest.* For example, the magic ring of the title represents some *interesting* ideas. The wizard Gandalf, the chief source of truth in the trilogy, gives the hero Frodo an *interesting* warning about the power of the ring: Anyone who uses the ring's power—even for good—will be inevitably and increasingly corrupted by it.

Passage with Precise Substitutions

The many *fascinating* concepts in J.R.R. Tolkien's trilogy *The Lord of the Rings* continue to *intrigue* me. The magic ring of the title illustrates one of the most *thought-provoking* ideas. The wizard Gandalf, the chief source of truth in the trilogy, *warns* the hero Frodo that anyone who uses the ring's power—even for good—will be inevitably and increasingly corrupted by it.

EXERCISE A: **Using Action Words and Active Voice.** Revise the following sentences by replacing linking verbs with action verbs, by rewriting noun/verb/noun constructions, and by changing passive voice to active. Make all necessary alterations in word order.

1. The passage of the bill was immensely pleasing to the lobbyists.
2. Sunshine was brighter and then was dimmer as clouds passed overhead.
3. Many hardships are suffered by the animals of the Everglades during the dry season.
4. A searing guitar solo was ingeniously played by Jimmy Page.
5. At a science fiction seminar, Isaac Asimov gave a presentation on his theories of time and space.
6. Lucy's interpretation of that incident was upsetting to me.
7. Sociologists took a survey of residents of New City to ascertain income levels.
8. The apartment residents were angry about the owner's mismanagement.
9. Only two questions were missed by me when I took my oral examination.
10. Hundreds of years ago people were of the belief that the sun circled the earth.

EXERCISE B: **Making Vivid, Specific Word Choices.** Replace any vague modifiers, overly general verbs and nouns, and overused words in the following sentences with more precise language. Use your imagination to supply missing details.

1. I have just finished reading a very good novel that takes place during the early years of our country's history.
2. Madge went out west for a while to see things and to have a pleasant change.
3. Michael was happy when he got his report card.
4. The tiny vibrations of the floor were so tiny that had I been even a tiny bit preoccupied I might never have noticed them.
5. Private Robinson saw something move near them and felt strange.
6. Brenda made an attractive garment for herself to wear for a special occasion.
7. The speaker gave her dramatic interpretation.
8. The lazy clouds drifted lazily out over the lake.
9. The fair offered many sources of fun and many kinds of unusual food.
10. The poor weather depressed him.

■ Choosing the Right Connotations

When you are choosing a word from several possibilities, you are probably considering synonyms. While synonyms have similar *denotations,* or literal meanings, they often have different *connotations,* subtler shades of meaning or emotional associations. For instance, the words *pleased* and *ecstatic* both denote strong pleasure, yet their connotations are different. You might use *pleased* to describe happiness or some kind of satisfaction, but you would probably choose *ecstatic* to suggest an even more intense and profound feeling, an emotion closer to joy. A dictionary, thesaurus, or dictionary of synonyms can help you determine the appropriate connotation for a particular context.

Connotations and Tone.   When you examine connotations, you should consider tone as well as clarity of meaning. You should try to choose words that best reflect your attitude toward your subject and audience. This attitude is revealed by the *tone* of your writing, which your audience can "hear" throughout a passage. In choosing among synonyms, you should listen carefully to the tone of each, to find the one that harmonizes with the rest of the passage.

Choose words whose connotations suit the tone of your passages.

In almost any group of synonyms, you will find a whole range of connotations with different tones. For example, *confused, disorganized, bumbling,* and *inept* all mean approximately the same thing. But clearly, *inept* has a strongly condemning tone, while *confused* and *disorganized* sound more neutral, and *bumbling* adds a small note of humor to the criticism. Depending on your attitude toward your subject, one of these words is likely to be more appropriate than the others to build and sustain the overall tone of the passage.

The following chart shows you how different synonyms can establish different tones in the same sentence.

CHOOSING CONNOTATIONS TO SUIT TONE	
Favorable, Admiring Connotation:	He is a *steadfast* man, and nothing can budge him.
Still Positive Connotation, but Moving Toward Neutrality:	He is a *strong-willed* man, and nothing can budge him.

Neutral Connotation Moving Toward Negative:	He is a *stubborn* man, and nothing can budge him.
More Negative Connotation, Suggesting Unreasonableness:	He is an *obstinate* man, and nothing can budge him.
Very Negative, Suggesting Ridicule:	He is a *pigheaded* man, and nothing can budge him.

Connotations and Levels of Language. When considering connotations of synonyms, you should also think about levels of language. Depending on your audience, you will usually choose either a formal or an informal level of language for your writing. Your style may be more scholarly in formal writing, whereas in informal writing you may choose more casual language. When deciding among synonyms, you should maintain the formality or informality of a passage.

Choose words whose connotations suit the level of language in your passages.

In the preceding examples, the words *steadfast* and *pigheaded* not only convey different attitudes; they also represent different levels of language. Your writing will sound inconsistent if you choose a word with a formal connotation for an informal, casual passage. The following chart demonstrates how different synonyms can either disrupt or suit the level of language of a sentence.

CHOOSING CONNOTATIONS TO SUIT LEVELS OF LANGUAGE	
Too Formal:	Under heavy gunfire and a barrage of blasting mortars, our soldiers had to *relinquish* their foxholes.
Revised:	Under heavy gunfire and a barrage of blasting mortars, our soldiers had to *abandon* their foxholes.
Too Informal:	Among the lemurs of Madagascar, biologists have found a *batch* of courtship rituals.
Revised:	Among the lemurs of Madagascar, biologists have found a *variety* of courtship rituals.

EXERCISE C: Finding Synonyms and Choosing Among Connotations. Use a dictionary, a thesaurus, or a dictionary of synonyms to help you list three synonyms for each underlined word in the following sentences. Consider the connotations of all synonyms, including the original word, and circle the one you think best suits the tone and level of language of the sentence.

1. Placed in the care of an adoption agency, the twins <u>asked</u> repeatedly not to be separated.
2. An important aspect of training race horses involves <u>guessing</u> their varied potentials.
3. A yellow car pulled ahead of the others and <u>moved</u> toward the finish line.
4. <u>High-and-mighty</u> remarks by the nation's ambassador earned censure from Security Council members.
5. My uncle bought a quaint rustic cabin <u>ensconced</u> in the White Mountains.
6. Resting in a <u>bad</u> position, the enormous boulder threatened cars that passed on the roadway beneath.
7. Apparently <u>tickled</u> by Joan's answer, Mrs. Caperonis smiled and then proceeded with the lesson.
8. Hoping that she had finally <u>found</u> the source of the problem, Dr. Malone began the complex experiment again.
9. Jasper made the poodle angry so that it began to <u>bark.</u>
10. We just wanted to spend a long, lazy day, lying on the beach, <u>perusing</u> the ocean.

■ Using Figures of Speech

Similes, metaphors, personification, and analogies are figures of speech that strengthen your writing by appealing to a reader's imagination.

Similes.   A *simile* is an imaginative statement that uses the words *like* or *as* to link two different items explicitly on the basis of certain shared qualities.

Use similes to emphasize the shared qualities of otherwise dissimilar items.

The effect of a simile depends on the fact that the two linked items are not normally associated with each other, so that the reader will be doubly struck by the similarities that *do* exist. Notice how the following similes give the reader a new way of looking at the destructive power of a colony of ants and the fragility of a broken umbrella.

SIMILE: *Like a wave of brush fires*, droves of army ants swept across hundreds of acres of grasslands.

SIMILE: The broken umbrella turned inside out *as limply as a flower.*

Metaphors.   Like a simile, a *metaphor* compares two unlike items. But unlike a simile, it draws the comparison by identifying one item completely with another. A metaphor *implies* a comparison between two items by imaginatively overstating the similarity and equating them: It says one item *is* another. For instance, in the metaphoric statement *The boat was a large white bird on the water,* the reader can read beyond the impossibility of the statement to understand that a comparison has been drawn between the boat's beauty, grace, and ease on the water and the beauty and grace of a bird.

> **Use metaphors to heighten an imaginative connection between two items.**

Metaphors are even more striking figures of speech than similes. They should therefore be used with great selectivity and care. The following sentences include metaphors. Notice how the first one rewords the brush fire/ants simile.

METAPHOR: Droves of army ants swept across hundreds of acres of grasslands, a brush fire that could not be contained.

METAPHOR: Her hair was a bridal veil around her face, shimmering, pale, and still.

Because metaphors are imaginative and forceful many writers try to work them in more subtly by *submerging* them in exact, graphic verbs, for instance. Here is a submerged version of the brush fire/ants metaphor.

SUBMERGED METAPHOR: Droves of army ants scorched the grasslands for miles around.

Personification.   *Personification* also works as a kind of metaphor by attributing human qualities to nonhuman things. This figure of speech lends itself readily to humor, but it càn also be serious in its emotional impact on a reader.

> **Use personification to endow an inanimate object with human traits for either humorous or vivid effects.**

Personifications can be fun to write, but you should develop them carefully and only for a clearly defined purpose. They can easily sound pretentious and even ridiculous when you want to be serious. The following examples demonstrate the use of personification.

PERSONIFICATION: The welcoming hands of sunlight touched my shoulders, and I looked up.

PERSONIFICATION: The old train wheezed into the station and stopped with a grateful sigh.

Analogies.   An *analogy* is an extended comparison, which develops and explains the various points of similarity between the things compared. Writers often use analogies to relate an unfamiliar experience or set of circumstances to some other condition that will be more familiar to readers.

Use analogies to clarify an item, experience, or set of circumstances by likening it point by point to another.

Usually an analogy begins with a simile and then offers some detail and occasionally some narration to illustrate the likeness between the two items or experiences. For example, an analogy that explains a free fall in terms of a ride in a glass elevator should list several points of comparison.

ANALOGY: A free fall toward earth is like descending rapidly in a glass elevator. If you lose sight of the structures holding the glass walls, and if you ignore the feel of the floor through your shoes, you will have some sensation of what it is like to float in space, the pull of gravity your only reality.

EXERCISE D: **Creating Similes and Metaphors.** Form ten sentences that express comparisons, using one noun from each of the following columns in each sentence. Five sentences should contain similes, and five should contain metaphors. Try to write at least two submerged metaphors. Avoid using the same noun more than twice. Finally, label the type of each comparison that you write.

EXAMPLES: Her voice was like a lifeline pulling me from unconsciousness.   simile

Her voice was a lifeline pulling me from unconciousness. metaphor

Her voice pulled me from engulfing unconsciousness. submerged metaphor

face	lifeline
fear	blessing
youth	satin
hands	weapon
air	thirst
beauty	mask
hair	trap
car	monument
friendship	perfume
voice	costume

EXERCISE E: Using Personification. Write five sentences, each containing personification, using an item from the following list in each sentence.

A telephone	A stuffed toy
A skyscraper	Clouds
Waves lapping	A computer
A signpost	A gasoline lamp
A weed	A car rushing

EXERCISE F: Creating Analogies. Choose one of the following pairs of items or think of a pair of your own. Compare the two items and develop the comparison into an analogy.

Studying for an exam—filling a shopping cart quickly
A job interview or date—a performance onstage
A person you know—some fruit or vegetable
Hosting a party—spinning plates
Talking to a shy person—running uphill

■ Creating Moods with Language

In addition to communicating ideas and pictures, you can use words to influence your readers' moods or states of mind. You can find words that capture sensory impressions, such as sights, sounds, smells, tastes, and touches, which your readers can identify with from their own experiences. You can also use symbols—words that suggest associations beyond their own literal meanings.

Sensory Impressions. *Sensory impressions* are words that appeal to a reader's senses of sight, sound, smell, taste, and touch. A passage rich in sensory detail can involve a reader with particular intensity because it recreates the experience.

Use sensory impressions to recreate particular experiences and help create moods for your audience.

To create a mood with words you must go beyond their surface meanings. You must use words to evoke an emotional response. Words that convey sensory impressions can make a reader remember or imagine specific experiences. The following passage recreates the melancholy feeling and sensations you might have on an autumn night by using details of sight, sound, and touch.

Passage with sensory impressions   The night was coolly lit by a crystalline full moon. As we crunched through the piles of leaves, we cast silver shadows on the ground before us. I shivered as a small sharp wind nipped at my face.

Symbols.   Within a description you can include a *symbol*— a person, place, object, or action that the writer invests with significance beyond its literal meaning. Certain actions or things are natural symbols because of their built-in associations—for example, the sea, the sun, and the change of seasons. But any object can work as a symbol if the writer can convincingly endow it with special meaning.

Endow a concrete thing with symbolic significance to enrich the mood of a passage.

Symbols have more impact if they grow naturally and subtly out of the situation described. The objects that take on deeper meanings should fit into the context of the passage. A writer lays the groundwork for the symbol by establishing a mood from which the symbol's special meaning can develop. Then the readers sense for themselves the deeper meanings of a particular object or action. In this sense, symbols often work well as concluding effects, culminations of the other details in a passage.

The description of a fall evening, given above, might take on more meaning. For example, the "small sharp wind" might, with more preparation through words like *waning, dead,* and *weak,* become a symbolic reminder of the passage of time and the inevitability of death.

Passage developing a symbol   The night was coolly lit by a waning crystalline moon. As we crunched slowly through the deep piles of dead leaves, we cast weak shadows on the ground before us. Autumn was almost over. I shivered as a small sharp wind touched my shoulder.

EXERCISE G: **Writing with Sensory Impressions and Symbols.** Use one of the following subjects or think of one of your own to write a passage of between 150 and 200 words. Include sensory impressions and, if possible, one or more symbols in your passage. At the bottom of your paper, list the senses you appealed to and any symbols you created.

1. Write about a young man or woman driving alone to visit a college. Describe his or her expectations and/or fears. Express these with symbols.
2. Write about a family member or close friend who has died, or whom you have not seen in a very long time. Include some details that symbolize your insights or feelings about the person.
3. Describe how a bus station or airport looks late at night. Build up sensory impressions to reveal the mood of the place.
4. Write about a person packing for a long-awaited vacation or special journey. Describe items that he or she considers for packing; these can serve as symbols of the person's attitudes and expectations about the trip.
5. Narrate a situation in which someone becomes lost, panics, and then finally conquers the predicament. Use shifting sensory impressions to show the change in his or her mind.

■ Using Professional Models

Reading the work of professional writers can improve your writing, especially if you study the devices used by the writers to create effective prose. Precise language, appropriate connotations, figures of speech, sensory impressions, and symbols are among the most useful tools of successful writers. Now that you can recognize such devices, you should look for them in your reading and demonstrate your increased sensitivity to them in your own writing.

Study the language used by professional writers in order to improve your own writing style.

When you encounter effective uses of language, identify the idea or feeling that the writer has captured and identify the devices used. You might even copy such passages for future reference, making a note of the source of your models.

Stephen Crane's *The Red Badge of Courage* contains the following passage. Notice the vividness and precision of the description and its use of such figures of speech as "the furnace roar of the battle."

Metaphor	He became aware that the furnace roar of the battle was growing louder. Great brown clouds had
Precise language	floated to the still heights of air before him. The noise, too, was approaching. The woods filtered men
Submerged metaphor	and the fields became dotted. —Stephen Crane

The following passage from "Flowering Judas" by Katherine Anne Porter illustrates another effective use of language. Porter makes a metaphoric connection between a young woman's clothing and her life.

Precise language	Her knees cling together under sound blue serge, and her round white collar is not purposely nun-like.
	She wears the uniform of an idea, and has renounced
Metaphor	vanities. She has encased herself in a set of principles derived from her early training, leaving no detail of gesture or of personal taste untouched, and for this reason she will not wear lace made on machines. She
Submerged metaphor	loves fine lace, and there is a tiny edge of fluted cobweb on this collar, which is one of twenty precisely alike, folded in blue tissue paper in the upper drawer of her clothes chest. —Katherine Anne Porter

The following passage from Nathaniel Hawthorne's *The House of the Seven Gables* employs several devices. Notice how personification, sensory impressions, and symbolism can create a ponderous mood and how the wind becomes a symbol of something ominous or foreboding that has entered the lives of those in the house.

	He tried the door, which yielded to his hand, and was flung wide open by a sudden gust of wind that
Personification	passed, as with a loud sigh, from the outermost portal through all the passages and apartments of the
Sensory impressions	new house. It rustled the silken garments of the ladies, and waved the long curls of the gentlemen's wigs, and shook the window hangers and the curtains of the bedchambers; causing everywhere a sin-
Symbol	gular stir, which yet was more like a hush. A shadow of awe and half-fearful anticipation—nobody knew wherefor nor of what—had all at once fallen over the company. —Nathaniel Hawthorne

From your study of professional works, you might write a vivid passage like the following.

Sensory impressions	The hot, harsh lights of the acting studio melted decades away from her cunning old face, and she glowed and fattened, growing ageless, beautiful, and
Precise language	larger than life on the star-worship of her students. They paid her to torture them into art. She bellowed at them, pounced on them, and throttled them like
Simile	an old medicine man trying to wake the dead.

EXERCISE H: Examining a Professional Model.

Read the following passage. List the strong action words, vivid modifiers, specific language, similes, metaphors, personification, analogies, sensory impressions, and symbols you find.

(1) Joel gazed at the girl, not much older than himself. (2) She leaned her cheek against the fiddle. (3) He had never examined a fiddle at all, and when she began to play it she frightened and dismayed him by her almost insect-like motions, the pensive antennae of her arms. (4) And quite clearly, and altogether to his surprise, Joel saw a sight that he had nearly forgotten. (5) Instead of the fire on the hearth, there was a mimosa tree in flower. (6) It was in the little back field at his home in Virginia, and his mother was leading him by the hand. (7) Fragile, delicate, cloudlike, it rose on its pale trunk and spread its long level arms. (8) Among the trembling leaves the feathery puffs of sweet bloom filled the tree like thousands of paradisical birds all alighted at an instant. (9) It seemed to be the mimosa tree that lighted the garden, for its brightness and fragrance overlaid all the rest. (10) Out of its graciousness this tree suffered their presence and shed its splendor upon him and his mother. (11) Then the vision was gone. —Eudora Welty

EXERCISE I: Collecting and Studying Professional Models.

Find three passages in professional works with effective words. Copy them and write down each source. Label the devices in each.

APPLICATION: Choosing Effective Language for Your Writing.

Write a passage of 150 to 300 words on one of the following topics or on some other. Use vivid and specific language, suitable connotations, figures of speech, and words that convey mood. Use any professional models as guides.

Your feelings—alone in your home on a rainy day
An interview for college or a job
A late night walk through a dangerous section of town
Working out for a sport
The place where you would least want to live

Sentence Style

In a composition, your sentences should be *more* than grammatically correct. They should please and interest the reader as well as communicate ideas. Using varied sentence lengths and structures can give you a more sophisticated writing style and can also help to hold the reader's attention.

This chapter discusses how you can improve your writing style by varying the lengths, structures, and patterns of your sentences and by learning from professional writers.

19.1 Identifying Problems in Sentence Length and Structure

Even the most original ideas will lose their impact if they are expressed in monotonous or confusing sentences. The best writing usually mixes long and short sentences and uses a variety of sentence structures. The sentences in your paragraphs and compositions can have flair and pleasing rhythms if you adopt some of the methods for varying your sentences discussed in this section.

■ Variety of Sentence Lengths

When all the sentences in a passage are the same length, the ideas are hidden by the repetitive rhythm. To achieve a pleasing variety of lengths, you must first examine whole series of sentences to hear their rhythm and test their effect.

Recognize when too many short, jerky sentences or too many long, tangled ones are weakening your writing style.

564

Too many short sentences in a passage will produce a halting effect, as in the following passage.

Passage with short, choppy sentences

> A busy airport vibrates with the comings and goings of many people. Taxis honk and huddle at the curb. They deposit and pick up passengers. Inside, escalators carry people up and down. The loudspeaker announces arrivals and departures. Some big planes inch toward and some back away from the terminals. They blast the air with their engines.

If too much information is packed into one sentence, however, as in the following long, rambling sentence, monotony and confusion result.

Passage with a long, rambling sentence

> A busy airport vibrates with the comings and goings of many people while taxis honk and huddle at the curb, depositing and picking up passengers, and, inside, escalators carry people up and down, and the loudspeaker announces arrivals and departures while some big planes inch toward and some back away from the terminals, blasting the air with their engines.

A satisfactory style will be neither choppy nor rambling. A variety of sentence lengths makes a passage more readable.

Passage with varied sentences

> A busy airport vibrates with the comings and goings of many people. Taxis honk and huddle at the curb, depositing and picking up passengers. Inside, escalators carry people up and down. While the loudspeaker announces arrivals and departures, some big planes inch toward and some back away from the terminals, blasting the air with their engines.

Improving a Series of Short Sentences.   A series of short, abrupt sentences often sounds awkward.

Eliminate choppy sentences by adding details or by combining ideas.

Sometimes sentences in a series are short and abrupt because they include too few details. These sentences are often plain and uninformative.

Short sentences with scanty information can be improved by fleshing them out with details. Modifying words and phrases, appositives, and clauses can lengthen these sentences while expanding their ideas. But be sure that the new information is relevant. The following examples illustrate the different kinds of details that you can add.

LENGTHENING SHORT SENTENCES BY ADDING DETAILS

Short Sentence: The worker hammered tiles onto the roof.

With Adjectives and an Adverb Added:	The worker *busily* hammered *fresh, green* tiles onto the *old* roof.
With Prepositional Phrases Added:	*For nearly an hour,* the worker hammered tiles onto the roof *of the old barn.*
With a Verbal Phrase Added:	*Defying the searing sun,* the worker hammered tiles onto the roof.
With an Appositive Phrase Added:	The worker, *an ancient ranch hand,* hammered tiles onto the roof.
With a Clause Added:	*Although the summer sun burned down all day,* the worker hammered tiles onto the roof.

Combining two or more short sentences can also eliminate choppiness and create a variety of lengths. Any sentences containing closely related ideas can be joined to form one longer sentence. For example, two short sentences can sometimes be joined by using a compound subject or verb or by making one sentence into a participial phrase, a prepositional phrase, or an appositive. Also, short simple sentences can be combined to form different sentence structures: compound, complex, and compound-complex sentences. The following chart illustrates these numerous possibilities.

FORMING LONGER SENTENCES BY COMBINING IDEAS

Short, Choppy Sentences	Longer, Smoother Sentences
In August, the Grossis hiked in the Sierra Mountains. The Dykes also hiked in the Sierra Mountains.	In August, the *Grossis* and the *Dykes* hiked in the Sierra Mountains. (Compound subject)
Edna parked the car. She brought packages into the building.	Edna *parked* the car and *brought* packages into the building. (Compound verb)
The small dog yapped frantically. It ran away from a large cat.	*Yapping frantically,* the small dog ran away from a large cat. (Modifying phrase)
Mrs. Kurtz became the new personnel director. She moved her office upstairs.	Mrs. Kurtz, *the new personnel director,* moved her office upstairs. (Appositive)

The police cars passed, flashing red lights. The fire engines screamed down the boulevard.	The police cars passed, flashing red lights, *and* the fire engines screamed down the boulevard. (Compound sentence)
He lost his grip on the ladder. He knocked over a can of paint.	*When he lost his grip on the ladder,* he knocked over a can of paint. (Complex sentence)
The strike continued. Some dock workers continued to appear on picket lines. Others sought new jobs.	*While the strike continued,* some dock workers continued to appear on picket lines, *but* others sought new jobs. (Compound-complex sentence)

Improving a Series of Long Sentences.   Long, rambling sentences can burden a reader with an overload of ideas. Because too much information is packed into a few sentences, the reader may have trouble absorbing the ideas.

Eliminate rambling sentences by separating and regrouping ideas into two or more simpler sentences.

You can often improve rambling sentences by dividing them into shorter sentences as in the following chart.

SEPARATING IDEAS IN RAMBLING SENTENCES	
Two Long Compound-Complex Sentences	**Four Shorter Varied Sentences: Simple, Compound, Complex, Simple**
Driving on long trips can be physically and mentally fatiguing because for hours drivers must sit in the same position, using the same muscles, and they must concentrate on the road. Unless they take regular breaks, their leg, back, shoulder, neck, arm, and hand muscles may stiffen or become numb, or even worse, the miles of monotonous macadam can lull their minds to sleep.	Driving on long trips can be physically and mentally fatiguing. For hours, drivers must sit in the same position, using the same muscles, and they must concentrate on the road. Unless they take regular breaks, their leg, back, shoulder, neck, arm, and hand muscles may stiffen or become numb. Even worse, the miles of monotonous macadam can lull their minds to sleep.

As you can see in the preceding chart, rambling sentences are unusually long compound, complex, or compound-complex sentences. They can become easier to follow if they are shortened to sentences with fewer clauses.

Long, rambling sentences can also be improved in another way. Often, when too much information is packed into a few sentences, the ideas sound awkward and confusing. To improve these sentences, you should regroup as well as separate ideas to vary the lengths and to achieve clarity.

The following chart shows how a long, rambling sentence can be separated into three shorter ones. Reorganizing as well as separating ideas improves both the rhythm and sense of the passage.

SEPARATING AND REGROUPING IDEAS	
A Long, Rambling Compound-Complex Sentence	Three Shorter Varied Sentences: Simple, Complex, Complex
Peter decided to approach the mess in the office, including advertisements, letters, and bills which had accumulated, by first dividing the mail into manageable piles for answering and processing, which Mr. Campbell, his boss, could help him with when he returned, but Peter hoped that he could complete the sorting beforehand.	Peter decided to approach the mess in the office including advertisements, letters, and bills by first dividing the mail into manageable piles. He hoped to complete this sorting before his boss, Mr. Campbell, returned. Then together they could answer the letters and process the bills which had accumulated.

EXERCISE A: **Lengthening Sentences by Adding Details.** Rewrite each of the following sentences, adding details to make them longer as well as more interesting. Underline your additions and label the kinds of structures you have added in each sentence: a modifying phrase, an appositive, and so on.

EXAMPLE: The cat meowed.

                Prep Phrase   Adj   Adj   Adv   Prep
        For three hours, the lost tiger cat meowed loudly on our

            Phrase
        doorstep.

1. Selma looked at each of her friends.
2. We wore purple caps and gowns.
3. Confusion as well as excitement filled the air.
4. We filed in.
5. He approached the foot of the stage.

EXERCISE B: Combining Short Sentences. Combine each of the following groups of sentences into one longer sentence. Vary your methods of combining, and label the method you have used in each sentence: modifying phrase, appositive, compound verb, and so on.

1. Rust is a popular color. It is often used in home decorating.
2. She had trouble building the fire. A brisk breeze was blowing.
3. Our local newspapers were the *Kensington Chronicle* and the *Orinda Record*. They merged last year.
4. The dog trotted down the main street. It paused in front of the meat market. It sniffed eagerly.
5. I ran to answer the phone. I slipped on a magazine. I tripped over the coffee table.

EXERCISE C: Adding Details and Combining Ideas. Rewrite the following passage to correct a series of short, choppy sentences. Add details to some sentences and join some ideas to make longer sentences.

(1) The race was over. (2) Sally stumbled to the post. (3) It had been a long five miles. (4) No one had expected her to finish, or even "place." (5) She had shown them. (6) She had worked out for weeks. (7) She had used her training. (8) She had depended on her confidence. (9) She had given all of her energy to this goal. (10) She had now won a personal victory as well as a public one.

EXERCISE D: Simplifying Long Sentences. Rewrite the following passage by eliminating the rambling sentences. In some of the sentences, separate the thoughts to form sentences with fewer clauses. In others, separate and regroup the ideas. Make sure that the lengths of sentences are varied.

(1) In moving, almost everything that is familiar to a child, except of course members of the family, disappears, leaving the child with a feeling of loss and perhaps without a sense of identity in the new surroundings, and many children at such times attach themselves to certain objects such as a blanket, stuffed animal, or favorite toy, which they have carried with them, because an object can serve as a source of comfort and security.

(2) Such attachments can be sensitive stages in a child's development because when the child has become dependent on one particular object, he or she may then resist new things, often holding desperately to the familiar old ones, fearing the type of loss first felt during the move to a new home.

■ Variety of Sentence Openers and Structures

Although the lengths of sentences may vary, sentences can still sound awkward or monotonous if too many of them have the same kinds of beginnings and structures. For example, a series of sentences all beginning with prepositional phrases may distract a reader. Similarly, a series of compound sentences may sound tedious.

Recognize monotonous writing styles caused by repeating the same sentence openers and sentence structures.

Repeating the same opener in sentence after sentence can create a dull rhythm and can cause a reader to lose interest.

The following passage sounds monotonous because all of the sentences begin in the same way: subject first, then the verb.

Monotonous passage with only subject/ verb openers

Tobias escaped quietly around the corner of the building, but he found that he was not alone. He retreated a few more steps back into the alley as he watched the two figures. They studied a paper and spoke in low voices. The taller one lit a cigarette and looked furtively about him. Tobias held still. He saw the man start and stare toward him through the dusk. Tobias crept backwards down the alley, his eyes never leaving the two men.

A passage can also sound awkward if the writer has overused any particular sentence structure, such as too many complex sentences with adverb clauses, as in the following passage.

Monotonous passage with only complex sentences

As Tobias escaped quietly around the corner of the building, he found that he was not alone. While he retreated a few more steps back into the alley, he watched the two figures study a paper and speak in low voices. When the taller one lit a cigarette, he looked furtively about him. As Tobias held still, he saw the man start and stare toward him through the dusk. When Tobias crept backwards down the alley, his eyes never left the two men.

An effective writing style makes use of varied sentence openers and usually includes some simple, some compound, some complex, and some compound-complex sentences.

Passage with varied sentence openers and structures	As Tobias escaped quietly around the corner of the building, he found that he was not alone. He retreated a few steps back into the alley, and he watched the two figures study a paper as they spoke in low voices. Before long, the taller one lit a cigarette and looked furtively about him. Tobias held still. When he saw the man start and stare toward him, Tobias crept backwards down the alley, his eyes never leaving the two men.

Improving Sentence Openers. In addition to the common and useful subject/verb opener, there are many ways to begin sentences to help you achieve a lively sentence style.

Use some of the many options for beginning different sentences in a passage.

In a series of sentences, you should vary your openers. Find the most appropriate sentence beginnings to match your ideas. The following chart shows many of the possibilities available to you.

DIFFERENT WAYS TO BEGIN SENTENCES	
Subject/Verb:	*Sightseers visited* the Great Pyramid.
Adjectives:	*Worn-out and exhausted,* we crawled toward the cave.
Prepositional Phrase:	*For entertainment,* the prince provided clowns and minstrels.
Participial Phrase:	*Gripping the rope tightly,* she completed her ascent to the crow's nest.
Infinitive Phrase:	*To finish the foundation,* we hired a contractor.
Subject with Appositive Phrase:	The *prophet, a small, withered man,* turned to address his assemblage.
Adverb Clause:	*Before the tide was at lowest ebb,* we returned the rowboats to the boathouse.
One-Word Transition:	*Eventually,* a point of light appeared on the horizon.
Transitional Phrase:	*As a result,* the sprinkler system engaged and fire doors closed.
Inverted Order:	*Within the cloud of galactic dust* appeared three huge asteroids.

Improving Structural Variety.   To achieve sentence variety you should also think about varying the structures of your sentences.

Use some simple, some compound, some complex, and some compound-complex sentences to avoid structural monotony.

Varying length and openers will have some effect upon the structures of your sentences, but you should also specifically check your sentence structures in a passage. Too many sentences of any one structure will stand out awkwardly and detract from your ideas.

In the following passage, the writer has used a variety of structures. Notice how four different sentence structures enhance the ideas expressed and help to establish an interesting rhythm.

(1) Simple sentence
(2) Complex sentence (Adverb clause)
(3) Compound sentence
(4) Simple sentence
(5) Compound-complex sentence

(1) Snorkeling in tropical waters opens a window on another world. (2) If snorkelers paddle gently above a coral reef, they will see a colorful garden just below them. (3) Lacy, lavender sea fans just like palm fronds wave lazily in the current, and orange, gold, red, and purple coral branches up toward the sunlight. (4) Among these underwater trees, fish colored metallic blue, aqua, purple, green, orange, yellow, red, and pink drift and flit. (5) When the snorkelers' bubbles and shadows momentarily disturb their world, some of the fish dart to coral caverns, and others swim closer or nibble seaweed nonchalantly.

EXERCISE E: **Varying Sentence Openers.** Each of the following sentences begins with its subject and verb. Vary the beginning of each sentence by rearranging its words. As you rewrite, use as many different sentence openers as you can, and identify the type of opener you have chosen in each case.

1. Many new houses in the West, in contrast, do not have attics or basements.
2. The child got lost in the crowd at the fair.
3. He sprained his ankle, dashing for a bus.
4. They felt that they could not leave the place until they had fulfilled their obligations.
5. The Red Cross in its Basic First Aid Course teaches three methods to stop bleeding.
6. You must take care with your plants to avoid rotting the roots.

7. A six-cylinder engine uses less fuel, not surprisingly, than does one with eight cylinders.
8. The dog, lonely and sad, watched its owner through the window.
9. Antique jewelry and furniture are smart investments because they appreciate in value rather than depreciate.
10. A faint glimmer appeared through the window.

EXERCISE F: Varying Sentence Structures. Rewrite the following passage so that you have a variety of sentence structures: simple, compound, complex, and compound-complex. In the margin of your paper, identify the structure of each sentence that you have written.

(1) I entered the forest as the sun began to set. (2) The shadows were long. (3) I followed a seldom-used path. (4) I felt restless. (5) I had started walking. (6) The forest was cool. (7) The dark branches drooped with the weight of green summer. (8) The leaves fluttered. (9) The brush crackled beneath my feet.

(10) I turned to the left. (11) I walked into a clearing. (12) The grass was short and peppered with dark-colored flowers. (13) I climbed onto a rock. (14) I faced the west. (15) The sun was disappearing into a honey sunset swirl. (16) The clouds shimmered orange. (17) A cool breeze blew the leaves, my hair, and the grass. (18) The sun melted into the trees and soon dropped out of sight. (19) My restlessness was gone. (20) I was at peace with the world.

APPLICATION 1: Achieving Variety in Sentence Lengths and Structures. Choose one of the following topics or think of one of your own, and write a composition of about ten sentences. As you write, vary the lengths of your sentences and use a variety of sentence openers. Check the structures of your sentences to ensure that your sentences are varied.

The worst day you ever had
A favorite toy you had as a child
Emotions you experienced facing a difficult assignment or task
Your personal stand on some political or social issue
A responsibility you wished you had never assumed

APPLICATION 2: Revising for Variety in Your Sentences. Use *three* of the following methods to check the lengths, openers, and structures of your sentences in the short composition you wrote for the preceding exercise. Revise your sentences to eliminate any weaknesses you discover.

1. Have another reader evaluate whether you have included enough or too much information in each of your sentences. If the reader cannot fully grasp your ideas, you may have to flesh out short sentences with more details or break up rambling sentences into simpler groupings of ideas.
2. Listen to the rhythm of your sentences as you read them aloud. If your sentences have a halting, sing-song, or faltering rhythm, adjust some of the lengths, openers, and structures to make the rhythm smooth and pleasing.
3. Identify the opener you have used in each of your sentences. If you have used only one or two kinds of openers, try to rephrase some of your sentences for variety.
4. Identify the structure of each of your sentences. Decide in each sentence whether you have tailored the structure to the idea and whether another structure would be more effective.

19.2 Experimenting with Sentence Types and Patterns

Your sentence style is partly determined by the lengths, beginnings, and structures of your sentences. It is also determined by how you mold sentences to fit the ideas you are expressing. Skilled writers create sentences that please the reader's ear with their rhythm as well as suit the ideas being expressed.

This section explains how to achieve special effects with your sentences. It discusses different ways to emphasize ideas and explores the use of similar and contrasting patterns. Finally, it shows some of the effects professional writers have achieved by experimenting with their sentences.

■ Using Different Types of Sentences

When you write sentences in a composition, one of your goals should be to create a variety that holds the reader's interest. Another should be to show your ideas to best advantage. Certain types of sentences—some that you probably use all the time—can highlight your ideas and can affect the speed at which your reader absorbs your ideas.

Consider using different types of sentences to achieve special kinds of emphasis for your ideas.

Different types of sentences can be used to achieve emphasis. In a *loose sentence,* for example, the writer draws the reader's attention to the main idea by placing it first and by placing all modifying phrases and clauses at the end. In a *periodic sentence,* the writer accents the main idea even more by placing it at the end of the sentence after the modifying phrases and clauses. In a *balanced sentence,* the writer emphasizes the difference between two or more ideas by using very similar grammatical structures to express them. And in a *cumulative sentence,* the writer emphasizes the exactness of modifying details by using certain kinds of modifiers and by placing them before, after, or both before and after the main idea. Many of the sentences you write will be loose, periodic, balanced, or cumulative while many others will have some characteristics of more than one of these types of sentences. The following paragraphs introduce each of these types of sentences and discuss their usefulness to you as a writer.

Loose Sentences.　A *loose sentence* follows the common subject-verb-complement order and may conclude with modifying phrases and clauses. A loose sentence can be simple, compound, complex, or compound-complex, but the main idea is always placed at the beginning of the sentence.

Use loose sentences to draw moderate attention to your main ideas.

In a loose sentence the main idea is presented first, where the reader will immediately notice it. This placement emphasizes the main idea to some degree. The details that follow the main idea add information to the main idea.

EXAMPLES:　The Great Depression left thousands desperate because their sources of income had disappeared overnight and because many banks collapsed. (Main idea—subordinate clause—subordinate clause)

The drought destroyed the area by shriveling the leaves and baking the ground until dust lay everywhere. (Main idea—modifying phrase—subordinate clause)

Because it is natural to think of the main idea first, you will write many loose sentences. Putting the main idea first seems logical to both writers and readers. Loose sentences can be read quickly. But you will naturally want to use other types of sentences as well. You should also try to add details at the beginning and in the middle of your loose sentences to give your writing variety.

Periodic Sentences. In a *periodic sentence* the main idea is presented at the end. The entire main idea can be presented at the end of the sentence, or just the verb and complement or even just the complement can be held back until the end. By beginning with modifying phrases and clauses and by withholding the main idea, the writer of a periodic sentence builds suspense and raises the reader's expectations.

> Use periodic sentences to lead a reader toward a main idea you want to emphasize strongly.

A periodic sentence builds to the main idea, which is revealed at the end where it will have a strong impact. The rest of the sentence prepares for the main idea by leading the reader up to it. Placing the main idea at the end of the sentence underscores that idea. The complex sentence, which begins with its subordinate clause and ends with its main clause, is a common example of a periodic sentence. Some other examples follow.

EXAMPLES: Abandoning reason and defying fear, the prisoner bolted toward the barbed wire fence. (Modifying phrases—main idea)

Her beauty, her talents, and her famous performances—these were the source of her pride and power. (Appositives—main idea)

Because a periodic sentence presents a crafted, packaged thought, it can have a dramatic effect. Consequently you should use long, intricate periodic sentences only to build to a high point and to emphasize that point. And you should regulate your use of shorter periodic sentences to prevent your writing from becoming heavy-handed.

Balanced Sentences. Another kind of sentence accentuates ideas by repetition and contrast. A *balanced sentence* presents two or more contrasting main ideas using similar grammatical structures. The similarity of the structures highlights the contrast in the ideas.

Use balanced sentences to emphasize contrasts between two or more main ideas.

A balanced sentence calls attention to its main ideas by presenting them in parallel phrases or clauses. These equal and repetitious grammatical structures set up a rhythm, which makes the ideas stand out. Often, the parts of a balanced sentence are joined by a coordinate conjunction or frequently by just a semicolon.

EXAMPLES: She appeared sullen and secretive; her twin seemed lively and open. (Main idea—main idea)

          The boy had all the money that he wanted but none of the love he needed. (Complement and modifying clause—complement and modifying clause)

Like a periodic sentence, a balanced sentence is a well-shaped thought. You can use balanced sentences to emphasize ideas, to present weighty thoughts with few words, or even to make ideas memorable for the reader, but you should use balanced sentences infrequently and only to achieve a particular effect.

Cumulative Sentences. A cumulative sentence is a variation of the loose sentence. It uses details to develop the main idea. A *cumulative sentence* consists of a main idea or base clause and layers of descriptive details added before or after the main idea. Sometimes these details are added both before and after the main idea. The modifying phrases and clauses that add descriptive details are free modifiers, which can be moved around in the sentence or removed entirely. These added modifiers make the main idea concrete and specific by providing details.

Use cumulative sentences to emphasize modifying details that develop a main idea.

In a cumulative sentence specific modifiers are added to expand a main idea. The modifiers can be adjectives in a series, prepositional phrases, appositives, verbal phrases, nominative absolutes (verbal phrases with their own subjects), adjective clauses, and adverb clauses. Grouped at the beginning and end of cumulative sentences, these colorful modifiers stand out for the reader.

EXAMPLES: The drier's drum circled monotonously, flinging the towels and sheets, the shirts and jeans against its moving metal walls, the buttons and zippers clicking with every toss. (Main idea—verbal phrase—nominative absolute)

Its tail arching in a gray plume, its paws clutching an acorn, the squirrel watched us, poised and ready to run. (Nominative absolute—nominative absolute—main idea—adjectives in a series)

As the bus pulled up, a gust of air blasted the curb, stirring up dust, leaves, and scraps in a dirty whirlpool, which stung the eyes of the waiting passengers. (Adverb clause—main idea—verbal phrase—adjective clause)

Cumulative sentences can give your writing a density of detail. They work particularly well when you are trying to express action or describe something exactly. They give your writing a varied pace and rhythm that can recreate the exact movement of the thing you are describing. You should use cumulative sentences when you want to elaborate on a main idea and convey exact observations to the reader. Interspersing cumulative sentences with the other types of sentences can make your writing sophisticated and interesting.

EXERCISE A: Identifying Types of Sentences. Identify each of the following sentences as loose, periodic, balanced, or cumulative. Remember that loose and cumulative sentences are similar, although in cumulative sentences, the writer's intention is to build up vivid, specific modifying details.

1. A sloop was loitering in the distance, dropping slowly down with the tide, her sail hanging uselessly against the mast. . . . —Washington Irving
2. Let us never negotiate out of fear [but] let us never fear to negotiate. —John F. Kennedy
3. Whenever the rain hangs a gray curtain around the house and pitter-patters on the leaves and dirt, I am lulled to sleep.
4. We chose to sit on the far side of the stadium for the big game because that side was in the shade.
5. He was standing there, one hand on his hip, the other holding out at an angle the wooden staff, as tall as he was, to the tip of which clung the soft will-o'-wisp. —Ursula Le Guin
6. The energetic came, eager to put their hands to work; the lazy [came], hoping to live with no work at all. —Eric Sevareid

7. Sitting at the counter in the coffee shop in patched jeans, dark glasses, and a cowboy hat, which was creased and smudged, was a movie star.
8. He would not have backed into the telephone pole, if the gutters had not been cluttered with broken branches and piles of leaves, if two delivery trucks had not blocked the loading zone, and if he had not been in such a hurry.
9. Their eyes sticking up, exposed and beady, three square-bodied crabs floated along the sand, sideways, like some outer space vehicles exploring the surface of a planet pocked with craters.
10. If the curb had not been cluttered with broken branches and piles of leaves, if two delivery trucks had not blocked the loading zone, and if he had not been in such a hurry, he would not have backed into the telephone pole.

EXERCISE B: Locating Different Types of Sentences. Examine several magazine articles and short stories to find examples of different types of sentences. Find *two* loose sentences, *two* periodic sentences, *two* balanced sentences, and *two* cumulative sentences. Write down these sentences as well as the writer, the title of the article or story, the title of the magazine or book, and the page where you found each sentence.

EXERCISE C: Practicing with Different Types of Sentences. Using the sentences in Exercise A and the ones you found in Exercise B as models, write *two* loose sentences, *two* periodic sentences, *two* balanced sentences, and *two* cumulative sentences. Label each of your sentences.

■ Employing Effective Patterns

Besides using different types of sentences, you can focus on patterns to make the ideas in your sentences stand out for the reader. Using a series of similar structures to set up a pattern and breaking a pattern by using a different structure are two ways to control and vary the rhythm of your sentences.

Consider using repetition of similar structures and contrast of structures to accentuate your ideas.

Structural Similarities. A series of similar grammatical structures, called parallelism, within sentences or within groups of sentences can set up a repetitious rhythm. This rhythm can draw the reader's attention to the ideas in the similar structures, indicating that the ideas belong together.

Use parallel structures within a sentence and in groups of sentences to point out relationships among ideas.

You have already learned that parallellism can emphasize contrasting ideas in a balanced sentence. Using parallel structures for items in a series within sentences can present items in categories or can have an intensifying effect. The rhythm underlines the ideas expressed in the repeated parts of speech, phrases, or clauses.

Parallelism within sentences

The chimpanzee *put on a pair of glasses, hopped up on the desk chair, rolled a piece of paper into the typewriter, turned on the machine,* and *began typing.* (Parallel verbs capture and list the chimpanzee's actions.)

If you want to go on that trip and *if you hope to find a place to stay,* you should make your reservations now. (Parallel clauses build intensity and emphasize the warning.)

Parallelism can also create effects in a series of sentences in a passage. Two or more consecutive parallel sentences can link the ideas they contain by indicating that the ideas are equal and similar or related in some other way. The following passage begins with a main idea about a medical facility. The writer presents three reasons in three parallel sentence structures. This kind of structural similarity emphasizes the idea that *many* reasons exist for keeping the medical facility open.

Parallelism within a group of sentences

Residents of the Dalewood district can't afford to allow the Dalewood Medical Clinic to close. *No similar facility exists near the residential area. No downtown hospital offers a ready local ambulance.* And *no other facility could replace the personalized service and treatment* that Dalewood residents have come to trust.

Structural Contrasts.   The deliberate breaking of a pattern—a structural contrast—within a sentence and especially within a group of sentences draws the reader's attention to the idea that is expressed in a different structure.

Use a contrasting structure to emphasize an idea or to present a concluding thought.

Contrast in rhythm—that is, in length and structure—can signal a new idea, an opposing idea, or a final idea. A reader becomes accustomed to the rhythm of similar structures so that when you break the pattern with a different structure you can heighten the impact of the idea through this contrast. The following periodic sentence builds intensity through parallel structures and then reaches a climax in the final contrasting structure.

Contrasting structures within a sentence	Angered by the constant yapping of her neighbor's dog, exhausted from too little sleep, and terrified by her friend's disappearance, *the old woman sat down on the sofa and cried.*

A structural contrast coming at the end of a series of sentences can please or startle a reader as well as announce a final important idea. The following passage, for instance, contains many sentences with compound parts and modifying phrases. The final sentence breaks the pattern with a short, direct structure that hits the reader with the main idea of the passage.

Ending a passage with a structural contrast	He ran across the slippery grass and disappeared under the ropy curtain of the willow branches. He had spent many hours in this hideout, playing card games, reading, and talking to imaginary friends. He took a deep breath to inhale the scent of the tree and scanned the lawn, the hedges, and the patio until he focused on the waiting car. *He would never return.*

EXERCISE D: Using Structural Similarities. Use any one of the following ideas or one of your own to write either a sentence or a passage that uses structural similarities to underscore relationships among ideas.

Sounds and sensations one night that terrified you
Unappetizing features of a dinner party that you attended
Spectacles at a sound and light show or a fireworks display
Unseasonable weather that left everyone surprised and uncomfortable
Reasons to vote for a particular political candidate

EXERCISE E: Using Structural Contrasts. Use any one of the following ideas or one of your own to write a passage. As you write, establish a pattern that readers will find appropriate and be comfortable with. Then break the pattern with a contrasting sentence structure.

A visit to an unfamiliar city
A drive through hill country, a desert, or mountains
The scene of an accident
The behavior of a crowd at a parade or rally
Your feelings and observations sitting in a doctor's or dentist's
    waiting room.

■ Using Professional Models

Professional writers have learned to craft their sentences to achieve precise effects—rhythms, emphasis, and subtle, successful patterns. Studying sentences written by professionals can show you options for your own sentences and can help you develop stylistic preferences.

Examine and learn from the kinds of sentences that professional writers use.

When you read, certain sentences and passages will occasionally impress you. You may notice the rhythm, the boldness or subtlety of ideas, or some striking pattern. By analyzing the kinds of sentences and patterns and their particular effects, you can gather some ideas for your own writing.

In the following passage, for instance, the writer slowly builds a feeling of relationship between a character and nature by using a series of loosely parallel clauses in the long second sentence. The change of structure that follows helps to carry the reader back from this extended comparison to the character's own human unhappiness.

Passage with loosely parallel clauses

How dreary the moonlight is! robbed of all its tenderness and repose by the hard driving wind. The trees are harassed by that tossing motion, when they would like to be at rest; the shivering grass makes her quake with sympathetic cold; and the willows by the pool, bent low and white under that invisible harshness, seem agitated and helpless like herself. But she loves the scene the better for its sadness: there is some pity in it. It is not like that hard unfeeling happiness of lovers, flaunting in the eyes of misery. —George Eliot

For practice, you can collect and analyze memorable passages. Notice the variety of kinds of sentences and the positioning of ideas and rhythm in the sentences in the following passage.

(1) Cumulative sentence	(1) Sparkling eyes, blond hair, bare little arms and legs—that imp of a Tina darted across the room to open the glass doors of the balcony, her childish laughter escaping in muffled giggles. (2) She had started to turn the knob when a hoarse growl, like that of a wild beast surprised in his lair, quickly stopped her. (3) Petrified with fear, she turned around to stare into the room. (4) Everything was dark. —Adapted from Luigi Pirandello
(2) Loose sentence	
(3) Periodic sentence	
(4) Short, loose sentence	

You might recreate the structures and rhythms of the passage in some of your own writing, as in the following example.

(1) Cumulative sentence	(1) Sneakers pounding on hard flooring, our books clutched tightly for quick flight, we raced for the nearest door to escape the dusk of the locker room and the soap drawing of Coach Barnes decorating the shower, our gasps and chuckles nearly doubling us over. (2) Jay reached the exit first while we bobbed nervously behind. (3) Piercing the gloom behind us, a shrill whistle issuing from the faculty room we had just passed caused us to turn in unison. (4) There stood Coach Barnes.
(2) Loose sentence	
(3) Periodic sentence	
(4) Short, loose sentence	

EXERCISE F: Locating Models of Professional Writing. Find passages that you have read and enjoyed. Make copies of *three* passages with striking sentence patterns. Write down the author, title of the book, publisher, copyright date, and pages of each. Then examine the types of sentences used and any structural similarities or contrasts in series of sentences.

EXERCISE G: Using Professional Models. Use any one of the models that you found in Exercise F to write a passage of your own on any topic. Use the types of sentences that the writer used, and follow a pattern similar to that in the model.

APPLICATION: Experimenting with Types of Sentences and Patterns for Effects. Use one of the following suggestions or one of your own to write a passage of about ten sentences. Use some loose, balanced, periodic, and cumulative sentences, and try to use parallelism and contrast among the sentences in your passage. Some of your professional models can help you.

Your opinion on some school, local, or national issue
A setting where something ominous is about to happen
Someone well-known you would like to meet
An event that brought people racing from their homes
Some discovery that you hope becomes reality

Chapter 20

Logical Thinking in Writing

The meaning of your sentences depends not only on the words you choose but also on the connections you make between *groups* of words. Because a reader must be able to follow a series of ideas, you must lead clearly from one idea to the next and from one sentence to another. To do this, you must use transitions and other connecting words, while grouping your ideas in logical patterns.

This chapter explains the specific words—such as transitions and coordinating and subordinating words—that you can use to link ideas logically. It also illustrates the pitfalls that can weaken logical connections among ideas. Finally, it discusses some new patterns of reasoning—such as inductive and deductive logic, cause and effect arguments, and so on—that you can sometimes use to give your ideas a logical framework.

20.1 Using Coordination, Subordination, and Logical Patterns

When you write, you will usually have in mind not only the sentence you are writing at the moment but also the one you have just written, as well as the ideas for the sentence you are about to write. As you work through all these ideas, you should also have in mind the words that will establish logical connections between them. Transitions will help to make relationships among ideas clearer, and coordinating and subordinating words will act similarly to guide your reader through your thoughts. When you are presenting a series of ideas, you should also organize them in a logical order that will seem sensible and natural to your reader. This section discusses ways to connect whole series of ideas logically.

■ Using Transitions Between Ideas

Because a reader will expect to follow your thinking from sentence to sentence through a passage, you must establish clear connections between every important step of your thinking.

Use transitions to establish relationships among ideas and to clarify the order of ideas.

You may not need transitions in every sentence, but most passages will need *some* transitions to guide the reader. Without transitions, a passage can sound clumsy and its ideas can be difficult to follow. For example, in the following passage the thought is complete but the sentences sound disjointed and confusing.

Passage
without
transitions
Trains and buses take about the same amount of time to travel from one place to another. The rides are very different. Riding on a bus is much like riding in a car. A bus is nothing more than a huge car traveling down the highway with twenty-five back seats. A train chugs and hums in a rhythm all its own. Trains are more self-contained than buses. Riding on a train is like entering a new world, complete unto itself.

Transitions can help clarify relationships. Adding transitions to the preceding passage sharpens the points of comparison and contrast and makes the passage flow more smoothly.

Passage
with
transitions
Trains and buses take about the same amount of time to travel from one place to another. The rides, *however*, are very different. *First of all*, riding on a bus is much like riding in a car. *In fact*, a bus is nothing more than a huge car traveling down the highway with twenty-five back seats. *On the other hand*, a train chugs and hums in a rhythm all its own. *Furthermore*, trains are more self-contained than buses. Riding on a train is like entering a new world, complete unto itself.

Transitions can establish several different kinds of relationships among ideas, as the following chart indicates.

TRANSITIONS AND THEIR PURPOSES

To Show Time Relationship		To Show Comparison or Contrast	
first	later	however	nevertheless
second	during	unlike	on the other hand
third	earlier	yet	
next	at that moment	likewise	in like manner
now	eventually	similarly	
soon	meanwhile	instead	on the contrary
before	afterwards	in contrast	
last	after		
finally	then		

To Show Spatial Relationship		To Show Cause and Effect	
outside	before	thus	so
inside	ahead	then	because of
beyond	there	therefore	on account of
here	overhead	as a result	
near	beneath	consequently	
behind	above		

To Show Addition of Ideas		To Show Emphasis	
also	second	indeed	in other words
besides	as well	in fact	
too	in addition	even	especially
moreover	furthermore		
first			

To Show Examples			
for instance	as an illustration	that is	also
for example		namely	in particular

The following groups of sentences demonstrate the difference between two thoughts isolated without transitions and those same thoughts linked by an appropriate transition. Notice that the sentences without transitions sound awkward and even confusing.

WITHOUT TRANSITION: He knew how to be a brilliant host. His cats looked happy to see us.

WITH TRANSITION: He knew how to be a brilliant host. *Even* his cats
(showing emphasis)   looked happy to see us.

WITHOUT TRANSITION: Doris hates to sing in public. She has a beautiful voice.

WITH TRANSITION: Doris hates to sing in public. *And yet* she has a
(showing contrast)   beautiful voice.

WITHOUT TRANSITION: She was a regal-looking woman. She carried herself in a queenly way.

WITH TRANSITION: She was a regal-looking woman. *In particular,* she
(showing example)   carried herself in a queenly way.

EXERCISE A: Choosing Transitions for Sentences. Rewrite each of the following pairs of sentences. In every case, add a transition that best connects the ideas. Then state the relationship clarified by your transition.

EXAMPLE: I waited for Marcello to meet me in the bus station. He walked through the door looking quite worried.

              I waited for Marcello to meet me in the bus station. <u>Eventually</u>, he walked through the door looking quite worried.   time relationship

1. We sat dejectedly by the window. Rain poured in torrents.
2. The announcer told fans not to enter the field of play. He instructed youths along the sidelines to take seats.
3. Reacting to soaring prices of gasoline and oil, many people will purchase smaller cars. Some will rebuild older cars and modify them to improve efficiency.
4. An unexpected strike by air traffic controllers kept planes on the ground and caused long delays. My father was unable to attend my brother's graduation.
5. John took the dog for a walk. He left to go to the theater.
6. I was so angry at Angela that I could not speak. I hoped never to speak to her again.
7. The Prime Minister was quite contemptuous of treaties. He never honored them.
8. Prospect Hill's football team has earned considerable public attention. Newton High's team has received a great deal of coverage in the media.
9. Intermissions provide important opportunities for stage managers. They can use the time to oversee costume changes, or they can attend to the change of scenery.

10. Horoscopes have offered intriguing, sometimes astounding, predictions. Little scientific evidence exists to explain why some are accurate.

EXERCISE B: **Improving a Passage with Transitions.** Rewrite the following paragraph, adding transitions where necessary to clarify relationships among the ideas and pieces of information.

(1) Last year, Detective Leonardo solved the robbery case out at the McGraw mansion. (2) He interviewed and searched servants and neighbors. (3) There was no trace of the missing items. (4) He checked for criminal records among the people he interviewed. (5) He found one promising lead. (6) He conducted a surprise "second search" of the estate to look for more clues. (7) He knew where to go. (8) He found the stolen goods and arrested the groundskeeper.

■ Using Coordination and Subordination to Join Ideas

In addition to transitions, coordinating and subordinating words can connect ideas for the reader. Using *coordination*, you can join related and equally important words, phrases, and clauses within a single sentence. A compound sentence is the result of coordination—the joining of two independent but related clauses into a single statement by means of a coordinating conjunction such as *and* or *but*. Using *subordination*, you can join related *but unequal* ideas by means of subordinating conjunctions such as *when* or *because* to form a complex sentence. Subordination enables you to show how one idea qualifies, supports, or explains another.

Recognize the need for coordination and subordination to connect related ideas within sentences.

Just as using coordination and subordination helps to provide logical connections between ideas in a sentence, so can it also improve an entire group of sentences. In the following passage, for instance, the absence of coordinating and subordinating words makes the writing sound awkward and repetitious; the ideas do not flow smoothly from sentence to sentence.

Passage lacking coordination

Bikers may find long distance bicycle racing an exhilarating and exhausting sport. It is not meant for the beginner. It is not for the "pleasure biker" either.

and subor- dination	The preparation for a typical race over a fifty mile course is grueling. Bikers must build their endurance. They must ride for several hours every day. They must train in all kinds of weather all through the year. These hardships are all accepted in the love of the sport.

When coordinating and subordinating words are added, the reader can grasp logical connections more easily, and the passage sounds smoother.

Passage with ideas connected using coordination and subor-dination	Bikers may find long distance bicycle racing an exhilarating and exhausting sport, *although* it is neither for the beginner nor for the "pleasure biker." The preparation for a typical race over a fifty mile course is grueling *because* bikers must build their endurance; they must ride for several hours every day, *and* they must train in all kinds of weather, all through the year. These hardships are all accepted in the love of the sport.

Coordination.   *And, but,* and other coordinating conjunctions can join equally important ideas within a sentence, telling the reader that a relationship exists between these ideas.

Use coordinating words to join equal and related ideas in a compound sentence.

The following chart lists the most frequently used methods of coordination: coordinating conjunctions, correlative conjunctions, conjunctive adverbs, and semicolons. Notice that conjunctive adverbs are also transitions. When they join two main clauses in compound sentences, they must be used with semicolons. Semicolons can also be used without conjunctive adverbs to show a close relationship between ideas. Notice the different relationships that can be shown with certain coordinating words.

COORDINATING WORDS		
Comparison and Contrast		**Addition**
but	either . . . or	and
or	neither . . . nor	not only . . . but also
nor	not only . . . but also	both . . . and
yet	; however,	; in addition,
; (by itself)	; on the contrary,	; for example,
	; otherwise,	; moreover,

Time		Cause and Effect	
and	; (by itself)	for	; therefore,
not only . . . but also		so	; consequently,
Emphasis			
; indeed,			; in fact,

When you use these words, be aware of the various relationships that they can establish, such as addition, contrast, and cause and effect. Always be precise in choosing the method of establishing the link between your ideas. Notice that halting, unconnected statements can be improved through the use of coordinating words, as in the following examples.

UNCONNECTED: Two hundred people waited patiently. The line would not move.

WITH COORDINATION: (showing contrast) Two hundred people waited patiently, *but* the line would not move.

UNCONNECTED: Ticket holders were warned that seats might not be available to everyone. Some people gave up and left the line.

WITH COORDINATION: (showing result) Ticket holders· were warned that seats might not be available to everyone; *therefore,* some people gave up and left the line.

UNCONNECTED: The ticket sellers were inexperienced and slow. The patrons seemed to be taking their time at the box office.

WITH COORDINATION: (showing addition) *Not only* were the ticket sellers inexperienced and slow, *but* the patrons *also* seemed to be taking their time at the box office.

Subordination. When ideas are not of equal importance but are still closely related, you can use subordinating words to link them in a complex sentence. Rather than give equal weight to all your ideas, you can emphasize the main points by putting them in the main clauses, while you subordinate the less important ideas by putting them in dependent (adjective or adverb) clauses. You will thus indicate to the reader the relative weight of your various ideas and increase the variety and fluidity of your sentences.

Use subordinating words to join ideas in a complex sentence and to clarify the relationships between ideas of unequal importance.

The following chart shows that different subordinating words are useful in establishing different relationships between ideas.

SUBORDINATING WORDS			
Comparisons		**Addition or Identification**	
as though	just as	that	where
as if	as much as	which	whom
as well as		who	whose
Time Relationships		**Cause and Effect**	
after	until	because	whether
whenever	when	so that	provided that
before	while	in order that	
since	as soon as		
Contrasts			
though	whereas	although	

When you connect ideas with subordination, remember the different relationships that you can establish and choose the word that best clarifies the connection. Also, indicate to the reader the importance of an idea by making it the main clause and by putting limiting and identifying details in the adjective or adverb clause, as in the following examples. Notice that the less important idea is always the one placed immediately after the subordinating word.

UNCONNECTED: I wrote to my sister. She lives on the West Coast.

WITH SUBORDINATION: (adding detail) I wrote to my sister, *who* lives on the West Coast.

UNCONNECTED: I entered the room. I smelled something burning.

WITH SUBORDINATION: (showing time) *As soon as* I entered the room, I smelled something burning.

UNCONNECTED: Fire trucks were delayed by traffic. The fire spread to
an adjacent building.

WITH SUBORDINATION: *Because* fire trucks were delayed by traffic,
(showing cause and effect)   the fire spread to an adjacent building.

UNCONNECTED: He is hot-tempered. I enjoy his company.

WITH SUBORDINATION: *Although* he is hot-tempered, I enjoy his com-
(showing contrast)   pany.

Problems with Coordination and Subordination.   When you
use coordinating and subordinating words, you must guard
against a few specific problems. You should not try to join too
many clauses in a single sentence; *excessive* coordination or
subordination can confuse a reader. You must also make sure
that the clauses you connect go together sensibly; *illogical* coordination or subordination can muddle your meaning. And finally, you should not use coordination where subordination
would be clearer. *Inappropriate* coordination can weaken the
presentation of your ideas.

**Use coordination and subordination in moderation, in logical
places, and at appropriate times.**

Excessive coordination or subordination creates more connections than readers can follow comfortably in a single sentence. Too many coordinating or subordinating words result in
tangled relationships among ideas and too many compound
and compound-complex structures. Notice how the following
passage rambles because too many ideas are strung together
with *and*'s, *but*'s, and *so*'s, and too many subordinating words
make connections that are simply unnecessary.

Excessive use
of coordinat-
ing and sub-
ordinating
words

> I sat in the coffee shop *because* I was expecting
> Carol to meet me, *but* she was late *so* I stirred my
> coffee mechanically *and* wondered what was keeping
> Carol, *who* is always prompt, *and* I knew that the
> shop would soon close, *and so* I walked to a pay
> phone, *where* I could call her, *because* by now I was
> worried.

Reworded with an appropriate number of coordinating and
subordinating words, the passage is easier to follow and
sounds less awkward.

Appropriate coordination and subordination	I sat in the coffee shop expecting Carol to meet me, *but* she was late. Mechanically, I stirred my coffee *and* wondered what was keeping her. She is always prompt. *Because* I knew that the shop would soon close *and because* by now I was worried, I walked to a pay phone to call her.

Illogical coordination or subordination can also burden a reader and obscure your meaning. When joining ideas in a compound sentence, you must make sure that the two ideas are equal and related. Then, you must choose the appropriate conjunction. Do not use *and* if you mean *but,* as in the following example.

WEAK USE OF COORDINATION:	Nobody expected Roger even to finish the race, *and* he surprised everyone by placing third.
IMPROVED COORDINATION:	Nobody expected Roger even to finish the race, *but* he surprised everyone by placing third.

Similarly, when you use subordination to form a complex sentence, you must set up a logical relationship between the clauses. Your main idea should be in the main clause, and your dependent clause should contain an idea that does indeed modify or explain the main clause. In addition, you should choose the subordinating word that most clearly establishes a logical connection so that the relationship between the clauses will be precise and sensible.

ILLOGICAL SUBORDINATION: (main idea subordinated)	Because her leaps and turns finally reached perfection, she studied under Dame Weston.
LOGICAL SUBORDINATION: (main idea in main clause)	Her leaps and turns finally reached perfection because she studied under Dame Weston.
ILLOGICAL SUBORDINATION: (inappropriate word)	Janice received an "A" for the course *since* she had been ill during the term.
LOGICAL SUBORDINATION: (appropriate word)	Janice received an "A" for the course *although* she had been ill during the term.

Still another problem involves depending too heavily on coordination to link related ideas and overlooking the opportunity to express more precise relationships through subordination. For example, in the following sentence, the writer has simply joined two related ideas together in a compound sentence without deciding whether one idea is more important than the other. The complete idea can be sharpened by subordinating one clause to show a cause and effect relationship.

WEAK COORDINATION: I exercised regularly for a month, *and* I made the tennis team for the first time in my life.

CLEAR SUBORDINATION: *Because* I exercised regularly for a month, I made the tennis team for the first time in my life.

EXERCISE C: **Using Coordination.** Rewrite each of the following pairs of sentences, joining equal and related ideas. Underline the coordinating word that you use to connect each pair.

EXAMPLE: Hastings yelled at the top of his lungs. We could not hear him over the sirens.

Hastings yelled at the top of his lungs, <u>but</u> we could not hear him over the sirens.

1. Richard must pitch our team to victory. We will be eliminated from the county championship game.
2. Michele is two inches taller than her mother. She is smaller than her sister.
3. Dr. Martin discovered a new technique for formulating molecules. She was awarded a government grant to continue her research.
4. Machiavelli urged the princes not to oppress the people. He believed that a prince should do whatever is necessary to retain his power and position.
5. Simon arrived late for the performance and realized that he had forgotten his glasses. He had forgotten his ticket.
6. Henry VIII married Catherine of Aragon. He divorced her to marry Anne Boleyn.
7. Jill walked to the field house. She asked to sign up for the soccer team.
8. Casey must construct a four-foot fence around the pond. A neighbor's child might accidentally wander near and fall in.
9. Selfishness is unattractive. It is contagious.
10. Dr. Werner was thankful and relieved to find a taxi. He tipped the driver handsomely.

EXERCISE D: **Using Subordination.** Rewrite each of the following pairs of sentences, using subordination to join unequal but related ideas. Underline the subordinating word that you use to join each pair.

EXAMPLE: My cousin lived in a noisy dorm at the university. He had trouble studying in his room.

My cousin, <u>who</u> lived in a noisy dorm at the university, had trouble studying in his room.

1. The airliner began to lose altitude rapidly. Passengers panicked.
2. My sister stepped through the door into the darkened room. Everyone jumped out and yelled, "Surprise!"
3. Modern dramas often contain scores of characters. Classical Greek plays included no more than a handful.
4. Thomas could not locate his keys. He became angry.
5. A specialist will treat only a certain set of problems. An internist practices general medicine.
6. The storm had passed and flood waters had receded. Rescue teams flew into the stricken valley.
7. The politician could not win the party's nomination. She was popular.
8. Mature trees can survive almost any weather condition or change. Saplings are much more vulnerable.
9. A quiche can turn out lumpy, or it can even "fall" in the oven. Use an electric blender to mix your ingredients.
10. We finally could sit down to dinner. The telephone rang.

EXERCISE E: Correcting Problems with Coordination and Subordination. Rewrite each of the following passages to correct excessive, illogical, or inappropriate use of coordinating or subordinating words.

1. Terry had reservations for a flight that was going to Houston, but first he had to catch a bus to Chicago, and since the bus was late, he missed the plane as a result.
2. After you check your gas gauge, start the engine and engage your gears.
3. The sun was brighter on the front of the building, and we decided to take the picture on the front steps.
4. The Pope recognized Petrarch's accomplishments as a poet, but Petrarch was designated "poet laureate."
5. Our teacher assigned us an additional problem until we could have more practice.
6. Since a fuse blew out, he connected two wires inside the television.
7. When my brother and I went hiking in the mountains so that we might enjoy ourselves, we wanted to hike fifty

miles, but not only did we find the hiking strenuous but also the weather became threatening.

8. The mayor instituted a curfew because we could not leave the house after 10:00 p.m.

9. Kristin was happy that Cynthia had offered to drive her into town, and she was not too sure whether or not to accept because she had planned to collect pond water along her walk so that she could bring paramecium samples to biology class when it met on Monday so she declined the offer even though she would have enjoyed Cynthia's company.

10. Our star player was benched for the remainder of the game, and the rest of us managed a slim victory.

■ Using Expected Orders

In addition to using transitions and coordinating and subordinating words to make your ideas flow smoothly, you can establish logical patterns to direct a reader through a series of ideas or items in a sentence or passage. You can structure a series of events by relating them in chronological order or by describing an object or scene by the position of items in spatial order. You can compare and contrast two items or set forth a series of reasons in the order of their importance. These logical orders are basic patterns of thinking that readers will recognize and follow easily, whether in a single sentence or in a series of sentences.

> **Whenever possible, use logical orders to make a series of ideas easier to follow.**

Your reader will expect you to maintain certain well-known patterns of thought when you present certain kinds of information. A series of events, for example, should be presented in the order in which they occurred. Notice the difference between the confusing sentence that fails to follow logical order and the meaningful one that does follow logical order.

ILLOGICAL ORDER: We ran for cover; rain began to fall; and the skies darkened.

LOGICAL ORDER: The skies darkened; rain began to fall; and we
(chronological order)   ran for cover.

An especially useful logical order is order of importance. In the next example, the suggestions for quitting smoking are related in no particular pattern; however, the revision makes more sense by listing the points in ascending order, from least to most important.

ILLOGICAL ORDER: To quit smoking, one can hold fast to self-discipline, chew gum as a substitute, and avoid the temptation for "just one."

LOGICAL ORDER: To quit smoking, one can chew gum as a substi-
(order of importance) tute, avoid the temptation for "just one," and hold fast to self-discipline.

When you are presenting a group of related ideas in a series of sentences, logical order becomes even more important. To avoid confusing and losing the reader, you should set up a logical order and carry the reader through by observing that order.

For example, to present visual details you should arrange them in a clear spatial order, such as from top to bottom, left to right, near to far, and so on. In the first of the following groups of sentences no logical arrangement exists and the reader must pause and reread the sentences. The revision, however, guides the reader from the bottom of the building to the top.

ILLOGICAL ORDER: Strips of shining steel gleamed like icicles on the upper floors of the building. The first twenty stories were quite ordinary—undecorated gray granite. The whole structure narrowed into a hat-like tower at the top, trimmed with rainbow arcs piled one on top of another. As the eye climbed higher, the architecture became increasingly ornate and fanciful.

LOGICAL ORDER: The first twenty stories of the building were quite
(spatial order) ordinary—undecorated gray granite. But as the eye climbed higher, the architecture became increasingly ornate and fanciful. Strips of shining steel gleamed like icicles on the upper floors of the building. The whole structure narrowed into a hat-like tower at the top, trimmed with rainbow arcs piled one on top of another.

You can use other logical orders as well. To compare and contrast two items, you should establish a consistent pattern, such as item A—item B, item A—item B, or else item A—item

A, item B—item B. To explain a process, present the steps in an order that the reader would logically follow were he or she to repeat the process.

EXERCISE F: Establishing Logical Patterns. Each of the following items contains information without a logical pattern. Choose a pattern for each, and then rewrite the item. Finally, identify the type of order you have chosen. In some cases, you may have to add words or make slight alterations as you revise the order of ideas.

1. I rose from my desk, finished my homework, and turned on the television.
2. Knowing that his big brother would accompany him to camp, Arnold felt proud, surprised, even glad.
3. On our drive across the country, we especially enjoyed Nevada, Pennsylvania, Montana, and Illinois.
4. Edward mixed the ingredients thoroughly, set the pan in the oven, assembled the milk, eggs, flour, and sugar, and poured the batter into a cake pan.
5. A dramatic economic slowdown, a brutal civil war, and foreign censure beset the nation almost immediately.
6. I could not stand my new dorm room. The floors were covered with linoleum of a faded floral pattern; several corners were chipped or upturned. The ceiling needed painting, and a single uncovered light bulb cast a clinical glare over the rest of the room. The walls were painted a sickly green, and the one small window was bare of shades or blinds.
7. The squirrels darted in ten different directions. We startled them when we opened the cellar door. They looked at us for a split second in nervous alertness.
8. The annual town meeting dealt with topics from the absurdly petty to the issue that frightened most residents. Almost everyone had something to say about the gruesome statistic: One household in three had been robbed or vandalized within the past six months. A few people spoke of the need for street repairs. One elderly gentleman reprimanded the Chief of Police for not finding a lost cat. Several people raised the issue of power shortages, which have become more frequent since summer and which have caused food to spoil.
9. Finally, he decided to run for office. Months before the primaries, his colleagues in the State House urged James Monroe to become a candidate. He knew that his credentials were sound, and support seemed available. At first he

discounted the notion, but slowly the advice of his friends and family began to sound plausible.
10. Skicrafts are engineered to glide over the surface with minimal water resistance. The major difference between skicrafts and Boston whalers lies in their purpose. Boston whalers are engineered for capacity. Designed for speed, skicrafts are excellent for racing. Unlike skicrafts, whalers hold a number of passengers, and their most popular uses are for moderate-speed cruising and for fishing.

APPLICATION: **Checking Your Writing for Clear, Logical Connections.** Select one of the following topics and write a brief passage of 150 to 200 words. When you have finished, read it over very carefully with the following questions in mind. Have you linked your ideas smoothly from sentence to sentence by means of transitions? Have you joined clauses containing related ideas with either coordinating or subordinating words? Have you used a moderate amount of coordination and subordination and have you used both logically and appropriately? Where you present a series of items or ideas, have you followed a logical order?

Describe the view from your front window.
Explain a process with which you are familiar (how to change a tire, put on makeup, paint a room, and so on).
Compare and contrast two magazine advertisements for competing products.
Offer reasons for voting for or against something.
Discuss a chain of events that led to a particular historical event.

Using Correct Forms of Logic in Your Writing   20.2

Once you feel confident about connecting and organizing your ideas within and between sentences, you can think about using whole patterns of reasoning as you develop a set of ideas.

In this section, you will explore new ways of presenting your ideas, and you will learn to avoid weaknesses in reasoning. Finally, you will examine the work of professional writers to give you ideas for your own compositions.

■ Thinking About the Direction of Your Ideas

In your writing, you will often have occasion to use three patterns of reasoning to provide a logical framework for your ideas: *induction*, which leads from specific information to a general conclusion; *deduction*, which leads from a general truth to a specific instance of that truth; and *cause and effect*.

Induction.   One method of presenting your main ideas and supporting evidence logically is the inductive approach.

Use an inductive approach by presenting concrete evidence before stating your conclusion or main point.

An inductive approach relies on evidence—facts, statistics, examples—that point to a logical conclusion. For example, if your phone is out of order, and your neighbor's phone is not working, if the people behind you have lost phone service, and the family across the street cannot use their phone, you might conclude *inductively* that phone service in your area has been cut off. You cannot prove your conclusion absolutely because you cannot sample every phone in the community, but you can be reasonably certain that your conclusion is correct. Induction allows for a fair sampling of evidence without complete, total proof.

In writing, you can sometimes arrange your information according to the inductive approach. Your passage might present a body of evidence or other related information, and your final sentence might present the conclusion that you reached on the basis of the evidence. The inductive conclusion, then, is usually a general truth based on specific supporting evidence.

Notice in the following passage how the first three sentences present evidence about student performance at different room temperatures. The last sentence presents a conclusion reached on the basis of the preceding information. The reasoning of this writer follows the inductive approach because it leads the reader through specific evidence to a general conclusion. Notice also that the evidence does not include *every* room in the school, only a fair sampling.

Inductive approach	The students in Room 121 seem to work more briskly at a temperature of 70°F. (21.1°C) than at the temperature of 75°F. (23.9°C) to which they had previously been accustomed. In Room 120, class discussions have become more animated at a room temperature of 65°F. (18.3°C) than they had been at 75°F.
Evidence	

Conclusion

(23.9°C). And in Room 113, test scores improved significantly at a daily temperature of 68°F. (20°C). As a result of this evidence, the superintendent of schools has concluded that moderately lower temperatures improve student performance.

Deduction. Another approach to presenting your ideas and information logically is the deductive method of reasoning. Deduction proceeds in the opposite direction from induction: While induction begins with specific cases and leads to general principles, deduction begins with general principles and leads to specific cases. You use deductive reasoning whenever you apply your knowledge and past experience to understanding a new experience. In your life so far, you have already observed many laws of nature, patterns of behavior, and other general principles that allow you to predict or deduce what will probably happen in a particular case under certain circumstances. For example, you know that the prefix *semi-* means *half;* when you come across an unfamiliar word beginning with *semi-*, you are able to *deduce* that the word means something that is half of something else.

Deductive reasoning, in the purest sense, is primarily a tool of thought, a way of applying known principles to new or unknown phenomena. But you can also use a form of the deductive method in your writing. You can begin with a basic principle, a generally accepted truth that does not need to be proven. You can then follow it with one or more specific examples that fulfill the pattern of the general principle. Finally, you can draw the conclusion that the specific examples all represent instances of the general truth.

Use a deductive approach by establishing a general principle and then drawing conclusions about specific examples of that principle.

In the following series of statements, a general observation about basketball players is followed by a reference to a specific basketball player. The conclusion predicts the behavior of the particular player, based upon the general observation.

GENERAL PRINCIPLE: Professional basketball players usually retire well before their fortieth birthdays.

SPECIFIC EXAMPLE: Matt Eliott, a professional basketball player, is thirty-eight years old.

CONCLUSION: Therefore, Matt Eliott's career as a professional basketball player is probably nearing its end.

If the reader accepts the truth of the general principle, and if the specific example fulfills the conditions stated in the general principle, then the conclusion can be logically deduced. Here are some other examples of the deductive method.

GENERAL PRINCIPLE: Oak is a golden brown hardwood with a pronounced grain.

SPECIFIC EXAMPLE: My desk is made of a hardwood that is golden brown and has a pronounced grain.

CONCLUSION: My desk is made of oak.

GENERAL PRINCIPLE: Most college teachers who hold the rank of professor have a doctorate.

SPECIFIC EXAMPLE: My next door neighbor is a professor at the City University.

CONCLUSION: My next door neighbor probably has a doctorate.

In using deduction, you should note that in some cases—with facts of nature, for example—the general truth is always and absolutely true. In other cases—with observations about human behavior, for example—the general truth is true *most* of the time. In these cases, as in the statements about the basketball player and the college professor, the conclusion should not be expressed as an absolute truth but rather as a probability.

In the following passage, you can see how the pattern of deductive reasoning can be used to structure the presentation of ideas.

Deductive approach: general principle

Specific examples

Conclusions made by applying the general principle to the specific examples

Sound travels at the speed of 1,080 feet per second, a rate much slower than the speed of light. Perhaps the best example of the comparatively slow speed of sound is found during an electrical storm. When the storm is directly overhead, you see a flash of lightning a split second before you hear the thunderclap. When the storm is further away, there is an even greater gap between the lightning and the thunder. Given the knowledge about the speed of sound and light, you can estimate the distance of the storm by counting the number of seconds between the lightning and the thunder. Since a mile is 5,280 feet, and sound travels at a rate of less than 1,100 feet per second, it takes slightly less than five seconds for the sound of thunder to travel one mile. You can also tell how fast the storm is approaching or moving away by paying attention to changes in the length of time between the lightning flash and thunderclap.

Cause and Effect.   *Cause and effect* is another pattern of reasoning that can help you establish order among your ideas. By stating that one condition or situation "causes" another and that another condition "causes" still another, you can set up a logical pattern of reasoning for your reader to follow.

Use a cause and effect approach by pointing out the logical cause and effect relationships among the ideas you are presenting.

Cause and effect reasoning is one of the most basic elements of logic. It appears most frequently in scientific and historical writing, but it can also be used in a number of other writing situations, as you can see in the following example.

STATEMENT OF CAUSE AND EFFECT: As a result of the injury that disabled the star quarterback for the first part of the season, our football team got off to a slow start and lost its first four games.

In using cause and effect reasoning to structure your writing, it is important to establish clear and convincing connections between the causes and effects. It is also important to remember that something that *precedes* something else does not necessarily *cause* it. Finally, you should feel free to mention the effect *before* the cause, as in the following example.

EFFECT STATED BEFORE CAUSE: Our football team got off to a slow start this year and lost its first four games largely as a result of the injury that disabled the star quarterback during the first part of the season.

The cause and effect structure does not need to be limited to a single sentence. You can develop a cause and effect pattern of reasoning throughout several sentences, or even throughout an entire passage. Notice how the following passage is developed largely through cause and effect reasoning. The first two sentences are each cause and effect statements. They are followed by a series of sentences that present a more gradual shift from cause to effect.

Cause
Effect   Whenever I am given time to pose for a photograph, I always end up looking frozen, with glazed eyes and a strained smile. On the other hand, when

Cause	I am caught in an absolutely candid shot, my mouth
Effect	is always gaping open and my eyes are closed in
	mid-blink. The happy medium seems to be a shot in
Cause	which I am given about one second's warning. That
Effect	second gives me time to shut my mouth and open my
	eyes, but not enough time to arrange my face into my
	usual painful grin. I manage to look natural but not
	uncouth, poised but not rigid.

EXERCISE A: **Using Induction.** Write a passage of 100 to 150 words in which you use an inductive approach to reach one of the following conclusions.

1. Ultimately, people pay for wrongdoings they commit.
2. Any ride in an amusement park will make me ill.
3. Well-trained dogs function as protectors for their owners.
4. Last-minute studying leads to academic dissatisfaction.
5. The police officers in our neighborhood are reasonable people.

EXERCISE B: **Using Deduction.** Use the deductive method to lead from one of the following general principles to a specific example of the principle and conclusions about the example.

1. Liquids freeze if the temperature drops sufficiently.
2. Cleanliness is important for good health.
3. In murder mystery novels, the most obvious suspect is seldom the real murderer.
4. Plants must be raised under the proper conditions if they are to grow.
5. Solids can be made to dissolve more quickly in water if the water is heated.

EXERCISE C: **Establishing Cause and Effect Relationships.** Rewrite both of the following series of statements to emphasize the connections between causes and effects.

1. The costs of construction have gone up tremendously. Fewer new buildings are being built. The prices of houses are escalating. People are finding it more difficult to buy their own homes. The demand for rental housing is increasing. Rents are rapidly going up.
2. The weather was hot and dry. A camper dropped a hot coal in a pile of leaves. A fire started. There was a high wind. The fire spread to the trees in the forest. The forest was almost entirely burnt down. Later that year, it rained heavily. Flooding occurred. There were no trees to hold the ground in place. There were many mudslides. A number of houses were swept away.

■ Avoiding Illogical Support for Your Ideas

Whenever you construct a series of ideas, you must provide all the information and mental connections that your reader will need to understand you. To write clearly you need to recognize and avoid a number of gaps, pitfalls, and errors in logic.

Avoiding False Assumptions.   Whenever you present a series of ideas, you risk overlooking a point that your reader might have to know to understand what you are saying. *You* know what you mean to say, but your reader can know only what you actually write. Thus you must not skip important steps or assume that a few words about a vital idea will convey the full meaning you have in mind.

> Avoid making false assumptions by clarifying all ideas and providing all information that your reader needs to follow your thinking.

A false assumption about the ideas and information a reader needs leaves a gap in the development of your ideas. It forces the reader to guess what you had in mind when you jumped from one idea to another.

To avoid this problem, you should check your writing for any unstated details or ideas that require explanation. To do this, you must reread your work from the reader's point of view. Pretend that you know nothing about the topic, and see if your sentences provide all the information and reasoning necessary to understand the ideas being presented.

In the following passage, a writer has left out an important connection. Notice that the first sentence mentions Mr. Jackson's appointment as vice president in charge of Marketing. The second sentence reports that the board of directors was not confident about the appointment because of Mr. Jackson's "record." The writer, in assuming that the reader knows about Mr. Jackson's record, has been negligent. The unstated idea creates a gap between the two sentences.

Unstated idea   Mr. Jackson was appointed vice president in charge of Marketing at the August meeting of the board of directors. Because of Mr. Jackson's record, board opinion was split evenly, but the president's vote broke the tie, and Mr. Jackson was promoted.

To correct a false assumption, you must add the ideas or information necessary to enable the reader to make all important mental connections and comprehend your meaning fully.

In a revision of the passage about Mr. Jackson, the writer has corrected the assumption by adding the connecting information.

Necessary information provided

Mr. Jackson was appointed vice president in charge of Marketing at the August meeting of the board of directors. *His achievement record, however, raised some doubts about his abilities. During his previous tenure as director of Marketing at the branch office, sales had dropped rather sharply in his area.* Because of Mr. Jackson's record, board opinion was split evenly, but the president's vote broke the tie, and Mr. Jackson was promoted.

Avoiding Hasty Generalizations.   A hasty generalization is an idea that is stated without sufficient information or reasoning to support it. Like false assumptions, hasty generalizations create gaps in the logical structure of your writing and therefore weaken what you say. Unless you are absolutely certain of your facts, try to avoid such words as *always, never, all,* and *none,* which weaken statements by leaving no room for exceptions.

Avoid hasty generalizations in your writing by stating your points precisely and backing them up with the necessary support.

By definition, a hasty generalization is untrue because it overlooks exceptions. Because of its lack of precision, it can misrepresent your actual intent by overstating the point you are trying to make.

To determine if you have written a hasty generalization, you must ask yourself if the idea is true as you have stated it. If not, it may need specific details or some qualifying words to allow for exceptions. Notice in the following passage that the statement *Nobody seems to care any more* is a hasty generalization. Some people *do* care. Also, the statement is too vague to add any helpful information to the other ideas in the passage.

Passage with hasty generalization

What has happened to that old slogan, "Service with a smile"? Nobody seems to care any more. It is very frustrating to bring a television set to a repair shop, to be kept waiting for fifteen minutes, and then to be told impatiently to leave it with no assurance of when it will be ready.

To improve the preceding passage, the hasty generalization can be left out or it can be altered. Whenever you are faced with the choice of omitting or rewriting a hasty generalization, try first to rewrite it. Your generalization may be a vague, hasty version of a worthwhile idea that could be valid if it were expressed in more precise terms.

In the preceding passage, the word *nobody* can be made specific. Perhaps the writer has a number of tradespeople or shopkeepers in mind. Also, the phrase *to care* might be rewritten in more concrete terms. Notice in the following example how the revision of a hasty generalization can clarify the message of the whole passage.

Statements made more precise	What has happened to that old slogan, "Service with a smile"? Too many tradespeople seem overworked and resentful. It is very frustrating to bring a television set to a repair shop, to be kept waiting for fifteen minutes, and then to be told impatiently to leave it with no assurance of when it will be ready.

Avoiding Non Sequiturs.   One of the most jarring and confusing mistakes in logic is the logical fallacy called a non sequitur. A non sequitur is an idea or a conclusion that does not follow logically from the preceding ideas.

Avoid non sequiturs by making sure that each new idea you present follows logically from the previous ideas you have presented.

The following passage contains a statement that simply does not belong in any logical sense. The third sentence is a non sequitur because it is not logically connected to the preceding ideas.

Passage containing a non sequitur	Teenagers who repeatedly fail their courses often become dropouts. They are then less likely to find satisfying work than their classmates who do graduate. My second cousin, who never finished the tenth grade, ended up as a burglar.

The first two statements in the preceding passage may be accurate, but the last sentence does not follow logically. It introduces irrelevant personal information and makes a misleading connection between dropping out of school and becoming a criminal.

To correct a non sequitur, you must eliminate it entirely, realizing that it is an unworkable idea. You may, however, replace it with a more reasonable idea, such as the one that follows.

Non sequitur eliminated	Teenagers who repeatedly fail their courses often become dropouts. They are then less likely to find satisfying work than their classmates who do graduate. As a rule, dropouts are eligible for fewer jobs and are also likely to earn less money over a lifetime than high school graduates.

Avoiding Begging the Question. Begging the question is the term generally used for the logical fallacy of circular reasoning. You "beg the question" or argue in circles when you simply restate the question instead of answering it.

Avoid begging the question by not mistaking restatements of questions for their answers.

Begging the question is most likely to occur when a writer is attempting to use the pattern of cause and effect reasoning. In begging the question, the writer ends up saying something like *I am happy because I am contented* or *He is wealthy because he has a lot of money.* You must answer any question you pose and not simply express it in slightly different language.

The following statement begs the question.

BEGGING THE QUESTION: I like *Star Wars* because it is my favorite movie.

In the preceding statement, the writer has not answered the question—has not given the reader a real reason for liking *Star Wars.* The circular reasoning can be avoided by giving a real reason for liking the movie.

CIRCULAR REASONING ELIMINATED: I like *Star Wars* because it contains exciting adventures, colorful characters, brilliant special effects, and many funny moments.

EXERCISE D: **Checking the Logic of Ideas.** Some of the following items contain ideas that are developed illogically or expressed unsoundly. Identify any errors in thinking as false assumptions, hasty generalizations, non sequiturs, or begging the question. If you believe the item to be logical, write *correct* on your paper.

1. Jerry ran well in the race, but he lost because of what his opponent did to him. Jerry's coach made an official com-

plaint to the Athletic Board, but the Board voted to sustain the other athlete's victory.

2. Statistics show that automobile accidents have increased on Highway 41. Among these accidents are those involving tractor trailers. My brother-in-law owns a tractor trailer that he often drives on Highway 41.

3. Trees do not grow above altitudes of 10,000 feet. It should not be surprising that Tibet contains no trees. The entire country is more than 10,000 feet above sea level.

4. Cheating is not right because it is immoral.

5. Newspapers always exaggerate stories in order to create sensations and increase their circulation.

6. Senator Allbright voted against that bill because he was opposed to it.

7. The speed limit was lowered to 55 miles per hour in 1973. Ever since the speed limit was changed, traffic fatalities have dropped sharply. It seems reasonable to conclude that there is a connection between slower driving speeds and the decline in highway deaths.

8. I tried to understand why Mary had left the city so quickly. And then I remembered what she had said to me about her brother. I realized why she had had to leave in such a hurry.

9. People who trap lobsters do not begin to catch full-grown lobsters in Maine until the second half of the summer. The lobsters hibernate until that time in soft shells and most of the lobsters that turn up in lobster traps are not full sized. The coast of Maine is especially attractive during the second half of the summer.

10. All television commercials insult the intelligence of the viewer. Commercial writers always assume that their audiences are not intelligent, and they always aim their commercials to appeal to the lowest common denominator.

EXERCISE E: **Revising for Logic.** Take another look at the items in which you found errors in logic in Exercise D. Rewrite them to form logical statements.

■ Using Professional Models

Professional writers often use logical approaches such as induction and deduction to report the facts behind a conclusion or observation or to develop some concept or theory. As you come across such logical presentations, take time to examine them. Notice if the writer has used an inductive or deductive line of reasoning, a cause and effect arrangement, or some other pattern that seems clear, deliberate, and precise.

Study the specific ways professional writers use logical thinking to find models for your own writing.

Viktor Frankl's book *Man's Search for Meaning,* for example, contains many passages developed through logical thinking. In one, the author tells how he believes that his friend became ill and died in a concentration camp. Notice in the following passage that the line of reasoning is deductive. The passage begins with a main point: A person's "loss of hope and courage can have a deadly effect." The information that follows this premise adds details about his friend's despair over the fact that the camp was not liberated when the prisoners had expected it to be. The passage ends with a conclusion that ties together the opening statement and the specific information about the friend. The inmate lost his hope and courage and fell victim to an illness that caused his death.

Main point	Those who know how close the connection is between the state of mind of a man—his courage and hope, or lack of them—and the state of immunity of his body will understand that the sudden loss of hope
Specific example	and courage can have a deadly effect. The ultimate cause of my friend's death was that the expected liberation did not come and he was severely disappointed. This suddenly lowered his body's resistance against the latent typhus infection. His faith in the
Conclusion	future and his will to live had become paralyzed and his body fell victim to illness. —Viktor E. Frankl

In another passage, the author uses an effect-cause arrangement to illustrate psychological conditions among inmates in a concentration camp. Notice that a statement of effect is followed by a statement of cause. Then, a statement of effect appears followed by two sentences describing a cause. Finally, the first two effects are summarized in a concluding effect, and the first two causes are summarized in a concluding cause. The passage proceeds logically, allowing the reader to follow a clear mental pattern.

Effect	The camp inmate was frightened of making decisions and of taking any sort of initiative whatsoever.
Cause	This was the result of a strong feeling that fate was one's master, and that one must not try to influence it in any way, but instead let it take its own course.
Effect	In addition, there was a great apathy, which contrib-

Cause

Concluding
effect

Concluding
cause

uted in no small part to the feelings of the prisoner. At times, lightning decisions had to be made, decisions which spelled life or death. The prisoner would have preferred to let fate make the choice for him. This escape from commitment was most apparent when a prisoner had to make the decision for or against an escape attempt. In those minutes in which he had to make up his mind—and it was always a question of minutes—he suffered the tortures of hell. Should he make the attempt to flee? Should he take the risk? —Viktor E. Frankl

If you collect good examples of logical reasoning, you will have a file of models and ideas for your own work.

EXERCISE F: **Locating Professional Models.** Find books and magazines that contain good models of logical arguments: for example, scientific books, journals, magazines, and nonfiction books on social issues. As you skim this material, look for ideas or arguments developed by induction, by deduction, and by cause and effect.

Copy three passages that you decide are good examples of clearly logical presentations and label the approaches used. Document your sources, recording author, title, and page number(s).

APPLICATION: **Using a Logical Plan in Your Own Writing.** Choose one of the following topics for a passage of 150 to 300 words. You may need to identify your main idea in one sentence, and you will have to gather information—facts, examples, reasons, and so on—to present your ideas logically.

Use an inductive or deductive approach, or arrange your ideas according to a cause and effect pattern. Give the reader the information needed to establish all necessary mental connections. Try not to write any hasty generalizations, non sequiturs, or other errors. To help you choose a logical plan, use any of the professional models that you found in Exercise F or that you read in the section.

Proper behavior in student meetings
The results of an opinion survey and a specific conclusion implied by the results
Patterns of human behavior as they are presented on television situation comedies
The reasons for the current standing of a team
Fluctuations in supermarket prices (gasoline prices, record prices, and so on) over a period of time

Chapter 21

Effective Paragraphs

This chapter explains the essential features of paragraphs and the problems to avoid when writing them. It discusses methods of planning, writing, and revising paragraphs and ways of finding your own workable approaches to writing.

21.1 Key Features of Effective Paragraphs

The standard paragraph is a unit of thought that has a main idea and an explanation or elaboration of that main idea. The main idea of the paragraph is usually expressed in a topic sentence. Supporting information develops the main idea. Effective paragraphs include several other features as well: unity of ideas, logical development, and smoothness and flow created by such devices as transitions, repetitions of main words, parallelism, and concluding sentences. This section explores the differences between strong paragraphs and weak paragraphs, between effective features and ineffective features, to show you what to strive for in writing your own paragraphs.

■ The Topic Sentence

The topic sentence indicates to the reader the limits of the paragraph by telling what the paragraph is about. It also suggests the purpose and tone of the paragraph. Learning to recognize topic sentences and the problems that can weaken them can improve your own writing.

Features of Good Topic Sentences.   A topic sentence should identify for the reader the significance of the entire paragraph.

The topic sentence expresses the main idea and defines the scope of the paragraph.

The topic sentence should indicate the topic of the paragraph and the range of ideas covered. It should also give the reader an idea of the purpose of the paragraph and of the attitude of the writer.

The position of the topic sentence will vary from paragraph to paragraph, although a high percentage of paragraphs begin with their topic sentences. A topic sentence may come first in the paragraph to prepare the reader for the supporting ideas that follow. It may come after some introductory statements and then lead into the supporting ideas. Or it may end the paragraph and act as a summary statement or completing remark. Some specialized paragraphs may not have stated topic sentences. Instead, the main idea may be implied throughout the paragraph. (For more information on specialized paragraphs, see Section 22.2.)

The following paragraph begins with its topic sentence, which shapes the reader's expectations for the information that will follow.

TOPIC
SENTENCE

Supporting
information

There are all manner of snows, both cruel and kind.
There is the snow that falls like needles and drifts in hard ridges on the dead cornfields, is bitterly cold, coming down from the northwest and driving into the earth like knives. And there is the snow that people think of as *snow*, that actually comes very seldom, but is the symbol of all snows, the childhood miracle that remains forever an image larger than all the dreary, bitter or halfhearted snows that come before and after. —Josephine Johnson

Unsuitable Topic Sentences.   To guide the reader's understanding, a topic sentence must cover the paragraph's range of ideas. If it covers too much information or if it fails to cover some portion of the paragraph, the topic sentence can mislead the reader.

Recognize topic sentences that are too general or too narrow, and revise them to suit the supporting information in the paragraph.

A weak sentence may be *too broad* or *too vague*. If a topic sentence is too general, it will lead the reader to expect more ideas than are actually covered in the paragraph. If the paragraph about snows, for instance, had begun with this sentence—*There are all manner of snows and rains*—this topic sentence would be too comprehensive. The reader would expect a discussion of rains, an idea not developed in the paragraph.

To correct an overly general topic sentence, you should eliminate any words and ideas that exceed the scope of the paragraph. Using more exact words or including fewer ideas can limit the main idea to the supporting information the writer intends to use in the paragraph. For instance, eliminating *rains* from the topic sentence about snows and reshaping the statement can make it appropriate for the rest of the paragraph.

A weak topic sentence may instead be *too narrow;* that is, it may fail to express the entire range of ideas in a paragraph and thus be unhelpful or even confusing. If the paragraph about snows had begun with this sentence—*Some types of snows are cruel*—this topic sentence would be unsuitably limiting because it fails to mention *kind* snows, which are also described in the paragraph.

To correct an overly narrow topic sentence, you should adjust the sentence to make sure that it states the main idea of the whole paragraph by adding the overlooked ideas. In the paragraph about snows, the topic sentence could be expanded to include both *cruel* and *kind* snows.

EXERCISE A: **Recognizing Good Topic Sentences.** Read each of the following paragraphs to find the topic sentence. Write the topic sentence of each paragraph on your paper.

(1) Everyone was agreed that Lincoln was a homely man. The President himself made jokes about it. He was gawky, and his voice was high-pitched and unimpressive. He cared little about appearances; as often as not his clothes did not fit. He made no pretense to fine family. He was the son of a restless farmer who had wandered from Kentucky, where Lincoln was born, to Illinois, where he spent most of his life. Lincoln was as nearly self-educated and self-made as a man can be. He was a village postmaster for a while, a lawyer, a member of the Illinois legislature at Springfield, an unexceptional member of the House of Representatives in Washington for a single term. Little about his life until the 1850's seems adequate to explain the towering person he became. —*American Literature*

(2) Photosynthesis, a complicated process that is part of the life cycle of both plants and animals, is the means by which green plants manufacture food from inorganic raw materials. Photosynthesis takes place in green plant cells containing chlorophyll, a complex substance composed of the elements carbon, hydrogen, oxygen, nitrogen, and magnesium. Under the proper conditions of temperature, this chlorophyll, with the aid of energy provided by sunlight, combines carbon dioxide and water

to form glucose, a simple sugar that is an essential food of animals as well as plants themselves. Oxygen gas, also essential to the survival of animals, is then given off as a by-product of the action.

(3) Although determining Congressional seats prompted the first national census, additional uses for the information have multiplied over the decades until the list seems endless. Federal and local agencies, businesses and individuals, all rely on census statistics for important information. The value of the census, according to one official, is not only that it provides statistics but that it breaks them down into very local neighborhoods, sometimes as small as a city block. Thus an orthodontist checks to see if a certain neighborhood has enough children of teeth-straightening age to warrant his setting up practice. A shoe-store owner uses census information to decide if he should specialize in running shoes or sensible oxfords. In Minnesota, Boy Scout leaders looked at census information to project how many camps might be needed to accommodate new Scouts. —Adapted from Carol Simons

(4) Selling talking birds to Octavian (later Emperor Augustus) became a minor industry in Rome. In addition to a talking raven, he bought at least two more birds, a magpie and a parrot that had been trained to salute him. An enterprising cobbler thought to cash in on the trend by training a raven to say the appropriate "Ave, Caesar victor imperator" (Hail, Caesar, victorious leader!), but the bird was painfully slow to learn the prescribed phrase. Many times the poor cobbler exclaimed in exasperation, "Opera et impensa periit!" (Work and money wasted!) When the bird had finally learned its line, the man presented it. The raven performed, but Octavian declined to buy it, explaining that he already had enough birds to salute him. At that point the raven said, "Opera et impense periit!" Octavian laughed and bought the bird. —Adapted from Peter Muller

EXERCISE B: Identifying and Correcting Topic Sentences. In each of the following paragraphs the writer intended the first sentence to be the topic sentence, but each of the topic sentences is weak. Label the topic sentence *too general* or *too narrow*. Then write a revised topic sentence on your paper.

(1) Beginners in almost any sport are not ready for competition or independent play without first having proper training and guided practice. Crowding the slopes of ski resorts every year, hundreds—maybe thousands—of novice skiers create more hazards for the competent and experienced than equal numbers of bumps, ruts, trees, and ice. Because too many "beginners" take to the slopes without adequate training, and sometimes without proper-fitting equipment, they are ill-prepared for the demands and usually lose control, veer unexpectedly into paths

of other skiers, or fall in the middle of a path or trail in everyone's way. Some beginners may be coordinated and agile, but without guidance and training their abilities are only raw materials, and, on the slopes, they can become dangerous—to themselves and to others.

(2) The American traveler will often choose the airplane to reach his or her destination. The most frequent mode of transport, of course, is the automobile. An extensive road network, including many transcontinental routes, encourages this, and many travelers prefer the independence afforded by motoring, even cross-country. Surprising to some, many people today prefer the leisure of train and bus service, which are viable alternatives for budget travelers. Surely, the quickest way to travel is by jet plane, a popular, fun choice, many times faster than the others, but sometimes financially beyond the reach of some.

■ Supporting Information

The topic sentence of a standard paragraph is developed by information that clarifies or explains the main idea. Supporting information should be specific and complete to satisfy the reader's expectations. Learning to recognize strong supporting information and problems in support that can weaken a paragraph can help you develop your own paragraphs.

Features of Good Supporting Information.   A paragraph should contain enough supporting information to develop the main idea fully and to fulfill the purpose of the paragraph whether it be to explain, persuade, describe, or some other purpose. Support can be different kinds of information.

Supporting information should consist of adequate examples, details, facts, reasons, or incidents.

At least five kinds of information can be used to develop a main idea. Some paragraphs use mainly one kind of supporting information while others use a combination. The following chart describes these possibilities.

SUPPORTING INFORMATION	
Kind of Support	**Explanation**
Examples	—provide particular instances of a general idea or principle —offer specific items or ideas as evidence

Details	—present the different parts of a person, place, thing, or idea —offer pieces of description
Facts	—provide concrete, verifiable pieces of information to support an idea —offer accurate evidence, such as statistics and other data
Reasons	—provide explanations, justifications, or causes of the main idea —answer the question *Why?* raised by the topic sentence
Incidents	—relate events to support the topic sentence —illustrate the main idea through a brief story

A paragraph should have enough supporting information to make its main idea understandable and interesting. Supporting information should meet the reader's expectations by answering the mental questions the reader may have about the main idea.

The following paragraph supports a main idea with details and facts.

TOPIC
SENTENCE

Details and
facts

The design of the Viking ship remains a marvel and feat of technical skill. The Viking ship astonishes us today with its grace and beauty of line. In its day it astonished because of its strength and flexibility. Long and slim, built of oak, with symmetrical ends, long true keel, and overlapping wood planks molded into the shell shape that allowed the Vikings to land without benefit of harbor in very shallow water, the ship was equipped with a vast painted sail amidships, a side rudder, and as many as thirty-four pairs of oars. With the mast topped with a bronze weather vane and often with a prow sculpture, such a ship must have been a magnificent sight setting forth from the fjords. It was this technological weapon, combined with superb seamanship, that gave the Vikings mastery of the sea. —Adapted from Maureen Green

The next paragraph is developed with an incident that illustrates the main idea in the topic sentence. Notice that the incident includes details and that the paragraph ends with a concluding statement and some final details of interest.

TOPIC
SENTENCE

Incident with
facts and
details

A classic example of a form of propaganda by censorship through doctored information is Bismarck's famous Ems telegram of 1870. The point at issue was whether Leopold of Hohenzollern should succeed to the Spanish throne, a candidature supported by Bismarck and opposed by the French. King William of Prussia and the French ambassador had strolled together in the pleasure garden at Ems discussing the problem, although by this time Leopold, alarmed by the fuss his candidature had aroused, had already resigned it and the threat of war seemed to have been averted. But Bismarck wanted war, and, when William sent a telegram in cipher describing the inoffensive discussion that had taken place at Ems, Bismarck and his colleagues were at first despondent at its unimportant nature. Then the chancellor suddenly saw how he could make use of it to save the situation. By cutting out a few words and sentences and then publishing the abrupt telegram as it was, he could make what had been a fairly polite interview appear as a truculent challenge and a consequent snub. The provocative alterations were made and published, and the press on both sides clamored for war. Thus began the Franco-Prussian War in which 141,000 men were killed. —J. A. C. Brown

Inadequate and Inappropriate Supporting Information.   Just as a topic sentence might not suit the support in a paragraph, so the supporting information might not properly develop the topic sentence.

Recognize inadequate or inappropriate support, and revise supporting information to develop the main idea fully and accurately.

Often, the problem with paragraph development is *inadequate support;* that is, too little information has been supplied to develop the main idea fully. The reader will expect specific material to support the topic sentence. One or two examples or ideas may not make the main idea clear or convincing, especially if the support is brief and general. Notice the incompleteness of the supporting information in the following paragraph.

TOPIC
SENTENCE

The people at a baseball or football game can be part of the entertainment. Eating seems to be the primary interest of some people. They spend much of

Inadequate supporting information	their time hailing the roving vendors or eating food brought from home. Some viewers become restless when the play slows down and walk up and down the aisles and stairs. All these kinds of spectators add to the flavor of the experience.

Even though this paragraph gives two examples, the supporting information does not justify the concluding statement "all these kinds of spectators." The paragraph has not gone into enough depth to elaborate on the main idea and therefore is flat and disappointing.

To improve inadequate supporting information, you should reexamine the topic sentence and reconsider your initial ideas. Additional supporting information can come from ideas mentioned in the topic sentence but overlooked in the paragraph, from further explanation and development of existing supporting information, or from thinking up more examples, details, facts, or reasons related to your main idea.

In the paragraph about people at a baseball or football game, the reader expects more examples of spectators' behavior. The paragraph becomes more interesting and convincing when a few specific details are added to the supporting information already there and when three more examples are included.

TOPIC SENTENCE Additional details Additional details Added examples	The people at a baseball or football game can be part of the entertainment. Eating seems to be the primary interest of some people. They spend much of their time hailing the roving vendors or *munching snacks that they have brought with them.* Some viewers easily become restless when the play slows down and walk up and down the aisles and stairs, *trying the view from other parts of the stadium. In contrast, some fans constantly peer through binoculars zooming in on the action the way the television cameras do. Some viewers imagine that they are Howard Cosell or another well-known sportscaster and give a running commentary on the game to those sitting next to them. Still other fans become so involved in the game that they try to tell the referees or coaches what to do by yelling out their opinions and responses to calls and plays and by jumping up and down.* Although some of these kinds of spectators may be distracting, all of them add to the flavor of the experience.

Another problem with supporting information is that it may be the wrong kind of material. Vague statements, generalizations, and weak opinions are inappropriate support. They take up space without furthering the reader's understanding of the main idea. These problems stem from laziness and haphazard or shallow thinking. Instead of giving relevant, specific information, the writer may skim over the surface of ideas, using unclear words, making broad, abstract statements, and presenting opinions without defending them with concrete information.

The following paragraph illustrates these weaknesses in supporting information.

TOPIC SENTENCE	A boating enthusiast, I attend boat shows as frequently as possible but usually find them poorly planned and poorly run, making them tiring, frustrating experiences. Right from the beginning, the show is usually a problem because of the way it is set up. I can count on waiting hours just to get in and on waiting even longer to see an individual exhibit. And the worst parts are the so-called "experts" at the exhibits. These people really don't know anything. Often, they are salespeople who say: "This beauty will build your image, let me tell you!" or "This one is the fastest little roughneck on the high seas!"
Vague statement	
Generalization	
Weak opinion and generalization	

To revise inappropriate support you must approach the paragraph from the reader's perspective. The reader needs clear, exact words to understand precisely what you mean. To be acceptable to a reader a generalization should be qualified or developed with specific, concrete information. And weak opinions should be eliminated or made into logical reasons by backing them up with facts and examples. Sometimes, all the inappropriate support will have to be replaced by strong, specific examples, details, facts, and reasons. Notice how the problems in the preceding paragraph have been corrected in the following version of the paragraph.

TOPIC SENTENCE	A boating enthusiast, I attend boat shows as frequently as possible but usually find them poorly planned and poorly run, making them tiring, frustrating experiences. The problems begin at the door— in a waiting line. Because such shows are seasonal, occurring in most cities once a year, and because they are scheduled for usually no longer than a week in *one* large building, often a convention center, long lines inevitably form first at the entrance and then later at the individual exhibits inside. Waiting for as long as forty-five minutes to two hours at an exhibit is not uncommon. And, of course, the size of the crowd sharply limits any chance of inspecting a particular craft or of gathering craft-specifications from
Clear, exact language	
Specific facts and details	
Specific facts and details	

Opinion and generalization supported with facts and examples	an expert. In fact, worst of all are the "experts" themselves. Often, the men and women in charge at exhibit sites are salespeople, not boating experts or builders. A viewer with serious questions will seldom receive comparative statistics and relevant specifications. Instead, the information one receives is sales promotion: "This beauty will build your image, let me tell you!" or "This one is the fastest little roughneck on the high seas!"

EXERCISE C: Recognizing Kinds of Supporting Information.
Reread each paragraph in Exercise A on page 614. On your paper, make a list of the supporting information in each. Then identify the supporting information as mainly examples, details, facts, reasons, an incident, or a combination of these.

EXERCISE D: Identifying and Correcting Weaknesses in Supporting Information. Read each of the following paragraphs. First, locate the main-idea in the topic sentence, and then examine the supporting information to identify weaknesses. On your paper, briefly describe the weaknesses in each paragraph and then rewrite each paragraph. If the problem is inadequate support, add enough information of your own to develop the main idea fully. If the problem is inappropriate support, alter and add material to make the paragraph clear and strong.

(1) Many television shows have tried to educate the viewer. Popular for years, *Sesame Street*, a children's show, has taught basic skills and employed real learning methods amid "catchy" situations and engaging characters. A big bird, named appropriately "Big Bird," is one character who teaches everything from numbers to manners. Because this creature is so memorable, children probably have learned his lessons.

(2) To work with children—as a tutor, playground supervisor, babysitter, or in some other role—you need a warm personality and a firm manner. If you are friendly and interested in them, children will trust you. All children like to be happy, and a smile will work every time. If you do not set down ground rules, however, children will take advantage of you. They will test you to see what they can get away with. Children can be irritating and uncooperative. They can nag you until they get their way or cause trouble just to get your attention.

(3) That old saying "Red sky at night, sailors delight; red sky at morning, sailors take warning" actually holds true on many occasions. More often than not, sailors can expect winds the next day to fill their sails. Scientists now know that the red sky indicates high levels of moisture in the atmosphere, a precursor to blustery or even stormy weather. Many superstitions have bases in fact.

■ Unity

All the ideas and all the words in a paragraph should belong together so that the paragraph represents one unit of thought. The topic sentence should present a main idea, and the supporting information in the rest of the sentences should relate to that main idea. In addition, the particular words the writer chooses to express ideas should maintain a consistent tone. You can improve the unity of your own paragraphs by learning to identify paragraphs that have unity and to recognize the ideas and language that disrupt unity in some paragraphs.

Unity of Ideas and Tone.   A paragraph should be limited to its main idea and the expansion or development of that main idea. It should also fulfill the particular purpose and maintain the tone suggested by its topic sentence. For example, a formal persuasive paragraph concerning swimming as the healthiest form of exercise should stick to that idea and should be formal and persuasive throughout.

> To be unified, a paragraph must contain only information relevant to the main idea and words consistent with the paragraph's overall tone.

Unity of ideas and consistency of tone help a reader absorb and comprehend the writer's thoughts. Unity in a piece of writing indicates that the writer has kept the reader in mind at all times. It also helps the reader to grasp the main idea of the paragraph by omitting distracting ideas and unsuitable words.

The following paragraph attempts to explain one scientific concept to the reader. All the supporting information enhances the reader's knowledge of that concept, either by giving an example of the concept or by further explaining an example. Note that all the words in the paragraph maintain an objective, informative, and informal tone.

TOPIC
SENTENCE

Paragraph
with unified
ideas and
tone

Sea snakes have some unusual adaptations to their life at sea. For example, their nostrils are equipped with valves that close tightly when they submerge. This snug seal enables some species to dive to 300 feet or more and remain there for hours. The reptile can stay under so long because its single large lung, which stretches from near the throat almost to the tail, functions as an aqualung—a combination of air storage sac and buoyancy regulator. Another marine adaptation is a permeable skin that helps the reptile breathe and avoid the bends, or nitrogen poisoning. Any excess nitrogen simply passes through the skin into the sea. There's even an adaptation to compensate for the difference between the salt content in the reptile's body fluids and its surroundings. Salt can be excreted by a gland in the mouth. —Adapted from Emily and Per Ola D'Aulaire

Disunity of Ideas and Tone. A paragraph will be weakened by information that strays from the main idea or by words that disrupt the tone of the paragraph. Disunity can confuse a reader about the writer's ideas, purpose, and attitude toward the subject and audience.

Recognize disunity in a paragraph caused by extraneous information and unsuitable words.

Disunity of ideas or tone can cause a paragraph to fall apart. If a writer mentions unrelated ideas, the paragraph can become difficult to follow. Or, if a writer elaborates too much on any one piece of supporting evidence, the paragraph can become unbalanced. In either case, the reader may question or lose sight of the main idea. Similarly, if a writer uses casual words in a formal paragraph or elevated, technical words in an informal paragraph, the paragraph will probably no longer hold together.

The unity of the following paragraph is broken both by unrelated ideas and by words that do not fit the overall tone.

TOPIC SENTENCE	In Joan Aiken's novel *Go Saddle the Sea*, the main character, a young boy named Felix, barely escapes death in a series of adventures when he runs away
Too informal. a word	from his grandfather's estate in Villaverde, Spain, in search of his *dad's* relatives in England. *Felix's paternal grandfather is a duke of great wealth, but he does*
Extraneous information	*not know that Felix exists and never comes to understand Felix because he is becoming senile.* First, Felix stumbles into an unseen bog and almost *expires.*
Too formal words	Then he is mistakenly accused of robbery and thrown into a *penitentiary.* When he escapes, he becomes lost in the mountains during a storm and is captured by primitive people who try to sacrifice him. *Joan Aiken*
Extraneous information	*enjoys doing research and likes to put these frightening historical facts into her novels.* Finally, Felix reaches the coast of Spain only to book passage on a ship
Too formal a word	that has a crew of pirates. But with the help of a few friends and with his own *intrepidity*, good sense, and determination, Felix survives to achieve his goal.

To revise a paragraph for unity of ideas, you should evaluate both the topic sentence and the supporting information. Examining each supporting idea against the main idea can help you identify and eliminate extraneous information, which does not contribute to the reader's understanding of the main idea or directly develop another supporting idea. Sometimes you may have to replace extraneous information with relevant supporting ideas.

To correct disunity of tone, you should change words that draw attention to themselves because they clash with the overall tone of the paragraph. Replace words that sound too folksy or casual, too self-important or elevated, too technical, or too opinionated, with words that suit the purpose and tone of the paragraph.

The preceding paragraph can be improved by removing the ideas that lead away from the main idea and by substituting appropriate words that suit the straightforward, explanatory tone of the paragraph.

TOPIC SENTENCE	In Joan Aiken's novel *Go Saddle the Sea*, the main character, a young boy named Felix, barely escapes death in a series of adventures when he runs away
Unified paragraph with improved supporting information and word choices	from his grandfather's estate in Villaverde, Spain, in search of his *father's* relatives in England. First, Felix stumbles into an unseen bog and almost *dies*. Then he is mistakenly accused of robbery and thrown into *jail*. When he escapes, he becomes lost in the mountains during a storm and is captured by primitive people who try to sacrifice him. Finally, he reaches the coast of Spain only to book passage on a ship that has a crew of pirates. But with the help of a few friends and with his *courage*, good sense, and determination, Felix survives to achieve his goal.

Occasionally, extraneous ideas removed from one paragraph can be used as the basis of other paragraphs, especially if you are writing a longer composition. For example, the statements about Felix's paternal grandfather and Joan Aiken's research could be developed in other paragraphs.

EXERCISE E: Recognizing Unity and Disunity. Read each of the following paragraphs and determine which has unity and which does not. On your paper, label the paragraphs *unified* or *disunified*.

(1) The principal cause of the unpopularity, and ultimately the bankruptcy, of the Hartley specialty stores was the inferior

quality of their merchandise. Despite a large selection of appliances priced below many other similar types on the market, the Hartley brands were characterized by lousy construction. A Hartley toaster, for example, contained filaments that easily broke—often during original shipments to the store. Once home, customers would frequently find their new toasters to be total wastes. Discourteous service also marred the Hartley reputation. Specialty stores like Hartley's have trouble competing with the larger department store chains. And perhaps the most notorious example of disappointing merchandise could be found in Hartley's clothing sections. Their low prices could not compensate for incredible tailoring and imperfections in materials used, particularly in suits, shirts, blouses, and dresses.

(2) Ever since Charles Dickens wrote the story *A Christmas Carol* it has appealed to the hearts and imaginations of readers. Generations of parents have read the story to their children, and both children and older readers have thought about the frightening warnings that change Ebenezer Scrooge. Scrooge is a miser, unable to see beyond his own needs and interests. But through "visitations" by ghosts, he sees visions of the past, present, and future. He discovers the harm his love of money has done to himself and others. *A Christmas Carol* convincingly illustrates the theme that helping others may be the most rewarding thing that a person can do.

EXERCISE F: **Achieving Unity of Ideas and Tone.** Using the paragraph you identified as disunified in Exercise E, list any extraneous information and any words that disrupt the tone of the paragraph on your paper. Then rewrite the paragraph, eliminating the unrelated information and replacing the disruptive words with words that suit the purpose and tone. You may decide to invent some ideas to replace the extraneous material.

■ Coherence

In addition to a strong topic sentence, solid supporting information, and unity, an effective paragraph has *coherence*; that is, the ideas are logically arranged and smoothly connected for the reader. You can learn to identify the features that make a paragraph coherent and to improve paragraphs that lack coherence.

Logical Orders for Ideas. Supporting information in a paragraph should be arranged in the clearest, most logical order. A number of different orders are possible. Your choice will depend on the main idea and purpose of the paragraph you are writing.

> In a coherent paragraph, supporting information should follow a logical order. Some of the most helpful orders are order of importance, chronological, spatial, comparison and contrast, and developmental order.

Usually, the main idea, the purpose of the paragraph, and the supporting information will determine the best logical order for the paragraph. *Order of importance* organizes ideas from least significant (noticeable, interesting, and so on) to most significant (noticeable, interesting, and so on). Order of importance particularly suits persuasive paragraphs in which you are building a case for an opinion. *Chronological order*, or time order, presents events in the order of their occurrence and is useful for relating incidents or explaining how something is done. *Spatial order* arranges details by their location and functions well in description. *Comparison and contrast order* organizes details and ideas according to similarities and differences. You can discuss all the features of one item and then all the features of another, comparing and contrasting the second with the first. Or you can compare and contrast two or more items, feature by feature. *Developmental order*, more loose and versatile than these other orders, simply develops out of a particular topic sentence and presents information according to an order mentioned in that topic sentence or according to the writer's logical pattern of thought about the main idea. When other orders do not fit, you can use developmental order.

A paragraph may follow only one of these orders or may use a combination of orders. The following paragraph uses comparison and contrast order to organize supporting information about the teeth of crocodiles and alligators. The supporting information is compared and contrasted feature by feature: the crocodile jaw, the alligator jaw, the crocodile's fourth tooth, the alligator's fourth tooth.

TOPIC SENTENCE	In basic physical structure, the crocodile and the alligator have one major distinguishing feature: their teeth. *Both* creatures have teeth, of course, *but* the crocodile's teeth are aligned as the jaws close, *whereas* the alligator's teeth overbite; the upper jaw juts out and over the teeth in the lower jaw. *Both* species have a fourth tooth on each side, measurably
Comparison and contrast AB	

Comparison and contrast AB	larger than the rest; however, in the crocodile this tooth fits into a notch in the upper jaw leaving it visible when the mouth is closed, *while* in the alligator this tooth fits into a pit in the upper jaw and is hidden from sight.

Transitions and Other Words That Aid Coherence. No matter what logical order you use to arrange ideas in a paragraph, you will probably need a few connecting words to link ideas, to underscore the order for the reader, and to make the writing flow smoothly from one sentence to the next.

Transitions, coordinating words, and subordinating words can clarify the order of ideas in a paragraph and can connect the ideas smoothly for the reader.

Although not all paragraphs will need these connecting words, using a few of these words can help make most paragraphs logical and clear. Transitions, usually placed at the beginning of sentences, sometimes at the end or in the middle, can guide the reader by pointing out the connections among ideas. Coordinating and subordinating words within sentences can also show the relationship between ideas. Some connecting words are more useful to highlight one logical order than another, as the following chart shows.

WORDS THAT AID COHERENCE	
Logical Order	**Transitions, Coordinating Words, and Subordinating Words**
Order of Importance	first finally for one reason second most even greater third last greatest next also most significant one (of) even more
Chronological Order	when first later formerly while next finally at last then as soon as meanwhile afterward before now after moments later immediately last soon
Spatial Order	outside inside beyond near overhead beneath under over in the distance ahead in front behind to the left (right)

Comparison and Contrast Order	but besides in addition
	just as . . . so also yet similarly
	however but . . . also or
	in contrast whereas on the contrary nor
	like too both on the other hand
	as well as
Developmental Order	also finally along with next
	furthermore for example therefore
	thus accordingly for instance
	as a result indeed consequently
	another in fact namely and

If you look back at the paragraph illustrating a logical order on the preceding page, you will see that the words in italics are transitions, coordinating words, or subordinating words. Note the use of *both, but, whereas, however,* and *while.*

Repetitions of Main Words, Synonyms, and Consistent Pronouns.   Other devices for achieving coherence involve the deliberate use of certain words within the context of the paragraph. Repeating the main words can ensure that the reader concentrates on the important ideas of the paragraph. Using synonyms and consistent pronouns for main words can form subtle links among ideas while adding variety.

Repeating main words, using synonyms for main words, and using consistent pronouns for main words can tighten the logical connections among ideas and guide the reader.

In the following paragraph about the Spanish artist Joan Miró, the writer purposely repeats the main word *survivor* through the use of the verb *survived* to accent her main idea. However, instead of repeating the words *eighties* and *middle seventies,* the writer uses *old age* in the last sentence, and instead of repeating the artist's name throughout the paragraph, she substitutes the pronouns *he* and *his.*

TOPIC SENTENCE

Paragraph connected by the repetition of main words, synonyms, and pronouns

Joan Miró, well into his *eighties,* is one of the great *survivors. He* has *survived* as a human being: Never has *he* been more alert, more spontaneous, more intense. *He* has *survived* as an upright citizen: In *his* middle seventies, *he* would put up with hardship and discomfort to manifest *his* solidarity with *his* fellow Catalans who were being persecuted by the Franco government. And *he* has *survived* as an artist: Like Claude Monet, Henri Matisse, Pablo Pi-

casso and George Braque, *he* seems to have met *old age* at the door and told it to come back another day.
—Rosamond Bernier

Parallelism and Concluding Sentences.   Supporting ideas in paragraphs can also be linked by parallelism or can be summed up by concluding sentences. Using parallelism—similar grammatical structures—can tell the reader that ideas are similar, related, or equal. For example, a series of sentences with parallel structures can be used to present examples or reasons of equal importance. A concluding sentence, a sentence that echoes the main idea, that brings the paragraph to completion, or that summarizes preceding ideas can also create coherence.

Parallelism and concluding sentences can aid coherence by showing relationships among ideas and by tying ideas together in a paragraph.

Notice both of these devices at work in the following paragraph. Most sentences in the support follow a subject/verb/complement pattern to signal similarities among ideas—in this case, examples of the loss of natural beauty. Notice, also, that a concluding sentence ties together the supporting details as well as the main idea and the persuasive purpose of the paragraph.

TOPIC
SENTENCE

Parallelism
in sentences
following a
subject/verb/
complement
pattern

Concluding
sentence

The mountainous area around the southern end of Lake Tahoe in California has lost some of its natural beauty in the last twenty years. Housing developments now dot the ridges and meadows where pine forests once stood. Tall hotels and casinos fringe the lake with commercial activity. Caravans of vehicles creep over the pass that leads to the lake. Traces of smog sometimes taint the once pure and refreshing air. The roaring of chain saws and car, motorcycle, plane, and boat engines echoes off the rocky ridges. And even the trails up the rugged mountains and into the more remote valleys are now traveled by packs of hikers. *Gradually, civilization with all its sights, smells, and sounds is invading the wilderness.*

Illogical Order and Poor Connections.   Even paragraphs with strong supporting information can be weakened by illogical order or by the absence of transitions and other connecting devices. If the ideas in a paragraph skip around or if they follow an order that contradicts their meaning, the reader will have difficulty comprehending that paragraph. Similarly, if the writer does not provide necessary connections, the reader may fail to see the relationships among the ideas in a group.

Recognize faulty coherence caused by an illogical order of ideas or the absence or misuse of connecting devices such as transitions, repetitions of main words, synonyms, consistent pronouns, and possibly parallelism and concluding sentences.

Incoherence can make a paragraph difficult to read. If the writer has not chosen the most natural logical order for the material, the reader may be confused about the writer's main idea. If either too few, too many, or inappropriate transitions are used, the paragraph may be disjointed or heavy-handed. If the writer has not made good use of other connecting devices, the paragraph may sound elementary or awkward.

The following paragraph discusses two famous baseball players, but the writer has neglected to order the supporting information logically or to make the writing flow from sentence to sentence; consequently, a reader has trouble following the ideas.

TOPIC SENTENCE	Most baseball fans agree that two of the greatest baseball players of all time are Ty Cobb and Joe DiMaggio. Joe DiMaggio was elected to baseball's
Illogical order	Hall of Fame in 1955. With the New York Yankees between 1936 and 1952, Joe became one of the greatest outfielders of all time, and his popularity soared
No transitions between examples	when he set a major league record of hits in fifty-six consecutive games, achieving a lifetime batting average of .325. Ty Cobb set a record for the most base hits while he played ball with the Detroit Tigers from 1905 to 1907. Ty Cobb became famous for base-
Unnecessary repetition of a name	stealing; in one season, Ty Cobb stole ninety-six bases. Ty knew how to slide with style, and he claimed that by watching the baseman's eyes rather than the ball, he could gauge his landing.

To revise a paragraph for coherence, you should reexamine the main idea and purpose of the paragraph. You should try to arrange supporting information according to a logical order suggested by the topic sentence or by the supporting information itself. Once you have rearranged the material, you should look for places—movement to a new supporting idea, a change in time or place, or addition of details—that would be clearer and smoother with transitions. Then you should choose the transition that matches and clarifies the particular ideas. To improve the continuity of the paragraph even more, you should look for main words that can be repeated or replaced by synonyms or pronouns.

When the paragraph about Ty Cobb and Joe DiMaggio is revised for coherence, the information on Ty Cobb comes first according to the topic sentence and to chronological order. Transitions clarify the arrangement of examples and add smoothness. The use of *he* for *Ty* eliminates the unnecessary repetitions of his name. A bridge idea forms a transition between the supporting information on Ty Cobb and Joe DiMaggio. Notice, too, that the material on Joe DiMaggio now follows a more logical time order, ending with his election to the Hall of Fame.

TOPIC SENTENCE	Most baseball players agree that Ty Cobb and Joe DiMaggio are two of the greatest baseball players of all time. *While* Ty Cobb played ball with the Detroit
Logical order	Tigers from 1905 to 1907, he set a record for the most base hits. He *also* became famous for base-stealing; in one season, he stole ninety-six bases. *In addition,*
Transitions and pronouns	Ty knew how to slide with style. He claimed that by watching the baseman's eyes rather than the ball, he could gauge his landing. *Joe DiMaggio's record also*
Bridge idea	*made him a favorite among fans.* When he played for the New York Yankees between 1936 and 1952, he became one of the greatest outfielders of all time, and his popularity soared when he set a major league record of hits in fifty-six consecutive games. Joe's other records and his lifetime batting average of .325 earned him his election to baseball's Hall of Fame in 1955.

EXERCISE G: Achieving Coherence. The following six sentences can be arranged to form a coherent paragraph. Decide on the best order for the sentences by recognizing introductory statements, the topic sentence, and a logical order for the supporting ideas. Write the paragraph so that it is coherent.

1. First, it failed to explain why the different planets travel at different angles and at different speeds in relation to each other and to the sun.

2. French astronomer Pierre de Laplace and German metaphysicist Immanuel Kant maintained that the planets in our solar system were formed from a central nebula.

3. Third, and most obvious to critics of the theory, a planet as massive as Jupiter could not have been spread out as a thin ring of matter surrounding the sun, because it would

have been impossible for that thin stream to have contracted into a huge spherical body.

4. Because of three major drawbacks, however, critics of the
theory found it incomplete and imperfect.

5. Second, centrifugal force alone would not have the power
to propel rings of matter outward into space.

6. According to this theory, as the nebula began to rotate, it
threw off rings of matter centrifugally, and each of these
rings contracted gravitationally to form the different
planets.

EXERCISE H: **Recognizing Devices That Aid Coherence.** Follow
these instructions to analyze the paragraph that you reordered
in Exercise G.

1. Identify the most apparent logical arrangement used in the
support, and list the transitions used to clarify this
arrangement.

2. List any other transitions, coordinating words, and subordinating words that clarified relationships between ideas
in the paragraph.

3. Identify a main word that has been repeated in the
paragraph.

4. Identify a synonym used for an important word or idea.
Write both the synonym and the original word on your
paper.

5. If the paragraph uses parallel structures, list these; otherwise, write "None." If the paragraph has a concluding sentence, copy it; otherwise, write "None."

EXERCISE I: **Improving Coherence in a Paragraph.** The following paragraph contains weaknesses in coherence, such as illogical order in the support, lack of transitions, and other awkward connections. Rewrite the paragraph to improve coherence.
Consider rearranging the supporting information, using devices that clarify order and improve smoothness, and, if necessary, rewrite any sentences to improve the flow of ideas.

(1) Justin had never been to an art auction before, so he entered the large hall nervously, overly conscious of his presence
among so many strangers. (2) Feeling out of place, Justin observed the entrances of others and decided to follow a course of
action that he thought would be proper. (3) Justin walked con-
fidently to a reception desk where he saw people signing a guest
register. (4) Justin waited a moment behind two women signing
their names, and Justin signed his own beneath theirs. (5) Finally, Justin took a seat in the last row, folded his hands in his
lap, and waited for the bidding to begin. (6) Before Justin sat

down, he walked to the other side of the entrance foyer to a coatroom where Justin hung his raincoat among at least fifty others.

APPLICATION: Recognizing Key Features and Improving Your Paragraphs. Select a paragraph that you have recently written and examine it to find the key features. Follow these instructions to analyze and record the features of your paragraph.

1. Copy the topic sentence of your paragraph onto your paper, and determine if it suits the paragraph or is too general or too narrow.
2. List the pieces of supporting information you have used in your paragraph and state whether you have used mainly examples, details, facts, reasons, an incident, or a combination of kinds.
3. Determine whether you have used enough supporting information and add supporting ideas if your material is inadequate. Also, remove any vague statements, generalizations, and weak opinions, and add specific, concrete replacements, if necessary.
4. Examine your paragraph for unity of ideas and tone. Write *unified* if your paragraph sticks to the topic and maintains a consistent tone. Otherwise, list any extraneous information you find and any words that disrupt the tone.
5. Identify the logical order you have used to arrange supporting information and list any transitions, repetitions of main words, synonyms, and pronouns you have used. If you have used parallelism and a concluding sentence, write these on your paper also.
6. If any part or all of your paragraph is weakened by lack of coherence, identify any problems in logical order, transitions, or other connecting devices.
7. Rewrite your paragraph to improve any of the weaknesses you may have discovered in items 1, 3, 4, and 6.

Planning, Writing, and Revising Paragraphs

21.2

An understanding of the key features of standard paragraphs and of the weaknesses that you should avoid can help you develop paragraphs effectively. This section discusses some planning, writing, and revising steps that you can follow and later modify to suit your own writing methods.

■ Preparing a Topic Sentence

Your first major planning step involves arriving at a main idea for the paragraph—one that limits the information to be covered in the paragraph and one that reflects a particular purpose. Your goal in this step is to complete a topic sentence.

Choosing and Narrowing a Topic.   The process begins with possibilities: topics that have been assigned or topics that you think of. As you think about different topics and as you imagine what you could write about each, you should consider topics that interest you and that you can support with plentiful information.

> **Divide possible topics into smaller ones, and choose a topic that is manageable and appealing.**

Usually, the topic you begin with will be too general for a single thorough paragraph. Therefore, you should narrow the topic by thinking of subcategories or smaller topics under the general topic. Then you should select the one you can handle well in a paragraph.

The following chart illustrates how the general topic *Human biology* can be narrowed to several smaller topics. One of the smaller topics can then be narrowed still further to several even more specific topics, one of which you may select as your paragraph topic.

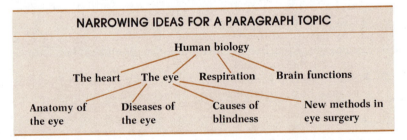

NARROWING IDEAS FOR A PARAGRAPH TOPIC

Human biology

The heart   The eye   Respiration   Brain functions

Anatomy of the eye   Diseases of the eye   Causes of blindness   New methods in eye surgery

Once you have followed this process of exploring and narrowing a general topic, you might choose *Anatomy of the eye* to be the topic of your paragraph.

Focusing a Main Idea to Fit Your Audience and Purpose. Once you have a manageable paragraph topic, such as the anatomy of the eye, you must decide what you want to say about it. Thinking about your audience—the people to whom you are writing—and your purpose, whether it will be to explain, persuade, describe, or tell a story, can also help you zero in on a main idea.

Consider audience and purpose as you focus a paragraph topic on a main idea and write a topic sentence.

One way to guide your thinking to find a main idea involves asking yourself questions about the topic. Your purpose, your audience, and your own interest in the topic can be the starting points for your questions. For instance, knowing whether your audience will be other students who are familiar with the topic, other students unfamiliar with the topic, a particular group within your community, your instructor or coach, or a general audience can help you ask significant, thought-provoking questions. For instance, you might ask yourself, "What can I tell my audience about this topic? What do I think the audience should know about it?" The answers to these and other similar questions can be possible main ideas. The next chart lists three questions you might ask yourself about the anatomy of the eye.

QUESTIONS SUGGESTING POSSIBLE MAIN IDEAS	
Paragraph Topic: Anatomy of the eye	
Questions	**Possible Main Ideas**
What interests me about this topic?	—The eye is a delicate instrument that is less complex than most people realize.
What do I know about the eye's anatomy?	—The eyeball structure contains three basic layers, each performing different functions that result in sight.
How does the eye "see"?	—The eye functions like a camera.

When you have a list of possible main ideas, you should examine each one to see which best suits the audience you want to address, the purpose you choose to have, and your own familiarity with the topic. Any of the possible main ideas in the chart would be suitable for an audience of students unfamiliar with the topic or for a general audience. The first main idea implies a persuasive purpose because it suggests that you will convince your readers of the simplicity of the eye, a task that may take some arguing. The second and third main ideas suggest that you will explain some factual information, the structure and function of the eye, to the audience.

You should choose the main idea for which you have the most information and which most closely suits your audience and purpose. Then you should try wording your main idea different ways to find the version of your topic sentence that you like best. Although experimenting with your topic sentence at this point will help you plan the rest of your paragraph, you should remember that you may still have to revise your topic sentence later on.

If you chose the second main idea in the preceding chart, you might write topic sentences like those in the following chart.

POSSIBLE TOPIC SENTENCES

Main Idea: The eyeball contains three basic layers, each performing different functions that result in sight.

1. The three basic layers of the eyeball perform different functions that result in vision.
2. The three basic layers of the eye—the sciera, the middle or choroid layer, and the retina—perform specific functions in creating sight.
3. The eyeball contains three basic layers which help to produce sight.
4. The eyeball consists of three basic layers, which contain the instruments of sight.

You could choose any of these statements to be your topic sentence because they all present the same main idea and have an explanatory purpose. Notice, however, that the wording of the first, third, and fourth sentences sounds simpler than the wording of the second sentence. You might decide that the paragraph would be more suitable for an audience unfamiliar with this topic if you saved technical terms for the body of the paragraph, where you can explain them. You might choose the fourth topic sentence because it gives the main idea the particular focus you would like to have.

EXERCISE A: Finding a Manageable Paragraph Topic. Choose one of the following general topics and write it on your paper. Beneath it, list at least four related smaller topics that you might write about in a paragraph. If these smaller topics still seem too broad for a single paragraph, you might divide them further. Then circle the paragraph topic that appeals to you the most.

A musical instrument
Necessary gear for a partic-
    ular sport
A book or movie
Major accomplishment of a
    painter, politician, or
    other famous person
Your attitudes regarding a
    type of clothing

Medical treatment for some
    disease
How to construct or set up
    something
A new or popular scientific
    theory
A social issue or problem
Oceanography

EXERCISE B: Choosing a Main Idea and Writing a Topic Sentence. Use the paragraph topic you selected in Exercise A to complete the following instructions.

1. Briefly identify the audience to whom you will write (for example, your friends, your neighborhood, the town council, an editor of a newspaper, and so on).
2. While thinking about this audience and your paragraph topic, write down at least three questions about your topic. Then write down short answers to these questions. Your answers should be possible main ideas for the paragraph.
3. Identify the suggested purpose of each main idea.
4. Select the main idea that best suits your knowledge of the topic, your audience, and your purpose.
5. Experiment with the wording of your main idea as you write at least three versions of your topic sentence.
6. Circle the topic sentence that seems most direct, carefully worded, and workable.

■ Gathering Supporting Information

Once you have a main idea and a topic sentence, you must think of specific information that will support the topic sentence. In this step, you must anticipate your readers' expectations and develop the main idea completely and satisfactorily. After gathering supporting information, you must consider the quality and relevance of your supporting ideas and choose only the information that clarifies your main idea, fulfills your purpose, and is meaningful to your audience.

Brainstorming for Supporting Information.   When you brainstorm for ideas for a paragraph, you should do some serious, creative thinking. You should use your imagination, and you may want to consult special sources of information, such as books, magazines, and other people. Of course, if you use unusual and original ideas from a book, you will have to give credit to the author for his or her ideas. Most often, brainstorming will involve carrying on a dialogue with yourself—recalling and thinking up material—to write the strongest possible paragraph on your topic.

> **Brainstorm for examples, details, facts, reasons, and incidents that will support and develop your main idea.**

To gather supporting information for your topic sentence, you might try free-associating from your main idea. Write down your topic sentence and then list every piece of related information that comes to mind. Try to write quickly and let one thought spark another like a chain reaction. Jot down all these ideas in the form of words, phrases, and even sentences. Do not sort your ideas at this stage. If you run out of ideas, reread your topic sentence to start your thoughts flowing again. You might also reread your topic sentence from time to time to prevent your thoughts from straying too far from your topic.

The question and answer method also works well to encourage your thinking about your main idea. Using this method, you can give yourself some thought-provoking questions to answer. You should anticipate the questions that your audience might ask after reading your topic sentence. When you think of those questions, you should write them on the left half of your paper. Then on the right, you should answer the questions with specific pieces of supporting information. Remember that readers might want to know about the meaning of any terms in your topic sentence. One final question might be "What other special information relates to the main idea?"

The following chart illustrates this question and answer method of brainstorming. Notice that the topic sentence appears at the top of the brainstorming sheet to focus the questioning and the listing of examples, details, and facts.

QUESTION AND ANSWER METHOD OF BRAINSTORMING

Topic Sentence: **The eyeball consists of three basic layers, which contain the instruments of sight.**

What are the basic layers of the eyeball?

—the three basic layers:
the sclera (outer layer)
the middle layer (mostly the choroid)
the retina (inner layer)

—eyelids which protect from exterior threats such as foreign matter and projectiles

—eye socket cushions the eyeball with fatty tissues and about 6 different muscles

—major muscles (levator palebrae, superior and interior recti) which hold the eye and guide eye movements

—the center of the eyeball, called the vitreous humor, consists of transparent, jelly-like substance

How are these layers instruments of sight?

—the sclera or outer layer has a transparent cornea, which allows light to enter

—the eye socket contains tear glands that keep the eyeball moist

—the middle layer or choroid layer contains the blood vessels that nourish the eyeball, also contains the iris and pupil, a hole in the iris which expands and contracts to allow light to pass through a lens

—eyelid muscles react involuntarily to protect the eyeball

—the retina is farthest inside the eyeball and contains nerve cells and light sensitive cells called rods and cones that receive the light, form images, and stimulate the nerve cells, which in turn transmit the images to the brain

What other special information pertains to the eyeball?

—the size of the eyeball—about one inch or 2.5 centimeters in diameter

—the eyeball structure is similar to the parts of a camera

—unlike a camera, the eye cavity contains protective mechanisms such as involuntary muscles and tear glands

Using either method of brainstorming, you will most likely gather too much information for a single paragraph. On closer examination you will probably find that some of the ideas you have jotted down do not really fit in your paragraph. If you have a long list of supporting information, you can choose from it only the most useful, significant information for the paragraph.

Checking the Unity and Completeness of Support.   Once you have a list of supporting information, you are ready to analyze the ideas on your list for unity and completeness. You should concentrate on your main idea, audience, and purpose as you decide which pieces of information to use, which to eliminate, and which to expand or alter.

> Examine all supporting information to eliminate irrelevant or unimportant ideas, to add or expand ideas, or even to revise the topic sentence to fit the supporting information.

This step gives you an opportunity to weed out those ideas that do not strengthen your paragraph and perhaps to write down other useful ideas that you may have overlooked. You should read over each item on your list to determine whether it is necessary and helpful to the audience. Cross out those ideas that do not relate to the main idea or directly develop another piece of supporting information. You may have to eliminate repetitious support, or you may find gaps in your supporting material or unanswered questions. You should then supply more examples, details, facts, or reasons.

At this point, you may also want to revise your topic sentence to match the supporting information. Or you may discover an introductory idea that could affect the wording or placement of the topic sentence.

The following chart shows this evaluation step for the list of information on the eyeball. Notice that some pieces of information have been crossed out. Possible introductory and concluding ideas have been circled.

EVALUATING SUPPORTING INFORMATION

Topic Sentence: **The eyeball consists of three basic layers, which contain the instruments of sight.**

What are the basic layers of the eyeball?

—the three basic layers:
  the sclera (outer layer)
  the middle layer (mostly the choroid)
  the retina (inner layer)

—eyelids which protect from exterior threats such as foreign matter and projectiles

—eye socket cushions the eyeball with fatty tissues and

about 6 different muscles

—major muscles (levator palebrae, superior and interior recti) which hold the eye and guide eye movements

—the center of the eyeball, called the vitreous humor, consists of transparent, jelly-like substance

How are these layers instruments of sight?

—the sclera or outer layer has a transparent cornea, which allows light to enter

—the eye socket contains tear glands that keep the eyeball moist

—the middle layer or choroid layer contains the blood vessels that nourish the eyeball, also contains the iris and pupil, a hole in the iris which expands and contracts to allow light to pass through a lens

—eyelid muscles react involuntarily to protect the eyeball

—the retina is farthest inside the eyeball and contains nerve cells and light sensitive cells called rods and cones that receive the light, form images, and stimulate the nerve cells, which in turn transmit the images to the brain

What other special information pertains to the eyeball?

—the size of the eyeball—about one inch or 2.5 centimeters in diameter

—the eyeball structure is similar to the parts of a camera

—unlike a camera, the eye cavity contains protective mechanisms such as involuntary muscles and tear glands

The topic sentence for this paragraph about the structure of the eyeball might be revised to include one of the particularly interesting pieces of information.

REVISED TOPIC SENTENCE: The eyeball, a sphere of about one inch or two and a half centimeters in diameter, consists of three basic layers, which contain the instruments of sight.

EXERCISE C: Developing Supporting Information.

Use the topic sentence that you wrote in Exercise B on page 637. Write the sentence at the top of your paper, and then, beneath it, list as many pieces of supporting information as you can. Use either of two methods—free-association or the question and answer method—to find and list appropriate examples, details, facts, reasons, and incidents. Use your imagination as well as any sources you think necessary to develop supporting ideas. If you use ideas from books, be sure to write down the author's name, the title of the book, and the page number.

EXERCISE D: Examining Your Support and Choosing the Best Information.

Use your lists of information from Exercise C. On your brainstorm sheet, cross out any pieces of information that you think stray from the main idea or that you find unimportant. Consider adding new information or altering the ideas in your list. Look for any information that could become introductory or concluding ideas. Then reexamine your topic sentence to see if it suits the body of information you have developed for the paragraph. If you think it is necessary, revise the topic sentence.

■ Organizing the Paragraph

The next major step is to organize the information you have gathered for your paragraph in a logical order so that a reader can follow your ideas easily. There are a number of ways to do this step but the goal is always the same: clarity and logical flow of ideas.

Arrange your supporting information in the most logical order.

Now you should look again at your list of supporting information to determine the most logical order in which to present your ideas to the reader. An organization, such as order of importance or comparison and contrast order, may be suggested by your main idea and list of support. In fact, you may already have jotted down the supporting information in a logical order. If none of these logical orders suits your paragraph, try to find a developmental order that presents your ideas naturally and smoothly.

You should also consider the most advantageous position for your topic sentence. For example, if you are using an incident in chronological order to illustrate a main idea, you may want your main idea to complete the paragraph. If you are presenting a series of examples in developmental order, you may choose to lead into your topic sentence with several introductory ideas. Often, you will plan to put your topic sentence early in the paragraph where it will prepare the reader for the information that follows.

The method you use to do this organizing step will depend on how you work best. For instance, you may rough out a plan for the paragraph on your brainstorming sheet by numbering pieces of support or by drawing circles and arrows. You may prepare a modified outline by listing your supporting information in the logical order you have chosen on another piece of paper. Or you may write a more formal topic outline. No matter which method you use for this step, you may want to refine your supporting information even further by adding, removing, or changing ideas.

By examining the list of information on the structure of the eyeball, you can see a spatial order emerge. The explanation of the eyeball can take the reader from the outer layer of the eyeball to the innermost layer, with details and facts explaining each layer. An introductory idea can lead into the topic sentence, and a concluding sentence can complete the paragraph. This logical order for the paragraph is shown in the following modified outline.

Introductory Ideas About the Eyeball
  1. Rests in a skull cavity
  2. Moves with help of different muscles and is kept moist by tear glands

Topic sentence: The eyeball, a sphere of about one inch or two and a half centimeters in diameter, consists of three basic layers, which contain the instruments of sight.

The Sclera or Outermost Layer
  1. Is the "white" of the eye
  2. Has a transparent cornea, which allows light to enter

The Middle or Choroid Layer Within the Sclera
  1. Contains the blood vessels that nourish the eyeball
  2. Contains the iris and pupil, a hole in the iris which expands and contracts to allow light to pass through a lens

The Innermost Layer, or Retina
  1. Contains nerve cells
  2. Contains light-sensitive cells called rods and cones
  3. Is the processing layer; rods and cones receive the light and form images and stimulate nerves cells, which in turn transmit the images to the brain

Concluding Idea Comparing Eyeball and Camera
  1. Resemble each other in structure
  2. Regulate and admit light and focus images on light-sensitive surfaces

EXERCISE E: **Organizing Supporting Information Logically.** Use the list of supporting information you prepared in Exercises C and D to follow these instructions.

  1. Analyze your topic sentence and your supporting information to determine the most appropriate logical order for the paragraph.

2. Consider whether you will begin or end the paragraph with your topic sentence or put the topic sentence in the middle after some introductory remarks.

3. Then either (1) organize your paragraph on your brainstorming sheet by using numbers or marginal notes; (2) write a modified outline in which you include your topic sentence and put the supporting information in the logical order you have chosen; or (3) make a topic outline that arranges your supporting information in logical order.

■ Writing the Paragraph

The planning and organizing you have done up to this point will help you in a number of ways as you write your paragraph. Because you have already worked out most of the paragraph, you will be freer to refine your ideas. As you express your ideas in complete sentences, you can consider the best way to communicate your ideas. You may even revise your paragraph as you write by thinking of new relevant ideas. While your logical order guides you, you can concentrate on making logical connections clear for the reader. And you can also think about the style of your writing.

> As you draft your paragraph from your plan or outline, concentrate on connecting your ideas for meaning and flow and on writing sentences with different lengths, openers, and structures for variety.

In addition to following the logical order you have chosen, you should concentrate on leading the reader along smoothly from idea to idea. Appropriate transitions and coordinating and subordinating words can clarify the logical order of your ideas and highlight the relationships among them for the reader. Using repetitions of main words and synonyms and consistent pronouns for main words can also tie your ideas together. You may even find parallelism useful in underscoring similarities or a concluding sentence helpful in bringing the paragraph to a smooth, logical close.

Varying the rhythm and pattern of your sentences can also help to make your paragraph readable and interesting. As you draft your sentences, you should consider using sentences of different lengths, beginning in different ways, and using a variety of simple, compound, and complex sentences. (For more information on sentence variety, see Sections 19.1 and 19.2.)

Writing on every other line or double spacing and leaving wide margins will give you room to make changes on your first draft.

EXERCISE F: **Writing a First Draft.** Use your plan or outline from Exercise E to write a first draft of your paragraph. When you are writing, if new ideas that support your main idea or clarify another piece of supporting information occur to you, include them. Try to use transitions and other linking devices to clarify the logical order of your ideas. In addition, try to express your ideas clearly in sentences of different lengths and with different structures.

■ Revising for Unity, Coherence, and Style

The final step, revising, allows you to look critically at your writing to find errors and to make improvements. You should put your paragraph aside for awhile and examine it and revise it when you can view it with some objectivity.

Use a checklist like the following to evaluate all parts of your paragraph and to help you revise.

The following checklist can guide you as you look for weaknesses in the topic sentence, supporting information, unity, coherence, writing style, and the grammar and mechanics of your paragraph.

CHECKLIST FOR REVISING A STANDARD PARAGRAPH

1. Does the topic sentence accurately state the main idea developed in the paragraph or is it too general or too narrow?
2. Does the topic sentence suggest your purpose and suit your intended audience?
3. Does the supporting information contain enough examples, details, facts, reasons, and/or incidents to develop the topic sentence?
4. Can you find any weaknesses among supporting ideas: vague statements, generalizations, or weak opinions?
5. Can any information be eliminated as extraneous or insignificant?

6. Does the supporting information follow the most logical order consistently throughout?

7. Have you achieved coherence by using transitions, coordinating and subordinating words, repetitions of main words, synonyms, and consistent pronouns to connect ideas?

8. Could you improve any confusing or awkward places by adding any of the above linking devices, parallelism, or a bridge idea?

9. Does the paragraph need a concluding sentence?

10. Are your sentences varied in their lengths, openers, and structures?

11. Are the word choices the best you can find for your ideas?

12. Can you find any errors in grammar, usage, punctuation, or spelling?

A completed, revised version of the paragraph about the eyeball follows. Notice that the transitions—*outermost, within,* and *innermost*—help the reader follow the spatial order, and other transitions—*like a camera* and *then*—tie the paragraph together. The repetition of the main words *eyeball* and *layer* and the use of the pronouns *it* and *its* for the different layers also help to link ideas for the reader. Notice that some of the sentences are simple, some are complex, and one is compound.

Introductory ideas	The human eyeball rests in a skull cavity, where it moves with the help of six different muscles and is kept moist by tear glands. The actual eyeball, a
TOPIC SENTENCE	sphere of about one inch or two and a half centimeters, consists of three basic layers, which contain the instruments of sight. The outermost layer is called
Supporting information in spatial order	the sclera; this is the "white" of the eye. Through its transparent cornea, a slight bulge in the front of the eye, light can pass to the interior. Within the sclera is the middle or choroid layer. This layer contains the blood vessels that nourish the eyeball, the iris, or colored part of the eye, and the pupil, a hole in the iris, which expands and contracts to allow light to reach the eye's lens and pass through. The innermost layer is the retina, which contains nerve cells and light-sensitive cells called rods and cones. The retina is the processing layer. It receives the light that has passed through the other layers, forms images, and stimulates nerve cells, which in turn transmit the
Concluding sentence	images to the brain. Like a camera, then, the eyeball with its various layers regulates and admits light and focuses images on a light-sensitive surface.

EXERCISE G: **Revising Your Paragraph.** Reread the first draft that you wrote for Exercise F. Use the checklist to examine all features of the paragraph. Make any corrections or revisions on your paper, and then write a good final copy of the paragraph.

APPLICATION: **Planning, Writing, and Revising a Paragraph.** Choose one of the following topics or one of your own. (Remember that some topics may need more narrowing than others.) Then carry out the planning, writing, and revising steps that follow the list of topics.

A famous battle
An unusual animal
An important organization
Outer space
Course requirements
Hazards of a certain
   place or thing

A riddle of science
Commuting or
   traveling woes
Botany or zoology
A particular singer's style
   of music

1. Narrow the topic.
2. Find a main idea by considering your audience and purpose.
3. Write several versions of your topic sentence expressing your main idea.
4. Brainstorm for supporting information and select support that is unified and thorough.
5. Organize your supporting information logically.
6. Write a first draft, concentrating on using connecting devices and varying your sentences.
7. Recheck your first draft and use a checklist for revisions.
8. Write a good final copy of the paragraph.

Finding Your Own Approach to Writing Paragraphs 21.3

Now that you have practiced one basic process of planning, writing, and revising paragraphs, you can experiment with the process. You can explore combining and reordering some of the smaller steps to find the process that is most natural, efficient, and successful for you.

In addition, this section will give you some suggestions for handling problems you may encounter as you write.

■ Adapting the Steps

As discussed in Section 21.2, one common way to compose and polish paragraphs is to use the steps in the following chart.

PLANNING STEPS
Choose a topic.
Narrow the topic to a main idea by focusing on audience and purpose.
Write a topic sentence.
Develop support through questioning or free-associating.
Check for unity.
Choose a logical order for your support.
Prepare a rough or modified outline.

WRITING STEPS
Follow your modified outline.
Compose full sentences for support.
Add transitions and main word repetitions.
Use other linking devices for coherence.

REVISING STEPS
Revise topic sentences that are too general or too narrow.
Add supporting information if support is sketchy.
Eliminate generalizations, opinions, and repetitions.
Eliminate insignificant or extraneous support.
Look for more logical arrangements of ideas.
Add transitions, repeat main words, and use synonyms, pronouns, bridge ideas, parallelism, and a concluding sentence as necessary.

These steps, however, do not always have to be followed in the exact order shown here.

The basic steps are useful in giving you guidance and direction—a place to begin and methods for proceeding toward a goal. However, writing is not always a linear process, first one step, then the next. Because it is creative, it is sometimes a forward and backward and forward process. Sometimes you will write with a burst of ideas and energy, and other times you will have to think long and hard to come up with ideas. No one knows exactly how a person's mind works during the writing process, and each person goes about writing in a slightly different way. One of your challenges as a writer should be to discover how you think and write best to create the best possible piece of writing. By adapting the writing steps you already know, you should be able to find a procedure that is practical for you.

Experiment with the planning, writing, and revising steps to find a process that works well for you.

You should strive to write paragraphs that have a focused, well-developed idea, a specific audience and purpose, and unity and coherence. The way in which you achieve these goals may affect the usual writing steps. For instance, you may find that doing the planning steps in a different order, drafting your paragraph directly from your list of support, or revising your work at every step works best for you.

As you examine new approaches, try to find a process that makes writing easier for you. You may use any of the following suggestions, or you may experiment further to find your own process.

Varying Planning Steps. Sometimes you may write with an audience and topic in mind but no focused idea. You may not even know if your topic is a good one for that writing situation, but you may want to pursue it to see if you do have something to communicate. Instead of formally narrowing the topic and shaping a main idea, you might want to brainstorm on the topic first and see what kinds of ideas emerge. If your potential supporting information looks promising after brainstorming, you can then determine and focus a main idea and express it in a topic sentence.

For instance, if you had recently tried canoeing for the first time, you might want to communicate your experience to your friends. With this general topic in mind, you might jot down as many ideas as occur to you.

BRAINSTORMING SHEET

Canoeing
—great way to enjoy outdoors
—see hills, forests, and river from a unique perspective
—can be as strenuous as you want—go as many miles as you want in a few hours or many hours

—white water (rapids) rated from 1 to 5—4 and 5 rapids most dangerous, fast, deep, rocky—take most skill

—2 people in a canoe—person in back steers and paddles—person in front paddles and watches for rocks

—to go straight—two riders paddle on alternate sides—to turn, both paddle on side opposite to direction canoe is turning

—aluminum canoes—not as tipsy as I expected

—vigorous exercise for arm, shoulder, and back muscles

—cool breeze on the river—especially over the rushing white water

—can float and slide with current

—can beach canoe—picnic and swim

—as a precaution all things in canoe should be waterproof and buoyant

—tie things to canoe so they won't float downstream if canoe tips over

—takes practice to dip paddle far enough into water to get power

—in summer purple heather, Queen Anne's lace, golden black-eyed susans, lavender thistles on the banks, dense trees covered with shaking leaves, rocky cliffs

—rope swing out into the water

—fish jumping, frogs perched on rocks

—ducks sleeping, camouflaged by resemblance to half wet rocks

—important to avoid getting caught on rocks in white water—canoe can be turned around by fast-moving water—riders helpless and canoe wobbly

—wear shoes that can get wet, hat and clothes that protect you from the hot sun—wear swim suit underneath

—rivers in the summer are warmer, lower, and slower than in the spring—good for learning to paddle a canoe

—in less populated areas, state parks rent canoes on the rivers

After you have produced a list of ideas, examples, facts, and details, you can examine your list. You will notice that you will probably have material for several paragraphs. The list of ideas for canoeing, for example, could become three paragraphs: one on equipment and things to take when you go canoeing, one on the pleasures of canoeing, one on how to paddle and how to handle white water. From these possible narrowed topics, you might decide to write on the pleasures of canoeing. You might limit the topic further by focusing on canoeing on a river in the summer. This paragraph topic would enable you to speak from your own experience and to include some ideas that would apply to most summer canoeing. You might then decide definitely that your audience would be your friends who have never gone canoeing and your purpose would be to persuade them to try it. Using your list of supporting information and these decisions, you might write several versions of your topic sentence.

POSSIBLE TOPIC SENTENCES: Canoeing on a river in the summer will reward you with good exercise, good views, and outdoor fun.

The pleasures of canoeing on a river in the summer are many: exercise, outdoor fun, and views of natural surroundings.

For exercise, outdoor fun, and a chance to be close to nature, you should try canoeing on a river in the summer.

When you have chosen a topic sentence that you like, you can then select the relevant support from your brainstorming sheet, and possibly add a few more ideas that occur to you. Then you can follow the regular writing steps you have learned.

Varying Drafting Steps.   A second adaptation of the writing process you might like to try is combining the steps for evaluating support and organizing support with the drafting step. Once you have a topic sentence and a list of support you might begin drafting directly from your list, deciding on unity and logical order of ideas as you write. Choosing this method may mean that you have to write several drafts to find the best supporting information and the best organization. However, this method has the advantage of allowing you to capture your ideas in paragraph form when they are fresh and of giving you more time to do the actual writing. As you try to write a paragraph with certain support in a particular order, you may discover that you have too many unrelated pieces of information and that your information should be organized in a better way. You can then make changes on your first draft before and as you write your second draft.

For example, if you were going to write a paragraph about the pleasures of canoeing on a river in the summer, you might have started by preparing a topic sentence and list of support as in the following chart, using the usual narrowing and questioning steps.

BRAINSTORMING FOR SUPPORT FOR A TOPIC SENTENCE

Topic Sentence: For exercise, outdoor fun, and a chance to be close to nature, you should try canoeing on a river in the summer.

What exercise does canoeing provide?

—paddling uses arm, shoulder, and back muscles

—can be as strenuous as you want depending upon how far and how fast you want to go

What outdoor fun can you have canoeing?

—floating and sliding with the current—relaxing

—canoe races with friends

—can beach canoe—picnic on bank or an island, and swim in river

—river bank might have rope swings from trees out into the water

—can sunbathe as you paddle and float

—can race through the white water (rapids)—scary and exciting—better than a ride at an amusement park

How does canoeing put you close to nature?

—see hills, forests, and rivers from the middle of it all

—purple heather, Queen Anne's lace, golden black-eyed susans, lavender thistles on the banks

—rocky cliffs

—dense cool trees covered with shivering leaves

—breeze ripples over water

—earthy smell

—can see fish swimming, frogs squatting on rocks, muskrats searching for food, ducks bobbing on the water

Why go canoeing on a river in the summer?

—in summer most rivers are warmer, lower, and slower than in spring

—calmer and less dangerous

—many state parks rent canoes at this time of year

—canoeing on a river gives you sense of journeying—current takes some of work out of paddling

From your list of support you might then begin to draft your paragraph without examining or screening support and without studying the support to find the most logical order. You could plan to do these steps as you write and after you write. Then you would probably have to write another draft.

Your first draft written directly from the support might resemble the following. Notice the ordering of information, the addition of a few ideas *not* on the list, and the omission of other ideas that were on the list.

First draft of
a paragraph

For exercise, outdoor fun, and a chance to be close to nature, you should try canoeing on a river in the summer. In the summer, when rivers are warmer, lower, and slower than in the spring, many state parks rent canoes to groups of people for day trips. River trips give you a sense of journeying and adventure, of a panorama unfolding, while the current on a river takes some of the work out of paddling. As you round each bend, you can see hills, forests, or cliffs on either side of you. From the middle of the river, you can watch banks of flowers, such as purple-tipped heather, creamy Queen Anne's lace, golden black-eyed susans, and lavender thistles slide by. You may also see fish swimming, frogs squatting on rocks, ducks bobbing on the water, and muskrats hunting for food. The breeze rippling over the water will surround you with the earthy smell of moist dirt, dense pine, and leafy trees. As you approach the shallows, where the water rushes over the rocks, you will hear splashing that sounds like waterfalls. When you tire of floating and sunbathing or paddling, you can beach the canoe on some sandy bank, picnic in the shade, or cool off with a swim in the river. Back on the river, you can have canoe races with your friends or shoot the canoe through the rapids, rushing through channels and dodging rocks on a ride more exciting than one in an amusement park. Throughout all this activity, you will be exercising. Paddling uses arm, shoulder, and back muscles. The amount of exercise you get, however, will depend upon how far and how fast you want to go and how much you swim and explore when you are not paddling.

Reading over this first draft of your paragraph, you might decide that it has a dull, disappointing ending. The paragraph might be stronger if you ended with comments about fun or nature. In fact, when you reexamine your topic sentence, you see that your reader will expect you to cover exercise first, then fun, and then nature. You could then do some deleting and organizing right on your first draft, as shown in the following model. You might notice groups of ideas within the paragraph, mark them, and number them for rearrangement according to the developmental order that you now see fits your topic sentence and support. You might also find some phrases and ideas that are not necessary as well as some transitions and bridge ideas that you do need.

First draft showing reorganizing and editing	For exercise, outdoor fun, and a chance to be close to nature, you should try canoeing on a river~~in the summer.~~ In the summer, when rivers are warmer, lower, and slower than in the spring, many state parks rent canoes ~~to groups of people~~ for day trips. River trips give you a sense of journeying and adventure, of a panorama unfolding, while the current on
(1)	
Bridge idea	*Besides providing exercise and fun, canoeing puts you close to nature.* a river takes some of the work out of paddling. As

hills,

you round each bend, you can see ~~hills,~~ forests, ∧or

or banks of flowers sliding by.

cliffs ∧~~on either side of you. From the middle of the~~

On an eastern shore, for example,

~~river,~~ ∧~~you can watch banks of flowers, such as~~ purple-tipped heather, creamy Queen Anne's lace, golden

line the banks with color.

black-eyed susans, and lavender thistles ∧~~slide by.~~ You may also see fish swimming, frogs squatting on

shadowed

∧rocks, ducks bobbing on the water, and muskrats

on a river ripples

hunting for food. The breeze ∧~~rippling~~ over the water

carrying

will ∧~~surround you with~~ the earthy smell of moist

the scent of   fresh, cool air.   In the shallows, the

dirt, ∧~~dense pine, and~~ ∧leafy trees. As ∧~~you approach the~~

river adds its splashing and rushing over rocky beds, surrounding

~~shallows, where the water rushes over the rocks, you~~

you in the middle of the river with the sounds as well as the sights

~~will hear splashing that sounds like waterfalls.~~ When

and smells of nature.   paddling or   as you float,

you tire of ~~floating and~~ ∧sunbathing ~~or~~ ∧paddling, you can beach the canoe on some sandy bank, picnic in the shade, or cool off with a swim in the river. Back

(3)   *race*

on the river, you can ~~have~~ ∧canoe ~~races~~ with your

small

friends or ~~shoot the canoe through the~~ ∧rapids, rush-

of the rapids   e

ing through channels ∧and dodg~~ing~~ rocks on a ride more exciting than one in an amusement park. ~~Throughout all this activity, you will be exercising.~~

will give your   a workout.

Paddling ∧~~uses~~ arm, shoulder, and back muscles. ∧The

(2)

> *canoeing on a river*
> amount of exercise you get, ~~however,~~ will depend
> upon how far and how fast you want to go, ~~and how~~
> ~~much you swim and explore when you are not~~
> ~~paddling.~~

After analyzing and marking your first draft, you should write a second draft showing your selection and rearrangement of ideas. As you rewrite your paragraph, you may even improve it further by your choice of words, phrases, and transitions. Notice how the second draft that follows differs from the first version of the paragraph on canoeing on page 653.

Second draft showing reorganization of the paragraph

For exercise, outdoor fun, and a chance to be close to nature, you should try canoeing on a river. In the summer, when the rivers have warmed up and have become more controlled than in the spring, many state parks rent canoes for day trips. As you travel down a river, you can paddle quickly or drift with the current, while you experience a sense of journeying and adventure and enjoy the scenery unfolding before you. The amount of exercise you get will depend upon how far and how fast you want to travel. However, paddling at any speed will exercise particularly your arm, shoulder, and back muscles. When you tire of paddling or sunbathing while drifting, you can beach the canoe on some sandy bank, picnic in the shade, or take a cooling swim. For pleasure, you can also race canoes with friends or rush through the channels of rapids, dodging rocks, on a ride more exciting then one in an amusement park. Besides providing exercise and fun, canoeing puts you close to nature. Rounding each bend, you can see forests, hills, cliffs, or banks of flowers slide by. On an eastern shore, for example, purple-tipped heather, creamy Queen Anne's lace, golden black-eyed susans, and lavender thistles may line the banks with color. You may also see fish swimming, frogs squatting on shadowed rocks, ducks bobbing on the water, and muskrats hunting for food. The breeze on a river ripples over the water, carrying the earthy smell of moist dirt, the scent of pines, and fresh, cool air. While you float in the deeper water, you can hear the rushing of the river over the rocks in the shallow stretches—the sights, fragrances, and sounds of natural beauty completely surround you.

When you have a second draft that is unified, complete, well-organized, and smoothly connected, recopy your paragraph in final form.

Varying Revising Steps.   Still another way to handle the writing process is to do extensive revising. If you plan to revise throughout the writing steps, you can get your ideas down on paper quickly. You will then spend most of your time revising. Your finished product will probably bear little resemblance to the first topic sentence and supporting information you had written. But at each point in the writing process you will always have something down on paper with which to work.

Essentially, revising throughout means thinking on paper— listing, expanding upon, crossing out, circling, and squeezing in ideas as you work on your paragraph topic, main idea, topic sentence, and list of support. You may have to do quite a bit of revising before you discover what you really want to say and how you want to say it. However, the changes you make as you revise show that you are concentrating on finding the best ideas and the best way to express those ideas.

If you use the method of revising throughout, your scrap paper and brainstorming sheets will show your changes, deletions, and additions at every step. The draft of your paragraph might resemble the marked up paragraph on page 654.

When you have reread your draft several times and made your last improvements, you can then make a final copy.

EXERCISE A: **Experimenting with Steps in Writing.** Choose one of the following topics or think of one of your own. Use the topic to begin writing a paragraph. Before you plan, write, and revise, choose one of the methods discussed in this section. Follow the method and show your work for each step. Be sure to keep track of the steps you follow.

Mysteries
Tipping
A popular style of
  clothing
Honesty
A famous artist (writer,
  sculptor, musician)

An unusual vehicle
The perfect summer job
Clever commercials or ads
A funny character from
  literature
Love

EXERCISE B: **Examining Your Approach.** Reexamine the approach you followed when you wrote a paragraph for Exercise A. Then list the steps that you followed. Briefly describe why you did or did not find the new approach helpful. Explain why you would use the method again, or speculate on what method might work better for you.

■ Overcoming Writing Problems

Writers of all ages—students, adults, professionals—can become frustrated when their ideas do not flow freely and when "writer's block" sets in. You may have experienced such problems. You may have wished that you could get started, or think of some new ideas, or gain some confidence in your work.

Try different techniques to help you begin writing, overcome writing "blocks," and look clearly and critically at your writing.

Writers have used the following techniques to stimulate their thinking and to gain perspective about their work. By experimenting with these techniques, you may find some that work well for you.

Getting Started.   Your first problem may be finding a topic when none has been assigned. If you have the freedom to write about anything, be open to all the possibilities from your own experiences and from the world around you. Suggestions in the following chart will show you some ways to do this.

SOME METHODS FOR FINDING A TOPIC	
Method	**How It Works**
Taking Action: Carry a pad and pencil with you as you walk around and discover ideas.	—Look around your room for objects such as a poster, postcard, memento, pair of shoes, or globe that might spark an idea.
	—Walk around your home. Think about events that have occurred there. Notice unusual features. Think about other people who once lived there and the interests, behavior, and ideas of guests who have visited.
	—Walk around your neighborhood. Look at buildings, landmarks, and vehicles. Study people and think about what might be on their minds, where they might be going, what their interests might be.

Going to Sources: Carry a pad and pencil with you as you flip through your own books, magazines, and newspapers or those in the library.	—Leaf through magazines and newspapers for any articles, pictures, or advertisements that might give you ideas for topics.
	—Browse through bookshelves at home or at the library. Look at titles and tables of contents that might suggest topics.
	—Use the card catalog in the library. Look for subjects such as Astronomy, Boating, or Crafts that might lead you to interesting topics.

Once you have a list of possible topics, you may not know which one to write about or what you want to say about a topic. You may need a push to get started on choosing and narrowing a topic. The suggestions in the following chart might help you over this hurdle.

SOME METHODS FOR CHOOSING AND FOCUSING A TOPIC	
Method	**How It Works**
Thought Associations	—Write a general topic on a piece of paper. Time yourself for a minute or so with a clock or timer. Write down as many smaller topics or related ideas as you can. Do not worry about whether or not they all make sense. Then select one of the smaller topics as your paragraph topic.
	—Ask someone to read one topic at a time to you, allowing you thirty seconds or a minute to list smaller related ideas for each. Select one of these smaller ideas for your paragraph topic.
Head-First Approach	—Take a number of possible topics and write each on a different sheet of paper. Beneath each, list all the smaller topics that occur to you. Then see which topic inspires you the most.

> —Begin writing sentences about different topics. Do not worry about organization or style. See which topic generates the most ideas. Choose that one.

Overcoming Blocks. Once you have begun writing, you may encounter "writer's block," the point at which you find yourself at a loss for words and ideas. Perhaps you have written only two or three sentences and cannot express the next idea, or perhaps you are more than halfway through the paper. In any event, you can try some of the following methods for "unstopping" your thoughts.

SOME METHODS FOR OVERCOMING BLOCKS	
Method	**How It Works**
Rereading	—Use the sentences you have written so far to help you express the next idea. Reread your sentences and concentrate on your main idea. Gather momentum for the next sentences. —Concentrate on the last sentence you have written. Certain words may help you with the next sentence by providing a bridge, a direction, or a point that needs explaining.
Talking It Over	—Ask someone to listen as you read aloud what you have written so far. Discuss where you intend the paragraph to go from there. —Ask someone to read your writing aloud. Listen to your work and frame the next ideas in sentences in your mind.
Going Back to Your Sources	—Reexamine the object or location that suggested your topic. Look at it, think about it, or talk about it with someone. See what ideas occur to you.

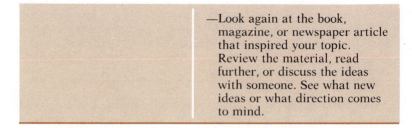

—Look again at the book, magazine, or newspaper article that inspired your topic. Review the material, read further, or discuss the ideas with someone. See what new ideas or what direction comes to mind.

Gaining Perspective. Sometimes during or after the writing of your first draft, you may feel unsure about what you have written. Does it communicate with your audience? Does it say what you want to say? Because you have been so involved in your writing, you will have to make a special effort to see your work as others do. If you can look at your work from a different point of view or from a fresh perspective, you should be able to identify any weaknesses. The following suggestions can help you evaluate your work objectively.

SOME METHODS FOR GAINING PERSPECTIVE	
Method	**How It Works**
Put Your Work Aside	—Put your work down and go on to some other activity. Think about something else for a while. Then return to your writing with a clearer head and immerse yourself in it again by rereading it.
Share Your Writing with Others	—Read your work to an audience of friends or relatives. Ask your audience to comment on strong points first and then on weaknesses and areas that need improvement.
Find an "Editor"	—Ask someone—a friend or relative—to inspect your work and to offer comments and constructive criticism. Discuss ideas for improving all aspects of the paragraph.

EXERCISE C: Preparing to Write. Use the following instructions to choose and narrow a topic.

1. Pretend that you have been told to write a paragraph about some kind of animal. Consult the chart on page 657 and list the specific activities that you could do to get started. Then use one of these activities to find a topic. Write down your topic. Afterwards, write one or two sentences commenting on how the activities helped you.
2. Once you have several possible topics, use two of the ideas in the chart on page 658 to help you narrow the topic.

EXERCISE D: **Overcoming a Writing Block.** The following paragraphs are incomplete because, in each case, the writer encountered a "block." Choose *one* of the paragraphs and decide what suggestions you would give the writer to overcome the block. Write three specific activities that the writer could perform to complete the paragraph.

(1) The effects of a dress code on students are more often negative than positive. If the code requires that all must wear identical uniforms, these suits can be depressing. Any dress code stifles individuality and prevents complete freedom of choice.

(2) Everyone should be prepared in at least four ways for power failures caused by storms or earthquakes. First, candles, matches, and flashlights should be readily available in case all electricity is cut off. A transistor radio should be handy so that people without electrical power can learn the extent of the damage and can estimate the time needed for repairs.

APPLICATION: **Using Your Own Approach to Writing.** Choose one of the following topics or think of a topic of your own on which to base a paragraph. As you prepare your paragraph, use one of the approaches you learned in this section or one of your own that works well for you. If you have difficulty getting started or if you encounter a "block" of ideas, try any of the suggestions in this section to overcome such problems.

A memorable quarrel	A bestselling record
A remarkable athlete	Physical fitness
A newly recognized sport	Types of testing
Sportsmanship	Carnivals, fairs, or circuses
Snobbery	Preparing a meal

Chapter 22

Paragraphs with Different Purposes

In addition to understanding the features of and steps for writing standard paragraphs, you should know about the different purposes paragraphs can have and the particular functions paragraphs can serve in longer works. The first section in this chapter discusses paragraphs with four different purposes: *expository paragraphs, persuasive paragraphs, descriptive paragraphs,* and *narrative paragraphs.* The second section in the chapter discusses special kinds of paragraphs often found in longer works. Understanding these paragraph variations will help you become a more versatile writer.

22.1 Expository, Persuasive, Descriptive, and Narrative Paragraphs

Your writing is always shaped by a purpose of some kind: You communicate with your reader for a reason. You may want to pass information along to your reader, or you may want to influence your reader's thoughts or feelings in some way. In any case, what you write will be shaped by your objective.

This section discusses the special features of paragraphs that serve four different purposes: *expository paragraphs*, which explain something to a reader; *persuasive paragraphs*, which attempt to change a reader's opinions or ideas; *descriptive paragraphs*, which attempt to recreate a person, place, object, or experience as fully as possible for a reader; and *narrative par-*

agraphs, which connect a series of events into a unified story. This section will give you practice in writing all of these paragraphs.

■ Writing Expository Paragraphs

Expository paragraphs are versatile: They can vary from scholarly discussions of difficult concepts to practical explanations of such matters as first aid and backpacking. You will be doing expository writing whenever you prepare a job application, answer an examination question, present a theory, write out a recipe, or direct a friend to your house. For this reason, you should understand expository writing and how you can do it effectively.

An Explanatory Purpose and an Informative Tone. Expository writing sets out to *explain* something to an audience. The subject may be a concept, a historical event, a process, or the meaning of a word. The audience may already be familiar with the topic or may never have heard of it. But whatever the topic and audience, all expository writing has a few recognizable characteristics.

> The main features of an expository paragraph are an explanatory purpose and an informative tone.

Since its main purpose is explanatory, an expository paragraph is factual, consisting of objective and verifiable information. It does not contain opinions. In the following statements of fact and opinion, note that the statement of fact is an indisputable matter of public record, whereas the statement of opinion offers an interpretation or a personal judgment, which could be challenged.

STATEMENT OF FACT: The English language is largely hybrid, mixing Anglo-Saxon roots with Latin and French borrowings.

STATEMENT OF OPINION: Because of its hybrid nature, the English language is the most versatile and flexible language on earth.

An expository paragraph should have a topic sentence that states a factual main idea, which can be explained with objective information—examples, details, facts, incidents. For example, an expository paragraph about tennis serves might establish the main idea that different serves can be effective in different situations and then might go on to explain the advantages of several different serves. Often, the supporting information can include references to documented sources, such as newspaper accounts, almanacs, encyclopedias, and other historical records. For example, the paragraph about tennis serves could include the recommendations of professionals or could refer to specific newspaper accounts of winning serves in particular tournaments.

The explanatory purpose of an expository paragraph should be apparent in its informative tone. The writer should make a deliberate and sustained attempt to instruct the reader about a particular topic. In order to do this effectively, the writer must decide how much the reader already knows about the topic and then choose supporting information and language that corresponds to the reader's knowledge. When the reader is unfamiliar with the topic, the writer should use uncomplicated information and language and should supply the reader with examples to clarify particularly difficult material. For more knowledgeable readers, the writer should go into greater depth or develop a more detailed aspect of the topic and should use more advanced language.

The following expository paragraph about hailstones presents factual information to a general audience. Notice that the paragraph begins with a statement of fact and then clarifies and develops this statement with specific examples and facts. The ideas and language are direct and appropriate for readers who may not be familiar with the topic.

Expository paragraph with an explanatory purpose and an informative tone	Hailstones vary greatly in size and shape. They can be as small as a pea or as large as a grapefruit. They can be conical, round, or oblate, dimpled or knobbed with protrusions. The largest stones weigh from one to two pounds and fall at a speed of some 100 miles per hour. People have been reported killed by hailstones in India and a 1977 plane crash in Georgia was attributed to hail. But the greatest damage from hail is to high-value crops such as fruit and vegetables and is caused by small stones that can blanket the ground and occasionally accumulate to a depth of several inches. —John Hallett

In addition to its basic explanatory purpose and informative tone, an expository paragraph may have a secondary purpose and tone. An expository paragraph might have a secondary purpose of defining a term or instructing the reader in some task. The writer might also want to entertain the reader in addition to explaining something. Similarly, expository writing can establish an informative tone while ranging from the serious and formal to the matter-of-fact and informal to the lighthearted and casual. For example, the following discussion of holography—three-dimensional photography—both informs and entertains the reader. The paragraph has a casual, enthusiastic tone.

Expository paragraph with an entertaining purpose and a casual tone	Essentially each holographic movie display in the Museum of Holography is a transparent, 120-degree, screen-like partition suspended in a smooth semi-circle against the wall. A lightbulb is fitted at the base against the wall and—presto!—an ethereal embodiment of a personality appears lurking in midair behind the screen. The uncanny motion comes into play as a viewer advances from one side of each display to the other. The speed of action is regulated by the rate at which a viewer walks around the screen. Hence, the viewer had delightful control over whether Joseph Papp appears to recite prose at a ridiculously super-animated pace or a lethargic one. —Adapted from Peggy Sealfon

Pointers for Writing Expository Paragraphs. When you write an expository paragraph, you should concentrate on explaining. You should focus your topic in a single sentence, gather and organize your supporting information, draft your paragraph, and revise it with the strong and clear intention of communicating information to a particular audience in order to expand that audience's knowledge.

Focus on explaining the topic to a specific audience as you select the content and language for an expository paragraph.

The following guidelines should help you apply what you already know about writing paragraphs to the specific requirements of expository writing.

SUGGESTIONS FOR WRITING EXPOSITORY PARAGRAPHS

1. Choose a topic that lends itself to factual treatment, that interests you, and that you can write about with authority.
2. Decide on any secondary purpose and tone.
3. Determine your audience and its knowledge of your topic.

4. Focus your topic by finding a main idea and write a factual statement expressing that idea.

5. Gather supporting information, and select those examples, details, and facts which best explain your main idea to your audience.

6. Organize your support logically for clarity.

7. Draft your paragraph, concentrating on your explanatory purpose, as well as your secondary purpose, if you have one.

8. Revise your paragraph for unity and coherence, and check your language to make sure that your tone is objective and informative throughout. If there is a secondary tone in your paragraph, it should also come through consistently. (See the checklist for revision on page 645 for additional suggestions.)

EXERCISE A: Recognizing the Features of Expository Paragraphs. Read the following expository paragraphs and identify in each (1) the topic sentence, (2) the pieces of supporting information, and (3) any secondary purpose and tone.

(1) If you are supposed to yawn [onstage], you must learn that the physical reason for yawning is a need for oxygen in the brain. Most of you will open your mouths wide and *ex*hale, and then jump to another action because exhaling felt so peculiar. Instead, you should *in*hale deeply as you push your jaw down and back until the mouth opens, and you continue to pull the air deeply into your lungs before forcing it up into your head as you exhale. You can create a yawn at will in this way so that your eyes may even water. —Adapted from Uta Hagen

(2) The neutrino is the nearest thing to nothing, being distinguished from the other elementary particles of matter mainly by what it does not have and what it does not do. The traditional theory of the neutrino describes it as a particle without mass and without electric charge. It interacts with matter only through the weakest of the basic forces of nature. The earth moves in a thick soup of neutrinos (there are estimated to be about 100 per cubic centimeter throughout the volume of the universe), but they are such ephemeral particles that they almost never leave any trace of their passage. —*Scientific American*

EXERCISE B: Planning, Writing, and Revising Expository Paragraphs. List *five* general topics in which you are interested and about which you could write expository paragraphs. Choose one and write an expository paragraph, following the steps you have learned for writing paragraphs, along with the suggestions on the chart above. When you revise your paragraph, refer to the checklist for revising on page 645.

■ Writing Persuasive Paragraphs

Persuasive writing attempts to convince the reader to accept the writer's opinion. It appears in its most obvious form in editorials, speeches, advertisements, and reviews of films, plays, and books, but many essays, letters, and other kinds of writing also involve persuasion. Because you will be doing persuasive writing whenever you write to express an opinion, interpret something, or argue in favor of a course of action, you should become familiar with the main features of persuasive paragraphs.

A Persuasive Purpose and Tone.   Persuasive writing attempts to change the reader's mind: to make the writer's opinion or interpretation so convincing that the reader agrees with it. In order to accomplish this goal, the persuasive writer must find arguments and language that attract the reader's interest and appeal to his or her reason.

> The main features of a persuasive paragraph are a persuasive purpose and a reasonable, convincing tone.

Because a persuasive paragraph attempts to convince the reader to agree with something, its topic sentence should be a statement of *opinion*, a matter of interpretation. Furthermore, the opinion should be one that the reader will find significant and that the writer can support with fact and logic. The following examples demonstrate the difference between appropriate and inappropriate topic sentences for persuasive paragraphs.

STATEMENT OF OPINION: The defendant's right to a fair trial should take precedence over the reporter's right to protect his or her sources.

STATEMENT OF FACT: The right of free speech and the right of a fair trial are both protected by the Constitution.

SIGNIFICANT OPINION: Nuclear power presents too great a hazard to public safety to be used as a major energy source.

INSIGNIFICANT OPINION: I don't like nuclear power.

SUPPORTABLE OPINION: Of all the Presidents of the nineteenth century, Abraham Lincoln faced the greatest problems.

UNSUPPORTABLE OPINION: No other President, past or future, can match Lincoln's greatness.

Every element of the persuasive paragraph should attempt to convince the reader to accept the writer's opinion. The topic sentence should be supported with specific examples, strong evidence, and logical arguments. Clear, relevant facts and other concrete information can engage the reader's interest and win his or her consideration of the writer's opinion.

The tone of a persuasive paragraph should be compelling but reasonable. It should express the writer's opinion forcefully while showing respect for the reader's possibly opposing views. Firm but reasonable language is more likely to be persuasive than emotionally loaded words, which could antagonize the reader. The use of exact, concrete language and relevant comparisons will also help to establish the writer's credibility and hold the reader's attention.

The following persuasive paragraph by Barbara Tuchman argues that there has been a decline in the quality of the goods produced for the mass market. Notice the writer's use of historical examples and logical arguments to make her opinion sound reasonable and worth considering.

Persuasive paragraph with a persuasive purpose and a reasonable tone

In former times, the princely patron had the resources in wealth and power to commission the finest workmanship, materials, and design. Since his motive was generally self-glorification, the result was as beautiful and magnificent as he could command: in crystal and gold and tapestry, in exquisite silks and brocades, in the jewelled and enameled masterpieces of Cellini, the carved staircases of Grinling Gibbons. The decline in quality that has since set in has a good historical reason: The age of privilege is over and civilization has passed into the age of the masses ... our culture has been taken over by commercialism directed to the mass market and necessarily to mass taste. De Tocqueville stated the problem, already appearing in his time [a century and a half ago], when he wrote: "When only the wealthy had watches they were very good ones; few are now made that are worth much but everyone has one in his pocket." —Adapted from Barbara Tuchman

While it is the basic objective of the persuasive paragraph to win the reader over to the writer's opinion, persuasive writing can vary in the *urgency* of its purpose and tone. The writer of a persuasive paragraph might want simply to offer the reader a fresh interpretation of a particular question or set of circumstances. On the other hand, the writer might want to spur the reader to take action: for example, to attend a meeting, to vote a certain way, to buy a certain product. The tone of persuasive writing can range from the compelling urgency of a political speech to the relaxed and amusing chattiness of a sports commentary or a movie review.

The following paragraph is a humorous commentary on the experience of camping today. Notice that the tone of the paragraph is casual and amused.

Persuasive paragraph with a humorous tone

Camping out has become so popular among travelers that campgrounds in summer are likely to be simply crawling with people, pets, vehicles, habitats, and implements, all piled onto one prime strip of the Great Outdoors. At a typical crowded campground, the variety of camping styles is in itself a thing of wonder. One family, visible only from the collective waist up, floats about a high pavilion made of canvas and mosquito netting, setting the table for dinner, just as if they had not left the screen porch back home. Only five feet away, another group prefers to rough it on the bare ground with a pup tent and campfire, somehow oblivious to the impressive technology that surrounds them. Everything and everybody is crammed into such close quarters that the campground could be mistaken for some sort of outdoor convention of recreation equipment vendors, if it were not for the scenic splendor hovering in front of the milling crowd, like a colossal television set.

Pointers for Writing Persuasive Paragraphs.   When you write persuasive paragraphs, work through the steps you have already learned for paragraph writing. Concentrate especially on presenting a definite opinion and on convincing your reader to accept it. You will write more persuasively if you assume that your audience disagrees with you and must be won over to your side.

Concentrate on defending your opinion to an unsympathetic or apathetic reader as you choose the content and language for your persuasive paragraph.

The material you use to support your opinion in a persuasive paragraph is crucial to your paragraph's effectiveness. In order to win your reader over to your side, you must defend your opinion with accurate, specific, and compelling examples, facts, and reasons. The more controversial your opinion, the more carefully you must build your defense.

One way to find strong support for your side involves considering the opposing arguments, so that you can counter objections that may occur to your reader. Such anticipation of opposing arguments can help you eliminate the weak spots in the defense of your opinion. For example, if you were opposing the absolute right of reporters to keep their sources confidential in a court of law, you might build a defense by listing points for and against your own position, and then by answering the other side's arguments, as the following chart demonstrates.

BUILDING YOUR DEFENSE		
Topic Sentence: The privilege of the reporter to protect his or her sources should be waived by the court when such information is crucial to the just outcome of a trial.		
Evidence For	**Evidence Against**	**Additional Evidence For**
—the defendant has a Constitutional right to a fair trial and should be protected against unfair accusation by unknown sources	—the reporter's right of free speech is also protected by the Constitution	—if the two Constitutional rights are in conflict, the judge must decide which takes precedence —reporter's right is not absolute
—the public's right to a just outcome in a trial should take precedence over the reporter's privilege	—the reporter cannot practice his or her profession under the threat of being forced to reveal sources in court	—the right of the reporter to earn a livelihood should not affect the judgment of a court case —the Constitutional protections interfere with the free practice of all kinds of professions

—the special privilege of reporters not to disclose confidential material is not more binding than those involving doctor-patient, attorney-client, or priest-penitent relationships; these are left up to the court to decide case by case	—rights of reporters are in a different category since they are guaranteed by the Constitution *explicitly*	—rights of reporters should not be waived except in those few *special* cases in which the court determines that the defendant cannot receive a fair trial without the privileged information —court has the power to make such a judgment

The process of building a defense for a controversial opinion by anticipating opposing arguments can also suggest ways of arranging your supporting material in the paragraph. You may want to acknowledge that the opposition has a few good arguments; *conceding a point* in this way will increase your credibility with your reader. It indicates that you are reasonable and have considered all sides of the issue. You might even approach your issue by answering the other side's major arguments with your own stronger ones in a con-pro—con-pro—con-pro arrangement, ending the paragraph with your own most powerful argument.

The following guidelines will help you write all kinds of persuasive paragraphs, whether they involve highly controversial questions or reactions and interpretations.

SUGGESTIONS FOR WRITING PERSUASIVE PARAGRAPHS

1. Think about an issue, question, or set of circumstances you know well and have a strong interest in. Determine your opinion on the topic.
2. Decide on the urgency of your purpose and your tone: How controversial is your opinion? And how intensely do you want to convince your reader?

3. Determine your audience and its expected response to your opinion: whether it is apathetic, unsympathetic, or strongly opposed.

4. Focus your opinion in a topic sentence that is clear, significant, and supportable.

5. Gather specific examples, facts, reasons, and incidents to support your opinion. For a highly controversial opinion, take the opposition into account and list the evidence for and against your side.

6. Organize your support by order of importance or interest, leading up to your most convincing argument. For highly controversial opinions, plan to concede one or more points, and organize your defense around the opposition's arguments.

7. Draft your paragraph in forceful but reasonable language, using specific, concrete words and making logical connections between ideas.

8. Revise your paragraph by looking for any weaknesses in your approach or any inconsistencies in your tone. (See the checklist for revision on page 645.)

EXERCISE C: Recognizing the Features of Persuasive Paragraphs. Read the following persuasive paragraphs and identify in each (1) the opinion in the topic sentence, (2) the supporting evidence, and (3) the urgency of the writer's purpose and tone.

(1) In every stage of these oppressions we have petitioned for redress in the most humble terms: our repeated petitions have been answered only by repeated injury. A prince whose character is thus marked by every act which may define a tyrant, is unfit to be the ruler of a free people. Nor have we been wanting in attentions to our British brethren. We have warned them from time to time of attempts by their legislature to extend an unwarrantable jurisdiction over us. We have reminded them of the circumstances of our emigration and settlement here. We have appealed to their native justice and magnanimity, and we have conjured them by the ties of our common kindred to disavow these usurpations, which would inevitably interrupt our connections and correspondence. They too have been deaf to the voice of justice and consanguinity. We must, therefore, acquiesce in the necessity which denounces our separation, and hold them, as we hold the rest of mankind, enemies in war, in peace, friends. —Thomas Jefferson

(2) One of the most insidious and dangerous of the many environmental problems is air pollution, particularly acid precipitation. It is one that simply cannot wait. Sulfur and nitrogen oxides from power and industrial plants are hurled high into the atmosphere. Carried by air currents hundreds or thousands of miles, these particles can be transformed into compounds which

contribute to respiratory diseases, sterilize lakes and streams, damage vegetation, and cloud the sky. Accelerating the use of coal for energy to replace oil promises to aggravate already serious situations in the Upper Midwest, Rocky Mountains, Southeast, and New England-Canadian regions. How much more can we take? —Thomas L. Kimball

EXERCISE D: **Planning, Writing and Revising Persuasive Paragraphs.** List *five* general topics or issues about which you could formulate opinions appropriate for a persuasive paragraph. Select one of these topics and write a persuasive paragraph, following the suggestions in the chart at the left. If your opinion is particularly controversial, take note of opposing arguments and use a chart to build your defense. Revise your paragraph, using the checklist for revising on page 645.

■ Writing Descriptive Paragraphs

Descriptive writing paints a picture of a topic in words that appeal to the reader's senses and imagination. Much of your own writing will involve description of some kind, ranging from your impressions of a vacation spot to your detailed word picture of the structure of a cell on an examination. Because you will often want to make someone else see something *exactly* as you saw it, you should learn to recognize and use the elements of effective description.

A Descriptive Purpose and Descriptive Language. A descriptive paragraph conveys a single dominant impression of a particular topic. The specific details and words are vivid enough to enable the reader to see or experience the topic as clearly and intensely as the writer saw or experienced it.

The main features of a descriptive paragraph are a descriptive purpose, which attempts to communicate a dominant impression, and descriptive language, which attempts to appeal to the reader's senses, imagination, and emotions.

A descriptive paragraph focuses on a *single* topic and creates a *single* dominant impression of that topic. The dominant impression may be the most outstanding quality of the topic—its heaviness, brightness, or vitality—or it might be a characteristic, which makes the topic different from all other things, such as a particular animal's mannerism. A dominant impression can also be a mood, a feeling created by the topic: for example, the terror of a storm or the joyousness of a spring scene. This dominant impression may be explicitly stated at the beginning, at the end, or in the middle of the paragraph. On the other hand, it may only be implied, that is, subtly revealed by the details and language of the paragraph.

To make a dominant impression real for the reader, a descriptive paragraph should include striking, specific details. These details can help the reader visualize or imagine the precise dimensions, colors, and distinguishing features of the topic. For instance, to make a particular street recognizable for the reader, you could mention details of the shapes, kinds, and colors of the buildings, the kinds of trees, the width of the street and sidewalks, the cars parked along the curbs, the mailboxes, and so on. To present these details and to make your description strong, you should use exact verbs, concrete nouns, and vivid adjectives. In contrast, weak description fails to provide enough specific details and fails to use accurate, vivid language. Instead, it consists only of general statements and vague, judgmental language: for example, adjectives such as *large, attractive, interesting, elderly.* In the following examples of weak and strong description, notice that the weak description gives the reader only a fuzzy picture of the person who is being described whereas the strong description helps the reader to see this particular man.

WEAK DESCRIPTION: The middle-aged hiker carried a strange collection of things, including binoculars and some pipes.

STRONG DESCRIPTION: The hiker, a man in his late fifties or early sixties, wore a Russian fur cap and carried binoculars and a small knapsack with an umbrella sticking out. Around the back of his belt in little loops hung twelve or more pipes, some of wood, some of horn, and some of ivory.

Effective description also involves the reader by using sensory impressions and figures of speech. Sensory impressions are specific details that appeal to the reader's sense of sight, smell, hearing, touch, or taste. For instance, a sensory impression could be the waxiness of a daffodil or the metallic smell of the dentist's drill. In addition, figures of speech—similes, metaphors, personification, and analogies—can help to depict the topic vividly. For example, the hills in fall colors might be *a patchwork quilt;* or the wind might nip at the house *like a pestering puppy.* Such imaginative comparisons allow the reader to share the writer's perceptions of the topic and perhaps even experience the shock of recognition of common experiences. (For a more detailed explanation of sensory impressions and figures of speech, see Section 18.2.)

The specific details, sensory impressions, and imaginative comparisons in a descriptive paragraph should be organized logically for the reader. The details should be arranged in an order that the reader can follow and that clarifies the dominant impression the writer wishes to communicate. Many descriptive paragraphs present their details in spatial order, such as from top to bottom, left to right, near to far, or outside to inside. Other descriptions, such as of an animal running, or of a train approaching, passing, and then disappearing, or of an ice cream cone melting might follow chronological order.

The following descriptive paragraph by Joan Didion presents a series of images of Bogotá, Colombia. The dominant impression is one of remoteness and aloofness. The details are organized in spatial order, from indoors to outdoors, and in order of importance, leading to the most memorable detail, that of the mountains in the distance.

Descriptive paragraph creating a dominant impression of aloofness

Of the time I spent in Bogotá I remember mainly images, indelible but difficult to connect. I remember the walls on the second floor of the Museo Nacional, white and cool and lined with portraits of the presidents of Colombia, a great many presidents. I remember the emeralds in shop windows, lying casually in trays, all of them oddly pale at the center, somehow watered, cold at the very heart where one expects the fire. I asked the price of one: "Twenty-thousand American," the woman said. She was reading a booklet called *Horoscopo: Sagitario* and did not look up. I remember walking across Plaza Bolivar, the great square from which all Colombian power emanates, at midafternoon, when men in dark European suits stood talking on the steps of the Capitol and the mountains floated all around, their perspective made fluid by the sun and shadow; I remember the way the mountains dwarfed a deserted Ferris wheel in the Parque Nacional in late afternoon. —Joan Didion

A writer can use descriptive details and language in different ways to produce many different kinds of responses in the reader. Through the selection of details, sensory impressions, and certain words, a writer can create different moods. In the preceding paragraph, the writer has chosen to emphasize coolness and aloofness—in the white walls of the Museo Nacional, the cool emeralds, the deserted Ferris wheel, and the mountains. The writer conveys her fascination with and detachment from the scene she describes. The paragraph leads a reader also to feel resignation and detachment, a mood which arises from the sense of distances and impersonality. By choosing different details and language, Joan Didion might have emphasized the city's buzzing life. The following paragraph by Charles Dickens from *Little Dorrit* describes another city scene and produces an entirely different mood. Dickens captures the oppressiveness of a hot Sunday evening in nineteenth-century London when there is nothing to do. Notice how he recreates the sounds that contribute to the mood.

Descriptive paragraph creating a mood of gloom and sadness

It was a Sunday evening in London, gloomy, close, and stale. Maddening church bells of all degrees of dissonance, sharp and flat, cracked and clear, fast and slow, made the brick-and-mortar echoes hideous. Melancholy streets in a penitential garb of soot steeped the souls of the people who were condemned to look at them out of windows in dire despondency. In every thoroughfare, up almost every alley, and down almost every turning, some doleful bell was throbbing, jerking, tolling, as if the Plague were in the city and the dead-carts were going round. Everything was bolted and barred that could by possibility furnish relief to an overworked people. Nothing to see but streets, streets, streets. Nothing to breathe but streets, streets, streets.
—Charles Dickens

Descriptive paragraphs may also have secondary purposes or may appear in longer works that have other purposes. For example, a description of a car or of a resort might have a secondary purpose of persuading the reader to buy the car or to vacation at the resort. A piece of expository writing might contain a scientific or technical description of the topic. Or a writer can use description in order to amuse a reader.

The following paragraph by zoologist Archie Carr details a mysterious and intriguing facet of snake behavior so that the non-expert can visualize and understand the "combat dance."

Descriptive paragraph that explains with technical description

Another overt piece of snake behavior that rewards a lucky snake-watcher is the combat dance between the males of some species. This is a balletlike posturing by two male snakes, a crossing and recrossing of necks as the two performers raise the foreparts of their bodies high above the ground until

they topple over backwards. The routine is punctuated by periods in which the snakes chase each other about at terrific speed. Then the neck crossing is resumed. No biting or constricting or other violence is involved, and the social function of the dance is not clear. Over and above its interest as an arresting instinctive behavior pattern, the occurrence of the ritual in such distantly related animals as pit vipers, rat snakes, and racers is quite extraordinary.
—Adapted from Archie Carr

Pointers for Writing Descriptive Paragraphs. While you are planning, organizing, drafting, and revising your descriptive paragraph, you should be focusing on making your topic concrete and recognizable for the reader. Your aim should be to express your dominant impression through your choice of details and vivid language.

Focus on making the reader sense, imagine, and respond emotionally to what you are describing as you choose the content and language for a descriptive paragraph.

The topic of your description will determine the kinds of details you choose. To describe a person, you might elaborate on physical and behavioral characteristics, such as facial features, height, weight, movements, voice, and habits. To describe an object, you might focus on size, shape, and use. To recreate a scene or experience, you could present the sights, sounds, smells, surroundings, people involved, and your own feelings.

The following chart offers additional guidelines for writing effective descriptive paragraphs.

SUGGESTIONS FOR WRITING DESCRIPTIVE PARAGRAPHS

1. Choose a particular person, object, place, or experience for your description. Your knowledge of your topic should be detailed enough to provide you with several strong, interesting impressions.
2. Determine a dominant impression of your topic and state it in a topic sentence.
3. Decide if your paragraph will fulfill a secondary purpose besides description and if it will create a specific mood.
4. Give yourself a time limit and list as many details, sensory impressions, and comparisons to describe your topic as you can. Express your details, sensory impressions, and

comparisons in exact language, using vivid verbs, nouns, and adjectives.

5. Organize your details, sensory impressions, and comparisons in the order which most clearly establishes your dominant impression.

6. While you draft your paragraph, try to appeal to the reader's senses, imagination, and emotions.

7. Revise your paragraph to strengthen your dominant impression and make the description as vivid as possible. (See the checklist for revising on page 645.)

EXERCISE E: Recognizing the Features of Descriptive Paragraphs. Read the following descriptive paragraphs and identify (1) the stated or implied dominant impression, (2) the specific details, sensory impressions, and figures of speech that develop the dominant impression, and (3) the mood created or any secondary purpose.

(1) The antique cash register glowed a pale greenish-gold, broken by sullen flecks of green tarnish. Its arching narrow decorated front curved gracefully downward to eleven long-stemmed, lotus-headed keys. It seemed to perch lightly and elegantly on the counter, but in truth the thing squatted there, unbudgeable, a dense, implacable weight. It was a product of a solider time, which lived on in the heavy little machine's solid frame, solid metal, solid wood, solid marble—in all the reassuring substance and solidity that money once could buy.

(2) Myers was the perfect type of rootless municipalized man who finds his pleasures in the handouts or overflow of an industrial civilization. He enjoyed standing on a curbstone, watching parades, the more nondescript the better, the Labor Day parade being his favorite, and next to that a military parade, followed by the commercial parades with floats and girls dressed in costumes; he would even go to Lake Calhoun or Lake Harriet for doll-carriage parades and competitions of children dressed as Indians. He liked bandstands, band concerts, public parks devoid of grass; sky writing attracted him; he was quick to hear of a department-store demonstration where colored bubbles were blown, advertising a soap, to the tune of "I'm Forever Blowing Bubbles," sung by a mellifluous soprano. He collected coupons and tinfoil, bundles of newspaper for the old rag-and-bone man (thus interfering seriously with our school paper drives), free samples of cheese at Donaldson's, free tickets given out by a neighborhood movie house to the first installment of a serial—in all the years we lived with him, we never saw a full-length movie but only those truncated beginnings. He was always weighing himself on penny weighing machines. He seldom left the house except on one of these purposeless errands, or else to go to a ball game, by himself. —Mary McCarthy

EXERCISE F: **Planning, Writing, and Revising Descriptive Paragraphs.** List *five* topics which you could describe in detail. Choose one of them and write a descriptive paragraph, following the guidelines in the chart at the left. Revise your paragraph, using the checklist for revising on page 645.

■ Writing Narrative Paragraphs

Narrative writing appears in novels and short stories, in memoirs, and in biographies, but it can be found in all kinds of writing—whenever a series of related events are told as a story. Even if you have not experimented with writing short stories, you have probably developed some narrative skill by relating experiences and anecdotes in your letters and even in your day to day conversations and jokes. The following pages will help you strengthen and practice the basic techniques of writing narrative paragraphs.

A Narrative Purpose and Graphic Language. A narrative paragraph presents a series of events in chronological order in a story or part of a story. It attempts to involve and usually to entertain the reader through the graphic language of action as well as the specific details and sensory impressions of descriptive language.

The main features of a narrative paragraph are a narrative purpose that tells a series of related events in story form and graphic language that conveys action and sensory impressions.

A narrative paragraph recounts a series of actions, mental, physical or both, occurring in sequence. It covers a limited period of time and has a beginning, a middle, and an end. The story related in the narrative paragraph may be complete in itself, or it may be part of a longer narrative. But in either case, the narrative paragraph presents events involving action and moves through time: Something happens between the opening and closing sentences.

The topic sentence of a narrative paragraph can be one of several kinds. It can simply set the scene and start the action of the story. On the other hand, if the story is intended to illustrate some general truth or to offer the reader a lesson that the writer has learned, the topic sentence may actually state that general truth or main idea. The topic sentence may appear at the beginning or end of the paragraph. In some narrative paragraphs that are part of longer narratives, the first sentence may simply continue the action from the preceding paragraph. Whatever form the topic sentence takes, it should arouse the reader's curiosity and make him or her want to read further.

Every story has a story teller or narrator. A narrative paragraph's *narrator*, also called *point of view*, is usually indicated by the topic sentence or first sentence of the paragraph. It is the narrator who tells the events and who determines through whose eyes the reader sees the action of the story. When writing a narrative paragraph, you can choose to write in the *first person*, using *I*. A first person narrator participates in the events of the story, tells them as he or she sees them, and can include his or her thoughts and feelings. Another point of view you may choose is *third person objective* observer. This third person objective narrator reports the visible actions in the story but does not participate in the actions and cannot see into any of the minds of the people involved. Still another possibility is the *third person partially omniscient* narrator, who does not participate in the story but who tells the story from the perspective of a single character in the story. This narrator can see into the mind of that one character and record his or her feelings and thoughts. Finally, the *third person generally omniscient* narrator does not participate in the action but can enter the minds of several or all of the characters. No matter which of these narrators you choose, you should maintain that point of view consistently throughout the narrative.

A narrative paragraph must consist of events arranged in chronological order. The events are the physical and/or mental actions of the story. The narrator determines the kind of actions your narrative paragraph can include. For example, a first person narrator can relate his or her own actions and other people's actions and can mention his or her own thoughts but not those of others. A paragraph with a third person objective narrator can include only observable actions. Whether the events of the narrative are primarily thoughts or observable actions, the events should be arranged in a time order. The paragraph might begin with the outcome of the story and then trace its development, but the body of a narrative paragraph still moves forward in time, drawing the reader along to what happens next.

The graphic language used to convey these actions should enable the reader to become involved in what is happening. Graphic language consists of precise action verbs, specific, concrete nouns, and colorful adjectives. It recreates the pace of the events and through the transitions and other connecting devices makes the story flow. Graphic language can also build suspense and mystery by hinting at what is to come and by making the reader want to read faster. Frequently, narrative paragraphs also make use of descriptive language—specific details, sensory impressions, and figures of speech—to make the action more real for the reader.

In the following narrative paragraph from a story by Arthur L. Campa, the topic sentence sets the scene and begins the action of this incident. The story is told from the third person partially omniscient point of view so that the reader knows the character's thoughts as well as sees his actions. Notice that the graphic language engages and holds the reader's attention, builds suspense, and makes the reader feel like a witness to the scene.

Narrative paragraph with a third person partially omniscient narrator

Halfway down the wall the scorpion lost its hold and fell the remaining distance to the earthen floor with a dull thud. Its menacing pincers went up immediately like the horns on a Texas longhorn, as it raised its grayish belly on four pairs of bony legs. José kept his eyes riveted on it and watched every move. Twelve inches of the most vicious spider known lay before him! The scorpion charged. José ran around the table. Again and again the spider raised its lance to deal the fatal blow, but the elusive prey jumped over it. More determined than ever, the scorpion tried to approach José by moving cautiously toward him. More than once José thought of stepping on the ugly monster, but the thought of touching such a dangerous hard-shelled creature with his bare foot was too revolting. The nocturnal spider snapped its pincers in defiance and made for its prey, poised on the tips of its stout legs. José backed slowly, watching his chance for a spring. Step by step he kept retreating until inadvertently he ran against the wall and stumbled. The scorpion saw its chance and charged, but José resorted to a machicueta, turning over his head with a handspring that cleared him fully six feet across the room. "Caramba!" he exclaimed, "That was too close a call!"
—Arthur L. Campa

Like descriptive writing, narrative writing can create a mood or serve a secondary purpose. A story may make a reader feel depressed, frightened, peaceful, or joyful. The mood evoked by the preceding paragraph is a combination of fear, exhilaration, and hope. In addition to creating various moods, a narrative paragraph can also function to amuse, to instruct, or to persuade the reader. Sometimes a passage of narrative writing can be part of a longer work of expository or persuasive writing, or sometimes narrative writing can have a secondary purpose, such as to inform or to convince.

The following nonfictional narrative by Dorothy Canfield tells how she developed an idea for a story she wrote. The narrative paragraph relates a series of events in order to explain as well as to entertain. Notice that it has a first person narrator and begins with a topic sentence that states a general truth or main idea, which the story then illustrates.

Narrative paragraph with a first person narrator

My story "Flint and Fire" hovered vaguely in a shimmer of general emotion, and then abruptly crystallized itself about a chance phrase and cadence of the voice which pronounced it. One evening, going on a very prosaic errand to a farm-house of our region, I walked along a narrow path through dark pines; beside a brook swollen with melting snow I found the old man I came to see, sitting silent and alone before his blackened small old house. The old man had been for some years desperately unhappy. I had known this, every one knew it. But that evening, played upon as I had been by the stars, the darkness of the pines and the shouting voice of the brook, I suddenly stopped merely knowing it, and felt it. It seemed to me that his misery emanated from him like a soundless wail of anguish. We talked very little, odds and ends of neighborhood gossip, until the old man, shifting his position, drew a long breath and said, "Seems to me I never heard the brook sound so loud as it has this spring." There came instantly to my mind the recollection that his grandfather had drowned in that brook, and I sat silent, shaken by that thought and by the sound of his voice. And I knew at the same instant that I would try to get that pang of emotion into a story and make other people feel it. —Adapted from Dorothy Canfield

Pointers for Writing Narrative Paragraphs. Writing a narrative paragraph involves using the familiar paragraph-writing steps while focusing on your particular purpose. Your principal concerns should be to connect a series of events in a continuous narrative that is unified by a consistent narrator and enlivened by the graphic language of action and description.

Focus on making your story realistic and captivating for the reader as you choose the content and language for a narrative paragraph.

When you are planning, writing, and revising a narrative paragraph, you should try to make each event as clear and vivid as possible and try to use the narrator to shape and connect events for the reader. The following chart gives additional suggestions for writing lively narrative paragraphs.

SUGGESTIONS FOR WRITING NARRATIVE PARAGRAPHS

1. Choose an idea or experience that you can develop into a story, or think about your own experiences to find an incident that you remember vividly. Choose a story that you can tell memorably in a paragraph.
2. Determine the point of view you will use in the story by considering the different narrators you could have.
3. Decide if your narrative paragraph will create a specific mood or have any secondary purpose, such as to amuse, instruct, inform, or persuade.
4. Decide whether your topic sentence will state a general truth or launch the story. Jot down a version of your topic sentence.
5. List the major events of your story. According to the point of view you have chosen, include the important physical and mental actions that make up the story. Jot down specific details, sensory impressions, and graphic language that will make the actions realistic.
6. Organize the events in chronological order, eliminating information that does not further the story and adding any information that could make the story clearer or more interesting.
7. When you draft the story, maintain a consistent point of view. Concentrate on involving the reader through graphic language and connections in the unfolding of the action.
8. Revise your narrative paragraph for clarity, vividness, and consistency of point of view. (See the checklist for revision on page 645 for further help in revising.)

EXERCISE G: **Recognizing the Features of Narrative Paragraphs.** Read the following two narrative paragraphs and in each one identify the following features: (1) the kind of topic sentence (Does it present a general truth or set the scene and start the action?); (2) the kind of narrator; (3) the main events in chronological order; (4) examples of specific details, sensory impressions, and graphic language; and (5) any specific mood or any secondary purposes.

(1) When my son and I arrived at the pigyard, armed with a small bottle of castor oil and a length of clothesline, the pig had emerged from his house and was standing in the middle of his yard, listlessly. He gave us a slim greeting. I could see that he

felt uncomfortable and uncertain. I had brought the clothesline thinking I'd have to tie him (the pig weighed more than a hundred pounds) but we never used it. My son reached down, grabbed both front legs, upset him quickly, and when he opened his mouth to scream I turned the oil into his throat—a pink, corrugated area I had never seen before. I had just time to read the label while the neck of the bottle was in his mouth. It said Puretest. The screams, slightly muffled by oil, were pitched in the hysterically high range of pig-sound, as though torture were being carried out, but they didn't last long: it was all over rather suddenly, and, his legs released, the pig righted himself.
—E. B. White

(2) Jerry dived, shot past the school of underwater swimmers, saw a black wall of rock looming at him, touched it, and bobbed up at once to the surface, where the wall was a low barrier he could see across. There was no one visible; under him, in the water, the dim shapes of the swimmers had disappeared. Then one, and then another of the boys came up on the far side of the barrier of rock, and he understood that they had swum through some gap or hole in it. He plunged down again. He could see nothing through the stinging salt water but the blank rock. When he came up the boys were all on the diving rock, preparing to attempt the feat again. And now, in a panic of failure, he yelled up, in English, "Look at me! Look!" and he began splashing and kicking in the water like a foolish dog. —Doris Lessing

EXERCISE H: Planning, Writing, and Revising Narrative Paragraphs. List *five* ideas or experiences which you could develop into a story—either real or imagined. Choose one and write a narrative paragraph, following the suggestions in the chart on page 683. Revise your paragraph according to the checklist for revision on page 645.

APPLICATION 1: Writing and Evaluating Expository and Persuasive Paragraphs. Choose one of the following general topics to serve as the basis for two separate paragraphs, one expository and one persuasive. Follow the guidelines for writing each kind of paragraph and write a first draft of each.

Then exchange papers with another student, and analyze his or her paragraphs, identifying purposes, topic sentences, any secondary purposes or tones, and supporting information. Write a two-sentence evaluation of each paragraph. Then revise your own paragraphs according to the other student's comments as well as the items in the checklist for revision. Recopy both paragraphs and submit them to your teacher.

A film, book, television   Status symbols
    program, or record album   Space travel/exploration

A prominent political figure
Student activism/apathy
Medical careers
Advertising

Weather
Newspapers
Physical fitness

APPLICATION 2: **Writing and Evaluating Descriptive and Narrative Paragraphs.** Choose one of the following ten general topics to serve as the basis for two *connected* paragraphs which combine description and narration. You may confine the description to one paragraph and the narration to the other, or you may mix description and narration in both paragraphs. Follow the suggestions in this section for writing description and narration to write a first draft of your paragraphs.

Then exchange papers with another student and analyze his or her writing, identifying moods and any secondary purposes. Make a note of the most striking details and uses of vivid language in the paragraphs as well as any language that is abstract, vague, or colorless. Write a four-sentence evaluation of the other student's work. Then revise your own paragraphs according to the other student's comments as well as the items in the checklist for revision. Recopy both paragraphs and submit them to your teacher.

Your reunion with an old
   friend
A discovery or revelation
A machine or gadget that
   caused problems
The first day of school
An experience buying a pet
A favorite elderly relative

A dangerous or frightening
   experience with nature
A sports accident
An experience while moving
A historical, mythical,
   fictional, or fairy-tale
   figure set down in today's
   world

Paragraphs with Special Purposes 22.2

Not all the paragraphs you read or all the paragraphs you write will be standard, with topic sentences developed by supporting information. Some paragraphs may differ from standard paragraphs in topic sentence, length, and development because they are performing a special function within a longer piece of writing. By learning to recognize and write these special kinds of paragraphs, you can increase your range and flexibility as a writer.

■ Introductory and Concluding Paragraphs

In longer works, such as articles, essays, and library papers, paragraphs operate in different ways, depending on whether they present, develop, or conclude the ideas in the piece of writing. The most specialized of these tasks involve the introduction and conclusion of a piece of writing. Because the paragraphs that perform these functions are especially shaped by their tasks, they can often be identified as introductions and conclusions, even out of context.

Introductory Paragraphs.   An introductory paragraph may differ from a standard paragraph in a number of ways: (1) It may or may not have its own topic sentence; (2) it may be one sentence or many sentences, depending on the length of the piece of writing it is introducing; and (3) it may mention several ideas without itself developing these ideas. An introductory paragraph usually consists of a series of remarks designed and structured to attract the reader's attention, to present the topic, and to suggest the point of the whole work.

> An introductory paragraph reveals and advertises the topic and often includes the main point of the composition. Its content and length vary according to the particular piece of writing it is beginning.

An introductory paragraph is not just a paragraph that comes first in a series of paragraphs; it prepares the reader for all the paragraphs that follow by serving as a preview, an overview, or a lure. Rather than start with a topic sentence and develop that idea to a satisfactory stopping point, an introductory paragraph is usually forward-looking, easing the reader into the topic or mentioning ideas that will be expanded in later paragraphs.

The content of an introductory paragraph should suit the purpose and content of the composition it introduces. An introductory paragraph may start with an attention-getting statement, a short description, a question, an incident, a quotation, or some general remark to make the topic seem appealing. Then it may specify the topic of the composition and indicate the direction of ideas to follow. Often it focuses on the main point the writer intends to develop at length. Thus, one common form of introductory paragraph can be seen as a funnel. The paragraph begins with general statements and grows more specific with each sentence as it draws the reader toward the main point. And like a funnel, an introductory paragraph is usually open-ended because it should make the reader want to read on to see how the main point is developed in the other paragraphs.

The length of an introductory paragraph usually depends on the length of the piece of writing it is introducing. A long essay or article of many paragraphs may have a long introductory paragraph. A short piece of writing, however, should have an introductory paragraph of just a few sentences.

The following paragraph introduces an essay about modern misuses of language. The first sentence presents a lively, general opinion, designed to interest and intrigue the reader. The second sentence introduces the topic, *American language*, and the third offers some background information. The last sentence presents the main point that the essay develops: *United States vocabulary seems to have shrunk to child size*. This introductory paragraph leads the reader to expect a critical discussion of instances of language abuse in this country.

| Introductory paragraph | The rich have always liked to assume the costumes of the poor. Take the American language. It is more than a million words wide, and new terms are constantly added to its infinite variety. Yet as the decade starts, the United States vocabulary seems to have shrunk to child size. —Stefan Kanfer |

Concluding Paragraphs.   Like an introductory paragraph, a concluding paragraph usually does not have a topic sentence, usually has a length that is in proportion to the piece of writing it is ending, and echoes or links ideas mentioned elsewhere in the work without expanding on them. It ties together and completes the information that has come before.

A concluding paragraph touches upon or relates ideas presented earlier in the composition and includes remarks that signal the completion of the work. Its content and length vary according to the particular piece of writing it is closing.

A concluding paragraph is built upon the paragraphs that precede it. It may not develop any of the thoughts it ties together, and it may not have its own topic sentence. Instead, it may begin with a transition and make references to the main point of the entire work or to the ideas in the preceding paragraph. It may summarize all of the ideas, if the piece of writing is long and complex. It may add a final illustration or bit of information; it may mention the implications or results of the preceding ideas; or it may restate the main point of the overall work in a striking way. Because it represents the writer's last chance to say something to the reader, the writer usually tries to create a memorable concluding paragraph. A quotation, incident, question, or play on words may help to implant the writer's main point in the reader's mind.

One frequently used form of concluding paragraph can be visualized as an upside-down funnel. The paragraph may begin narrowly with a rephrasing of the work's main point or other references to the preceding discussion. Then it may widen to include more general remarks and to suggest the broader meaning of the main point. For short pieces of writing, a concluding paragraph may be just a few sentences, but for a long work it may be a series of sentences. No matter how long it is, the concluding paragraph indicates to the reader that the discussion has come full circle and is nearing completion.

The following concluding paragraph ends the essay about language. Notice that the writer uses a quotation to help anchor his ideas in the reader's mind. The paragraph has no topic sentence of its own, but the second to last sentence rephrases the main point of the essay. The final sentence echoes the clothing metaphor used in the introductory paragraph on page 687.

| Concluding paragraph | In fact, since its beginning, our native tongue has been maligned and mauled, invaded by foreigners and abused at home. No one has ever succeeded in making it uniform, and no one ever will. But then, as Henry Thoreau observed more than a century ago, "Where shall we look for standard English but to the words of a standard man?" As the '80's begin, Americans and their vernacular can be put down as fractious, infuriating, untidy, overbearing, cacophonous— but never as standard. The United States vocabulary may be dressed in blue jeans and work shirts, yet it cannot disguise one of the country's truest and most unassailable treasures: the American language. |

—Stefan Kanfer

EXERCISE A: **Recognizing Introductory and Concluding Paragraphs.** Each of the following paragraphs functions in a longer work as either an introductory or concluding paragraph. Read each carefully and identify its function. On your paper write down *two* reasons why you think each paragraph is an introductory paragraph or a concluding paragraph.

(1) One year out of every eleven, the mysterious star that controls our lives does something even more baffling than usual. For reasons imperfectly understood, its magnetic forces build to a peak and discharge in a pyrotechnic display. Great tongues of flame leap hundreds of thousands of miles into space and violent, erratic flashes of energy stream out from its surface to cause all sorts of weird happenings on earth. —Adapted from Lillian Borgeson

(2) Congress may be equally stingy about funding high-speed Amtrak routes. "It must be something that a significant portion of the American public will perceive as a reasonable and practical course," says Boyd, "and we are not there yet." Given the time and expense involved, a significant improvement in American rail-passenger service is still a long way down the track. —*Newsweek*

(3) Javelinas eat them. Deer eat them. Bears, bugs, and birds eat them. And some people eat them, too. They're acorns, which, of course, are the fruits of the 80 or so species of oaks native to the United States. Many animals prefer them all year round, but during late fall and winter, when other foods are scarce, acorns are especially important for *all* wildlife. In fact, these nuggets of nourishment affect the lives of many animals in some really surprising ways. —Bill Vogt

(4) It was Edouard de Laboulaye's idea. He had always loved America, her people, and her customs. Even Abraham Lincoln had sent him a note congratulating him for his work as the leader of the French Anti-Slavery Society. Laboulaye wanted France to construct and present the largest statue in the world to the United States; this monument would honor the nation's first century of freedom and would symbolize America's image to the peoples of other nations.

(5) No one is certain how gold will fare as an investment or as a support for the economy. If a practical way to extract the estimated ten billion tons of gold in the water of all the world's oceans is ever discovered, the price may plummet. But gold will always be the most beautiful metal known on earth. It will always possess an allure as mysterious and powerful as the pull of the tides and there will always be a buyer for it somewhere, somehow, someday. —Adapted from Joy DeWeese-Wehen

EXERCISE B: **Writing an Introductory and a Concluding Paragraph.** Choose a general topic that interests you and that would be appropriate for a composition. Focus it to a main point, as you would for a paragraph, by considering audience and purpose. Then think of an appealing way to introduce your topic and main point and write a short introductory paragraph. Finally, write a short concluding paragraph of three to five sentences in which you refer to the main point mentioned in the introductory paragraph and supposedly developed in the middle of the composition. Include a quotation, an incident, a question, or some final general remarks on your topic in this concluding paragraph.

■ Other Special Kinds of Paragraphs

Between the beginning and end of a piece of writing, other kinds of paragraphs are used to develop ideas. Many of these paragraphs will be standard, beginning with topic sentences followed by sentences presenting supporting information. But a writer can also use paragraphs with different lengths and content.

Paragraphs in a longer piece of writing may have a development that suits the progression of ideas in the overall work instead of being well-developed units of thought in themselves. For example, newspapers and some magazines favor short paragraphs and may divide paragraphs into units of two or three sentences for the sake of appearance on the page. Or a writer may extend the development of one main idea over several paragraphs so that two or three paragraphs actually develop one topic sentence. Sometimes a paragraph can simply connect the ideas in the paragraph before it with the ideas in the paragraph after it. And other paragraphs may imply rather than state their topic sentences. The following subsections explain how these other kinds of paragraphs can be useful.

Continuing Paragraphs.   A continuing paragraph does not contain a topic sentence of its own but rather continues the development of an earlier main idea. It presents additional supporting information to elaborate on some main idea in a preceding paragraph. Such a paragraph is unified and coherent because its information follows a logical order. Furthermore, it contributes to the unity and coherence of the piece of writing as a whole because it builds on and is clearly linked to the paragraph that precedes it.

A continuing paragraph continues the support of the topic sentence from an earlier paragraph through unified, coherent development.

Continuing paragraphs give a writer flexibility in supporting main ideas with specific information. A writer may decide to build on a main idea by starting a new paragraph rather than by making the first paragraph still longer. The additional supporting material receives more emphasis when it is placed in a paragraph of its own, and the first paragraph does not become so long that it loses the reader's attention. Sometimes a writer may set forth a main idea and define terms in one paragraph and develop this main idea in the next two or three paragraphs. A continuing paragraph may begin with a transition that connects it with and yet makes it distinct from the preceding paragraph.

For example, the following passage from an article on Nigeria includes a continuing paragraph that might easily have been part of the paragraph that precedes it. Notice that the first paragraph is a standard paragraph containing a topic sentence and supporting examples and details. The second paragraph simply provides additional examples and details to develop the topic sentence of the preceding paragraph.

Standard paragraph with a topic sentence	A livelier, more responsive people I have never met. I was hustled, jostled, even threatened by Nigerian citizenry, but so was I gently cared for by strangers when I lay ill. I was turned away from meetings with public officials sensitive about publicity, but I was never turned away from a home.
Continuing paragraph	I saw fights break out over traffic incidents and arguments erupt in grocery lines, but most outspoken confrontations seemed to subside as suddenly as they mounted. Seared by northern heat, parboiled by coastal humidity, feelings seemed ever ready to surface into kindness or violence, charity or self-interest. —Noel Grove

Transitional Paragraphs.   A transitional paragraph is usually brief, often containing only one or two sentences as a bridge or link between two other paragraphs. It often has neither a topic sentence nor developed ideas of its own.

A transitional paragraph acts as a bridge to lead the reader from one group of ideas to another.

Transitional paragraphs may resemble continuing paragraphs or extended transitions or both, depending on the writer's needs and style. Sometimes a transitional paragraph reads as if it could be attached to the paragraph it follows or to the one it precedes. But usually the transitional paragraph consists of one or two sentences written to stand by themselves so that they emphasize the change in thought that the composition is making at that point. Occasionally, a transitional paragraph may be a single sentence, possibly even the topic sentence of the paragraph that follows it. The following transitional paragraph from the article about Nigeria follows the preceding paragraphs, emphasizes a shift in ideas, and presents the topic sentence for the next paragraph.

Transitional	Emotion is one thing, efficiency is often quite an-
paragraph	other. The experience of my friend Anthony Akinduro
	is a case in point. —Noel Grove

Paragraphs with Implied Topic Sentences.   Unless a paragraph acts as an introduction, conclusion, or transition between other paragraphs, it is usually based on one main idea. In a standard paragraph, the main idea is stated in the topic sentence. In a continuing paragraph, the main idea is stated in the preceding paragraph. But in some paragraphs, the main idea is never stated at all; instead, it is *implied* by the information within the paragraph, and the reader infers the main idea from this material.

A paragraph may imply its main idea with its supporting information rather than state it directly in a topic sentence.

A paragraph may develop a main idea without ever expressing that idea in a straightforward manner. The main idea may be implied throughout the paragraph rather than expressed in a topic sentence. Sometimes writers think that the main idea is sufficiently clear in the material and that spelling it out might make the paragraph sound repetitious or simple-minded. Occasionally, writers may want to appeal to readers' imaginations by challenging them to infer the main idea from the rest of the material in a paragraph. Other times a direct statement of the main idea might interrupt the flow of details or action. Descriptive and narrative paragraphs often imply rather than state their main ideas.

The following paragraph makes its point by implication, rather than with a single topic sentence. Notice how the individual details contribute to a unified and coherent dominant impression of coldness, even though that impression is not stated explicitly in a topic sentence.

Paragraph
with an
implied main
idea
The wind zipped through the frozen weeds in the vacant lot. Three people stood separately, shifting from foot to foot. Three pairs of eyes peered brightly above thick woolen scarves, anxious for a glimpse of the bus in the distance. No one spoke, for the air burned in the nose, the throat, the lungs.

EXERCISE C: Recognizing Special Kinds of Paragraphs. Look through several magazines and books to find examples of special kinds of paragraphs. Locate five special paragraphs, including at least one example of each of these: a continuing paragraph, a transitional paragraph, and a paragraph with an implied topic sentence. Copy or reproduce each model and label each one. Be sure to indicate the writer, title of the article, magazine, or book, and page number for each paragraph.

APPLICATION: Using Special Kinds of Paragraphs in Your Writing. Write a composition of about 350 to 500 words in which you include several of these special paragraphs: an introductory paragraph, a concluding paragraph, a continuing paragraph, a transitional paragraph, and a paragraph with an implied topic sentence. Your composition may include standard paragraphs as well. Exchange papers with another student and identify and label the special kinds of paragraphs in the composition. You can use one of the following general topics or think of one of your own.

A danger you have learned to avoid
An experience traveling alone or with your family
The most unusual person you know
Your most ordinary or extraordinary day
An experience meeting someone famous

Essays

An essay is a composition made up of a group of related paragraphs. All of these paragraphs focus on a main point and, together, the paragraphs support and develop the main point.

This chapter discusses the structural features that are essential to good essays and examines the ways in which unity and coherence contribute to the overall presentation of ideas. It also provides steps for planning, writing, and revising standard essays. Finally, it introduces the informal essay, which allows you to experiment with new patterns of organization and style.

23.1 Key Features of Good Essays

An important step toward writing essays of all types involves recognizing and understanding the features common to *any* essay. This section explains the parts of an essay and shows how they work together to serve different purposes. It also discusses methods a writer can use to make an essay a unified and coherent piece of writing.

■ Structural Features of Standard Essays

A standard essay has a number of structural features, each of which has a particular function. The *title* suggests the topic and main point of the essay. The *introduction,* or first main part of the essay, further acquaints the reader with the topic, establishes the essay's purpose and tone, and leads into the thesis statement. The *thesis statement* usually comes at the end

694

of the introduction and defines the main point and scope of the essay. The *body,* or middle, is the second main part of the essay. It contains two or more well-developed paragraphs, each exploring some aspect of the essay's main point with examples, details, facts, reasons, and incidents. The third and final main part of an essay is the *conclusion.* It is usually a paragraph at the end, which completes the essay by reminding the reader of the essay's main point. It may include a summary of the ideas in the body of the essay and any final observations or closing remarks. The following diagram illustrates this three-part structure and shows the position of the title and thesis statement.

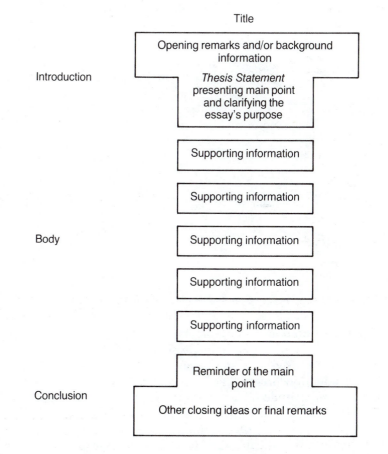

Understanding these structural features will prepare you for planning and writing your own essays.

The Title.   A reader gains his or her first impression of an essay from the title. For this reason, a title should grab the reader's attention.

> The title of an essay should reflect the main point and purpose of the essay and should capture the reader's interest.

The title should give the reader a preview of the essay. It can reveal the writer's slant or focus on the essay's topic. It can point up the engaging qualities of the topic, or it can simply attract the reader's attention.

No matter how informative the title is, however, it should not be too long and it should suit the tone of the essay. The following chart gives some topics for essays with titles that would be appropriate for them.

SAMPLE ESSAY TITLES	
Topics	**Titles**
Recent discoveries by archaeologists	"Unearthing New Worlds"
The adventures of skin diving	"Frolicking Among the Fish"
Why the government and people of Australia are worried about the kangaroo population	"Warning: I Brake for Kangaroos"
How to create an herb garden in your own back yard	"Herb Farming at Home"
Ways that new drivers sometimes abuse the rules of the road	"Learning to Keep Your Driver's License"

Introduction and Thesis Statement.   The introduction of the essay usually consists of a single paragraph, although two or more may be used in a long essay. The opening statements of the introduction present the topic to the reader and establish the writer's attitude toward both the subject and the audience. Most important, the introduction prepares the reader for the thesis statement. The thesis statement specifically presents the main point and indicates the purpose of the essay.

> The essay's introduction offers opening remarks on the topic and establishes the tone of the essay. It zeroes in on and includes the thesis statement, which states the essay's main point.

The following introductory paragraph captures the reader's attention and informs the reader of the essay's topic: the stars in the heavens. Word choices in the opening remarks establish a serious but friendly tone and guide the reader to the thesis statement at the end of the paragraph. The thesis statement identifies the essay's main point—the differences among stars in the universe—and indicates an expository purpose: to explain the differences among these stars.

Introduction to an expository essay	In the daytime, we see only one star—our own sun. But when we gaze up into the evening sky, we see thousands and thousands of stars—or suns. And from our earthly vantage point, we see few, if any, differences among them. However, according to astronomers, if we could travel through space, we
Thesis statement presents a factual main point	would be surprised to find that huge differences characterize the millions of suns in the universe. We would find that while some are quite similar to our own sun, most are vastly different, particularly in size and temperature.

The following example shows how an introduction can establish an entirely different tone and work toward a persuasive purpose. The following introduction from a persuasive essay begins with some examples taken from the writer's personal experience, moves toward a statement of the problem, and culminates in an opinion, a proposed response to the problem. The tone is concerned, slightly casual, and insistent. The thesis statement expresses an opinion in a straightforward manner and declares its persuasive purpose: to convince the reader of the need for and effectiveness of stricter penalties for negligent driving.

Introduction to a persuasive essay	After being on the road for just ten minutes one day, I observed the following driving maneuvers: Without warning a van turned right from the left lane, causing the car behind it to jerk to a halt; a station wagon backed up the entire distance of a highway's entrance ramp; a sports car stopped in the middle of a residential street just around a bend while its driver conversed with a pedestrian; and a sedan ran a red
Thesis statement: an opinion that establishes a persuasive purpose	light and barely missed the cross traffic. The accident statistics and rising insurance rates confirm what any driver can observe firsthand: The number of negligent drivers is increasing. To combat this menace, our state should institute stricter penalties for negligent driving and moving traffic violations.

The most important sentence in any introduction is the *thesis statement* because it states the controlling idea, or main point. It also clarifies the purpose for the essay and helps to set the tone. In addition, the thesis statement can set up a plan for the body of the essay if it includes subtopics, or natural divisions of the main point. Thus, the thesis statement is the keystone of an essay in the same way that the topic sentence is the keystone of a paragraph.

The main point in a thesis statement can be a statement of fact, a statement of opinion, a dominant impression, or a general truth, depending on the purpose of the essay. Usually, however, a standard essay will be expository or persuasive; that is, it will seek to explain or to convince.

A thesis statement for an *expository* essay should be factual and objective. It may reveal that the writer intends to report information, to explain something, to instruct the reader, or to define a concept. It should convey the writer's purpose to increase readers' knowledge, *not* to change their minds.

The following examples illustrate thesis statements suitable for expository essays. Notice that some statements include subtopics while others do not.

THESIS STATEMENTS FOR EXPOSITORY ESSAYS		
Thesis Statement	**Purpose**	**Subtopics**
Public libraries in many communities offer special programs for preschoolers, young adults, and adults.	To explain	Programs for 1. preschoolers 2. young adults 3. adults
To make an aquarium, you must purchase several important pieces of equipment and choose fish that are compatible in a single environment.	To instruct	1. Buying the necessary equipment 2. Choosing compatible fish
Integrity means acting according to a consistent standard of ethical behavior.	To define	None

A thesis statement for a *persuasive* essay should be a debatable or even highly controversial opinion. It should reveal the writer's intention to convince readers to consider or accept some interpretation, opinion, or stand on an issue. A persuasive thesis statement should sound both reasonable and force-ful. It should indicate that the writer intends to try to influence the reader's thinking and actions.

The following thesis statements illustrate main points appropriate for persuasive essays. Again, notice that some have subtopics.

PERSUASIVE THESIS STATEMENTS	
Thesis Statement	**Subtopics**
If you master kite-flying, you will open a new world of fun.	None
Swimming should be a required course because swimming is one of the best forms of exercise and is a necessary survival skill.	Swimming is 1. one of the best forms of exercise 2. a necessary survival skill
Television stations should devote more viewing time to fine arts programs, documentaries, and dramatizations of classics.	1. Fine arts programs 2. Documentaries 3. Dramatizations of classics

Body Paragraphs.   The body paragraphs provide the development of the essay. These take up most of the essay and elaborate on the main point with relevant examples, details, facts, reasons, and incidents. If the thesis statement includes subtopics, the body paragraphs will support and develop each subtopic in order.

> The body of an essay contains two or more paragraphs that develop the main point (and any subtopics) with relevant and complete supporting information.

The number of body paragraphs an essay should have depends on the complexity of the thesis statement, the number of subtopics into which the writer divides the main point, and the quantity of available supporting information. Sometimes an essay can have one paragraph for each subtopic. Other times two or more paragraphs will be needed to develop each subtopic. The body paragraphs should always cover the main point thoroughly.

Conclusion.   Usually no more than one paragraph, the conclusion wraps up the essay with a reminder of the main point as well as any other closing remarks or ideas. The conclusion leaves the reader satisfied that the topic introduced at the beginning has been fully explored.

> The conclusion of an essay should refer to the main point, remind the reader of the ideas that have been covered, and bring the essay to a satisfying resolution.

The conclusion is the writer's final word to the reader. It may offer a summary of the ideas in the essay, one last example or observation, or some reference to the introduction. On no account, however, should it repeat whole parts of the essay or go off on an entirely new topic. The reader should sense that the essay is winding down to a fitting close. Sometimes the final sentence of a conclusion will be a witty or otherwise noteworthy statement to make the entire essay more memorable.

The Complete Essay. All key features should work together to create a unified, logical essay focused on a main point. The following is the complete essay about suns in the universe. As you read it, notice the key features, and examine how each part contributes to the thought and structure of the whole.

Suns in All Sizes and Colors

Introduction	In the daytime, we see only one star—our own sun. But when we gaze into the evening sky, we see thousands and thousands of stars, or suns. And from our earthly vantage point, we see few, if any, differences among them. However, according to astronomers, huge differences characterize the millions of suns in the universe. While some of them are quite similar to our own sun, most are vastly different, particularly in size and temperature.
Opening remarks	
Thesis statement with two subtopics	
First body paragraph	Stars range in size from smaller than the earth's diameter to about 1,000 times our sun's diameter. The star group Alpha Centauri, for example, has a star nearly identical in size to our own. (Actually, scientists calculate the size of this star as 1.1 times that of our sun.) Yet elsewhere in the universe there are differences in the sizes of stars. Cygnus X-1, for instance, has shrunk to a black hole fifteen miles (twenty-five kilometers) across. Our own sun, almost one million miles across, dwarfs this tiny star, and yet our sun is dwarfed in turn by much bigger stars. For example, Betelgeuse, a mere pinpoint in our night sky, is actually a monster nearly 300 million miles wide (480 million kilometers)—300 times the size of our sun.
(develops first subtopic)	

Second body paragraph

(develops second subtopic)

Just as stars differ greatly in size, so they also vary enormously in temperature. The surface temperature of stars can be determined by their amount of blue and red light. By passing starlight through color filters and through a photometer or by using a spectograph to measure the spectrum of the star's light, astronomers can figure out the dominant color and then calculate the temperature. Our own sun is white/yellow, and its color indicates that its temperature is about 10,000° Fahrenheit (5,500° Celsius). Other stars also have our sun's color. The double star system Capella, for instance, consists of two yellow stars with approximately the same surface temperature as the sun. The hottest stars burn blue, while the coolest have more red light, with a variety in between ranging from blue/white to orange/red. Rigel, a supergiant star with a surface temperature of 17,000° Fahrenheit (9,400° Celsius) is blue. Sirius B, a dwarf star, still quite hot at 12,500° Fahrenheit (6,900° Celsius), emits a blue/white light. Red stars, such as the supergiants Betelgeuse and Antares in the constellation Scorpio, are cooler, with surface temperatures of less than 5,500° Fahrenheit (3,040° Celsius). Our own sun will, over the eons, change its color. It will consume its present fuel source, cool down, and swell to 100 times its present size. As a result of this drop in temperature, it will emit a correspondingly cooler red light. Some day, our skies will be dominated by a huge red ball, our own sun in its old age.

Reference to main point

Our sun is merely one among trillions of diverse celestial bonfires called stars. If the old nursery rhyme were written to reflect the actual state of the universe, it would have to read in the following manner:

Conclusion

Twinkle, twinkle little (medium, giant) star
How we wonder *which* you are,
Up above the world so high
Like a diamond (sapphire/topaz/ruby) in the sky.

EXERCISE A: **Examining the Features of a Standard Essay.** Read the following essay on foreign languages written by a student. Then follow the instructions given after the essay.

The Monolingual American

You are in a foreign country and your traveler's checks are stolen. Naturally, you go to the authorities—only the authorities do not speak English. Your luggage is lost in the Paris airport. You complain loudly in English, but the French porter only gives you a blank stare. In a Spanish restaurant you try to order veal and are informed that you have just propositioned the waiter. These common painful episodes can be easily eliminated by one thing: knowlege of foreign languages.

This type of verbal faux pas is in no way limited to the ordinary American tourist. Both a President of the United States and the General Motors Corporation have experienced similar losses of face overseas. Who can forget the Polish people's surprise when Jimmy Carter's interpreter stated that the President was "abandoning" the United States? Mr. Carter's own attempts at speaking Spanish, his "Bway-nōs Dee-ahs," could not have endeared him to the people of Mexico. Perhaps the example most illustrative of America's ignorance of foreign languages is that of General Motors' marketing debacle. The corporation tried to market its economy car, the Nova, in Latin America with repeated failure. Finally someone pointed out that in Spanish, "no va" means "doesn't go."

These national and international fiascos are merely the latest evidence of America's ignorance concerning foreign languages. The average European student learns at least two foreign languages. The average American student does not learn any foreign language. According to the *Hartford Courant*, less than twenty-five percent of high school students in the United States study a foreign language. The nation's school systems seem to be adding to the problem. Ninety percent of all colleges have dropped their language requirements for admissions, and one quarter of all high schools do not teach any foreign languages. As a result of these deficiencies, nine out of ten Americans today cannot effectively comprehend any language but English. Of those Americans who have been taught another language, only seventeen percent can use that second language easily.

It is to our own advantage to repair these flaws in our educational system. In today's international economic market, a business person has an automatic edge when he or she speaks a client's language. This is true here in the United States. With the high concentrations of Hispanic people in certain areas of the country, a Spanish-speaking professional would obviously have a jump on the competition. Ms. Elona Vaisnys of Mount Carmel, a member of the Presidential committee appointed to try to revive America's flagging foreign language system, struck at the heart of the problem when she said, "You can buy anything anywhere in the world in your own language, but you can't sell."

Americans can no longer—if we ever could—assume that everyone will speak English. We are no longer in the unique position of being able to demand special treatment. In a world where many high-level technological articles are written in German and Russian, the days of "English" supremacy are over. America must realize that knowledge of foreign languages is a vital part of international relationships. It is time we acknowledge what the rest of the world seems to have accepted: the importance of learning foreign languages. —Marcia Pentz

1. Explain why the title suits the essay.
2. Examine the introductory paragraph to complete each of the following items.

a. Identify the tone and list words or phrases that help to establish it.
b. Identify the thesis statement and the purpose it implies.
c. Identify the audience for whom the writer is writing.
d. Briefly explain whether you think the introduction is effective.

3. Examine the body paragraphs of the essay to complete each of the following items.
   a. Identify the topic sentence of each body paragraph.
   b. List the supporting information contained in each paragraph.
   c. Explain how any *one* of the body paragraphs develops or supports the thesis statement.

4. Examine the conclusion of the essay to answer each of the following items.
   a. Identify the references to the thesis statement.
   b. List any pieces of information that have been saved for the conclusion, and briefly explain how they contribute to the impact of the essay.
   c. Explain how the conclusion signals that the essay is complete. List any changes or additions you would make in the conclusion.

■ Unity and Coherence

Like any good writing, an essay must be unified and logically ordered from beginning to end. The longer and more complicated a piece of writing is, the more important unity and coherence become to both the writer and the reader. An essay must sustain a focused discussion over many paragraphs. Thus, the qualities of unity and coherence are vital both within an essay's individual paragraphs and throughout the essay as a whole. In a unified essay, all ideas belong together and develop the thesis statement, and the tone is consistent throughout the whole essay. In a coherent essay, all the parts of the essay—every sentence and every paragraph—are arranged in a logical order, and the ideas and information flow smoothly from the introduction to the conclusion.

Unity of Ideas and Tone. Unity in an essay concerns both content and style. All the information included in the essay should be relevant to the main point as it is expressed in the thesis statement. In addition, the writer's attitude toward the subject and the audience, as revealed by the words the writer chooses, must be consistent throughout the essay if it is to be unified.

An essay has unity if each of the paragraphs is unified, if all the paragraphs develop the thesis statement and belong together, and if the writer maintains a consistent tone throughout the essay.

The thesis statement and its subtopics are some of the main unifiers in an essay because they form the skeleton of ideas. By clearly stating the main point of the essay, the thesis statement becomes a focus, which should guide the writer in choosing significant supporting information. If the writer has the thesis statement in mind at all times, ideas that do not contribute to the main point—that would distract a reader—will appear noticeably out of place. In addition, the subtopics can function as a guide to distinguish related information from irrelevant material. Whether the subtopics are stated directly in the thesis statement or chosen after the thesis statement is written, they should be natural divisions, or logical categories of the main point, which are also related to each other. If these relationships are strong and clear, by choosing supporting information and developing each subtopic well, the writer will simultaneously develop the thesis statement and stick to the main point. For example, a thesis statement about the efficiency of the Wankel engine could suggest four subtopics—the four stages of the engine's power cycle. Each of these stages and only these stages would then be discussed in the body of the essay, ensuring that the essay expands and explains the main point without including extraneous information.

The writer can also consciously use the introduction and conclusion to unify the essay. The introduction should narrow the topic to the thesis statement and indicate the scope of the entire essay. Then by referring to the thesis statement and perhaps picking up a few other important words or ideas from the introduction, the conclusion can help to tie together all the ideas and information in the essay. The conclusion should imply to the reader that the purpose of the essay has been accomplished, that all the ideas have been treated thoroughly.

Just as all of the essay's ideas must belong, so all the words must create a tone that is consistent from the beginning to the end. The writer must establish and sustain a clear attitude toward the subject and the audience. For example, if the opening paragraph is casual and friendly, the rest of the essay should not shift to a formal, distant tone. Or if the introductory paragraph establishes a matter-of-fact, informative tone, the writer should not offer opinions and personal reactions in the body of the essay. Furthermore, the level of language should not vary. Informal or formal, conversational or scholarly, language should be used consistently in all parts of the essay so that all the paragraphs sound as though they belong together.

Coherence Through Logical Order and Connecting Devices. In addition to having unity, a good essay has coherence. All the information follows a logical order and the essay flows smoothly from idea to idea.

> An essay has coherence if all the ideas within each paragraph and all the parts of the essay follow a logical order and if connections between ideas are clear and smooth.

Information in an essay should be logically organized within each paragraph and within the body of the essay as a whole. Ideas in each paragraph and subtopics in the body should follow one of the logical orders: order of importance, chronological order, spatial order, comparison and contrast order, or developmental order. (For more information on logical orders, see Section 21.1, page 625. Often the main point and the subtopics—whether they are steps, categories, arguments, and so on—will help determine the most sensible order for supporting information. The following chart illustrates how a main point and its subtopics can suggest a logical order for the body of an essay.

POSSIBLE ORDER FOR SUBTOPICS	
Subtopics of a Main Point	**Possible Order for the Support**
Three reasons why a proposed law should be defeated	Order of Importance
Rewards that motivated the fifteenth-century Spanish explorers	
Events of an exploration through a cave	Chronological
Stages in the metamorphosis of a caterpillar	
Original structures of Rome's Colosseum	Spatial
Sights along Alaska's Yoho Falls	

Crime statistics in two cities Team versus individual sports	Comparison and Contrast
Specific use for common products Effects of radiation poisoning	Developmental

Because an essay consists of many paragraphs, it usually needs connecting devices to show the reader the relationships among the ideas: for instance, between subtopics or between paragraphs developing the same subtopic. Transitions, repetitions of main words, and synonyms and consistent pronouns for main words can link ideas and can underscore the important thoughts for the reader. Concluding sentences, used occasionally at the ends of paragraphs, can point out the completion of a thought, and parallelism, used within paragraphs, can signal that ideas in a series are equal and related. Using a transition at the beginning of a paragraph can link that paragraph with the preceding one. The following diagram shows how the parts and paragraphs of an essay can be connected.

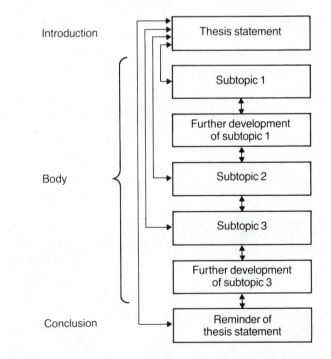

An essay about the Wankel engine could be made coherent through its organization and use of transitions. The subtopics, the four stages of the engine's power cycle, could follow chronological and spatial order. Because the essay is explaining a process, the development of each subtopic could also follow chronological and spatial order. The essay could achieve unity as well as coherence by developing each subtopic with information on that particular stage only. In the following excerpt from an essay by a student, notice the transitions in italic type and the other connecting devices that clarify the relationships among ideas within each paragraph and from paragraph to paragraph.

Thesis Statement: Basically, what makes the Wankel engine efficient is its four-step power cycle.

Body paragraphs	The *beginning* step is intake of fuel: gasoline and air. The rotor is positioned so that a gas-air mixture can enter the housing through a valve and fill the
Paragraphs arranged in chronological and spatial order	cavity *between* the wall of the housing and one face of the rotor. *As* the fuel fills the cavity, the rotor *then* moves *past* the valve, shutting off the flow but capturing the fuel to use it for power.

The *second* step is compression. *Once* the housing contains a pocket of fuel, the rotor is forced to change its position. It *now* shifts, turning its rounded face *toward* the fuel pocket, decreasing the size of the fuel cavity, and *thereby* compressing the mixture into a smaller volume. *Such* compression makes the fuel mixture more volatile and greatly aids its burning, a principle which increases the engine's efficiency.

The *third* step, ignition, is the most important part of the engine's operation. *When* the rotor moves to compress the fuel, it prepares the mixture for an explosion. *As soon as* the gas-air mixture is at its point of greatest compression, a spark plug *inside* the housing fires and ignites the mixture. *Instantly,* the explosion drives the rotor in its clockwise motion with a force that creates the power for the whole engine.

The *end* result of ignition is the engine's *fourth* step: exhaust. In *this final* movement, the rotor must sweep the used fuel *out* of the housing and prepare for *another* cycle. *After* ignition of the fuel mixture, the rotor is pushed to a *new position: Still* pushing a pocket of gases (*now* in the form of used fuel), the rotor's new position uncovers an exhaust valve and allows the waste to leave the chamber. *At this point,* the rotor uncovers the intake valve, allowing a new gas-air mixture to enter the housing. The cycle *then* begins again. —Thomas Wu

EXERCISE B: Reorganizing a Jumbled Essay to Achieve Unity and Coherence.

The following essay paragraphs are not unified, nor are they in logical order. However, by removing extraneous information from some of the paragraphs and by rearranging the paragraphs in a logical order, you can create a unified, coherent essay. Read and analyze the paragraphs carefully and then complete each of the instructions that follow to produce an essay that is both clear and logical.

A second example of courage is an old fisherman's struggle with the sea, in which he faces nature on its terms. In Ernest Hemingway's *The Old Man and the Sea*, an aged peasant catches an enormous fish and must tow it to shore. But an angry sea, including maruading sharks, presents obstacles that the peasant must fight. *Moby Dick* is another novel in which the sea serves as a testing-ground. Calling upon every ounce of his strength and spirit, the old man battles to save his catch. He grows fond of his fish and talks to it from time to time, charming the reader. And despite his age and exhaustion, the man finally manages to reach shore and complete a valiant struggle. Even though his catch has been destroyed by sharks, the old man emerges the victor; this is more a story of courage than of tangible success. In bravery, the old man succeeds because he has battled not only the forces of nature but also the exhaustion and despair within himself.

Courage, or bravery, is not simply an end in itself. On the other hand, goodness and compassion are. Courage leads one to higher levels of attainment and awareness. By battling opponents, even when the opponent is one's own feelings, one gains something. Young Henry learns something important about himself, that he can fight and survive of his own will. And the old fisherman gains or perhaps regains, faith in himself.

In Stephen Crane's *The Red Badge of Courage*, a young man must struggle to be brave in battle. Stephen Crane wrote many short stories about the West. Henry, a soldier on the Union side during the Civil War, at first has difficulty restraining himself from flight when danger is near. He sees death for the first time, and rather than break down with grief and terror, Henry wants to run away. However, he does not permit himself such indulgence, and he becomes aware of the horrors of war. By so doing, he finds that repeated contact with both his fears and the brutalities of battle numbs him. He no longer trembles at the sight of the wounded and the dying. He resembles Shakespeare's heroes who grow in battle—particularly Prince Hal. Then, he finds that he can numb his fears so that he can act as a part of a fighting unit. As a result, Henry discovers that he has developed courage to fight in battle, despite the obvious physical dangers.

Courage, or bravery, is the human quality of willfully facing obstacles, often frightening ones. Characters in a wide variety of literature call upon their courage to combat an enemy or to battle against seemingly unfair forces in society or nature. This happens in many films and plays as well. And sometimes the most private form of courage is the kind that a person must find to battle feelings within him- or herself. In particular, Henry, the main character of *The Red Badge of Courage*, and the fisherman in *The Old Man and the Sea* display courage when they confront different kinds of obstacles.

1. Identify the thesis statement, what part of the essay each paragraph represents, and the logical order suitable for the subtopics.
2. Copy the paragraphs in logical order, eliminating any material within each paragraph that does not belong because it does not contribute to the development of the thesis statement.
3. Underline and label the thesis statement and all other major parts of the essay (introduction, subtopics, and so on). Then add a title.
4. For one body paragraph, label the logical order in which supporting information is arranged and circle any transitions, repetitions of main words, and synonyms or pronouns for main words.
5. Underline the statement in the conclusion that reminds the reader of the main point of the essay.

APPLICATION: **Analyzing Features of an Essay.** Select an essay from a magazine, newspaper, anthology, or nonfiction book. Or you may use an essay that you have written recently. Read the essay carefully to answer these questions and follow these instructions.

1. How is the title related to the essay?
2. Identify the thesis statement and any subtopics that it may contain. What purpose does the main point imply?
3. Identify the essay's tone and list words or phrases that help establish it.
4. What are the subtopics in the body?
5. How many paragraphs form the body?
6. Identify supporting information in each paragraph.
7. Is the essay unified? What, if any, supporting information strays from the main point?
8. What logical order do the subtopics follow? Is this order effective? What logical order does each paragraph follow?

9. What words or phrases act as transitions? What, if any, repetitions of main words, synonyms or pronouns for main words, concluding sentences, or examples of parallelism contribute to the coherence of the essay?
10. Does the conclusion satisfactorily complete the essay? What sentence or part of the conclusion refers to the thesis statement?
11. To what extent is this essay complete, unified, and coherent?

23.2 Planning, Writing, and Revising Essays

Now that you are familiar with the structure of a standard essay, you are prepared to plan and write successful essays of your own. The process of planning the essay is an important phase of writing. This section offers suggestions for finding an appropriate essay topic, focusing it into a thesis statement, generating support for it, and organizing that support. Further suggestions are offered for drafting and refining the essay. Following this sequence of steps will help you create a cogent, clear, and polished essay.

■ Planning an Essay

The planning stages are vital to your essay. From choosing and narrowing a topic to writing a sharply defined thesis statement, following a few basic steps can help you channel your thinking for the entire writing process.

Choosing an Appropriate Essay Topic.   Often, you will begin writing an essay with a general idea or topic of your own or one that has been assigned to you. To make sure that your essay will have a specific point, however, you must narrow your area of interest to a topic that you can discuss satisfactorily in a single essay.

> Choose a general topic that suits your interests and knowledge and narrow it to a manageable topic that you can cover thoroughly in an essay.

Unless a topic has been assigned to you, you can find topics by using your imagination and exploring your interests, as well as by examining books and other sources of ideas. Write down possible essay topics as you come across them. Although you may find that some are narrow enough to be starting points for essays, in most cases you will have to narrow the idea still further in order to be able to cover it. Remember that the broader your topic is, the more superficial your treatment is likely to be; it is always best to define your topic sharply.

The following chart shows an example of brainstorming for an essay topic. It lists topics that might emerge from a survey of your interests and from your reading. While generating possible topics, you might jot down some that are somewhat narrowed already, such as *The use of animals in space exploration in the 1960's, Early American painters,* and *Popular American myths.* During your brainstorming, you might also break down some general topics into smaller ones, more suitable for essays.

BRAINSTORMING FOR AN ESSAY TOPIC

The use of animals in space exploration in the 1960's

Student employment
—full-time career opportunities
—the minimum wage
—starting your own service business

Early American painters

Popular American myths

The Renaissance
—development of Italian art
—the expansion of scientific knowledge

What to do in the Scottish Highlands
—Loch Ness
—Scottish castles
—surrounding islands (Orkneys, Isle of Skye, and so on)

Hockey
—development of the game
—how to shoot properly
—the importance of a goalie

Once you have listed a number of smaller topics, you can select one from among them. After thinking about the topics in this list, you might decide to write on *Starting your own service business* because of your interest in and knowledge of the topic.

Determining Audience, Purpose, and Main Point.   Once you have found a topic, you have a starting place. You now need to find a main point—something to say about your topic. This main point is what you will explain, expand, or argue for in your essay. Deciding on your audience can help you sharpen your topic to a main point as can thinking about your purpose.

Turn your essay topic into a thesis statement by deciding on your audience, purpose, and main point and by stating the main point in a concise sentence.

Thinking about the readers with whom you plan to communicate and your purpose—to explain, persuade, describe, relate events—can guide your selection of a main point. An essay about starting your own service business, for example, could be written for an audience of other students who have had experience with self-employment or for adults who are skeptical about the idea. Or it could be aimed at students who know little about the topic.

Suppose you decided to write for the students who are unfamiliar with the concept of starting a business. With this audience in mind, you could ask yourself questions about your topic, to find some possible main points.

ASKING QUESTIONS TO FIND A MAIN POINT

Question	Main Point
What kinds of service businesses can high school students start?	—High school students can start businesses that involve handywork around the house and yard, special skills such as typing and tutoring, and creative projects such as catering children's parties and recycling.
What are the advantages for high school students of starting a service business?	—The advantages that starting a service business gives you are the opportunity to make more money than in some conventional jobs and flexibility in your working hours.
What single idea do I most want to communicate to the audience?	—Working for yourself should be considered as a real alternative to "regular" after-school jobs.

Each of these main points focuses on some aspect of the topic of high school students working for themselves, but each suggests a different purpose and emphasis. The first point explains some of the service businesses that students can start; its purpose would be expository. The second and third points, on the other hand, are persuasive; they are both directed toward selling the idea of starting your own service business to an audience who may not have given it much thought. The second point focuses on the benefits to be derived from working for yourself while the third point merely states an opinion about working for yourself.

Any one of these main points could be written as a thesis statement by expressing it as a complete sentence and by polishing it a little. You should always experiment with the wording of your thesis statement by writing several versions to find the appropriate emphasis for your ideas. In addition, several of your potential thesis statements might be preferable because they might include subtopics, which could guide your planning of the body of the essay.

If you were writing for an audience unfamiliar with the topic of starting your own service business, you might choose to have a persuasive purpose and to express the second main point as your thesis statement. The following chart shows some versions of the thesis statement that you might write using this main point.

POSSIBLE THESIS STATEMENTS

Main Point: The advantages that starting a service business gives you are the opportunity to make more money than in some conventional jobs and flexibility in your working hours.

1. Working for yourself has the advantages of giving you the opportunity to make more money than you would in some conventional jobs and of giving you flexible working hours.
2. Hang up that gas pump and crumple that grocery bag; become your own boss so that you can make more money and choose your own hours.
3. Starting your own service business can provide lucrative wages and the independence of a flexible work schedule.
4. If you do some thinking, you might discover a number of valuable services you can perform that pay more than some conventional jobs and that give you flexible working hours.

Each of these four possible thesis statements has a slightly different meaning and a different tone. The first is the most direct and plain, clearly stating the idea of advantages. The second is the most casual and striking, resembling a high-powered sales pitch. The third is direct and slightly more formal than the others, and the fourth includes the idea of valuable services and creative thinking. After considering the four statements, you might decide that you favor the first thesis statement because it is straightforward and yet has a personal tone.

EXERCISE A: Selecting and Narrowing a Topic for an Essay. Choose one of the following general topics or think of one of your own. Beneath the topic, list at least three or four smaller topics that would narrow the general topic to the scope of a single essay. Then circle the one narrowed topic that you prefer to write about.

Professional sports	A career or college major
The history of a game	Ancestry
A political stand	Victims of crimes
Amateur photography	An extinct or near-extinct
Vitamins or nutrition	species of animal
Home computers	

EXERCISE B: Shaping a Topic into a Main Point and Thesis Statement. Using the topic you selected in Exercise A, follow these instructions.

1. Briefly describe the audience for whom you are writing.
2. Keeping this audience in mind, write down at least three questions about your topic. Write brief answers that will be possible main points for your essay.
3. Examine each possible main point to determine its implied purpose, and decide what purpose you want your essay to have. Choose the main point that strikes you as an intriguing one for your essay.
4. Phrase this main point in three or four different thesis statements and choose the one you like best.

■ Developing Support for a Thesis Statement

Having formulated your thesis statement, you can begin planning the rest of the essay. Even though you may still revise your thesis statement at some later point, it can now establish the scope and direction of your essay and guide you in your search for supporting information. When you brainstorm for support, you should continue to keep your purpose and audience in mind.

Have your thesis statement in front of you as your brainstorm for examples, details, facts, and reasons to support and develop your main point.

You can follow at least two methods of brainstorming. In one, you can generate supporting material through a process of free association. You should write your thesis statement at the top of your paper and jot down everything that comes to your mind that might be usable in the development of this main point. Or you might want to use a question and answer method, writing down questions that a reader would naturally raise about your main point and then jotting down all the material you know that answers these questions. If your thesis statement contains subtopics, these can be part of your questions and can lead you to appropriate answers.

Whatever method you use for brainstorming, your goal should be to gather as many related examples, details, facts, reasons, and incidents as possible from your own experience, knowledge, and recent reading. If your essay seeks to explain a concept or event, you should gather factual information and give credit to any books, magazines, or newspapers that supply you with relevant material. If your essay is trying to persuade your reader of something, list all the arguments and evidence that support your case. If your essay is descriptive or narrative, concentrate on specific details, sensory impressions, and actions and events. Your goal at this point in your preparation is quantity; you can refine and screen your ideas once they are down on paper.

The following chart applies the question and answer method of brainstorming to gather strong, thorough supporting information. Notice that it makes use of the subtopics in the thesis statement and also incorporates some of the methods for building a defense for an opinion because this is a persuasive essay.

BRAINSTORMING FOR SUPPORTING INFORMATION

Thesis Statement: **Working for yourself has the advantages of giving you the opportunity to make more money than you would in some conventional jobs and of giving you flexible working hours.**

What are some of the valuable services that high school students can perform that pay more than conventional jobs?

—typing for as much as $.75 a page for about $5.00–$7.50 an hour

—tutoring—can charge $4.00– $5.00 an hour, if you're a good tutor

—work for older people
　—walking their dogs
　—shoveling snow
　—running errands
　—could pay about $4.00 an
　　hour
—household work for working
　people
　—cleaning
　—washing windows
　—polishing floors

—home improvement
　projects
—cleaning eaves
—painting indoors and
　outdoors
—people willing to pay for
　services they don't have
　time or skill to do
　themselves

How does running a service business give you flexible hours?

—you can work as much as
　you want
　—grooming pets
　—collecting aluminum cans
　　for recycling
　—refinishing furniture
　—hauling away trash
—you can work just on
　weekends
　—organizing and
　　publicizing garage sales
　—catering children's
　　birthday parties
—you can work only over
　long weekends or holidays
　—bringing in people's mail,
　　watering lawns, caring for
　　pets

—you can schedule your work
　around your studying and
　school activities
　—tutor a few afternoons a
　　week
　—offer private classes for
　　children in sports, crafts,
　　piano, or guitar in a few
　　afternoons a week
—teach a few evening classes
　at a community center in
　folk dancing, crafts, sewing,
　weight training
—work when you want

What are some arguments against running your own service business?

—requires a lot of planning,
　developing customers
—takes advertising

—might require investment in
　equipment

What are some counter arguments on the pro side?

—planning pays off
—find contacts in your
　community through
　parents' friends and work,
　through clubs, and religious
　organizations
—free advertising by using
　bulletin boards at grocery

stores, community centers,
local businesses
—neighbors might lend
　equipment; parents might
　help in the investment;
　local hardware stores might
　rent the equipment
　reasonably

EXERCISE C: Gathering Supporting Information. Write down the thesis statement you developed in Exercise B, and then use *one* of the following methods for gathering support.

1. Use free association to list beneath your thesis statement all the supporting information that comes to mind.
2. Write down questions that a reader would expect you to answer about your thesis statement. Then write all the answers—all the examples, details, facts, reasons, and incidents—that you can think of.

■ Organizing an Essay for Unity and Coherence

Once you have a thesis statement and plentiful supporting information, you have the raw materials for your essay. Now you must organize your information, examine it for unity and completeness, and prepare a plan to guide you as you write.

Group your supporting information according to logical subtopics of your thesis statement, eliminate or add information as necessary, and develop a rough plan or outline for the body of the essay.

Each writer usually discovers a preferred way of doing the organizing step in writing, but there are a few guidelines that can be helpful. Early in the organizing step you should identify subtopics of your main point, if your thesis statement does not include them already. These subtopics should be natural categories, steps, divisions, or outgrowths of your main point. Your essay should have two or more subtopics. If your thesis statement does not contain subtopics, you may find, by examining your supporting information, that the material divides logically into two or three groups or parts. Once you know your subtopics, you should decide which will come first, next, and last in the body of your essay. Can your subtopics follow a chronological or spatial organization? A comparison and contrast order? Can you use a developmental order or order of importance? Consider your purpose here. If your essay is persuasive, which subtopic is your most convincing? If it is expository, what sort of organization would be most helpful to your reader?

The essay on starting your own service business is already partially organized by its thesis statement, which contains subtopics—the two advantages of working for yourself: (1) the opportunity to make more money than in some conventional jobs and (2) flexible working hours. However, if you examine the list of supporting information and if you consider the persuasive purpose of the essay, you can see that you might include another subtopic in which you mention the arguments against the thesis statement and then counter with arguments in favor of it. This way you can dispose of the negative points at first and move on to your important reasons and examples. Thus, the essay would have three subtopics, one refuting some opposing points, one discussing opportunities to make money, and one discussing flexible working hours. You might decide that the flexible working hours are more important than the money so that the second and third subtopics would follow order of importance.

All your supporting information should be sorted and grouped under an appropriate subtopic and should be evaluated for unity at the same time. Pieces of information that do not fit under a subtopic and support the thesis statement should be eliminated. Support that is repetitious or vague can also be deleted. To fill in any gaps, you may have to think up additional supporting information so that each subtopic of your thesis statement is covered thoroughly. You can complete this organizing and sorting right on your brainstorming sheet by circling ideas that belong together or by using a numbering system, marking all the ideas to go under the first subtopic with 1's and all the ideas to go under the second subtopic with 2's and so on.

You may find it necessary now to revise your thesis statement to reflect any important ideas that have appeared during your brainstorming and organizing.

The only other organizing you will need to do is to decide on a logical order for pieces of supporting information under each subtopic. Again, the orders for coherence—order of importance, chronological order, spatial order, comparison and contrast order, and developmental order—can be useful.

The blueprint or rough plan from which you will write your essay should show all of your organizing decisions. Your plan may simply be your brainstorming sheet marked and numbered. It may be a modified outline with subtopics as headings and supporting material listed in logical order under each heading, or it may be a formal topic outline that shows the relative importance of your supporting information as well as the order.

For the essay on working for yourself, you might write a topic outline like the following. The thesis statement has been revised slightly for smoothness. Notice that the first subtopic is organized like a debate with a few of the opposition's arguments admitted and three pro arguments presented. The second and third subtopics are also actually pro arguments. They follow order of importance. The information under all three subtopics follows developmental order.

Thesis Statement: Working for yourself has advantages: You can make more money than you would in some conventional jobs and you can have flexible working hours.

I. Not difficult to start your own service business
   A. (Con arguments) Impractical to start your own business
      1. Takes a great deal of planning
      2. May require some financial investment for advertising and equipment
   B. (Pro argument) Possible to find customers easily
      1. Make contacts through the community
      2. Make contacts through parents and their work
      3. Make contacts through clubs and religious organizations
   C. (Pro argument) Possible to advertise inexpensively
      1. Run one initial ad in newspaper
      2. Place ads free on bulletin boards in stores, businesses, and community centers
   D. (Pro argument) Possible to obtain equipment
      1. Borrow from neighbors
      2. Buy with parents' help
      3. Rent from local stores
II. Making more money on your own than in some conventional jobs
   A. Possible to do household work for working people
      1. Clean houses for $6.00 an hour
      2. Wash windows, polish floors, shampoo rugs
   B. Possible to help out older people
      1. Work for at least $4.00 an hour
      2. Garden, walk dogs, shovel snow, do laundry, shopping, and errands
   C. Possible to do home improvement projects
      1. Receive good wages from people who don't want to pay high professional fees
      2. Paint houses indoors and out
   D. Possible to tutor for $4.00 to $5.00 an hour
   E. Possible to type for $7.50 an hour
      1. Type papers and manuscripts
      2. Make much more than an office employee at $3.50 an hour
III. Having flexible working hours
   A. Set own hours to fit school and other activities

    B. Possible to work only on long weekends or holidays by taking care of people's houses, lawns, pets
    C. Possible to work only on weekends
        1. Cater children's birthday parties
        2. Organize and publicize garage sales
    D. Possible to work only on a few afternoons
        1. Tutor
        2. Teach private classes for children
    E. Possible to work as much as you want doing assorted jobs

EXERCISE D: **Arranging and Sorting Supporting Information.** Use your brainstorming sheet from Exercise C to plan the order of ideas for your essay. Follow these steps.

1. Examine your thesis statement and list of supporting information and identify two or more subtopics of your thesis statement.
2. Choose a logical order for these subtopics.
3. Decide the order of information under each subtopic and, at the same time, delete repetitious, irrelevant, or vague pieces of information. Add information if necessary to cover each subtopic completely.
4. Examine your thesis statement and revise it if it no longer exactly fits your ordered and unified supporting information.
5. Finally, show your organizing decisions on your brainstorming sheet, in a modified outline, or in a topic outline.

■ Writing the Essay

By the time you write an outline or plan, your preparatory steps are completed. You can now think about writing a first draft of the entire essay in which you should strive for a unified tone and smooth connections among your ideas. Before you actually begin to write, you should think about your introduction and make note of a few ideas for your title and conclusion, if you have not done so already.

    Plan your introduction and jot down some ideas for your title and conclusion. Then use your outline to guide you in writing a unified, coherent version of the complete essay.

If you have not already thought of some ideas for your introduction, you should do so now. Often the introduction is the most challenging part of the essay to write because it has to spark the reader's interest, provide background information, establish the tone of the essay, and lead into the thesis statement. You might experiment with several different ways of attracting the reader's attention and of introducing the thesis statement. While you are thinking of provocative beginnings, you might also jot down ideas for your conclusion. You might discover ways to tie the beginning and end of the essay together by a unity of tone and ideas. Knowing where you want to end up will also help you when you begin to draft the whole essay. In addition, you might think up a few titles. Sometimes the title can give you insight into the tone you wish to maintain and can launch you into the writing.

When you actually write your draft, use every other line to allow room for revisions or alterations later on. Think about your purpose and audience as you write, and establish and maintain an appropriate and consistent attitude toward your subject and reader. Do you want to sound friendly or scholarly? Formal or informal? Casual or serious? In addition, as you compose sentences, make a deliberate effort to link your ideas smoothly by using transitions, repeating main words, using synonyms for main words, or employing other connecting devices. Vary the length and structure of your sentences to make your writing more interesting and to emphasize important ideas. Choose precise words, and try to maintain a consistent level of language.

EXERCISE E: **Creating an Introduction, Title, and Conclusion.** Refer to your original list of supporting information or brainstorm for new ideas for your introduction. Then sketch out an introduction that includes your thesis statement. Jot down three different titles for your essay, and choose the best one. Finally, think up two or three ideas for your conclusion.

EXERCISE F: **Writing a First Draft.** Use your rough version of your introduction and your plan or outline to write a complete version of your essay, ending with the ideas you listed for your conclusion and any others that come to mind. Try to maintain the tone you set in the introduction and thesis statement. As you write, attempt to achieve a fresh, readable style. Use transitions and other connecting devices to clarify your ideas for the reader. Write in complete sentences and double space or skip every other line.

■ Revising the Essay

Checking and revising your first draft gives you a chance to rethink your ideas and refine your writing. It is a creative step in the writing process as well as a technical one that allows you to make improvements and corrections.

Checking Content and Organization.　If possible, you should set your first draft aside for a while before you begin to revise. After a short interval, you can take a fresh look at your writing to gain some objectivity. When you reread your essay, look for places where you can improve the content and organization; feel free to change anything if it will make your essay clearer, more forceful, more interesting, more unified, or more coherent.

Go over your essay carefully for any problems in the development or organization of ideas.

Now that the writing is essentially finished, you can afford to be objective about your essay, to eliminate and change things that do not work. Use some of the questions in the checklist for revising on page 723 to help you identify any problems with your ideas or with the logic in your presentation of them.

Polishing for Language and Style.　When you are rexamining your essay, you should also pay attention to the words you have chosen and the construction of your sentences. You might read your writing aloud to yourself or to someone else and try to hear your words and sentences as if you were the audience.

Reread your essay to check word choices, consistency of tone, and variety of sentence lengths and structures.

While your word choices should be precise, they should also suit the tone of the whole piece. Check for inconsistencies in tone and for words whose connotations create misleading impressions of your attitude. Also consider your purpose as you check your word choices. In an expository essay, your words should be direct and forceful but not emotional or offensive. And, finally, check your word choices with your audience's knowledge in mind. Specialized or technical language would not be appropriate for an audience just learning about a topic, and overly simple language would seem dull to an audience of experts.

To check your sentence style, you might try reading and rereading a single paragraph at a time. Listen to the rhythms created by a series of sentences. If you detect monotonous patterns, rambling sentences, or awkward places, you should adjust sentence lengths, sentence openers, and other structures. Adding transitions, coordinating words, or subordinating words might help, also. Make sure that each paragraph reads smoothly and carries the reader forward.

Checking the Essay Overall.   In addition to reconsidering the content and style of your essay, you should proofread your essay for technical errors and any other weaknesses that you might not have noticed before. Because you have invested considerable effort in this work, you should not allow easily correctable mistakes in spelling, punctuation, grammar, or usage to undermine the effectiveness of what you have written.

Use a checklist for revision to improve and correct your essay.

Throughout your revising and during your final review, you can use a checklist to direct you to specific problems. Do not just answer each question with a yes. After reading each question, go back to your essay and examine it closely for that particular feature. View your essay as a reader would, and try to make your writing stronger and clearer.

CHECKLIST FOR REVISING A STANDARD ESSAY

1. Is the title appropriate to the ideas and style of the essay? Is it appealing?
2. Does the introduction catch the reader's interest, provide necessary background information, set the tone, and lead toward the essay's main point?
3. Is the main point clearly stated in the thesis statement, with or without subtopics?
4. Do the body paragraphs expand and support significant subtopics of the thesis statement? Is the main idea of each paragraph clear?
5. Have you included enough supporting information—examples, details, facts, reasons, and incidents—to develop each subtopic thoroughly for the reader?
6. Are the subtopics arranged in logical order: order of importance, chronological order, spatial order, comparison and contrast order, or developmental order?
7. Is the information within each paragraph arranged logically and connected by transitions and other linking devices?
8. Does the conclusion refer to the main point and complete the essay?

9. Do your word choices convey the tone you intend? Does the tone remain consistent throughout the essay?

10. Do your sentences have varied lengths, openers, and structures?

11. Can you find errors in grammar, usage, punctuation, or spelling? If you are not sure, check a dictionary or the grammar, usage, and mechanics units of this book.

12. Does the essay communicate with your audience and fulfill its purpose?

Once your revision work is done, you should prepare a neat final copy of the essay.

If you were to complete the essay on working for yourself, you might produce a finished version like the following. The marginal comments point out the essay's structure, and some of the transitions are italicized. Notice the repetition of main words and the use of synonyms throughout the essay to link ideas: *working for yourself, performing some useful service on your own, running your own service business,* and others.

Title	Becoming Your Own Boss
Introduction	The thought of doing part-time work during the school year may conjure up for you images of bussing dishes, pumping gas, bagging groceries, or standing behind a cash register. These jobs are all ways to make money while you are going to school, but there are other ways as well. You might consider becoming your own employer by starting your own service business to do such things as paint houses, garden, or
Thesis statement	tutor. Working for yourself has advantages: You can make more money than you would be able to in some conventional jobs, and you can also have flexible working hours.
Subtopic 1: arguments against the drawbacks	Some people might argue that working for yourself is impractical because it takes a great deal of planning and may even require some financial investment in advertising and equipment. Although these drawbacks have some validity, they are actually surmountable: Establishing your own service business is not that difficult. You should be able to find customers through contacts in your community, through your parents' friends and business acquaintances, and through clubs and religious organizations. You can advertise the service you are offering by investing a small amount of money to run an ad in a local newspaper. *Or better yet,* you can place ads

without charge on bulletin boards in grocery stores, community centers, local businesses, and maybe even schools. To acquire any necessary equipment such as floor polishers or lawn edgers, you probably will find that neighbors will lend equipment, that parents will help in the investment, or that local stores will rent the equipment reasonably. Sometimes you can pick up secondhand machines quite inexpensively by searching the want ads in newspapers. *And* once you set up your business, your efforts will reward you with profitable and convenient work.

Subtopic 2: making more money than in some conventional jobs

By performing some useful service on your own, you can usually earn more than minimum wage. An increasing number of people today will pay others to do household work that they don't have time to do themselves. Many working people, *for example*, will pay someone as much as $6.00 an hour to do their housecleaning. These same customers will pay at least equally well for such strenuous household work as window washing, floor polishing, and rug shampooing. Many older people would probably contract with you for at least $4.00 an hour to handle such tasks as gardening, walking their dogs, shoveling snow, or doing their laundry, shopping, or errands. *And* some homeowners lack the interest or skill to do special home improvement projects. *Consequently,* they would prefer to pay hard-working students very well to do indoor or outdoor painting than to engage a professional service at a much higher fee, if such a service even exists in your community. *Or,* if you are a good tutor, you can charge from $4.00 to $5.00 an hour. *And* an accurate typist might be able to make as much as $7.50 an hour typing papers for college or graduate students or manuscripts for writers or publishing companies. This wage is well above the $3.50 an hour you might make as a part-time office employee.

Subtopic 3: having flexible working hours

Perhaps the greatest advantage of running your own service business is that you can work when you want to and as much as you want to. You can set your own working hours and adjust them to fit your schedule, including your studying time and extracurricular activities like sports or student government. You might choose to work only on long weekends or holidays, *for instance. Then* you might offer your services minding people's houses, collecting their mail, watering their lawns, or caring for their pets. You might choose to work just on weekends, catering children's birthday parties or organizing and publicizing garage sales. If afternoon work would suit your schedule, you might tutor on one of your free afternoons or conduct small private classes in crafts, sports, or music for children. *Or,* if you want to work many hours, you might set up a service grooming pets, refinishing furniture, tailoring, or collecting aluminum cans, newspapers, and bottles for recycling.

Reminder of thesis statement

Conclusion

When you consider working for yourself, you can see that the possibilities for making the most money in the time you have to work are numerous, depending on how creative, enterprising, and conscientious you are. You might even find your service business so lucrative that you could expand it and share the work with other students, or increase your part-time work to a full-time job in the summer. Rather than be discouraged or frustrated about the part-time job market for students, remember that clerking in a store, flipping hamburgers, or answering phones are not your only choices.

EXERCISE G: **Evaluating, Revising, and Rewriting the Essay.** Check the draft you wrote in Exercise F. Reread it carefully, looking first at your content and organization, then at your word choices and sentence style, making any alterations right on the paper. Use the checklist on page 723 to review and polish any features of the essay that you think require improvement. When you are satisfied, write a neat final copy of the essay and submit it to your teacher.

APPLICATION: **Planning, Writing, and Revising an Essay.** Choose another topic for an essay from the following list, from the list in Exercise A, or think of one of your own. Follow the steps for narrowing the topic, developing support, organizing, and writing a first draft. As you plan and write the essay, use other students in class as your audience. If you wrote an expository essay, write a persuasive essay this time (or vice versa).

When you have written a first draft, exchange essays with a classmate and use the checklist on page 723 to evaluate the other student's essay. Revise your own essay according to the comments you receive. Then write a neat final copy of the essay.

Language	Politics
Traffic laws	Beauty
Dancing	Conservation
Spectator sports	Newscasting
Comedy	Insects

Key Features of Informal Essays

You may notice as you read essays written by professional writers that not all essays exactly fit the pattern of the standard essay. Essays that have looser, more individual structures are called informal essays.

This section explains some of the variations of form and structure found in informal essays and some of the options you have in writing these essays.

■ Characteristics of Informal Essays

Like standard essays, informal essays must be unified and coherent, flowing logically from thought to thought and sentence to sentence. Like a standard essay, an informal essay should develop a focused main point and avoid distracting the reader with irrelevant ideas and information. An informal essay should have a consistent tone throughout to unify it. Logical order and transitional devices should guide the reader from idea to idea and from paragraph to paragraph.

What distinguishes the informal essay is the presentation of the main point and the development of support. An informal essay has a topic and a main point or controlling idea. But the main point may or may not be expressed directly in a thesis statement, and it may not always appear in the first paragraph. Similarly, the body paragraphs may not be a distinct group; introductory ideas may blend with paragraphs that develop the controlling idea so that you cannot separate the introduction from the body, or even the body from the conclusion. Despite this variable form, there should be a logic behind the presentation, and some closing remarks should signal the end or resolution of the essay.

The following informal essay by Gerald Durrell does not contain a distinct introduction and body. Rather, it seems to plunge right into its topic—an interesting garden wall that contains so many layers and varieties of life that it seems to be a world unto itself. The essay is ordered by a process of discovery, which takes the reader deeper and deeper into the wall, revealing layer after layer of life in it. It is not until the third paragraph that the writer mentions what he finds to be the most interesting inhabitants of the wall: the scorpions, which live almost invisibly in its cracks. These creatures are described in closest detail and are given the greatest emphasis. Notice that the controlling idea, which is that the wall represents a little world of its own, is explictly stated only in the title, but it is clearly implied and developed throughout the entire essay.

Title

The World in a Wall

Background idea and description

First indication of main point: wall seen as world in miniature

Subtopic 1: landscape

    The crumbling wall that surrounded the sunken garden alongside the house was a rich hunting ground for me. It was an ancient brick wall that had been plastered over, but now this outer skin was green with moss, bulging and sagging with the damp of many winters. The whole surface was an intricate map of cracks, some several inches wide, others as fine as hairs. Here and there large pieces had dropped off and revealed the rows of rose-pink bricks lying beneath like ribs. There was a whole landscape on this wall if you peered closely enough to see it; the roofs of a hundred tiny toadstools, red, yellow, and brown, showed in patches like villages on the damper portions; mountains of bottle-green moss grew in tuffets so symmetrical that they might have been planted and trimmed; forests of small ferns sprouted from cracks in the shady places, dropping languidly like little green fountains. The top of the wall was a desert land, too dry for anything except a few rust-red mosses to live in it, too hot for anything except sunbathing by the dragonflies. At the base of the wall grew a mass of plants, cyclamen, crocus, asphodel, thrusting their leaves among the piles of broken and chipped roof-tiles that lay there. This whole strip was guarded by a labyrinth of blackberry hung, in season, with fruit that was plump and juicy and black as ebony.

Subtopic 2: creatures of this world in the wall

    The inhabitants of the wall were a mixed lot, and they were divided into day and night workers, the hunters and the hunted. At night the hunters were the toads that lived among the brambles, and the geckos, pale, translucent, with bulging eyes, that lived in the cracks higher up the wall. Their prey was the population of stupid, absentminded craneflies that zoomed and barged their way among the leaves; moths of all sizes and shapes, moths striped, tessellated, checked, spotted, and blotched, that fluttered in soft clouds along the withered plaster; the beetles, rotund and neatly clad as businessmen, hurrying with portly efficiency about their night's work. When the last glow-worm had dragged his frosty emerald lantern to bed over the hills of moss, and the sun rose, the wall was taken over by the next set of inhabitants. Here it was more difficult to differentiate between the prey and the predators, for everything seemed to feed indiscriminately off everything else. Thus the hunting wasps searched out caterpillars and spiders; the spiders hunted for flies; the dragonflies, big brittle, and hunting-pink, fed off the spiders and the flies; and the swift, lithe, and multicoloured wall lizards fed off everything.

Subtopic 3: the scorpions, the most interesting creatures of this small world

But the shyest and most self-effacing of the wall community were the most dangerous; you hardly ever saw one unless you looked for it, and yet there must have been several hundred living in the cracks in the wall. Slide a knife-blade carefully under a piece of the loose plaster and lever it gently away from the brick, and there, crouching beneath it, would be a little black scorpion an inch long, looking as though he were made out of polished chocolate. They were weird-looking things, with their flattened, oval bodies, their neat, crooked legs, the enormous crablike claws, bulbous and neatly jointed as armor, and the tail like a string of brown beads ending in a sting like a rose-thorn. The scorpion would lie there quite quietly as you examined him, only raising his tail in an almost apologetic gesture of warning if you breathed too hard on him. If you kept him in the sun too long he would simply turn his back on you and walk away, and then slide slowly but firmly under another section of plaster.

I grew very fond of these scorpions. I found them to be pleasant, unassuming creatures with, on the whole, the most charming habits. Provided you did nothing silly or clumsy (like putting your hand on one) the scorpions treated you with respect, their one desire being to get away and hide as quickly as possible. They must have found me rather a trial, for I was always ripping sections of the plaster away so that I could watch them, or capturing them and making them walk about in jam-jars so that I could see the way their feet moved. By means of my sudden and unexpected assaults on the wall I discovered quite a bit about the scorpions. I found that they would eat bluebottles (though how they caught them was a mystery I never solved), grasshoppers, moths, and lacewing flies. Several times I found them eating each other, a habit I found most distressing in a creature otherwise so impeccable.

By crouching under the wall at night with a torch, I managed to catch some brief glimpses of the scorpions' wonderful courtship dances. I saw them standing, claws clasped, their bodies raised to the skies, their tails lovingly entwined; I saw them

Closing
remarks

waltzing slowly in circles among the moss cushions, claw in claw. But my view of these performances was all too short, for almost as soon as I switched on the torch the partners would stop, pause for a moment, and then, seeing that I was not going to extinguish the light, they would turn round and walk firmly away, claw in claw, side by side. They were definitely beasts that believed in keeping themselves to themselves. If I could have kept a colony in captivity I would probably have been able to see the whole of the courtship, but the family had forbidden scorpions in the house, despite my arguments in favour of them. —Gerald Durrell

Topics of Informal Essays.   When writing an informal essay, a writer has a wide range of topics to choose from and only a few restricting considerations. An informal essay can be expository, persuasive, descriptive, or narrative. It can discuss a political event, reflect on a scientific discovery, present an observation or general truth, relate a personal experience, or even do a combination of these. There are only a few restrictions on a writer's choice of topics. Like standard essays, informal essays should treat only those topics that are narrow enough to be covered satisfactorily with plentiful supporting information within the limits of an essay. Secondly, although an informal essay can be about almost anything, the topic should be one that the writer cares about and knows well from study or personal experience.

The topic of an informal essay should be narrow enough to be developed thoroughly in an essay and should be of great personal interest to the writer.

Because an informal essay allows great freedom for personal expression, the writer's own interests are the major determinants of the topic. Informal essays are often descriptive or narrative or often contain substantial amounts of description and narration: for example, the writer's own impressions, experiences, and responses to something in the environment. Gerald Durrell, for instance, was fascinated by an unusual wall and in particular by the scorpions, so he described in great detail the plants and animals of the wall. But informal essays might consider larger social or political issues as well, or might treat aesthetic or ethical questions. Or they might combine personal impressions with social or political issues. For example, the British essayist George Orwell expresses his opinions about colonialism in his account of a personal experience in the essay "Shooting an Elephant." And Joan Didion offers several separate personal impressions of incidents in the late 1960's to characterize the spirit of that time in her essay "The White Album."

Often, the title of an informal essay will indicate the topic and even the writer's particular angle or main point. The title of Durrell's essay, "The World in a Wall," prepares the reader for the topic. It suggests that every detail in the essay will show how the wall is a microcosm. Some titles directly state their topics, while others take a more fanciful or clever approach. The first title, in the following chart, for instance, "The Noblest Instrument," playfully treats the writer's childhood memories of violin practice. The second and third titles reveal their topics in a more straightforward manner. On the other hand, the fourth and fifth titles have a special appeal to certain audiences. Joan Didion's "The White Album" is directed at a certain group of people who would connect the Beatles' *White Album* with a particular period of recent history. And Pauline Kael's "Raising Kane" makes a playful pun on the title of the very famous film, *Citizen Kane*, and implies that the making of that movie was a lively and difficult experience.

TITLES AND TOPICS OF INFORMAL ESSAYS	
Topics of Some Informal Essays	**Titles of the Essays**
Violin lessons (the writer's childhood memories)	"The Noblest Instrument" by Clarence Day
Frustrations of planning a vacation (the writer's personal experiences)	"On Vacations" by G. Jean Nathan
Reasons why young men and women should consider a college education (social issue)	"Why Go To College" by Robert M. Hutchins
Observations of society in the late 1960's—title refers to Beatles' album (social issue)	"The White Album" by Joan Didion
Process of making the movie *Citizen Kane*	"Raising Kane" by Pauline Kael

Controlling Ideas for Informal Essays.   Like a standard essay, an informal essay should always have a controlling idea or main point, whether presented explicitly in a thesis statement or simply implied throughout the essay. In other words, in an informal essay the method of presenting the controlling idea depends on the writer's choice and the nature of the topic.

An informal essay should have a controlling idea. It may resemble a standard thesis statement, may be presented in different sentences, may appear anywhere in the essay, or may be implied rather than stated.

In an informal essay, the main point may be stated in a thesis statement in the introduction, or it may be revealed gradually to the reader. For instance, the main point may be spread out over several sentences, perhaps even over different paragraphs. It may not appear until the middle or final paragraphs of the essay. It may grow throughout the essay and appear several times, each time more complete as the writer adds ideas. On the other hand, it may never be stated at all but instead be implied by the examples, details, facts, reasons, and incidents in the essay. The Durrell essay suggests the controlling idea in the title and then begins to expand this main point in the first paragraph and continues to elaborate on it without ever stating the complete main point in a single sentence. Still, the idea that a little world exists in the wall is unmistakable from the writer's treatment of the material as he shifts from an overview of the wall to a closer look at the plant and animal life and finally describes the scorpions in detail.

Sometimes the controlling idea in an informal essay may be even more subtly presented. Readers may have to infer the main point from all the pieces of information provided in the essay by forming their own decisions about the essay's underlying meaning. Such an approach works well in an informal essay that is largely descriptive or narrative. The writer may feel that the essay will have greater impact if readers must interpret its meaning for themselves. These informal essays resemble works of literature in which the message is not "spelled out."

EXERCISE A: Analyzing the Topics of Informal Essays. Find *three* informal essays in books, magazines, or anthologies. You might look for works by any of the following professional writers. Read each of the informal essays you choose and then write the three titles on your paper. Along with each title, write a brief description or statement of the essay's topic.

Montaigne	George Orwell	Erma Bombeck
Charles Lamb	E.B. White	George F. Will
Francis Bacon	Nora Ephron	Jean Kerr
Susan Sontag	James Baldwin	Joan Didion
Henry David	Doris Lessing	Pete Axthelm
Thoreau	James Thurber	Lillian Hellman
Virginia Woolf	Pauline Kael	Judith Crist

EXERCISE B: Determining Controlling Ideas. Use the essays that you found for Exercise A. Reread each essay, if necessary, and decide if the controlling idea is formulated in a thesis statement, is spread out over two or more sentences, is placed in the middle or at the end of the essay, or is implied by the rest of the essay. Write the controlling idea for each essay on your paper.

■ Structural Possibilities for Informal Essays

The parts of an informal essay may be arranged similarly to those in a standard essay, but they often have a more individualistic, flexible structure. You might think of the standard essay as a typical, traditional house while the informal essay might be envisioned as a house with experimental or unusual architecture. Both buildings are identifiable as houses and both function as houses, but one has a predictable, readily apparent form, and the other does not.

In order to be identifiable as an essay and to function as an essay, an informal essay must be unified and coherent; however, the connections among the ideas in an informal essay may be more subtle than those you would expect to find in a standard essay.

Flexibility of Structure. The key to an informal essay's structure is flexibility, and one informal essay may differ greatly from another. The introductory material may flow inseparably into the development in the body, which may in turn wind down gracefully to a concluding sentence instead of a concluding paragraph. The normal functions performed by the introduction, body, and conclusion in a standard essay *do* appear in the informal essay, but they are not necessarily performed within the limits of certain specified paragraphs, as they are in the standard essay.

The structure of an informal essay is flexible: The introduction, body, and conclusion may not be distinct from each other or confined to separate paragraphs.

The informal essay is frequently used as a form of highly personal expression, and therefore its form is usually dictated by the particular needs and tastes of the writer. The entire essay should be based on a controlling idea, and it should have a beginning, a middle, and an end, but in an informal essay these parts may not be neatly contained within certain paragraphs. The introduction may be only *part* of the opening paragraph with the rest of the paragraph beginning to develop the stated or unstated main point. Or the introductory material may be carried over into a second or even a third paragraph. Body paragraphs may not form a clearly defined unit; instead, they may blend with introductory remarks at the beginning of the essay, and they may taper down to concluding remarks at the end. The paragraphs in an informal essay, besides performing several different structural functions within the essay, may be one of several special kinds of paragraphs—transitional, continuing, and so on—and may not contain topic sentences.

Unity and Coherence. Even though the boundaries of the parts in an informal essay may often be indistinct, all ideas should still be unified and should follow a clear, logical order.

Informal essays should be unified in ideas and tone and should be coherent throughout.

The tone and internal organization of an informal essay may be unique, rather than common and easily recognizable. Unlike a standard essay, an informal essay may have a personal, introspective, casual, or conversational tone. In some cases, an informal essay will use its tone to lead readers to inferences about the controlling idea. The tone should always be consistent and should hold the ideas in the essay together. And coherence in an informal essay may be more subtle than in a standard essay; in other words, the reader may have to infer the relationships among ideas. Often an informal essay will follow a developmental order of its own rather than one of the more structured and noticeable logical orders, such as chronological order or order of importance. Furthermore, the connecting devices in an informal essay may be woven into the ideas, consisting of repetitions of main words and synonyms, the use of consistent pronouns, and parallelism, rather than the more usual and obvious transitions.

Because the features, meaning, and structure of an informal essay are not explicit, an informal essay demands more from a reader than a standard essay does. A reader may have to infer the main point from the reader's clues or make judgments that are not openly stated in the essay. To understand the ideas that are suggested, a reader may have to read closely and think deeply in order to pin down the writer's meaning.

EXERCISE C: Analyzing the Structure of Informal Essays. For this exercise, use the same informal essays that you found in Exercise A. Try to identify an introductory part for each, a development or body part, and a concluding or closing part, keeping in mind that the parts may blend with one another and may not be confined to separate paragraphs. In a few sentences, write *why* you think each writer has chosen a particular structure and organization: why, for example, one essay might have only one sentence of introductory material, or why another might have an introduction several paragraphs long. Try to imagine the essay in a more traditional form: What, if anything, would be lost if the structure were less flexible?

EXERCISE D: Examining Informal Essays for Unity and Coherence. Again, use the essays found in Exercise A. Choose one and evaluate its unity and coherence. Decide if any ideas seem to stray from the controlling idea. Identify the tone of the piece, and decide if it remains consistent throughout. Can you spot any overall pattern of organization for the essay as a whole? Look at *one* paragraph. Do the ideas flow smoothly? Does the writer connect his or her ideas through transitions? Repetitions of main words? Synonyms? Parallelism?

APPLICATION: Practicing Writing Informal Essays. Find a topic for your own informal essay by drawing on your experience or convictions or by using your memory and imagination. Follow some of the steps for writing the standard essay and vary others. Zero in on a controlling idea (which you can state or imply in your essay), and gather ideas to develop your main point. As you plan your informal essay, experiment with structure and logical order. Consider blending the introduction with the body or having the body gradually become the conclusion. Try a developmental order. Concentrate on maintaining a consistent tone and on linking ideas smoothly and subtly for the reader. Finally, revise for clarity, unity, and coherence.

Chapter 24

Research and Writing

A library paper is a formal composition based on research on a specific topic. In style and structure, it is similar to an essay, but it is usually longer and somewhat more complex. Because a library paper contains information from research sources, it also has some features that an essay does not. A library paper contains citations of sources, or footnotes, as well as a list, or bibliography, which includes all sources used to prepare the paper.

The first section of the chapter examines the key features of library papers, particularly the methods of documenting and incorporating research. The second section offers steps that can help you plan, organize, write, and revise a library paper. The purpose of the chapter is to improve your ability to incorporate your research in your writing.

24.1 Special Features of the Library Paper

High school teachers, college professors, and many employers may expect you to know how to expand your knowledge of a subject through careful, thorough research. Doing research involves investigating a topic and familiarizing yourself with other people's ideas and discoveries. It also involves arriving at your own ideas on the topic after you have gained some knowledge of it. A composition that is based on this research and that combines your ideas with other people's knowledge is a library paper. Like an essay, a library paper has an introduction, a body, and a conclusion. It must be unified and clearly organized and it can be written for a number of different purposes: to explain, to inform, to instruct, to define, or to persuade.

It differs from a standard essay, however, in that it draws heavily on material gathered through research. It integrates your ideas developed through reading and thinking about a topic with information found in research sources. The use of sources influences the content, style, and structure of a library paper, as you will see in this section.

■ The Documentation and Use of Sources

The researching of a library paper usually begins with checking material on your topic in the card catalog, *The Readers' Guide to Periodical Literature*, and sometimes the vertical file. These research tools can guide you to books, articles in magazines and newspapers, and specialized reference works that contain information on your topic. (For an explanation of the use of the library and reference materials, see Sections 17.1 and 17.2.) By reading widely on your topic, you can become enough of an expert to have some ideas of your own. Your own ideas and especially the main point you make in the thesis statement of your paper will form the skeleton of the paper. The information you have gathered through research will provide much of the development of your ideas.

Because a good portion of the material in a library paper derives from outside sources, you must know how to include this information and how to give credit to other people for their ideas. The following pages explain how to credit and use information from sources.

Documentation of Research.   The correct documentation of sources makes your paper authoritative, believable, and useful to readers interested in learning more about the topic. Citing sources throughout your paper identifies the origin of quotations and ideas that you found through your research. There are two different methods that can be used to cite sources.

> To document information from research sources, use informal citations, which give the source in parentheses within the text of the paper, or footnotes, which give the source at the bottom of the page on which the information is used or in a group at the end of the paper.

Informal citations appear immediately after the borrowed quotations or information. To write informal citations, include in parentheses the author's name, the title of the source, and the page number where the information can be found. The following passage illustrates informal citations. In this case, the same source is used twice. Notice that the second reference to the same source is abbreviated; only the last name of the author, the title of the book, and the page number are given.

Passage with
informal
citations

(Second reference to
same work)

> The buffoon, clown, or fool, a dramatic figure popular since the Golden Age of Greece, has rarely been used to such an extent or with such great success as in the plays of William Shakespeare. The fool is a "nearly indispensable personage ... with a many-sided social, theatrical, and literary tradition behind him" (Leo Salinger, <u>Shakespeare and the Traditions of Comedy,</u> p. 15). Shakespeare's buffoon plays a major role in both comedy and tragedy, serving as entertainer, explainer, and illuminator of the truth, as well as providing the audience with a temporary escape from reality (Salinger, <u>Shakespeare and the Traditions of Comedy,</u> pp. 15–16).

Footnotes, the more formal and usually the preferred method, can be used instead to cite the same information. To write footnotes, place a small number above the line immediately following the borrowed information. Each succeeding footnote on the page should be given a higher number. Then, at the bottom of the page, the same number appears with the source documented: the author's name, the title of the work, publishing information, and the page number of the borrowed information. Again notice that a second reference to the same work is abbreviated.

Passage with
footnotes

> The buffoon, clown, or fool, a dramatic figure popular since the Golden Age of Greece, has rarely been used to such an extent or with such great success as in the plays of William Shakespeare. The fool is a "nearly indispensable personage ... with a many-sided social, theatrical, and literary tradition behind him."[1] Shakespeare's buffoon plays a major role in both comedy and tragedy, serving as entertainer, explainer, and illuminator of the truth, as well as providing the audience with a temporary escape from reality.[2]

---

[1] Leo Salinger, <u>Shakespeare and the Traditions of Comedy</u> (London: Cambridge University Press, 1974) p. 15.

[2] Salinger, <u>Shakespeare and the Traditions of Comedy,</u> pp. 15–16.

The footnote method can also be modified. Instead of placing the sources at the bottom of pages, you can group them on one *footnote page* following the last page of the paper. Sources should be listed according to the raised numbers in the text of the paper. No matter which method of citing sources is chosen, that method should be used consistently throughout the paper.

To write informal citations and footnotes, you can use the following chart as a guide. Notice that different types of sources require some different pieces of information.

FORMS FOR CITING SOURCES		
Kind of Source	**Informal Citation**	**Footnote**
Book	(Olga Connolly, The Rings of Destiny, p. 63)	[1]Olga Connolly, The Rings of Destiny (New York: David McKay Company, Inc., 1968), p. 63.
Book (with two authors)	(Albert Goldman and Lawrence Schiller, Ladies and Gentlemen, Lenny Bruce, p. 379)	[1]Albert Goldman and Lawrence Schiller, Ladies and Gentlemen, Lenny Bruce (New York: Random House, Inc., 1971), p. 379.
Magazine article (signed)	(Richard Wolkomir, "Hypnosis: Peephole into the Mind," Kiwanis, September 1980, p. 30)	[1]Richard Wolkomir, "Hypnosis: Peephole into the Mind," Kiwanis, September 1980, p. 30.
Magazine article (unsigned)	("Why More Bureaucrats Are Being Sued," U.S. News and World Report, September 8, 1980, p. 44)	[1]"Why More Bureaucrats Are Being Sued," U.S. News and World Report, September 8, 1980, p. 44.
Encyclopedia article (signed)	(The Jewish Encyclopedia, 1902 ed., "Bannaah, Bannay, Bannayah," by Louis Ginzberg)	[1]The Jewish Encyclopedia, 1902 ed., "Bannaah, Bannay, Bannayah," by Louise Ginzberg.
Encyclopedia article (unsigned)	(The New Columbia Encyclopedia, 1975 ed., "Religion")	[1]The New Columbia Encyclopedia, 1975 ed., "Religion."
Newspaper article (signed)	(Ann Crittenden, "Growers' Power in Marketing Under Attack," The New York Times, March 25, 1981, p. A1)	[1]Ann Crittenden, "Growers' Power in Marketing Under Attack," The New York Times, March 25, 1981, p. A1.
Newspaper article (unsigned)	("Drought Slows Mozambique's Recovery Program," The New York Times, October 26, 1980, p. 13)	[1]"Drought Slows Mozambique's Recovery Program," The New York Times, October 26, 1980, p. 13.

Collected or selected works of a single author	(Mark Twain, <u>The Complete Humorous Sketches and Tales of Mark Twain</u>, ed. Charles Neider, p. 312)	[1]Mark Twain, <u>The Complete Humorous Sketches and Tales of Mark Twain</u>, ed. Charles Neider (Garden City, N.Y.: Doubleday and Company, Inc., 1961), p. 312.
Collected or selected works of several authors	(John W. Bachman and E. Martin Browne, eds., <u>Better Plays for Today's Churches</u>, p. 21)	[1]John W. Bachman and E. Martin Browne, eds., <u>Better Plays for Today's Churches</u> (New York: Association Press, 1964), p. 21.
Translated work	(Francoise Sagan, <u>Sunlight on Cold Water</u>, trans. Joanna Kilmartin, p. 82)	[1]Francoise Sagan, <u>Sunlight on Cold Water</u>, trans. Joanna Kilmartin (Harmondsworth, Middlesex, England: Penguin, 1978), p. 82.
Work in several volumes	(Thomas Paine, <u>The Writings of Thomas Paine</u>, vol. 1, ed. Moncure Daniel Conway, p. 33)	[1]Thomas Paine, <u>The Writings of Thomas Paine</u>, vol. 1, ed. Moncure Daniel Conway (New York: AMS Press, Inc., 1967), p. 33.

Correct Use of Sources. In addition to documenting sources in a consistent manner throughout your paper, you should know for what kinds of information from sources you must provide informal citations or footnotes. Including information from other writers without giving credit to them is *plagiarism*, or literary theft, and should always be avoided.

Avoid plagiarism by citing the sources of any words, ideas, or little-known facts that you have used.

The use of someone else's words, theories, ancedotes, or other specific ideas without giving credit for this information constitutes plagiarism. When exact words or a particular writer's ideas are taken from a source, this borrowing of information must be acknowledged. Only when the ideas are common knowledge because they can be found in several sources can this information be incorporated into a library paper without a reference to any *one* source.

There are a number of ways to avoid plagiarism. If you use information in another person's words, put quotation marks around this information, and then list the source in an informal citation or footnote. If you mention the idea of a particular writer and rephrase it in your own words, you do not need to use quotation marks, but you must cite the source of the idea in an informal citation or footnote. Or if you include a fact that is not generally known—in other words, that does not appear in many sources on the topic—you should specify where you found the information.

If you were writing a paper about trade wars, for instance, you might consult the following article from the magazine *Archaeology*.

Passage from
a magazine
article

Salt has always played a curious role in the history of human affairs. Widely available to most people, salt can be transported easily and requires relatively little energy for its exploitation. Accessible at low cost in most world markets, it is hardly surprising that societies, past and present, have always taken this resource for granted—ironic because a salt scarcity can threaten the very life of a community and disrupt the affairs of an entire nation.

At the bare minimum, people need two grams of salt a day. Failure to maintain this level for a relatively short span of time is fatal. In very humid tropical regions, where laboring people require a great deal more than two grams a day, consumption levels of up to 30 grams daily have been reported. Today in Middle America—the ancient home of the Maya—an individual needs a minimum daily intake of approximately eight grams of salt. A community of 50,000 people requires at least 400 kilograms a day or 146 tons of salt a year. Most communities, however, consume several times the minimum requirement of salt for both dietary and other purposes. When the supply is reduced or cut off, there can be drastic repercussions. It is at this point that salt becomes a critical factor in human affairs.

A sudden shift in supply or demand can create havoc within the trading networks of empires. Competition to obtain salt can even lead to wars. There are many regions in the world where salt has played a crucial role in the history of human events: None is more famous than the great Maya empire. For over 2,000 years, salt was a major trade item throughout the Maya area of southern Mexico and northern Central America. Salt trade figures prominently in both the development and demise of Maya civilization.
—Anthony P. Andrews

The following passage uses material from the preceding article incorrectly. It both borrows word for word and rephrases some of the ideas without giving the source of each quotation, idea, and fact. The plagiarized material is underscored.

Passage from an unacceptable library paper

Plagiarism

Of all the economic causes of wars, competition for salt is perhaps one of the least known, but <u>salt has played a curious role in the history of human affairs.</u> People's health has always demanded a daily dosage of salt—anywhere from <u>two grams of salt a day up to thirty grams daily. Accessible at low cost in most world markets, it is hardly surprising that societies, past and present, have always taken this resource for granted.</u> When societies have suffered from shortages or cuts in trade supplies of salt, this <u>sudden shift in supply or demand has created havoc within the trading network of empires. Competition for salt has even been the cause of wars.</u>

As you can see in the preceding passage, plagiarism not only constitutes a serious error but also makes writing sound padded, unnatural, and patched together. To avoid these problems, you should learn when to include a particularly well-stated idea by quoting it word for word and placing it in quotation marks and when to state a writer's ideas in your own words—preserving your own writing style—and then give the source of the ideas.

Notice in the following passage that the writer has incorporated and cited a fact from the article in an informal citation and has used a quotation from the source correctly with quotation marks and a citation.

Passage from an acceptable library paper

Fact cited

Quotation cited

Of all the economic causes of wars, competition for salt is perhaps the least known. Humans have always needed a daily dosage of salt—anywhere from two grams to thirty grams a day (Anthony P. Andrews, "The Salt Trade of the Ancient Maya," <u>Archaeology,</u> July/August 1980, p. 24). Because salt is a necessity for human life, many societies have suffered when faced with shortages or cuts in trade supplies of salt. For example, "salt trade figures prominently in both the development and demise of the Maya civilization" (Andrews, "The Salt Trade of the Ancient Maya," p. 24).

When you use and cite sources, you must also make sure that your readers will understand any ideas and terminology in the borrowed material. For this reason, you may have to translate technical ideas into simpler language for your reader, or you may have to provide explanations when you include certain material from sources in your paper.

Bibliography. The sources that have been used in the preparation of the paper and within the paper itself must also be acknowledged in a formal list at the end of the paper, called a *bibliography*.

List all the sources that you consulted during the research and other planning steps in a bibliography at the end of your library paper.

The bibliography shows the extent to which you researched your topic by including all the sources that you used in researching and writing the paper. It enables readers to locate any of your sources if they are interested in reading more about your topic.

In your bibliography, the sources should be listed alphabetically, according to the last name of the author or the title of the work if no author is given. The entries should give complete information about each source: the author, title of the work, place of publication, name of the publisher, and date of publication. Page numbers are not necessary in a bibliography, unless the source is a magazine or newspaper article.

The following chart illustrates sample entries for a bibliography, covering the kinds of sources you are likely to use.

	ENTRIES FOR A BIBLIOGRAPHY
Kind of Source	**Bibliographic Entry**
Book	Connolly, Olga. <u>The Rings of Destiny</u>. New York: David McKay Company, Inc., 1968.
Book (with two authors)	Goldman, Albert and Schiller, Lawrence. <u>Ladies and Gentlemen, Lenny Bruce</u>. New York: Random House, Inc., 1971.
Magazine article (signed)	Wolkomir, Richard. "Hypnosis: Peephole into the Mind." <u>Kiwanis</u>, September 1980, pp. 30–38.
Magazine article (unsigned)	"Why More Bureaucrats Are Being Sued." <u>U.S. News and World Report</u>, September 8, 1980, pp. 44–45.
Encyclopedia article (signed)	<u>The Jewish Encyclopedia</u>. 1902 ed. "Bannaah, Bannay, Bannayah," by Louis Ginzberg.

Encyclopedia article (unsigned)	The New Columbia Encyclopedia. 1975 ed. "Religion."
Newspaper article (signed)	Crittenden, Ann. "Growers' Power in Marketing Under Attack." The New York Times, March 25, 1981, p. A1.
Newspaper article (unsigned)	"Drought Slows Mozambique's Recovery Program." The New York Times, October 26, 1980, p. 13.
Collected or selected works of a single author	Twain, Mark. The Complete Humorous Sketches and Tales of Mark Twain. Edited by Charles Neider. Garden City, N.Y.: Doubleday and Company, Inc., 1961.
Collected or selected works of several authors	Bachman, John W. and Browne, E. Martin, eds. Better Plays for Today's Churches. New York: Association Press, 1964.
Translated work	Sagan, Francoise. Sunlight on Cold Water. Translated by Joanna Kilmartin. Harmondsworth, Middlesex, England: Penguin, 1978.
Work in several volumes	Paine, Thomas. The Writings of Thomas Paine, vol. 1. Edited by Moncure Daniel Conway. New York: AMS Press, Inc., 1967.

EXERCISE A: **Preparing Informal Citations and Footnotes.** Choose one of the following topics or think of one of your own. Then find *five* different kinds of sources on your topic in the library (for example, a book with two authors, an unsigned magazine article, a signed encyclopedia article, a work in several volumes, and a collected works of a single author). Then, for each source, pretend that you are citing a specific piece of information and write both an informal citation and a footnote.

A famous artist, athlete, or
  writer
One of the world's great
  religions
An archaeological discovery
The history of a game or
  sport

Psychology
Tuberculosis
The Alaskan pipeline
New Zealand's mountains
The history of trains
Child labor in the
  nineteenth century

EXERCISE B: **Using Information from Sources Correctly.** Read a short magazine article on a topic you know well. Copy the article from the magazine and write down the complete publishing information you need to cite this source in a library paper:

the author, the title of the article, the title of the magazine, the date of the magazine, and the page number.

Then write an expository, persuasive, or descriptive paragraph combining your knowledge of this topic with some information from the article. In your paragraph you should use (1) a direct quotation from the article, (2) an idea from the article, and (3) a little-known fact from the article. Be sure to place all quoted material in quotation marks and to give the source for each quotation and piece of information you include from the article. Finally, submit both your copy of the article and your paragraph to your teacher.

EXERCISE C: **Preparing a Bibliography.** List the five sources you located on one topic in Exercise A in a bibliography, using correct form for each entry and arranging the entries in alphabetical order.

■ The Structure and Features of a Library Paper

While a library paper follows the introduction-body-conclusion structure used for standard essays, it is usually longer than an essay. It will often have at least six paragraphs, frequently more, depending on the amount of information necessary to cover the topic and the amount available from research. A few other features also are characteristic of this kind of paper.

A library paper has a title, an introduction with a thesis statement, a body, a conclusion, citations of sources throughout the paper, and a bibliography at the end.

The *title* of the paper is designed to catch the reader's interest, to reveal the topic, and sometimes to indicate the paper's purpose.

The paper's *introduction* closely resembles that of an essay in that it reveals the tone and purpose of the paper. Opening remarks and background information should lead to a thesis statement, often the last sentence of the paragraph. Usually, the introduction to a library paper is only one paragraph long, but sometimes two or more paragraphs are necessary to prepare the reader for the discussion of the topic. In this event, the thesis statement usually comes at the end of the final introductory paragraph.

The *body* of the paper supports and develops the thesis statement with any relevant examples, facts, details, and other information, much of it taken from research sources. The body may contain any number of paragraphs, and these should develop ideas in a logical sequence for coherence. If the body section is long, *subtopic headings* can be used to guide the reader.

The paper's *conclusion* summarizes the main point and any subtopics. It brings all of the information presented in the body to a logical close, and it can refer to ideas in the introduction or end the paper smoothly in some other way.

Throughout the paper, informal citations or footnotes identify the sources used, and a bibliography at the end of the paper lists all of the works read and used in the preparation of the paper.

NOTE ABOUT OTHER FEATURES: A library paper will usually begin with a title page, a separate page that lists the title of the paper, the writer's name, the date, and the class for which the paper is written. Some library papers also include formal outlines after the title page and before the actual paper.

The following library paper is written in three-part essay structure and includes the documentation and proper use of sources.

Picasso's Turning Point

Pablo Picasso, probably the greatest artist of our century, enjoyed an extremely long and fruitful career until his death in 1973 at the age of ninety-one. He contributed an unequalled number of masterpieces to the art of the modern period. But perhaps his very greatest work is one that he produced relatively early in his career at the age of thirty-six.[1] Les Demoiselles d'Avignon, painted in 1907, offered a startling new way of looking at "reality." It was new to Picasso's own work and to the world of painting in general. A look at the work of Picasso that led up to this masterpiece shows both how Les Demoiselles d'Avignon grew from his work and how it grew beyond it.

Picasso began his career, like most artists, by imitating others. Copying at first the large, realistic, and sentimental paintings popular at the end of the nineteenth century, Picasso moved in his late teens to Paris, where he began to imitate the more original masters of the time—Cézanne, Gauguin, and Toulouse-Lautrec.[2] In a relatively short period, he absorbed these influences and began to develop his own style, the first of many styles that he would discover for himself. He took the blue line that Gauguin had used to define his figures and began to color whole paintings of pathetic figures with it.[3] But these images of poverty and melancholy in Picasso's so-called "Blue Period" changed within a few years to the happier mood paintings of his "Rose Period." And while the figures of the "Blue Period" were thin and starved, those of the "Rose Period" were tremendous and very solid, almost like pieces of sculpture.

This early phase of his career came to a close when Picasso began to be influenced by ancient African and Iberian (Spanish) art. His famous portrait of Gertrude Stein, which looks more like a statue than like a portrait, has a blank face that resembles a mask. In the portrait, one can see his growing interest in the bold and more abstract art of these ancient cultures.[4]

These influences led to a breakthrough in Picasso's art and opened up an entirely new channel in his imagination. Following ancient models, his new works tended to flatten three-dimensional reality as it had been pictured in Western art for centuries.[5] And even more important, Picasso's interest in ancient masks introduced new images into Western paintings, images that distorted the human form and imposed animal faces on human bodies. This influence appears most dramatically in Picasso's 1907 painting <u>Les Demoiselles d'Avignon</u>, a work which many regard as his greatest single painting.

<u>Les Demoiselles</u> depicts five women. Three of them are painted in highly simplified and distorted, but still recognizably human, terms. But the other two are grotesquely contorted and have frightening animal faces. The whole painting looks as if it is made up of angular blocks and wedges, all jammed together. Its effect is that of a bad dream or nightmare. The painting is a very powerful expression of the unknown side of life, with its subjects changing, almost disintegrating, from human beings into twisted geometrical figures.

<u>Les Demoiselles d'Avignon</u> produced a strange reception among Picasso's colleagues in the art world. The great Henri Matisse hated the painting.[6] Picasso's own friends thought that he had gone mad.[7] Picasso had not gone mad, but he had broken through to a mad vision of human life. He had broken through his various influences, using them but changing them to produce a distinct and revolutionary style, painting "reality" as no one had ever done before.

---

[1]John Ashbery, "Picasso: The Art," <u>New York</u>, May 12, 1980, p. 29.

[2]Robert Hughes, "The Show of Shows," <u>Time</u>, May 26, 1980, p. 70.

[3]Hughes, "The Show of Shows," p. 71.

[4]<u>Encyclopedia Britannica</u>, 1971 ed., "Picasso, Pablo Ruiz."

[5]Mark Stevens, "Picasso's Imperial Eye," <u>Newsweek</u>, May 19, 1980, p. 85.

[6]H.W. Janson, <u>History of Art</u> (Englewood Cliffs, N.J.: Prentice-Hall, 1962), p. 522.

[7]Hughes, "The Show of Shows," p. 73.

BIBLIOGRAPHY

Ashbery, John. "Picasso: The Art." <u>New York</u>, May 12, 1980, pp. 28–31.
<u>Encyclopedia Britannica</u>. 1971 ed. "Picasso, Pablo Ruiz."
Gedo, Mary M. <u>Picasso: Art as Autobiography</u>. Chicago: University of Chicago Press, 1980.
Hamill, Pete. "Picasso: The Man." <u>New York</u>, May 12, 1980, pp. 34–38.
Hughes, Robert. "The Show of Shows." <u>Time</u>, May 26, 1980, pp. 70–78.
Janson, H.W. <u>History of Art</u>. Englewood Cliffs, N.J.: Prentice-Hall, Inc., 1962.
Smith, Margaret. <u>Pablo Picasso</u>. Minneapolis, Minn.: Creative Education, Inc., 1975.
Stevens, Mark. "Picasso's Imperial Eye." <u>Newsweek</u>, May 19, 1980, pp. 80–85.

EXERCISE D: Examining the Structure of a Library Paper. Answer the following questions about the library paper on Picasso.

1. How does the title suit the paper?
2. How does the introduction lead the reader into the body of the paper? What are the tone and purpose of the paper?
3. What is the thesis statement of the paper? What subtopics does it include?
4. How many body paragraphs does the paper have? What is the topic sentence of each?
5. How has the writer organized the supporting information in the body of the paper?
6. How does the conclusion refer to the main point of the paper? What other closing ideas help to end the paper?

APPLICATION: Analyzing the Features of a Library Paper. Answer the following questions about the use of research material in the library paper on Picasso.

1. Which of the two methods of documenting sources has the writer used?
2. How many different sources does the writer cite?
3. What kinds of information are incorporated in the paper? Quotations? Ideas? Little-known facts?
4. How varied are the sources (books, magazine articles, and so on) from which the writer has taken information?
5. How many sources are listed in the bibliography? Which of these were not cited in the paper?
6. What other sources might you have considered if you had written a paper on Picasso? Locate *four* additional sources in a library, and list them alphabetically.

From Research to Final Paper 24.2

Once you are familiar with all parts of a library paper, you can begin the process of writing one. Writing a library paper is similar to writing an essay, but it also includes research steps, which begin early in the planning stages. This section discusses the steps you can follow in preparing a library paper and provides guidelines for your research.

■ Selecting an Appropriate Topic

Because a library paper is the product of much time and work, the preliminary steps of selecting a topic and locating sources are crucial.

Choosing and Narrowing a Topic.   An appropriate topic for a library paper is both manageable and researchable. It should also arouse your curiosity and hold your interest.

> Investigate the sources of information available on possible topics. Then choose the topic that interests you, that seems important to your studies, and that is adequately covered by sources.

One approach to choosing a topic is to think of several areas of interest and then check out the library's resources on these potential topics. You might list these general topics at the top of your paper, making a column for each. Then look through the card catalog, *The Readers' Guide to Periodical Literature*, and other indexes for sources—books, magazine articles, newspaper articles, and so forth—that contain information about each general topic. If only a few sources are available on a topic, you probably should avoid it; on the other hand, if numerous sources are available, you will have to choose a smaller category of the topic. Remember that you may be able to find only newspaper and magazine articles on very recent discoveries or events.

Surveying the available sources can guide you to a manageable topic that you can research and develop well in a library paper of three to ten pages. For instance, if one of your areas of interest was dolphins, you might discover from the numbers of books and articles available that this general topic is too broad. After skimming the tables of contents of a few books and the titles of articles, you might make a list of more specific topics, such as those in the following chart.

NARROWING A GENERAL TOPIC	
General Topic:	Dolphins
More Specific Topics:	The intelligence of dolphins
	How dolphins communicate
	Feeding and migration patterns
	Anatomy and physiology
	Kinds of dolphins

As you examine possible specific topics, you might choose only one to be the focus of the entire paper, or you might combine two ideas. From the list in the chart, you might decide to combine the first two possibilities into a paper topic: *Dolphins' intelligence and communication.*

Making Your Initial Bibliography Cards.   When you have selected and narrowed a topic, you should prepare a list of sources.

> For every source that you intend to consult, record all information necessary for footnotes and bibliography entries.

Maintaining orderly bibliography cards will help you to be organized during your research and later during your writing. The following chart offers suggestions for making bibliography cards.

GUIDELINES FOR PREPARING BIBLIOGRAPHY CARDS
1. Write each source on a separate note card or piece of paper.
2. For a book, write the author's complete name, the title, the city of publication, the publisher, and the date of publication, just as you would for a bibliography entry. For a magazine article, write the author's complete name, the title of the article, the magazine, the date, and the page numbers of the article. (For the exact form for these and other kinds of sources, see the chart on page xxx in Section 24.1.)
3. Make note of the location symbol or call number and any illustrations, maps, charts, or tables that the source contains.

The number of sources you should consult will depend on the assignment and the required length of the paper. Usually, it is a good idea to list many more sources on your bibliography cards than you actually need because some of these sources may not prove helpful.

EXERCISE A: Finding a Suitable Paper Topic. Follow these instructions.

1. List four general topics that interest you.
2. In the library, consult at least the card catalog and *The Readers' Guide to Periodical Literature* and make note of the material available on each general topic.
3. Then select a promising topic—one that will provide you with at least four sources. Narrow this topic, if necessary, to one you can cover in a single paper by breaking the topic down into categories with the help of the card catalog, the subheadings in *The Readers' Guide,* or the table of contents of one of the books on the topic.
4. Choose one or combine several specific topics to pursue in your research.
5. Make a bibliography card with complete publishing information for each source you intend to consult.

■ Researching the Library Paper

Gathering information for your paper involves several steps. First, you should map out the research you are planning to do. Next, you should locate the books and other material listed on your bibliography cards and begin reading them and taking notes on note cards.

Directing Your Research.   Before you plunge into reading your sources, you should think about your topic enough to have some ideas you want to verify and one main point to concentrate on.

Guide your research with several significant questions about your topic and a preliminary thesis statement.

Preparing some questions on your topic can stimulate your research. For a paper on *Dolphins' intelligence and communication,* for example, you might pose questions like those in the following chart.

SAMPLE QUESTIONS TO DIRECT RESEARCH ON A PARTICULAR TOPIC

---

1. How intelligent do scientists think dolphins are?
2. What tests have scientists made of dolphins' intelligence?
3. How do dolphins communicate with each other?
4. How long have people known about dolphins' abilities?
5. What specific behavior of dolphins indicates their intelligence or communication abilities?

Your research will go more smoothly if you make some preliminary decisions about the scope and purpose of your paper. Using your knowledge of the topic, consider the audience for whom you will write the paper. You probably already have a few ideas, facts, or opinions about your topic that can suggest a purpose for your paper. By giving some thought to your audience and purpose and by using your knowledge and interests, you can choose a tentative main point and express it in a sentence as a preliminary thesis statement. Throughout your actual note-taking and planning of your paper, you may refine or even change this thesis statement. For now, however, this main point can focus your research by helping you zero in on important information on your topic and weed out unrelated information. For the topic *Dolphins' intelligence and communication*, you might formulate the following rough version of a thesis statement based on some facts you know. Notice that it is noncontroversial and intended to explain the topic to an uninformed audience.

PRELIMINARY THESIS STATEMENT: Dolphins have remarkable intelligence and methods of communicating.

Taking Notes on Your Sources.   You are now ready to begin a serious investigation of the sources you listed on your bibliography cards. You should study and sort through the information that addresses your thesis statement and answers your questions. Your goals should be to increase your knowledge and to gather relevant examples, details, facts, incidents, and quotations.

Take accurate notes from your sources to answer your research questions and to develop your thesis statement. Make note of exact sources, page numbers, and direct quotations.

A few simple procedures can simplify the researching process. First, you should get an overview of all the sources listed on your bibliography cards, selecting the ones most likely to contain useful information. Begin taking notes from the sources that appear to have the most relevant, thorough information for your paper. These sources, rich in information, will give you a good grasp of your specific topic and will speed up your note-taking. You should skim each source first and then reread it more slowly while you take notes.

Although note-taking is an individualistic matter, following some suggestions can help you produce notes that are accurate, well-organized, and easy to use.

SUGGESTIONS FOR TAKING NOTES

1. Use a different note card for each different source. Also, use a different note card for each new subject or major idea on your paper topic.
2. In the upper right-hand corner of each note card, write a subject heading to indicate what information the card covers. Eventually, you can organize all your cards according to these subject headings.
3. In the upper left-hand corner of each note card, write the information necessary for citing the source: author, title, and publishing information. If you have many cards for the same source, you may want to abbreviate this information and just write the author and title on the second, third, and later cards.
4. Keep track of the pages from which you record each fact, idea, and quotation.

The actual notes on your note cards can be in several different forms: modified outlines, summaries, and direct quotations. For detailed examples, case histories, and thorough explanations, you may want to take notes in modified outline form, paraphrasing the important ideas from the source and indicating the pages that your notes cover. For sources that have information that is either lengthy or interesting but not specific, you may want to take notes in summary form, again rephrasing the ideas in your own words and noting the pages covered. For ideas or facts that are particularly useful or well-stated, you may want to copy the quotation word for word, enclosing the material in quotation marks and indicating the page of the source. From one source, on one note card, you might use several or all three of these forms.

The following sample note cards from sources about dolphins' intelligence show some of the different methods of recording information.

Subject heading ────────────────────────────────

Author, title, publishing information

> Eleanor Devine and Martha Clark, eds., *The Dolphin Smile, 29 Centuries of Dolphin Lore* (New York: The Macmillan Company, 1967)
>
> ***Dolphin Feats***
>
> Dolphins save a woman from drowning. (pp. 141–143)
> —Florida swimmer caught in a dangerous undertow (p. 142)
> —Woman believed she would never make it back to shore; began to lose consciousness. (p. 142)
> —Someone gave her "a tremendous shove," she reported. (p. 142)
> —As she grappled toward the beach, onlookers reported the "someone" who pushed her to be a dolphin. (p. 143)

Paraphrased information in a modified outline

Subject heading ────────────────────────────────

Author, title, publishing information

> Robert Stenuit, *The Dolphin* (New York: Sterling Publishing Company, Inc., 1968)
>
> ***Dolphins in Folklore, Myths, and Legends***
>
> "There was Taras, for example, a demigod, son of Poseidon, saved from the briny deep by a dolphin who brought him to the shore...." (pp. 4–5)

Exact quotation

While you are taking notes, you should be thinking ahead to your paper. Make sure that your notes are complete and neat enough to be usable later. At the same time, attempt to digest and sift information so that the notes you take concentrate on your research questions and pertain to your preliminary thesis statement. If the same information appears in several sources, you do not have to take notes on it every time. If most of your sources do not relate to your thesis statement, you should formulate a new one that reflects the information you are finding. Or if all your information centers on one small aspect of your topic, you should locate and take notes on additional sources.

EXERCISE B: **Planning Research and Taking Notes.** For the topic you selected and for which you listed sources in Exercise A, follow these instructions.

1. Think of four or five important questions on your topic that can guide your research.
2. Formulate a preliminary thesis statement.
3. From the sources listed on your bibliography cards, decide which ones look the most useful and which ones look the least related to your thesis statement. Plan to consult the most complete sources first.
4. Take notes from your sources by skimming them first and then rereading them. Make your note cards well-labeled, orderly, and clear, and adapt your note-taking form—modified outline, summary, exact quoting—to the specific material.

■ Planning and Organizing the Library Paper

Once you have thoroughly researched your topic and discovered information that answers your research questions, you can reexamine your thesis statement and envision the organization of ideas in the entire paper: Your paper is ready to take shape.

Refining the Thesis Statement.   Now that you have a body of notes on your specific topic, you can polish your thesis statement.

> Write a revised thesis statement that precisely states your main point.

When you revise your thesis statement, you should reword it, lengthen it, or shorten it to reflect any important information you uncovered during your note-taking. In addition, revise it to clarify your purpose and to include any subtopics that can further define the focus of the paper. The words you use to express your main point should be appropriate for your audience's level of understanding.

After researching the topic of dolphins' intelligence and ability to communicate, you might decide to include a subtopic about their accomplishments. You might reword the thesis statement so that it includes two subtopics.

REVISED THESIS STATEMENT: Dolphins have remarkable intelligence and ability to communicate as well as a natural capacity to learn tricks and to perform other amazing feats independently.

Organizing the Paper in an Outline.   The task of organizing a library paper entails grouping, ordering, and sorting the information you have gathered. Your thesis statement and your own ideas that you have developed on your topic should become the framework of your paper, and your research should explain or substantiate your main point and other thoughts. Preparing a topic or sentence outline can help you figure out how you are going to build your paper from your ideas and your research.

Organize your own ideas and the information from your notes into a unified, logical outline that sketches the development of your thesis statement.

To group, sift, and arrange the material for your paper, you can follow several steps.

STEPS FOR ORGANIZING A LIBRARY PAPER

1. If your thesis statement does not include subtopics, determine two or more smaller divisions of your main point from your thoughts and your notes.
2. Group your note cards according to subtopics. Put aside those notes that do not seem to fit naturally under any subtopics.
3. Choose a logical order for the subtopics in the body of the paper. Then decide the order of supporting information under each subtopic. Arrange your note cards according to this order (order of importance, chronological, spatial, comparison and contrast, or developmental order). Again put aside information that does not belong in your plan for the development of each subtopic.

When you have completed these steps, you are ready to write your outline. The more complete your outline is, the easier it will be for you to write the paper. Include your own ideas in the outline, and list the material from your research that will support them.

Beginning with the introduction, you should list all introductory ideas as well as your revised version of the thesis statement. Then, to outline the body of the paper, write down each subtopic, listing under each the appropriate information you have selected and ordered from your notes. Finally, outline your ideas for the conclusion, including any information from your research that might help bring the paper to a close.

The following skeleton topic outline for the paper on dolphins shows you a common, functional plan for a library paper.

1. Introduction
   A. ⎫
   B. ⎬ Introductory ideas and background information
   C. Thesis Statement: Dolphins have remarkable intelligence and ability to communicate as well as a natural capacity to learn tricks and to perform other amazing feats independently.
II. Subtopic 1: Dolphin intelligence and ability to communicate
   A. ⎫
   B. ⎪
   C. ⎬ Information—facts, details—about dolphin intelligence and ability to communicate
   D. ⎪
   E. ⎭
III. Subtopic 2: Dolphin feats
   A. ⎫
   B. ⎪ Information—examples, facts, details—about tricks
   C. ⎬ that dolphins can perform as well as special feats
   D. ⎪ credited to them
   E. ⎭
IV. Conclusion
   A. ⎫
   B. ⎬ Reference to the thesis statement and closing remarks
   C. ⎭

If you plan to use any diagrams, charts, or other graphics in your paper, you may want to indicate in your outline where these will go.

When you have prepared an outline for your paper, reread it to see if you have weak spots that need more information and if the order of information will indeed clarify your topic for a reader. Make any necessary changes or additions.

EXERCISE C: Revising Your Thesis Statement. Compare your notes and your preliminary thesis statement, and adjust the thesis statement by adding subtopics or altering the wording so that the thesis statement expresses the main point that your material can best support. Consider your audience and purpose as you make changes.

EXERCISE D: Arranging the Information in Your Library Paper. With your revised thesis statement and your notes before you, follow the steps for organizing a paper in the chart on page 756. Then, write a complete topic outline of your paper's introduction, body, and conclusion, including your ideas and the information from your research in the logical order you chose.

■ Writing and Revising the Library Paper

The last stage of preparing a library paper involves writing a complete first draft, revising it, and making a final copy with accurate footnotes and a complete bibliography. Throughout these steps you should try to make your paper a solid piece of research and an interesting, effective composition.

Writing a First Draft. When you are satisfied with the quality and amount of your information and the organization of your ideas in your outline, you should write a complete first draft.

Use your outline and notes to guide you in writing a first draft of the paper.

As you write the paper, you should put your ideas, research, and the parts of the paper together in complete sentences and unified, coherent paragraphs. Follow the arrangement of ideas in your outline and the grouping and order of your note cards, but be open to new ideas, better arrangements, or other refinements as you compose your draft. For example, you may find that one subtopic can divide into two or more paragraphs. Use transitions and other connecting devices to help you combine your own ideas with material gathered from research and to make your paper read smoothly. If your paper is long and you do include subtopic headings within the body, make sure that these are accurate and helpful guides for the reader. Finally, choose one method of citing sources and use it consistently. Be sure to cite a source for every fact, idea, or quotation you use from a source. (For the correct forms for documenting sources, see Section 24.1.)

If you write rather than type the paper, use every other line to leave room for revisions, corrections, and alterations later on. If you type your first draft, double-space.

Checking and Revising the Draft. When you have completed the first draft, you have the opportunity to assess the paper for weaknesses and possible improvements.

Reread your first draft, looking for ways to improve and refine it. Use a checklist to examine all parts of the paper.

The following checklist can guide your examination of the paper. Make any revisions or corrections right on your paper and, if necessary, rewrite any parts to achieve greater clarity or a better style.

CHECKLIST FOR REVISING A LIBRARY PAPER

1. Have you included enough background information and other opening statements to acquaint your reader with the topic and to lead into the thesis statement?

2. Does the thesis statement clearly present the paper's main point and suggest the paper's purpose?

3. Does the information in the body thoroughly support and develop the subtopics of the main point?

4. Is the main idea of each body paragraph clear?

5. Do the body paragraphs develop your main point and subtopics in a logical order? Have you arranged all examples, facts, and other pieces of information logically within each paragraph?

6. Do transitions and other connecting devices link ideas within and between paragraphs?

7. Does the conclusion contain a restatement or summary of the paper's main point and subtopics? Does it complete the paper?

8. Have you used complete citations for each fact, idea, or quotation from a source? (For correct forms of documentation, see Section 24.1.)

9. Are direct quotations exact and enclosed in quotation marks?

10. Is your method of citing sources (footnotes or informal citations) consistent throughout the paper?

11. Do the word choices throughout the paper suit your audience and purpose? Are sentences varied in length and structure?

12. Can you find any errors in grammar, usage, punctuation, or spelling?

Writing a Final Copy. When you have answered all the questions on the checklist, proofread your paper and made any necessary revisions and corrections, you should prepare a final copy of the paper.

Write a revised, corrected final copy of the paper, add a title on a title page, and attach a complete bibliography.

The final copy should be prepared carefully, either completely handwritten or completely typed. Include your name on each sheet of paper, and number each page beginning with page two of the actual paper. (Do not count the title page.)

Add a title that reflects the content and main point of your paper. The title should go on a title page, the first page of the paper. Center the title on the page, and beneath it place your name, the title of the course for which you are submitting the paper, and the date of submission. (Your teacher may require a special format.)

The final step is to prepare a complete bibliography from your bibliography cards. Make an alphabetical listing by last name of the authors, or by the titles if no authors are given, for all sources that you have consulted in the planning and writing of the paper. (For the exact form for bibliography entries, see the chart on page 743 in Section 24.1.) The bibliography should be on a separate page at the end of the paper. Note in the bibliography on page 764 that for two books by the same author, a blank line takes the place of the author's name in the entry for the second work.

The final version of the library paper on dolphins follows. The annotations at the sides of the paper point out the use of research materials and the organization of the paper.

Those Amazing Dolphins

Introduction Background ideas Raised number indicates the use of footnotes	For at least 2,500 years, the dolphin has appeared in folklore, myth, and legend. "There was Taras, for example, a demigod, son of Poseidon, saved from the briny deep by a dolphin who brought him to shore. . . . Aesop already knew about dolphins' friendship with humans when he wrote the fable, 'The Monkey and the Dolphin.' It went without saying: If a castaway is struggling in the water, and suddenly a dolphin appears, the castaway is brought to land, safe and sound, by the dolphin."[1] Why have dolphins caught people's fancy for centuries? Why have even Ireland and France minted coins with dolphins' heads pictured prominently?

Dolphins, if not unique, are at least unusual animals. They are also mysterious, largely because they live in the sea, where, until recently, they have been difficult to observe at any length. But in this century,

More
background
information

dolphins and humans have become closer, brought together by marine life centers and scientific advancements in techniques of study. In the past twenty years alone, many scientists and other people have been captivated by tales of dolphins and by allegations of dolphins' abilities. Many people want to believe that these creatures are "benign, philosophical, and gifted with the patience and wisdom of the sea."[2]

Now, with results of close observations and studies of dolphins, we can dispel some of the myths and legends—but only some. Old tales of dolphin heroism may well have bases in fact. As we learn more about dolphins, we uncover more evidence of their extraordinary capabilities. Dolphins have remarkable intelligence and ability to communicate and a natural capacity to "learn" tricks and to perform other amazing feats independently.

Thesis
statement
with two
subtopics

Optional
heading
introduces
first subtopic

Dolphin Intelligence and Communication Abilities

The first studies of dolphins' intelligence were examinations of their brains. The French scientist Cuvier revealed in his "Leçons d' anatomie comparée" that "the ratio between the weight of the (dolphin's) brain and that of the body is some 25 to 1."[3] And many scientists today believe that just such a ratio indicates dolphins' capacity for advanced thinking.[4] An American scientist, Dr. John C. Lilly, showed that the dolphin's brain has a complex structure, containing a density of cells as well as folds and convolutions that indicate a high degree of intelligence.[5]

But since dolphins cannot take IQ tests, scientists use other means of measurement to determine how intelligent dolphins really are. Close observation is one method of investigation. One extraordinary example of dolphin ingenuity was observed at Marineland of the Pacific. Two fun-loving dolphins wanted a new play-partner. Selecting a stubborn moray eel, one dolphin tried in vain to dislodge it from its hiding place by pulling its tail while the other dolphin attempted to snare it from the other end of the hole. Taking a few moments' break on the surface, one of the dolphins killed a spine fish with its beak. Holding it carefully, the dolphin stung the eel with the spines, and as the eel attempted to flee, the dolphins caught it and played with it until they lost interest. Finally, the friendly dolphins allowed the eel to go its own way.[6]

As a result of these and other observations, scientists have noted the adeptness with which dolphins communicate with one another. By using a type of sonar, dolphins are able to differentiate objects by the sound waves that they send and receive. Then, to communicate discovery of the object to another dolphin, a dolphin reproduces the original echo.[7] This ability to differentiate between sound waves reveals the complexity of the dolphin's brain. Scientists believe dolphins use a "Doppler effect" system for describing complicated movements to other dolphins; that is, dolphins can recreate sounds rising and falling in pitch to communicate messages to other dolphins.[8] In effect, "dolphins may use their sonar sounds to project images into other dolphins' brains."[9]

An experiment conducted by Dr. Jarvis Bastieu at the University of California offers concrete evidence of dolphins' ability to communicate. Using a male and a female dolphin, Dr. Bastieu began by showing each how to push levers in sequence. When the levers were pushed accurately, a reward of small fish would reach the dolphins. Only by seeing flashing or continuous light could the dolphins know how to push the levers. After both dolphins were able to use the lights to figure out the device, a curtain was placed between them so only one dolphin would be able to see the light. When the experiment was repeated with the curtain between them, the first dolphin could be heard sending a sound signal to the second dolphin who then pushed the proper level. Bastieu repeated the experiment fifty times; the dolphins communicated successfully forty-eight times, earning a 96 percent competency rating.[10]

Heading introduces the second subtopic

Dolphin Feats

In addition to their use of a sound system to communicate with each other, dolphins are known for their ability to master complex tricks and for their untaught feats. They shake hands (flippers), catch footballs, race, dive through rings of fire, solve puzzles, and have rescued humans in trouble at sea, earning them distinction as a kind of underwater Red Cross.

For many years and in locations around the world, people have harnessed the intelligence of the dolphin for their own entertainment. Under the guidance of experts, dolphins have been trained to perform the most amazing stunts. One such expert is André Cowan who trains dolphins at Marineland in St. Augustine, Florida. Cowan uses the "food-technique" method, in which an audible signal tells the dolphin to receive a reward when the trick has been successfully completed.[11] Other approaches to signal dolphin tricks include loudspeakers and flashing lights. In some cases, dolphins are trained to respond to a rap on the side of the tank. The dolphin's memory enables it to associate a certain learned behavior with a certain sound. In this way, a trainer can instruct a dolphin to perform different tricks by presenting different signals.

While many dolphins have performed a variety of different tricks, from shaking flippers to catching footballs, some have been trained to perform complex series of tasks. Splash, a dolphin at Marineland, is just such a performer. Splash's trainer can put one fist over the water in the tank, and Splash will take the hand in his mouth and remain motionless until the hand is removed. Then the dolphin knows to swim backwards and on his side, moving away from the trainer but keeping eye contact. At the same time, Splash will make a clicking noise that simulates a human laugh.[12]

While we can marvel at the performances of dolphins in captivity, their activities in the wild have fostered accounts—some questionable, others documented—of heroic dolphin rescues of drowning swimmers and persons imperiled at sea. In one documented case, six American airmen were shot down over the Pacific Ocean during World War II. Landing in the ocean, the men inflated a rubber raft and drifted for a while aimlessly at sea, vulnerable to storms or enemy ships and planes. However, a dolphin appeared and saved them from possible death by towing their raft onto the sand of a tiny island.[13] In another documented case, a woman was caught in a dangerous undertow while swimming off the coast of Florida. Believing that she would never make it back to shore, she began to lose consciousness when someone gave her "a tremendous shove," enabling her to reach the beach. That "someone" was a dolphin, according to witnesses on the shore.[14]

Reference to main point

Summary of the paper's ideas

Conclusion

Dolphins continue to impress scientists, trainers, and other observers with their ability to decipher and transmit information, to learn, and to act intelligently. It is their potential—still unmeasured, still the source of speculation—that remains for scientists to gauge. Just the dolphins' ability to use a form of sonar to project mental images is still beyond scientists' full understanding. Scientists continue to study dolphins, not just to train them for performing tricks. In the future, who knows what secrets will be learned about dolphins?

---

[1]Robert Stenuit, The Dolphin (New York:Sterling Publishing Company, Inc., 1968), pp. 4–5.

[2]Michael Parfit, "Are Dolphins Trying to Say Something, or Is It All Much Ado About Nothing?" Smithsonian, October 1980, p. 73.

[3]Stenuit, The Dolphin, p. 60.

[4]Parfit, "Are Dolphins Trying to Say Something, or Is It All Much Ado About Nothing?" p. 74.

[5]Stenuit, The Dolphin, p. 62.

[6]Stenuit, The Dolphin, p. 132.

[7]Karl-Erik Fichtelius and Sverre Sjolander, Smarter than Man? (New York: Pantheon Books, 1972), p. 72.

[8]Fichtelius and Sjolander, Smarter than Man?, pp. 72–73.

[9]Parfit, "Are Dolphins Trying to Say Something, or Is It All Much Ado About Nothing?" p. 76.

[10]Stenuit, The Dolphin, pp. 56–57.

[11]John C. Lilly, M.D., Man and Dolphin (New York: Doubleday and Company, Inc., 1961), p. 114.

[12]Lilly, Man and Dolphin, p. 116.

[13]Stenuit, The Dolphin, p. 11.

[14]Eleanore Devine and Martha Clark, eds., The Dolphin Smile, 29 Centuries of Dolphin Lore (New York: The Macmillan Company, 1967), p. 142.

BIBLIOGRAPHY

Cousteau, Jacques-Yves. Dolphins. New York: Doubleday and Company, Inc., 1975.

Devine, Eleanore and Clark, Martha, eds. The Dolphin Smile, 29 Centuries of Dolphin Lore. New York: The Macmillan Company, 1967.

Fichtelius, Karl-Erik and Sjolander, Sverre. Smarter than Man? New York: Pantheon Books, 1972.

Lilly, John C., M.D. Communication Between Man and Dolphin. New York: Crown Publishers, Inc., 1978.

——————. Man and Dolphin. New York: Doubleday and Company, Inc., 1961.

McIntyre, Joan. Mind in the Waters. New York: Charles Scribner's Sons, 1975.

Nayman, Jacqueline. Whales, Dolphins, and Man. London: Hamlyn, 1973.

Parfit, Michael. "Are Dolphins Trying to Say Something, or Is It All Much Ado About Nothing?" Smithsonian, October 1980, pp. 73–80.

Stenuit, Robert. The Dolphin. New York: Sterling Publishing Company, Inc., 1968.

EXERCISE E: Writing a First Draft. Use every other line of your paper and leave margins as you write a first draft of your library paper. Follow the outline you developed in Exercise D and use your notes. Try to write with transitions and other connecting devices. Use a consistent form for citing sources: informal citations or footnotes. If you wish, you can use headings for the subtopics in the body of your paper.

EXERCISE F: Revising and Writing the Final Copy. Reread your first draft using the checklist on page 759 as a guide. Make all revisions and corrections right on the paper. Then write a neat final copy, adding a title page and a bibliography.

APPLICATION: Analyzing the Process of Writing a Library Paper. Think about the library paper you completed in the preceding exercises as you answer the following questions.

1. What other topics did you consider before you chose the one you used for your paper? What, if any, problems did you encounter in selecting a topic?
2. How many of the sources listed in your bibliography cards proved helpful?
3. Approximately how many hours did you spend researching your topic?
4. To what extent did your questions and preliminary thesis statement help you while you were taking notes?
5. How closely did your revised thesis statement resemble your preliminary thesis statement?
6. How complete was your outline? How closely did your final paper follow it?
7. Would you handle the use and documentation of sources differently if you wrote another library paper?
8. What *three* specific ways could you improve your approach to writing a library paper?

Papers Analyzing Literature

Often, in English classes, you are expected to read literary works. At times, you may also be asked to write about what you have read. To do this, you can apply many of the skills you have learned in writing paragraphs and essays. In addition, you will have to apply your reading and thinking skills to understand and interpret what you have read. Once you have interpretations and observations to make in a paper, you can concentrate on communicating your ideas to someone else.

The first section in this chapter explains some of the characteristics of literary analysis papers and some of the possible variations in topics, purposes, and forms. The second section explains some practical steps you can follow as you write about literature.

25.1 The Literary Analysis Paper

A literary analysis paper is a composition in which a writer communicates an understanding of and often interpretations of or opinions about one or more works of literature. Writing a literary analysis can often help you to better understand what you have read.

In this section, you will learn to recognize the key features of literary analysis papers. The section will focus first on the elements in a work of literature that can be analyzed. It will then explore the variety of purposes you can have in writing a literary analysis, the kinds of support available to you, and the forms or structures your paper can take.

■ Key Features of Literary Analysis Papers

Literary analysis can sharpen and reinforce your understanding of a particular work of literature as well as teach you to read other works more closely and thoughtfully. It can also help you to understand your preferences for certain writers or kinds of literature.

Topics for Literary Analysis Papers.   When you analyze literature, there are a number of points and elements that you can explore.

The topic of a literary analysis paper can be based on theme, character, conflict, plot, point of view, setting, imagery, symbols, tone, a combination of any of these elements, or the entire work.

In any work of literature these elements overlap and interconnect, creating a complex piece of writing that can usually be interpreted a number of ways. These elements resemble threads of different colors woven by the author into a detailed tapestry. Like woven threads, one element can never be examined completely apart from the rest. Yet often if you focus on one element, it becomes easier to understand the entire work. One prerequisite for writing an analysis, then, is an understanding of the elements and the ability to identify them in the work you are studying. The following chart briefly explains these elements.

RECOGNIZING LITERARY ELEMENTS FOR ANALYSIS	
Element	**Explanation**
Theme	A central idea or general truth dramatized or implied; for example, the love of money can destroy a person's humanity; a great part of human suffering comes from the fear of being misunderstood and unloved. A work can have a number of themes.
Character	A person in a story, poem, or play. Characters act out an author's theme; characters are presented to the reader through their actions, dialogue, what other characters say about them, the characters' effects on other characters, and often through the narrator's comments on the characters.

Conflict	A struggle between two opposed forces. A conflict can be external: a character and another character, a character and society, a character and nature, or a character and God or Fate. A conflict can be internal, between forces within a character. Conflict helps to create the interest and action of stories, poems, and plays.
Plot	The planned ordering of actions in the story so that the actions grow out of character and conflict. In most works, the plot builds toward a crisis or climax where the conflict is resolved.
Point of view	The voice and consciousness that is telling the story; the narrator. The narrator determines how much the reader sees and knows about the characters. In *first person point of view*, a major or minor character in the story tells the story, using "I," and reporting events as she or he observes or experiences them. In *third person omniscient point of view*, the narrator is outside the story but can see into the minds of all the characters, revealing the thoughts and feelings of all. In *third person partially omniscient point of view*, the narrator is outside the story and can see into the mind of one character. The narrator tells the thoughts and feelings of that character and the reader understands that character best. In *third person objective point of view*, the narrator tells the events as they happen to a character in the story but reports only factual observations that can be made objectively, not from inside the mind of the character.
Setting	The time, place (physical location), and general background of a story or other work of literature.
Imagery	The use of words to create sensory impressions and figures of speech, or imaginative comparisons; the use of words to create pictures, moods, impressions.
Symbols	Something that stands for itself and represents something else beyond itself; a thing that has a literal, surface meaning, and deeper, suggested meanings.
Tone	The author's attitude toward the subject and the audience.

For each work you plan to write about, you should examine the theme or themes, characters, conflicts, point of view, setting, imagery, symbols, and tone. These are tools for getting at the meaning, structure, and style of a work. Then once you understand these elements as they are used in the work, you can select one element as a topic that you will explore in depth, you can explore two or more of them, or you can write about the entire work in less detail. Remember that any literary work can be analyzed from numerous angles.

If you wanted to treat one element in a work, you could choose character. Your focused topic might then be how the author makes a character believable, how a character changes in the course of the story, or why the author makes two characters exact opposites. You can choose to focus on the author's treatment of a character or on your response to a character. For example, after reading the play *The Miracle Worker* about Helen Keller and Annie Sullivan, you might choose to analyze the characteristics that made Annie Sullivan an excellent teacher. With any of these topics concerning character, you would want to include specific examples of the character's thoughts, actions, and speech to support your ideas.

If you choose a broad topic, such as the entire work, you would still draw on your understanding of the elements in the work. You might highlight a number of the elements that you find the most interesting or that you think other readers might want to know about.

The following chart illustrates some of the choices for topics for a literary analysis paper on one work, Anne Frank's *The Diary of a Young Girl.*

SAMPLE TOPICS FOR A PAPER ON ONE SPECIFIC WORK	
Element or Elements	**Possible Topics from This Work**
Theme	The human spirit is invincible.
Character	The qualities that made Anne Frank's father a natural leader
Point of view	The impact and effectiveness of Anne's telling her own story (first person)
Setting	How living in the hiding place affected the different people
Whole book	Why the book is worth reading and considered a modern "classic"

Purposes for Literary Analysis Papers. As with any writing, the topic and purpose of literary analysis papers are closely related. Often the purpose will grow out of the topic and your general intention. You can choose to focus on explaining or persuading, but sometimes a paper that is devoted to explaining the features of a work will end with an opinion and recommendation. Many of the papers you will write on literature, however, will involve some degree of persuasion because you will be offering your own conclusions, interpretations, and observations.

> A literary analysis paper can concentrate on explaining and informing a reader about a work, on persuading a reader to consider or accept a particular interpretation or recommendation, or on a combination of these purposes, with either one dominant.

The following chart shows some of the general intentions you can have when you write literary analysis papers and some of the purposes these general intentions imply.

INTENTIONS AND PURPOSES OF LITERARY ANALYSIS	
General Intention	**Purpose**
To explain some of the elements in a work	to explain
To inform the reader of the content or ideas in a work	to explain
To explain the work's effect on you	to explain
To evaluate the significance or effectiveness of particular elements	to persuade
To interpret and draw conclusions about the work's meaning	to persuade
To evaluate and judge the work's relation to other works or to real life	to persuade

A literary analysis paper can be *expository;* that is, it can be devoted solely to explaining what is in the work by discussing elements and ideas with which no one would disagree. This kind of paper would show that you know the work by including many facts, details, and examples from it. The paper should not retell the story although it might include a short summary of some of the action or ideas. In an expository paper, you should remain objective, explaining one or more elements of the work so that the reader can better understand it or draw his or her own conclusions. If your purpose is to explain, you can assume either that the reader has not read the material or that you have studied it more thoroughly than the reader, and therefore can elaborate on it for the reader's benefit. Sometimes you will be asked to write this kind of paper primarily to show your own familiarity with the material. Even in a paper that makes no attempt to interpret or criticize, you will have to select certain aspects of the work to explain. You will also have to impose your own organization on your explanation.

A literary analysis paper can instead be *persuasive.* Just how persuasive it has to be will depend on how controversial your interpretation, criticisms, judgments, or recommendations are. This kind of paper should also show that you know the work, but it should go a step further to show that you have come to your own decisions about its meaning, value, or quality. It should include evidence from the work to back up your opinions and to explain the reasons behind those opinions. If your purpose is to persuade, you might assume that the reader has not read the work, in which case you can offer reasons why a reader should or should not read it. Or you might assume that the reader has read it and either has not thought about it as much as you have or actually disagrees with you. In this case, your goal might be to make the reader accept or at least consider your interpretation as the one that is closest to the author's intentions.

Instead of stressing one purpose, a literary analysis paper might have two purposes: A first purpose might be to explain what the work is about, how it is organized, or some of the elements; and a second, later purpose might be to evaluate, interpret, criticize, or recommend.

Kinds of Support for Literary Analysis Papers. A literary analysis paper should draw much of its supporting material from the work being discussed. Support for a literary analysis paper should always show that you have read and comprehended the work.

Support for literary analysis can include short summaries, specific examples, details, and facts from the work being analyzed, and often direct quotations from the work.

One kind of support is the *brief summary* that recounts some of the important events or ideas for the reader. Summaries should never be a major part of your paper, but they can provide the reader with useful information that will make the rest of the paper more understandable. Summaries should be written in your own words, should be completely accurate, and should not include interpretations or opinions.

Specific examples, *details*, and *facts* form a major portion of the support in any literary analysis paper. The main point or main ideas in your paper should be your own generalizations or opinions, but much of the information that develops your ideas should come from the work itself. For instance, by mentioning a character's actions or thoughts in a specific part of the book to show the validity of your idea, you can clarify and verify your idea for the reader. Specific pieces of support from the work put the reader in touch with it. Still, the reader should not be given simply a list of examples. Rather, these should be woven together with your ideas and explained or interpreted for the reader throughout the paper.

One of the most effective kinds of support is the *direct quotation* from the work. Quotations give the reader the flavor of the work. While quotations can be helpful and interesting, they should be used with care. They should illustrate or back up your own ideas; they should be short; and they should not function as padding or as the main substance of your paper. Direct quotations are always put in quotation marks. They are usually accompanied by page and publishing information within the line, at the end of the page, or the end of the paper. The forms are the same as those used for citing quotes in a library paper. (For more explanation of citation form, see Section 24.1.)

Many literary analysis papers will include a combination of these kinds of support, but you should not think that you must have either summaries or direct quotations in a literary analysis paper.

EXERCISE A: Identifying Topics for a Literary Analysis Paper. On your paper, write the name of a short story, novel, poem, play, or nonfiction book you have read in the last month or one that is still very fresh in your mind. Then using the chart on page 767, identify the different literary elements of the work, such as theme, characters, conflicts, point of view, and so on. (For some nonfiction books, substitute central idea and other main ideas for theme.) Then circle or star three elements you would be interested in analyzing in a literary analysis paper.

EXERCISE B: Choosing a Purpose for a Literary Analysis Paper. Using the three topics you circled in Exercise A, decide on (1) a general intention and (2) a purpose for each and write them on your paper.

EXAMPLE: General intention—to evaluate why the third person omniscient point of view is the author's best choice for this story and why it is essential to the meaning of the story
Purpose—to persuade

EXERCISE C: Identifying Support for a Literary Analysis Paper. Using the work you chose for Exercises A and B follow these instructions.

1. Write a summary of the work that is no more than one paragraph long. The summary should be accurate and should not contain subjective interpretations.
2. List and briefly explain *three* specific examples, details, or facts from your work that would develop one of the elements you chose in Exercise A, while following the general intention and purpose you chose in Exercise B.
3. Find *two* short quotations that could be used to elaborate on one of the elements you chose in Exercise A. Write down the direct quotations exactly and indicate the page (or line for a poem) of the quotations.

▪ Structures of Literary Analysis Papers

Two of the possibilities for the organization of a paper about literature follow. You might use a standard three-part essay structure in a paper that is unified and based on a thesis statement. Or you might write a literary review that includes a series of coherent paragraphs unified by their common general topic but not linked by a controlling idea.

A Three-Part Essay Structure.   A literary analysis paper that is either expository or persuasive can follow the organizational plan of an essay.

A literary analysis paper can have a standard three-part essay structure: an introduction with a main point expressed in a thesis statement, body paragraphs containing supporting information, and a conclusion.

Using this structure, your topic, purpose, and support will function as they do in an essay. The following diagram shows the structure of a literary analysis paper written as an essay on a character in Anne Frank's *The Diary of a Young Girl*. The paper's intention is to present conclusions about one of the characters in order to win the reader's agreement.

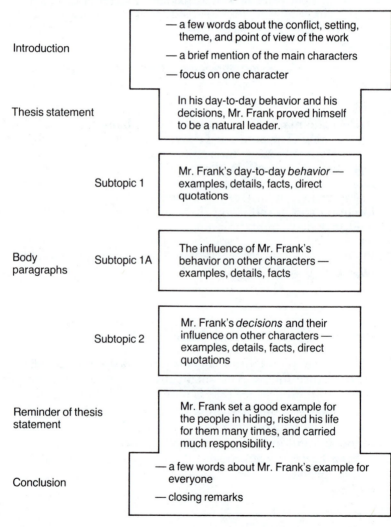

Introduction
— a few words about the conflict, setting, theme, and point of view of the work
— a brief mention of the main characters
— focus on one character

Thesis statement
In his day-to-day behavior and his decisions, Mr. Frank proved himself to be a natural leader.

Subtopic 1
Mr. Frank's day-to-day *behavior* — examples, details, facts, direct quotations

Body paragraphs   Subtopic 1A
The influence of Mr. Frank's behavior on other characters — examples, details, facts

Subtopic 2
Mr. Frank's *decisions* and their influence on other characters — examples, details, facts, direct quotations

Reminder of thesis statement
Mr. Frank set a good example for the people in hiding, risked his life for them many times, and carried much responsibility.

Conclusion
— a few words about Mr. Frank's example for everyone
— closing remarks

As you can see in the diagram, the introduction should pre- pare the reader for the thesis statement, which should present the topic focused in a main point. The thesis statement should suit your purpose and audience. The body paragraphs should develop subtopics of your main point with plentiful supporting information in the form of summaries, specific references to the work, or direct quotations, and sometimes all three. A con- cluding paragraph should remind the reader of the main point and give the essay an appearance of completeness with closing remarks on the main point or the entire work. Finally, an orig- inal title should provide a clue to the content of the paper.

A Literary Review Structure. Sometimes you might choose to present your analysis of a work as a literary review. A liter- ary review has a beginning, a middle, and an end and consists of several paragraphs, each highlighting a different element of the work. Although a literary review is less formal and structured than an essay and does not have a thesis state- ment, it should be unified and coherent with a number of well- developed paragraphs.

> A literary analysis paper can take the form of a literary review: a series of related, but loosely connected, paragraphs focus- ing on a few elements in a work, including introductory remarks and usually a final evaluation and recommendation.

A literary review usually has five parts: a title, introductory remarks, a summary of the contents of the work, a discussion of several of the elements, and final statements. The title should suggest your purpose and approach to the work. Intro- ductory remarks consisting of a few sentences should identify the work, the author, and the author's intentions in writing the work. A summary or description should give the reader an idea of the contents or main ideas of the work. The amount of detail you include in the summary will vary, but you should give readers enough information so that they will understand your later comments on the work. Often, when you write a literary review, you assume that the reader has not read the work. Sometimes the introductory remarks and the summary can form the first paragraph.

The succeeding paragraphs might cover any of the literary elements. In these paragraphs, you should discuss a few of the interesting or significant elements, including specific support- ing information from the work. For instance, one paragraph might discuss one of the themes of the work, another might discuss an important character, and another might give some details about the tone.

The final statements in the last paragraph should summarize your ideas presented in the review. In addition, this paragraph will usually include your evaluation of the meaning, effectiveness, or significance of the work. You might conclude with a recommendation to the reader.

A literary review written on Dorothy L. Sayers' mystery *The Nine Tailors* might use the structure presented in the following diagram.

Introduction with summary of work	Introductory remarks ending with a summary of the plot (without giving away the identity of the criminal)
Significance of title	"The nine tailors" — a descriptive name for the way church bells are rung to announce a death; science of church-bell ringing is woven throughout the book
Setting	Vivid setting in a small farming town in East Anglia, England, the fen-country, between the two world wars; old Norman church; dangerous sluices
Main character	Lord Peter Wimsey's concerned involvement in the townspeople's problems
Recommendation	Book is worth reading: — fascination of the eery bells, the old church, and the menacing sluices — exciting mystery

EXERCISE D: Evaluating a Literary Analysis Paper. The following literary analysis paper is based on Henrik Ibsen's play *A Doll's House*. Read it carefully and then answer the questions that follow the paper. As you write your answers, you may need to refer to the paper.

The Doll's Dance

Henrik Ibsen's play <u>A Doll's House</u> presents the conflict of a woman who has been treated like a child for nearly thirty years and who both longs for and fears full adulthood. The heroine, Nora Helmer, an apparently frivolous and childlike woman, is married to a rather overbearing and overprotective banker. Torvald Helmer treats his wife as an adorable but irresponsible pet and calls her his little squirrel, his skylark. He does not know that ten years earlier, when he had been very ill, Nora bravely, if foolishly, forged her father's signature on a promissory note to finance a rest-cure for him. Over the course of the play, the man who lent Nora the money tries to blackmail her. Nora tries desperately to prevent Torvald from learning the truth, but at the same time she imagines fondly that he will step forward heroically and save her when he does learn it. In a crucial scene at the end of the second act, Nora dances the tarantella for Torvald, to prevent him from opening their mailbox and discovering a letter from the blackmailer. This dance represents the play's most powerful expression of Nora's conflict, her dread of and desire for Torvald's recognition of her one independent act.

Throughout most of <u>A Doll's House</u>, Nora behaves like a dependent child-woman. She is always the butterfly, the frivolous one among a group of rather sober adults. And yet, at the same time, she expresses admiration and even envy for her schoolfriend, Mrs. Linde, a widow who has been bowed down by many cares and responsibilities. Nora is also very proud of her secret debt—proud that she "had the wit to be a little bit clever"[1] and save her husband's life. One part of Nora <u>wants</u> the truth to be known, and it is this part that is released in the turbulence of the tarantella.

The tarantella is a dance that supposedly resembles the violent attempt of a person bitten by a tarantula to rid the poison from his or her system. In the plot of <u>A Doll's House</u>, Nora's performance of the tarantella has a clear and simple function. Planning to dance at a party the following night, Nora deliberately does a wild and inaccurate rehearsal of the tarantella for Torvald in order to distract him from opening his mail and to persuade him to direct her performance. Nora dances in a frenzy, which Torvald finds both inappropriate and unsettling. He says to her afterward, "Come, come don't be so wild and nervous. Be my own little skylark, as you used to be."[2] And while she is dancing, he tells her, "My dear darling Nora, you are dancing as if your life depended on it," to which Nora replies, "So it does!"[3]

But although Nora may regard her tarantella as a desperate ploy to buy time for herself, it is clear from her feverish performance that much more is going on in her than either she or her husband is aware of. The dance is her outlet for the emotion that has been building up in her ever since she learned of the blackmail threat. In this sense, Nora's situation is like that of the person stricken by a tarantula's poison: She too has been infected with something like poison, and she too dances feverishly for release. Dancing the tarantella allows her to express a wildness that would otherwise not be appropriate for a middle-class wife and mother. Just as the dance gives her a day's reprieve from Torvald's discovery of her wrong-doing, so its fury allows her to escape from herself, her present troubles, and the boundaries and conventions that she has accepted all her life.

Even more important, however, is the function of the scene within Nora's development in the play. Just before she dances, she tries to get the damaging letter out of the mailbox before Torvald can see it. She sends her friend Mrs. Linde to beg the blackmailer to withdraw his letter and continues to fight against her husband's discovery of her action. Even the dance itself is one more strategy to prevent the inevitable. But after the dance, Nora seems to have changed. Calmly and without panic, she accepts Mrs. Linde's report that she has failed to reach Krogstad:

> Mrs. Linde: Gone out of town.
> Nora: I could tell from your face.
> Mrs. Linde: He is coming tomorrow evening. I wrote a note for him.
> Nora: You should have let it alone; you must prevent nothing. After all, it is splendid to be waiting for a wonderful thing to happen.
> Mrs. Linde: What is it that you are waiting for?
> Nora: Oh, you wouldn't understand. Go in to them, I will come in a moment.[4]

In other words, the tarantella leaves Nora in a new frame of mind. Still fearing what will happen to her when Torvald learns the truth, she has begun to be fascinated with it. She even begins to look forward to it. Romantically, Nora expects that Torvald will take the responsibility for her action and that he will repay her risk with a selfless act of his own.

What happens is actually quite different. When Torvald eventually reads the letter, he turns on Nora angrily and seems concerned only with the effect of her action on his reputation. He forgives her when the blackmailer repents and returns the incriminating evidence to them. But Nora, shocked and disappointed by Torvald's first reaction, packs a suitcase and leaves their home. The "wonderful thing" that she both dreaded and longed for after her tarantella takes a form quite different from what she expected. Belatedly, she realizes that she has been a child for decades, living in a doll's house, playing at life. This tragic recognition has lain underneath her action throughout the play, beneath her envy of Mrs. Linde's maturity and her great pride in her own single act of courage. This recognition is the fate that has awaited her, the fate that she both avoided and embraced when she danced the tarantella.

---

[1]Henrik Ibsen, A Doll's House, trans. R. Farquharson Sharp in Four Great Plays by Ibsen, with an Introduction by John Gassner (New York: Bantam Books, Inc., 1959), act 1, p. 12.

[2]Ibsen, A Doll's House, act 2, p. 48.

[3]Ibsen, A Doll's House, act 2, p. 47.
[4]Ibsen, A Doll's House, act 2, p. 48.

1. What is the topic of the paper?
2. What intention and purpose does the writer have?
3. What kinds of support are used?
4. What are *five* pieces of support used in the paper?
5. Does the paper follow a three-part essay structure or a literary review structure?
6. What features in the paper identify the structure that is used?
7. How effective is this paper in fulfilling its intention and purpose?
8. What if anything would you change, add, or delete in the paper?

APPLICATION: **Locating and Examining a Literary Analysis Paper.** Look in magazines such as *Newsweek, Time,* and *The New Yorker,* in the Sunday sections of the newspapers, or in a book of critical essays about literature for a literary analysis paper or a literary review to analyze. Read the paper or review carefully. Then use the questions in Exercise D to evaluate it. Refer to the paper or review as you write your answers to the questions.

Writing the Literary Analysis Paper   25.2

A literary analysis paper should be well thought out, carefully developed, and clearly and logically organized. The structure of the paper can be an essay or a literary review. This section will explain some practical steps for writing a literary analysis paper as an essay. You will probably find that many of the steps can be varied and adapted to writing a literary review as well.

■ Analyzing the Work of Literature

To write a literary analysis paper you must examine the different elements and general meaning of a piece of literature. Your understanding of the work should grow through your analysis.

Once you know a work and can recognize its elements, you can choose a topic and shape it to a main point. As you will see, this process requires reading and making inferences about the work as well as narrowing your ideas to a manageable topic for a paper.

Examining the Elements in a Work.   As you read a work for the first time, you should jot down notes about important or memorable passages, the development of a character, your reactions, and any questions you might have. Taking notes will help you remember, observe, and react to the work.

Prepare to analyze a work of literature by reading it carefully, by studying its parts, by asking yourself questions, and by taking notes.

One way to examine and ponder a work of literature is to pose some questions about the elements of the work, the author's intentions, and your responses to the work. During a discussion in class, the teacher or other students usually ask questions for you to think about and answer. In your preparation for writing a literary analysis paper, however, you will often have to ask *and* answer the questions yourself. You can ask a question about every literary element, explore one element to a greater extent, or probe the "why's" behind your own responses to the work. The following chart presents sample questions like those you can use in your own thinking and analyzing.

POSSIBLE QUESTIONS TO PROMOTE UNDERSTANDING OF A LITERARY WORK

General Questions

1. Do the characters seem realistic? Is the work enjoyable, thought-provoking, upsetting?
2. Who is (are) the main character(s) in the work?
3. What characters or external or internal forces are opposed to the main character?
4. What is the crisis or climax of the work? What main events lead up to the climax?
5. What point of view has the author used in the work? How would using another point of view change the work?
6. What is the setting? Does it change? Is it strongly felt throughout the work or simply a backdrop?

7. Is the imagery rich and dense or sparse? Are there any patterns of imagery, such as sights, smells, sounds?

8. Do any characters, objects, places, or names function as symbols in the work?

9. What is the dominant tone of the work?

10. What is one major theme of the work?

More Specific Questions

1. What scenes in the work particularly illustrate and dramatize the theme?

2. Does the main character change in the course of the work?

3. With which character or characters in the work does the author sympathize most? What makes you think so?

4. Can you identify with any of the characters? With whom do you sympathize?

5. Which of the methods of revealing character (action, dialogue, thoughts, author's comments, other characters' reactions, and other characters' words) does the author use most in the work?

Every kind of literature lends itself to special types of questions. For instance, if you were examining a poem, you might want to consider the speaker of the poem, the number and kind of sensory impressions, the number of adjectives in comparison to the number of verbs, and the number of imaginative comparisons (figures of speech) in proportion to the number of direct statements. For a play, you might want to explore how the playwright conveys background information, how much of the setting is presented in the words and how much through props and scenery, how the playwright controls tension and suspense, and many other points peculiar to drama. Part of the success of your analysis will depend on how imaginative your questions are and how carefully you read to answer them.

Suppose, for instance, you had read Eudora Welty's short story "A Visit of Charity." One way you might approach the analyzing step is to jot down ideas that occur to you or reactions that you have as you read. Next, you might pose a series of questions for yourself to answer. You might then reread and examine the story as well as use your rough notes to help you answer the questions. Using some of the questions given above and a few more, some rough notes, and some ideas you had come up with on "A Visit of Charity," you might produce answers similar to the answers in the following chart.

ELEMENTS FOR ANALYSIS OF "A VISIT OF CHARITY"

General Questions About the Work	Your Specific Answers from the Work
What is the story about?	—teen-age girl visits two elderly women at a nursing home and brings them a plant to earn points for Campfire Girls; frightened by the crowded room and the unattractiveness and strange behavior of the women, she runs away from the lonely old women
What are my impressions?	—very lifelike characters; story is thought-provoking, depressing
Who are the main characters?	—Marian—14-year-old Campfire Girl, blond hair, bright clothes, concerned about getting points
	—First Old Woman—friendly, tries to talk with Marian, rocks wildly in the rocking chair, and asks Marian for a present—arms, hands like bird's claws
	—Second Old Woman (Addie)—lies bundled up in bed, contradicts other old woman, cries, refuses to tell her age, looks like a sheep
	—Nurse—strong, impersonal, mannish, unfeeling—like a guard
What are the external or internal conflicts?	—youth against age; the supposed reason Marian visits the nursing home (charity) versus the real reason (self-interest); healthy, vigorous, independent people (Marian, nurse) against sickly, helpless people (the old women)
What point of view has the author used?	—third person partially omniscient; through Marian's eyes and mind; Marian = viewpoint character
What is the setting?	—mid-morning, winter day, Old Ladies' Home, slightly run-down, cold, damp place, residents crowded two to a small room
What is the dominant tone?	—critical, cynical, slightly humorous
What is one major theme?	—self-interest and indifference often hide the needs of others and leave people helpless and neglected.

The analyzing you have done so far might lead you to even more specific questions. For the story "A Visit of Charity," you might wonder about some of the following ideas.

MORE SPECIFIC QUESTIONS ON "A VISIT OF CHARITY"	
With whom do I sympathize?	—somewhat with Marian because the place and the women are unpleasant and scary but more with the women because no one cares for them or sees them as people with feelings and needs; Marian puts herself first and sees them only through her own selfishness
How does the author imply criticism of Marian?	—through Marian's words "I have to pay a visit to some old lady" (p. 245) —by revealing Marian's thoughts—she didn't even look at or think about the plant she was giving the women —Marian's unthinking question about age —Marian is so unprepared for the visit she hasn't realized these are human beings —Marian dashes out; she has things of her own—the hidden apple, freedom to leave, health to run for the bus; she feels only relief at escaping the Home —she doesn't understand the idea of charity, love for others at all

Once you have analyzed the work and listed ideas about it you can choose one or more elements that especially interest you. Remember that your paper can focus on one element or on the relationship between two or more elements, or it can give an overview of the entire work, highlighting a few features. Think about how much information you can find to develop a paper on the topics you are considering.

For a paper on "A Visit of Charity," you might decide to write on a theme of the story: People's self-interest and indifference often blind them to the humanity and needs of others.

Deciding on General Intention, Purpose, Audience, and Main Point.   The next step in preparing a literary analysis paper involves shaping and refining your topic and deciding what you will attempt to do in your paper.

Determine your general intention, purpose, audience, and main point. Then write a thesis statement that suits and reflects these decisions.

Your first decision concerns determining your general intention and purpose. You should consider the assignment, the notes you have taken, the thinking you have done so far, and your audience. If everyone in your class has read the same work, you may choose either to explain a part of the work simply to show your understanding or to offer your own interpretation and defend it with examples from the work. On the other hand, if you have selected the literary work independently, you may decide to explain some part of it to readers unfamiliar with it or to present some conclusions you have drawn from your study of it. You could then develop these ideas to interest the reader in the work as well as to provide helpful insights.

If you were writing about a theme in "A Visit of Charity," for example, you might want to convince the reader that it is a major theme of the story by showing what elements dramatize and convey the theme. Your audience might be other students in the class who have read the story but who may not have thought about it as deeply as you have. Your purpose might then be to persuade your audience to consider and agree with your interpretation.

When you have made these decisions, you should shape your topic into a main point and your main point into a thesis statement. All the thinking you have done so far can help you formulate a thesis statement that (1) suits your general intention, purpose, and audience; (2) accurately reflects the work and your understanding of it; and (3) limits your paper to analysis that is thorough and significant.

One or more additional questions may help you arrive at a workable main point.

QUESTIONING TO TURN A FOCUSED TOPIC AND GENERAL INTENTION INTO A COMPLETE MAIN POINT	
Question	**Ideas to Complete Main Point**
What elements in the story develop this theme and indicate that it is the major one?	—Setting—shows by many details that old women are neglected and, in many ways, dehumanized

—<u>Character</u>—main character, person through whose eyes action is shown—Marian; Marian acts out the theme in her encounter with the women

When you have a main point, which will frequently include subtopics, you should try to write a thesis statement. You should write at least two versions to find one that most clearly states your controlling idea for the paper. Some possible thesis statements for the preceding main point are shown in the following chart. Notice that sometimes in literary analysis papers you may want to phrase your thesis statement in two sentences.

POSSIBLE THESIS STATEMENTS

1. The major theme of "A Visit of Charity" is that people's self-interest and insensitivity can blind them to the humanity and needs of others. Welty dramatizes this theme through her choice of setting and her characterization of Marian.

2. In "A Visit of Charity," the setting and the characterization of Marian illustrate the theme that people's self-interest and insensitivity can blind them to the humanity and needs of others.

3. Welty's depiction of the setting and her portrayal of Marian dramatize the theme that people's self-interest and insensitivity can blind them to the humanity and needs of others.

From the different versions of your thesis statement you should choose the one that has the most concise, clear wording and that appeals to you the most. After examining these thesis statements, you might decide the third one would work best.

EXERCISE A: Doing Preliminary Analysis. Choose a piece of literature—a novel, short story, nonfiction book, play, or poem—that you are reading for pleasure or for class. As you read or review the work, jot down ideas and reactions. Note important places in the work. Then adapt or simply answer the questions in the chart on page 780 for your specific work. In addition, write *three* specific questions on your particular work and answer them. From your paper with your answers, select a topic that appeals to you and that is supportable.

EXERCISE B: **Writing a Thesis Statement.** Using the topic you selected in Exercise A, determine your general intention, purpose, audience, and main point. If you need to, ask yourself further questions about your focused topic to find subtopics and to complete your main point. Then write *two* versions of your thesis statement and choose the one you think is best.

■ Gathering Support for a Literary Analysis Paper

Finding adequate, appropriate support will lead you back to your notes and the literary work itself. You must use your ability to interpret to find examples, details, and other pieces of information from the work to support your main point.

> Reexamine the work and your notes to find appropriate examples, details, facts, and possibly direct quotations to develop your thesis statement.

Gathering support for a paper of this kind involves both additional analysis and brainstorming. You may have to return to the work several times. You may also have to locate relevant support in your notes and your answers to the questions you asked earlier. Furthermore, you may have to brainstorm for more insightful ideas and information using the notes you already have as departure points.

Your literary analysis based on your thesis statement should be expanding as you flesh out points on paper. One approach to this stage of writing is to continue your dialogue with yourself on the work. You can think out loud, on paper, or any way you choose. Jotting down ideas, however, ensures that you will not forget the good insights that you have.

Questioning and answering can help you once again at this stage. You might begin with your thesis statement at the top of your paper and several specific questions about your main point. Your answers to these questions will become your body of supporting material. You should not worry about the order of the information as you jot down ideas to support your interpretation or to explain your main point. If you include direct quotations, place them in quotation marks and write down the page numbers.

For the paper on "A Visit of Charity," your support sheet might include the following information.

SUPPORT SHEET FOR A PAPER ON "A VISIT OF CHARITY"

Thesis Statement: Welty's depiction of the setting and her portrayal of Marian dramatize the theme that people's self-interest and insensitivity can blind them to the humanity and needs of others.

What is the setting? How does it illustrate the theme?

—mid-morning, winter day, Old Ladies' Home

—"prickly dark shrubs" (p. 245) outside—unfriendly—no beauty or softness

—"whitewashed building reflects sunlight like a block of ice" (p. 245)

—"loose, bulging linoleum on the floor" (p. 246)

—"smell like the interior of a clock" (p. 246)

—silence—old lady sounds like bleating of a sheep

—tiny room—too much furniture

—everything smells wet—window shade down—dark medicine bottles on the bedstand

—conditions suggest that society has shut up and neglected these elderly ladies without privacy, space, freedom; deprived them of their humanity

How does the characterization of Marian dramatize the theme?

—Marian is a member of the society that has dehumanized these old people

—Welty undercuts the reader's sympathy for Marian by presenting Marian's shallow, insensitive thoughts

—Marian thinks of the women as things and animals

—"I have to pay a visit to some old lady" (p. 245) "any one of them will do" (p. 246)

—she dashes out at the end

—thinks only of herself—her apple, her ride home

—feels only relief and freedom catching the bus, eating the apple

—Marian didn't prepare for her visit at all—didn't even notice the plant she was giving the women

—she only thinks about what she will get out of it—she wants to leave the whole time she is there

—she sees one woman as a bird with claws: "short, gradual jerks" (p. 246) "a hand quick as a bird claw" (p. 247)

—other woman resembles a sheep—sounds like a sheep—"bunchy white forehead and red eyes like a sheep" (p. 248)

—she doesn't want to become involved, can't think, won't share herself or give her name or show genuine interest in the women

While you continue to develop your literary analysis paper, new ideas will probably occur to you, and you will probably think of additional strong examples or details. However, having produced this rough list of the ideas and material for your paper, you are now ready to move on to evaluating, organizing, and shaping your support into the clear, logical form your paper should have.

EXERCISE C: Developing Support for a Literary Analysis Paper. Using your notes, thought work, and thesis statement from Exercises A and B, gather supporting information by listing ideas, examples, details, facts, and possibly direct quotations with page numbers on a piece of paper under your thesis statement. Either use the question and answer method or some other that you think will help you produce a strong list of support. Remember to draw much of your material from the work. Concentrate more on capturing your ideas at this point than on evaluating and sorting them.

■ Organizing a Literary Analysis Paper

Organizing a literary analysis paper using the essay structure is similar to organizing any essay. You should group supporting information logically, delete information that seems weak or otherwise extraneous, and add new pieces of support and ideas that will strengthen your analysis.

Arrange supporting information for the body of the paper and evaluate the quality and quantity of supporting information. Add and eliminate support as necessary; then prepare a plan or rough outline.

The supporting information in the body of your paper should be grouped according to subtopics of your thesis statement. If you have stated these subtopics in your thesis statement, your supporting information may already be in basic groups. If you must now choose subtopics, find natural divisions or parts of your main point, and rearrange your support. You can do this ordering step right on your support sheet. You should also order the supporting information under each subtopic.

If you were preparing the paper on "A Visit of Charity," you would notice that your supporting information is already grouped by the subtopics: setting and portrayal of Marian. Because you have more information about Marian than about the setting, you might want to divide your analysis of Marian into a discussion of what she thinks, what she says to the old women, and what she does. Each of these subdivisions should build your interpretation of the theme.

Either before or after you have a basic plan for the body of your paper, you should consider the unity and completeness of your support. Check your supporting information to make sure it is accurate. Then ask yourself, "Do I have enough support for each subtopic? Is every example, quotation, or detail I have listed relevant and necessary? Have I found the best support?" You should respond to these questions critically and go back to your notes or to the work, if necessary. Delete information that will take up space without furthering the reader's understanding of your main point.

As the last stage of organizing, you should create a working plan or an outline from which to write. Your plan can be your support sheet marked and annotated, a rough outline, or a topic outline. (For more information on outlining supporting information for an essay, see Section 23.2.)

EXERCISE D: **Arranging and Evaluating Your Supporting Information.** Use the list of supporting information you prepared in Exercise C. Order the information by subtopics of your thesis statement and, under each subtopic, check for complete coverage of each subtopic. Eliminate information that does not strengthen and develop your thesis statement. Finally, prepare a working plan or outline of the body of your essay.

■ Writing the Paper

By the time you have analyzed the work, developed your analysis, and organized your paper, you are ready to write. This writing stage involves two major steps: writing a first draft and then checking and revising the paper and completing a final copy. As you complete these steps, keep in mind that new ideas may occur to you, especially if you continue to think about and refer to the work.

Completing a First Draft.   When you draft your paper, you should concentrate on communicating your understanding of the work to the reader. Your paper should give the reader insights into the author's craft or ideas and thus lead the reader to appreciate the work. To achieve these goals, the paper should be unified and coherent in its parts and as a whole. Your thesis statement and the plan or outline you developed for the body of the paper will help you while you write. The analysis and thought work you have done should also contribute background information and additional ideas for the introduction, conclusion, and title of your paper.

Consider your audience and use your analysis of the work, your notes, and your outline to write the introduction, body, and conclusion of your paper.

An introduction should serve several special functions as well as suit your particular paper. In the introduction, you should identify the work and author and give the audience a capsulized version of the story or main ideas. You should prepare the audience for the elements that you have chosen for your analysis. Often you will end the introduction with your thesis statement, which then leads into the body.

As you write the body of your paper, you should keep several points in mind. Clarify your analysis by using transitions, possibly bridge ideas, or even transitional paragraphs between subtopics. Often strong topic sentences, which relate supporting information under a subtopic to your overall point, can help the reader follow your ideas. Repeating main words and using synonyms and consistent pronouns can also promote coherence and smoothness. Be sure to put all direct quotations in quotation marks and to give the source and the page for each quotation either as an informal citation or as a footnote. (For more information on citing sources, see Section 24.1.) If a short work has been reprinted in many books, be sure to identify which version you are using. The second reference to the same source does not need to be as complete as the first.

In your conclusion you should at least wrap up the main point of your analysis and the ideas presented in the paper. You may also bring in related material from the work to expand your interpretation, or you could mention other similar works. However you choose to end your paper, your conclusion should round out your analysis and leave the reader with a sense of completion.

The title of a literary analysis paper in essay form should indicate the topic of the paper or arouse curiosity about it and should reflect the thesis statement.

Revising and Rewriting.   When you have completed your first draft, you should reread it carefully, looking for any weaknesses you can improve.

Use a checklist to guide you in making any corrections or revisions of your first draft.

The following checklist can help you reexamine your paper and look specifically at the key features that should be part of a literary analysis paper.

CHECKLIST FOR REVISING YOUR LITERARY ANALYSIS PAPER

1. Have you chosen the best title for your paper?
2. Do introductory statements provide enough background and summary information about the work to suit the audience?
3. Does the thesis statement present your main point and indicate the paper's purpose—to report, to explain, or to persuade?
4. Do subtopics develop the main point with sufficient examples, details, and direct quotations as well as your ideas about the work, if appropriate?
5. Have you identified and provided pages for all direct quotations? Have you used one method for citing sources consistently throughout the paper?
6. Does your conclusion include a reminder of the main point and then bring the paper to a satisfying close?
7. Have you used transitions and other devices for coherence to help the reader follow your analysis?
8. Throughout the paper, is your analysis centered on the work and presented clearly for the audience's understanding?
9. Are sentences varied in length and structure, using a mature, smooth style?
10. Can you find errors in grammar, spelling, usage, or mechanics?

After you have spent time proofreading and checking your first draft, you might have another person read it to make constructive suggestions. Then you should prepare a final copy.

If you wrote the literary analysis paper on "A Visit of Charity" discussed throughout this section, your paper might resemble the following. Notice the development of the subtopic that focuses on setting and the three-part development of the subtopic that treats the character Marian. Notice, also, that the topic sentences and ideas throughout the paper link setting and character to theme. A transitional paragraph leads the reader from the first subtopic to the second. A few short, direct quotations give the flavor of the work and support the main point. Quotation marks and page numbers in footnotes identify these quotations for the reader.

Title	A Scarcity of Charity
Introduction	In the short story "A Visit of Charity" by Eudora Welty, a fourteen-year-old girl visits two women in a home for the elderly to bring them a plant and to earn points for Campfire Girls. Welty implies through this story, however, that neither the society that supports the home nor the girl, Marian, knows the meaning of the word "charity." The dictionary defines "charity" as "the love of man for his fellow men: an act of good will or affection." But instead of love, good will, and affection, self-interest, callous-
Thesis statement with two subtopics	ness, and dehumanization prevail in this story. Welty's depiction of the setting and her portrayal of Marian dramatize the theme that people's selfishness and insensitivity can blind them to the humanity and needs of others.
Subtopic 1: setting	Many features of the setting, a winter's day at a home for elderly women, suggest coldness, neglect, and dehumanization. Instead of evergreens or other vegetation that might lend softness or beauty to the place, the city has landscaped it with "prickly dark shrubs."[1] Behind the shrubs the whitewashed walls of the Old Ladies' Home reflect "the winter sunlight like a block of ice."[2] Welty also implies that the cold appearance of the nurse is due to the coolness in the building as well as to the stark, impersonal, white uniform she is wearing. In the inner parts of the building the "loose, bulging linoleum on the floor"[3] indicates that the place is cheaply built and poorly cared for. The halls that "smell like the interior of a clock"[4] suggest a used, unfeeling machine. Perhaps the clearest evidence of dehumanization is the small, crowded rooms, each inhabited by two older women. The room that Marian visits is dark, with a drawn shade and too much furniture. No colors, decorations, or beauty brighten this room, which is packed with beds, a chair, a wardrobe, a washstand, a rocker, and a bed table. The wet smell of everything and the wet appearance of the bare floor suggest that this cramped room is more like a stall in a barn, a place for animals, than a home for human beings.
Transitional paragraph	The character Marian represents the society that has confined old women to this dismal, neglected home. Specifically through Marian's thoughts, words, and actions, revealed by the third person partially omniscient narrator, Welty shows how selfishness and indifference can obscure the needs of the less fortunate.

Subtopic 2A:
Marian: her
thoughts

Throughout her so-called visit of charity, Marian perceives the old women she meets sometimes as things and sometimes as animals. She refers to an old woman as an object to be used and discarded when she announces the purpose of her visit: "I'm a Campfire Girl. . . . I have to pay a visit to some old lady."[5] These words and her frequent thoughts about the points she will get for the visit reveal her real reason for coming: self-gain. An old woman—"any of them will do"[6] she says—is an impersonal thing with no identity or personality. Clearly, her concern is focused on her progress in Campfire Girls. During her brief stay at the Home, Marian thinks of the first old woman as a bird and the second as a sheep. In her eyes, the first woman moves in "short, gradual jerks"[7] like a bird, has "a hand quick as a bird claw,"[8] and grabs her with the grip of a talon. The other woman, bundled up in bed with a quilt, appears to Marian to resemble a sheep. When Marian first sees her, she describes her mentally as having "a bunchy white forehead and red eyes like a sheep."[9] When this second woman clears her throat or talks, she sounds to Marian like a sheep bleating or a lamb whimpering. Marian's unconscious dehumanization of the women, her reduction of them to objects and creatures, reveals her own insensitivity.

Subtopic 2B:
Marian: her
words to the
women

Welty also dramatizes the blinding power of self-interest through Marian's lack of preparation for her visit and her inability to talk with or listen to the old women. Marian is so preoccupied with the points she is earning that she never thinks beyond her task to deliver the potted plant to some old woman. When the first woman takes the plant, Marian realizes that she has not even looked at it. Nor has she thought that during her visit she would be interacting with human beings in need of warmth, concern, and cheer. From the moment she finds herself in the dark, tiny room, her uppermost thought is escape. She is so stunned by her surroundings and the strange, lonely women that she cannot remember her own name or answer the questions that the first woman asks her. She identifies herself only as a Campfire Girl and never learns the names or histories of the women. A few of the remarks Marian blurts out do not even make sense, and the one question she asks, "How old are you?"[10] only serves to remind the bedridden woman of her helplessness and age. If Marian had had a different purpose or had let herself become involved in the lives of these women, she might have seen beyond their squabbling. She might have realized that emptiness and despair led the one to contradict and deny her roommate's identity, past, and meager memories while it led the other to give away her roommate's birthday secret. But Marian only hears and does not understand. Her one flash of interest in the old woman's age quickly fades when the woman refuses to answer the question.

Subtopic 2C:
Marian: her
actions

Finally, Welty illustrates the theme of self-interest and callousness through Marian's actions, particularly at the end of the story. Even before her visit she was thinking about herself when she hid her apple under a bush before entering the building. Marian came to give a thing, a potted plant, not herself. She even gave less time than another Campfire Girl who read the Bible to the old women. Throughout her visit she is uncomfortable, until finally her desire to escape overwhelms her. When the first old woman begs Marian for a penny or a nickel to buy something of her own, Marian does not even speak to her. Instead, she exerts all her strength to free herself from the woman's grasp and run away. Marian is stylishly dressed, indicating her social standing. She could have given the old woman something, something for the woman's sake and not just something to buy herself points. Even after her rapid and rude departure, she is untouched by the raw needs and emotional vacuum that have been revealed to her. As she yells for the bus to wait for her, leaps on, and chomps on her apple, she shows her untouched feelings and undisturbed ignorance. She is young, vigorous, and free. She has her points, and nothing else matters.

Reminder of
the thesis
statement

Conclusion

Neither the maintenance of the Old Ladies' Home nor Marian's delivery of a potted plant qualify as an act of charity. In fact, as an analysis of the setting reveals, the Home is inhumane in many ways. Marian indicates by her thoughts, words, and deeds that she is opportunistic and indifferent to the feelings and needs of the aging women. Welty further suggests in this story that pseudo-charity can destroy the very humanity it pretends to acknowledge and uphold. People like Marian acting either out of duty or for personal advantage have created the Home and the conditions that have made the inhabitants cranky, clutching, and unlovable. Marian left the women more lonely and distraught than she found them. This kind of charity is uncharitable indeed.

Footnotes
credit source;
shorter
subsequent
references

[1]Eudora Welty, "A Visit of Charity" in <u>Modern Satiric Stories: The Impropriety Principle</u>, ed. Gregory Fitzgerald (Glenview, Illinois: Scott, Foresman and Company, 1971), p. 245.
[2]Welty, "A Visit of Charity," p. 245.
[3]Welty, "A Visit of Charity," p. 246.

[4]Welty, "A Visit of Charity," p. 246.
[5]Welty, "A Visit of Charity," p. 245.
[6]Welty, "A Visit of Charity," p. 246.
[7]Welty, "A Visit of Charity," p. 246.
[8]Welty, "A Visit of Charity," p. 247.
[9]Welty, "A Visit of Charity," p. 248.
[10]Welty, "A Visit of Charity," p. 251.

EXERCISE E: Drafting a Literary Analysis Paper. Using your work from preceding exercises, write your analysis by preparing an introduction, writing from your plan or outline, drafting a conclusion, and thinking up a title. Pay special attention to presenting your ideas clearly and smoothly with transitional devices. Be sure to cite the sources of all direct quotations, either in informal citations or in footnotes.

EXERCISE F: Revising a Literary Analysis Paper. Put the paper you wrote in Exercise E aside for at least ten minutes. Then reread it and use the checklist on page 791 to help you make corrections and revisions. Prepare a final version of your paper.

APPLICATION: Using Your Analytical Skills and Writing Skills. Choose a work entirely unlike the one you used in the exercises in this section. Then analyze it using some of the questions in this section and at least *five* of your own more specific questions on the work. Then follow the thinking and writing steps in this section. Before you revise your paper, find someone who will read it, comment on how clearly it expresses your analysis of the work, and suggest changes. Then revise your paper, making any necessary alterations, and recopy it. Submit your evaluator's comments along with your final version to your teacher.

Chapter 26

Letters and Applications

At various times throughout your life, you will need to write letters or brief compositions for college and job applications. You may need to correspond with friends and business acquaintances, to respond to invitations, or to order merchandise. And when applying for a job or for admission to college, you may be required to write a paragraph or essay.

This chapter provides some guidelines for these different types of writing.

26.1 Writing Social and Business Letters

You have probably been writing letters for some time. Many of your letters are likely to be personal; others are probably business-related. To be successful at letter writing, you should know the different styles and features of both personal and business letters, and you should understand the purposes of the different types of letters.

■ Writing Social Letters

Personal letters are used to correspond with distant friends and relatives, invite people to social gatherings, and so forth. To write *any* type of personal letter, you must be familiar with the structural features and the proper procedures for writing and mailing the letter.

Basic Structure of the Letter.   A personal letter should have five basic parts. You must understand these different parts, and you must know how to arrange them on paper.

A personal letter should include five basic parts arranged properly: a heading, salutation, body, closing, and signature.

Place a *heading* in the upper right-hand portion of your letter. Include your street address on the first line, your town or city, state, and zip code on the second line, and the date of writing on the last line.

Follow the heading with a *salutation* placed at the left margin of the letter, below the heading. These are words that greet the person who receives the letter. The salutation you choose may vary depending on the nature of the letter's contents and upon your familiarity with the recipient. The following are some possible salutations.

FORMAL SALUTATIONS:	Dear Steve,	Dear Miss Lynch,
	Dear Aunt Greta,	Dear Mrs. Hopper,
	Dear Dr. Gray,	Dear Ms. Assali,

LESS FORMAL SALUTATIONS:	Hi, Pal,	Howdy, Bruce,
	Hey, Cora,	Greetings,

The middle section, or *body*, of your letter starts several lines below the salutation. It can include as many sentences and paragraphs as you like and will contain all ideas, feelings, and other personal information that you wish to communicate.

Following the body should be a *closing*, which signals the end of the letter. Normally, you will place the closing two or three lines beneath the body on the right-hand side. Be sure to capitalize only the first word of your closing, and place a comma after the last word, as in the following examples. Notice that many different choices of words are available. The words you choose for a closing should suit the particular tone of your letter.

CLOSINGS:	Very truly yours,	Love,
	Sincerely,	So long for now,
	My best wishes,	Yours,

One or two lines directly beneath the closing, your *signature* will end the letter. Use the name by which the receiver normally addresses you, and write it in ink, even if you have typed the rest of the letter.

The very last item may be an *R.S.V.P.* if you have written an invitation. This abbreviation, placed in the very lower left-hand corner of the invitation, stands for the French words *répondez s'il vous plait (respond please)* and asks the reader to accept or decline in response.

Possible Letter Styles.   You should include these five basic parts in any personal letter; however, the style of the letter is your choice. You may select either of two styles.

Use either indented or semiblock style for writing a personal letter.

If you choose the *indented style,* you will indent the lines of the heading, closing, and signature, along with the first line of each paragraph in the body. Using *semiblock style,* you will still indent the first line of each paragraph, but all other lines of writing will follow directly beneath one another. The following diagrams illustrate these two styles.

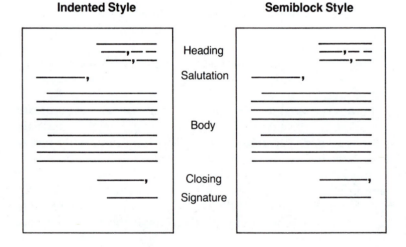

Procedures for Mailing.   Preparing your letter and envelope for mailing are simple but important parts of personal correspondence.

Fold your letter properly and prepare an envelope.

To *fold the letter,* you can create a single fold or a double fold, depending on the size of your paper or stationery. If you have written on a small piece of paper, you can probably fold the letter in half and slip it into the envelope. With standard-size paper (8½ × 11 inches or 21.6 × 27.9 cm), you may need to fold it into thirds, as in the following diagram.

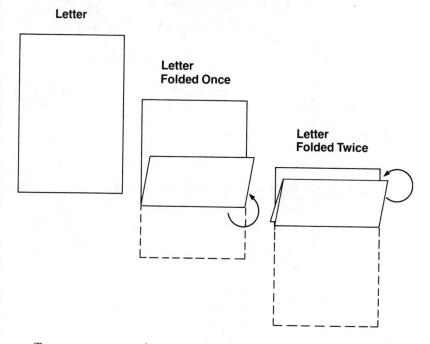

Letter

**Letter
Folded Once**

**Letter
Folded Twice**

To *prepare an envelope,* you should follow the same style (indented or semiblock) that you chose for the letter. Write the lines of the address and your return address in either of the following ways.

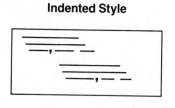

Indented Style

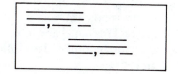

Semiblock Style

In addition to following the style of the letter, you should also follow a few more guidelines.

GUIDELINES FOR PREPARING ENVELOPES

1. Type the envelope if you have typed the letter, or handwrite it if your letter is handwritten.
2. Include your name, address, apartment number (if necessary), and zip code in the return address.
3. Avoid such titles as Mr., Miss, or Ms. when you write your own name, but use a title with the name of the person to whom you are writing.
4. Avoid any abbreviations that will not be immediately clear to anyone who reads the envelope.
5. Check the address of the person to whom you are writing; make sure the address is complete and correct. *Always* include the zip code.
6. Check for mistakes in spelling or punctuation.
7. On small envelopes, you may have to write your return address on the reverse side, but check with the post office to see if the envelope is large enough for mailing.

Types of Personal Letters. As you write personal letters, you should be aware of the different purposes that your correspondence can serve.

Understand the characteristics of different types of personal letters: friendly letters, invitations, letters of acceptance and regret, and other kinds of social notes.

A *friendly letter* is probably the most informal. Writing to a friend, acquaintance, or family member, your purpose may be to share current events in your life, to continue the communication of an earlier letter or phone call, and probably to encourage additional correspondence. You should try to include ideas and information that you think your reader will find interesting.

As you compose the letter, the organization and tone will be entirely up to you, but you should obey the rules of usage, mechanics, and spelling. Certainly, the ideas should be sensibly ordered and easy to read, but you might also enliven your letter with descriptive language and elements of story-telling to relate an incident, for instance. The following is a brief model of a friendly letter.

16 Westward Lane
Cambridge, Mass. 02138
October 15, 1981

Dear John,

I've been away from Omaha for only six days, and I miss it already. Of course, I've had many things to do to get over my homesickness and have seen so many fascinating things. Dad and I have visited two colleges so far, and each has impressed me with its stately brick buildings and park-like campuses. Boston manages to honor and preserve its history and prosper as a modern, cosmopolitan city. I loved identifying the landmarks and parts of the city from the top of the John Hancock Building.

I hope that I am accepted by one of the colleges near Boston, but even if I don't go to school here, I would enjoy another visit to this city. You should consider applying to one of the schools here. You are a city-person, too, and you would probably find Boston as intriguing as I have.

Even so, after a week of interviews and sight-seeing, I am looking forward to returning home. Dad changed our flight reservations for next Tuesday. If you can come to the airport, call my mother and ask for the flight time (and a ride). Give my regards to your family.

Love,
Cheryl

An *invitation* is a brief note to ask someone to attend a special event you are planning. An informal invitation is typed or handwritten, not engraved. It should include certain specific details: the time, date, and location of the event; the nature of the event; and possibly a suggestion about what the person should wear. Your invitation should answer any questions that the recipient might ask. If you need an advance response from the person, you can include an R.S.V.P. at the bottom of the invitation. The following is an example.

146 Sanford Boulevard
Mt. Vernon, N.Y. 10550
November 30, 1981

Dear Leona,

My family and I are sponsoring a party on December 13 for the exhange students from Spain who have recently arrived. As representatives of the American Field Service, we want to welcome these two young men and two young women to our country and to our city and school.

We plan to begin our reception at 6:30 p.m. and to follow with dinner at 7:30 p.m. Dress will be casual, and one gift will be presented to each of the four students on behalf of the A.F.S.

I'm sure that we will all enjoy the party, and I hope that you will be able to attend.

Sincerely,
Lester Freeman

R.S.V.P.

A *letter of acceptance or regret* is a response to an invitation. If you are accepting an invitation, your letter should begin with your positive response, and you should repeat the date, time, and place to avoid any misunderstanding. On the other hand, if you must decline the invitation, you should offer a reason for being unable to attend. Both types of letters should express your appreciation for the invitation. The following is an example of a letter of acceptance.

6 Carole Circle
Mt. Vernon, N.Y. 10550
December 5, 1981

Dear Lester,

    I will be happy to attend your party on December 13. I know I will find it interesting to share information about our school and other activities, and I welcome a chance to practice my Spanish.

    I plan to arrive at 6:30 p.m. Thank you for inviting me.

Sincerely,
Leona Lewis

Other social notes may include thank-you letters for gifts and entertainment, letters of congratulations, and letters of condolence. Like other personal letters, these notes should be gracious, timely, and direct, concisely fulfilling their specific purpose.

EXERCISE A: Practicing with the Features of Personal Letters. Use two separate pieces of paper or stationery to sketch two skeleton letters. Use lines to represent the body paragraphs, and use your own address for the heading and someone else's name for the salutation. Follow indented style for one skeleton letter, and follow semiblock style for the other.

EXERCISE B: Preparing Personal Letters for Mailing. Prepare an envelope for each of the skeleton letters in Exercise A. Match the style of each envelope with the style of its corresponding letter. Fold each letter properly and place it into its envelope. Leave the envelope unsealed.

EXERCISE C: Writing Different Types of Personal Letters. Use any one of the following ideas to write a personal letter. Be sure to include all five parts of the letter, and use your own name and address for the heading. Make up all necessary details. When you complete the letter, prepare an envelope for it.

1. Your cousin in another state has won a scholarship. Write an appropriate letter expressing your reaction to this news.
2. You have been invited to the wedding of your best friend's brother. Respond either positively or negatively.
3. You are planning an after-prom party at your home. Write an invitation and address it to someone in your class.
4. Write a letter sharing information with a good friend or close relative who lives in another state.
5. A friend or relative living in another state is in the hospital recovering from an operation. Write an appropriate letter.

■ Writing Business Letters

Business letters, like personal letters, should have certain structural parts. They can be written in any of three styles, and can serve different purposes, for instance, ordering merchandise, applying for a job, and expressing a complaint.

Basic Structure of the Letter.   A correct business letter has six basic parts. You should know what these parts are and how to arrange them on plain paper or business stationery.

Your business letter should include six basic parts arranged properly: a heading, inside address, salutation, body, closing, and signature.

Place the *heading* in either the upper right-hand section of the paper or at the left margin, depending on the style you are following. Include your complete address and the date, and locate the heading about one inch down (2.54 cm) from the top of the paper.

Follow with an *inside address* about two or three spaces beneath the heading. Located at the left margin of the paper, the inside address should include the complete address of the person or business to whom you are writing. If the addressee has a title, such as President or Director of Personnel, this should follow the name.

INSIDE ADDRESSES: Mr. John Hanson, President
Hanson Motors, Inc.
1550 States Avenue
Milwaukee, Wisconsin 53233

Richardson Furniture Store
1400 Kings Road
Pittsburg, Kansas 66764

Two or three lines beneath the inside address you should place your *salutation* to the reader. Writing to a business or to a business person, your salutation should be formal, as in the following examples. Notice that each salutation is followed by a colon.

SALUTATIONS: Dear Sir: Gentlemen:

Dear Sir or Madam: Dear Mrs. Simon:

In the *body* of your business letter, you will present all the information necessary to conduct your business. You might be requesting merchandise or information, applying for a position, complaining, expressing an opinion, or continuing an on-going business transaction. The body should be single-spaced if typed and should begin two lines below the salutation.

The *closing* ends your communication. Placed two or three lines beneath the body, the closing should be a formal sign-off, as in the following examples. Notice that each begins with a capital letter and ends with a comma.

CLOSINGS: Sincerely yours,   Cordially,

Very truly yours,   Respectfully,

Your *signature*, always written in ink, should follow a few lines beneath the closing. If you have typed the letter, you should also type your full name beneath your signature. Titles should not be included in the signature; however, to indicate how women prefer to be addressed in return correspondence, they sometimes will write Miss, Mrs., Ms., Dr., and so on, in parentheses before the typed name.

Possible Letter Styles.   Your business letter can follow any of three styles.

Use block style, modified block style, or semiblock style for your business letter.

In some ways, the *block style* is the simplest of the three styles. In block style, all parts of the letter are aligned at the left margin. No lines are indented, not even the first line of a paragraph. Notice in the following diagram that spacing is used to set off each of the six parts of the letter and each paragraph in the body of the letter.

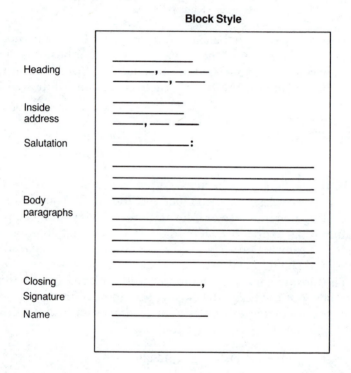

Block Style

In *modified block style,* the heading is placed, not in the upper left-hand portion of the letter, but in the upper right-hand portion of the letter. The closing and signature are aligned in a similar right-hand position at the end of the letter. Between these parts, the inside address, salutation, and body paragraphs all begin at the left margin, as in the diagram at the top of the next page. *Semiblock style,* also shown on the next page, resembles modified block style, except that the first line of each body paragraph is indented, just as it would be in a personal letter. This is the only business style that calls for indented paragraphs.

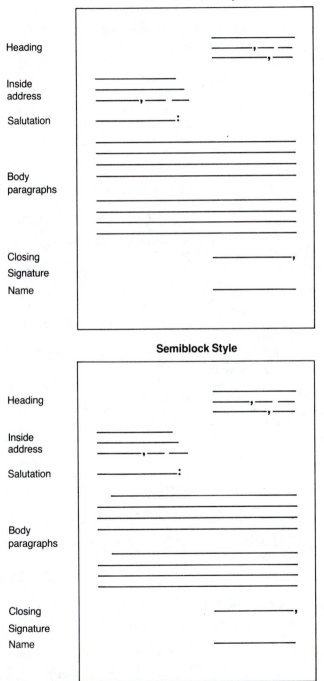

Modified Block Style

Heading

Inside address

Salutation

Body paragraphs

Closing
Signature
Name

Semiblock Style

Heading

Inside address

Salutation

Body paragraphs

Closing
Signature
Name

The *second page* of any business letter should have a heading of its own. In this case, you should place the name of the recipient of the letter, the page number of the letter, and the date of writing at the top of the paper.

Other features of business letters include letterhead stationery, which you may use if you write for a specific company, or standard-sized white paper ($8\frac{1}{2} \times 11$ inches, or 21.6×27.9 cm). It is usually better to type business letters, if possible. Your margins should be at least one inch on all sides of the paper. And you should double- or triple-space between paragraphs and other parts of the letter.

Procedures for Mailing.   Just as you prepare personal letters for mailing, you should follow some simple guidelines for mailing business letters.

Fold your business letter correctly in thirds and prepare an envelope following business style.

Your business envelope should be standard business size, matching your stationery. Your return address in the upper left-hand corner should contain your name (without any title) and address. And the mailing address should match the inside address on the letter. All business envelopes should follow the style of the following diagram.

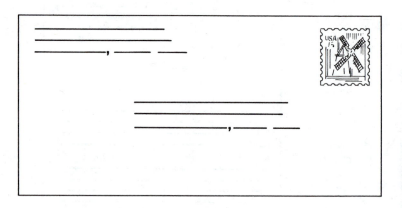

Types of Business Letters.   Different types of business letters will serve different, specific purposes.

Understand the characteristics of some different types of business letters: request and order letters, letters of application, and letters of complaint and opinion.

Request and order letters are written to obtain information or merchandise. The body should be explicit and to the point. You should begin by stating your specific request; that is, the particular items of information you want or certain pieces of merchandise in the quantity you want. Include any information that your recipient will need to know in order to help you: the reason for your request, for instance, or order numbers and other identifying information for your order. If you send money with such a letter, be sure to state the amount of the enclosure as well as the form in which you have sent the money. The following is an example of an order letter.

310 Monterey Avenue
Los Angeles, California 90007
March 27, 1981

Order Department
Fresh and Salt - Fish and Tackle, Inc.
Whittier, California 90054

Dear Sir:

I would like to order the following items from your 1980/81 Outdoorsman catalogue. To complete my order, I have enclosed a money order for $45.00, which includes postage and handling costs.

Amount	Item	Price
1	Deluxe Golden Rod fishing pole Order Number: 037	$23.00
15	Pack sets of assorted lures Order Number: 050	22.00
		$45.00

Sincerely,

Phyllis Porter

Phyllis Porter

To seek employment or to answer an advertisement for a job, you might write a *letter of application*. In such a case, a letter is generally preferable to a phone call since it gives the employer a chance to reply at his or her leisure. The following is an example of a letter of application written by a student who is seeking summer employment as a waiter.

```
                          16 Timpson Street
                          Providence, Rhode Island 02908
                          May 2, 1981

Manager
The Thruway Diner
Route 1
Providence, Rhode Island 02908

Dear Sir or Madam:

        I will be spending this summer at home, and
I am seeking employment for the period beginning
June 1, 1981, through September 1, 1981. I am 18
years old and will be a freshman at Brown Univer-
sity in the fall.

        I have worked on Long Island for the last
three summers, first as a busboy and then as a
waiter at the Silver Sun Inn, Greenvale, New York.
My former employer is available to offer a
reference:

                Mr. Ted Wilson, Manager
                The Silver Sun Inn
                Greenvale, New York 11548

        I can be reached at home if you need addi-
tional information. My phone number in Providence
is (401) 555-1036.

                    Sincerely,

                    Stephen M. Zook
                    Stephen M. Zook
```

Notice that the preceding letter contains the six basic parts of a business letter and includes certain special details. First, it identifies the reason for which the letter is being written. Then, it provides background information, such as work experience, that may help qualify the letter writer for a job. Finally, it provides a reference as well as other information that the recipient may need to know. It also supplies a telephone number at which the letter writer can be reached. Letters of application can also include relevant enclosures, such as résumés and other records.

You may have occasion to write other types of business letters, such as *letters of complaint and opinion.* For instance, to exchange faulty merchandise, to remedy poor services, or to indicate that you have not received something you ordered, you may need to write a letter of complaint. To solve a problem of this kind, you should present your point clearly and objectively at the beginning of the body of the letter, and you should supply any information that will help the recipient understand and help you.

When you want to voice your opinion or take a stand on something, such as a local issue or a program that you have seen, you may want to write a letter of opinion. In such a letter, you should begin the body with your particular opinion or stand and then develop or support it logically, using appropriate methods of persuasion. In both letters of complaint and letters of opinion, you should be as reasonable and polite as possible, while still taking care to communicate your point thoroughly and clearly.

EXERCISE D: Practicing with the Parts of Business Letters. Use two separate pieces of business-sized stationery to sketch two skeleton letters. Use one style for the first letter and another style for the second. Label each letter with the style you are following. Use lines to represent the body paragraphs. Use your own address for the heading and a local business address for the inside address and salutation.

EXERCISE E: Preparing Business Letters for Mailing. Prepare an envelope for each of the skeleton letters in Exercise D. Follow proper business form for the envelope, and then fold each letter correctly before placing it inside. Leave the envelope unsealed.

EXERCISE F: **Writing Different Types of Business Letters.** Use any one of the following ideas to write a business letter. Be sure to include all six parts of the letter and to use your own name and address. When you have completed the letter, prepare an envelope for it.

1. Think of some television show or commercial that you have seen recently. Write to someone who is involved, such as a writer, director, or programmer, expressing your particular stand or opinion. You should have the name of a specific person and a correct address.
2. Find a catalog from any store and choose merchandise that you might order. Write a letter ordering more than one piece of merchandise and include any necessary information.
3. Recall a situation in which you were disappointed by some service you did or did not receive, or else imagine an experience that would cause you to complain. Write an appropriate letter.
4. Write a letter of application. Identify a position you would like to hold and find the necessary application and mailing information.
5. Write to a college or other school requesting some specific piece of information. Offer a reason for your request. Again, you will have to locate the necessary information for addressing and mailing your letter.

APPLICATION: **Writing a Personal or Business Letter.** Think of a real purpose you might have for writing a letter at this time. Determine the type of personal or business letter you want to send. Review the guidelines for this type of letter and then write it. After your letter is written, prepare an envelope.

26.2 Completing the Essay Portion of Applications

When you answer essay questions on college or job application forms, you may encounter a number of different types of questions on diverse topics. Your first step will be to understand the specific requirements of the question. Then your other writing skills will help you present yourself and your ideas clearly to make a good impression.

■ Understanding Questions on College and Job Applications

Most college applications for admissions and for scholarships will require samples of your writing in response to some questions. On a single college application, you might be asked to write several paragraph answers as well as an essay answer. Job applications, also, may require a writing sample, usually only a paragraph-length answer. In all instances, the people who read your answers will look at your organization, style, and knowledge of grammar, mechanics, and usage, as well as your ideas.

To begin any response on a college or job application, you must examine the question closely and try to envision the length and form (paragraph or essay) of your answer.

Determine the specific requirements of an essay question on an application.

The purpose of almost any application question is to find out several important things: (1) the quality of your ideas about certain topics, (2) special knowledge that you may possess, or (3) personal information about you. And *all* applications seek to determine how well you can express yourself in writing.

Writing on College Applications.   College admissions officials often need to determine how well applicants write. In addition, they may seek information about such things as your extracurricular activities and your educational goals. Usually, the wording of the question will indicate how long your response should be.

College applications will often contain any of three types of questions, as illustrated in the following chart.

QUESTIONS ON COLLEGE APPLICATIONS	
Type of Question	**Sample Question**
1. *Topical* questions ask you for your understanding, interpretation, or stand on some idea of general interest.	Discuss a problem that faces your country, state, city, home, or school. In your answer, include the origin and some possible solutions to the problem.

2. *Goal* questions ask for specific ideas that you have about your future, both as a future college student and after graduation.	Describe at least one educational objective, interest, or professional goal that has led you to apply to this school.
3. *Personal* questions ask for background information about your school and personal life.	Tell us about one or more of your interests or skills—in or out of high school—explaining how you acquired and developed them.

The directions or the question itself will generally indicate the length for an appropriate answer. The topical question in the chart, for example, might best be answered in an essay with separate paragraphs to identify the problem and to discuss its origin and possible solutions. Other questions may require answers of only one paragraph each. The goal question in the chart, for instance, might be covered in a paragraph that describes your "educational objective, interest, or professional goal." This goal could be stated in the topic sentence, and the support could provide relevant explanations.

A sample essay answer to the topical question in the chart follows. Notice how the labels on the left point out the structure.

Essay answer on a college application

Introductory remarks (origin of the problem)

Thesis statement

First body paragraph (solutions to the problem)

Because my home town lies near a large city, many people drive to the city for work, cultural activities, and even recreation. As a result, our town is often a boring, uneventful place. Many senior citizens and young people have little to do, and most young people cannot wait to leave. Yet the residents who are using their ideas, energy, and money elsewhere could change the mentality of our town. If interested residents and local government officials would turn their talents toward this community, they could give our town a new identity.

Homeowners, members of the school board, and local merchants could create numerous cultural, creative, and athletic activities. Working through the schools, for example, local residents could organize an acting group, art shows (featuring local talent), "white elephant" sales, performances of local musicians, and community courses, which could be conducted in the schools or in one of the churches. These courses could feature exercise, auto mechanics, dancing, guitar, yoga, gourmet cooking, creative writing, and many other subjects. Adults could also become more involved in athletic events. The community could have a soccer team or hold a yearly tennis or golf tournament. With some cooperation from local merchants, the empty warehouse could be converted into a roller skating rink. By sponsoring events such as picnics and bazaars that coordinate with varsity football or baseball games, residents would help to draw larger crowds, both for the games and for the activities.

Second body
paragraph
(solutions to
the problem)

Town officials could also encourage the participation of residents. With planning and publicity, officials could initiate events such as a Founders' Day celebration, which could include barbecues and a band. And the town could plan a spring or autumn carnival that could have field activities, rides, game booths, and refreshment stands. The town board could encourage local merchants to donate prizes and gifts, to advertise "specials," and to display products of interest. Surely, school and religious groups would gladly become involved.

Reminder of
the thesis
statement

Conclusion

If people in our town, especially the local government officials, would decide to develop and expand the activities in our town, the results could only be positive. What now appears to be a sleepy suburban town might become a lively, energetic community full of people who enjoy living here and who have fun together.

Writing on Job Applications.   For the most part, a job application will require one- or two- sentence answers for each question. Most of the writing that you would submit to a job interviewer would be on your résumé, an outline of your educational background and job experiences. Yet, occasionally, you will encounter an application that requests a longer writing sample. These samples provide the interviewer with information about your writing ability and any special knowledge, abilities, or experience you might bring to the job.

The following chart offers examples of three types of questions most often found on job applications.

QUESTIONS ON JOB APPLICATIONS	
Type of Question	**Sample Question**
1. *Specialized* questions ask for special knowledge that you might have to offer a business.	Describe three different business machines often used in a secretarial office, and explain how each is operated.

2. *Problem-solving* questions present a difficult situation or other problem that you might encounter on the job.	As a social worker, you might be asked to help an impoverished family of four budget their small income. How would you proceed?
3. *Personal* questions ask for background information about you. Often, such questions seek proof of your suitability for a particular job.	Describe past experiences that you feel qualify you for work with the Recreation Commission.

Depending on the amount of information requested and on the complexity of the question, you may write a paragraph answer or essay answer. The preceding *specialized* question might be answered in an essay having a brief introduction, three body paragraphs (one for each business machine), and a brief conclusion. The *personal* question, on the other hand, might be answered in a single paragraph, as in the following model. Often, businesses require complete but short answers; a good solid paragraph will often suffice.

Paragraph answer on a job application

I seek employment as an assistant recreation director because of my experiences in the field. I have been working in local recreation departments for the past two years, or since my sophomore year in high school. I started as a playground supervisor, and by the time I was a junior, I was working with the local director on programming and planning. I helped to initiate new programs, such as our Apple Cider Field Day, in which townspeople picked apples and made cider. I also helped update the old programs, making them more suitable to the people they were serving. For example, I supervised the reconditioning of an old horseshoe field. In addition, I have taken courses in first aid, health, sociology, psychology, music, art, and physical education, which have prepared me to perform any nonrecreational responsibilities that I may encounter.

EXERCISE A: **Becoming Acquainted with Questions on College and Job Applications.** Find at least five applications for college admission, scholarship, and employment; you should collect at least one of each type. To find these, visit your school's guidance office as well as local colleges and business firms. From these applications, list any five questions that require answers of either paragraph or essay length.

EXERCISE B: **Recognizing the Requirements of Application Questions.** Using the five questions that you found in Exercise A or the following sample questions, interpret the requirements of the application questions. For each question, identify its type (*topical, specialized, personal,* and so forth). Then determine the requirements of the question, decide on the best length for an answer, and rough out a possible organization for the answer.

1. (College) What personal experience has had a significant impact on your life?
2. (College) To get to know you as well as possible through this application, we would like to know about your special interests and achievements and how these have influenced your life.
3. (College Scholarship) Discuss Daniel Webster's statement: "Liberty exists in proportion to wholesome restraint."
4. (Job) What jobs or work-related experience have you had during the last two years?
5. (Job) If you were interviewing someone for this position, how would you describe the job requirements to him or her?

■ Planning and Writing a Response

Once you understand what an application question is asking and the length and form your answer should take, you should follow some thinking and organizing steps. Then you should write, check your answer, and rewrite it in final form.

Follow the steps for planning, writing, and revising a paragraph or essay.

Writing a composition on an application follows a process similar to the writing process discussed in previous chapters.

Focusing Your Main Idea. After you have identified the requirements of an application, limit your topic to something fairly specific that you can write about in a paragraph or an essay. Often questions on applications are broad and open-ended. It is up to you to focus a topic to an idea you can cover well in the space you are given. You should consider both the complexity and scope of the question and your own ideas, and then zero in on a manageable topic and main idea. For a paragraph, shape your main idea about the question into a topic sentence. For an essay, choose a slightly larger main point and shape it into a thesis statement, possibly with subtopics. Your topic sentence or thesis statement should give your basic response to the application question and indicate your expository or persuasive purpose.

The following diagram shows the thinking process you can follow, using the initial planning of the topical question essay on page 814 as an example.

FROM ANALYZING A QUESTION TO FOCUSING AN ANSWER	
Analyze question	Discuss a problem that faces your country, state, city, home, or school. In your answer, include the origin and some possible solutions to the problem.
↓	↓
Decide on length	Essay length
↓	↓
Write thesis statement —include subtopics —indicate purpose	If *interested residents* and local *government officials* Subtopic A Subtopic B would turn their talents toward this community, *they could give our town a new identity.* (statement of opinion indicates a persuasive purpose)
↓	↓
Think about support	What can interested residents do? What can local government officials do?

Brainstorming and Outlining.   When you have a topic sentence or thesis statement, you should list all ideas and information that you have for the support. Try to find specific examples, details, facts, and reasons that will make your answer concrete and interesting. Weak, vague, or rambling answers give a bad impression of the writer.

Once you have a substantial list of supporting material, you should organize the material logically. For an essay, group your ideas into paragraphs according to subtopics of your thesis statement. Then group information under each subtopic. Be sure to eliminate ideas that repeat or stray from your main point. When you have chosen the order and content of your answer, you might jot down a modified outline to guide you as you write.

Writing and Revising Your Answer.   Before you write or type your answer on the application, you should write a first draft. Follow your outline, but feel free to make additions, deletions, or alterations. As you write, concentrate on sticking to the point and on connecting your ideas smoothly. Also, try to write concisely by stating your ideas directly and clearly. Write on every other line of your paper so that you can make revisions.

Finally, you should check and polish your answer. You should reread your answer carefully, and use a checklist such as those in Section 21.2, page 645, and Section 23.2, page 723, to inspect all key features of your paragraph or essay.

When you are satisfied with any corrections and revisions that you have made on the first draft, write a good final copy. If space has been provided on the application, place your answer there if it will fit; otherwise, add a sheet of your own paper to the application, and, in the space provided for your answer, indicate that a page has been added.

If possible, type your paragraph or essay answer. Anyone who reads the application will appreciate one that is typed.

EXERCISE C: Focusing a Main Idea to Answer an Application Question. Choose one of the questions that you worked on in Exercise B. Write this question on the top of your paper. Beneath the question, indicate whether you will write a paragraph- or essay-length answer. Then write a thesis statement or topic sentence to express your basic answer. Be sure to focus your purpose and clarify any subtopics for a thesis statement.

EXERCISE D: Developing and Organizing Your Answer. Beneath the topic sentence or thesis statement that you wrote in Exercise C, list as many ideas as you can to develop and support your answer. When you have completed your list, prepare a modified outline or rough plan of your answer.

EXERCISE E: Completing Your Answer. Use your modified outline from Exercise D to write a first draft of the paragraph or essay. Follow the outline, but incorporate any good ideas that occur to you. Write concisely and connect your ideas smoothly for the reader. Also, write on every other line of your paper. Then reread the first draft. Make all corrections and revisions, using a checklist to guide you, and write a final copy.

APPLICATION: Planning and Writing a Response to an Application Question. Choose another question from a college or job application. Then follow the steps in this section for planning, writing, and revising a response. If you wrote a paragraph for Exercise E, now write an essay.

Chapter 27

Précis and Essay Examinations

You will always need to know how to write compositions to meet the requirements of particular situations. In your classes and in many occupations, you may be asked to write a *précis*, a summary of material you have read. And you will also be called upon to write compositions of different lengths in response to examination questions, usually with specified time limits. This chapter will help you apply what you have already learned in studying paragraphs, essays, and other compositions to the specialized tasks of writing précis and examination answers.

27.1 Writing Précis

A *précis* is a synopsis or summary of a piece of writing, typically of an essay, article, or chapter of a book. Written in your own words, the précis condenses the main ideas and major details into a shortened but accurate version of the original.

Your teachers may ask you to write a précis to test your comprehension of reading assignments or to help you remember important ideas in certain short works. On your own, you might find the précis a valuable study and writing aid, helping you to express main ideas precisely as well as to record and store information you have gathered in preparing a speech or library paper. For these reasons, learning to recognize and to plan, write, and revise précis can be a useful skill. This section presents certain key features you should consider when writing a précis. It also contains original articles and précis of them for you to compare. Then you will be ready to plan, write, and revise a précis of your own.

■ Key Features of a Précis

Before you can write a précis, you should understand the makeup and purpose of a précis. A précis is a summary of another piece of writing. In this sense, it differs from a composition that you would plan and organize entirely on your own. It does not contain any analyses, interpretations, opinions, or other ideas of yours. Rather, a précis preserves the main ideas, purpose, organization, and tone of the original. In writing a précis, your aim should be to reduce the original by eliminating the less important ideas and expressing the basic content in your own words.

A précis is a well-written condensation or abridgement of an original work, which preserves the original's main ideas and major details, its purpose and basic organization, and even its tone, but uses different language from the original.

The following example illustrates the relationship between an original article and a précis of it. Notice that the précis, which follows the original, is shorter than the actual article because minor details have been omitted and the main ideas have been compressed. The précis preserves the original's tone and, except for the repositioning of a few details, follows its basic organization. The précis also finds new words to express the original's ideas and is a coherent, well-written composition.

ARTICLE:

Locked in the steamy Guatemalan jungle, the three huge mounds had long intrigued archaeologists. But it was not until 1978 that a major expedition began excavating the swampy site known as *El Mirador.* Experts are now convinced that their findings will dramatically rewrite the history of Mayan civilization.

In the first two digging seasons, teams from Brigham Young University in Provo, Utah, and Washington's Catholic University of America turned up pottery shards older than the earliest known cities in the New World. These fragments showed that El Mirador flourished in the three centuries before Christ—one thousand years before the rest of the Mayan empire reached its zenith. The scientists also began to uncover extensive reservoirs, public plazas, and clusters of residential buildings. This suggested that El Mirador supported diverse political, social, and economic activities.

Archaeologists didn't understand the full extent of El Mirador's lost glory until this season. The most spectacular discovery was the great stone pyramid. It rises twenty stories high from a base 1,000 feet across, making it one of the largest buildings of

antiquity. Such immense size means that someone had authority to order thousands of workers to quarry and carry great
stone blocks. "It requires the organization of a state," says Ray-
mond Matheny of Brigham Young. Most experts had doubted
that Mayan civilization in 300 B.C. was so advanced.

The latest expedition unearthed other examples of sophistication. At the top of a staircase, archaeologists found a perfectly
preserved stucco figure of a jaguar—a 20-foot-long, anthropo-
morphic cat that is probably a deity. The early inhabitants of El
Mirador also were skilled scientists. The structures radiating
from the great pyramid seem to provide a kind of celestial compass, pinpointing such events as the summer solstice. And there
are hints of Mayan class structure: Some homes, outfitted with
built-in beds and separate kitchens, undoubtedly belonged to
the Mayan elite.

The great mystery of El Mirador remains its collapse. After
sampling soil for clues to past climates, Catholic University's
Bruce Dahlin now suspects that a severe drop in rainfall—combined with a booming population—may have doomed the me-
tropolis. Ironically, drought may also have triggered the birth of
El Mirador: A dry spell coincided with its founding, perhaps
forcing the Mayans to band together to build reservoirs to store
water. But after the population growth, not even the reservoirs
could prevent the disaster. —*Newsweek*

PRÉCIS:

Long a source of mystery to archaeologists, three large
mounds in the Guatemalan jungle called El Mirador have been
discovered to be the remnants of an advanced Mayan civilization dating from 300 B.C. This dramatic relevation suggests that
Mayan civilization reached a high level of sophistication at an
earlier date than had previously been supposed.

Archaeologists from Brigham Young University and Catholic
University were especially impressed with a stone pyramid
twenty stories high and one thousand feet across, a building
whose monumental proportions imply the surprisingly early existence of a state with the authority to complete such a massive
undertaking. In addition, reservoirs, plazas, and elaborate residences imply the existence of a complex and organized society,
one which probably had a distinct class structure.

Archaeologists are still puzzled over the fall of this advanced
civilization, speculating that drought combined with overpopu-
lation may have brought an end to El Mirador. In an ironic parallel, some experts believe that an earlier drought had caused
Mayans to found the city in the first place, as a means of conserving water.

When you examine a précis closely, you should find five key
features: A précis should substantially *shorten* the original,
should accurately *represent* the original's main ideas, purpose
and tone, should *observe the order* of the original's information,

should *reword* the original, using fresh language, and should be a *skillfully written* composition in its own right.

Reduction.   A précis reduces the original work to its major points by eliminating less significant material. It may be as brief as one-tenth the length of the original, or it may be one-half its length, depending on the nature of the materials and the amount of detail the précis-writer decides to include.

The précis of the article on El Mirador, for instance, is about two-fifths the length of the original. It has condensed the article to its essential ideas and significant facts, while omitting the less important points and details. For example, where the original describes several structures and artifacts besides the great stone pyramid, the précis focuses only on the pyramid and summarizes other details. The précis also combines the ideas of two or three sentences into a single sentence. A précis of a longer article might even reduce several paragraphs to a sentence or two.

Accurate Representation of Main Ideas, Purpose, and Tone.   The main ideas of the original should become the main ideas of the précis. And the most important details should support these points with all vital information accurately taken from the original. You should not add material or alter the meaning, purpose, or tone of the piece you are reducing, nor should you interpret, analyze, or draw your own conclusions. Instead, the précis should accurately reflect the content, purpose, and tone of the original. For instance, in the preceding example, an explanatory article with an informative but somewhat informal tone is reduced to a précis that captures that purpose and tone.

Observance of Order.   The original follows its own basic organization and logical order of ideas, and the précis should reflect these as closely as possible. For instance, if the original follows chronological order, the précis should also use this order. If one idea is given more attention in the original than another idea, this emphasis should be reflected in your précis. If the précis includes clearly defined parts or sections, such as a distinct introduction, body, and conclusion, you should not depart greatly from this pattern, although of course, your précis will be shorter.

Rewording.   In a précis, you must use your own words to express the significant ideas and details of the original. You may have to repeat certain words from the original, such as specialized terms, but you should use new words wherever you can. Furthermore, you should always try to find exact equivalents for the shades of meaning and level of language used in the original. Actually, rewording is a helpful exercise because it makes you process the information mentally and helps you to find ways of condensing the original.

Skillful Writing. As with any other type of composition, you should write a précis in a smooth, clear style, choosing your words carefully, and varying your sentence lengths and structures. A précis should be a coherent, well-written composition that makes sense on its own, rather than a disjointed list of the points in the original. You may not always be able to produce an exact equivalent of a particularly clever or eloquent original article, but you should create a composition that is gracefully and intelligently written and enjoyable to read.

EXERCISE A: Examining the Key Features of a Précis. The following is an article about rodents and a précis of the article. Read each carefully and then answer the questions that follow. You may need to refer to both article and précis as you write your answers.

ARTICLE:

We rarely see most of them, but they are all around us, day and night: the animals that belong to the order Rodentia. We know them as rats and mice, squirrels and chipmunks, woodchucks and prairie dogs. In numbers of individuals and species, this order is the largest group of mammals in North America—and on earth.

How many are there: We do not know. We can only guess that of the 4,200 living species of animals, nearly 40 percent belong to the order Rodentia. Even though we may know of some of them by their common names, they are all rodents (from the Latin word *rodere*—to gnaw). For gnaw is what they all do to stay alive.

They live in more land areas than any other order—in forest and in desert, on farm and in city. Some places have more rodents than other places. California, Oregon, and Washington, for instance, have about twice as many species as are found in all of western Europe. And, though we think of them as small, they do come in many sizes. The South American capybara—a giant relative of the guinea pig—weighs about 100 pounds. Some mice weigh less than an ounce. In North America, the largest rodent is the beaver. The smallest is the pygmy mouse, whose body is only two inches long.

Rodents are of considerable economic importance to every one of us—particularly as pests that feed on our crops, stored grains, and trees. Some rodents serve as hosts for fleas, lice, and other parasites that transmit disease to people or domestic animals. The classic example is bubonic plague, or "black death," which is transmitted by a flea that lives on the black rat. A similar plague is harbored in the western United States by ground squirrels, prairie dogs, and some voles. The disease, which is often fatal, has been transmitted to humans, probably by fleas.

On the positive side, the native beaver and muskrat, along with the introduced nutria, annually yield furs worth millions of dollars. Laboratory rats and mice have been used extensively in medical research on human diseases and in studies of basic biology. Hunters derive enjoyment from hunting squirrels, which, early in our history, were a valuable food resource. — *Wild Animals of North America.*

PRÉCIS:

Although we are hardly aware of them, members of the order Rodentia, or rodents, which includes rats, mice, squirrels, chipmunks, and woodchucks, are populous and pervasive. Nearly 40 percent of all living mammals on earth are classified as rodents—which makes them the largest class of mammals.

In addition to their large numbers, rodents inhabit more areas of land than any other species. Rodents are found in just about any habitable place, although their numbers may be highly concentrated in certain areas such as the Pacific Coast states.

The sizes of rodents also vary widely. In South America, the capybara, a relative of the guinea pig, can weigh as much as 100 pounds, while some mice can weigh less than an ounce.

Rodents can be dangerous, but they are also valuable to people for many reasons. While some rodents carry parasites that cause diseases and plagues, others provide economic benefits. Beaver and muskrat are valuable for clothing and provide their breeders with ample profits. In medicine, rats and mice are useful to scientists who study diseases and biology.

1. By how much does the précis reduce the original? Should the précis be longer or shorter and why?
2. What main ideas from the original are included in the précis? What major details have been chosen to support them? Would you have eliminated any of the supporting details?
3. To what extent does the précis accurately represent the ideas and intent of the original? What other main ideas or major details in the original would you have included in the précis?
4. Compare the order of ideas in the précis with the order in the original. Where has the order of the original been altered?

5. What main words from the original are repeated in the précis? What words are substituted for main words in the original?

6. How varied and smooth are the sentences in the précis? What alterations or refinements, if any, would you make in the style of the précis?

■ Planning, Writing, and Revising a Précis

Creating a précis draws as heavily upon your reading and note-taking skills as it does on your writing skills. You must read and reread the original, analyze, select, and express its ideas in your own words, and finally polish your condensation for conciseness, accuracy, and style.

Planning the Précis.   Your first step in writing a précis involves reading the original carefully several times and taking accurate notes.

> Begin by reading the original several times to understand its content, purpose, and tone and then take notes on the main ideas and major details in your own words.

Planning requires several different activities presented as steps in the following chart.

PLANNING THE PRÉCIS

1. Read the original several times to absorb as much information about it as you can. First, determine the main point and the author's purpose and tone. Then, take note of any subtopics, other main ideas, major details, and the organization of ideas.

2. Figure out the meaning of all words in the original by using a dictionary or other reference work if necessary.

3. Decide on the length of your précis to determine how much nonessential material to omit. If your précis is going to be much shorter than the original, you will have to mention only the most prominent ideas. If the original contains a great deal of information, you should probably expect to write a longer précis.

4. Take notes logically. Select only the most important information in each paragraph, expressing it in your own words. Decide which pieces of less vital information and which details you can summarize generally; identify other details that you can omit altogether. Include in your notes main words from the original that you must use, and try to preserve the tone of the original with your other word choices.

5. Check your notes for accuracy; see if you have followed the organization of the original as closely as possible, without adding any comments of your own.

Writing the Précis. To write the précis, you should use your notes and focus both on doing justice to the original and on producing your own shortened version.

> Write a first draft by grouping and phrasing your notes into well-structured sentences that reflect the original's main content, purpose, tone, and organization and that reduce the original.

As you write, pull the information you listed in your notes together into coherent sentences and paragraphs, aiming for the length you tentatively set in your planning step. Do not draw conclusions or otherwise go beyond the original material. Find language that captures the tone and purpose of the original. Be prepared to experiment with your wording; write several versions of a sentence, if necessary, to express an idea accurately and to condense points into a few phrases. Look for ways of joining ideas in your sentences and for words and phrases that could be used to cover several items in the original. You should try to make your précis both unified and coherent.

Revising the Précis. When you revise, you should check your draft for length, accuracy, and organization.

> Revise your précis by looking for ways to shorten it further and by checking the accuracy and quality of your writing.

You should particularly evaluate the length and exactness of your précis. You can do this by comparing your précis with the original, side by side. If your précis is too long, you should look for details to omit. You should also check your précis with the original, paragraph by paragraph, to see whether you have neglected any important ideas or included anything that was not necessary. Make sure that you have not changed facts or ideas or misrepresented the purpose or tone of the article you are reducing.

Finally, you should check the smoothness, clarity, and style of the writing by reading your précis out loud to hear the rhythm of your sentences. Consider adding transitions to improve coherence, and look for ways to vary your sentence openers and structures.

The following checklist provides guidelines for revising your précis. When you answer each question, go back to your précis, read it, and examine the particular feature under consideration.

CHECKING AND REVISING YOUR PRÉCIS

1. Does your précis reduce the original to a significantly shorter piece of writing? Have you met a desirable length?
2. Have you included all of the main ideas and major details of the original?
3. Have you reproduced the ideas and purpose of the original without adding opinions or outside pieces of information?
4. Do your own word choices accurately reflect both the purpose and the tone of the original?
5. Have you followed the basic organization and any particular arrangements in the original?
6. Have you used original language in your précis while maintaining the writer's level of language and shades of meaning?
7. Can your précis be understood without the original?
8. Is your précis free of grammatical, mechanical, and spelling errors?

EXERCISE B: Planning a Précis. Read the following article carefully in order to write a précis of it. Make sure you understand its main ideas and major details, and then decide on a length for your précis. Take notes in your own words, using the chart on page 826 as a guide.

ARTICLE:

Two-thirds of the Atlantic's commercially valuable fish and shellfish rely on the salt marsh for food. Crabs and mussels make the creeks a permanent home. Flounder are winter residents, coming into the marsh to feed and to spawn. Bass and menhaden use the warm tidal waters as a summer nursery. For others—smelt, alewives, and shad—the marsh is an important way station on the route to fresh-water spawning grounds.

The ebbing and flowing tides are the farmers of the marsh, watering the grasses, feeding the fish and shellfish, and cleaning away the waste.

The salt marsh is one of our country's most fertile resources, more productive than fields of wheat and hay. Each year, the salt marsh produces up to ten tons of organic material per acre.

During the same time, an acre of hay produces only four tons; an'acre of wheat, two tons. Wheat and hay require extensive cultivation, expensive fertilizers, and deliberate pest control. The salt marsh yields its bountiful harvest year after year, without depleting its resources or reducing its productivity.

The rhythm of life on the marsh is constant, tuned to the nourishing tides. The harvest, begun in autumn as the grasses die, continues all year. By the end of winter, most of the marsh hay will have disappeared. Anything left by the insects or bacteria sinks into the marsh as a rich peat, ready to fertilize the new grass in the spring.

Many years ago, the salt marsh was a barren ice field. When the glacier melted and the ocean rose, the wind blew in the first seeds of marsh grass. Over six million acres of salt marsh grew behind the newly formed barrier beaches and tidal rivers. Today, fewer than two million acres of salt marsh remain on the Atlantic coast. The rest have been lost to development—to housing, marinas, causeways, and dump sites. What we have thrown away through ignorance and selfishness is not only an aesthetic pleasure, a reassuring contrast to our congested highways and polluted cities, but also an invaluable resource, critical to our food supply. We have the means to protect our salt marshes—through local conservation commissions, state wetlands-protection laws, and Federal coastal-zone management policies. All we need is the will. —Adapted from Deborah Cramer

EXERCISE C: Writing a Draft of Your Précis.

Using your notes from Exercise B, write a first draft of your précis. Compose varied sentences that condense and join the information in your notes. Concentrate on smoothness and style and try to match the length you decided on. Be sure to preserve the main ideas and major details of the original article, to use your own words, and to avoid inserting your own opinions.

EXERCISE D: Revising the Précis.

Comparing your précis to the original article and using the checklist on page 828, correct and improve your draft in whatever way you can. Delete ideas or add information and replace words as you see necessary. When you are satisfied, write a good final copy.

APPLICATION: Planning, Writing, and Revising a Précis.

By looking through magazines, collections of essays, and other works, find an article—no longer than a page—for which you could write a précis. Then write a précis, following the planning, writing, and revising steps in this section.

Writing Answers to Essay Exam Questions

27.2

As you take exams now and in future years, you will often be required to write paragraph- and essay-length answers to examination questions. Certainly, you will adapt the skills you have developed in writing paragraphs and essays to this task. But writing with a time limit on an exam adds a particular kind of pressure, and in addition, different kinds of essay questions call for specific types of answers. This section will give you practice in handling the challenges involved in answering essay questions.

■ Budgeting Your Time

On most exams, you will have a limited amount of time. The examination may include only essay questions, or it may also have objective questions. You must learn to budget your time so that you can finish all portions of any exam; in particular, you must allow enough time to complete all of the steps that are involved in planning and writing your answers to essay questions.

Before you actually begin an exam, allot blocks of time for the different parts of the exam, allowing enough time for all steps involved in answering essay questions.

First, you should skim the exam to see how many and what kinds of questions you must answer. You should rapidly determine the difficulty of each part and assess the amount of time you might need to complete each part satisfactorily. Quickly sketch out a schedule for yourself. The following chart offers an example.

SAMPLE SCHEDULE FOR A ONE HOUR EXAM (10:00 - 11:00)		
Activity	**Time**	**Breakdown**
20 multiple choice questions	20 minutes —finished by 10:20	1 min. for each

1 essay	40 minutes —be ready to write by 10:30 —stop writing at 10:55 to check	10 min.: plan and outline 25 min.: write 5 min.: check and revise

Determine approximately when you need to finish each part of the exam and each step in order to complete the exam on time. You should try to keep to your schedule as closely as possible by checking the time occasionally.

EXERCISE A: Practicing with Budgeting Your Time. Each of the following items represents a possible examination. For each, sketch a schedule showing how you would divide your time in each situation. Pay special attention to the steps you would follow in writing an essay.

1. Sixty minutes for ten multiple choice questions and two essays
2. Forty minutes for ten true-false questions and one short essay
3. Sixty minutes for ten fill-in questions, two short essays, and one more difficult essay
4. Forty-five minutes for two essays, one more difficult than the other
5. Forty-five minutes for ten short answer (one sentence each) questions and one essay

■ Understanding the Question

As you read an essay question, determine its specific requirements so that you can plan an accurate answer.

Identify the specific requirements of an essay question by finding clues to the types of support you will need to supply.

Different essay questions will make different demands. You must identify the requirements of each in order to write concise, appropriate answers in the time given. Your first step is to look for word clues that indicate the kinds of information that each question requires. If you can recognize these clues, you will find it easier to plan a suitable answer. The following

chart explains some common kinds of questions and lists word
clues that identify them. The chart also shows the type of support each kind of question calls for.

WORD CLUES IN ESSAY EXAM QUESTIONS		
Kind of Question	**Word Clues**	**Support Needed**
Compare	*compare, similarities, resemblances, likenesses*	Specific examples and details that show similarities
Contrast	*contrast, differ, differences*	Specific examples and details that show differences
Definition	*define, explain*	Examples and details to explain what something is or means
Description	*describe*	Specific examples and details to present the main features of something
Diagram	*draw, chart, diagram, plot*	A drawing or chart with labels and explanations
Discussion	*discuss, explain*	One or more general statements and supporting facts, examples, and details
Explanation	*explain why, what, how, to what extent, in what ways*	Examples, details, and facts that show how something happens, what it is, why it is so
Illustration	*illustrate, draw*	Concrete examples with explanations to demonstrate the significance or truth of an idea
Opinion	*assess the validity, what do you think, defend your idea, state your opinion*	A clear statement of your opinion supported by facts, examples, reasons

| Interpretation | *significance, meaning of (quotations or events), influence, analyze* | Your idea about the overall meaning of something, with examples, facts, reasons to support your idea |
| Prediction | *If . . . then* *What . . . if* | Your prediction or other statement of the logical outcome; information and arguments in support |

EXERCISE B: **Interpreting the Requirements of Essay Questions.** Each of the following questions might be found on an examination. Read each carefully, looking for word clues. For each one, identify the kind of question and briefly indicate the kind of support you might need to answer it. Try to limit yourself to three minutes for each question. Do not be concerned about finding actual pieces of support or about actually answering the questions.

1. What are the principal differences between the Articles of Confederation and the Constitution?
2. If a cure for all fatal diseases were found and life expectancy were doubled, predict how society might change.
3. Charles Dickens included events from his own life in his novel *David Copperfield*. Illustrate the validity of this statement by citing specific events both from the novel and from the biography you have read.
4. Describe a method used by refineries to produce gasoline from crude oil.
5. In *Lord of the Flies* what is the significance of the two radically different sides of the island?

■ Planning the Essay Answer

Your understanding of the essay question will enable you to plan an effective answer. Whether your answer will be as short as a single paragraph or as long as a whole essay, you can follow certain planning and organizing steps, always keeping your time limit in mind.

Determining Your Main Idea or Main Point and Support. When you begin to plan your answer, you should try to answer the whole question in a single sentence. This sentence can become the main idea or main point of your answer. You may have to rough out several versions, but once you have a suitable one, you can plan your support.

> State a main idea or main point as your answer, express it in one sentence, and then list relevant supporting ideas and information.

Reducing your answer to one main idea or one main point in one sentence provides you with a topic sentence for a paragraph answer or a thesis statement for an essay answer. It offers you a focus around which you can organize your answer. In a paragraph answer, your topic sentence would be followed by a number of other sentences containing supporting information. In an essay answer, you would introduce your thesis statement with a few sentences, develop the thesis statement with a few paragraphs of support, and end with a short conclusion. But in either case, your single sentence represents the core of your answer. It should take into account the requirements of the question and respond to the question as fully and as specifically as possible. You might want to restate some portion of the original question in your sentence. The following chart offers a few examples of one-sentence answers. One is appropriate for a topic sentence, and the other two are appropriate for thesis statements.

STATING A MAIN IDEA OR MAIN POINT FOR A PARAGRAPH OR ESSAY ANSWER

Question	Answer
Explain the cause of the Northern Lights or Aurora Borealis.	The flickering, multicolored lights known as the Aurora Borealis are believed to result from the collision of atomic particles from the sun with particles in the earth's atmosphere. (Topic sentence)
Discuss the economic conditions that enabled the Industrial Revolution to take place in England between 1780 and 1840.	Between 1780 and 1840, England had the money, the labor, the markets, the government's encouragement, and the engineering ideas needed to launch the Industrial Revolution. (Thesis statement)

Is Hamlet sane or insane? Defend your opinion.	Hamlet is not insane; rather, his statements and actions reveal a rationality that is both cunning and determined. (Thesis statement)

Once you have come up with a topic sentence or thesis statement, you can brainstorm for the support you will need in your answer. You might use scratch paper or the blank side of the exam itself to list as many relevant facts, examples, details, reasons, and other pieces of information as you can think of within the time limit you have set for yourself. Try to remember the material you have studied on the subject, and draw on your own ideas as well. Write down your ideas freely as they occur to you, but always try to relate them to the one-sentence answer that is the focus of your paragraph or essay.

Organizing the Answer.   Keeping as close as possible to your schedule, you should have at least three or four major items of support listed before you begin to arrange your ideas. Once you are ready to organize your answer, group your items of support into a modified outline.

Sort and organize your supporting information in a modified outline.

As you organize all of your supporting material, keep the original question in mind. Remember that your supporting information must develop your topic sentence or thesis statement. Eliminate any items that do not seem to fit into your answer, and look for any logical groupings among your ideas and information. A logical order—order of importance, chronological order, spatial order, comparison or contrast order, or developmental order—can be particularly helpful to you in writing a coherent paragraph or essay under the pressure of a time limit. A logical order will make the answer you write sound more authoritative and will simplify and speed up the writing step.

Once you have decided on the organization of your answer, prepare a rough outline, either by numbering your pieces of support or by arranging them in a modified outline. Incorporate any new and relevant ideas that occur to you as you organize. For a paragraph-length answer, list your support in the most appropriate order. For an essay-length answer, think about the number of paragraphs you will have and the information you will include in each. You might also jot down a few thoughts about your conclusion.

The following chart shows sample modified outlines, one for a paragraph-length answer and one for an essay-length answer on the Hamlet question, calling for the defense of an opinion with examples, facts, and reasons.

SAMPLE MODIFIED OUTLINES	
Paragraph Answer	**Essay Answer**
<u>Topic Sentence:</u> Hamlet's actions indicate that he is both rational and determined.	<u>Thesis Statement:</u> Hamlet is not insane; his statements and actions reveal a rationality that is both cunning and determined.
—Behavior toward Ophelia to make her think he is overcome with love, thereby disguising his real anguish —Feigning insanity helps him gather clues and find a means to seek revenge —His plot to face his uncle with the crime is clever	<u>Hamlet's Statements</u> —Tells his friends Horatio and Marcellus that he will feign madness —Admits in a soliloquy that he must find a way to prove his uncle's guilt
<u>Concluding Idea:</u> Even with his heavy burden of grief, Hamlet's mind remains sharp enough to plan his actions and to manipulate other characters.	<u>Hamlet's Actions</u> —Chooses to appear insane to disguise his grief while finding answers —Manipulates Ophelia and her father —Masterminds a plot to face his uncle with the crime
	<u>Conclusion:</u> Hamlet's behavior is coherent, even ingenious; although burdened by grief, he can weigh his options, manipulate other characters, and plot and execute a course of action.

EXERCISE C: Planning Your Answer. Find an essay question from one of your classes, consult the study questions at the ends of chapters in a textbook, or use one that your teacher provides. Choose a question that you have not answered before. Give yourself about ten minutes to plan an essay-length answer. Follow these steps.

1. Identify the requirements of the question.
2. In one sentence, write as complete an answer as possible to the whole question. Use this as your thesis statement.
3. Gather and list as much of the appropriate kind of supporting information as possible, and list it beneath your thesis statement.
4. Group your supporting information according to a logical order, and prepare a modified outline for the answer. Include your thesis statement as well as any ideas for the introduction and conclusion.

■ Writing and Checking Your Answer

At this point, you should still have about two thirds of your budgeted time remaining to write and check your answer. Write quickly and legibly, fleshing out your outline, concentrating on making your ideas flow logically. Allow a few minutes to proofread and correct your answer.

> As you write, follow your outline, filling in details, and then proofread to make all final corrections and revisions.

After planning your thoughts, you should be able to write a complete and satisfactory answer within the time you have left. Follow your outline: It will keep you on the track of the question and will guide you from point to point as you write. If you remember additional information, include it in your answer if it expands your main idea or main point or the supporting information in your outline. Fill out the ideas listed in your outline with complete sentences, and try to make each sentence flow logically into the next. You may find that using transitions and other connecting words will help you establish a logical and focused train of thought under the pressure of a time limit, especially when you are writing a long answer. Repeating main words or phrases from your topic sentence or thesis statement throughout your answer will also help to keep your paragraph or essay focused on the requirements of the question. Your careful planning should enable you to write quickly, but make a special effort to keep your writing legible. You might leave wide margins or skip lines in order to make your answer more readable and to allow for last-minute changes and corrections.

When you have covered all the material in your outline and completed your answer, reread it carefully. This final check represents your last chance to correct any mistakes, to add anything that is missing, and to fix any stylistic flaws or technical errors that might count against you. Ask yourself questions such as those in the following chart.

CHECKING YOUR ANSWER

1. Does the paragraph or essay have a clear topic sentence or thesis statement presenting a basic answer to the question?
2. Have you answered the question fully and provided the right kinds of supporting examples, facts, details, and reasons?
3. Do you still need to add specific support?
4. Does your answer end clearly and logically?
5. Can you find any errors in grammar, mechanics, or spelling?
6. Is your paper legible?

Following is an example, written by a student, of an essay-length answer to a question about Hamlet's sanity. Notice that it fits the standard essay form, generally following the modified outline on page 836. The ideas have been fleshed out, and some new ones have been added. The essay contains three body paragraphs, an introduction, a conclusion, and transitions that help make the essay flow.

Essay-length answer to an essay question

A central problem of Shakespeare's *Hamlet* is the question of the main character's sanity. Is Hamlet driven insane by the message of the ghost that his Uncle Claudius has killed his father in order to usurp the throne and marry Hamlet's mother? Hamlet is understandably upset by the ghost's accusation and confused for a time about the wisest course of action. But he is *not* insane: His statements and actions reveal a rationality that is both cunning and determined.

Hamlet's behavior often appears wild and tortured throughout the play. But it is important to recognize that he is torn by conflicting feelings. He is by nature gentle and fair, and yet he is bound by his love for his father and by honor and duty to avenge his father's murder. Furthermore, if the ghost's message is true, Hamlet's own life is probably in danger. And Hamlet cannot even be certain that the ghost's message *is* true. Given his painful and difficult situation, Hamlet's behavior in the play is the intelligent attempt of a sensitive man to deal with a heartbreaking and confusing set of circumstances. He decides to *seem* mad to the rest of the court in order to buy himself time to decide what to do.

Hamlet's own statements indicate his rationality. Early in the play, Hamlet tells his friends Horatio and Marcellus that he will feign madness, and he makes them promise not to break their oath of silence even if they see him act strangely. Shortly afterward, Hamlet admits in a soliloquy that he cannot simply act on the ghost's accusation. He needs to prove his uncle's guilt before avenging his father's death.

Throughout the rest of the play, in almost every case of irrational behavior, Hamlet *chooses* to appear insane for a reason. He wants to confirm what the ghost has told him without arousing his uncle's or the court's suspicion. His behavior to Ophelia allows her father, Polonius, to believe that Hamlet has been driven mad by unrequited love. Knowing that word of his lovesickness will reach his uncle, Hamlet can disguise the real cause of his suffering from his enemy, and thereby remain free to investigate the truth of the ghost's statements. In addition, if others at the court believe him insane, Hamlet may be able to gather clues to help him confirm his uncle's guilt. For example, he convinces his former friends Rosencrantz and Guildenstern of his insanity and is able to use them to uncover more evidence of his uncle's treachery. Finally, Hamlet's shrewdness and clarity of mind are most evident in the plot that he eventually develops to prove his uncle's guilt. He directs a band of traveling actors to recreate his father's murder in a play. Hamlet knows what he is doing: It is his purpose to confront his uncle with a reenactment of his crime in order to "catch the conscience of the king." He can then prove to himself that the ghost's horrible message is true.

Although Hamlet's actions appear erratic and irrational when viewed separately, his behavior is coherent, and, in some instances, ingenious. Any sane person would be deeply grieved and confused in Hamlet's situation. His burden is heavy, but his mind is not overwhelmed by his grief. He can weigh his options, manipulate other characters, and plot and execute a course of action. Hamlet is brokenhearted, but he is not insane. —Richard Supple

EXERCISE D: **Writing and Checking Your Answer.** Use your outline from Exercise C to guide your writing of the answer. Allow yourself about forty minutes to write, and then leave a few minutes to check your answer and make any corrections and improvements. Use the checklist on page 838 to proofread and revise.

APPLICATION: **Planning, Writing, and Checking an Answer to an Exam Question.** Take another question from a recent exam or a question that your teacher supplies. Follow the steps and suggestions in this section for planning and writing the answer. Budget your time wisely, and allow a few minutes to check and revise.

Manuscript Preparation

The most important part of any writing you do is, of course, the ideas that it contains. The composition unit offers many suggestions for developing, organizing, and expressing your ideas in clear and interesting language. However, when you hand in a paper there are also certain technical things that you should provide. The following pages give suggestions for basic manuscript preparation, for dealing with mechanical and other technical aspects of writing, for giving credit to your sources, and for understanding and using correction symbols.

Basic Preparation

Whether handwritten or typed, your manuscript should follow certain basic rules. The following chart shows the suggested procedures for each style.

PREPARING A MANUSCRIPT	
Handwritten	**Typed**
1. Use white 8½ × 11 inch (21.5 × 28 cm) lined paper, but never pages ripped from a spiral binder.	1. Use white 8½ × 11 inch (21.5 × 28 cm) paper.
2. Use black or blue ink only.	2. Use a clear black ribbon.
3. Leave a margin of 1 inch (2.54 cm) on the right, using the paper's own rules as your margin on other sides.	3. Leave a margin of at least 1 inch (2.54 cm) on all sides.
4. Indent each paragraph.	4. Double-space all lines and indent each paragraph.
5. Use only one side of each paper.	5. Use only one side of each paper.
6. Recopy if necessary to make your final copy neat.	6. Retype if necessary to make your final copy neat.

You must also identify your manuscript, following either an elaborate or simple style. For long and important papers, such as library papers, you will probably want an elaborate style. Set up a title page as shown on page 842. The next page and all the other pages should carry only your name and the page number, beginning with page one.

With Title Page

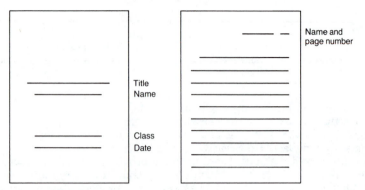

For shorter papers, use the simple style. Basic identification appears on the first page, while the second page still carries your name and the page number, beginning with page two.

Without Title Page

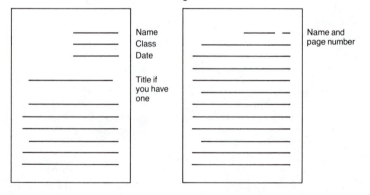

Dealing with Mechanics

The following chart offers basic guidelines for using punctuation marks and other mechanical items that seem to cause most manuscript problems.

CHECKING MECHANICS		
Item	**Basic Guidelines**	**Further Reference**
Capitalization	Use common sense in capitalizing proper nouns, proper adjectives, and first words.	Section 11.1, pages 302–318

Abbreviation	Avoid most abbreviations in formal writing. Feel free, however, to use abbreviations such as Mr. and Mrs., a.m. and p.m., and well-known abbreviations for organizations such as NATO and VISTA.	Section 12.2, pages 339–354
Commas	Take care not to overuse commas. Also check to make sure you are not dividing compound verbs with commas.	Section 12.2, pages 339–354
Hyphens	Check compound words in the dictionary. Hyphenate at the end of the line only when absolutely necessary and only at a syllable break.	Section 12.6, pages 381–385
Apostrophes	Avoid using apostrophes incorrectly in personal pronouns such as *its* and *theirs*.	Section 12.6, pages 385–391

Handling Other Technical Matters

Other technical matters should also be checked to make your paper more readable and more persuasive.

CHECKING OTHER ITEMS		
Item	**Basic Guidelines**	**Futher Reference**
Spelling	Keep a dictionary at your side and check it whenever you are in doubt.	Section 14.2, pages 420–430
Usage	Take special care to make sure your subjects and verbs agree.	Section 7.1, pages 206–220, for subject-verb agreement; Section 9.2, pages 252–281, for a list of one hundred common usage problems.
Sentence Faults	Check for fragments, run-ons, problems with modifiers, and faulty parallelism or coordination.	Chapter 4, pages 128–145

| Numbers | Spell out most numbers that can be written in one or two words and all numbers at the beginning of a sentence. Use numerals, however, for lengthy numbers, for dates, and for addresses. | Section 11.2, pages 327–330 |

Giving Credit to Sources

Whenever you are quoting the words or using the ideas of another writer, make sure you have given credit to that person. The chart in Section 24.1 on pages 739–740 shows the different forms for these kinds of citations.

Using Correction Symbols

You may find the following symbols very useful when you are proofreading your own manuscript. Your teacher may also choose to use these or similar marks when grading your papers.

USING CORRECTION SYMBOLS

Symbol	Meaning	Example
⟑	delete	The colors is red.
⌒	close up	The color is reᗡd.
∧	insert	The color ∧ red.
#	add space	The coloris red.
∿	transpose	The colro is red.
¶	new paragraph	¶ The color is red.
no ¶	no paragraph	no ¶ The color is red.
cap	capitalize	the color is red.
lc	use small letter	The Color is red.
sp	spelling	The colar is red.
us	usage	The colors is red.
frag	fragment	The red color and the blue.
ro	run-on	The color is red the house is blue.
mod	problem modifier	Newly painted, I saw the house.
awk	awkward	The color is, I think, kind of red.

Index

Bold numbers show pages on which basic definitions and rules can be found.

Acknowledgments

The authors and editors have made every effort to trace the ownership of all copyrighted selections found in this book and to make full acknowledgment of their use.

The dictionary of record for this book is *Webster's New World Dictionary*, Second College Edition, copyright © 1980 by Simon & Schuster, Inc. The basis for the selection of vocabulary words appropriate for this grade level is *The Living Word Vocabulary: The Words We Know* by Edgar Dale and Joseph O'Rourke, copyright © 1976.

Citations follow, arranged by unit and page for easy reference.

Usage: Pages 284 Barbara Tuchman, *A Distant Mirror* (New York: Alfred A. Knopf, Inc.). **285** Flannery O'Connor. Reprinted by permission of Farrar, Straus and Giroux, Inc. Selection from THE HABIT OF BEING: LETTERS BY FLANNERY O'CONNOR, edited with an Introduction by Sally Fitzgerald. Copyright © 1979 by Regina O'Connor. **288** James Bordley, *Two Centuries of American Medicine* (Philadelphia, PA: W.B. Saunders Co., 1976).

Mechanics: Pages 367 John McPhee. Reprinted by permission of Farrar, Straus and Giroux, Inc. Excerpt from "The Keel of Lake Dickey" from GIVING GOOD WEIGHT by John McPhee. Copyright 1975, 1976, 1978, 1979 by John McPhee. This material first appeared in *The New Yorker*. **368** Suzanne Charlé. From an article in *Travel and Leisure Magazine*.

Study Skills: Pages 447, 448 Edward B. Fry, *Reading Drills*, 1975. Reprinted by permission of Jamestown Publishers, Providence, Rhode Island. **472** Adapted from Michael McRae, "Survival of the Fastest," OUTSIDE (September 1980). **477–478** FROM JULIA CHILD'S KITCHEN by Julia Child. Copyright © 1975 by Julia Child. Reprinted by permission of Alfred A. Knopf, Inc. **479** Selma H. Fraiberg, *The Magic Years*. (New York: Charles Scribner's Sons, 1959). **480** J.P. Jones, *The Money Story* (New York: Drake Publishers, Inc, 1973). **480** Elizabeth Gaskell, *Wives and Daughters* (New York: Penguin, © 1969). **502** *The Encyclopedia Americana 1980*, Vol 30, p. 560. Reprinted with permission of The Encyclopedia Americana, copyright 1980, The Americana Corporation. **507** From ROGET'S INTERNATIONAL THESAURUS, Fourth Edition (Thomas Y. Crowell Company). Copyright © 1977 by Harper & Row, Publishers, Inc. Reprinted by permission of the publisher. **511** *Essay and General Literature Index* copyright © 1978, 1979 by The H.W. Wilson Company. Material reproduced by permission of the publishers. **516** *Readers' Guide to Periodical Literature* Copyright © 1980 by The H.W. Wilson Company. Material reproduced by permission of the publisher. **517** *The New York Times Index* © 1980 by the New York Times Company. Reprinted by permission. **523** Ray Walters, "Paperback Talk" *The New York Times Book Review*, November 9, 1980. © 1980 by The New York Times Company. Reprinted by permission. **524, 533** (second item) By permission. From *Webster's Third New International Dictionary* © 1976 by G. & C. Merriam Co., Publishers of the Merriam-Webster Dictionaries. **525** *Oxford English Dictionary*, 1979. (Oxford, England: Oxford University Press). **526** By permission. From *Webster's New Collegiate Dictionary* © 1980 by G. & C. Merriam Co., Publishers of the Merriam-Webster Dictionaries. **528, 531, 532, 533** (first item), **534** with permission. From *Webster's New World Dictionary*, Second College Edition. Copyright © 1980 by Simon & Schuster, Inc.

Key of Major Concepts